The *The* BEST PLACES TO KISS

in NORTHERN CALIFORNIA

KATE CHYNOWETH

EDITION 6

SASQUATCH BOOKS
SEATTLE

Printed in the United States of America
Published by Sasquatch Books
Distributed by Publishers Group West
14 13 12 11 10 09 08 07 06 05   6 5 4 3 2 1

Cover and interior design: Stewart A. Williams
Cover photograph: Peter Beck/CORBIS
Interior maps: Lisa Brower/Green Eye Design
Project editor: Kris Fulsaas
Production editor: Kurt Stephan
Copy editor: Donna Stonecipher
Proofreader: Karen Parkin
Indexer: Michael Ferreira

ISBN 1-57061-409-1

Sasquatch Books
119 South Main Street, Suite 400
Seattle, WA 98104
(206) 467-4300
www.sasquatchbooks.com
custserv@sasquatchbooks.com

CONTENTS

GREATER NORTHERN CALIFORNIA

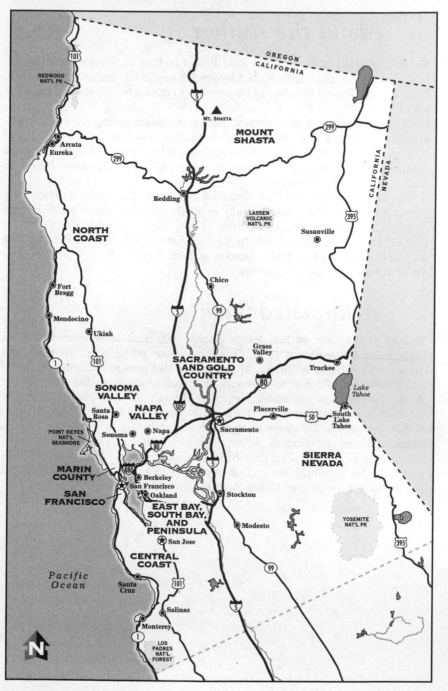

OREGON
CALIFORNIA

REDWOOD
NAT'L PK.

MT. SHASTA

MOUNT
SHASTA

Arcata
Eureka

Redding

LASSEN
VOLCANIC
NAT'L PK

Susanville

NORTH
COAST

Fort
Bragg

Chico

Mendocino

Ukiah

Grass
Valley

SACRAMENTO
AND GOLD
COUNTRY

Truckee

Lake
Tahoe

SONOMA
VALLEY

Santa
Rosa

NAPA
VALLEY

Placerville

South
Lake
Tahoe

POINT REYES
NAT'L
SEASHORE

Sonoma

Napa

Sacramento

SIERRA
NEVADA

MARIN
COUNTY

Berkeley

San Francisco

SAN
FRANCISCO

Oakland

Stockton

EAST BAY,
SOUTH BAY,
AND
PENINSULA

Modesto

YOSEMITE
NAT'L PK

San Jose

CENTRAL
COAST

Pacific
Ocean

Santa
Cruz

Salinas

Monterey

LOS
PADRES
NAT'L
FOREST

CALIFORNIA
NEVADA

N

About the Author

For this updated edition of *The Best Places to Kiss in Northern California*, freelance writer and editor **Kate Chynoweth** explored romantic hideaways, from the windswept beaches of Mendocino to the decadent spas of the wine country.

Chynoweth, who spent several formative years living in a cramped-but-charming San Francisco Victorian, is now based in Seattle. Her latest project involves traveling and puckering up in pursuit of new romantic destinations as the editor of the upcoming edition of *The Best Places to Kiss in the Pacific Northwest*.

She is the author of *The Bridesmaid Guide: Etiquette, Parties, and Being Fabulous* (Chronicle Books) as well as other books on food and entertaining. She is also the editor of *The Risks of Sunbathing Topless* (Seal Press), a humorous anthology of women's travel essays. Her writing on travel, food, and lifestyle appears in *Real Simple*, *Sunset*, and various other newspapers and magazines.

Acknowledgments

Thanks to the team at Sasquatch Books, including series editor Terence Maikels, project editor Kris Fulsaas, production editor Kurt Stephan, and designer Stewart A. Williams. Appreciation also goes to Suzanne de Galan and Cassandra Mitchell for helping the book along from the start. A big thank you goes to Christina Henry de Tessan for her contributions to the Bay Area chapters, and thanks also to David Griffith and Richard Wilson for their willingness to stomach so much talk of romance. To Lisa Taggart, whose encyclopedic knowledge of Northern California and savvy advice earned my unending gratitude, all I can do is raise my glass. Finally, gratitude for invaluable services rendered goes to copy editor Donna Stonecipher, proofreader Karen Parkin, and indexer Michael Ferreira.

About Best Places® Guidebooks

PEOPLE TRUST US. *Best Places®* guidebooks, which have been published continuously since 1975, represent one of the most respected regional travel series in the country. We are proud to have incorporated the best-selling *Best Places to Kiss* guidebooks into our publishing series. This sixth edition (our first) of *The Best Places to Kiss in Northern California* has earned a special place in our hearts and aims to do the same in yours. Our reviewers know their territory. They have your romantic interests at heart, and they strive to serve as reliable guides for your amorous outings. The *Best Places to Kiss* guides describe the true strengths, foibles, and unique characteristics of each establishment listed. *The Best Places to Kiss in Northern California* specifically seeks out and highlights the features of this region that harbor romance and splendor, from restaurants, inns, lodges, and bed-and-breakfasts to spectacular parks, pristine beaches, and romantic drives. In this edition of *The Best Places to Kiss in Northern California*, couples will find all the information they need, including the best times to visit a place for the most privacy, where to find the most intimate restaurants, which rooms to request (and which to avoid), and how to find each destination's most romantic activities.

NOTE: *The reviews in this edition are based on information available at press time and are subject to change. Romantic travelers are advised that the places listed herein may have closed or changed management and, thus, may no longer be recommended by this series. Your romantic feedback assists greatly in increasing our accuracy and our resources, and we welcome information conveyed by readers of this book. Feel free to write to us at the following address: Sasquatch Books, 119 S Main St, Suite 400, Seattle, Washington, 98104. We can also be contacted via e-mail: bestplaces @sasquatchbooks.com.*

Lip Ratings

The following is a brief explanation of the lip ratings awarded each location.

◐◐◐◐	*Simply sublime*
◐◐◐	*Very desirable; many outstanding qualities*
◐◐	*Can provide a satisfying experience; some wonderful features*
◐	*Romantic possibilities with potential drawbacks*
UNRATED	*New or undergoing major changes*

Price Range

Prices for lodgings are based on peak season rates for one night's lodging for double occupancy (otherwise there wouldn't be anyone to kiss!). Prices for restaurants are based primarily on dinner for two, including dessert, tax, and tip, but not alcohol. Peak season is typically Memorial Day to Labor Day; off-season rates vary, but can sometimes be significantly lower. Because prices and business hours change, it is always a good idea to call ahead to each place you plan to visit.

$$$$	*Very expensive (more than $100 for dinner for two; more than $250 for one night's lodging for two)*
$$$	*Expensive (between $65 and $100 for dinner for two; between $150 and $250 for one night's lodging for two)*
$$	*Moderate (between $35 and $65 for dinner for two; between $85 and $150 for one night's lodging for two)*
$	*Inexpensive (less than $35 for dinner for two; less than $85 for one night's lodging for two)*

Romantic Highlights

The Romantic Highlights section of each chapter guides you to the most romantic activities in each region. These include pursuits that are intimate and relaxing for couples, such as strolling to a lighthouse, taking an easy guided kayaking tour, or enjoying an alfresco lunch. It is our firm belief, however, that during any romantic getaway, doing away with the notion of an itinerary (and, of course, sleeping in!) is part of the fun. In Romantic Highlights, the establishments or attractions that appear in boldface are recommended and addresses and phone numbers are supplied. Every attempt has been made to provide accurate information on an establishment's location and phone number, but it's always a good idea to call ahead.

Lodgings

Many romance-oriented lodgings will require two-night-minimum stays throughout the year (especially on weekends); during some holiday weekends or high-season periods, this requirement may be extended to three nights. It is a good idea to call in advance to check the policy at your lodging of choice. In the spirit of romance, popular family lodgings are mostly not included in this guide; however, some accommodations included do allow children, particularly those over age 12. Many of these have safeguards for your privacy, such as separate breakfast times (one seats children, the other is adults-only) or detached suites for those traveling with children. If having a kid-free environment is critical to your intimate weekend away, call ahead to find out an establishment's policy. For more information about where to find pet-friendly rooms, see "Puppy Love" in the Carmel and Carmel Valley section of the Central Coast chapter, or refer to the pet index at the back of this book.

Indexes

In addition to the index of pet-friendly accommodations mentioned above, this book also features a wedding index. Organized by region, this index lists romantic lodgings with facilities able to accommodate wedding parties of at least 50 people. (Since, after all, one of the most auspicious times to kiss is the moment after you exchange wedding vows, we felt this was a good idea.) Additionally, all restaurants, lodgings, town names, and major attractions are listed alphabetically in the back of the book.

Credit Cards

Many establishments that accept checks also require a major credit card for identification. Note that some places accept only local checks. Credit cards are abbreviated as follows: American Express (AE); Bravo (B); Carte Blanche (CB); Diners Club (DC); Discover (DIS); Enroute (E); Japanese credit card (JCB); MasterCard (MC); and Visa (V).

*"As usual with most lovers in the city, they were
troubled by the lack of that essential need of
love—a meeting place."*

—THOMAS WOLFE

The Fine
Art of Kissing

THIS IS THE SIXTH EDITION of *The Best Places to Kiss in Northern California*, and we are delighted to be publishing this book in a new, improved format that provides better-than-ever coverage of this region's most romantic destinations. This expanded edition includes features that are entirely new for *The Best Places to Kiss in Northern California*, including a Romantic Highlights section at the start of every chapter that lets you in on the most romantic activities in each region. We have also expanded the Romantic Wineries sections (featured in our wine country chapters) that highlight which of each region's hundreds of wineries have the most appeal for amorous couples. In addition, we have detailed access and information, added maps, and expanded coverage of the northern mountains, Central Coast, and growing wine regions of Carmel Valley and California's Gold Country. As ever, our research is enthusiastic, our investigations are thorough, and our criteria increasingly more restrictive (disappointment can approach disastrous proportions where the heart is concerned). We are proud of our unique position as one of the few travel books to review romantic properties with a candid and critical eye, and we treasure the feedback we get from readers who report that our reviews offer a breath of amorous fresh air.

It's no secret that Northern California is, simply put, a splendid part of the world. Its diverse regions brim with romantic potential and provide terrific inspiration to those of us who kiss and tell for a living. From the sparkling city of San Francisco and the towering peaks of the Sierra Nevada to the redwood forests, rolling vineyards, dramatic shorelines, and sandy beaches throughout the region, there is probably no more diverse yet compact place in the world in which to pucker up. The coastal climate is temperate throughout the year and marked by misty mornings, sultry afternoons, and cool evenings; in the mountains, snowy winters and brilliant, hot summers prevail. We recommend the most romantic times of year to visit particular regions. For example, Yosemite National Park is especially delightful in spring when the waterfalls are at their roaring peak and summer crowds have not yet arrived; San Francisco, which tends to be cold and foggy in summer, lends itself better to exploration during the usually sunnier autumn months. No matter the weather, however, this region's romance and vitality are contagious, as you'll discover each time you visit one of the legendary wineries, excellent restaurants, charming bed-and-breakfasts, alluring beaches, scenic hiking trails, or world-famous San Francisco landmarks. With your kissing companion at your side, the only challenge you'll find in Northern California will be choosing from among so many wonderfully intimate options.

Any travel guide that rates establishments is inherently subjective—and our *Best Places to Kiss* series is no exception. We rely on our professional experience, yes; and we also rely on our reporters' instincts to evaluate the romantic quotient of each establishment or region. Three major factors influence our decisions on which places to include: setting, privacy, and ambience. Setting is straightforward—we mean simply location and view; but the latter two categories deserve a bit of clarification. In regard to privacy, our preference is for cottages and suites set at a distance from main buildings: such locations allow amorous couples to say or do as they please without fear of being overheard or of disturbing others. However, many truly heart-stirring bed-and-breakfasts and hotels require guests to share space; in these cases, we look both for modern soundproofing techniques and for expert innkeepers who know how to provide guests with a sense of intimate seclusion. We also applaud the notion of private breakfasts, whether delivered straight to your suite or served at an intimate table for two in the dining room. (Our ideal: a warm and friendly greeting, knowledgeable and helpful service, and the ability of the staff to become nearly invisible when the two of you lock eyes across the table.)

Ambience, the final major criterion, includes a multitude of factors. It takes more than a four-poster bed and lace pillows or a linen-draped table set with silver and crystal to create romantic ambience. Ambience relates more to the degree of intimacy and comfort provided and the number of gracious appointments in a place than to froufrous and frills. We also look for thoughtful details such as appropriate music, fresh flowers, and candles. Ambience is created in part by innkeepers, and if you are traveling to celebrate a special romantic occasion, we highly recommend informing them in advance. With notice, the best innkeepers will take extra care to ensure that an intimate ambience welcomes you and your loved one. They can also inform you of any special-occasion packages, which might include chilled champagne, breakfast in bed, or thoughtful touches during turndown service, such as dimmed lights and your beloved's favorite music playing softly to set the right romantic mood.

If a place has all three factors going for it, inclusion is automatic. But if one or two of the criteria are weak or nonexistent, the other feature(s) must be superior in order for the location to be included. For example, a place that offers a breathtakingly beautiful panoramic vista but is also inundated with tourists and children on field trips would not be featured. A fabulous bed-and-breakfast in a less-than-desirable setting might be included, however, if it boasts a wonderfully inviting and cozy interior that outweighs its location. Of course, we also consider myriad other factors, including uniqueness, excellence of cooking, cleanliness, value, and professionalism of service. Luxuries such as complimentary champagne, handmade truffles, or extraordinary service frequently determine the difference between a lip rating of three and a half or four. In the final analysis, keep in mind that every place listed in this book is recommended. When you visit any of the places we include here, you should look forward to privacy, a beautiful setting, heart-stirring ambience, and access to highly romantic pursuits.

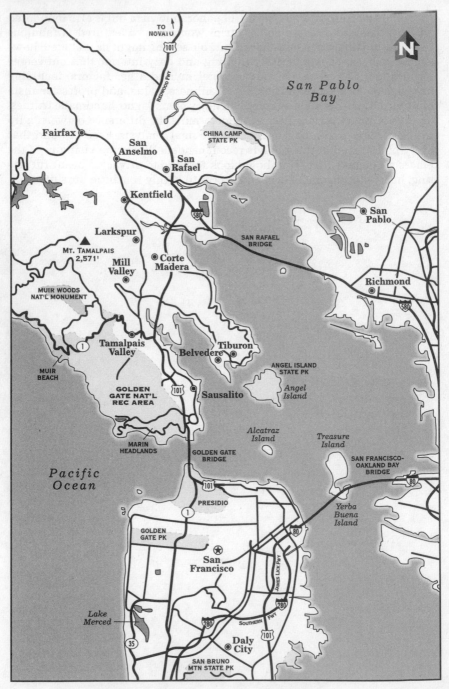

> *"You may conquer with the sword, but you are conquered by a kiss."*
>
> —DANIEL HEINSIUS

♡ SAN FRANCISCO

Shrouded in fog one moment, glittering in sunlight the next, dynamic and intriguing San Francisco is romance itself. At the heart of "the City," as locals call it, are its diverse neighborhoods—many of which offer scenic views of the Pacific Ocean and San Francisco Bay. Colorful Victorian-style homes dot the dramatic hillsides, while the swooping cables and spires of the landmark Golden Gate Bridge rising from the mist provide a constant reminder of the city's iconic beauty. On sunny days, the city's waterfront and many lovely parks come alive with walkers, picnickers, and bicyclists; its neighborhoods filled with bakeries, cafés, and restaurants and its sleek, sophisticated downtown beckon in any weather. In spring and fall, however, tourists are fewer and the often crisp, clear weather provides a stunning backdrop for hand-in-hand exploration.

Options in such a diverse city are endless when it comes to luxury hotels and cozy bed-and-breakfasts, while restaurants run the gamut from neighborhood gems to glitzy downtown showstoppers. Of course, such big-city plenty doesn't come without big-city drawbacks, which in San Francisco can range from crowded restaurants to high prices to incessant traffic. Because parking spaces aren't easy to come by, we highly recommend leaving your car behind whenever possible: for example, if you are downtown or near it, do yourselves a favor and catch a cab, a bus, or a cable car—or simply go on foot (bring comfortable walking shoes for climbing those famous hills). No matter how you get around, you will be constantly rewarded, from the verdant gardens and pathways in beautiful Golden Gate Park to the cultural destinations such as the theater, opera, symphony, and world-class museums. Whether you're riding up the hills on a cable car, exploring the bustling international district, or sipping espresso in the Italian enclave of North Beach, San Francisco's sights and sounds are certain to energize your hearts and minds—not to mention your lips.

1

DOWNTOWN SAN FRANCISCO

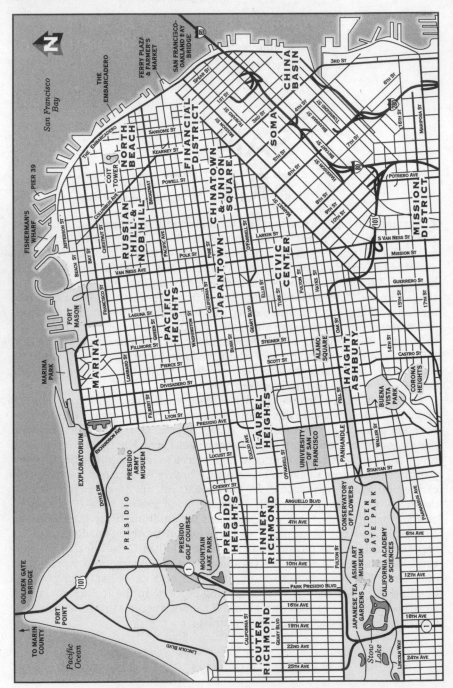

SAN FRANCISCO

ROMANTIC HIGHLIGHTS

An enchanting day in San Francisco can take many different forms. Whether you explore the Victorian mansion–lined streets of Pacific Heights, visit downtown's glamorous Union Square to enjoy the glitzy shops, or hop aboard the famous cable car, the City by the Bay will reward you with its nearly endless number of places in which to kiss. The famously hilly landscape, bordered by the sparkling Pacific and San Francisco Bay, and the beautiful parks and beaches make San Francisco also one of the world's best cities for kissing alfresco.

An excellent place to start your excursion is **Golden Gate Park** (415/831-2700; www.parks.sfgov.org), whose 1,017 acres feature museums, lakes, and flower-lined pathways. Visit the tropical wonderland at the **Conservatory of Flowers** (John F. Kennedy Dr, near Conservatory Dr; 415/666-7001; www.conservatoryofflowers.org), an exquisitely restored 1879 Victorian hothouse. Or tour the famed **Japanese Tea Garden** when the cherry blossoms and azaleas are abloom in March and April (to avoid the distinctly unromantic crowds, visit early or late or wait until it's raining). If you simply walk westward through the park, you'll eventually come to the perfect place to watch the sunset: on the brink of the majestic Pacific. Even on a foggy day, the ocean view is romantic from a window-side table at **The Beach Chalet** (1000 Great Hwy at Ocean Beach; 415/386-8439; www.beachchalet.com), located above the Golden Gate Park Visitor's Center, right where the park meets the turbulent ocean.

North of this stretch of shoreline, known as Ocean Beach, is verdant **Lincoln Park**, home to what is surely California's most romantic museum, the **California Palace of the Legion of Honor** (near 34th Ave and Clement St; 415/863-3330 or 415/750-3600; www.thinker.org). Set high above the pounding Pacific surf and overlooking the Golden Gate Bridge, this stunning French neoclassical building features a grand outdoor courtyard dominated by the famous Rodin sculpture *The Thinker*. Inside, the impressive collection offers more than 4,000 years of fine art, including works by Monet, Cézanne, and Rembrandt. After musing upon the artwork and stopping into the café for refreshments, go outside to enjoy the sweeping views and the fresh ocean breeze. You're more likely to have the place to yourselves if you visit on a weekday and arrive when the doors open.

If there is a lovers' lane in San Francisco, it would have to be the **Golden Gate Promenade**, one of the most astounding scenic walks the city has to offer. This 4-mile stretch extends from Aquatic Park at Fisherman's Wharf past the Marina Green and Crissy Field to historic Fort Point, nestled under the south end of the Golden Gate Bridge. On chilly mornings, you can stop

3

to enjoy a hot drink and a bite to eat and browse the bookstore at the **Crissy Field Warming Hut** (www.crissyfield.org; 9am–5pm every day). Views of the sparkling bay, the Golden Gate Bridge, and Marin's golden rolling hills in the distance continue to unfold and become ever more inspiring as you walk.

Of course, the **Golden Gate Bridge** is also a destination in itself. You can walk across the monumental structure, which offers astonishing views. From this exhilarating vantage point, you can survey both the city's skyline and the endless blue of the Pacific Ocean, 260 feet below. The gusts of wind up here can cause even the reinforced steel cables to sway; this is one place where, even without a kiss, you can really feel the ground move beneath your feet. On a clear, sunny day, put on your walking shoes, don your jackets, and discover the thrill for yourselves.

Also in this beautiful northwest corner of the city, you'll find the Palace of Fine Arts and the Presidio, two wonderfully romantic destinations. Built in 1915 for the Panama-Pacific International Exposition, the **Palace of Fine Arts** (3301 Lyon St, between Jefferson and Bay Sts; 415/563-6504) is a cherished San Francisco landmark. Its stunning Romanesque rotunda, supported by mammoth Corinthian columns and flanked by majestic colonnades, overlooks a park and a lagoon filled with ducks and swans. During the afternoon, you're likely to encounter a wedding party as well as couples enjoying picnics on the grass. This setting, ethereal at any time of day, is especially romantic at night, when the building is lit up by spotlights, or in the early morning, when you can have the views all to yourselves.

The Presidio (415/556-0560) is a vast 1,480-acre former military base now part of the Golden Gate National Recreation Area (like Crissy Field and the Marina Green). Begin by driving the grounds on roads lined with redwood and eucalyptus trees. Next, park the car, clasp hands, and go for a long, leisurely walk. Stroll by some of the historical sites and displays, or take in some of the superb views of the Golden Gate Bridge and the Pacific Ocean.

To outfit yourselves for a romantic picnic, don't miss a visit to the restored historic **Ferry Building** (on the Embarcadero at the foot of Market St; www.ferrybuildingmarketplace.com; open every day). An emporium of Northern California's finest purveyors of gourmet food, this bustling spot has everything your hearts could desire, from organic produce to gourmet cheese to fresh, crusty bread. Or forget the picnic and simply linger at **Hog Island Oyster Company** (415/391-7117) over a glass of chilled white wine, impeccably fresh oysters (remember, they're an aphrodisiac), and sweeping water views. The **Ferry Plaza Farmer's Market** (415/291-3276) draws large crowds, particularly on Saturdays, but it's an exciting place to catch the pulse of this gourmet-minded city. (For a quieter atmosphere, visit the market on Tuesday, Thursday, or Sunday; eventually, the market is slated to become a daily affair much like the Pike Place Market in Seattle.) The location on the waterfront means that you can always step away from the bustle, gaze out at the boats crossing the water, and kiss.

San Francisco's waterfront tourist mecca, **Fisherman's Wharf**, is too crowded to offer much intimacy. However, it makes a lovely jumping-off point for a boat trip with the **Blue & Gold Fleet** (415/705-5555; www.blue andgoldfleet.com), which ferries passengers to Sausalito and Tiburon (see the Marin County chapter). Perhaps the most romantic idea is to become castaways for a day on **Angel Island**, the gem of San Francisco Bay. On the island, stop by the **Angel Island Company** (415/897-0715; www.angelisland .com; seasonal services) to rent mountain bikes or sign up for an all-day guided kayak tour. There's even an hourlong tram tour of the island's historic sites available for history buffs. However, if you're kissing buffs first and foremost, climb until you discover your own private panorama of the San Francisco skyline or Marin's forested hills. Bring along a picnic lunch to enjoy while relaxing in a sunny meadow. With its 6-mile perimeter trail and rugged climb up to a 360-degree view of the Bay Area, Angel Island is sure to yield several secluded kissing spots.

Back on the mainland, visit one of San Francisco's dizzying number of neighborhoods, each of which has its own undeniable charms. What you don't want to miss is an afternoon spent soaking up the bohemian ambience of the city's Italian-accented **North Beach** neighborhood. If you don't mind a tight squeeze, it doesn't get much more authentic than dinner at the tiny **L'Osteria del Forno** (519 Columbus Ave; 415/982-1124). North Beach also harbors one of the city's loftiest viewpoints, from the iconic **Coit Tower** (415/362-0808) atop **Telegraph Hill**. The serious stair-climbing yields a bird's-eye view from the bone-white, fluted column built in 1933. Alas, you won't have the tower to yourselves, and the other sightseers may obscure the vistas and dash your hopes of a romantic moment. But then again, when you share the dazzling view from this pinnacle, you may find that the crowds around you fade rapidly into the background.

Access and Information

Two major airports serve the city—**San Francisco International Airport** (SFO; 650/821-8211; www.flysfo.com) and **Oakland International Airport** (OAK; 510/563-3300; www.oaklandairport.com). Most travelers use SFO, which is located 14 miles south of downtown San Francisco via Highways 101 or 280; fares can vary depending on which airport you fly into, so it's worth checking both airports before making your reservations. From SFO airport, **Bay Area Rapid Transit** (BART; 510/464-6000; www.bart.gov) trains run every day from the SFO terminal to downtown San Francisco and cost only about $5 one way; BART also services the OAK airport, but you'll need to take a free shuttle from the airport to get to the station.

When planning your trip, consider carefully whether you actually need to bring or rent a car. San Francisco is a great city for walking, and there's plentiful public transportation on the **San Francisco Municipal Railway** or **MUNI** (415/673-6864; www.sfmuni.com) as well as BART (routes run to the East Bay, including Berkeley and Oakland). Also, parking is a notorious hassle: many neighborhoods limit nonresidents to only two hours, and most downtown meters have a maddening maximum half-hour time limit. If you do drive, come forewarned about the vigilant meter readers (almost 30 percent of all parking tickets statewide are issued in San Francisco), the expensive downtown parking garage fees, and the often unbearable traffic (avoid the highways at rush hour like the plague). There's simply nothing less conducive to kissing than sitting in traffic, searching for a parking space for an hour, getting an expensive ticket, or having your car towed.

Changeable weather is the norm in San Francisco. Afternoons can be sunny and spectacular, but they are often preceded by foggy mornings or followed by cool evenings. The climate is mild, rarely rising above 70°F or falling below 40°F, but bring a sweater or coat—chances are, you'll need it. Spring and fall months are warmest, as the fog makes its most frequent appearances in summer (August can be downright cold). For more information, contact the **San Francisco Convention and Visitors Bureau** (900 Market St; 415/391-2000; www.sfvisitor.org; open every day).

Romantic Lodgings

THE ARCHBISHOP'S MANSION
●●●●

1000 Fulton St / 415/563-7872 or 800/543-5820
Located on Alamo Square along with San Francisco's "Painted Ladies"— the famous row of pastel Victorian homes that are backed by the city skyline—this mansion embodies old-world elegance. Built in 1904 for the archbishop of San Francisco, its regal facade encloses an opulent interior. The formal parlor, where you'll enjoy complimentary wine and cheese each evening, holds two of the inn's most noteworthy features: a triple-vaulted, hand-painted ceiling and, for film buffs, a chandelier that was used on the set of *Gone with the Wind*. A stained-glass dome crowns the formidable three-story staircase in the lofty foyer, whose historic appointments include English actor Noel Coward's grand piano. Each of the 15 lavish guest rooms is named after a well-known opera. All of the accommodations are superbly designed for intimacy, but a few stand out as particularly kiss-worthy. In Carmen's Suite, the claw-foot tub in the spacious bathroom faces an elaborately carved fireplace, for a double dose of romance. The bright and cheerful Der Rosenkavalier Suite, once the archbishop's library, is a soothing oval room with curved wooden closet doors and a book collection; the spacious bathroom has a Jacuzzi tub for two. Yet nothing compares to the grand Don

Giovanni Suite, with its separate sitting room with fireplace, mahogany four-poster French bed, and seven-headed shower; you won't want to leave this extraordinary room. In fact, we're told many people don't—preferring to have dinner delivered via a local gourmet caterer for a candlelit meal in-room. All guest rooms feature choice antiques, comfortable sitting areas, embroidered linens, and partial or full canopies gracing queen-size feather beds (except for La Traviata and the Gypsy Baron Rooms, which offer king-size beds). Several rooms have city views; many have fireplaces; and two boast Jacuzzi tubs, while others have soaking tubs for two. At the hour of your choice, a simple continental breakfast is brought to your door along with the newspaper. Though the location on the square is lovely, the streets a few blocks away aren't, so you may want to consider a cab for nighttime excursions. However, you also may just want to stay put in your regal room and enjoy feeling like royalty.
$$$ AE, DC, MC, V; checks OK; www.jdvhospitality.com.

ARGONAUT HOTEL
♥♥♦

495 Jefferson St / 415/563-0800 or 866/415-0704
Fisherman's Wharf, too touristy and crowded to make for an intimate get-away, has never been an ideal kissing destination. Yet this impressive new hotel, which opened in fall 2003 at the wharf's western edge, has upped the area's romance quotient considerably. Housed in a handsomely refurbished 1900s warehouse building, the hotel's major selling point is the views: many rooms enjoy beautiful vistas of the bay and the Golden Gate Bridge. And if you don't mind the busy wharf right outside, the location—within the San Francisco Maritime National Historic Park at Hyde Street Pier—has some perks: for one, it's right next to the cable-car turnaround, so hopping aboard for the beautiful ride to Union Square couldn't be easier. The hotel is too large to be considered intimate—there are 252 guest rooms, including 13 suites; furthermore, since it's kid-friendly, you'll be joined by parents with strollers and children in the large, bustling lobby. Fortunately, the stylish, cozy rooms outweigh such minor drawbacks, and you'll be charmed by the hotel's "harbor style," which reinvents nautical-theme decor with very chic results. Rooms feature elements such as white-and-yellow striped wallpaper, blue carpeting scattered with gold stars, and Frette linen–draped beds with nautical headboards and crimson, blue, and gold bed skirts. Many rooms have a small sitting area, too, with palm-tree-printed-fabric upholstered easy chairs and captain's-style desk chairs. The building's history shows up in some decorative elements, too—ranging from original exposed-brick walls to warehouse-style steel doors. Clever pocket doors to the bathrooms help create a tad more space; step inside and you'll be charmed by the exposed wood beams, granite counters, and luxury massage showerheads. You can open the soundproof windows to soak up the sights

and sounds of the bay or close them for peace and quiet. If you can afford a splurge, consider the suites, which have additional space, wonderful spa tubs, and DVD/CD stereo systems. The handsome lobby, with soaring 16-foot ceilings, a large fireplace for warming up on foggy mornings, and exposed columns of Douglas fir, hosts a complimentary wine reception each evening. Morning brings a complimentary newspaper and coffee. Guests also have access to an exercise room, as well as room service from the hotel's casual restaurant, the Blue Mermaid Chowder House. Ask about specifics when you book a room; only those on the second, third, and fourth floors have unobstructed views, so be sure to indicate if your kissing is contingent upon gazing at the bay or the Golden Gate Bridge. You might be equally pleased with an overview of gleaming Coit Tower in North Beach and the pointy TransAmerica Pyramid.
$$$–$$$$ *AE, DIS, MC, V; checks OK; www.argonauthotel.com.* &

CAMPTON PLACE HOTEL
◐◐◐◐

340 Stockton St / 415/781-5555 or 800/235-4300
From its marble lobby with Asian accents to the rooftop fitness gym to its extravagant restaurant, the Campton Place Hotel offers full-service luxury in every sense of the word. The valet service will unpack your baggage, bring fresh bouquets to your room, and provide shoe shines; the maid service occurs twice daily; and complimentary limousine service is at the ready on Tuesday through Saturday evenings. Such luxury, of course, has its price: the rooms are phenomenally expensive. But the hotel doesn't take any false steps. A $15 million renovation completed in 2002 knocked down the building's old walls, and the new rooms are lovely, if compact: each is decorated on a sleek contemporary theme, with furnishings in light maple and dark pear wood, champagne-hued cushioned headboards on the luxurious down comforter–topped beds, and sandblasted glass doors opening to elegant bathrooms fitted out with limestone counters, soft knit robes, and oversize soaking tubs (along with bath salts and scented candles). Double-paned windows in each room help screen out the noise of busy Union Square. The 110 rooms are spread out over 17 floors in order to ensure privacy, and from the 9th floor up, there are only 4 rooms per floor. For the best views, ask for one of the larger deluxe corner rooms on the upper floors; the view from room 1501, which overlooks Union Square, is particularly stunning. The 17th-floor luxury suite, with chandelier-graced bedrooms and a formal dining room, is a study in opulence. You'll be delighted by the hotel's convenient central location and stylish decor, and the newly revamped and highly acclaimed Campton Place Restaurant downstairs (415/955-5555). The sublime cuisine, rich with French and Mediterranean influences, is considered among the finest in the city. The elegant, refined, and intimate dining room, filled with extravagant floral arrangements, gilt-framed mirrors, and tables

set with crystal and freshly cut flowers, is designed for romance and the service is seamless. At breakfast, the predominantly business-suit crowd creates a less formal but nonetheless pleasant atmosphere. Of course, room service is available should you find yourselves too busy kissing to leave your sumptuous quarters.

$$$$ AE, DC, MC, V; checks OK (for lodgings only); www.campton place.com. &

EDWARD II BED AND BREAKFAST
●❶

3155 Scott St / 415/922-3000 or 800/473-2846
The endless procession of cars on Lombard Street is enough to make you want to pass this one up, but if you're willing to contend with intense traffic noise, the Edward II is one of San Francisco's best romantic bargains. While its prices are comparable to those at a plethora of nearby economy motels, the Edward II is in a class by itself in every other respect. The pink stucco exterior belies the property's authentic English feel, enhanced by the adjacent London-inspired pub, ornamented with beautiful green tile work. Although 10 of the inn's 32 guest rooms are reminiscent of European hostel accommodations, with shared baths, the remaining rooms offer many of the essentials for a romantic getaway. If you can afford it, book one of the three large suites in the main building, all of which feature spectacular beds and whirlpool bathtubs. (There are also four suites across the street in the pink "Carriage House Annex" that resemble apartments; while these are pleasant and private, we prefer the more charming main-house accommodations.) If the suite prices are too steep, bargain hunters in love will find satisfaction in the Queen Bedrooms with private baths. The corner rooms get the most light; however, you'll need earplugs at night to drown out the traffic noise. The decor throughout is conjured from a mix of styles and includes hunter-green carpeting, floral wallpaper, wicker furniture, and wooden shutters. If you're traveling with your own car, know that designated parking spaces are limited and metered street parking is scarce. The inn is not located near the downtown core, but it's an easy ride by taxi; and if you're up for a little fresh air and exercise, you can walk to the wealth of great shops and restaurants along Union and Chestnut Streets. Greet the morning together over a continental breakfast served in the simple dining room.

$-$$$ AE, MC, V; no checks; www.edwardii.com.

FAIRMONT HOTEL & TOWER
●●❶

950 Mason St / 415/772-5000 or 800/527-4727
You may recognize the legendary 1907 Fairmont Hotel even if you've never been here—it's one of the most fabulous, and most photographed, classical hotel facades in the country. The hotel's extravagant lobby instantly

transports you to a bygone era with its original marble floors, crimson velvet couches and settees, extraordinary Corinthian marble columns trimmed with gold, and crystal chandeliers hanging from the vaulted ceiling. An $85 million renovation completed in 2001 restored the lobby to its original opulence and refurbished the 591 rooms. New furnishings and luxurious touches include goose-down pillows and large walk-in closets. The tasteful color schemes vary from charming French country–style yellow and blue to a pretty combination of pale green and melon; all are lovely. Not all rooms have views, however, so if you desire one, be sure to request it (as always, the more expensive the room, the better the view). Of the hotel's wealth of options, the newer Tower Rooms are the most romantic. Most have large picture windows that showcase stunning views of the distant bay. The inviting, pristine bathrooms have marble soaking tubs and glassed-in showers. The rooms in the main building are part of the hotel's designated historic area and thus have smaller bathrooms, but the ambience is authentic and the decor is undeniably charming. Within the hotel, there's a beauty salon, a barbershop, a shopping arcade, and even a pharmacy (yes, this place is big). For refreshments, head for the hotel's Polynesian-style Tonga Room for exotic tiki-bar cocktails or the Laurel Court Restaurant for fine dining. While the hotel's size means there is no dearth of cell-toting conference types roaming the halls, it's an easy proposition to carve out your own romantic niche in such a historic and beautiful setting.
$$$$ *AE, CB, DC, DIS, MC, V; checks OK; www.fairmont.com.* &

HOTEL DRISCO
❂❂❂❂

2901 Pacific Ave / 415/346-2880 or 800/634-7277
Perched at the peak of the regal Pacific Heights neighborhood, this lovely boutique hotel is the gem of any San Francisco trip. The exquisitely appointed rooms and suites, intimate yet relaxed atmosphere, and quiet residential location make this hotel extremely easy to fall in love with. Lovers can stroll hand in hand through the peaceful neighborhood while enjoying breathtaking city vistas, exploring nearby parks and shopping streets, and admiring the gilded mansions along the way. Afterward, return to the hotel's lovely sitting room for a wine and cheese reception, held each evening. The views from the rooms are certain to inspire kisses: depending on which room you choose, you'll be looking out onto the Golden Gate Bridge, the East Bay, or everything in between. All 43 guest accommodations were designed by the same interior decorator, who outfitted the sublime Ritz-Carlton (see review), so expect only the best. A tasteful color scheme of butter yellow, white, and pale green brightens the nicely sized rooms, which come equipped with classical European furnishings, CD stereos, plush robes, and two-poster beds covered with the softest of linens. Bright, private bathrooms grace most of the rooms, except for six that have

Dinners à Deux

In yet another boon for couples in search of the perfect San Francisco date, 2004 ushered in a resurgence of glamorous dining in the city, with a number of new restaurant openings not seen since the days of the dot-com boom. Of the highly anticipated destinations opening to fanfare just as this book was going to press, two spots struck us as especially promising for romance. **Tartare** (550 Washington St; 415/434-3100), set in the cozy, golden-lit intimate space that was formerly the beloved Elisabeth Daniel, offers a quiet, upscale dining backdrop for its wildly innovative French-inspired cuisine. **Frisson** (244 Jackson St; 415/956-3004) is a cosmopolitan supper club–style restaurant with a dazzling modernist interior dressed in luxe crimson and gold, a menu of small plates that meld French and California cuisine, an enticing list of cocktails, and late-night dining and music until 1:30am for couples who don't want the fun to end.

Of course, there are also many San Francisco restaurants that have proven their worth time and again—too many to list here, in fact, although we can mention a few more of our amorous favorites. If you want to lock lips over the city's best martinis, step into the sexy supper-club ambience of **Bix** (56 Gold St; 415/433-6300), decorated with retro 1920s charm, massive silver columns, art deco–style lighting, and exquisite hand-carved Honduran mahogany; request a table on the quiet intimate mezzanine if you decide to stay for an indulgent (and expensive) dinner. For some of the city's most ornate French haute cuisine and an exclusive, sexy, candlelit ambience, put on your best date outfits and adjourn to the Hotel Palomar's (see Romantic Lodgings) intimate **Fifth Floor** (12 4th Street; 415/348-1555), where an appetizer of frothy lobster cappuccino (lobster broth emulsified with chestnuts, prawns, and sautéed lobster) indicates the inventiveness of the cuisine to come.

When the mood is more casual and what you have on your mind is simply excellent food, there are many options. The ever-popular Mission District restaurant, **Delfina** (3621 18th St; 415/552-4055), is a mainstay for its flawlessly fresh regional Italian cuisine; while the sleek, often noisy interior lacks intimacy, the pristine flavor of the food is pure romance. In North Beach, the acclaimed **Rose Pistola** (532 Columbus Ave; 415/399-0499) also serves up delicious Italian fare with a slightly more rustic bent, and an even more bright and gregarious atmosphere. The tables in the back of the restaurant are more intimate, and if you want to linger and kiss for hours, go ahead—the menu is served until 1am on weekends.

Continued on next page

For more old-fashioned fare and views that go on for miles, visit the **Carnelian Room** (555 California St; 415/433-7500), set 52 stories above street level at the top of the Bank of America Building. Go at dusk, order champagne and enjoy the dizzying views of the city (men, wear your sports coats). More sky-high seats are found at the elegantly appointed, glass-walled **Top of the Mark** lounge (Mark Hopkins Hotel; 999 California St; 415/392-3434), with live music Tuesday, Wednesday, Friday, and Saturday that ranges from romantic jazz piano to big six-piece bands that will entice you to dance the night away.

Come back to earth and journey west to the modest Richmond neighborhood to discover the city's most exotic and romantic Moroccan restaurant, **Aziza** (5800 Geary Blvd; 415/752-2222). Settle into a cobalt-blue alcove nestled beneath carved arches while the servers douse your hands with warm water in Moroccan tradition before you dine; belly dancers undulate to strains of Arabian music for your entertainment. Share Moroccan-spiced prawn tagine or lavender-honey braised squab, chased with "fez fizz" cocktails (champagne with pomegranate puree), and finish with house-made walnut–cardamom crunch ice cream (and a kiss in the candlelight).

For the ultimate prelude—or conclusion—to any romantic evening on the town, visit **Bubble Lounge** (714 Montgomery St; 415/434-4204), where the extensive selection of bubbly from around the world is served in candlelit salons furnished with satin couches, overstuffed chairs, rich mahogany, and marble tables.

detached bathrooms across a semiprivate hallway. (Guests are compensated for the inconvenience with either outstanding views or discounted rates.) Room 404A, a corner suite with an extraordinary view of Pacific Heights' mansions and the surrounding neighborhood, is particularly enchanting. In the morning, venture down to the elegant dining room, find a table for two, and enjoy a complimentary continental breakfast. Later, you can pay a visit to the nearby health club with indoor swimming pool or head into town via the complimentary drop-off limousine service (available mornings only). This beautiful hotel is the best reason yet we've found for visiting San Francisco without motorized transport: parking here is a real challenge. Even if you're lucky enough to find a spot, you'll have to move the car every three hours (8am–6pm Mon–Fri). Of course, once you ensconce yourselves within the Hotel Drisco's regal appointments, leaving may be the last thing on your minds.

$$$ *AE, DC, DIS, MC, V; no checks; www.hoteldrisco.com.* &

HOTEL MAJESTIC
◐◐◐

1500 Sutter St / 415/441-1100 or 800/869-8966
Located in posh Pacific Heights, this gleaming white five-story hotel, formerly the home of a turn-of-the-20th-century railroad magnate, is as grand as the surrounding neighborhood. The lobby instantly sets a mood of old-world elegance with towering ceilings, antique tapestries and lighting, beautifully framed oil paintings, and French Empire furnishings. You may want to stop at the Avalon Bar, sip a cocktail at the genuine 19th-century French mahogany bar, and admire the exquisite (and rare) butterfly collection adorning the walls. But don't flutter here too long—the real romance is waiting for you upstairs in the 57 elegantly historic rooms. The centerpiece of each of the One Bedroom Suites is a four-poster king bed made up with plump feather pillows, fine linens, and a plush down comforter. The sleeping arrangements become less ornate as the rooms descend in price: the Junior Suites offer canopy queen beds, and the basic Superior Rooms offer full- and queen-size beds without posters or canopies. Lace curtains, subtle color schemes, large and light marble bathrooms (many with claw-foot tubs), and beautiful antiques and antique reproductions create an upscale, turn-of-the-century ambience, while the gas fireplaces in some of the rooms add an instant glow. Small crystal chandeliers hang in every room, and bay windows allow in ample sunlight, especially in the corner rooms, each of which features a semicircular wall of tall windows. Only two points detract from the elegance of this architecturally stunning hotel. First, busy Gough Street runs beneath it, and the windows aren't soundproof. (Of course, the latter tends to be the case in most places you stay in San Francisco.) To avoid undue traffic noise, we recommend the rooms that face somewhat quieter Sutter Street. Also, there are occasional decor slip-ups, such as exposed extension cords or less-than-perfect paint jobs in the rooms; fortunately, recent renovations in some of the guest rooms and bathrooms have put some wrongs right. After breakfast in the dining room, stroll through Lafayette Park, at the corner of Octavia and Sacramento, a few blocks north of the hotel. Panoramic views of San Francisco await you, along with well-tended gardens and sloping lawns.
$$$–$$$$ AE, DC, DIS, MC, V; no checks; www.thehotelmajestic.com.

HOTEL MONACO
◐◐◐◐

501 Geary St / 415/292-0100 or 800/214-4220
As you cross the threshold of this French-inspired luxury hotel, conveniently located around the corner from the theater district, Union Square, and the cable car, you'll feel truly transported, and not just because the hotel's front desk mimics an old-fashioned steamer trunk. In every detail, large and small, the designers of this hotel have created a showpiece. In the front

lobby, you'll find a sweeping marble staircase, leafy potted palms, and an ornate chandelier hanging from a cathedral ceiling frescoed with a painting of hot-air balloons aloft in the clouds. Unwind in one of the plush armchairs set next to the blazing fireplace. Or adjourn to the cozy common room richly decorated with flamboyant fabrics, where modern artwork graces the terracotta walls and a fireplace casts a warm glow; wine and cheese are served every afternoon in this handsome room. The 201 extravagant guest rooms are works of art in themselves, full of exotic details: boldly striped bed canopies, Chinese-inspired armoires, bamboo writing desks, old-fashioned decorative luggage, and wallpaper in green and yellow pin-stripes are just a few examples. Seventeen suites offer jetted two-person Jacuzzi tubs; showerheads with massage options are in the rest of the rooms. The Grand Cafe, which serves trendy California-French cuisine, is set in a boldly redesigned former ballroom with spherical chandeliers—but the open kitchen and echoing cathedral ceilings, while lovely, create unwelcome noise and distraction. A full-service fitness center and spa are available to guests; newspaper delivery, morning coffee, afternoon tea and cookies, and evening wine reception are provided; and Nintendo is featured in every room—although we can think of better games to play in such surroundings. $$$–$$$$ AE, DC, DIS, MC, V; no checks; www.monaco-sf.com. &

HOTEL PALOMAR
◐◐◐◖

12 4th St / 415/348-1111 or 877/294-9711
Not only does this glamorous, modern hotel offer a terrific central location at the crossroads of downtown (great for walking, and only two blocks from Tiffany & Co., should you want to breakfast there), its mood is surprisingly intimate given its 198 guest rooms. The rooms are located between the fifth and ninth floors of the building to create a feeling of lofty urban refuge. Hotel Palomar's signature leopard-print carpeting adds a wild, sexy touch to the elegant rooms, where subtle color schemes enlivened with rich splashes of emerald and ruby invite you to relax. Polished wooden headboards adorned with velvet squares along with plush down comforters give the beds extra appeal. In the sparkling-clean bathrooms, you'll find plush robes, tile floors, granite countertops, and ivory and silver wallpaper. Upgrade to a luxury room, and you'll enjoy a separate glassed-in shower stall and deep Fuji spa tub as well. Spa tubs are also featured in the large and expensive suites, and sofas beckon in their stylish lounging areas (although the formal dining tables seem more suited to conference calls than to kissing). In all the rooms, televisions are hidden away in armoires, and you'll also find CD players and the usual business-traveler amenities, such as high-speed Internet connection. Other amenities include a fitness center, 24-hour room service, valet parking, in-room spa services, and complimentary morning coffee and the daily paper. Modern French haute cuisine (read: deciphering the menu

can take some work) and intimate, exotic surroundings are found at the hotel's acclaimed restaurant, the Fifth Floor (415/348-1555; www.fifthfloor .citysearch.com). The dark wood paneling and candlelit ambience at the restaurant bar make it a romantic spot for an aperitif, or, better yet, an early nightcap (book well in advance if you wish to stay for dinner). $$$-$$$$ *AE, MC, DIS, V; checks OK; www.hotelpalomar.com.*

HOTEL TRITON
❍❍❍

342 Grant Ave / 415/394-0500 or 800/433-6611
If Alice had stayed in a hotel room in Wonderland, it might have looked something like the Hotel Triton. This establishment's bazaarlike, jewel-colored interior simply must be seen to be believed. From curvaceous chairs shimmering in gold silk taffeta to a pastel mural portraying mythic images of sea life, triton shells, and human figures, every detail here is part of the pageant. Even the in-house phones are bedecked with faux jewels. The colorful modern exotica continues in the 140 guest rooms, where beds are strewn with oversize pillows and have upholstered headboards adorned with anything from fluffy clouds to bold navy-and-khaki stripes. Walls are splashed with checkerboard patterns or sponge-painted pink and iridescent gold. All of the rooms have up-to-date amenities to make your stay exceedingly comfortable, if amusingly eccentric. On the seventh floor, otherwise known as the EcoFloor, the ecologically minded meets the superchic. Here, everything that can be is made from recycled, biodegradable, or organically grown materials: rooms come equipped with water- and air-filtration systems and all-natural linens, as well as biodegradable soaps and shampoos. Hotel Triton also offers seven stellar designer suites. The Jerry Garcia Suite is a studio-style room filled with the musician's autographs, favorite colorful silks, and a DVD of a live performance. The Wyland Suite boasts colorful seascapes and a tropical-fish aquarium; and Suzan Briganti's Love Letter Suite might inspire you to pen a few of your own. Freshly baked cookies, along with complimentary wine and beer, are served in the lobby each evening. Once in a while, a Tarot card reader shows up to tell fortunes. $$$ *AE, DC, DIS, MC, V; checks OK; www.hoteltriton.com.* &

HUNTINGTON HOTEL
❍❍❍❍

1075 California St / 415/474-5400 or 800/227-4683
The elegant Huntington Hotel, perched on the upper tier of Nob Hill, earns our highest recommendation for kissing in San Francisco. This isn't just because the fabulous on-site Nob Hill Spa offers by far the most incredibly romantic couples' massage in the city. It's also due to the Huntington's peerless grown-up ambience, untainted by the commotion and crowds that can so quickly ruin the mood when you're seeking romance. Originally

built as a luxury apartment building, the Huntington has 140 commodious, wonderfully quiet rooms marked by individuality and romantic flair. An independently owned hotel with no corporate-set standards on decor, its owners have invited noted designers to transform the guest rooms into works of art. Styles range from contemporary Asian to English classical, all with luxurious touches at every turn: marble foyers and bathrooms, large windows that let in the crisp San Francisco air, ultracomfortable beds, and enough space to make these rooms some of the largest in town. Large mirrors, artwork fit for museums, minibars or kitchenettes, and TVs hidden within armoires are other pleasing features. Guests are offered complimentary tea or sherry service in their rooms upon arrival—perfect for unwinding in privacy. Many of the rooms enjoy views of well-groomed Huntington Park, across the street, where the sight of locals doing tai chi in the morning inspires guests to slow down their pace, too. For a dazzling vista, book a city-facing room and see the skyline in all its glory. The Huntington's room rates may be high, but you truly get what you pay for here. You'll want for nothing, and the gracious staff ensures that your stay will be private and thoroughly comfortable. Don't miss the chance to dive into the spa's indoor pool and Jacuzzi, accessible to all guests and overlooking city views through floor-to-ceiling windows. An intimate outdoor deck shares this same sparkling vista. (On our visit, we spotted a couple who'd just had a swim lounging outside while having a spa lunch delivered; it was plain to see that kissing was in their immediate future.) Come evening, get cozy at the Big Four Restaurant (415/771-1140), where the "gentleman's club" look of mahogany walls, deep green leather banquettes, and historical photos is given a romantic twist with soft lighting and elegant appointments. The best spot for cuddling is next to the crackling fire in the cozy lounge. In this alluring location, listen to the soft piano music and enjoy a nightcap before retiring to your marvelous accommodations.
$$$$ *AE, DC, DIS, MC, V; checks OK; www.huntingtonhotel.com.* &

THE INN SAN FRANCISCO
❂❂❂
943 S Van Ness Ave / 415/641-0188 or 800/359-0913
When you see the rather gritty urban neighborhood surrounding this hotel, you may want to turn your car in the other direction. But the moment you cross the threshold of this pristine Italianate Victorian mansion, you'll forget the less-than-inspired sights outside: it actually takes several moments to soak up the truly opulent mood in the front parlors, furnished with antiques, medallion ceilings and chandeliers, hunter green walls, marble fireplaces, and glowing white orchids and freshly cut flowers. The location away from the city's downtown core even has some benefits: the chance to stay in the lively Mission District, where San Francisco's trendiest restaurants and bars share space with taquerias and markets that reflect its Latino heritage; and

the value—rooms this beautiful could easily be twice the price at a fancier address. Polished dark wood wainscoting and historical photographs and maps in the hallways accompany you on the journey to your room, where you'll find antiques, marble sinks, and polished brass fixtures. For romance, choose one of the well-appointed "master bedrooms," where special touches include claw-foot tubs, fireplaces, and bay windows. (Those on the second floor are especially spacious.) Two of these are "Jacuzzi suites" equipped with whirlpool tubs; the pale blue Oriental Suite is especially elegant, although its location above a busy street means that passing cars are audible. The largest accommodation is the Garden Cottage, with two bedrooms, a gas fireplace, a Jacuzzi tub in the bathroom, glowing hardwood floors, and an old-fashioned stove in the fully equipped kitchen. The "cozy" or "intermediate level" rooms are budget-friendly but simply not as romantic (some lack private baths and most are quite small indeed); it's worth the step up to get the additional amenities. If street noise bothers you, request a room in back overlooking the garden. Chocolate truffles, fresh flowers, and feather beds are just a few of the extra-special touches. Equally memorable is the redwood hot tub set in a fern-trimmed gazebo in the gorgeous back garden (it's in plain sight, so you'll need to wait for cover of darkness to kiss). A generous breakfast buffet of freshly squeezed juice, fruit, home-baked breads, and other goodies is served in the parlor. What's least impressive is the parking situation; spaces are limited, and if you aren't lucky enough to get one, you'll have to park on the street (remove the valuables from your car). But it's all just part of the experience at an establishment that prides itself on being a "city inn" rather than a "country inn."
$–$$$ *MC, V; checks OK; www.innsf.com.*

MANDARIN ORIENTAL
❂❂❂
222 Sansome St / 415/276-9888 or 800/622-0404
We debated over whether to include this exclusive business-oriented hotel in our listings, but not for long. The Mandarin Oriental has million-dollar, mile-high views: how could it not, after all, when guest rooms start on the 38th floor? With such unparalleled scenery from your windows, you'll quickly forget the Financial District location and the suit-and-tie crowd down in the lobby. You can also overlook the outrageous room rates if you visit on Friday and/or Saturday nights, when rates tend to drop. Unobstructed city and bay views from huge windows are standard in all of the ample 158 rooms and suites, so just choose your preferred compass point, and you'll be able to gaze at it to your hearts' content with the in-room binoculars. (Some rooms even have peekaboo ocean views—when the weather cooperates.) The rooms are decorated with soothing sage, crimson, gold, and cream colors; luxurious marble baths delight the senses, while extra touches such as Thai silk slippers presented at turndown, silk-covered headboards,

260-thread-count Egyptian cotton sheets, and plush robes make clear why the Mandarin Oriental is a first-class hotel. If you want to soak in more than just the view, book one of the Mandarin Rooms, where the bathtub fronts a floor-to-ceiling window. Better yet, enjoy the views from your private terrace in the Taipan or Oriental Suites. If the height of these suites doesn't make you dizzy, their price tags certainly will. Descending from cloud nine can be difficult, but back on earth you'll find a state-of-the-art fitness center and the hotel's restaurant, Silks (415/986-2020). The exceedingly formal dining room tends to cater to executives, but the subdued decor is brightened by lavish floral arrangements, bold modern art, and colorful handblown-glass wall sconces and chandeliers. The California cuisine is excellent and, best of all, the tables are set far enough apart to encourage intimacy. *$$$–$$$$ AE, DC, DIS, MC, V; checks OK (for lodgings only); www.mandarinoriental.com.* &

NOB HILL LAMBOURNE
◐◐
725 Pine St / 415/433-2287 or 800/274-8466
After a day spent exploring the city and walking up and down hills, you'll be happy to return home to this boutique hotel, which offers soothing relief from the world outside with only 14 rooms and 6 suites. Guests are ensured privacy and attentive service that is concentrated on your health, both mental and physical. An on-site spa treatment/massage room, a complimentary healthy continental breakfast, organic minibars in the rooms, and all-natural, chemical-free cleaning products are just a few of the "wellness" touches here. Quiet, serene, and simple in its decor, the Nob Hill Lambourne offers pleasing neutral color schemes of white, ivory, and beige along with comfortable, contemporary furnishings, as well as kitchenettes, TV/VCRs, and high-tech stereos. Although standard in style, bathrooms come equipped with features designed to promote relaxation and romance: temperature-controlled deep tubs, waffle-weave robes, homeopathic remedy bars, and built-in stereo speakers. The hotel's six suites offer even more perks. Each suite features a separate parlor, in-room exercise equipment, and a hard-to-find amenity in San Francisco: a tiny (no view) veranda off the bedroom that perfectly fits two. There's also a wine and cheese reception every evening and evening turndown service (with antioxidant vitamins instead of chocolates). Best of all, the central location three blocks from shopping in Union Square and two blocks from the top of scenic Nob Hill makes it convenient to explore the city on foot. *$$$ AE, MC, V; checks OK; www.jdvhospitality.com.*

PETITE AUBERGE
●●

863 Bush St / 415/928-6000 or 800/365-3004
All of the 26 guest rooms at this cheerful downtown hotel—even the 8 smallest—are endowed with French country–inspired charm and comfort. Lace window treatments, floral wallpaper, and muted color schemes inspire serenity, and the staff's attention to detail guarantees satisfaction. Eighteen rooms feature fireplaces, and the deluxe Petite Suite has its own private entrance, Jacuzzi tub, and patio (of course, don't be expecting a petite price). The largest rooms face Bush Street and, thus, are more subject to street noise. Fairly effective soundproofing efforts have been made throughout the inn, but the smaller rooms at the back of the hotel are still the quietest. Evening turndown brings chocolates on your pillow, and in the morning, the scent of freshly baked goodies wafts up from the kitchen. The generous full breakfast is carefully prepared and served buffet-style in the French country dining room. (Late-afternoon wine and hors d'oeuvres are also offered here.) In the parlor, comfortable sofas and a glowing gas fireplace invite you to rest your weary feet after a long day of walking—which you'll surely be doing, given that Union Square and many other attractions are nearby. Once you feel refreshed, you can step out again to enjoy dinner at one of the countless downtown restaurants. If all the rooms are booked, ask about openings at the equally charming White Swan Inn (415/775-1755 or 800/999-9570), under the same ownership and also located on Bush Street, just a few doors down.
$$$ AE, MC, V; checks OK; www.jdvhospitality.com.

THE PRESCOTT HOTEL
●●●●

545 Post St / 415/563-0303 or 800/283-7322
While the Prescott is a bit too large to be considered truly romantic, the management succeeds at creating an intimate ambience nonetheless. A fire glows in an immense stone hearth in the hotel's elegant "living room," where beautiful flower arrangements, antique writing desks, comfortable chairs, and a collection of early California arts and crafts welcome guests. The hotel's 164 rooms are spread out between two connecting buildings. For a splurge, book one of the 46 rooms or 23 suites on the Executive Club Level, where you'll find the "hotel within a hotel" concept in full swing, with a private concierge, complimentary continental breakfast and evening cocktail reception, and free morning limousine service within the general area. You can even have stationary bicycles and rowing machines delivered to your room. And if that's not enough, complimentary head and neck massages are available from 5pm to 7pm in the Executive Club's lounge. Rich color schemes of hunter green, eggplant, and taupe, as well as cherrywood tables and antique-style armoires, decorate the Executive Club's guest rooms.

Bathrooms, while standard, are beautifully appointed with tasteful black and taupe colors, marble accents, and gold and pewter fixtures. Executive Club Suites are slightly more expensive but are larger and feature the added luxury of whirlpool tubs. The remaining 83 regular rooms and 9 deluxe suites are all impeccably stylish and comfortable and come equipped with every imaginable modern convenience, including color TV/VCRs, stocked bars and refrigerators, hair dryers, and terry-cloth robes. You'll have a newspaper delivered to your room, as well as access to the adjacent and newly renovated fitness facility. Roosting at the top of the Prescott is possibly the most extraordinary suite in the city: the Mendocino Penthouse (one of three luxury suites on the seventh floor). Its unbelievably high price tag is a little easier to swallow once you eye the rich Edwardian furnishings and hardwood floors in the parlor and bedroom, the grand piano in the formal dining room, the two wood-burning fireplaces, and the rooftop deck with its Jacuzzi tub and garden. But unless you're planning on breaking the bank, you might do better to save your splurging for Postrio (see Romantic Restaurants, below), located just off the hotel's lobby. Hotel guests get priority seating at this chic eatery with acclaimed California cuisine—a plus when things get busy.

$$$ AE, DC, DIS, MC, V; checks OK (for lodgings only); www.prescotthotel.com. &

THE RITZ-CARLTON, SAN FRANCISCO
ᴏᴏᴏᴏ

600 Stockton St / 415/296-7465 or 800/241-3333
The crème de la crème of San Francisco hotels, the Ritz is nothing short of fabulous. This neoclassical-style hotel on Nob Hill is quite simply the ideal destination when you're in the mood to be waited on, catered to, and delightfully spoiled. The moment you step into the polished marbled lobby, filled with rare china collections, exquisite 18th- and 19th-century furnishings, and soaring, dramatic floral arrangements, you'll feel inspired. From the expansive rose garden to the Persian carpets and Bohemian crystal chandeliers, everything is first class; the surroundings, service, and amenities embody old-fashioned elegance. Just off the foyer is the Lobby Lounge, a regal room with ornate chandeliers, floor-to-ceiling windows, and life-size portraits of aristocratic women. Here, guests can savor afternoon tea accompanied by the soothing melodies of a classical harp. Come evening, a sushi chef appears with an accompanying sushi cart and rolls out made-to-order delicacies for your enjoyment. All 336 rooms and suites feature antique-style furnishings, elegant window treatments, richly upholstered furniture, and Italian marble bathrooms with double sinks. Beds draped in silky 300-thread-count sheets, fully stocked honor bars, thick terry-cloth robes, high-speed Internet access, and in-room safes round out the amenities. Some rooms (though not many) have wonderful views of the city and the bay, but

your best bet is one of the quieter rooms overlooking the landscaped court-yard. The 42 spacious suites are the grandest, with separate dining, living, and sleeping rooms and private balconies, some of which offer glimpses of the city. In the 52 Ritz-Carlton Club rooms that line the eighth and ninth floors, guests are provided with a dedicated concierge and continuous culinary treats: a complimentary continental breakfast, midmorning snacks, an afternoon tea, cocktails and hors d'oeuvres, and late-evening cordials and chocolates. Should you want to combat any overindulgence, head for the in-house fitness center, complete with a fully equipped workout room, heated indoor pool, whirlpool, and spa. Massage therapy is also offered. Everything your hearts desire is at your fingertips when you stay at the Ritz, including two restaurants: the opulent Dining Room at the Ritz-Carlton (see Romantic Restaurants), and the more casual Terrace (415/773-6198), which serves excellent Mediterranean fare in a pleasant dining room adorned with handsome oil paintings. On sunny days, enjoy lunch or Sunday brunch in the Terrace's charming courtyard, complete with greenery, umbrellas, and white wrought-iron chairs and tables: this is one of the loveliest alfresco dining experiences in the city and a worthwhile stop even if you aren't staying overnight at the Ritz.
$$$$ *AE, DC, DIS, MC, V; no checks; www.ritzcarlton.com.*

Romantic Restaurants

ACQUERELLO
♥♥♥♦

1722 Sacramento St / 415/567-5432
In a city full of ritzy, trend-setting restaurants where showiness is taken to extremes, it's refreshing to find a place that allows elegance to speak for itself. At Acquerello, a lovely, upscale Italian hideaway, the round, two-person tables are simply adorned with linens, crystal, and china, while the butter-colored walls are softly illuminated by wall sconces and graced with watercolors of Italy. Pay attention to the details here, and you'll notice that Acquerello is housed in a former church. Ornate ironwork, a round stained-glass window, and vaulted ceilings that retain their original rustic wooden beams add a sense of history and serenity. Just as notable as the surround-ings is the service, which ranks close to flawless. Special touches include a complimentary aperitif and tableside decanting service for the restaurant's outstanding selection of Italian reds. You can't go wrong choosing any of such hearty, innovative pasta and entrée courses as decadent truffle-scented pasta with foie gras, fresh pappardelle with succulent rabbit ragout, seared venison loin chop with white polenta and fig sauce, or saffron-sauced grilled sea bass and mussels—all are superb. For an especially indulgent night, sample the enticing tasting menu of four courses paired with wines. End

the meal with the heavenly almond panna cotta adorned with caramel-Frangelico sauce.
$$$–$$$$ *AE, DIS, MC, V; no checks; dinner Tues–Sat; reservations recommended; full bar; www.acquerello.com.*

ANA MANDARA
◍◍◍

891 Beach St / 415/771-6800
With its exotic ambience and excellent, French-influenced Vietnamese cuisine, Ana Mandara, which opened in 2000, has blessed San Francisco's touristy Ghirardelli Square with a true taste of elegant romance. High ceilings, lush potted palms, ornate dark wood accents, and servers wearing traditional Vietnamese attire evoke the beauty of Vietnam, while cozy dining nooks and soft lighting create intimacy. The most romantic tables for two are on the slightly elevated terrace against the restaurant's back wall, where ornately carved wooden screens and shutters offer a sense of seclusion and privacy; tables for larger parties occupy the restaurant's main floor. The exquisite food seems only natural after you've been enjoying the elegant ambience. Start with the tender fish ceviche with toasted coconut and peanuts or the crispy spring rolls stuffed with crabmeat, shrimp, and shiitake mushrooms. Seafood dominates the entrée selections, and dishes such as seared lobster with lobster roe–cognac sauce served with ginger sticky rice are especially delicious; other choices, such as the grilled lemongrass chicken, are a bit less extraordinary. Side dishes, such as stir-fried snow pea sprouts or grilled Japanese eggplant, are priced separately but are worth ordering. Portions are more gemlike than generous—but that only helps justify the heavenly desserts, such as fried bananas served with a small pitcher of warm caramel-walnut sauce. Before dinner, consider heading to the elegant exposed-brick upper-level bar for live jazz and the signature Ana Mandara cocktail, flavored with refreshing lemongrass and mint. The restaurant's name is taken from a centuries-old Vietnamese love story in which a courageous warrior and a beautiful princess find refuge in a serene tropical sanctuary; in such surroundings, your own evening might just become a romantic legend.
$$$ *AE, DIS, DC, MC, V; no checks; lunch Mon–Fri, dinner every day; full bar; reservations recommended; www.anamandara.com.* ⅙

BOULEVARD
◍◍◍◍

1 Mission St / 415/543-6084
It takes more than an avalanche of praise from nationwide food critics to make a restaurant romantic. Fortunately, Boulevard's legendary food is served in an elegant and dynamic atmosphere, which makes it a fabulous place to wine and dine a date. Just don't arrive expecting coziness, because

the restaurant is big, bustling, and glamorous: after a spin through the revolving entrance door, you'll find yourselves standing under an impressive domed brick ceiling offset by a dizzying array of details, including hand-blown art nouveau glass light fixtures and thousands of brightly colored mosaic floor tiles. The dark wooden walls and chairs fit nicely with the decorative ironwork. In fact, the chic interior is classic San Francisco, from the well-heeled clientele to the windows that survey a sweeping view of the Embarcadero and the Bay Bridge. The tables by these windows are by far the most romantic. Alas, specific tables can only be requested, not actually reserved or guaranteed. (It doesn't hurt to mention to the reservationist if you're coming in for a romantic occasion such as an anniversary.) During the evening, the dining room's sheer size makes noise a factor (as does the adjacent open kitchen) so if you're partial to quiet, try to arrive early or late. But for gourmet-minded couples, the enticing fare will doubtless outweigh such drawbacks. Incredibly fresh ingredients characterize the well-chosen mix of seasonal California-style cuisine with inspired French and Italian influences. Fresh Dungeness crab salad, oysters, and sautéed foie gras with blood orange salad and Sauternes vinaigrette highlight the extensive appetizer list; the crispy calamari stuffed with piquillo peppers are also a showstopper. For main courses, you'll find classic dishes with exotic touches, from a wood oven–roasted pork chop with pistachios and pomegranates to a smoked bacon–wrapped duck breast served with apples, chestnuts, and an Italian chestnut soup. To cap off the evening, order the exotic tangerine cardamom crème brûlée and smooch your way through dessert.

$$$ *AE, DC, DIS, MC, V; no checks; lunch Mon–Fri, dinner every day; full bar; reservations recommended; www.boulevardrestaurant.com.* &

CAFÉ JACQUELINE
♥♥

1454 Grant Ave / 415/981-5565
Finding parking isn't an easy feat in North Beach, and in the interest of romance, we suggest that you arrive by taxi when dining in this famously charming neighborhood. (Nothing kills the mood like searching fruitlessly for a parking space.) Once you've arrived, you can sit back, relax, and enjoy the peaceful ambience at this unique restaurant, where the menu is comprised entirely of soufflés for two. What could be more romantic? The leisurely pace of the dinner, in addition to sharing the meal, creates an intimate mood. There's lots of time to whisper sweet nothings as you wait for your soufflé to be whipped up from scratch in the kitchen. (Try not to arrive absolutely starving, or the leisurely pace might get on your nerves.) The clean, somewhat sparse interior radiates simple charm, with high ceilings, closely spaced tables for two, and worn wood floors. Although the decor is a bit haphazard, the soft lighting creates a warm and inviting mood. You'll have no difficulty deciding what to order. The more goodies you want added

to your build-your-own soufflé—leeks, broccoli, prosciutto, mushrooms, extra Gruyère cheese—the more you pay. Some may find the prices a little high for a single soufflé dish, but keep in mind that each does serve two. Desserts keep the soufflés coming; you can choose from among such classic fillings as chocolate, Grand Marnier, lemon, and seasonal fresh fruit. $$$ *AE, DC, DIS, MC, V; no checks; dinner Wed–Sun; beer and wine; reservations recommended on weekends.*

CLEMENTINE
♥♥

126 Clement St / 415/387-0408
Set on predominately Asian Clement Street, where dozens of Japanese and Chinese restaurants and greengrocers share space, this darling French bistro is a tiny bit of France in the midst of San Francisco's Inner Richmond neighborhood (and not at all inconvenient for kissing couples who have spent the day exploring nearby Golden Gate Park). Unlike many of the big names downtown, this restaurant caters mainly to a neighborhood crowd, drawing them in with reasonable prices, consistently delicious food, and an elegant, inviting atmosphere. A copper bar, large gold-framed mirrors, and photographs of France all contribute to the tasteful decor, while butter-yellow walls and delicate wall sconces add softness. Banquettes lining the long walls create a slightly cramped seating area, and the tables are too close together; however, the smooth, unobtrusive, and excellent service more than compensates. Given this city's weather—which tends toward fog, rain, mist, and more fog, year-round—the French-inspired comfort food on the seasonally changing menu always hits the spot. Certain nights of the week bring an affordable and appealing (under $25) prix fixe menu if you dine before 7pm. Delicious entrées include the chicken stuffed with rosemary and anchovies served alongside a helping of delicate-yet-rich gratin potatoes *dauphinois*; sage-perfumed veal shank; juicy rack of lamb; and an outstanding dish of sautéed halibut with lobster risotto and matelote, a delicious red-wine reduction sauce. End the meal with the dainty but luscious warm chocolate cake crowned with coconut sorbet.
$$–$$$$ *AE, MC, V; no checks; dinner Tues–Sun; full bar; reservations recommended.*

THE DINING ROOM AT THE RITZ-CARLTON
♥♥♥♥

600 Stockton St / 415/773-6198
As we did, you may wonder if this dining room could possibly live up to the stellar reputation of the hotel in which it resides (see Romantic Lodgings). Well, after a meal here, you will wonder no more. You can be assured of service beyond reproach, peerlessly elegant surroundings, and some of the finest presentations of California cuisine in the Golden State. Although

formal, the mood is far from stuffy. All the right touches are in place—plush chairs, beautifully adorned tabletops, classical oil paintings, flowing fabrics, soft harp music, and glowing candlelight—yet somehow the atmosphere is warm and intimate rather than pretentious. Blond wood–paneled walls set off the rich red and gold interior. The gracious service, along with the kitchen's willingness to be flexible, demonstrate that the Dining Room aims to please. If it's a very special occasion, sample some bubbly from the custom-made champagne cart, which offers an array of champagnes and sparkling wines by the glass. You may order à la carte or choose from one of two chef-designed, six-course menus, one of which is vegetarian. The portions are generous for haute cuisine, and each course brings a new array of sensational flavors to the table. Under the guidance of the acclaimed former chef of Masa's, the cuisine is modern with a Japanese influence. Asian-inspired plates like sashimi of kampachi with abalone and watermelon radish are presented alongside traditional French offerings like sweetbread medallions or two types of foie gras. Characteristic courses for the six-course meal might include a salmon tartare with squid sashimi and sake gelee, decadent Maine lobster with sautéed heirloom tomatoes and basil oil, and veal tenderloin with wild mushroom risotto and shallot jus. Lucious yet light desserts such as cherry sorbet with muscat gelee provide a bright finish to an utterly sophisticated meal.
$$$–$$$$ *AE, DC, DIS, MC, V; no checks; dinner Tues–Sat; full bar; reservations required; www.ritzcarlton.com.*

FARALLON
◐◑◖

450 Post St / 415/956-6969
With 160 seats, this designer restaurant's mood isn't exactly intimate, but the seafood dishes are as innovative as the aquatic-themed decor, and couples might enjoy diving into its undersea world. Giant, handblown jellyfish chandeliers with glowing tentacles seemingly float beneath a sea-blue ceiling in the Jelly Bar cocktail lounge, where sculpted strands of kelp climb up illuminated pillars. The dining room continues the marine motif with huge sea-urchin chandeliers dangling from the arched ceiling with its elaborate painted design of bathing beauties. This dramatic backdrop sets off the upscale coastal cuisine. For starters, consider the delectable asparagus bisque with cardamom cream; truffled mashed potatoes with crab and salmon caviar artfully stuffed into a real sea-urchin shell; or the outstanding giant tiger prawns. Entrées change daily and might include ginger-steamed salmon and sea-scallop pillows with a prawn mousse or sautéed gulf prawns with potato risotto. While seafood dominates the menu, meat lovers will enjoy dishes such as a juicy grilled fillet of beef served with a potato galette, haricots verts, and black-truffle aioli. The well-trained staff can be slightly aloof, noise levels can detract from the ambience, and the prices on the

300-item wine list might make your head swim (if so, consider the two dozen–plus wines available by the glass). But despite such drawbacks, this restaurant is unique and should offer a memorable dining experience. $$$ AE, DC, DIS, MC, V; no checks; lunch Tues–Sat, dinner every day; full bar; reservations recommended; www.farallonrestaurant.com. &

FLEUR DE LYS
❤❤❤❤

777 Sutter St / 415/673-7779
Although an electrical fire damaged this hallowed establishment and closed it down for nearly a year, the original charm of this traditionally romantic French restaurant was restored for its 2002 reopening. Utterly secluded from the busy street outside, the impressive dining room is a perfect place to spend an enchanted evening together. The only possible drawback to dining here (if you can afford the indulgence) is that, on some weeknights, the corporate crowd can seem a bit prevalent. Fortunately, on the weekends, this is not true. Stepping into the dining room is an experience in plushness: 900 yards of floral fabric in rich hues of pomegranate and deep green drape the ceiling and walls, creating the illusion of dining beneath a big, beautiful tent. In the center of the room, a Venetian chandelier hanging from the pinnacle of the fabric spotlights a towering floral arrangement. Ornamental mirrors surround the dining room, reflecting the solicitous work of the highly professional staff. Some of the contemporary French dishes you'll taste here are near-miracles. Unlike a lot of celebrity chefs, the acclaimed chef here still works in his own kitchen, and this shows on the plate. Each intriguing dish is more decadent than the last. Begin by indulging in beluga caviar with parsnip blinis or curried cauliflower and lobster vichyssoise; continue with entrées such as seared scallops with melted leeks, caviar, and corn sauce with vanilla bean; foie gras and summer truffle–stuffed squab breasts served with squab confit ravioli and Sauternes-ginger sauce; or peppered filet mignon on braised endives with oven-roasted pears and pecans. For the finale, try an assortment of French cheeses served with tasty fig spread or a sweet dessert such as caramelized rum and chocolate crème brûlée or a classic Grand Marnier soufflé. Whether you opt for the three-, four-, or five-course menu—all of which allow you to select from the many different appetizers and entrées—each course is cooked to perfection and beautifully presented. There's even a stunning four-course prix fixe option for vegetarians. Just remember to make the required reservations well in advance of your projected dinner date—and to reconfirm them two days prior to dining. $$$–$$$$ AE, DC, MC, V; no checks; dinner Mon–Sat; full bar; reservations required; www.fleurdelyssf.com. &

FOREIGN CINEMA

⚫⚫

2534 Mission St / 415/648-7600
The eclectic Mission District is the barometer of what's hip in the world of San Francisco restaurants, and most of its dining destinations are too crowded and bustling to encourage intimacy. Yet even though Foreign Cinema isn't traditionally romantic, it is, in our opinion, one of the city's most intriguing and unique spots for a date. The concept behind this contemporary Mediterranean-inspired restaurant is to combine "dinner and a movie" in a single location: on one wall in a center courtyard, classic foreign films such as Fellini's *La Dolce Vita* and Bergman's *The Seventh Seal* are projected in all their grainy black-and-white glory. Not surprisingly, urban hipsters come here to check out each other as much as the films. The surroundings are industrial chic, with deliberately unfinished walls, exposed mechanical systems in the ceiling, a stark open kitchen, and hard surfaces throughout that don't exactly help combat the noise. You'll be able to hear the film, nevertheless, as drive-in-movie-style speaker boxes are placed at each table. It's the food and the cocktails, however, that take center stage here. While some of the dishes feel rushed and a bit uninspired (read: go with the wait staff's suggestions), there is much to entice you on the menu, from appetizers such as grilled calamari with green charmoula sauce or fresh oysters to entrées such as grilled rib-eye steak with romesco sauce and organic shell beans to the Spanish paprika–roast chicken and crispy Yukon potatoes. Ingredients are fresh and seasonal. For dessert, order the chocolate pot de crème with two spoons—now there's a happy ending.
$$–$$$ *MC, V; no checks; dinner every day; full bar; reservations recommended; www.foreigncinema.com.* ⚫

GARY DANKO

⚫⚫⚫⚫

800 North Point / 415/749-2060
For couples who enjoy gourmet indulgence, Gary Danko offers the most sought-after seats in the city. Situated in an unobtrusive building on the northern slope of Russian Hill, this upscale establishment serving French–New American cuisine has earned rave reviews for its outstanding food and service since its opening in 2001. We are happy to add our voice to the din of praise. A fresh, clean, modern aesthetic is visible everywhere in the restaurant, from the sleek banquettes to the stylish, silver-rimmed china. There's a wonderful sense of intimacy in the two small, adjoining dining rooms, which are trimmed with dark wood and ornamented with mirrors and impressive original paintings. Exquisite floral arrangements and tables topped with fresh roses and candles enhance the mood, which feels like a happy meeting of a ritzy gentleman's club and an elegant French restaurant. Service is truly impeccable, and recessed pinpoint lights over the table

illuminate your meal as it unfolds, contributing to the sense of showmanship. Given the surroundings, you might expect to encounter a fair amount of pretentiousness here, but the mood is actually quite friendly and warm. The only possible drawback is that the tables are close together, which might discourage you from sharing heartfelt sentiments; fortunately, you'll have plenty to discuss even if you just stick to what's on your plates. Diners may choose from the three-, four-, or five-course tasting menus, all of which offer an enticing array of seasonally changing dishes. For a decadent start, order an appetizer such as foie gras and duck confit terrine brightened with a Meyer lemon chutney. Entrées include a Moroccan-inspired dish of pan-fried snapper with saffron, olives, couscous, and harissa; olive-crusted lamb served with goat cheese polenta; or seared beef fillet with nettle risotto, asparagus, and morel mushrooms. Chocolate lovers won't want to miss the delicious chocolate desserts, although the flambéed bananas with dark rum and toffee ice cream, prepared tableside, offers the sweetest—and most theatrical—finish. Reservations—not easy to come by—are accepted up to two months in advance, so be sure to plan ahead.

$$$ *AE, DC, DIS, MC, V; no checks; dinner every day; full bar; reservations recommended; www.garydanko.com.* &

JARDINIÈRE
❍❍❍❶

300 Grove St / 415/861-5555
Champagne, so some say, is the elixir of love, and at this lively, swanky Civic Center restaurant, you'll be fairly swimming in it. An inverted "champagne-glass" dome twinkling with tiny lights that resemble bubbles sets the mood above the grand, two-story dining room, while the balcony railing posts are adorned with unusual lit-glass pewter-colored champagne buckets. You almost can't help but feel celebratory in such surroundings. Upstairs, away from the crowded entrance and busy cocktail bar, is where you'll find the highest romantic quotient. Lush aubergine velvet drapes, exposed-brick walls, and rose-colored wall sconces create a mood of timeless elegance, while booths and tables are spaced far enough apart to afford privacy for those sweet nothings the champagne will encourage you to whisper. Unfortunately, the music from the speakers can be a bit deafening, but later in the evening, when a jazz duo takes over, the decibel level drops and a sultry mood prevails. The kitchen's French-California cuisine is quite simply smashing. Appetizers are a strong point, especially the flavor-packed lobster, leek, and chanterelle strudel and the delicate kabocha squash ravioli with chestnuts and sage brown butter. For the main course, the seared scallops surrounded by mashed potatoes and a black-truffle sauce bring comfort food to a whole new level; other choices, such as loin of venison with juniper sauce or red wine–braised short ribs, are equally satisfying. Save room for one of the divine desserts, including a brown-butter walnut cake with crème fraîche

and homemade ice creams and sorbets. "Flights" (multiple tastings) of almost any specialty liquor your hearts could desire, including an impressive array of champagnes and sparkling wines, will make your celebration complete. $$$ *AE, DC, DIS, MC, V; no checks; lunch Mon–Fri, dinner, late-night menu every day; full bar; reservations recommended; www.jardiniere.com.* &

KHAN TOKE THAI HOUSE
♥♥

5937 Geary Blvd / 415/668-6654
If you're in the mood to play footsie with your beloved, this beautiful Thai restaurant in the Richmond District is the place to do it. It also happens to be one of the few restaurants in San Francisco where you can enjoy an exotic date at prices that won't melt your credit card. Following Thai tradition, you'll be asked to remove your shoes at the entrance (be sure to wear your best socks!). Although a chaotic mood often prevails in the tiny entryway, where patrons are piling up their shoes and waiting for their tables (even with reservations, it's not unusual to wait), any awkwardness is washed away when one of the gracious servers arrives to escort you to your table. After wending your way through the lavishly decorated dining room—complete with carved teak furnishings, Thai statues, and hand-woven Thai tapestries—you'll settle onto large pillows set on the floor around a low table (although you sit on the floor, most of the tables have space carved out beneath them so you can stretch out and don't have to sit cross-legged for the whole meal). There are also tables in the garden out back. Start with the fragrant *tom yam gong*, a delicious soup made with lemongrass, shrimp, mushrooms, and cilantro. Other appealing dishes include the prawns with hot chilis, mint leaves, lime juice, and lemongrass; the chicken with cashew nuts, crispy chilis, and onions; and the ground pork with fresh ginger, green onion, peanuts, and lemon juice. If the vast menu has you bewildered, simply opt for the multicourse dinner, which includes appetizer, soup, salad, two main courses, dessert, and coffee. An evening in such unique surroundings is likely to create more than a little heat, especially with all that shoeless playtime under the table. Couples should consider visiting on a weeknight when you can make a reservation; on busy Friday and Saturday nights, reservations are accepted only for parties of three or more.
$$ *AE, MC, V; no checks; dinner every day; beer and wine; reservations recommended.*

LA FOLIE
♥♦

2316 Polk St / 415/776-5577
You can't help but fall in love at first sight with this enticing, festive French restaurant. From outside, a soft glow illuminates the mullioned windows, and boxes of flowering plants hang from the second story. Inside, dreamy

white clouds adorn the sky-blue ceiling, a massive mirror frames the bar, and textured golden walls are hung with whimsical French marionettes, many posed within painterly frames. Snug tables for two are packed a little too close for comfort in the all-too-common San Francisco fashion. Thankfully, half-curtained windows help conceal the bustling sidewalk outside. Seating is also offered in the Green Room, a new addition with towering ceilings, hunter green walls, and more closely packed tables. The fabulous French food is exquisitely presented. If you're in the mood to splurge and want to sample a bit of everything, consider the Discovery menu, which allows you to choose five courses à la carte. There's also an enticing vegetarian's menu—a prix fixe feast of the freshest seasonal produce. Appetizers such as the velvety corn-and-leek soup or stuffed rabbit loin and entrées such as wild black bass with a leek and truffle-oil risotto or roasted venison served with a chestnut-celery root flan and caramelized apples won't fail to please. A classic French finish of assorted gourmet cheeses or a sweet fruit clafouti with chocolate sauce is bound to set the stage for kissing later on.
$$$–$$$$ *AE, DC, DIS, MC, V; no checks; dinner Mon–Sat; full bar; reservations recommended; www.lafolie.com.* &

LE CHARM
♥♥€

315 5th St / 415/546-6128
This intimate bistro south of Market Street offers one of the best values in French cuisine in the city—there simply aren't many places that offer an expertly prepared, professionally served three-course prix fixe menu for the price. Best of all, the interior ambience is romantic to boot (so you won't mind looking past the location on busy, industrial Fifth Street). Soft lighting illuminates the ocher and saffron walls in the dining room, while fresh flowers brighten the tables. Appetizers might include fricasee of escargot, a perfect French onion soup, or a seasonal salad of glazed figs with arugula and Roquefort cheese. For the entrée, your options might include duck confit, pan-roasted halibut with mussels and saffron velouté sauce, or a hearty leg of lamb. Desserts, which must be ordered with your meal so the kitchen has time to prepare them, are superb—but the tarte Tatin and the chocolate roulades are both especially kiss-worthy. The tiny but lovely outdoor patio is our hands-down favorite spot in San Francisco for an affordable alfresco lunch on a sunny afternoon. You'll linger for hours over the perfect plate of mussels and *pommes frites* or savory quiche Lorraine with green salad and perhaps a glass of chilled sauvignon blanc. Since San Francisco's warmest days are more apt to arrive in April or October than in August, you don't even have to wait for summer to seize this romantic opportunity.
$$ *AE, MC, V; no checks; lunch Mon–Fri, dinner Mon–Sat; wine and port only; reservations recommended; www.lecharm.citysearch.com.*

MASA'S
❂❂❂
648 Bush St / 415/989-7154 or 800/258-7694
Masa's reputation as one of the most romantic restaurants in San Francisco is well earned. It simply doesn't get more formal (or more expensive) than this. In fact, dining here is such a formal production that it may even distract you from each other—the only caveat we'd add to this restaurant's towering romantic reputation. Rich chocolate brown walls and shirred red Chinese silk lanterns set off well-spaced tables elegantly appointed with crystal, china, and silver. The moment you take your seat—on beautifully upholstered toile-covered chairs or a dark-chocolate mohair banquette—you'll find yourselves indulged and catered to almost to excess. With glasses of wine that cost more than your average entrée and entrées that cost more than the price of a good bottle of wine, this is to be expected. Luckily, if you're splurging, you won't be disappointed in the elegant French-California cuisine. To get a sense of Masa's idea of indulgence, note just a few of the characteristic offerings on the prix fixe menu: sautéed Bellwether Farm baby lamb chops accompanied with potato gnocchi and spring onions; farm-raised Davenport abalone served with hand-cut linguine; lobster ravioli with fava beans and beech mushrooms in a lobster-cream sauce; and potato-crusted Japanese halibut served with cinnamon-cap mushrooms and baby leeks. Desserts are equally astonishing, especially the decadent dark chocolate cake. You'll need to book your reservation several months in advance and back it up with a credit card. (And if you don't show or forget to cancel 48 hours prior, you'll be charged $50 per person and afterward sent a gift certificate for that amount.) If you're willing to pay these kinds of prices for three-, six-, or nine-course tasting menus, we can't think of a sexier, more polished place to wine and dine your beloved.
$$$ *AE, DC, DIS, MC, V; checks OK; dinner Tues–Sat; full bar; reservations required; www.masas.citysearch.com.* ♿

PANE E VINO
UNRATED
1715 Union St / 415/346-2111
This delightful Italian trattoria moved to a new location from its longtime address on Steiner Street just as this book was going to press. While we cannot vouch for the romantic quotient of the new dining room, we have every confidence that the new destination will maintain all the charm of the original (the ownership has not changed). It also offers the added benefit of more space, as well as an outdoor covered patio for alfresco dining. The menu will remain the same, with its emphasis on simple Italian classics: this means the food will remain delicious. The fresh pastas and the risotto of the day are always a good bet; you can also expect to find some excellent entrée choices, ranging from rack of lamb marinated in sage and rosemary

to the whole roasted fresh fish of the day. Desserts such as the luscious crème caramel or white chocolate pistachio gelato are the crowning touch. At its former location, we held the opinion that this restaurant should be renamed Pane e Vino e Amore! It remains for you to decide whether the new space can live up to the original, although our hunch is that the wonderful food and wine at this authentic Italian restaurant will sway you in its favor.
$$ *AE, MC, V; no checks; lunch, dinner every day; beer and wine; reservations recommended.* &

PLUMPJACK CAFE
●●◖

3127 Fillmore St / 415/563-4755
The whimsical name might lead you to assume this is a bright and silly place, but in fact it's just the opposite: a sophisticated dining room known for its showy clientele and stylized decor. If you like to kiss and be seen, this is the place for you. Decorated in a tasteful taupe and olive color scheme, the dining room features gold-leafed lights, ornate window treatments, and a towering central arrangement of elegant flowers. The large windows overlook fashionable Fillmore Street, and the closely spaced tables are draped with white linens. Even with such impressive decor, it's PlumpJack's Mediterranean-influenced California cuisine that will win your hearts. To start, sample a duck confit and lentil strudel or bruschetta topped with roasted beets, goat cheese, and garlic. Entrées are well-balanced and flavorful, whether you choose a pasta with caramelized onions, sun-dried cherries, and smoked chicken; risotto with smoked salmon and shiitake mushrooms; or perfectly roasted herb chicken breast with foie gras, hedgehog mushrooms, and spinach. The wine list is also impressive, but if you notice that your favorite vintage is missing, walk one block to the café's namesake wine store. Buy there, and the café will waive the corkage fee. With the delicious food, excellent wine selection, and innovative decor, PlumpJack is often plumb full; reservations for romance here are a must, even for lunch.
$$$ *AE, MC, V; no checks; lunch Mon–Fri, dinner every day; beer and wine; reservations recommended; www.plumpjack.com.* &

POSTRIO
●●

545 Post St / 415/776-7825
Postrio, located in the Prescott Hotel (see Romantic Lodgings, above), is an upbeat dinner spot for couples looking for a bit of excitement rather than quiet togetherness. Diners make their entrance down a grand sculpted-iron and copper staircase that fits in perfectly with the dramatic and colorful decor. The abundance of curvaceous metal accents, orb-shaped chandeliers, and bright fabric–finished booths are characteristic of the early-'90s style staked out by the restaurant's world-famous owner, Wolfgang Puck.

The quietest tables are on the mezzanine level, away from the often-noisy main dining room. The kitchen crafts an excellent hybrid of California-Asian-Mediterranean cuisine that includes such creations as grilled quail accompanied by spinach and a soft egg ravioli with port wine glaze; sautéed salmon with plum glaze, wasabi mashed potatoes, and miso vinaigrette; Chinese duck with mango sauce; and roasted leg of lamb with garlic potato purée and niçoise olives. The showstoppers on the dessert list range from a rich potato-pecan pie to a caramel pear tart with Grand Marnier crème fraîche. While this may not be the coziest and quietest spot, you can always kiss post-Postrio.

$$$ *AE, DC, DIS, MC, V; no checks; full bar; reservations recommended; www.postrio.com.* &

ZUNI CAFE
❂❂❂

1658 Market St / 415/552-2522
Zuni's two-tiered, exposed-brick dining room can get noisy, and the copper-topped bar in the glass-walled lounge downstairs is often surrounded by a swinging cocktail scene, but though it might not sound like a place for romance, it is: few restaurants in the city deliver a terrific date night as reliably as this time-honored establishment. Its surefire charms include outstanding food and a casual elegance that captures San Francisco at its best. The talent in the kitchen is exacting, yet the dishes are free of the exotic ingredients and fussy techniques that can make fine dining in this town a hit-and-miss proposition. Instead, the upscale Mediterranean-influenced food on the menu somehow manages to be both divinely simple and supremely sophisticated. The Caesar salad is the best you'll find anywhere, and the perfectly roasted chicken for two on a bed of delicious Tuscan bread salad is a natural for kissing couples; it might just turn out to be the best chicken you've ever tasted. Other savory delights include the plate of mild, house-cured anchovies sprinkled with olives, celery, and Parmesan cheese; polenta with delicate mascarpone; and the grilled rib-eye steak accompanied by sweet white corn seasoned with fresh basil. At lunchtime and after 10pm, you can get some of the best burgers in town here, served on focaccia with aioli and house pickles (be sure to order a side of the perfect shoestring fries). Service is professional if not always warm or friendly. Just don't arrive expecting to find quiet—even on the least busy weeknights, Zuni draws an enthusiastic crowd. Night owls can find some degree of quiet with a late dinner (served until midnight Tuesday through Saturday).

$$$ *AE, MC, V; no checks; lunch, dinner Tues–Sun; full bar; reservations recommended.* &

MARIN

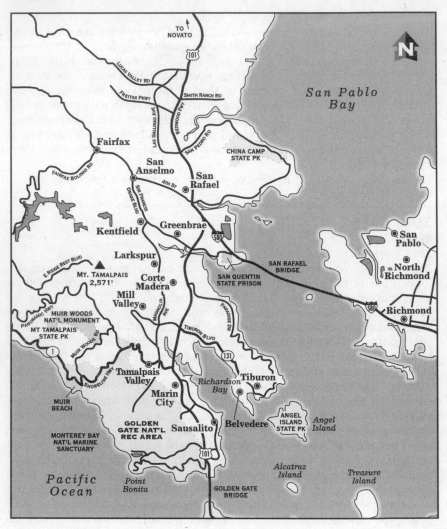

"To be thy lips is a sweet thing and small."
—E. E. CUMMINGS

# MARIN

Good things come in small packages, and as the third-smallest county in California, Marin is a small, beautifully wrapped package full of good things—and romantic surprises. If your starting point is San Francisco, the journey brings its own rewards, including unparalleled views as you travel across the famously scenic Golden Gate Bridge. If you avoid rush hour, it takes less than 30 minutes to drive from the crowded urban streets of San Francisco to the picturesque waterfront towns of Sausalito and Tiburon or the forested hills of Mill Valley and Larkspur. From luxurious establishments such as spas and chic boutiques to hiking trails in the beautiful Marin Headlands—which feature breathtaking views of the Pacific and San Francisco—Marin County's offerings are generous and diverse. The region encompasses the Golden Gate National Recreation Area, which contains more than 70,000 acres of protected coastline, pristine woodland, mountains, rugged hillsides, and meticulously maintained city parks. It is hard to believe that such a massive nature refuge exists so close to San Francisco; the urbanites do make good use of it, though, so come prepared for traffic and crowds on beautiful summer weekends. One way to get to Marin without getting stuck in traffic is to take the Golden Gate Ferry (see Access and Information in the Sausalito and Mill Valley chapters), which departs from the San Francisco Ferry Building at the foot of Market Street and terminates in either Larkspur or Sausalito. Take the ferry during off-peak hours on weekdays—although even when the boat is crowded with commuters, the outdoor ferry deck provides a delightful vantage point from which to view the Bay Area.

Marin enjoys a temperate climate year-round, but the weather changes quickly from one location to the next. Expect cool, foggy mornings near the bay and the ocean; the central part of the county is located in a sun belt. Spring and fall can be the best seasons of the year along the coast: southern Marin might be socked in with fog while the sun shines brightly over West Marin beaches. Dress in layers, and bring comfortable walking shoes.

SAUSALITO AND TIBURON

ROMANTIC HIGHLIGHTS

Just a short drive or romantic ferry ride from San Francisco, the quaint seaside villages of Sausalito and Tiburon beckon with the promise of a pleasant escape. This region also boasts some of the Bay Area's most romantic outdoor attractions, including the scenic Marin Headlands and many beautiful and secluded waterfront parks and beaches.

The town of **Sausalito**, with its hillside mansions and paved promenade, is reminiscent of a Mediterranean-style village—but one that also offers spectacular views of Angel Island, Alcatraz, and the San Francisco skyline. In summer, hordes of visitors descend on the town's main street, which is lined with expensive boutiques, upscale art galleries, and T-shirt vendors and ice cream shops. However, the calming sight of ferries and kayakers crossing the bay, the joyful noise of frolicking seals, and the chance to enjoy the fresh air more than compensate for the touristy backdrop.

You're more likely to find quiet moments in the smaller hamlet of **Tiburon** (although on summer weekends it too can draw crowds). Even better, it has the reputation for being the Bay Area's sunny spot. Often when other parts of San Francisco and Marin County are veiled in fog, Tiburon is basking in sunshine. You'll want to explore the town's winding streets for some upscale shopping, have an alfresco lunch at **Guaymas** (see Romantic Restaurants, below), or visit the **Windsor Vineyards** tasting room (72 Main St; 800/214-9463; www.windsorvineyards.com; open every day).

To really enjoy the fresh air and the views, go for a hand-in-hand stroll. Near the Tiburon ferry landing (the Blue and Gold fleet docks right in town; see Access and Information, below) Shoreline Park offers benches with a gorgeous view. If you're seeking more seclusion and plenty of strolling and picnicking turf, continue northeast of the ferry landing along Paradise Drive to reach **Paradise Beach Park**. This quiet, wooded little corner of the world overlooks the distant hills beyond the bay and the San Rafael Bridge. Depending on the time of day and the season, this place could be yours alone.

For a scenic outdoor stroll laced with birdsong, visit the **Tiburon Audubon Center and Sanctuary** (376 Greenwood Beach Rd; 415/388-2524; www.tiburonaudubon.org; 9am–5pm Mon–Fri, call for weekend hours). A short, self-guided trail leads up to the crest of a hill for a scenic panorama of Angel Island, San Francisco, Sausalito, and the coastal mountains. The center is also home to the Lyford House, a charmingly restored Victorian by the water that hosts weddings.

For the ultimate in outdoor romance, explore some of the attractions in the 15-square-mile **Golden Gate National Recreation Area**. The Marin

Headlands **Visitor Center** (415/331-1540; www.nps.gov/goga; open every day; from Hwy 101 traveling north or south, take Alexander Ave/Marin County exit) has maps and touring ideas and can tell you everything you need to know to plan your outdoor excursion. We have two favorite kissing spots here. First is the **Marin Headlands**, where you can soak up outstanding views of the famous Golden Gate Bridge. Intrepid romantics can walk a winding road that leads to the water's edge or hike inland to find secluded picnic spots on the grass. Another wonderfully romantic spot is **Rodeo Beach**; on weekdays before summer vacation releases eager kids from the classroom, you might even have this marvelous place to yourselves. Dozens of hiking trails lead over the varied terrain, ultimately leading to breathtaking views of rolling hills and dramatic cliffs. Bird Island, just a short distance from shore, is often blanketed with fluttering white seabirds.

To expand the variety and terrain of your day hikes, you might also consider an outing to **Mount Tamalpais State Park** and **Muir Woods National Monument** (for more information, see Romantic Highlights in the Mill Valley chapter). We have only one reservation about these spots: you must be prepared to contend with crowds on weekends—particularly on clear summer days.

Access and Information

Two major airports provide access to Marin County. **San Francisco International Airport** (SFO; 650/821-8211; www.flysfo.com) is 34 miles away, and **Oakland International Airport** (OAK; 510/563-3300; www.oakland airport.com) is 19 miles from Marin. **Marin Door to Door** (415/457-2717; www.marindoortodoor.com) provides daily 24-hour service to San Francisco and Oakland airports.

Two major bridges connect Marin to the greater Bay Area. The **Golden Gate Bridge** provides access to and from San Francisco (pedestrians and bicyclists can use the bridge's sidewalks); the southbound toll is $5. **The Richmond–San Rafael Bridge** connects the county to the East Bay; the westbound toll is $2. Most Marin visitors travel north to south using **Highway 101** (the central artery) or coastal **Highway 1**, with its near-legendary grades, narrow winding roads, and gorgeous views.

If you're driving to Sausalito from San Francisco, immediately after crossing the Golden Gate Bridge, turn right on Alexander Avenue, which after about a mile turns into Bridgeway, the main drag through the center of town. For more information contact the **Sausalito Visitor Center** (415/332-0505; www.sausalito.org).

Travel by water is also an option: ferry service is offered by the **Golden Gate Transit System** (415/455-2000; www.goldengate.org). Ferries run daily between the Larkspur Landing Terminal and Sausalito to San Francisco's

Ferry Building and Fisherman's Wharf. The **Blue and Gold Fleet** (Pier 41, Fisherman's Wharf; 415/705-5555; www.blueandgoldfleet.com) runs to and from Sausalito and Tiburon.

The **Marin County Convention & Visitors Bureau** (1013 Larkspur Landing Circle, Larkspur, CA 94939; 415/499-5000; www.visitmarin.org) is an excellent resource for information on all destinations in Marin County.

Romantic Lodgings

CASA MADRONA HOTEL & SPA
●●●●

801 Bridgeway, Sausalito / 415/332-0502 or 800/567-9524
Casa Madrona's impressive property spreads out over a large portion of a residential hillside overlooking sparkling Sausalito Bay. As you climb to your accommodations—or the full-service luxury spa—on tiered walkways enfolded by greenery, this terraced hotel will set you dreaming. Describing all 63 rooms here would almost require a book in itself, so suffice it to say that most of the accommodations offer romantic amenities such as fireplaces, private decks with brilliant sunlit harbor views, and seductive soaking tubs. A major renovation in 2002 added a new wing of 31 contemporary guest rooms and suites, all with sunken tubs and most with private balconies overlooking the Sausalito waterfront. The better the view, the higher the rates: the garden and courtyard rooms are the least expensive, followed by the bay-view rooms and the one-bedroom suites. If you find extraordinary sweeping bay views as romantic as we do, it's worth it to reserve one of the newer bay-view rooms. For maximum privacy, the hillside casitas are a good choice, although their Victorian style could use a little sprucing up (also, the rooms are accessed by two long flights of stairs, so come prepared for a little workout). You'll find adventurous room themes in the Victorian mansion: the 1,000 Cranes Room artistically incorporates wood and lacquer Asian-style design; and the Katmandu Room comes complete with purple carpeting, oversize lounge cushions, lots of mirrors, secret alcoves, artifacts from the Far East, a fireplace, a soaking tub for two, and a king-size bed set beneath a skylight. A complimentary continental breakfast comes with your stay, and for dinner, try the mesmerizing Italian-themed restaurant Poggio (see Romantic Restaurants, below), which opened in 2003.
$$$$ *AE, DC, DIS, MC, V; no checks; www.casamadrona.com.* &

THE GABLES INN
●●●

62 Princess St, Sausalito / 415/289-1100 or 800/966-1554
Built in 1869, this nine-room historic inn may not be the center of attention in town, but it definitely should be for romance. Subtle beige, cream, and

green hues lend a soothing, California-contemporary touch to each room, while Indonesian furnishings add an exotic feel. Our top romantic picks are the three suites on the third floor, each of which has vaulted ceilings, a private balcony, and a king-size bed fronting the fireplace; the Lilac Suite offers the ultimate in bubbles with a view—from the two-person jetted tub, you can gaze out upon San Francisco's brilliant skyline. Although the two adjacent suites, the Willow and the Magnolia, lack two-person tubs, the views are stunning and you'll simply have to take turns. For romance on a budget, you might try the garden-level Sycamore Room; the fringe benefit is that this least-expensive room also happens to be prime privacy territory (read: no shared walls). There are no views, but the room does feature a cozy reading nook and a gas fireplace set at a height that allows you to gaze into the flames from the queen bed. The inn's common area turns into a wine-tasting room in the evening, and guests can sample cheese and fine vintages from Napa and Sonoma Valleys. Come morning, return to the same room for an expanded continental breakfast. After that, it's all downhill (literally, not figuratively) to Sausalito's sights and shops.
$$–$$$$ *AE, D, DC, MC, V; local checks only; www.gablesinnsausalito.com.* &

HOTEL SAUSALITO
◒◒◖
16 El Portal, Sausalito / 415/332-0700 or 888/442-0700
This boutique hotel bills itself as a French Riviera–style retreat in Sausalito and, happily, delivers the goods. Finding the entrance to this hideaway, however, is a bit tricky; only a small doorway indicates the hotel's presence among the storefronts. (To truly appreciate the hotel's exterior—a 1915 Mission Revival building—view it from across the street in the waterfront park.) The 16 rooms are on the small side, but all are bright and inviting—painted in soft tones of apricot, moss green, or raspberry—and the management exudes a sunny charm. All of the rooms are located off the second-floor hallway, where nicely framed Matisse and Van Gogh reproductions hang on the lemon-colored walls. Furnishings such as pine armoires, hand-forged wrought-iron beds, and exquisite mosaic tile work increase the chic European charm of this hotel; all of the rooms have private baths with glass-sided showers. Although the location is just steps from the water, views aren't a selling point here. The two spacious suites (rooms 201 and 203) have views of town and the bustling street below. The street-facing rooms can be noisy during the day, but since Sausalito isn't usually a happening place come nightfall, things usually quiet down. Come morning, a coupon for a hot drink and pastry is redeemable at the café adjacent to the hotel. If mingling with the café crowd isn't your cup of tea, take your goodies to the hotel's small terraced patio and enjoy your meal in relative privacy.
$$–$$$$ *AE, DC, MC, V; checks OK; www.hotelsausalito.com.*

THE INN ABOVE TIDE
◐◐◐◖

30 El Portal, Sausalito / 415/332-9535 or 800/893-8433

Aptly named, The Inn Above Tide does indeed sit directly above San Francisco Bay. Built with views in mind, the inn's 30 guest rooms have floor-to-ceiling picture windows that give panoramic views of the water and the distant San Francisco skyline. Guests can take advantage of the provided binoculars to home in on the seabirds and sailboats passing by. Nautical-themed fabrics and contemporary furnishings accentuate the inviting guest rooms, most of which feature waterfront decks with teak lounge chairs and potted rosebushes—perfect for watching San Francisco emerge from the fog while seals frolic just a stone's throw away. The Superior Rooms, the most basic option, do not have private decks, so request a Queen or King Deluxe Room with deck, definitely worth the small step up in price. Fireplaces stylishly tucked into rounded brick turrets in most of the rooms are equally welcome. All accommodations come with elegantly appointed private bathrooms, many of which feature deep circular soaking tubs. If you're into views, we recommend the Grand Deluxe Rooms: these have superlative vistas, the private decks we find so romantic, plus wood-burning fireplaces and spa tubs. For the ultimate splurge, the Vista Suite is extraordinary: this incredibly spacious corner suite offers stunning panoramic views of the water and city in the distance, a large wraparound deck, an elegant interior in champagne hues, and a king-size bed swathed in champagne raw-silk curtains that offers views of the city lights glittering in the distance. All guests can sample local vintages on the communal sundeck during the afternoon wine hour. In the morning, a generous complimentary breakfast is set out in the front common room or, if you crave privacy, delivered to your doorstep. For a special occasion, look into the romance packages, with extras such as chilled champagne, sunset wine service, in-room or deckside massages for both of you, and late checkout so you can sleep in as long as your hearts desire.

$$$$ AE, DC, MC, V; no checks; www.innabovetide.com. ♿

WATER'S EDGE
◐◐◖

25 Main St, Tiburon / 415/789-5999 or 877/789-5999

Opened in 2000, this boutique hotel is the first lodging in Tiburon to warrant real romantic interest. Given its waterfront setting on a historic dock, however, it's unfortunate that more of the 23 rooms don't offer vistas. On the upside, the location in the heart of town is just steps from a host of restaurants and boutiques. Just two rooms have unobstructed views of San Francisco across the bay, and these sport a very hefty price tag. However, there's much to make you comfortable in the standard guest rooms, all of which boast wood-burning fireplaces, plush feather beds, CD players,

and cable TVs with VCRs. We applaud the elegant, subdued decor, which includes dark wood headboards, champagne-colored armchairs and sofas, and taupe walls adorned with botanical prints. The tiled bathrooms are less inspired but offer plenty of space, full tub and shower, and spa robes. The heavy industrial doors on all the rooms provide adequate soundproofing, although they give the hallways a less-than-inviting dormitory look. Fortunately, where it counts—inside the rooms and downstairs in the elegant lobby—you will find plenty of charm. Perhaps the best part of the hotel is its pleasant (if small) oceanfront deck, which all guests have access to: it's the perfect place to watch the sunset during the wine and cheese hour every evening. In chillier weather, you'll be just as happy to relax in the lobby, a spacious room with glowing hardwood floors and a large, inviting fireplace. Complimentary continental breakfast and a newspaper are delivered to your door in the morning.
$$$–$$$$ AE, D, MC, V; no checks; www.jdvhospitality.com. &

Romantic Restaurants

THE CAPRICE
❂❂❂
2000 Paradise Dr, Tiburon / 415/435-3400
With its breathtaking views of Angel Island, San Francisco, and the Golden Gate Bridge, Caprice offers vistas that could be outdone only if you dined aboard your own private yacht. On Friday nights between April and October, the tables even provide ringside seating for local sailboat races. All who dine in this restaurant, perched sturdily above the swirling waters of Raccoon Strait, come away enamored. Tables spaced well for privacy hug the windows, ensuring that everyone has a share of the incredible scenery. Old-fashioned glass lanterns glow atop every table in the softly lit restaurant, and jazz music plays in the background. The celebrated chef offers creative California-influenced European cuisine. Appetizers such as pan-fried Dungeness crab cakes or savory cheese-filled crepes topped with wild mushroom–cognac cream are just the beginning. Try anything from the varied menu: seared sea scallops with ginger beurre blanc, lamb shank pot-au-feu, or roasted Sonoma duck. For a decadent finish, try the chocolate trio: truffle cake, a mousse tower, and chocolate ice cream all served on one plate. (Inform the staff in advance on a special romantic night such as a birthday or anniversary, and the kitchen will write a salutation in chocolate on the dessert plate.) Caprice is very popular on weekends, so reservations are a must. If you happen to arrive early—which we recommend—you can

enjoy a glass of wine beside the hearth in the entryway or downstairs next to a massive rock fireplace.

$$$ *AE, MC, V; no checks; dinner every day; full bar; reservations recommended; www.thecaprice.com.*

GUAYMAS
♥❤

5 Main St, Tiburon / 415/435-6300
Named for a Mexican fishing town, this waterfront restaurant is a perfect place to savor south-of-the-border flavors and enjoy a casual, relaxed meal. The wide array of authentic Mexican fare includes roasted duck with pumpkin-seed sauce, green-corn tamales with cactus and plantain, and grilled fresh fish served with chili-tomato butter. Don't miss the house specialty: poblano chilis stuffed with chicken and raisins accompanied by a walnut and pomegranate sauce. When the weather cooperates, catch the rays while you sip margaritas on one of the two waterfront decks. The upper deck has the best vantage point, but either way, you'll enjoy terrific bay and San Francisco vistas. (Not surprisingly, on a warm day, crowds congregate here.) Blooming bougainvillea climbing over whitewashed log beams, potted cacti, and pastel colors all create a beachy mood. Warmed with gas heaters, the patios are still pleasant even after the sun dips below the hills. During the cold months, enjoy the spicy food in the casual adobe dining room, accented with brightly colored paper flags hanging from the ceiling. Guaymas may not offer fine or intimate dining, but you'll find that here it is very easy to sit back, enjoy the view, and relax. And if you're staying in San Francisco, you can avoid the stress of driving over the bridge by taking a ferry to dinner in Tiburon—now that's romantic.

$$$ *AE, DC, MC, V; no checks; lunch, dinner every day; full bar; reservations recommended.* &

POGGIO
♥♥♥

777 Bridgeway (Casa Madrona Hotel), Sausalito / 415/332-7771
The recently opened Italian-themed Poggio is stylishly filling the shoes of the glamorous Casa Madrona Hotel's previous restaurant, the charming Mediterranean-style Mikayla. In the dining room, you'll find mood lighting, tables set with white linen and crystal, and cozy brick-red velvet booths, along with glowing wooden paneling and hardwood floors and elegant architectural touches such as a mahogany wine rack built into one wall. Ask for a table for two by a window so you can watch the world go by. As you dive into the basket of fresh rosemary rolls delivered promptly to your table, you'll remember that this elegant restaurant was opened by the man who started the renowned Il Fornaio chain of restaurants (known for its fabulous breads). The daily changing menu offers delicious Italian-inspired

fare, with an emphasis on fresh, high-quality, local ingredients; many of the dishes are prepared in the wood-fired oven or on the wood-fired grill. Starters include wood-roasted white shrimp in soffrito, prosciutto, and radicchio or endive and Gorgonzola salad with walnuts, figs, and honey. For the main event, select from delicious options such as local petrale sole with buttered spinach, poached potatoes, and lemon caper sauce; seared day boat scallops with creamed leeks, butter lettuce, peas, and Meyer lemon; fresh pappardelle (wide pasta) with braised rabbit, peas, and fava beans; or linguine with local fresh squid braised in red wine and leeks. Dessert might be a rustic apple and almond tart, gelato or sorbet, lemon and tangerine layered mousse, or chocolate cake. The appealing, old-fashioned bar may just seduce you into having a nightcap.

$$$ *AE, D, DC, MC, V; no checks; breakfast, lunch, dinner every day; full bar; reservations recommended; www.casamadrona.com.*

SCOMA'S
♥€

588 Bridgeway, Sausalito / 415/332-9551
Its dynamite location on the shores of Sausalito should make Scoma's a sure thing for romance, but, as with many highly touristed spots, the dining room is anything but intimate on a busy weekend night. The tables in both of the nautically inspired dining rooms are packed in far too tightly for any degree of privacy, and your best bet is to wait for one in the sunny glass-enclosed dining area, where you will have a little more elbow room and can soak up the magnificent views. The restaurant, which also has a location on San Francisco's Fisherman's Wharf, is known and loved for its classic seafood dishes, such as traditional cioppino or steamed clams in white wine and garlic, and your best bet here is to stop in for a casual lunch. Service is efficient but hurried (when you see the volume of people going in and out of here, you'll understand why). After your meal, enjoy a stroll along the shore.

$$-$$$ *AE, D, DC, MC, V; no checks; lunch, dinner Wed–Mon; full bar; reservations recommended; www.scomassausalito.com.* ♿

THE SPINNAKER
♥€

100 Spinnaker Dr, Sausalito / 415/332-1500
Situated on a rocky point next to the Sausalito Yacht Harbor, the Spinnaker's floor-to-ceiling windows spanning the entire length of the restaurant provide a tremendous view of Sausalito, with the distant cityscape of San Francisco sparkling in the background. Such views are especially dazzling at dusk on clear evenings. Reserve a window table so you can watch sailboats and ships slipping by against the picturesque backdrop of the city skyline, and always remember to schedule dinner to coincide with sunset.

The dining room's uninspired and dated decor makes the experience considerably less romantic on a foggy day, and while the array of seafood, pasta dishes, sandwiches, and burgers are usually satisfying, the vast, standard menu lacks any seasonal focus, and the food remains secondary to the splendid waterfront location. The true reason to spend an evening here is to enjoy the work of nature—in a place this beautiful, it's certainly worth celebrating.

$$–$$$ AE, D, DC, MC, V; no checks; lunch, dinner every day, brunch Sun; full bar; reservations recommended; www.thespinnaker.com.

MILL VALLEY AND ENVIRONS

ROMANTIC HIGHLIGHTS

There are many faces to Marin, and the forested hills around **Mill Valley**—with its outdoor attractions of Mount Tamalpais and Muir Woods—are as romantically intriguing as the popular seaside hamlets of Sausalito and Tiburon. In these wooded settings, red-tailed hawks soar above the rolling hills, and nearby historic towns beckon with lovely parks, antique shops, and gourmet restaurants. Take your pick: any of these towns would make an excellent base of operations for exploring the wondrous nature all around you.

For an inspired scenic drive, take the winding route to **Mount Tamalpais State Park** (415/388-2070; www.parks.ca.gov; from Hwy 101 in Sausalito, take Stinson Beach/Hwy 1 exit heading west and follow signs). The road hugs the windswept highlands, and each curve exposes another view of the golden, cascading hills. You can either keep driving or park the car and venture out into the hills with a picnic in hand. (Bring cash for parking fees.) The aptly named 2-mile **Steep Ravine Trail**, which begins at the Pan Toll Ranger Station on the Panoramic Highway (from Hwy 1, watch for sign for Mount Tamalpais State Park, turn right onto Panoramic Hwy, drive 5 miles, then turn left into Pan Toll Ranger Station parking lot). This strenuous but magnificent deep-forest journey ends in views of the ocean and bay. Here, in the midst of the earth's simple gifts, a loaf of bread, a jug of wine, and your beloved will be all you could possibly need.

Muir Woods National Monument (415/388-2595; www.nps.gov/muwo; from Hwy 101 in Sausalito, take Stinson Beach/Hwy 1 exit heading west and follow signs; 8am–sunset; $3 per person) is also a four-lip experience. Donated to the federal government in 1908, this well-preserved parcel of redwoods was declared a national monument by President Theodore Roosevelt. Set in the hushed splendor of Redwood Canyon, Muir Woods boasts 560 acres of undisturbed forest and 6 miles of walking paths. Sunlight filters through the leafy canopy, and you may even spot black-tailed deer on the fringes of the shaded forest. On weekends in summer, finding a secluded spot can be a challenge. Whatever you do, avoid holiday weekends such as the Fourth of July. Picnicking is not allowed, although a snack bar and gift shop are at the entrance.

You can picnic to your heart's content on the beautiful beaches along Highway 1. Three miles west of Muir Woods, you'll find **Muir Beach**, one of our favorite romantic stopovers. The small crescent-shaped cove, strewn with bits of driftwood and numerous tide pools, is more romantic and private than the popular Stinson Beach farther north. In addition, if hunger strikes, you're right by the cozy English-style pub **The Pelican Inn** (10 Pacific Way, Muir Beach; 415/383-6000; www.pelicaninn.com); the tables by the fireplace make a perfect spot to hold hands and warm up over hearty fare if the chilly coastal fog rolls in early.

Nature is not the only attraction in these hills, however, and each of the historic towns in Marin has its own distinctive appeal. The best known is the upscale hamlet of **Mill Valley**, which harbors luxurious accommodations, gourmet restaurants, art galleries, and boutiques. Browse the stacks at the **Mill Valley Book Depot and Cafe** (87 Throckmorton Ave; 415/383-2665), site of the town's last railway depot, or visit the original Banana Republic store, which still calls Mill Valley home. Any romantic weekend will be off to a fabulous start with a soothing couples' massage at the luxurious spa **Tea Garden Springs** (38 Miller Ave; 415/389-7123; www.teagardensprings. com). A leisurely espresso in one of the cafés overlooking the town's pretty central plaza or a casual Italian meal at **Piazza D'Angelo** (see Romantic Restaurants, below) is a pleasant way to wind up the day.

The town of **Larkspur**, which got its name from the blue flowers that in the late 1800s grew on hillsides that are now part of the town, is as charming as its name. Stroll down quaint Magnolia Avenue, lined with old-fashioned lampposts, and stop for espresso, biscotti, and an authentic Italian café experience at the beloved **Emporio Rulli** (470 Magnolia Ave; 415/924-7478; www.rulli.com; closed Mon). At the Bay Area's most charming tea parlor, **Chai of Larkspur** (23 Ward St; 415/945-7161; www.chaioflarkspur.com), enjoy high tea in the cozy indoor parlor or outdoors on the lovely patio, and afterward browse the fine teapot collection and appealing boutique. For dinner, the obvious romantic choice is the sublime **Lark Creek Inn** (see Romantic Restaurants, below), but if something more casual is on your minds, check out **Left Bank** (507 Magnolia Ave; 415/927-3331). This often crowded and casual bistro is a little too busy for any traditional notion of romance, but the phenomenal French bistro-style fare will make up for it.

To explore farther afield, visit some of Marin's less well-known towns. In **San Rafael**, the oldest, largest, and most culturally diverse city in Marin, visit the **Mission San Rafael Arcangel** (1104 5th Ave; 415/454-8141), Marin's

oldest historic site. Just 4 miles east of downtown San Rafael, enjoy a walk
at **China Camp State Park** (from Hwy 101, go east on N San Pedro Rd for
5 miles until it enters the park) amid 1,640 acres of natural watershed and
15 miles of hiking trails; this is a great place to spot wildlife, but be forewarned that on summer weekends the wildlife is likely to be wearing hiking
boots. If an afternoon of shopping tempts, explore the sleepy town of **San
Anselmo,** with its fun array of old-fashioned antiques and collectibles stores
along San Anselmo Avenue. If you linger in town for supper, consider **Bistro
330** (330 San Anselmo Ave; 415/460-6330; www.eatdish.com); the efficient
service, French-inspired menu, and sleek interior warmed by reds and golds
make this a pleasant spot for an evening out.

Access and Information

Two major airports provide access to Marin County. **San Francisco International Airport** (SFO; 650/821-8211; www.flysfo.com) is 34 miles away, and
Oakland International Airport (OAK; 510/563-3300; www.oaklandairport
.com) is 19 miles from Marin. **Marin Door to Door** (415/457-2717;
www.marindoortodoor.com) provides daily 24-hour service to San Francisco and Oakland airports.

Two major bridges connect Marin to the greater Bay Area. The **Golden
Gate Bridge** provides access to and from San Francisco (pedestrians and
bicyclists can use the bridge's sidewalks); the southbound toll is $5. **The
Richmond–San Rafael Bridge** connects the county to the East Bay; the west-
bound toll is $2. Most Marin visitors travel north to south using **Highway
101** (the central artery). **Highway 1** travels along the coast and is famous for
its steep grades, narrow winding roads, and gorgeous views.

Good resources include the **Mill Valley Chamber of Commerce** (85 Throckmorton Ave, Mill Valley, CA 94941; 415/388-9700; www.millvalley.org) and
the **Marin County Convention & Visitors Bureau** (1013 Larkspur Landing
Circle, Larkspur, CA 94939; 415/499-5000; www.visitmarin.org).

Romantic Lodgings

GERSTLE PARK INN
◐◐◐◖

34 Grove St, San Rafael / 415/721-7611 or 800/726-7611
Built in 1895, the Gerstle Park Inn was once a traditional English-style estate;
today its timeless charms draw romantics seeking luxury in a peaceful setting. This wonderful inn is ensconced on 1.5 acres in a pleasant residential
neighborhood overlooking the sleepy town of San Rafael. Redwood trees,
oaks, and cedars lend ample shade to the expansive gardens and orchards, in

which deer can frequently be seen. With its small size, romantic amenities, and emphasis on privacy, the inn strikes the right balance between intimacy and professionalism. Inside the lovely house, leaded-glass doors lead to enticing common rooms with gleaming hardwood floors and plush carpets; the walls are adorned with beautiful Asian artwork gathered during the owner's extensive travels. On chilly evenings, enjoy the roaring fire at the large marble hearth in the living room, where wine and cheese are set out every evening for guests. Four buildings on the property—the main house, the carriage house, and two cottages—house 12 guest rooms, and each one is uniquely exquisite, with bright, tasteful decor and furnishings, fresh bouquets of flowers, and private baths. Four rooms feature Jacuzzi tubs, and most have serene views of either the gardens or San Rafael's hills. Harbored on the lower floor of the main house, the Lodge Suite is a favorite with honeymooners. An outdoor stairway winds down to the suite's private entrance and lovely deck appointed with wrought-iron furniture. Tiled steps in the bathroom climb up to an enticing Jacuzzi tub for two, surrounded by classical pictures of beach-bathing scenes. In the Gerstle Suite, French doors open onto a private patio and flower gardens. An immense shower and steam bath are unexpected luxuries in its cozy bathroom, where Oriental rugs warm the tiled floor. A private staircase winds upstairs to the elegant Redwood Suite, where green-striped wallpaper, beautiful antiques, a luxurious king-size bed, a Jacuzzi tub, and a private deck overlooking the gardens add up to a perfect hideaway. Also very private is the Oak Suite, a second-floor room with a king-size bed, a separate parlor, a Jacuzzi tub, and a private deck. The Carriage House holds two beautiful suites, and the two French country–style cottages are perfect for those wanting a fully equipped and romantic place to call home for a while. Trust us: whichever room you stay in here, you will be pleased. Breakfast includes gourmet specialties such as orange French toast, a five-cheese scrambled-egg dish, and homemade granola, all served at cozy two-person tables in the snug breakfast room. If you're still hungry after this feast, you'll find cookies and fresh-picked fruit available in the kitchen area. After your indulgent breakfast, go for a walk in neighboring Gerstle Park, where trails crisscross the wooded hills. Or, if you'd rather lay low, relax on the front veranda and simply watch the day go by. $$$–$$$$ *AE, DIS, MC, V; checks OK; www.gerstleparkinn.com.* &

MILL VALLEY INN
❂❂❂
165 Throckmorton Ave, Mill Valley / 415/389-6608 or 800/595-2100
Mill Valley's one and only "downtown" inn is set near the foot of Mount Tamalpais and surrounded by redwood, eucalyptus, and oak trees. The 25 guest rooms are located throughout four buildings: the European-style main building, a renovated Victorian, and two cottages tucked in a forest

of redwoods. The inn is advertised as a European-style pension, and the main building fits this description, with its wrought-iron balconies overflowing with flowers and its tiled entryways, natural wood accents, and Tuscan yellow stucco exterior. Half of the rooms in this building face the street and have narrow balconies, while the other half offer wider balconies overlooking a forested area (we recommend these, not only for better views but also for less traffic noise). The two private and roomy cottages front a gentle creek and are well suited for those wanting complete privacy. Nearby, the restored Victorian home holds seven rooms, our favorite being Room 22 with its roomy veranda facing the creek. No matter which room you choose, you'll be completely comfortable. Most have queen- or king-size beds, tiled bathrooms (some with skylights), and French doors leading to the balconies or patios; many also have fireplaces or Franklin woodstoves. Warm, neutral colors suffuse the rooms, where the beds are covered in crisp white linens and the furnishings are of natural wood handcrafted by local artisans—including "distressed-wood" armoires and sleigh beds. The overall effect is truly charming, especially when you discover that many of the rustic furnishings have been created from leftover materials, such as old window frames turned into bathroom mirrors and coat racks crafted from antique doorknobs. Other nice touches include chocolates in the rooms and a wine and cheese hour every evening. This is served on the main building's second-floor Sun Terrace, a partially covered deck furnished with teak tables that overlooks tall redwoods and the creek below. The extensive continental breakfast is also served in this lovely setting; if you prefer privacy, simply load up a tray with goodies and take it back to your private patio. The cheerful staff will be happy to assist if you'd like champagne waiting in the room to add a romantic surprise to your getaway.
$$$ *AE, DC, MC, V; no checks; www.millvalleyinn.com.* &

MOUNTAIN HOME INN
❍❍❰

810 Panoramic Hwy, Mill Valley / 415/381-9000
Views just don't get much better than this. Set high above the trees on a ridge of Mount Tamalpais, the Mountain Home Inn surveys all the beauty Marin County has to offer. Hawks soar by, and the only sound you'll hear is the wind rustling through the surrounding trees. The inn's handsome wooden lodge-style exterior gives way to a stunning lobby with towering ceilings and rustic columns of redwood. Appropriately enough, a mountain-lodge motif appears in the inn's 10 guest rooms, which feature soft carpeting and wood-paneled walls. All have private decks and boast views of the breathtaking setting (except for Room No. 6, which is tucked into the redwoods). The rooms are equipped with varying amenities: some have their own fireplace, while others feature either a whirlpool or large soaking tub. Even the smallest guest rooms are worth staying in, since the views

are equally terrific. Our favorite kissing accommodation is the secluded Canopy Room, appointed with a king-size four-poster canopy bed made of tree trunks and topped with a pillowy down comforter. Natural light filters in through an overhead skylight set in the cathedral ceiling, and the whirlpool tub has views of the forested hillside. Another choice accommodation here is the Mountain View Room, but you have to walk through the lower dining room to reach it, and this dining room is often extremely busy, as the restaurant is open to the public. In fact, it fairly becomes a madhouse on sunny weekends, when hikers and mountain bikers descend for après-trek drinks and snacks or a late brunch on the deck. The New American cuisine served in the dining room (lunch, dinner Wed–Sun) is adequate, but the real reason to dine here is the views. As guests, you'll get to enjoy them in relative peace during the bountiful breakfast, which might include entrées such as French toast or homemade bagels with smoked salmon. $$$–$$$$ *AE, MC, V; no checks; www.mtnhomeinn.com.* ⅄

Romantic Restaurants

EL PASEO
●●●●
17 Throckmorton Ave, Mill Valley / 415/388-0741
This culinary jewel is one of the loveliest, most intimate French restaurants in Northern California. Don't be fooled by the Spanish name *El Paseo;* it means "the passageway" and simply refers to a charming path of red brick by which you reach the front door. Inside, the ambience captures a very romantic variety of dimly lit coziness, with imposing dark wood beams, exposed-brick walls, and richly colored decor—tables are swathed in red linen. (For the most privacy, request one of the tables adjacent to the windows.) Bottles of wine are tucked into nooks and crannies around the restaurant, and candles flicker at every table. The authentic French offerings, presented on hand-painted china, are delicious; the atmosphere is designed to soothe; and the service makes you feel coddled and indulged. You can't go wrong with pork tenderloin confit accented by apple marmalade, a dish of roast salmon served on a bed of leeks, or roasted lamb chops served alongside wild mushrooms in a thyme-scented red wine sauce. Be sure to save room for the decadent and outstanding desserts. It's not surprising that El Paseo has won a number of culinary and wine-list awards, not to mention numerous awards for best romantic atmosphere. It is equally deserving of its four-lip rating for romance in our book (literally). We simply can't think of a better environment in which to express your love while enjoying marvelous food. $$$$ *AE, D, MC, V; checks OK; dinner Tues–Sun; beer and wine; reservations recommended.*

LARK CREEK INN
●●●
234 Magnolia Ave, Larkspur / 415/924-7766
Set in a beautiful, century-old Victorian inn nestled in a stately redwood grove, the Lark Creek Inn is one of Marin's most renowned dining spots. The main dining room features hardwood floors, crisp white linens, and a glass ceiling; fabric tastefully covers the glass and diffuses warm light throughout the interior. Colorful abstract artwork adds a contemporary touch to the creamy white walls, while a towering flower arrangement dominates the center of the room. The second dining room feels like an elegant sunporch, with wraparound windows, a color scheme in crisp green and white, and lots of sunshine. When the weather warms up, the restaurant's garden patio, situated near a brook, is a plum spot. Unfortunately, this restaurant is no secret, and it ranks among the Bay Area's most popular destinations in which to celebrate, so you'll have to contend with the hustle and bustle created by the sheer number of fellow diners. However, the unforgettable food and enticing, seasonally changing menu more than outweigh this minor drawback. Basic American cooking is the jumping-off point, but an imaginative touch is visible in each entrée, from the tender Yankee pot roast with roasted vegetables and horseradish mashed potatoes to the roasted free-range chicken with lemon and herbs or tender grilled pork chops with sweet braised red cabbage. For dessert, try the melting chocolate cake with hazelnut ice cream or the classic strawberry shortcake with cheesecake ice cream. If you come for Sunday brunch, you'll find delicious dishes such as orange soufflé cakes or nectarine-stuffed brioche French toast. From appetizers to dessert, the food presentation is as beautiful as the surroundings, making a visit to the Lark Creek Inn an all-around wonderful experience.
$$$$ *AE, DC, MC, V; no checks; lunch Mon–Fri, dinner every day, brunch Sun; full bar; reservations recommended.* &

PIAZZA D'ANGELO
●€
22 Miller Ave, Mill Valley / 415/388-2000
Though it is exceedingly casual and rather noisy, Piazza D'Angelo offers an appealing combination of authentic Italian fare, stylish decor, and lively ambience. The restaurant's dining rooms are accented with terra-cotta floors, Italian tile, modern artwork, and colorful low-hanging lamps. Bottles of wine, Tuscan pottery, and other Italian knickknacks adorn a partition that runs through the center of the busy, and often crowded, restaurant. Favorite romantic perches include the semicircular booths hugging the restaurant's perimeter and the tables for two fronting the large fireplace. In the warmer months, sit in the open-air section of the dining room or on the tiled outdoor patio. The entrées are moderately priced, and the portions are so generous you might consider sharing. Good choices include the

spaghetti sautéed with kalamata olives, chili pepper, baby spinach, onions, sun-dried tomatoes, white wine, and pecorino cheese; roasted meat dishes from the rotisserie; and calzones stuffed with fresh ingredients such as ricotta, spinach, caramelized onions, mozzarella, and sausage. Desserts are made fresh daily, and the crème brûlée is a standout. An extensive wine list features a respectable selection of California and Italian labels (about 150 bottles), including 10 wines poured by the glass.

$$ *AE, DC, MC, V; no checks; lunch Mon–Fri, dinner every day, brunch Sat–Sun; full bar; reservations recommended.* &

EAST BAY, SOUTH BAY, AND THE PENINSULA

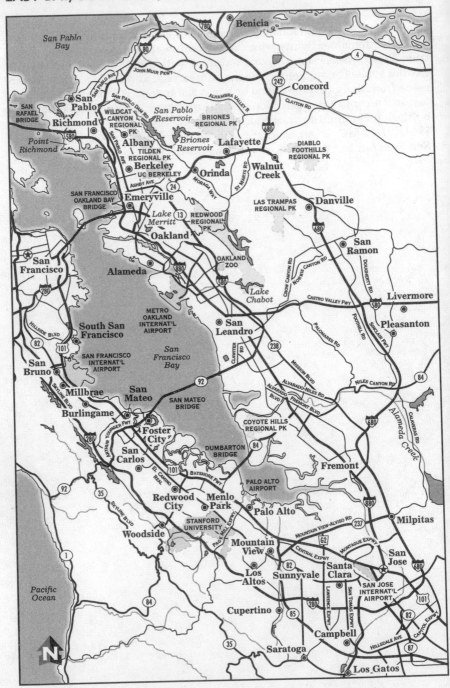

> *"The sound of a kiss is not so loud as that of a cannon, but its echo lasts a great deal longer."*
> —OLIVER WENDELL HOLMES

♡ EAST BAY, SOUTH BAY, AND THE PENINSULA

San Francisco is a famously romantic destination, but it's certainly not the only place in the Bay Area to enjoy an intimate evening out or a weekend getaway. Across the Bay Bridge from San Francisco lies the East Bay, which harbors a surprising number of romantic establishments worth your consideration, making for an extremely convenient weekend getaway. The East Bay stretches from Point Richmond south to the Livermore Valley. In between are Berkeley, home of the well-known University of California at Berkeley campus, and the sprawling metropolis of Oakland.

Drive south of San Francisco and you'll reach a verdant stretch of land referred to as the Peninsula—the Pacific Ocean is on one side, and San Francisco Bay is on the other. The posh communities in this region include Palo Alto, home of Stanford University, and Woodside, a scenic wooded hamlet. The world-renowned Silicon Valley is beyond the Peninsula, capping the bottom tip of the bay; it incorporates the sprawling city of San Jose along with smaller, quieter towns such as Saratoga and Los Gatos. Although Silicon Valley is better known for harboring tech types than kissing couples, we found some wonderfully romantic destinations. With the number of upscale inns, great restaurants, and glorious outdoor gardens in these parts, you can easily craft an amorous weekend getaway.

The Bay Area's weather is moderate most of the year; the East Bay is often two to four degrees warmer than San Francisco, and San Jose can run a couple of degrees warmer still. Savvy residents whose schedules take them to more than one locale in the course of a day will leave the house dressed in layers—they are ready to shed or add a layer at a moment's notice. In winter and spring, you can expect some rain, and summer is temperate. The real treat comes in early fall. Then you can expect temperatures to rise—it's as if summer is offering everyone a last hurrah before disappearing into a mellow autumn.

EAST BAY

ROMANTIC HIGHLIGHTS

There is no better place to kiss than in the great outdoors, and the East Bay's beautiful regional parks—which total more than 91,000 acres—beckon with plenty of opportunities for romantic exploration. One of Berkeley's most beloved getaways is **Tilden Regional Park** (510/562-7275; www.ebparks.org; several entrances located along Grizzly Peak Blvd), where you'll find more than 2,000 acres of forested trails, gardens, and picnic grounds. Enjoy a hand-in-hand stroll at its **Botanical Garden** (510/841-8732), where peaceful pathways wind through terraced plantings of native California flowers and trees; ardent hikers can find their own private paradise along the more rugged trails. It's a good idea to pack a gourmet lunch to enjoy at one of the many beautiful **picnic spots.** Attractions such as the Herschell Spillman merry-go-round and Lake Anza tend to draw crowds on summer weekends but, fortunately, there is plenty of acreage to explore—as well as secluded nooks where you can find a welcome respite from nearby civilization.

The **Berkeley Rose Garden** (Euclid Ave between Bay View and Eunice Sts) offers another lovely outdoor excursion. As you descend the stairs lined with lush, terraced beds of roses, you'll encounter flowers in a seemingly endless colorful array. This is prime kissing territory, especially in the summer when the fragrant blossoms are at their peak. You can usually find an empty park bench to call your own and spend a few moments (or a few hours) enjoying this earthly paradise. For a garden walk with an exotic twist, visit the 30-acre **University of California Botanical Garden** (200 Centennial Dr, Berkeley; 510/643-2755) and stroll amid the stunning New World Desert collection of cacti—you'll feel like you're kissing in a Dr. Seuss book. If you haven't seen enough roses yet, hike up to the Garden of Old Roses to enjoy the blooms and, on a clear day, the lovely views of the Golden Gate Bridge.

The charming, idiosyncratic neighborhoods of the East Bay harbor an array of chic shopping districts. **Fourth Street** in **Berkeley** is the perfect place to find little romantic gifts for each other, and it's easy to while away the afternoon browsing in the gorgeous boutiques, with stops for espresso and snacks at one of the upscale gourmet shops. While **Telegraph Avenue,** the student thoroughfare, is not exactly either picturesque or romantic, it is lined with fantastic independent bookstores such as **Cody's** (2454 Telegraph Ave; 510/845-7852) that will make book lovers swoon. The nearby University of California at Berkeley campus can make for a scenic stroll—particularly in the summer, when you won't have to share the shady pathways with hordes of students.

In the genteel **Rockridge** neighborhood in North Oakland, you'll find **Rockridge Market Hall** (5655 College Ave; 510/655-7748), a trendy multivendor market offering gourmet cheeses, chocolates, fresh-cut flowers, delicious deli sandwiches, exquisite produce, and a wide selection of wine. If you've got a gourmet picnic on your wish list or you're hoping to find that perfect celebratory bottle of champagne, this is the place. You can also enjoy an espresso here, browse the neighborhood's assortment of quirky, appealing shops, or stay for an upscale supper at nearby **Oliveto** (see Romantic Restaurants).

Amid the tall buildings and heavy traffic of downtown **Oakland**, **Lake Merritt** offers a pleasant oasis for couples who want to steal a quiet moment together. The lake is surrounded by 155 acres of parkland, and this is a perfect spot for an urban walk, especially in autumn when the leaves turn vibrant shades of gold and orange. Should you want to get out on the water, paddleboat and canoe rentals are available. Oakland's premier tourist destination, **Jack London Square** (866/295-9853; www.jacklondonsquare.com), is enticing only if you don't mind the crowds that flock here for the waterfront restaurants, retail stores, old-fashioned museums, and Jack London Village (10am–2pm), a series of specialty shops in a turn-of-the-twentieth-century setting. Sundays bring a delightful farmers market overflowing with fresh fruits, vegetables, and flowers; other appealing events are held year-round. An evening at **Yoshi's** (510 Embarcadero Wy; 510/238-9200; www.yoshis.com), the famous jazz club and restaurant, makes a sizzling date for music lovers.

To escape the urban streets of the East Bay, travel farther afield to **Pleasanton** and the scenic **Livermore Valley** wine region (from I-680 S, exit onto eastbound I-580 and then exit at Livermore Ave). Unlike Napa or Sonoma, this area has remained relatively undeveloped, and it harbors a number of wineries nestled among rolling hills sprinkled with oak trees and cattle. A mere hour's drive from nearly anywhere in the Bay Area, the Livermore Valley makes for an easy kissing excursion. If the weather is not cooperating for a romantic wine-country picnic, consider dining at the casually chic **Wente Vineyards Restaurant** (see Romantic Restaurants). The appealing fare, excellent wine list, affable service, and exquisite views through the floor-to-ceiling windows of the surrounding hillsides and vineyards set the stage for an evening of romance.

For the best views in the region, head east through **Lafayette** and Walnut Creek to visit **Mount Diablo**, a landmark that once guided pioneers coming down from the rugged Sierras into this part of the valley. The entrance to the mountain is in **Diablo Foothills Park** (1700 Castle Rock Rd, Walnut Creek; 510/562-7275; www.ebparks.org), which has no developed facilities but offers plenty of trails for hiking—and, if your timing is right, good wildlife- and bird-watching. When the green hillsides are dotted with spring wild- flowers or when autumn foliage adorns the trees with color, it's especially pretty, but midsummer afternoons can be a bit hot and dusty. Also, crowds descend on sunny weekends for all kinds of recreation, so hit the trails early if you are craving solitude in nature. Having the views to yourselves is worth it. On a clear day, the panorama includes everything from the rolling hills of Napa to the distant jagged peaks of the Sierra Nevada.

Access and Information

Oakland International Airport (OAK; 510/563-3300; www.oaklandairport. com) is the most convenient place to fly into if your destination is the East Bay. Driving is the most popular way to get around, but the main highways in this region are often clogged with traffic. On the main highways to and from San Francisco and San Jose, there are only a few precious hours on a weekday—sometimes even on a weekend—when you can actually get up to the speed limit. Another option is the public transit system known as **Bay Area Rapid Transit**, or **BART** (510/465-2278), which provides relatively stress-free travel between the East Bay and San Francisco. An even more enjoyable and scenic form of transportation is the ferry: the **Oakland/ Alameda Ferry** (510/522-3300) runs between Alameda, Oakland, and San Francisco every day.

The East Bay tends to be a little warmer and sunnier than San Francisco; whether you're hiking or just strolling, wearing layers and having your sun- glasses on hand will help you adapt to the changeable weather. For more information, contact the **Oakland Convention and Visitors Bureau** (475 14th St, Ste 120; 510/839-9000; www.oaklandcvb.com) or the **Berkeley Conven- tion and Visitors Bureau and Film Commission** (2015 Center St; 510/549- 7040; www.visitberkeley.com; between Shattuck Ave and Milvia St).

Romantic Lodgings

THE CLAREMONT RESORT AND SPA
🌸🌸
41 Tunnel Rd, Berkeley / 510/843-3000 or 800/551-7266
Surrounded by statuesque palm trees and gleaming with white cupolas and towers, this glamorous hotel could just as easily be set in the Mediterra- nean as here in the Berkeley Hills. Just don't come here looking for a small or intimate getaway, since the hotel's overwhelming scale can feel more

impersonal than romantic. Large resorts like the Claremont lend themselves to conventions and tour groups—and feeling like part of a software association's annual meeting doesn't exactly foster romance. Nevertheless, large resorts have their benefits, of course, and at the Claremont they are dazzling: tennis courts, swimming pool, lap pool, saunas, hot tubs, a full-service spa, a state-of-the-art exercise room, and a nearby golf course. This isn't the place to come, however, if you want to lock yourselves away in a luxurious room for some indoor sports. The 279 rooms have a standard, rather dreary feel, and many of the windows are quite small—especially considering the fantastic scenery outside. Some suites do have views of Berkeley's hills, the lovely grounds, or the distant San Francisco skyline, but they do not justify the cost given the nondescript interiors. Those are the pros and the cons, and, with so much at your fingertips, the Claremont certainly has its appeal. There's also the "Spa Romance" package if you want an easy (if not exactly affordable) getaway. The Claremont's most romantic restaurant, Jordan's (510/549-8510), offers some of the most breathtaking views around, especially of the San Francisco skyline during sunset. After you regain your breath, enjoy the standard California cuisine with Pacific Rim influences. $$$ *AE, DC, DIS, MC, V; checks OK; claremontresort.com.*

EAST BROTHER LIGHTHOUSE
🏵🏵

117 Park Pl, on East Brother Island, Point Richmond / 510/233-2385
If ringside seats for the bay's fabulous scenery are on your wish list, set your course for East Brother Lighthouse, one of Northern California's most uniquely situated bed-and-breakfasts. This destination, open Thursday through Sunday only, is located on the rocky shores of East Brother Island, which lies in the strait separating San Francisco Bay from San Pablo Bay. The 1873 lighthouse is on the National Register of Historic Places, and income from the bed-and-breakfast is used to preserve the island's buildings and boats. The accommodations are tucked away in a creamy white Victorian house connected to the lighthouse, as well as an additional structure called the Fog Signal Building. Breathtaking views of the water are definitely the highlight of each guest room; you can spend hours surveying the comings and goings of boats crossing over the bay from San Francisco. All four rooms in the Victorian home are sparsely decorated, with brass-frame queen-size beds and standard linens. Unless you don't mind sharing a bathroom with a neighboring couple, request one of the two upstairs rooms with private baths. The fifth accommodation, known as the Water's Quarters, is in the Fog Signal Building and features a double bed and a nautical theme. From the Victorian home's common area, ascend a spiral staircase to the light tower, where you can enjoy magnificent views of Mount Tamalpais and the San Francisco skyline. The island offers plenty of restful activities, including fishing and watching wildlife. Included in the price of overnight

accommodations are a 10-minute boat ride from the Point San Pablo Yacht Harbor to and from the island, hors d'oeuvres and champagne upon arrival, a four-course dinner highlighting local wines, and a hot breakfast. (Lunch is served only to guests staying two or more nights.) There are a couple of aspects to a stay here that some couples may view as romantic drawbacks. First, due to the island's limited water supply, showers are reserved for guests staying more than one night. Second, the U.S. Coast Guard's electronic fog-horn operates 24 hours a day between October 1 and April 1. Earplugs are provided for guests, but light sleepers might be awakened throughout the night. Keep in mind that even if you don't stay here, you can make a scenic outing to the lighthouse (Sat only May–Sept; reservations required). $$$$ *AE, DIS, MC, V; checks OK; lodging Thurs–Sun only; www.ebls.org.*

EVERGREEN

◗◗◗◖

9104 Longview Dr, Pleasanton / 925/426-0901

The community of Pleasanton has it both ways: it is close enough to the city to be convenient and far enough away to make urban pressures seem a distant dream. At Evergreen, you can have a taste of this good life. This impressive cedar and oak home sits on a hillside, with trees and shrubbery enclosing the property. Large windows and high ceilings highlight the sunny entryway and allow the natural splendor outside to complement the interior. Polished hardwood floors in the living room are warmed by a crackling fire, and plush couches provide a relaxing place to sit and discuss dinner plans. All four guest rooms exude the same comfortable elegance found in the living room. Of particular romantic interest is the top-floor Grandview Suite, a spacious, extremely comfortable room with a corner fireplace, a king-size sleigh bed, and a tiled bathroom with a two-person Jacuzzi tub and double-headed shower. From the private deck, you can enjoy serene views of the surrounding treetops. Hideaway, the other romantics' retreat, features a pine four-poster king-size bed, cream and beige accents, and an oval Jacuzzi tub for two. This room also has a deck, but it faces the driveway, so it is not as private as the Grandview Suite's. The two remaining guest rooms are smaller and less expensive and feature queen-size beds and simple bathrooms without Jacuzzi tubs. The Retreat Room has a cozy country interior, and the Library Room features rich, dark fabrics and a more tailored look. Even if you choose one of these rooms, you can bubble away with your sweetheart in the large communal spa on the sizable deck. There's also an exercise room on the second floor, complete with TV; com-plimentary goodies fill your room's refrigerator. A generous cooked-to-order breakfast with fresh fruit and baked goods is served in the sunny breakfast room, furnished with stone-topped tables and wrought-iron chairs. For more privacy, take your tray out to the deck or up to your room. You can walk off the morning's indulgence at the nearby Augustin Bernal Park (8200

Golden Eagle Wy), where 45 minutes of uphill hiking leads to the top of Pleasanton Ridge—and awe-inspiring views.
$$$–$$$$ AE, MC, V; no checks; www.evergreen-inn.com.

LAFAYETTE PARK HOTEL
❤❤

3287 Mount Diablo Blvd, Lafayette / 925/283-3700 or 800/368-2468
From the freeway, the Lafayette Park Hotel looks like an impressive European chalet—but because we *could* see it from the highway, we were worried. After all, a love nest that borders a busy road is potentially too noisy for a romantic retreat. In this case, however, our skepticism was unfounded. Once you enter this graceful accommodation, those speeding cars might as well not exist. The smart design isn't surprising considering that the hotel is part of the Woodside Hotel chain, which operates a handful of consistently romance-friendly facilities, including the Bodega Bay Lodge and Spa (see the North Coast section). In the lovely open lobby, a profusion of fresh flower arrangements brings soft color to the elegant decor, while skylights illuminate a hand-carved staircase that serves as the room's architectural centerpiece. Soundproofed and spacious, the 140 guest rooms are elegantly appointed with cherrywood furnishings, granite countertops, and wet bars. The quarters are full of light, and many rooms feature vaulted ceilings, wood-burning fireplaces, king-size beds, and cozy window seats. Exploring the grounds, we found three charming courtyards to kiss in: one built around an Italian marble fountain, another surrounding a stone wishing well, and a third with a large swimming pool and whirlpool spa. We highly recommend requesting a room with a pool or courtyard view (otherwise you might catch glimpses of the freeway). The recently completed spa offers even more luxury, with options such as couples' massages; spa packages are also available, as well as romance and weekend getaway packages. The cost is considerable (as are the regular rates), but you won't fail to feel pampered. Adjacent to the lobby, the Duck Club Restaurant (925/283-7108) offers New American cuisine including dishes such as lobster three ways (butter poached, shellfish cappuccino, and lobster corn fritter), "freeform" seafood ravioli, and grilled flatiron steak with zinfandel sauce. The Sunday brunch is among the best in town, with award-winning Bloody Marys. The dining room, with its warm yellow walls, intimate lighting, and linen-clad tables, is a pleasant spot to relax over a meal. After dinner, snuggle up near the cobblestone fireplace in the adjacent lounge for a latte or cappuccino, a wonderful way to round out the evening.
$$$–$$$$ AE, D, DC, MC, V; checks OK; www.woodsidehotels.com.

NORTH BERKELEY COTTAGE
⬡⬡

Milvia St, Berkeley / 510/898-1145

This sweet little retreat fits in perfectly with the idiosyncratic mood of its North Berkeley neighborhood—the owners do things their own way. Only cash is accepted as payment, and guests are responsible for their own breakfast. Nonetheless, a quiet, convenient location, simple charm, and affordable rates make this clean cottage a good choice for lovebirds seeking a low-key getaway. Nestled amid a beautiful, tree-shaded garden behind the owners' shingled home, the cottage can accommodate four if necessary—but we think it's just right for two. To experience quintessential Berkeley, the location could not be more perfect. You're just two blocks from the fondly named "Gourmet Ghetto," the North Berkeley neighborhood that harbors the famed Chez Panisse (see Romantic Restaurants) and other fine restaurants, plus excellent cafés and numerous lunch spots. It's also an easy 10-minute walk to the University of California–Berkeley campus. The cottage is filled with a hodgepodge of comfortable furnishings, but the overall effect is pleasantly simple and not overloaded by flowery decor. Inside, you'll find a spacious living room with queen sofa-bed, cable TV, and private phone; a small separate bedroom with queen bed; a straightforward full bath; and a private deck. Bring goodies to stock in the full kitchen, which includes an old-fashioned white enamel stove and quaint breakfast nook. The best places to kiss are outside, on the benches and chairs scattered around the well-tended garden—once featured in a "Secret Gardens of the East Bay" garden tour. You can't fail to relax here on a sunny morning, enjoying coffee and pastries (picked up at a nearby café) amid the chirping birds and blooming flowers.

$ *MC, V; checks OK; www.bbonline.com/ca/northberkeley.*

PURPLE ORCHID INN RESORT AND SPA
⬡⬡⬡⬤

4549 Cross Rd, Livermore / 925/606-8855 or 800/353-4549

Quiet—peace and quiet. That's exactly what you'll find way out here in the country, where the wind caresses the golden grasses and a dusty road leads to this fabulous inn. Built of hand-hewn logs, the Purple Orchid looks much like a rustic mountain lodge that has been set down among acres of olive trees and rolling hills. The 10 luxurious accommodations here have enough romantic features to keep any couple kissing through their getaway. Most noteworthy are the jetted tubs (varying in size) in each guest room, spacious quarters that create a welcome sense of seclusion, and outdoor patios perfect for enjoying the region's sunshine. Room decor varies, ranging from a Western lodge motif to a jungle safari theme, but all are tasteful and not overbearing. A few standout rooms include the main-floor Double Eagle Suite, which boasts a two-person jetted tub and enclosed porch where you

can enjoy a lavish morning meal in privacy. (Only the four suites offer the option of in-room breakfast.) Upstairs, we're partial to Uncle Howard's Adventure Retreat, which has a king-size bed, heart-shaped Jacuzzi tub for two, and semiprivate patio overlooking the countryside. Two vast and luxurious new Patio Suites, completed in 2003, take your retreat to an even higher level. Each features more than 1,000 square feet of space and every imaginable amenity, including Jacuzzi tubs for two and private outdoor patios. Especially romantic is the Celestial Moon Patio Suite, with elegant Asian-influenced decor, enticing king-size bed, 17-foot ceilings, and beautifully framed artwork. In addition to the lovely rooms, this inn offers many other treats. A pebble-tiled pool and waterfall out back help cool you off when it's hot; a full-service day spa meets all your relaxation needs; the concierge can arrange anything from a horseback ride to a tour of nearby wineries; and afternoon wine and hors d'oeuvres are served daily. Lavish breakfasts are served poolside, weather permitting, or in the magnificent dining room with cathedral ceilings and views of the olive groves. Best of all, whatever you want for breakfast is yours for the asking. The creative chef can whip up anything from old-fashioned biscuits and gravy to fancy Grand Marnier French toast—you won't find this feature at most bed-and-breakfasts! But then, the Purple Orchid is a special place, one definitely worth the trip out to the countryside.
$$$ *MC, V; checks OK; www.purpleorchid.com.*

ROSE GARDEN INN
❤❤
2740 Telegraph Ave, Berkeley / 510/549-2145 or 800/992-9005
Telegraph Avenue may not be the most romantic street in Berkeley, but it does harbor an amorous secret in the form of this Victorian-style inn. Consisting of five buildings hidden from the road by mature trees, this inn is especially beautiful when the English country gardens, complete with hundreds of rosebushes, are in magnificent summer bloom. There is a wide variety of styles and amenities among the 40 guest rooms. Accommodations in the historic Faye House, built in 1906, and in the Main Building—both restored mansions with elegant dark wood paneling—exude turn-of-the-20th-century elegance. Flowery wallpaper, period furnishings, claw-foot tubs, stained-glass windows, and working fireplaces distinguish these rooms. Room No. 9 on the third floor of the Faye House boasts a fabulous patio with views of the distant bay. The ivy-draped Lott Building (formerly the Carriage House) features four comfortable rooms, including a large "junior suite," with cathedral ceilings, rose-colored walls, hand-painted tiled fireplaces, and terra-cotta-tiled floors. The Garden and Cottage Buildings are similar, with the addition of gas fireplaces in several of the rooms. It would be nice if you could reserve a specific room, since not all of them have private baths, enticing views, balconies, and fireplaces; unfortunately,

the management can't guarantee a specific room number. It certainly doesn't hurt to make your preferences known, particularly if certain amenities are necessary for your romantic interlude. In the morning, enjoy the full buffet-style breakfast, which includes everything from eggs and bacon to freshly baked breads and homemade preserves, served in the country-Victorian dining room. If California's famous sunshine is on full blast, take your morning repast out to the patio or head for the gardens, where the scent of roses is sure to sweeten your morning.
$$ AE, DC, DIS, MC, V; local checks only; www.rosegardeninn.com.

WATERFRONT PLAZA HOTEL
◐❢

10 Washington St, Oakland / 510/836-3800 or 800/729-3638
A romance package is the year-round specialty at this waterfront hotel on Jack London Square, one of Oakland's most popular attractions. See if this doesn't inspire a kiss: chilled bubbly and keepsake champagne flutes are the prelude to an amorous stay in one of the spacious waterfront-view rooms; then, a continental breakfast is delivered to your door in the morning, saving you the trouble of calling room service or venturing to the hotel's restaurant. Whether or not you splurge for the romance package, rest assured that you will enjoy the waterfront location. (Be sure to request a room with a water view—not all of them have one.) The 144 rooms are standard but cheerful, with pine furnishings and floral linens; one perk is that many of them feature gas fireplaces. Corner suites with wraparound balconies and gorgeous water views are particularly enticing. TV/VCRs, minibars, coffeemakers, and access to a public fitness center, sauna, and pool take care of all your needs. Ironically, in spite of the waterfront views and romance packages, this hotel draws an almost exclusively business-oriented clientele, particularly on weekdays. You are likely to be the only two people here with something other than business on your minds.
$$$ AE, DC, DIS, MC, V; no checks; www.waterfrontplaza.com. ♿

Romantic Restaurants

BAY WOLF RESTAURANT
●●●

3853 Piedmont Ave, Oakland / 510/655-6004
With its unique setting in a charming Victorian home and its excellent food, this wonderful East Bay restaurant has been a favorite date destination for more than three decades. Though the interior does show its age in places and could use a fresh coat of paint, the dark wood wainscoting and pale yellow walls are a refreshing change from the cold brushed steel and polished wood interiors so common in trendy restaurants. Whether you enjoy dinner in

one of two softly lit, cozy dining rooms or outside on the veranda in warm weather, this restaurant enfolds you in its pleasant ambience—in typical East Bay fashion, you will feel comfortable here regardless of whether you are dressed up for a special occasion or casually attired. Ingredients are faultlessly fresh, and the carefully prepared seasonal dishes keep pace with many of the region's best restaurants. Typical first courses might include a spiced scallop and endive salad or a rich, smoky asparagus and hazelnut soup with lemon cream. Main courses vary from tender duck with Meyer lemon confit, green olives, and a gratin of turnips to crisp and savory horseradish-crusted wild steelhead with artichokes, lentils, and tangerine vinaigrette. Desserts change every two weeks, but offerings might include an irresistible berry pudding chock-full of seasonal berries or a warm chocolate pudding cake drizzled with crème anglaise and cocoa sauce. The carefully selected wine list offers a number of moderately priced vintages, and more than 10 wines are available by the glass. The mood is formal in the evening but less so during the day—the less expensive ticket for lunch also gives a midday outing here a great deal of romantic appeal.
$$$$ *AE, MC, V; checks OK; lunch Mon–Fri, dinner every day; beer and wine; reservations recommended; www.baywolf.com.*

CÉSAR
♥♥♥

1515 Shattuck Ave, Berkeley / 510/883-0222
One romantic drawback to this small, wonderfully authentic tapas bar is that it is perennially packed; another is that, if you're looking for privacy, much of the seating is at a large communal table in the center of the room. The third strike? The restaurant doesn't take reservations. So why, you might wonder, does such an establishment belong in the pages of this book? Well, simply because the food is delicious. And for couples who don't mind joining the fray for an evening, diving into the convivial European atmosphere is nearly as much fun as selecting dishes from the outstanding menu. You can't go wrong here, as most of the 20 or so items are superb. Start with the salty roasted almonds and a cool cucumber gazpacho. The salt cod and potato *cazuela* (Spanish version of brandade), which is served with slices of crunchy baguette, is not to be missed. The *papas fritas* (fried potatoes) seasoned with cumin and garlic are delicious, as is the ham with sweet grilled figs. Dessert selections include a honey-sweetened creamy fromage blanc served with peaches; bread pudding; and a rich *crema de chocolate*. For the best results, arrive early or late and avoid the weekend.
$$ *AE, MC, V; no checks; lunch, dinner every day; full bar; no reservations.*

CHEZ PANISSE
✪✪✪✪
1517 Shattuck Ave, Berkeley / 510/548-5525 / 510/548-5049 (café)
A small, hand-carved sign in front of a charming vine-covered fence is all
that identifies Northern California's most legendary restaurant. The unobtrusive exterior belies the epic status of this culinary institution, which
helped spark the California cuisine revolution more than three decades ago.
Chez Panisse has two dining rooms with separate menus, each offering innovative and seasonal fare. The first option is the lively Arts and Crafts–style
café upstairs, which offers a casual à la carte menu. Our favorite dining
spot in this room is a cozy alcove set aglow with lanterns and filled with a
handful of tables. Here, you might sample cherry-tomato salad with fava-
bean crostini; light and sweet *sopa de nopales* (cactus soup); king salmon
with grilled polenta and summer bean ragout delicately accented by a
cherry-tomato, cucumber, and chervil vinaigrette; and finish with an outstanding seasonal dessert (in summer, you will sigh with pleasure over the
fresh nectarine and raspberry crisp). More formal and expensive is the quiet,
elegant, and slightly stiff downstairs dining room, which has similar decor,
fewer tables with more candlelight, and two dinner seatings per night. The
inspired three- or five-course dinner menu changes daily, but a characteristic offering could include a salad of grilled leeks with toasted hazelnuts
and anchovies; handmade garden-herb ravioli in a wild-mushroom broth;
ragout of Maine lobster, scallops, and striped bass with spring vegetables,
new potatoes, and chardonnay butter; and, for dessert, candied tangerine
ice cream profiteroles with fresh strawberry coulis. Ultimately, which dining
room you choose will depend on your budget and your mood. Due to Chez
Panisse's towering reputation, it takes a bit of effort to book a table (don't
be shocked by the request for a credit-card guarantee). You can make reservations for dinner at the restaurant (downstairs) or for lunch or dinner at
the café (upstairs) only as far ahead as one calendar month in advance; we
recommend calling as early as possible.
$$$–$$$$ *AE, DC, DIS, MC, V; local checks only; restaurant: dinner Mon–
Sat; café: lunch, dinner Mon–Sat; beer and wine; reservations required;
www.chezpanisse.com.*

CITRON
✪✪✪
5484 College Ave, Oakland / 510/653-5484
A darling of restaurant critics and well-heeled East Bay couples, this cozy
destination in the Rockridge neighborhood serves delicious and satisfying
French-Mediterranean fare in an intimate setting. Noise can be a factor
on very busy evenings, and the tables in the small dining room are not far
enough apart to enable truly private conversation, but the lemon-yellow
walls, beautiful flower arrangements, and tables adorned with linen and

crystal all add up to create a romantic mood. The newly completed patio with vine-covered trellises offers an ideal place to linger on a warm evening (which, given the East Bay weather, is just as likely to arrive during late fall as during the summer months). The menu changes every two weeks, and starters might include grilled corn and sorrel soup with soft-shell crab or yellowtail carpaccio with a citrus–red onion salad. Main courses range from roasted chicken with 40 garlic cloves to lamb osso buco served on a bed of flageolet bean–and–sun-dried tomato ragout with a sprinkling of pistachio gremolata garnish. Desserts stray into the realm of the old-fashioned, with options such as a decadent bourbon pecan tart or a chocolate peppermint sundae. If you don't mind even more of a din and a trendy dining crowd, consider the next-door A Côté (510/655-6469), under the same ownership but opened more recently (2001), which serves delicious French tapas in a warm and beautifully lit dining room.
$$ *AE, DC, DIS, MC, V; dinner every day; full bar; reservations recommended; www.citron-acote.com.*

LA NOTE
◖◗

2377 Shattuck Ave, Berkeley / 510/843-1535
The East Bay might seem like a far cry from the south of France, but an evening at this friendly, charming restaurant may convince you that Provence is just a state of mind. La Note isn't fancy, but its red-flowered tablecloths, relaxed bistro ambience, and tasty, authentic French fare make it a wonderful spot to enjoy a casual night out. The restaurant's cheerful interior features pretty blue wainscoting, yellow walls, and appealing bright artwork, although the tables are rather cramped (those along the side wall or toward the front have a little more elbow room). The most romantic tables by far are situated on the gorgeous outdoor garden patio. Start dinner with a glass of *vin rouge* and one of several choices of pâté or country bread with a tasty assortment of homemade olive tapenade, tomato goat cheese, and eggplant caviar. Then it's time to mull over the selection of enticing dishes neatly written on the board of daily specials or the appealing French classics on the menu. Main-dish options include a classic braised chicken with garlic, lemons, fresh thyme, and white wine or traditional seafood bouillabaisse bubbling with shrimp, scallops, and chunks of sea bass in a saffron broth. Every meal of the day satisfies here: at the popular weekend brunch, you can savor chocolate croissants, toasted cinnamon brioche, or classic ham-and-cheese omelettes; weekday lunches bring delicious salads and baguette sandwiches. The restaurant, which takes reservations only for five or more, can sometimes feel too bustling for romance, especially during brunch. Fortunately, the evening meal brings a more intimate mood. No

matter what occasion brings you to La Note, the result will be a charming French affair to remember.

$–$$ AE, MC, V; breakfast, lunch Mon–Fri, dinner Thurs–Sat, brunch Sat–Sun; beer and wine; reservations for 5 or more only.

OLIVETO CAFE AND RESTAURANT
●●●

5655 College Ave, Oakland / 510/547-5356
The mood at this upscale Italian restaurant is more sophisticated than cozy, but gourmet-minded couples will find plenty to kiss about at Oliveto. Polished granite, olive wood, and custom ironwork create an impressive backdrop, while subtle lighting, magnificent flower arrangements, and linen-covered tables set the stage for an intimate meal. The menu is a study in careful interpretations of rustic Italian cuisine, and the food, though spendy, is delicious. Meats are treated with care in the wood-fired rotisserie or grill, with options ranging from lamb and house-made pork sausage to tender grilled rabbit. You can also count on the seafood to satisfy, with dishes such as petrale sole piccata served on a bed of sautéed spinach and topped with a caper, white wine, and butter sauce. Don't let the tempting entrées distract you from enjoying a first course of house-made pasta, such as ravioli stuffed with salt cod and new potatoes or savory fettuccine with duck liver, pancetta, and sage. For dessert, try the bittersweet chocolate cake or home-made biscotti while you sip an expertly made espresso. Downstairs, the more casual café serves small, crisp pizzas and sophisticated salads—such as the panzanella with cherry tomatoes and fresh mozzarella—and becomes a lively cocktail bar on the weekends.

$$$–$$$$ AE, DC, MC, V; no checks; café: breakfast, lunch, dinner every day; restaurant: lunch Mon–Fri, dinner every day; beer and wine; reservations recommended; www.oliveto.com.

SCOTT'S SEAFOOD GRILL AND BAR
●●

No. 2 Broadway (Jack London Square), Oakland / 510/444-3456
This popular seafood palace has marvelous waterfront views—watch a veritable parade of sailboats, tugs, motor yachts, and even seals pass by in the estuary just outside during the course of your meal. Just be sure to request one of the tables lining the windows; that way you'll be far from the noisy kitchen but close enough to the lounge area to appreciate the live piano music (every evening) or jazz trio (Sunday brunch only). Lanterns and white tablecloths top each table, while gold dome-shaped chandeliers hang from the maroon ceiling. Fish and more fish is what you'll find on the menu here, and the restaurant is consistently chosen as a favorite destination for seafood dinners in the East Bay. On any given night, a different fish might be highlighted, which means you'll find more than nine different specials on

that theme—in the case of salmon, options might range from smoked salmon ravioli to baked salmon Florentine. The main menu offers a wide array of choices that include charbroiled ahi tuna topped with tropical fruit salsa, grilled whole Pacific sand dabs (a type of flounder), and a deep-fried seafood platter featuring prawns, snapper, and scallops. Light eaters can easily fill up on the generous appetizers: the Dungeness crab cakes spiced with a mustard sauce are divine, and as for the steamed Manila clams, you'll fall for them hook, line, and sinker.
$$ *AE, DC, DIS, MC, V; no checks; lunch, dinner every day, brunch Sun; full bar; reservations recommended; www.scottseastbay.com.*

WENTE VINEYARDS RESTAURANT
☆☆☆
5050 Arroyo Rd, Livermore / 925/456-2450
Set among the vineyards and rolling hills of the 1,200-acre Wente estate, this beautiful Spanish Colonial–style restaurant is a romantic surprise. The lush gardens and open architecture create a portrait of wine-country grandeur, and this theme continues in the dining rooms and terraces, which have views of the vineyards and distant hills. In the two main dining rooms, you'll find large windows, French doors, and well-spaced tables. The larger room at the front of the restaurant is located across from the bar; we prefer the smaller Veranda room located at the back of the restaurant, with pretty views of the emerald lawns. Larger groups can take advantage of the Wine Cellar dining room, downstairs and adjacent to the restaurant's wine cellar. The seasonal menu changes daily, and dishes often star herbs, vegetables, lettuces, edible flowers, and citrus grown in the estate's own gardens. Start off with one of the enticing appetizers, such as fresh Hog Island oysters on the half shell served with a sparkling wine mignonette or roasted–butternut squash soup with crème fraîche and sage. House-smoked meats and fresh fish are presented with intriguing, tangy sauces and exotic chutneys, and Wente's trademark beef dishes, such as rib-eye steak with a fire-roasted onion and portobello relish, are delicious. The wine list has won numerous awards, so you are certain to find the right bottle to celebrate your special occasion.
$$$ *AE, DC, MC, V; checks OK; lunch Mon–Sat, dinner every day, brunch Sun; wine and wine-based spirits only; reservations recommended; www.wentevineyards.com.*

ZATIS
☆☆☆
4027 Piedmont Ave, Oakland / 510/658-8210
With its reasonable prices and intimate dining room, Zatis is a great place to celebrate a special occasion—without breaking the bank or fighting the well-heeled crowds that dominate the more upscale East Bay restaurants. The restaurant is tucked into a narrow spot near a bagel shop and a Peet's

coffeehouse on Piedmont Avenue; it's hardly noticeable during the day. At night, the elegant ice-blue neon light will entice you to step through the doors and take in the aromas of roasted garlic and olive oil. The light seduces, and the jazz soothes. About 15 tables are scattered around the small dining room, where the mood is akin to that of an intimate Italian trattoria. Start with the savory filo triangles stuffed with perfectly seasoned chicken and spinach, or dip into the roasted garlic with Gorgonzola and flatbread. Then try the vegetarian eggplant entrée stuffed with kalamata olives, jalapeños, and artichoke hearts and baked in a spicy tomato sauce; the grilled fillet of wild salmon served with red potatoes and fresh seasonal vegetables; or any of the chef's specialties of the day. Desserts, such as the chocolate-truffle mousse pâte with raspberry sauce or the crème caramel, provide tempting conclusions to a meal that will surely end up as a prelude to a kiss. $$ *AE, MC, V; no checks; lunch Mon–Sat, dinner every day; beer and wine; reservations recommended; www.zatisrestaurant.com.* &

SOUTH BAY AND THE PENINSULA

ROMANTIC HIGHLIGHTS

The glittering boutiques and restaurants of **Palo Alto**'s main drag make for a pretty picture, until you spend an afternoon fighting the traffic, as well as the students from Stanford and the hordes of shoppers for space on the sidewalk. The truth is, as pretty as this university town can be, it's not intimate. For true romance on the Peninsula, we recommend escaping the well-heeled crowds and traveling to the quiet towns of **Menlo Park** and **Woodside.** In the latter, you'll discover one of the Bay Area's most scenic drives, along breathtaking **Skyline Boulevard,** where towering coast redwoods line the gently curving road and a thin veil of mist creates a magical mood.

Our favorite romantic destination in Woodside is the **Filoli Estate and Gardens** (86 Cañada Rd; 650/364-8300; www.filoli.org; open Tues–Sat), where you'll discover 16 acres of stunning formal gardens that evoke passion in all who visit. The sumptuously designed Italian-French landscape, where terraces, lawns, and pools form a succession of garden "rooms," receives an annual infusion of more than 10,000 plants to ensure year-round splendor. Don't miss the Chartres Cathedral Garden, designed to evoke a stained-glass window with its roses and boxwood hedges, or the exquisite Woodland Garden. Give yourselves at least a couple of hours to explore the surroundings and the beautifully preserved mansion draped in wisteria, where original furnishings and items from the Getty and de Young

Museums recall an era of grand luxury. If you feel a sense of déjà vu, it may be because you have seen Filoli portraying the classy Carrington estate on the '80s television drama "Dynasty." Or perhaps you kissed here in your most pleasant dreams.

The sprawling city of **San Jose**, the South Bay's largest city and the urban core of this region, may not possess quite as much romantic charisma as its northern neighbor, San Francisco, and you may even be forgiven for wondering why anyone would go to the silicon capital of the world for anything other than computer software. We actually wondered the same thing, until we stumbled across several very romantic finds—and, amazingly, there wasn't a computer in sight. The **Japanese Friendship Garden** (in Kelley Park at 1300 Senter Rd; 408/277-2757; www.sjparks.org) is a pleasant place for a picnic and a stroll. The large, tranquil ponds connected by narrow streams and arched bridges, plus walkways framed in springtime by a profusion of gorgeous pink blossoms, will surely put you in the mood for romance. For a dress-up date, attend a performance by one of the thriving theater, ballet, and opera groups associated with the **San Jose Center for the Performing Arts** (255 Almaden Blvd at Park Ave; 408/277-3900).

San Jose enjoys a happy proximity to the small and charming towns of Saratoga and Los Gatos, which beckon with the chance for a romantic escape. In **Saratoga**, tall trees shade picturesque streets lined with delightful storefronts and well-tended gardens and homes. The town's main thoroughfare, Big Basin Way, is short but sweet, with plenty of pleasant restaurants and cafés. Saratoga is unique in boasting two venues where you can experience the most heavenly date night possible: enjoying beautiful live music in a splendid outdoor setting. At **Villa Montalvo** (15400 Montalvo Rd; 408/961-5858 for tickets, 408/961-5800 for information; www.villamontalvo.org), the concerts are oriented to classical music listeners, which fits well with the perfectly manicured lawns punctuated by Greek statues and an aristocratic villa. Classical strains aren't the only music you'll hear at Villa Montalvo; wedding bells chime here, as well. But even without music or weddings, the arboretum grounds and nearby hiking trails (open every day) are worth a visit. The villa isn't open for viewing, but there is an art gallery (open Wed–Sun). The other outdoor-music venue is **Mountain Winery** (see Romantic Wineries, below).

For the simplest of pleasures—a romantic walk—visit **Hakone Gardens** (21000 Big Basin Way; 408/741-4994; www.hakone.com; open every day). Discovering this traditional Japanese garden among the towering redwoods and fragrant eucalyptus trees is a delight, especially in the early morning when the birds chirp, the breeze is soft, and the crowds haven't arrived. At the center of the 15-acre garden is a clear pond where colorful carp, a Japanese symbol of love and longevity, sparkle in the still water. White water lilies float on the surface, and a cascading waterfall fills the air with tranquil music. Turtles basking in the sun look like statues until they suddenly slide into the water. The garden is edged with wood-fenced walkways adorned by sweet-smelling flowers. Several picnic tables are situated outside the gardens, where you can enjoy a cold drink from the gift shop or your own picnic.

A side trip to **Los Gatos**, located off Highway 17 just before the Santa Cruz Mountains, offers you sophisticated shopping in a charming, small-town atmosphere. All you need to do is find a place to park, which could take a while, as parking is mostly of the on-street variety. In the town's stylish boutiques, exclusive gift shops, and home-accessory stores, plenty of opportunities to find keepsakes and mementos of your romantic interlude await. With comfortable accommodations available at the sparkling new **Hotel Los Gatos** (see Romantic Lodgings, below), a handful of much-admired restaurants, and proximity to wine-tasting in the nearby Santa Cruz Mountains (see Romantic Wineries), you could easily kiss your way through a weekend getaway in this polished gem of a town.

Access and Information

The city of San Jose is served by the **San Jose International Airport** (408/501-7600; www.sjc.org). If you're visiting the Peninsula with a destination of, for example, Palo Alto, **San Francisco International Airport** (SFO; 650/876-2377; www.flysfo.com) is your best bet. Especially during rush hour, traffic is an important factor to consider in your travels in the region. Flying into the airport closest to your destination will help you avoid hours of sitting in traffic. **Caltrain** (800/660-4287; www.caltrain.com) provides service from Silicon Valley to San Francisco. On the Peninsula, everyone travels by car.

San Jose enjoys the distinction of almost always being several degrees warmer than the rest of the Bay Area, regardless of the season, while the Peninsula is often cooler. With this in mind, think layers, even in summer. For more information on San Jose, contact the **Visitor Information Bureau** (150 W San Carlos St and 333 W San Carlos St, Ste 1000; 408/977-0900; www.sanjose.org). If your destination is on the Peninsula, contact the **Palo Alto Chamber of Commerce** (250 Hamilton Ave; 650/324-3121; www.city ofpaloalto.org).

Romantic Wineries

BURRELL SCHOOL VINEYARDS
♥♥♥
24060 Summit Rd, Los Gatos / 408/353-6290
A restored turn-of-the-20th-century red schoolhouse, trimmed in white and complete with a quaint cupola, is at the heart of this scenic winery set high

up in the Santa Cruz Mountains. Step into the white gazebo in the midst of vineyards and surrounded by miniature pink rosebushes, and see if you can resist a kiss. This is a small working winery, so you'll spot equipment scattered about, and the tasting room is a modest affair. Nonetheless, the small terrace—with spectacular views of the surrounding vineyards and mountains—makes a lovely spot for a picnic. Sip wines such as chardonnay, merlot, cabernet franc, and zinfandel, and soak up the sunshine and the view.
11am–5pm Sat–Sun; www.burrellwine.com.

BYINGTON VINEYARDS AND WINERY
◐◐◐◑
21850 Bear Creek Rd, Los Gatos / 408/354-1111
This winery's grand, Italian-style villa, surrounded by manicured gardens and vineyards, makes for one of the most picture-perfect winery settings in the region. Ascend the red brick staircase trimmed with hedges to the winery's exquisite Wedding Lawn, adorned with a beautiful wisteria-draped arbor, for beautiful views of the Santa Cruz Mountains. Inside the villa's tasting room, you can sample an array of red and white wines, ranging from viognier and sauvignon blanc to pinot noir and cabernet franc. In August and September, Jazz Sundays are the perfect excuse to sip wine while relaxing to live music. If you're looking for a special place to celebrate Valentine's Day, call ahead and reserve space for the winery's romantic candlelit dinner in the wine cave.
11am–5pm every day; www.byington.com.

DAVID BRUCE WINERY
◐◐◑
21439 Bear Creek Rd, Los Gatos / 408/354-4214 or 800/397-9972
The mountaintop road that leads to this winery is decidedly rural, but the pinot noir here is nothing short of world-class. Since the industrial winery and tasting room will not inspire raptures—although a spacious terrace does offer sweeping views of the vineyard-covered hillsides—it's fortunate that plenty of romance resides in the *vino*. The tasting room usually offers at least four different types of superlative pinot noir, as well as cabernet sauvignon, petite sirah, and zinfandel. Select a favorite vintage to bring home, and you'll have a great excuse to celebrate once your trip is just a wonderful memory.
12–5pm Mon–Fri, 11am–5pm Sat–Sun; www.davidbrucewinery.com.

MOUNTAIN WINERY
❂❂❂
14831 Pierce Rd at Hwy 9, Saratoga / 408/741-2822
Perched above the idyllic town of Saratoga and reached by a long and winding country road, this winery encompasses some of the most exquisite, sun-drenched earth in the entire South Bay. The scene here looks almost too perfect. Graceful trees rustle in the soft breezes, and grapevines curve across the rolling hillsides. The only flaw in the majestic setting is that the winery is not open to the public, aside from once-a-month wine tastings and special events; happily, such events take place throughout the spring, summer, and early fall, so it is easier than you might think to get in the door. Each year, the winery presents a spectacular summer concert series featuring entertainers with wide appeal. (To maximize your comfort, come prepared for the conditions—on a summer day, sitting in an unshaded spot can lead to meltdown; at night, the mountain breezes can be cooler than you might expect.) Regardless of what musicians are performing, there is something miraculous about listening to music in the mountains with a clear sky and the sweeping countryside as the only backdrop. You will surely be inspired to kiss here—as have the many lucky couples who've tied the knot in this charmed setting. In 2004, construction began on a wine center that, upon completion in 2006, will feature an array of local wines and a tasting room that will be open to the public. We can't wait.
Open for special events only; www.mountainwinery.com.

THOMAS FOGARTY WINERY & VINEYARDS
❂❂❂
19501 Skyline Blvd, Woodside / 650/851-6777
Just when you think the rolling, mist-draped hills of scenic Woodside can't get any prettier, you come upon this charming winery. As you sip wines in the tasting room on this pleasant estate—which sprawls across 320 acres of forested, mountainous terrain—you'll enjoy breathtaking views of the lower San Francisco Bay. You can choose between five- or ten-dollar tasting menus that include an array of wines, ranging from chardonnay to pinot noir, merlot, and cabernet. One sip of the sparkling blanc de blanc should be enough to inspire you to lock lips—as do the couples who hold their nuptials in this beautiful mountaintop setting.
11am–5pm Thurs–Sun; www.fogartywinery.com.

Romantic Lodgings

THE FAIRMONT
◐◐

170 S Market St, San Jose / 408/998-1900 or 800/527-4727
In 2003, this giant landmark hotel got even bigger, with the addition of a grand 13-story tower that includes 264 additional rooms and 74 luxurious suites, bringing the total capacity to 805 rooms. You might see this staggering number of rooms as a drawback—and it can be, considering that the hotel's size makes it popular with convention goers and business types. Fortunately, this 20-story establishment in the heart of San Jose's downtown has plenty of benefits, starting with the fact that it's part of the Fairmont chain, which knows how to do luxurious basics right—all the way down to the Supercale cotton sheets on the beds. With guest rooms and public areas recently refurbished and with newly added niceties in the rooms including marble bathrooms, plush robes, electric shoe polishers, desks, walk-in closets, custom-made mattresses, minibars, and nightly turndown service, this hotel certainly puts everything you might want or need at your fingertips. During the summer months, the cabana rooms that directly face the 58-foot-long swimming pool and feature small, private sundecks are especially popular. You're in Silicon Valley—what would you expect besides high-speed modem links for computers and fax machines and interactive TV sets that let guests do everything from ordering up a movie to checking out of the hotel? Though these features might be of little interest when your only business is romance, other features, such as the elegant afternoon tea served in the hotel's lobby on weekends, will appeal. Three restaurants on the property make for convenient spots to tuck into a meal or snack: the Pagoda (408/998-3937) serves Chinese food at lunch and dinner; the Fountain (408/998-3982) is a casual spot for breakfast, lunch, and dinner; and the lobby-level Grill on the Alley offers hearty steakhouse fare and an extensive wine list.
$$$ AE, DC, DIS, V; checks OK; *www.fairmonthotels.com.* ⅙

GARDEN COURT HOTEL
◐◐◖

520 Cowper St, Palo Alto / 650/322-9000 or 800/824-9028
Escape the hustle and bustle of downtown Palo Alto in this Mediterranean-style villa built around an enclosed courtyard. All 62 guest rooms here have charming little balconies, many of which overlook the courtyard below. Though the courtyard view is appealing, come forewarned that the courtyard is not all you'll see, as these rooms directly face the rooms on the opposite side of the hotel. (For the utmost privacy, you'll have to shut the curtains.) However, even the rooms that face the busy street are infused with sunlight and laden with luxurious appointments, such as large arched

windows, pastel motifs, contemporary furnishings, and canopied beds made up with luscious fabrics and plush down comforters. Other amenities, such as CD players with a selection of CDs, morning newspaper delivery, and complimentary coffee and fruit, help set this hotel apart from others in town. The six suites with fireplaces and Jacuzzi tubs all offer loads of romantic potential. Breakfast is not included in your stay, but plenty of coffee shops just steps from the hotel can satisfy your morning cravings. Il Fornaio (650/853-3888), the restaurant on the hotel's main level, serves breakfast, lunch, and dinner. This chain Italian restaurant is too noisy and crowded to be romantic—and business types often overrun the place during weekday lunch—but the garden courtyard is a lovely place to enjoy a meal. Il Fornaio also delivers to guest rooms, and those private balconies double as wonderful dinner spots. Unlike most hotels these days in Northern California, this one offers smoking rooms; to ensure that you don't end up breathing in the unwanted scent of stale cigarettes, be sure to request a nonsmoking room.
$$$$ *AE, DC, MC, V; checks OK; www.gardencourt.com.* &

HOTEL DE ANZA
❤❤❤

233 W Santa Clara St, San Jose / 408/286-1000 or 800/843-3700
Few large hotels are as romance-friendly as this beautifully restored 1931 grande dame. The hotel's public spaces, such as the De Anza Room and the Hedley Club, boast art deco details and richly colored and refurbished Moorish ceilings. You'll find fewer decorative distinctions in the 101 rooms, but each is comfortable nonetheless, with pleasant lighting, modern furnishings, and blond wood accents. For an amorous encounter, consider splurging on a Junior Suite, a spacious corner room that features a king-size bed and comfortable sitting area. If you want even more room, consider the two-room Parlor Suites; each includes a separate parlor and has the romantic addition of a Jacuzzi tub in the spacious bathroom. Ask for one of the south-facing rooms to enjoy a sweeping view of downtown. Amenities include high-speed Internet access, an armoire with an honor bar, and a TV/VCR (you can check out movies gratis from the video library downstairs). The hotel's flagship restaurant, La Pastaia (408/286-8686), serves some of the best Italian food in town, and the place is always packed with locals as well as travelers. The stately Palm Court Terrace is a favorite place to meet for drinks in the warmer months, and a live jazz band performs in the Hedley Club on Wednesday through Saturday nights, where you can unwind in front of the beautiful wood-burning fireplace or sip a nightcap at the marble and cherrywood bar. The romance package, which includes in-room chilled champagne and dinner for two at your choice of one of several romantic restaurants, will take care of all the amorous details.
$$$ *AE, DC, MC, V; checks OK; www.hoteldeanza.com.*

HOTEL LOS GATOS
✿✿✿

210 E Main St, Los Gatos / 408/335-1700 or 866/355-1700
The sunny and sophisticated town of Los Gatos got an infusion of romance
with the arrival in 2002 of this luxurious, Mediterranean-style boutique
hotel. At the center of the lovely property is an elegant tiled courtyard,
complete with lush gardens and fountains and an aquamarine jewel of a
swimming pool (heated, of course), as well as a hot tub. Soak here together
while steam rises from the water's surface on a cool night or, on a warm day,
settle in poolside on the inviting cushioned chairs and nap in the sun. For
the ultimate pampering, visit the on-site spa, which offers an impressive
array of relaxing massages and beauty treatments (certain selected services
are even possible to have in your guest room). A sense of luxury will envelop
you from the moment you step inside the hotel. With its wrought-iron chandeliers, polished floors, inviting plush furniture, and earthy color scheme,
the lobby combines the charm of an old-world mansion with the elegance
of a Tuscan villa. The 72 rooms have opulent color schemes with crimson,
rich green, and topaz tastefully incorporated into the linens, drapes, and
custom furnishings. Every room has a king-size bed and an elegant stone-
tiled bathroom. The standard "deluxe" room features a combined shower
and tub; in the one-bedroom suites and the "junior grand" suites, wooden
shutters in the bathroom can be opened or closed to the bedroom, as your
hearts desire. In the one-bedroom suite, a wall separates the bedroom from
the spacious sitting area; the junior grand suite has an open floor plan.
The on-site restaurant Kuletos (408/354-8290; www.kuletoslosgatos.com),
a highly regarded Italian restaurant with locations in San Francisco and
Burlingame, serves well-prepared Northern Italian fare. In summer, the
restaurant's pretty, spacious courtyard is an ideal spot to enjoy a romantic
alfresco meal.
$$$$ AE, DC, DIS, MC, V; checks OK; www.jdvhospitality.com.

INN AT SARATOGA
✿✿

20645 4th St, Saratoga / 408/867-5020 or 800/338-5020
Nestled in the heart of picturesque Saratoga, this handsome inn strikes a
balance between the intimate warmth of a bed-and-breakfast and the comfortable practicality of a hotel. All 45 guest rooms feature private balconies
and windows that overlook Saratoga Creek as it flows through a small
forest of sycamore, maple, and eucalyptus trees. Upscale hotel furnishings,
king-size beds, double vanities, and a host of amenities provide everything
romantics yearn for, including luxurious tiled Jacuzzi tubs in seven of the
rooms. Don't be surprised if you see newlyweds locking lips here—there
is an abundance of wedding and reception venues in the greater Saratoga
area but few lodgings, making this centrally located spot popular with

newlyweds and their guests. Perhaps the hotel's monopoly in this area helps explain the prices, which range from expensive to outrageously expensive. You may want to stick with the average deluxe room with king-size bed, since the cost for the more spacious one-bedroom suite, equipped with additional sofa-bed and dining room, quickly climbs into the stratosphere. Complimentary wine and refreshments are served every afternoon in the plush lobby downstairs, and in the morning, a complimentary buffet-style continental breakfast is offered here; however, there aren't always enough tables to go around and, if you're late sleepers, the pickings can be slim. Consider waking up early and taking breakfast back to the privacy of your own room—you can always go back to bed after you eat. If you are really late sleepers and miss the morning offerings altogether, simply step outside—all of Saratoga's coffee shops, restaurants, and cafés are at your fingertips. $$$-$$$$ *AE, DC, V, MC; no checks; www.innatsaratoga.com.*

STANFORD PARK HOTEL
♥♥

100 El Camino Real, Menlo Park / 650/322-1234 or 800/368-2468
A hop, skip, and jump away from beautiful Stanford University is this pleasant and contemporary 163-room hotel, fronted by palm trees and a towering fountain. Though it's located next to a major arterial, this hotel has many redeeming features for those seeking a city getaway, including nearby shopping and easy access to university sights and activities. Plus, the popular town of Saratoga is only a 20-minute drive away. The lobby, furnished with a large fireplace surrounded by overstuffed sofas and high-backed chairs, is the gateway to what we consider the hotel's centerpiece: the garden courtyard. Adorned with modern sculptures, the inner yard is a delightful place to sit together and enjoy the California sunshine. Beyond is a small but tantalizing heated pool and a modest exercise studio. As for the rooms, those on the third floor are prime kissing spots; in addition to not having anyone above you, you'll also appreciate the high, vaulted ceilings. (Unfortunately, even with the extra space and large windows, the lighting isn't terribly bright. That's not a requirement for romance, of course, although it is for reading or finding things in your suitcase.) Try booking a third-floor courtyard-facing room if possible. Although the windows are soundproofed (quite well, we might add), the road-facing rooms lack view charisma. Many rooms have king-size beds fronting wood-burning fireplaces, and every room features a private bathroom with elegant granite and tile work, plus the added luxury of plush robes. Evening turndown service; pleasant color schemes of dark green, beige, and rose; and plenty of elbow room put this hotel in the above-average category for service and style. The menu at the on-site Duck Club Restaurant (650/322-1234) features classic California cuisine; dinner might include appetizers such as crab cakes or grilled portobello mushroom and entrées such as wild mushroom pasta

or rack of lamb for two. Tables in the recently remodeled dining room are set rather close together, but leafy potted plants and soft lighting create a pleasant ambience.

$$$$ *AE, DC, DIS, MC, V; checks OK; www.stanfordparkhotel.com.* &

Romantic Restaurants

BELLA MIA
◐◖
58 S 1st St, San Jose / 408/280-1993
Twenty thousand square feet of romantic possibilities await you at this sophisticated yet casual eatery in downtown San Jose. Polished wood and exposed brick lend a handsome air to the downstairs dining room, although noise from the open kitchen can intrude on quiet conversation. In fact, the overall ambience here is more that of an upscale bar scene than of an intimate restaurant, but the lively see-and-be-seen atmosphere is at least as much of a draw for most of the patrons as the food. If you're serious about wining and dining, head to the beautiful back room warmed by a fireplace and accented with candles; or, better yet, journey upstairs, where tables are arranged beneath skylights and sounds from the kitchen diminish. The lengthy and rather standard Italian menu has something to please even the pickiest palate. You might start by sampling one of the wines by the glass (there are more than two dozen) along with a starter such as freshly baked focaccia or almond prawn cocktail. The vast selection of hearty entrées includes everything from a long-simmered seafood cioppino or wood-grill spit-roasted chicken to cannelloni and eggplant parmigiana roasted in a hot oven. Bella Mia is one of the largest dining venues in San Jose; on the one hand, this may detract from intimacy, but on the other hand, it means you can usually get a table without a reservation. It's a rare treat to enjoy an impromptu romantic supper in the bustling Bay Area without having to plan it several weeks in advance—here is your opportunity.
$$ *AE, DC, DIS, MC, V; no checks; lunch, dinner every day, brunch Sat–Sun; full bar; reservations recommended; www.bellamia.com.*

EMILE'S
◈◈◈
545 S 2nd St, San Jose / 408/289-1960
The formal and stylish dining room at Emile's is appointed with wall mirrors, an ornate sculpted ceiling, and tapestry-covered chairs; at its center, sleek track lighting puts the spotlight on an impressive floral arrangement. This longtime local favorite offers a creative mix of contemporary European cuisines. Due to its extreme popularity and consequent crowds, the setting doesn't exactly feel intimate, but the food more than compensates.

The seasonally focused menu changes weekly; whatever the time of year, the entrées are appealing and creative, from fresh seafood dishes such as seared macadamia-crusted salmon on a bed of wild-mushroom risotto to more traditional fare, such as rack of lamb served with butternut squash gratin. Many things on the menu are made on the premises, from the house-cured gravlax that appears in an appetizer to the house-made sausage that features in a hearty entrée alongside braised cabbage, mashed potatoes, and caramelized onions with a veal reduction sauce. Though the dinner menu frequently changes, Emile's is known for one staple on its dessert list: the Grand Marnier soufflé. Don't miss it.

$$$ AE, DC, DIS, MC, V; no checks; dinner Tues–Sat; full bar; reservations recommended; www.emiles.com.

I GATTI
❍❍❍

25 E Main St, Los Gatos / 408/399-5180
The casual charm of the Tuscan countryside is effectively evoked at this small Los Gatos restaurant, which serves simple and satisfying Italian cuisine. The interior has a pleasant earth-toned decor, with sponge-painted mustard and red-brown walls and rustic yet elegant touches such as weathered wooden shutters and terra-cotta floor tiles. Despite the less than spacious quarters, the tables don't feel crammed together. Soft lighting and tables set with white linen and wine glasses complete the mood. A glass of your favorite *vino* is just the thing to accompany a plate of goat-cheese ravioli with a rich chianti-wine glaze or tender gnocchi with a creamy tomato-vodka sauce. You might also be tempted by the intriguing salads, such as the mixed greens with roasted walnuts, goat cheese, and caramelized onions drizzled with a balsamic pancetta dressing, or by a thin pizza brushed with olive oil and baked until tender and crisp. Main courses such as roasted filet mignon with a Barolo wine and wild-mushroom sauce, braised lamb shank, and lightly breaded breast of chicken served with a champagne, lemon-herb, and caper sauce are hearty and satisfying.

$$$ AE, MC, V; checks OK; dinner every day; beer and wine; reservations recommended.

L'AMIE DONIA
❍❍❍

530 Bryant St, Palo Alto / 650/323-7614
This bustling French bistro and wine bar is a popular choice with locals looking for an amorous evening out. The first sign that your evening will be a success comes when you step inside the pleasantly decorated space, where cushioned banquettes covered in burgundy and green fabric evoke the mood of a wine-country harvest, and a zinc bar adds a touch of urban chic. Everything about the interior encourages you to relax. The imaginative

yet unintimidating wine list offers several well-priced choices available by the glass, and the seasonally changing menu features an array of traditional favorites such as onion soup, galantine of duck, and steak bordelaise with *pommes frites*. But unlike some French restaurants, where you feel weighed down after a meal overloaded with creamy sauces, this fare is made with a light touch, so you can still exchange lighter-than-air kisses after dinner. It also means you'll have room for one of the superb desserts, such as the classic tarte Tatin with vanilla ice cream.
$$$ *AE, DIS, MC, V; no checks; dinner Tues–Sat; beer and wine; reservations recommended.*

LA FONDUE
♥♥

14510 Big Basin Wy, Saratoga / 408/867-3332
La Fondue lives up to its reputation as a unique restaurant. The two dining rooms are more unusual than romantic, with colorful and whimsical decor. The Blue Room draws its theme from Greek mythology and features moons, suns, and stars, while the Red Room tends toward a medieval theme. Who would guess that in a setting like this, the menu would offer nothing but fondues? The air is laden with delicious aromas, and the fondue selection is extensive, ranging from classic Swiss cheese to more unusual selections such as pesto and Cognac fondue. Of course, you can't leave a fondue restaurant without indulging in a "dunk-your-fruit-into-chocolate" dessert. Several dipping selections should entice your taste buds, including a velvety white chocolate and an old-fashioned milk chocolate—some people book here for dessert only. Reservations are accepted up to one month in advance, and our advice is to call early if you have your heart set on the experience. Corkage fees are waived on certain nights, so if you plan in advance, you can open your special bottle of wine at no additional fee. If you're wondering whether fondue is really all that romantic, take notice of the restaurant's "fondue rules," which state: "If a lady loses her cube in the fondue, she pays with a kiss to the man on her right." Just make sure you're not seated next to any strangers.
$$–$$$ *AE, MC, V; no checks; dinner every day; beer and wine; reservations recommended; www.lafondue.com.*

LA FORÊT
♥♥♥

21747 Bertram Rd, San Jose / 408/997-3458
La Forêt is just a short drive away from the high-tech world of San Jose, but its romantic interior will take you much farther away. Located outside the city limits, the restaurant sits next to a creek in what was the first two-story adobe hotel in California. White tablecloths cover intimately spaced tables topped with red roses in the restaurant's three dining rooms, which enjoy

scenic views of the wooded landscape; soft candlelight casts a gentle spell. The sublime French menu focuses on meat but includes everything from pheasant and duck breast to rack of lamb and wild game. Best of all, these hearty entrées tend to showcase the delicious sauces that are so essential in French cuisine: tender medallions of elk topped with delicate tarragon cream sauce; poached salmon served with a rich port wine sauce. A dish of pasta dressed with olive oil, herbs, garlic, wild mushrooms, and Gouda cheese or an appetizer of escargot with garlic butter is an appealing way to begin your meal. The service, like the food, is outstanding. Don't miss the chance to share one of the tempting cakes, cheesecakes, and exotic soufflés on the dessert list.

$$$ *AE, DC, DIS, MC, V; no checks; dinner Tues–Sun, brunch Sun; full bar; reservations recommended; www.laforetrestaurant.com.*

MADDALENA'S RESTAURANT
✪✪✪

544 Emerson St, Palo Alto / 650/326-6082
This luxuriously old-world restaurant, a Palo Alto romantic institution for decades, offers the sort of formal night out that can be hard to come by in the world of modern restaurants. The menu is a classic continental affair, and the swift and efficient tuxedo-clad waiters anticipate diners' every whim. The downstairs dining room exudes an intimate ambience. Well-placed screens between the tables create private space and separate you from your neighbors, giving you a wonderful sense of seclusion. Start the meal with a classic Caesar salad or grilled pancetta-wrapped prawns. Entrées are hearty yet elegant, and there is something to satisfy every craving: steak au poivre, tender veal, crisp duck with juniper berries and cassis, delicate poached salmon with a mustard-and-white-wine cream sauce, and pheasant with Grand Marnier. Pasta is also on the menu in creative preparations; the signature dish of fettuccine with smoked duck, spinach, and garlic in a light roma tomato sauce is a favorite, as is the fettuccine with lobster. The rich and decadent desserts include a wonderful house-made cheesecake and a three-layer chocolate mousse cake. The wine list, tipped toward expensive vintages, offers mostly Italian and California selections. For a romantic surprise, book the beautifully appointed art deco private room for two upstairs. If you'd like to sample this Palo Alto classic but your budget is a little tight, try Cafe Fino, the less-expensive yet still extremely elegant Italian bistro next door, which has the same management and shares Maddalena's kitchen. Cafe Fino's art deco–inspired dining room features a grand piano and every evening brings live jazz at 7:30pm—the perfect backdrop for intimate conversation.

$$$ *AE, DC, MC, V; checks OK; lunch Tues–Fri, dinner Mon–Sat; full bar; reservations recommended; www.maddalenasrestaurant.com.*

MANRESA
✿✿✿
320 Village Ln, Los Gatos / 408/354-4330

Opened in 2002 by the former proprietor of Sent Sovi, a Saratoga restaurant that received many kissing accolades in previous editions of this book, Manresa is designed for couples who hope to reach new culinary heights together. At this impressive destination, the sky is the limit when it comes to cost, and even the most jaded wine lover is bound to be impressed by the 17-page wine list. The dining room's muted color scheme of taupe, ocher, and blond wood accents does have elegant touches in the form of champagne silk shantung draperies and Oriental carpets, but overall the decor is more modern and sleek than romantic and intimate. Then again, it's not the decor that has turned this spot into a restaurant reviewers' darling, but the surprising combinations of flavors in the contemporary American cuisine with French and Spanish flair. Starting with refreshing granita of lychee nut, mint, and condensed milk is just the beginning of a meal that might last up to three hours—so come prepared to stay for a while. Select from one of three prix fixe menu options or, for the ultimate splurge, try the "seasonal and spontaneous" chef's tasting menu. A recent menu included a remarkable egg dish with fleur de sel and a soft egg topped with maple syrup and sherry vinegar; black-olive madeleines sweetened with molasses; an unusual strawberry gazpacho topped with chives; and grilled duck breast surrounded by gold beets and plums. As the exotic desserts are baked to order, you are requested to choose one at the start of the meal; whether you opt for the caramel coconut-mango tart with passion-fruit ice cream or chocolate fondant with cherry compote, you won't be disappointed.

$$$$ *MC, V; no checks; dinner Wed–Sun; beer and wine; reservations recommended; www.manresarestaurant.com.* &

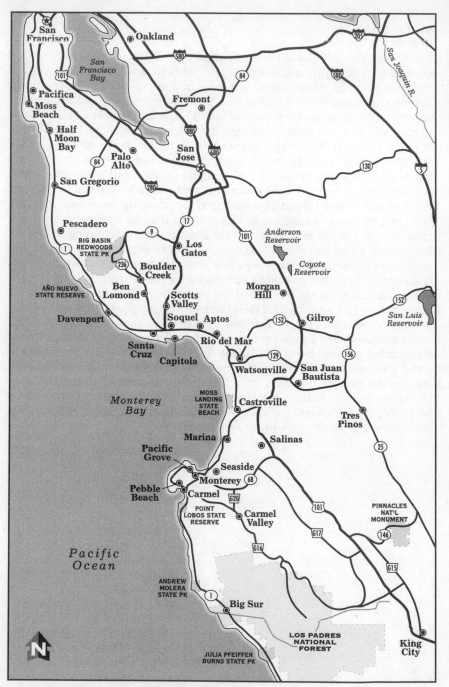

"A kiss can be a comma, a question mark, or an exclamation point. That's basic spelling that every woman ought to know."

—MISTINGUETT

♡ CENTRAL COAST

Traveling the coastline of California is an unforgettable experience. For literally hundreds of miles, the power of the ocean and the majestic scenery are staggering in their beauty. Each region along the coast also has its own personality, and the Central Coast—which begins south of San Francisco and stretches to Big Sur's famously beautiful and rugged stretch of shoreline—has a feel distinctly different from the North Coast, for example, where remote seaside towns are surrounded by little but crashing waves and scenery. In contrast, the Central Coast is densely populated and offers wonderfully diverse options for a romantic getaway.

The Central Coast's best-known communities are chic and expensive. Towns such as Carmel, Monterey, and Pebble Beach are the most upscale and cosmopolitan in all of Northern California; these are ideal destinations for urbane getaways involving dinners in upscale restaurants and shopping in stylish boutiques. The more casual destinations of Capitola-by-the-Sea and Santa Cruz (the latter is home to a University of California campus) offer more outdoorsy activities—yet there are still plenty of good restaurants and romantic accommodations to discover. A true small-town getaway is also yours to be had along this stretch of coast, if you visit Half Moon Bay or one of the handful of scenic towns that dot Highway 1 south of San Francisco.

No matter what you're in the mood for, there's a destination on the Central Coast that will more than live up to your dreams—and the region's numerous accessible beaches and unforgettably dramatic views of the mighty Pacific will earn a lifelong place in your memories.

HALF MOON BAY REGION

ROMANTIC HIGHLIGHTS

When the rest of the world heads to Stinson Beach and other points along the exquisite northern coastline, you can wind your way south to Half Moon Bay and beyond. The weather is often blustery, and it can be difficult to predict the behavior of the fog, but with miles of sandy beach at every turn, it's difficult to find a place that isn't suitable for kissing.

Access to all sorts of marine wonders can be found in **Moss Beach**, a tiny town between Pacifica and Half Moon Bay. Its highlight is the **James V. Fitzgerald Marine Reserve** (415/728-3584), where couples can trek along oceanfront trails and observe tide pools teeming with aquatic life. This rocky intertidal habitat is sheltered from the crashing surf by a series of offshore terraces. You will *ooh* and *ahh* as you tread—lightly and respectfully, of course—on the 30 acres of reef exposed during low tide. The shoreline here is a picture-perfect spot to observe the sun's nightly dip into the ocean. You can also head to the **Moss Beach Distillery** (see Romantic Restaurants) for lunch or an early supper with a lovely ocean view.

In the small town of **Princeton-by-the-Sea** you'll find **Pillar Point Harbor** (4 miles north of Half Moon Bay), a popular launching point for deep-sea fishing trips; more romantic are the whale-watching trips offered between January and March by such local outfits as **Captain John's Fishing Trips** (650/726-2913 or 800/391-8787). For an even closer look at marine wildlife, including harbor seals and marine birds, book a half-day paddling tour of Pillar Point Harbor with **California Canoe & Kayak** (Pillar Point Harbor at Half Moon Bay Yacht Club; 800/366-9804; www.calkayak.com). You can wind up your romantic outing with supper at **Mezza Luna** (459 Prospect Wy; 650-728-8108), a charming Italian restaurant with a sunny Tuscan interior housed in a historic hotel.

Half Moon Bay, a mere 25 miles from San Francisco, is the best-known romantic getaway in the region. This quaint hamlet hugging the seaside along the rocky Highway 1 feels worlds away from big-city life (despite the fact that it has become something of a satellite to neighboring Silicon Valley—real estate prices having risen accordingly). Originally, the town's main attraction was its annual **Pumpkin Festival**, but today, the quaint Main Street is busy year-round, with enough inviting shops and good restaurants to keep you occupied from dawn to dusk.

Outdoor adventurers can plan biking, hiking, and even whale-watching trips in the area. Renting beach cruisers at **The Bicyclery** (101 B Main St at Hwy 1; 650/726-6000) and going for a leisurely bike ride along the shoreline is a serene way to spend the afternoon together. Be sure to ask one of the staffers about the best biking trails. If a hike is your hearts' desire, visit

Purisima Creek Redwoods (650/691-1200; drive south from Half Moon Bay on Hwy 1 to Higgins Purisima Creek Rd, turn left, then continue 4.5 miles to the small gravel trailhead). This little-known sanctuary, frequented mostly by local hikers, mountain bikers, and equestrians, is a sublime spot for a little privacy amid lush redwood forests, fern-lined creek banks, and fields full of wildflowers and berries.

If you are in a more decadent mood and want to sleep late and partake of the finer things in life, enjoy a leisurely outing to the scenic **Obester Winery's Wine-Tasting Room** (12341 San Mateo Rd; 650/726-9463; www.obester-winery.com; 10am–5pm every day), located just a few miles from Half Moon Bay up Highway 92. The pleasant drive winds past fields of flowers—and pumpkin patches in the fall—and in the rustic tasting room, you and your sweetie can sample award-winning wines. Behind the tasting room, a small picnic area makes a perfect spot for an afternoon lunch break.

The stretch of coastline between Half Moon Bay and Santa Cruz provides spectacular ocean scenery—and little else, aside from the tiny town of **Pescadero** and the unique nature lovers' paradise known as **Costanoa** (see Romantic Lodgings). Even if you are continuing down the coast and not planning on spending the night, Costanoa makes a good stop. Plan a romantic hike on the **Pampas Heaven Loop Trail** (from main trailhead at Costanoa, cross Whitehouse Creek Bridge and follow Whitehouse Creek Trail to the loop), or simply stop for a tasty lunch or gourmet picnic items at the **Costanoa General Store and Café**.

Bird lovers will want to explore one of the few remaining natural marshes left on the central California coast, the **Pescadero Marsh Natural Preserve**. The 600 acres of wetlands—part of the Pacific flyway—provide refuge for approximately 230 bird species, including the majestic great blue herons that nest in the northern row of eucalyptus trees. The preserve is across the highway from **Pescadero State Beach** (650/879-2170; www.parks.ca.gov), a milelong sandy shoreline that's lovely for a romantic beach stroll.

Within a short drive of Pescadero is **Big Basin Redwoods State Park** (21600 Big Basin Way; 831/338-8860), a magical place filled with awe-inspiring ancient trees—even those accustomed to Northern California's magnificent natural beauty will find something to kiss about on these trails.

Access and Information

The quickest way to get to the Half Moon Bay region from San Francisco is to take Interstate 280 south to the Highway 92 exit, which leads straight into town. For a more scenic route, however, drive along Highway 1. The entrance to Half Moon Bay's Main Street is located about two blocks (east) up Highway 92 from the Highway 1 intersection. Head toward the Shell station, then turn right (south) onto Main Street until you cross a small bridge.

Romantic couples, beware: there are some very appealing inns in the towns of Moss Beach, Princeton, and Half Moon Bay, but—particularly if you visit midweek—it's not unusual to run into gaggles of conference types yakking into cell phones. Many of the areas here have facilities for small business conferences, so if you don't find the corporate atmosphere romantic, call the inn ahead of time to find out if any conferences will be going on during your stay.

Another source of information is the **Half Moon Bay Visitors Bureau** (520 Kelly Ave at Hwy 1; 650/726-8380; www.halfmoonbaychamber.org or www.coastsidelive.com; 9am–4pm Mon–Fri, 10am–3pm Sat).

Romantic Lodgings

BEACH HOUSE INN AT HALF MOON BAY
◐◐◖

4100 Hwy 1, Half Moon Bay / 650/712-0220 or 800/315-9366
We highly recommend splurging for a room with a view at this oceanfront getaway, set just a few miles north of the town of Half Moon Bay. The Nantucket shingle-style inn, with fabulous unobstructed views of the water, opened in 1997 and offers refreshingly modern rooms with upscale amenities. The 54 suites are similar in design and size; it's the views that determine price—and romantic potential. In the ocean-view rooms, a California king-size bed faces the sea, and you'll forget all about the highway on the other side of the inn. Each comfortable guest room includes a sandstone fireplace, a lovely step-down sitting area separate from the bedroom, a granite-accented kitchenette, and a sparkling white bathroom with oversize tub and shower. Sitting on your private balcony or patio, you can listen to the waves lapping against the barrier rocks and the sea grass rustling in the wind. The only unnatural sound you might hear is the honking of a distant foghorn. If you can tear yourselves away from your comfy quarters, you'll find a small swimming pool and communal but roomy Jacuzzi spa on the south-facing terrace, which affords views of Surfer's Beach and its namesake surfers. If this puts you in the mood for even more relaxation, schedule some indulgent treatments at the Beach House Day Spa, or arrange for an in-room massage. A continental breakfast is served in the lobby each morning. The property draws business conference types to its handful of large meeting rooms; if you wish to avoid such company on your romantic adventure, inquire whether any conferences are scheduled to take place during your stay.
$$$$ AE, DC, DIS, MC, V; checks OK; www.beach-house.com.

COSTANOA
❂❂❂

2001 Rossi Rd, Pescadero / 650/879-1100 or 800/738-7477

Lovers of the great outdoors have gained a new one-word definition for romance: Costanoa. Set in a pristine wilderness area bordering four state parks and 30,000 acres of hiking trails, this lovely eco-resort contains a comfortable lodge, 12 stylish wooden cabins, and more than 50 canvas tent bungalows: you decide exactly how much you want to rough it. The fullest amenities are to be found in the striking cabinlike lodge, the only place where guests are provided with their own entirely private bathroom. The lodge's 40 simple and pleasant guest rooms are decorated with a tasteful mix of eco-friendly materials and colors: polished wood, slate tile, and pale earth-toned hues. Room amenities, in addition to the private baths, include Bose stereo systems, refrigerators, robes, private decks, and access to the lodge's spa facilities and outdoor hot tub. Many rooms also have fireplaces and soaking tubs. One step lower on the luxury ladder are the six duplex cabins, which don't have private bathrooms; however, it's just a short walk to one of the six "comfort stations"—sleek and upscale communal bathrooms with heated floors, large showers, and dry saunas—which are shared by all guests except for those in the lodge. The charms of the cabin rooms cannot be denied: each features a vaulted ceiling, fireplace, and deck with porch swing that overlooks wild, lush terrain. Another step lower on the luxury ladder—but many steps higher on the adventure ladder—are the deluxe tent bungalows, one of California's most unusual lodging experiences. Their queen-size beds, down comforters, heated mattress pads, and retro-style furnishings put a new twist on "roughing it." As with Costanoa's other accommodations, continental breakfast is part of the deal. (A variety of less-luxurious tent bungalows is also available, as is a small area in which guests pitch their own tent or park their RV.) The small spa offers Swedish, deep tissue, or Shiatsu massage; aromatherapy; a sauna; and a steam room; and activities include hiking, on-site mountain bike rentals, and horseback riding. Couples should come forewarned: Costanoa is family-friendly rather than romance oriented. Fortunately, even at summer's peak, there are plenty of deserted hiking trails and stretches of beach where you can find romantic seclusion. Also, due to its rural location (on Highway 1 between Pigeon Point Lighthouse and the Año Nuevo State Reserve—9 miles south of Pescadero), there are no romantic restaurants to speak of in the immediate area. Happily, the Costanoa General Store and Café is delightfully gourmet and offers everything from enticing salads and sandwiches to hearty entrée specials such as fresh local fish—not to mention homemade desserts and an espresso bar. Plenty of specialty picnic items are also on hand, should you want to retreat to your room with goodies and picnic indoors.

$–$$$$ AE, DC, DIS, MC, V; no checks; www.costanoa.com.

CYPRESS INN ON MIRAMAR BEACH
●●●●

407 Mirada Rd, Half Moon Bay / 650/726-6002 or 800/832-3224
The rhythm of crashing waves, the telltale cries of gulls, and the invigorating smell of salty sea air are all part of the sensory package at this picturesque inn, whose three contemporary beach houses sit directly across the street from the ocean. The Lighthouse Building, completed in 2001, houses six new luxury suites that are loaded with romantic amenities such as Jacuzzi tubs and oceanfront decks and offer partial or spectacular full oceanfront views. The inn's original building showcases a colorful collection of hand-carved Mexican sculptures and artwork. The eight smallish rooms in this building offer breathtaking ocean views and incorporate the elements, with names like La Luna (the moon), Las Nubes (the clouds), and El Cielo (the sky). Vividly colored stucco walls, terra-cotta tile floors, and natural-fiber furnishings lend the rooms a simple yet sophisticated distinction. Luxurious white linens accent the fluffy feather beds, and a gas fireplace glows in every room. Although the spacious Penthouse Suite is the only room with a Jacuzzi tub (built for two), all of the rooms have private bathrooms and private balconies where you can kiss to a soundtrack of crashing waves. Four luxury suites occupy the second beach house, set directly behind the original inn. Located a little farther from the water, these rooms compensate for the lack of direct ocean views with pretty beach-theme decor that features color schemes in sand and coral and seashell-motif fabrics; the amenities include gas fireplaces, elegant bathrooms, and extradeep jetted tubs in two of the suites. The Dunes Beach room, which boasts an expansive deck with an ocean view, is the largest. When it comes to romantic amenities, however, there's no doubt that the new Lighthouse Building is the place to set up camp, with six bright, contemporary rooms each uniquely decorated with prints of famous California lighthouses. The four King rooms are the most splendid, with king-size beds and fireplaces. One of the most spectacular vistas is from Maverick's room, which overlooks the famous Maverick's surfing beach. The remaining two rooms offer partial ocean views, queen beds, and whirlpool tubs. In the morning, enjoy a bountiful breakfast brought directly to your room or served family-style in the inn's cheery dining room. Choices might include peaches-and-cream French toast, meat-free eggs Benedict with steamed asparagus, or light yogurt parfait. Wine and hors d'oeuvres are served in the twilight hours, and later on in the evening, you'll find a sweet treat on your pillow.
$$$$ AE, DIS, MC, V; checks OK; www.cypressinn.com. &

MILL ROSE INN
◆◆◆◆
615 Mill St, Half Moon Bay / 650/726-8750 or 800/900-7673
Surrounded by a classic white picket fence, a lush garden bursting with brilliant colors welcomes you to the Mill Rose Inn. The longtime owners of this English country inn have given every detail their full attention, from the lovingly tended rose garden in the courtyard to the luscious chocolates and liqueurs found in every room. Antiques and photos of the owners' prized poodles fill the cozy common areas, where guests can take in the ambience of bygone days while sampling wine, cheese, and decadent desserts in the early evening. Ornate and flowery decor reigns in the six intimate guest rooms, where you'll discover extravagant bouquets of silk and fresh-cut flowers, elaborate Bradbury & Bradbury wallpaper, and ultraplush window treatments. The furnishings, equal parts comfort and ornament, include plush European feather beds, claw-foot tubs, European antiques, and hand-painted tile fireplaces (in all but one room). TVs, VCRs, and stereos are hidden in armoires; mini-refrigerators are stocked with complimentary beverages. Each suite has its own private entrance, and you can expect turndown service and morning newspaper delivery. An ample whirlpool tub (large enough for two) highlights the Bordeaux Rose Suite, but all guests have access to a flower-shielded gazebo that encloses a Jacuzzi spa enhanced by lush greenery, more flowers, and a bubbling fountain. Don't worry about finding a crowd in the spa—you can reserve time here for a private, steamy soak of your own. After a good night's sleep, enjoy a champagne breakfast at your own private table in the dining room or, better yet, have it delivered to your room or to a table in the peaceful rose garden. Breakfast treats along the lines of apple-cranberry crunch, frothy banana-orange frappé, and artichoke frittata served with spicy salsa will keep you going until dinnertime. Mill Rose Inn also prides itself on extra thoughtful touches, such as offering you the use of blankets, coolers, and a handy picnic basket (you supply the food and drinks) for your beach outings.
$$$–$$$$ *AE, DIS, MC, V; checks OK; www.millroseinn.com.*

OLD THYME INN
◆◆
779 Main St, Half Moon Bay / 650/726-1616 or 800/720-4277
Spicing up your love life is a snap at this traditional bed-and-breakfast situated in downtown Half Moon Bay. A blend of modern and old-fashioned touches is apparent in each of the seven rooms of this delightful Queen Anne Victorian, handsomely renovated and well maintained by its owners. Works from the owners' art collection adorn walls painted in soothing solid colors, luxurious designer linens cover the beds, and claw-foot tubs and authentic stained-glass windows highlight some of the bathrooms. Other rooms are equipped with those romantic staples, fireplaces and whirlpool tubs. Extra

touches include fresh flowers brightening the rooms and a video library overflowing with "snuggling-up" movies that will entice you to stay put. By far the most romantic and spacious room is the Garden Suite, with its own private entrance off the herb garden, a double Jacuzzi tub set beneath a large skylight, and a canopied bed fronting the fireplace. A subtle Japanese motif is woven throughout this simple yet comfortable retreat, in which you have the indulgent option of having breakfast delivered, at your leisure. Savory morning meal options include warm tortillas stuffed with scrambled eggs or eggs Florentine served with harvest-grain bread. Special treats such as lemon-rosemary crumb cake showcase delights from the inn's productive herb garden, which contains dozens of aromatic varieties, all available for tasting by inquisitive guests. Breakfast is served at a common table in the living room or on the garden patio, when weather permits. It is easy to see how love—not to mention hundreds of flowers and herbs—can bloom so easily at the Old Thyme Inn.

$$$-$$$$ *AE, DC, DIS, MC, V; checks OK; www.oldthymeinn.com.*

PILLAR POINT INN
◐◐◑

380 Capistrano Rd, Princeton-by-the-Sea / 650/728-7377 or 800/400-8281
Escape to Cape Cod for the weekend without ever leaving the West Coast at this comfortable seaside inn that looks like a transplant from a New England fishing village. Despite its location on a well-traveled street, this inn's soundproof windows and sprawling architectural design make each room here a little haven unto itself. Ten of the 11 rooms feature bay windows with spectacular views of the ocean. Recline together in the window seat and stop kissing long enough to watch the fishing boats as they enter the harbor with the day's catch. The only room that does not face the ocean overlooks a meadow and a well-kept hedged garden. Each room features a beautifully tiled fireplace, a downy European feather bed, and amenities such as telephone, refrigerator, and concealed TV; all have private, standard baths. Vaulted ceilings in several of the upstairs rooms add a light, airy feel, and the best vistas are to be found in the corner rooms, Half Moon Bay (No. 6) and the Sybil Easterday (No. 10). The glowing fireplace in the breakfast room is complemented by large windows allowing you to bask in the morning sunshine as you enjoy delicious homemade granola, fresh muffins, coffee cake, Belgian waffles, chili-pepper quiche, or cheese blintzes. After you've had your fill, don your jackets, walk to the wharf, and see what the fishing boats have brought home; then head back to the inviting parlor for a fireside glass of sherry (available at all hours). Come evening, it's only a short walk to the lively Italian restaurant Mezza Luna (see Romantic Highlights), housed in a historic hotel nearby.

$$$ *AE, MC, V; local checks only; www.pillarpointinn.com.* &

THE RITZ-CARLTON
❂❂❂❂
1 Miramontes Point Rd, Half Moon Bay / 650/712-7000 or 800/241-3333
Perched on the edge of the gleaming Pacific, this glamorous Ritz-Carlton
hotel opened in 2001. The large golf and spa resort, with 261 rooms and
suites, is simply too large to feel cozy or intimate; however, its location on
a rugged ocean bluff with sweeping views of the coastline, as well as its
upscale amenities, exquisite luxury spa, and fabulous restaurants, provide
more than enough romance (more than 100 weddings take place here each
year). Best of all, the 19th-century-inspired shingled hotel isn't ostentatious
or grandiose, just luxurious: tucked into an oceanfront hillside, it fits beautifully into the natural surroundings. Inside, all rooms offer marble bathrooms and pleasing decor with color schemes in white and pale yellow, with
rosy floral linens and carpets. Amenities include feather beds with duvets,
silky 300-thread-count Egyptian cotton sheets, and plush robes; there's
also twice-daily maid service, evening turndown service, and 24-hour room
service. Two-thirds of the rooms offer ocean views (request a Deluxe Ocean/
Coastal View Guestroom), and many feature a fireplace, balcony, or window
seat. Up on the fifth floor, the Ritz-Carlton Club Level offers 50 rooms in a
private haven that includes an ocean-view lounge, personal concierge staff,
plus complimentary afternoon tea, hors d'oeuvres, and evening cocktails.
For the ultimate in pampering, book one of the seven luxurious garden-level
Spa Rooms, completed in 2004: Fresh flowers, candles, special ultraluxe
linens, your own private "spa bar" in the bathroom, soothing music, and
an aromatherapy diffuser make each room its own serene oasis. Glass doors
lead to your alfresco patio; you can simply pad down the hall to the spa
without ever stepping out of your robe and slippers. Of course, you don't
have to stay in one of the Spa Rooms to take advantage of the 16,000-square-
foot Spa, complete with calming views of the Pacific Ocean, candlelit co-ed
Roman Mineral Bath, and an oceanfront Jacuzzi, along with 16 treatment
rooms, including one designed especially for couples. If activities are more
your game, take advantage of the 36 holes of championship golf right outside, visit the fitness center with perks such as daily classes in the heated
yoga studio, or ask the concierge for tips on tide pooling, horseback riding,
or wine tasting. When it's time to wine and dine your beloved, visit one of the
property's three restaurants: At Navio (650/712-7040), enjoy sophisticated
coastal cuisine with breathtaking ocean views; in The Conservatory, peek
through telescopes to view the sea over cocktails; or at The Salon, indulge
in traditional English afternoon tea. When you're ready for some outdoor
kissing, stroll to the beach on the scenic trail that traverses the seaside bluffs
just outside the hotel.
$$$-$$$$ *AE, DC, DIS, MC, V; checks OK; www.ritzcarlton.com.* ♿

SEAL COVE INN
✿✿✿✿

221 Cypress Ave, Moss Beach / 650/728-4114 or 800/995-9987
The owner of this distinctive property is a well-known travel writer, so it's not surprising that the details at Seal Cove Inn are all so beautifully rendered. Everything you could possibly want for an amorous escape from city life is here, a mere 30 minutes south of San Francisco. Surrounded by herb and flower gardens, the expansive inn enjoys narrow glimpses of the ocean beyond a dense stand of lofty cypress trees. Guests can walk through the property to the rugged coastal bluffs and spend hours exploring the neighboring marine reserve and tide-pool beaches. In each of the 10 guest rooms, simple and pleasing country decor prevails, accented by homey touches such as grandfather clocks and watercolor paintings. The spacious rooms feature an abundance of romantic assets, from the luxurious linens gracing the wood-framed beds to wood-burning fireplaces that warm up cozy seating areas. TV/VCRs are tucked away in armoires. Fresh flowers, towel warmers, complimentary beverages, evening turndown service, and morning newspaper and coffee delivery to your door are nice touches. Each room has a private bath and a deck or terrace that overlooks the property's resplendent gardens. Vaulted ceilings lend a feeling of spaciousness to the upstairs rooms, and Jacuzzi tubs in the Cypress and Fitzgerald Suites are well worth the extra expense. If privacy is your priority, a continental breakfast can be delivered to your room; otherwise, start your day with hot entrées such as Grand Marnier French toast or blueberry pancakes in the formal, sun-filled dining room. After a day of exploring tide pools or beachcombing, return to enjoy wine and appetizers in the comfortable living room, complete with a blazing fire.
$$$–$$$$ AE, DIS, MC, V; checks OK; www.sealcoveinn.com. &

Romantic Restaurants

MIRAMAR BEACH RESTAURANT
✿

131 Mirada Rd, Half Moon Bay / 650/726-9053
Known more for its incredible views than for its ambience, the main draw of the Miramar Beach Restaurant is its location on the Pacific: many of the wooden tables are positioned next to windows that offer unobstructed views of spectacular sunsets and crashing waves. However, the interior does not live up to the scenery; table lamps and wall sconces are the only attempt to dress up the otherwise uninspired dining room, which has the further drawback of worn carpeting. While the oceanfront seating should not be missed, a romantic small table in back next to the fireplace can be reserved if privacy is your first priority. Live music from pianists and, sometimes, singers pro-

vides entertainment on Saturday evenings and all day Sunday. The broad menu of continental cuisine includes typical dishes such as filet mignon and pasta primavera in merely average incarnations. Fortunately, the seafood is more inspired, especially the generous crab cakes and the "fresh catch of the day," delivered by local fishermen. The scenic coastal trail that winds north of Half Moon Bay passes by here, making the restaurant a convenient stop for lunch should you be hiking or riding bikes.
$$ *DIS, MC, V; no checks; lunch, dinner every day, brunch Sun; full bar; reservations recommended; www.miramarbeach.com.*

MOSS BEACH DISTILLERY

140 Beach Wy at Ocean Blvd, Moss Beach / 650/728-5595
During Prohibition, this historic restaurant was used by bootleggers to store illicit liquids, but today it draws a more law-abiding crowd: hungry couples seeking dinner with a view. With its blue-painted walls, cozy dining alcoves, windows affording magnificent ocean vistas, and massive patio, the cliff-side landmark retains a beguiling 1920s beach-house atmosphere. The menu offers an assortment of creative California-Mediterranean dishes, such as grilled portobello mushrooms with cabernet sauce, shrimp tempura with ginger vinaigrette, and a fork-tender pork chop enlivened by a mustard-shallot sauce and leek-buttermilk mashed potatoes. And if the views, historical setting, and good food aren't enough, the Distillery also lays claim to a couple of resident ghosts, including the famous Blue Lady, a flapper-era beauty who is said to haunt the place searching for her faithless lover. All the more reason to get cozy over your table for two.
$$ *DC, DIS, MC, V; no checks; lunch Mon–Sat, dinner every day, brunch Sun (patio menu available all day); full bar; reservations recommended; www.mossbeachdistillery.com.*

PASTA MOON

315 Main St, Half Moon Bay / 650/726-5125
Set among the small boutiques that line Main Street, this inviting restaurant offers sophisticated Italian fare in a refined café atmosphere. Glowing candles, white tablecloths, and soft music contribute to the warm ambience. Most of the tables are spaced reasonably far enough apart to keep conversations private; the best table choices are next to the large picture windows, where noise from the open kitchen is less audible. The once-traditional Italian menu has taken a lighter, more creative turn with the arrival of a new chef from San Francisco: dishes now feature lots of locally grown, organic produce and fresh fish. Start with an appetizer of Half Moon Bay artichokes *à la grecque,* served with Italian butter beans, arugula, and lemon vinaigrette, or house-smoked salmon with pickled pearl onions and

parsley salad. *Secondi piatti* include a wood-oven-roasted veal chop stuffed with portobello mushrooms, Parmesan polenta, and endive with thyme-infused olive oil; and pan-seared sea bass with asparagus and risotto and a lemon, garlic, and shrimp vinaigrette. Pastas, breads, and pastries are all made on the premises; the focaccia is heavenly, the house-made pasta seldom disappoints, and pizza lovers can select from a wide range of thin-crust creations.

$$ AE, DC, DIS, MC, V; *local checks only; lunch, dinner every day, brunch Sun; full bar; reservations recommended; www.pastamoon.com.*

SAN BENITO HOUSE
ØØ€

356 Main St, Half Moon Bay / 650/726-3425
There's a touch of Europe in this candlelit dining room set inside a pastel blue Victorian on Main Street. Arrive early and enjoy a cocktail before dinner in the old-fashioned saloon, which gleams with polished wood and brass. The dining room is delightfully romantic, filled with tables set with crystal and linen and adorned with country antiques, vases of fresh flowers, and paintings by local turn-of-the-20th-century artists. And the food lives up to the ambience. The kitchen prepares such tempting fare as homemade ravioli stuffed with fennel, fontina, and toasted almonds with creamy leek sauce; fillet of beef with Gorgonzola and herb butter; and salmon topped with lemon-caper vinaigrette on a bed of lentil ragout. Desserts are terrific and may include a strawberry-rhubarb crepe served with crème anglaise and strawberry sauce, chocolate-espresso custard with Chantilly cream, or a pear poached with ginger and port wine. Thursday night is "Casual Menu" night; all entrees are $9 or less. At lunch, the deli café turns out top-notch sandwiches on fresh house-made bread, perfect for a picnic in the garden or on one of the nearby beaches. The dozen or so guest rooms located upstairs are cheerful but not terribly romantic.

$$ *AE, DC, MC, V; no checks; lunch (deli café only) every day, dinner (main restaurant only) Thurs–Sun; full bar; reservations recommended; www.sanbenitohouse.com.* &

SANTA CRUZ AND CAPITOLA-BY-THE-SEA

ROMANTIC HIGHLIGHTS

Santa Cruz is best known as a place where surfers ride big waves, locals spike volleyballs on the beach, and summer tourists flock to ride the oceanfront boardwalk's famous roller coaster. Add to the mix an eccentric University of California campus, and you have a colorful picture, if one not tailor-made for romance. Fortunately, Santa Cruz and the quaint neighboring town of Capitola-by-the-Sea have more than their fair share of romantic attractions. In a word: beaches. The varied and gorgeous settings in which you can enjoy the sand and the sun in this region are seemingly endless. In addition, both towns enjoy a handful of sophisticated restaurants and shops, enticing proximity to the 30-plus wineries in the Santa Cruz Mountains (see the San Jose and the Peninsula chapter), and enough outdoor adventure to keep nature lovers, and lovers in general, kissing for quite a while.

One of the best ways to take in the incredible **Santa Cruz** scenery is a hand-in-hand walk on the 2-mile paved trail running along **West Cliff Drive**, which hugs the coast. At sunset, the views are extravagantly romantic. It's also a good route to travel by bike, and **The Bicycle Shop of Santa Cruz** (1325 Mission St; 831/454-0909; www.BicycleShopSantaCruz.com) rents everything from cruisers to mountain bikes. West Cliff Drive and the trail conclude at **Natural Bridges State Park** (831/423-4609; www.scparkfriends .org), where the warm sandy beach, graced by a dramatic archway-shaped rock formation carved by the ocean waves, is a lovely place to explore. In colder months, the park's shady eucalyptus grove is transformed by a natural phenomenon, when some 50,000 beautiful orange-and-black monarch butterflies gather to engage in their annual winter roosting and mating. The best time to view the butterflies is midday, between late November and early February.

The Santa Cruz coast is gorgeous to look at the from the vantage point of the water, especially at sunset. If you are staying on land, such a view is easily gained by a stroll down the **Santa Cruz Wharf**, a scenic wooden walkway lined with seafood restaurants. Going out on the water is also a treat: for an elegant boat tour of the bay, board the *Chardonnay* (831/423-1213; www.chardonnay.com), a 70-foot luxury yacht that sails year-round on sunset, ecology, and wine-tasting tours and offers whale watching between January and March. The adventurous-at-heart can paddle away together with **Vision Quest Kayaking** (northeast end of Santa Cruz Wharf; 831/427-2267; www.kayaksantacruz.com), which even offers guided moonlight tours.

Or, for the quintessential California experience, learn to surf in two-hour group sessions or private lessons with **Club Ed Surf School** (831/459-6664 or 800/287-SURF; www.club-ed.com).

If browsing in shops is more your fancy, head for downtown's **Pacific Avenue**, which is lined with sculptures, benches, inviting cafés and restaurants, and colorful boutiques. Steal a kiss among the stacks at **Bookshop Santa Cruz** (1520 Pacific Ave; 831/423-0900), or sample locally made gourmet chocolates in the bookstore's café. To escape the crowds altogether, head up the hill toward campus to the **University of California Santa Cruz Arboretum** (1156 High St; 831/427-2998; www2.ucsc.edu/arboretum; 9am–5pm every day). This is a marvelous spot for concerts in the warmer months, and the newly constructed outdoor performance stage, completed in 2004, draws notable performers. After treating your ears to beautiful sounds, treat the rest of your senses to the fragrant flower and herb gardens.

Of course, there are also plenty of kiss-friendly pursuits inland; in the nearby Santa Cruz Mountains, forests provide shady grounds for romantic escapes; you'll discover some unforgettable hiking trails and splendid waterfalls if you drive about 23 miles north of Santa Cruz to the 18,000-acre **Big Basin Redwoods State Park** (21600 Big Basin Wy, off Hwy 236; 831/338-8860; www.bigbasin.org). Here, in California's first state park and its second-largest redwood preserve, you'll be inspired by giant redwoods that soar more than 300 feet high.

The town of **Capitola-by-the-Sea**, just south of Santa Cruz, is also a sunny haven for kissing couples. It's a true—if upscale—beach town, complete with Mediterranean-style buildings, curved streets, white-sand beaches, and outdoor cafés. The slow traffic and tight parking (take the first spot you see, and bring lots of quarters to feed the meter) are a minor drawback, but once you've parked and are happily browsing in the inviting boutiques or relaxing at a beachside patio restaurant, the breezy and informal ambience here will catch you up in its spell. At the west end of town, you'll find the **Capitola Pier**, a great place from which to admire the town and, on weekends, to listen to live music. A short drive south of Capitola leads to the more secluded and sandy stretches of **Sunset** and **Manresa State Beaches** (831/763-7063; www.parks.ca.gov). Pick up gourmet picnic goodies from **Gayle's Bakery & Rosticceria** (504 Bay Ave; 831/462-1200) first, and you'll be tempted to wander all day along the water's edge.

Nearby and inland, the towns of **Soquel, Aptos,** and **Rio del Mar** also offer a certain amount of rural charm. One of the highlights here is **The Forest of Nisene Marks State Park** (4 miles north of Aptos on Aptos Creek Rd; 831/763-7062; www.parks.ca.gov), a wonderful wooded paradise. Nature-loving romantics will discover a number of uncrowded picnic areas here, as well as more than 30 miles of hiking trails offering suitable challenges for both casual walkers and hard-core hikers. If you're not outdoorsy types, opt for a scenic drive through the tunnel of arching trees that line the main road.

Access and Information

Highway 1 and scenic but highly trafficked Highway 17 lead right to the center of Santa Cruz. Just "over the hill" is **San Jose International Airport** (408/501-7600; www.sjc.org), with plenty of major airlines and car rental companies. From Santa Cruz, Highway 1 continues on south with direct access to Soquel, Capitola, and Aptos.

The excellent **Visitors Information Center** (1211 Ocean St, Santa Cruz; 831/425-1234 or 800/833-3494; www.santacruzca.org) boasts a friendly staff and lots of information about area attractions and events.

Romantic Lodgings

THE BABBLING BROOK INN
●●

1025 Laurel St, Santa Cruz / 831/427-2437 or 800/866-1131
An acre of greenery is the backdrop for this rambling wooden inn anchored by a massive waterwheel that churns in the inn's namesake babbling brook. The surroundings include meandering paths and picturesque footbridges that offer close-up views of breathtaking redwoods, pines, and flowering gardens. This happens to be the oldest bed-and-breakfast in town, and the ambience is more Northern California funky than fancy. But the location is convenient: the boardwalk, the wharf, and the sparkling Pacific Ocean are a mere 10-minute stroll from the inn. Eight of the property's 13 guest rooms and cottages are named after famous painters. The simple but pleasant decor includes crisp white walls and floral accents, with simply framed prints by artists such as Cézanne, Van Gogh, and Monet establishing the theme in each room. A 10-foot-tall white wrought-iron bed from the University of California at Santa Cruz's production of *Romeo and Juliet* is the highlight of the Degas Room. A private deck in the hidden Fern Grotto Room offers close-up views of a small cascading waterfall and the inn's trademark waterwheel. (An extra benefit of all this musical trickling of water is that it helps drown out the traffic noise—most noticeable during the day and early evening—that results from the inn's location on a very busy street.) The Artist's Retreat boasts the property's quietest and most private location, high in the treetops, and has an outdoor hot tub on the deck to boot. Individual entrances, private decks, and wood-burning stoves in every room help keep the fires of romantce burning, and the double whirlpool tubs in two of the rooms are bonuses. In the morning, a generous country repast is served buffet-style in the parlor; wine and hors d'oeuvres are also served here in the evening, before a glowing fire.
$$$ AE, DC, DIS, MC, V; checks OK; www.babblingbrookinn.com.

BLUE SPRUCE INN
♥♥❀

2815 S Main St, Soquel / 831/464-1137 or 800/559-1137
As the saying goes, good things come in small packages, and that is indeed the case with the unpretentious and heartwarming Blue Spruce Inn. Enclosed by a white picket fence, this beautifully renovated Victorian farmhouse is fresh and endearing. Enjoy freshly baked cookies in the colorful parlor before retiring to one of the six guest rooms located throughout the main home and adjoining garden area. The accommodations tend to be on the smaller side, but most offer private entrances and patios. Romantic luxuries in some of the rooms also help to compensate: four rooms have Jacuzzi tubs, and all offer either gas fireplaces or rustic potbelly stoves, as well as skylights that let in plenty of sunshine. Seascape, a first-floor room decorated in ocean blues and greens, features wicker chairs, an inviting feather bed, a gas stove, a bow-shaped double Jacuzzi tub, and a private entrance. The teeny Victorian room is a second-story hideaway with cozy sloping ceilings and a tiny rose-colored bathroom with a four-jetted massage shower (dubbed, perhaps not very romantically, "The Human Car Wash"). The three Garden Rooms located in a separate structure behind the main house offer more space and elegance, particularly the sophisticated Orchid Room, decorated with a restful color scheme of white, beige, and gold. The king-size poster bed, gas fireplace, and whirlpool tub with shower offer plenty of romantic enticement. The tucked-away Secret Garden Room, which offers a private outdoor hot tub for soaking beneath the stars, is also a good romantic choice. Decorated with plaid accents, the Carriage House Room is handsome and spacious, with a two-person Jacuzzi tub set in the living room. (Now that's living!) In the morning, a full breakfast, complete with waffles or savory egg dishes, a fruit dish, and freshly baked goods, is served in the cheery dining room.
$$$ *AE, DIS, MC, V; checks OK; www.bluespruce.com.*

HISTORIC SAND ROCK FARM
♥♥♥

6901 Freedom Blvd, Aptos / 831/688-8005
From the moment you catch sight of the sun-dappled outdoor terrace of this beautifully restored Craftsman home set in a grove of towering redwoods, you'll have the feeling of entering a storybook romance. The mood continues as you step inside to the cozy redwood-beamed sitting room, where the polished wood floors, stained glass, antique furnishings, gorgeous flower arrangements, and upright piano reflect the elegance of a bygone era. Each of the five tastefully furnished guest rooms includes luxurious touches such as pillow-top feather mattresses. All three rooms on the main home's second floor boast Jacuzzi tubs, but the Honeycomb Suite promises the most romance, with truly elegant furnishings, an enticing queen-size sleigh bed,

and a two-person Jacuzzi tub cleverly built into one corner and surrounded by white curtains. The two downstairs rooms, set in an adjacent wing, offer the most privacy; they also share access to a large, private outdoor hot tub. Our favorite is the Hidden Garden Suite, which offers the most secluded location of all and features towering ceilings, large windows overlooking greenery, and polished wood floors. Farmhouse antiques and a queen pine sleigh bed with grapevine-motif wrought-iron scrollwork round out the pretty picture. The Sun Porch Suite, also downstairs, earns its name with a private, sunshine-drenched indoor seating area (there are plans to add a Jacuzzi to the bathroom of this suite as well). The beautiful terraced rose garden is for all to enjoy, as are the meadows, gardens, and woods on the property (which was originally a 1,000-acre ranch and winery built in the 1880s by a doctor's family). Every detail at the inn reveals the good taste and expertise of the mother-daughter team who run it: the mother was formerly an innkeeper in Sonoma, and the daughter was formerly a chef at several renowned San Francisco restaurants. Accordingly, breakfast is an astonishing gourmet delight, served outdoors on the redwood deck or, in chilly weather, in the cozy wood-paneled dining room between 8 and 9am. A summer morning's repast might include warm homemade cinnamon rolls; a dish of raspberries, strawberries, and figs with honey yogurt; and a light and savory goat cheese soufflé on a bed of fresh corn and summer tomatoes. Ask about the romance package, which has all the right extras, including a bottle of chilled champagne, gourmet chocolates, and fresh flowers. $$$ *AE, MC, V; no checks; www.sandrockfarm.com.*

THE INN AT DEPOT HILL
❀❀❀❀
250 Monterey Ave, Capitola-by-the-Sea / 831/462-3376 or 800/572-2632
If ever an inn deserved to enter the romance hall of fame, this one does. If we could extend our kiss rating we would, because the Inn at Depot Hill deserves 10 lips, possibly even 11. Built in 1901, this opulent establishment once served as a railroad depot—in the dining room, a hand-painted mural depicting a train window and a pastoral landscape beyond recalls the building's past life. Hop on board and select one of the lavishly decorated rooms, each of which evokes one of the world's most romantic destinations. You can kiss in a Parisian pied-à-terre, in a Mediterranean retreat on the Côte d'Azur, in a simple Japanese hideaway in Kyoto, or in an Italian coastal villa in Portofino. No matter which "destination" you choose, prepare yourselves for luxury and pampering along the route. The 12 spectacularly decorated rooms are magazine material, with gorgeous touches such as domed ceilings, handsome wallpapers and paintings, and two-sided fireplaces. Sumptuous fabrics drape unbelievably plush canopied feather beds, and magnificent antique furnishings enhance the authentic foreign flair in every room. A blue-and-white Dutch-tiled hearth warms the Delft Room, where

a cushioned window seat overlooks a private garden. Frescoed walls in the Portofino Room create the impression of a coastal Italian villa. Decorated in royal red, the Railroad Baron's Room is fitted out with handcrafted furniture covered in silk. The simple Kyoto Room, fronted by a serene Japanese garden, offers a deep soaking tub and a shower with a window. The spacious marble bathroom in each room comes equipped with all the amenities you could possibly need (and many more). Each room also features a wood-burning fireplace, an irresistible two-person shower, a stereo system with music complementing your room's decor, TV/VCR (concealed in a cabinet), and plenty of fresh flowers. We could fill a book with descriptions of each room, and we haven't even begun to tell you about the lovely courtyard or the deliciously cozy common areas. Four guest rooms have private outdoor Jacuzzi tubs; all guests can reserve time in the communal soaking tub set behind a latticed fence in the garden courtyard. Full breakfasts, afternoon wine with appetizers, and evening desserts, all prepared by the inn's executive chef, ensure energy for nonstop kissing. All aboard, indeed.
$$$$ AE, DIS, MC, V; checks OK; www.innatdepothill.com.

PLEASURE POINT INN
🌀🌀🌀
2-3665 East Cliff Dr, Santa Cruz / 831/469-6161 or 877/557-2567
This sleek, upscale bed-and-breakfast, which opened in 2001, offers many pleasure points—and many oceanfront places to kiss—for couples seeking a sophisticated getaway. The renowned Pleasure Point surfing beach, the inn's namesake, is just steps from your door. Set in a quiet residential neighborhood, this nicely renovated former home offers sunny living and dining areas, an inviting roof deck with unobstructed views of the sparkling Pacific, and four rooms decorated in warm minimalist style, with gleaming hardwood floors, crisp white walls, and blond wood accents. Cozy gas fireplaces, inviting love seats, plush down comforters on the beds, private patios, and immaculate bathrooms with hand-painted wall tiles complete these little love nests. Dimmer switches, heated bathroom floor tiles, and Jacuzzi tubs add to the luxury in some of the rooms. Each accommodation has its own appeal, but we're particularly taken with the Coral Room, the only room on the second floor, and the Pelican Room, a spacious first-floor abode featuring a king-size bed and an enticing bathroom with two-person Jacuzzi tub and skylight. A complimentary basket of goodies welcomes you upon check-in, and room amenities such as digital cable, a private phone, refrigerator, microwave, coffeemaker, and safe will make it hard to leave. On the inn's rooftop deck, you and your loved one can bubble your cares away in the large eight-person hot tub, soak up the sunshine on a chaise lounge, or stay cozy under the heated gas lamp as the sun sinks in the west. In the mornings, enjoy an expanded continental breakfast while viewing the ocean from either the spacious dining room or the deck. If you're looking for an

indulgent weekend and don't want to fuss over the arrangements, check out the inn's appealing packages for couples, one of which includes in-room massage for both of you as well as reservations for tours and wine tasting at local wineries.

$$$–$$$$ *MC, V; checks OK; www.pleasurepointinn.com.*

SEASCAPE RESORT

🌀🕯

1 Seascape Resort Dr, Aptos / 408/688-6800 or 800/929-7727
First impressions count for a lot, but, as another saying goes, you can't judge a book by its cover. This is especially true at Seascape Resort. At first glance, there is nothing remotely romantic about the resort's sprawling, apartment-like buildings. But the spectacular location atop a series of oceanfront bluffs and unexpected romantic touches in the otherwise standard hotel rooms make for a surprisingly kiss-worthy ambience. You can enjoy the lovely natural setting from a cushioned fireside window seat in the hotel's expansive, elegant lobby; although the water is partially hidden behind a dense grove of cypress trees, a steep footpath winds through a tree-laden ravine right to the ocean—and 5 miles of soft, sandy beach. Of Seascape's 285 guest rooms, those in the north wing are particularly enticing because of their wonderful views of the water beyond the trees. Fireplaces, private balconies, fully equipped kitchens, upscale linens, and comfortable but ordinary furniture are standard. Most (but not all) rooms have ocean views, so be sure to ask ahead. Surprisingly, for a resort this large, only six rooms have Jacuzzi tubs, but there are three heated pools, three outdoor Jacuzzi tubs, tennis courts (for a fee), and complimentary use of the sports club across the street. For a special treat, opt for the beach bonfire special for two ($49 per couple). A staff member will transport the two of you, via golf cart, to the beach, build a bonfire, and then leave so you can smooch for as long as the fire stays lit. (S'mores included.) Distant water views are the main attraction at the property's restaurant, Sanderlings (831/662-7120), which is decorated with tall green plants, white linens, and cloth umbrellas suspended from the high ceilings. Casual outdoor patio seating is available during warm weather. The kitchen serves up better-than-average California cuisine, including local Monterey Bay cioppino, roasted-vegetable ravioli, and a tempting tempura trio of nori-wrapped ahi, soft-shell crab, and prawns. Not surprisingly, given all the amenities and the beachfront location, this is a popular place for families. If you are traveling with children but want some grown-up time, the resort offers a Kids' Club program, in which plenty of activities will keep the young ones entertained while you pursue more amorous adventures.

$$$$ *AE, DC, MC, V; checks OK; www.seascaperesort.com.* ♿

Romantic Restaurants

BITTERSWEET BISTRO
✪✪

787 Rio Del Mar Blvd, Rio Del Mar / 831/662-9799
If you love chocolate *almost* as much as you love your sweetheart, Bittersweet Bistro will be a dream come true. Chocoholics come from miles around for the dessert creations here, most of which are perfectly sized for two. Of course, there's more to life than dessert, and the kitchen is also known for its fresh and hearty continental cuisine. Inside the restaurant, the various dining areas are all decorated with a warm Mediterranean theme. Wrought-iron sconces and bold modern prints fill the walls; fresh flowers and candles adorn butcher paper–topped tables (crayons supplied). The main dining room, near the entrance, is too crowded to be romantic, so opt for the room in the back or, as a last resort, hide yourselves in a bar booth. The outdoor patio is pleasant in warm weather. Many of the pasta, seafood, and meat dishes are satisfying but merely standard; we recommend trying the more intriguing nightly specials. If in season, the towering asparagus salad, topped with shaved Parmesan cheese, is a must. The seafood special of roast escolar topped with a mushroom sauce offers a fine alternative to predictable preparations of chicken and pork. When the grand finale arrives—whether it's a decadent chocolate mousse with crème anglaise or a chocolate walnut bread pudding with bittersweet chocolate sauce—all heads will turn to watch your mile-high prize as it's transported to your table. Don't linger too long trying to choose among the many tempting desserts; whatever you order, the result is quite likely to be more sweet than bittersweet.
$$$ *AE, MC, V; local checks only; late lunch, dinner every day, brunch Sun; full bar; reservations recommended; www.bittersweetbistro.com.* ᓚ

CAFE SPARROW
✪✪

8042 Soquel Dr, Aptos / 831/688-6238
Treat yourselves to a taste of the French countryside at Cafe Sparrow. Food this good is usually found in more refined settings, but the casual, rustic ambience is a refreshing twist. Blue and pink sponge-painted walls, floral tablecloths, Impressionist-motif seat cushions, and a worn wood floor give the restaurant its quaint feel. Although they are similarly decorated, the two dining rooms have distinct personalities: the airy main room is warmed by cheerful yellow walls, whimsical paintings, and large windows that let in the sunshine, while the second room is darker and more formal, with a ceiling of flowing fabric that gathers into a centerpiece of hanging baskets. The proximity of the open kitchen makes this second area less desirable. Cafe Sparrow offers a variety of savory French dishes prepared with California flair. The *fromage* baguette, with its delicate blend of cheddar,

Gruyère, and Brie, is nothing short of a cheese lover's dream come true. As for the albacore cheese puff, tuna just doesn't get any better than this. Dinner entrées include filet mignon and rack of lamb. For dessert, indulge in profiteroles—light pastries filled with your choice of ice cream or pastry cream and sprinkled with chocolate. Our only hesitation about Cafe Sparrow is that the casual atmosphere seems to have rubbed off on the wait staff; the service may be a little too leisurely for city dwellers.

$$ *MC, V; checks OK; breakfast Sat, lunch Mon–Sat, dinner every day, brunch Sun; beer and wine; reservations recommended; www.cafe sparrow.com.*

CASABLANCA RESTAURANT
⬢⬢

101 Main St, Santa Cruz / 831/426-9063
If you're looking for a good restaurant with a water view, Casablanca's just the ticket. Set directly across the street from the beach, the dining room has tall, stately windows that overlook the busy boardwalk and the crashing ocean surf. Candle lanterns at every table illuminate the small dining room, which is decorated with leafy palm trees, cushioned rattan chairs, and crisp white linens. Starters such as fried calamari with a spicy lime dipping sauce or Blue Point oysters on the half shell make an appealing prelude to classic continental dishes updated with a California accent, such as grilled salmon with citrus vin blanc or filet mignon with wild-mushroom whole-grain demi-glace. Local wines join selections from Italy, Germany, France, and Australia on a book-length wine list. The only difficulty you might encounter during your meal is choosing whether to gaze at the lights sparkling on the ocean waves just outside the window or into the candlelit eyes of your dinner companion. The inn attached to the restaurant is just your basic motel—don't be tempted to book a room.

$$$ *AE, DC, DIS, MC, V; checks OK; dinner every day; full bar; reservations recommended; www.casablanca-santacruz.com.*

OSWALD
⬢⬢⬢

1547 Pacific Ave, Santa Cruz / 831/423-7427
With its fresh California-French bistro cuisine and its spare, artful dining room, Oswald is a sophisticated gourmet gem in this beach-casual town. Located off a charming little courtyard, the restaurant holds just a handful of tables, with a few scattered upstairs on a petite wrought-iron balcony. Bold still-life paintings adorn the brick and pale yellow walls, while high ceilings and wooden banquettes add a touch of elegance. What will truly make your hearts race, however, is the food: the small seasonal menu is supplemented nightly by specials that take good advantage of the freshest local produce, meats, and seafood (organic whenever possible). Good options

include the sherry-steamed mussels with fried garlic and parsley; poached foie gras with port wine reduction and toasted hazelnuts; and a butter lettuce salad with citrus and creamy herb dressing. Entrées include the crispy yet moist "chicken under a brick" (while cooking, the chicken is flattened by the weight of foil-wrapped bricks to yield crispier skin), served with sweet pepper and potato hash. Good news for vegetarians: there's always a very reasonably priced entrée of carefully cooked vegetables. You won't have any trouble finding the right bottle to toast the occasion, since the wine list features a good lineup of both California and French offerings. The servers are helpful and ready to answer all your questions. And whether you finish with a seasonal fruit tart, the chocolate soufflé, a classic crème brûlée, or a Basque almond custard torte, don't miss the desserts—these heavenly creations are almost as sweet as a kiss.

$$ *AE, DC, MC, V; local checks OK; dinner Tues–Sun; beer and wine; reservations recommended.* &

SHADOWBROOK RESTAURANT
🍴🍴🍴

1750 Wharf Rd, Capitola-by-the-Sea / 831/475-1511
Located on the banks of Soquel Creek amid dense, lush foliage, this unique—and exceedingly popular—restaurant has an enchanting storybook appearance. The lodge-style chalet is reached via a steep, winding footpath surrounded by greenery—or you can hop aboard a little red cable car that rolls down its tracks to drop you at the restaurant's front door. Multilevel dining rooms scattered throughout the enormous restaurant offer a variety of views and surroundings in which to enjoy a romantic repast. The Greenhouse and Main Dining Room both have the ambience of an atrium, with ivy and ferns, flowing waterfalls, and windows looking out to the creek. The Wine Cellar is a small room tucked in back and surrounded by handsome wood walls, a beautiful tapestry, and wine bottles neatly arranged in racks. A table set in front of the massive brick fireplace is *the* spot to nab in the cellar. Our favorite room, however, is the Garden Room, famous for the redwood tree that grows right through it. Here you'll enjoy garden and creek views, as well as more privacy than in the other rooms. Despite the restaurant's vastness, things can get bustling, and you are almost guaranteed to hear at least one rendition of "Happy Birthday" in this quintessential celebration spot. If you can't get reservations (not uncommon), opt for having dinner, a drink, or a light supper in the bar area—the Rock Room—which is the most handsome room of all. Redwood cathedral ceilings and a sprawling rock wall adorned with plants and a waterfall easily entertain the eye. Copper pots above the wood-burning fireplace, reasonably comfortable teak furniture, and plenty of small tables make this a great place to romance the night away. And for those on a budget, happy hour is the bargain du jour. For all the restaurant's extraordinary ambience, the traditional California-style cuisine, focusing

on grilled meats and fresh seafood, is merely ordinary in both its delivery and presentation. Starters might include Dungeness crab-stuffed portobello mushrooms, steamed artichokes with lemon aioli, or a classic shrimp cocktail. Main courses show a bit more creativity—including dishes such as salmon surrounded by a spicy wasabi-ginger sauce or a stuffed organic pork chop with apple-spinach-pine nut stuffing and cider reduction sauce alongside Gorgonzola bread pudding. For a sublime finish, don't miss desserts such as the vanilla custard wrapped inside two crepes and surrounded by a pool of caramel sauce.

$$-$$$ *AE, DC, DIS, MC, V; local checks only; dinner every day, brunch Sun; full bar; reservations recommended; www.shadowbrookcapitola.com.*

THEO'S
❍❍❍

3101 N Main St, Soquel / 831/462-3657
Everything about Theo's reflects understated elegance, from the warm decor to the beautifully presented food and the refined service. Nestled in a quiet residential neighborhood, this charming bungalow-turned-gourmet-restaurant will enchant you from the moment you set eyes on its quaint courtyard and terra-cotta and brick exterior. The two dining rooms feature contemporary artwork, peaked ceilings, and linen-draped tables; the main dining area is made even cozier by its large stone fireplace. French doors open onto a rock patio that wraps around to the back of the house, and guests are encouraged to retreat here, wine glass in hand, to enjoy the cool evening breeze or explore the herb garden, which contributes fresh flavors to the chef's inspired creations. During warm weather (or when the heat lamps are on), guests can dine on the back patio overlooking an expansive lawn. The menu changes frequently to incorporate the freshest seasonal organic produce; only top-quality meats find their way onto the menu. Fresh salmon, homemade ravioli stuffed with goat's-milk ricotta, and roasted Muscovy duck breast are just a few of the consistently well-prepared main courses. Specials—such as an assortment of three Hawaiian fish bathed in a coriander and ginger broth—consistently prove to be exceptionally light and flavorful. Desserts are much more decadent: the deep-fried chocolate truffles served with vanilla-bean ice cream, for example, are certain to elicit some *oohs* and *aahs*. The mascarpone cheesecake atop a pistachio crust is equally extraordinary.

$$$ *AE, MC, V; no checks; dinner Tues–Sat; full bar; reservations recommended; www.theosrestaurant.net.*

MONTEREY

ROMANTIC HIGHLIGHTS

The barking of seals rises from the blue-green waters of Monterey Bay and an adjoining marine sanctuary to echo throughout this well-known seaside town. Pelicans, seals, and otters frolic in the gentle surf, the rocky beaches are bathed in year-round sunshine, and the meticulously maintained waterfront parks burst with flowers. Picturesque **Monterey** has a rich heritage that is reflected in its Spanish-style adobe homes. In December, many of the town's historic sites are decorated for the holidays and opened to the public for fascinating self-guided tours. But the most legendary event here is without doubt the annual **Monterey Jazz Festival** (925/275-9255 for tickets, 831/373-3366 for information; www.montereyjazzfestival.org), held the third weekend in September. (If you'd like to attend, be forewarned that tickets and hotel rooms get snapped up more than six months in advance). The rest of the year, Fisherman's Wharf and the Monterey Bay Aquarium are the prime tourist attractions. But escaping the crowds isn't difficult in this pretty town, and its excellent location, just a short drive from Pacific Grove, Pebble Beach, Carmel, and Big Sur, makes it a perfect base for exploring the attractions of the Monterey coast.

Kissing in the great outdoors is especially enjoyable in beautiful Monterey. It's nothing short of a four-lip experience to kayak together through the gentle waters of **Monterey Bay**, with a little help from **Adventures by the Sea** (299 Cannery Row; 831/372-1807; www.adventuresbythesea.com). The outfitter also rents bikes or in-line skates for landlubbers. Should you opt to paddle, however, you're in for a treat. Frolicking otters loop in and out of the kelp, sometimes even sliding playfully right up onto your kayak! The sun illuminates the bright orange and gold starfish in the water, sparkling like jewels down in the blue.

Thanks to its oceanfront location, **Fisherman's Wharf** is definitely worth visiting for an hour or two on a sunny afternoon—despite the crowds. You and your loved one can amble down the boardwalk, watching pelicans and seagulls soar overhead and boats rock gently in the nearby harbor. The wharf is home to the usual souvenir shops and stands selling fried seafood—if the smell of the sea makes you hungry, we suggest avoiding the mediocre sit-down restaurants at the end of the wharf in favor of tasty **Cafe Fina** (see Romantic Restaurants).

Monterey's **Cannery Row**, which was originally in the business of catching and canning sardines, is now a mall full of shops and restaurants in the business of catching tourists (who, we might add, are often packed as tight as sardines). Though Cannery Row is not the most romantic place in Monterey, take the opportunity to browse the endless array of boutiques, art galleries, and gift stores here, or visit the tasting room at **A Taste of Monterey** (700 Cannery Row; 831/646-5446) for sips of local vintages and a helpful information center that can fill you in on everything you need to know for a winery tour of the region. When you're ready to pedal away from the crowds, rent a bicycle built for two at **Bay Bikes** (640 Wave St; 831/646-9090) and, if you're in an athletic mood, ride all the way to Carmel (about 14 miles).

At the end of Cannery Row is the city's main tourist attraction, the **Monterey Bay Aquarium** (866 Cannery Row; 831/648-4888 or 800/756-3737; www.montereybayaquarium.org). Scores of visitors mean the experience is hardly intimate, but this is a not-to-be-missed opportunity to experience one of the world's largest and finest aquariums. The illuminated jellyfish exhibit is especially stunning, as is the kelp-forest display. Hold hands and brave the crowds for a few hours. You'll be even more pleased with yourselves if you purchase advance tickets by phone (highly recommended during holidays and the summer) or from participating hotels and bed-and-breakfasts—and breeze ahead of the long ticket line at the front door.

Driving might not be your idea of romantic fun, but you might change your minds after tooling about in a **Rent-a-Roadster** (229 Cannery Row; 831/647-1929; www.rent-a-roadster.com; $30–$40 per hour per vehicle). With a toot of the *ah-ooga* horn, you'll be off to tour the coastline in a reproduction 1929 Model A roadster—with the top down, the sun shining, the waves crashing, and onlookers waving as you trundle by in all your retro glory. This unusual company also offers a 1929 Mercedes and a 1930 Phaeton for rent—all of them are very easy to drive, with modern engines capable of doing 55 miles per hour—but why hurry? Be sure to allow yourselves enough time to stop and explore the seashore along **Lovers Point** (made for you, after all) in Pacific Grove, just a few minutes from Monterey, or for a tour of **17-Mile Drive** (see Romantic Highlights in the Pacific Grove and Pebble Beach chapter).

If a hand-in-hand hike away from the crowds sounds heavenly, head for the delightful **Jacks Peak County Park** (831/755-4899 or 888/588-2267; head north on Hwy 68 and follow signs; 11am–dusk every day). Explore the 8½ miles of riding and hiking trails (each trail is roughly a mile long) or simply indulge in some goodies at one of the many picnic areas. Ridge-top views overlooking the Monterey Peninsula are to be found throughout the 525-acre park; for an especially extraordinary vista, however, follow the Skyline Self-Guided Nature Trail to the summit of Jacks Peak.

Access and Information

Highway 1 provides direct access to Monterey. From Highway 101, take the Highway 156/Monterey exit, which merges with Highway 1. The **Monterey Peninsula Airport** (831/648-7000; www.montereyairport.com; Hwy 68 off

Holsted Rd, 4 miles from Monterey) has nearly 100 arrivals and departures daily, with connections to all domestic and foreign airlines. The car rental offices of **Avis**, **Budget**, and **National** are also located here. **Amtrak's Coast Starlight** (800/USA-RAIL; www.amtrak.com) route stops in Salinas at the junction of Hwys 68 and 101; free bus service is provided for the 30-minute ride into downtown Monterey.

The **Monterey Peninsula Visitors and Convention Bureau** (831/649-1770 or 888/221-1010; www.monterey.com) has two visitor centers: one is located in the lobby of the Maritime Museum at Custom House Plaza near Fisherman's Wharf, and the other is at Lake El Estero on Camino El Estero. Both are open every day and offer an array of maps, free pamphlets, and visitors' guides. Additional information is available online at monterey-carmel.com. The **Monterey County Vintners Association** (831/375-9400; www.monterey wines.org) can provide information on the area's wineries, many of which have public tasting rooms and picnic grounds.

Romantic Lodgings

HOTEL PACIFIC
◐◐◐
300 Pacific St / 831/373-5700 or 800/554-5542
With so many cozy bed-and-breakfasts and charming inns to choose from on the Monterey Peninsula, it's hard to believe anyone would elect to stay at a big hotel. Hard to believe, that is, until you lay eyes on some of the exceedingly chic and lavish hotels that have been developed in this area. Hotel Pacific is one of them, and it certainly qualifies as a romantic retreat. Plus, it goes one step further than most by paying homage to the flavors of Monterey's rich past, starting with the decor. A circular fountain fronts the entrance to the Spanish Colonial–style building, and dense flowering vines line the pathways that meander through two fountain-filled brick courtyards. Set in a historic section of town, Hotel Pacific gives little indication that it is any newer than the century-old buildings surrounding it. Terra-cotta tiles, cream-colored stucco walls, and Santa Fe–style fabrics accent the 105 guest rooms, in which you'll also find gas fireplaces, cushy feather beds, separate living areas with comfortable furnishings, and private patios or balconies facing either the inner courtyard or the surrounding neighborhood. The top-floor rooms are particularly appealing, with high beamed ceilings and curtained, canopied beds made from sandblasted pine logs. Although the hotel is not far from Monterey's fascinating sights and sounds, don't be surprised if you're tempted to spend the duration of your visit ensconced in the comfortable confines of your suite. A complimentary continental breakfast and evening appetizers are served buffet-style in a small, plush lobby filled with overstuffed couches and chairs, but there aren't enough seats in this

cramped room to accommodate so many guests. A much better idea is to bring your pastries, fruit, and coffee out to the garden-trimmed courtyard and sit at the fountain's edge while you plan your day in peace.
$$$$ AE, DC, DIS, MC, V; checks OK; www.hotelpacific.com. &

THE JABBERWOCK
♥☖

598 Laine St / 831/372-4777 or 888/428-7253
At first glance, this 1911 Craftsman-style home looks like any other bed-and-breakfast, but once you venture "through the looking glass" and into the Jabberwock, you'll find yourselves in the topsy-turvy world of *Alice in Wonderland*. Don't be surprised to discover a breakfast menu listing items such as "snarkelberry flumptuous" (crepes) and "deleeksious tweedledumps" (quiche), as well as a "burbling" room for private telephone conversations. Overall, the ambience is more homey and friendly than romantic, and the hodgepodge style of the interior is best described as eclectic. But each of the seven rooms is comfortable and has a private bath. The larger, more expensive rooms offer such romantic embellishments as Jacuzzi tubs, and these are the best choice for couples making an intimate getaway (the small rooms are exactly that and are decorated less appealingly). You're likely to forget this home was formerly a convent when you see the sun-filled Mome Rath Room, with its two-person Jacuzzi tub and enormous king-size bed. The Borogove Room has absolutely gorgeous views of the bay, plus a charming fireplace and sitting area. The highlight of Jabberwock, however, is outside: the lovely gardens are wound through with brick walkways, dotted with iron benches and chairs, and embellished with a soothing waterfall. If you can't enjoy the garden due to bad weather, the enclosed wraparound sundeck is the next best thing. Each morning, you'll start off the day with a sweet and savory gourmet breakfast. After imbibing some "jabber juice" and engaging in some "jabbertalk" with others in the dining room, you can look forward to spending the day whispering sweet nothings to each other in the garden. If you want to avoid all the gibberish completely, have breakfast delivered to your room. The only thing missing in this wonderland is the Cheshire cat, but you will see plenty of grins nonetheless.
$$$ DIS, MC, V; checks OK; www.jabberwockinn.com.

MONTEREY PLAZA HOTEL & SPA
♥♥☖

400 Cannery Row / 831/646-1700 or 800/368-2468
The Monterey Plaza Hotel is so large, it hugs both sides of Cannery Row—with a skywalk connecting buildings on opposite sides of the street. The ocean panorama is the primary attraction here, and when making a reservation, be sure to request a room with a water view. The white stucco exterior is made quaint by wrought-iron balconies filled with potted plants, while

polished elegance reigns inside. The expansive lobby dazzles with Italian marble floors, Brazilian teakwood walls, candle-style sconces, and a grand piano. The expansive outdoor terrace, popular with lovers and tourists alike, overhangs the water so effectively it feels like part of the jagged coastline. You can sit here to admire the blue water dotted with sailboats and kayaks. The 290 guest rooms and suites have a luxury hotel feel and are tastefully decorated in green, cream, and rose hues. All feature classic mahogany and walnut Biedermeier-style furnishings and leather chairs, marble bathrooms, and European duvets covering king-size beds. Corner rooms in Building 1 offer the best views of the bay, thanks to their extra windows and large decks. Rooms in Building 2 directly face the water but, unfortunately, many take in noise from the often-crowded terrace below. No matter which waterfront room you choose, you're guaranteed to hear the cries of seagulls and the gentle sound of lapping waves below. The balconies, with seats for two, are wonderful places to sit, snuggle, and watch the tide roll in. After an afternoon of sea-gazing, head downstairs to dine at the Duck Club Restaurant (831/646-1701). Well-spaced tables with handsome leather and wood chairs are complemented by cherrywood paneling, plants, art and statues on a wildlife theme, and enormous windows commanding waterfront views. The open kitchen serves a standard but tasty array of homemade pastas, seafood, and wood-roasted specialties (including, not surprisingly, several duck preparations). If you're lucky enough to nab a seat near the windows, you can watch the shimmering moon reflected in the bay as the lights of the city sparkle in the distance.
$$$$ *AE, DIS, MC, V; checks OK; www.woodsidehotels.com.*

OLD MONTEREY INN
◐◐◐◐
500 Martin St / 831/375-8284 or 800/350-2344
Set on a quiet hillside far from the bustle of town, the Old Monterey Inn is the kind of place you fall in love with the moment you enter the garden gate. Terra-cotta pots bursting with flowers hang like jewels from majestic trees surrounding the property, and meandering paths crisscross the lovingly tended gardens sprinkled with secluded niches. Attention to detail is equally evident inside the 1929 English Tudor inn, where every room offers something special for those seeking romance. The 10 rooms—9 of which have fireplaces and 4 of which have jetted tubs—strike a balance between handsome and pretty that is sure to please. Each room features a luxurious, pillowy, fine linen-swathed bed and peerless decor that includes original woodwork and English-style antiques. In the main house, the two recently enlarged and refurbished suites are the most suited to romantic occasions: The Mayfield Suite is a bright French-country paradise with soothing wheat-stalk-yellow walls, plush rose-patterned armchairs where you can sit cozily in front of the fireplace, and a sparkling two-person air-jet spa tub. The

Ashford Suite is equally spacious; its separate sitting room has a luxurious daybed and fireplace, and its large bathroom has an extralong soaking tub. Book lovers will be delighted by the handsome Library Room, with its bed tucked into a windowed alcove; this second-floor room even has a private patio where you can sit and read to each other from one of the many novels provided. Hidden behind the house are other appealing rooms, including the Chawton Room, which, although it's small and doesn't have many windows, warms the heart with whimsical cherub art, hand-stenciled walls, and a marble two-person jetted tub situated so you can gaze at the fireplace. The most private room of all (and the most expensive) is the Garden Cottage, which has its own entrance, a tiled fireplace in the sitting room, and a linen-and-lace crown canopy above the bed. Visit the inn's inviting fireside parlor for a lavish spread of wine and cheese in the afternoon and port and sweet treats in the evening. A delicious gourmet breakfast is served each morning. You can savor the meal on hand-painted china in the elegant dining room overlooking the gardens, indulge in breakfast in bed, or enjoy the meal on the brick patio, surrounded by roses, wisteria, and boxwood hedges. For couples seeking an intimate and luxurious overnight experience, there is virtually no better place to kiss in Monterey than at this outstanding inn. $$$$ *MC, V; checks OK; www.oldmontereyinn.com.*

SPINDRIFT INN
◐◐◐◐

652 Cannery Row / 831/646-8900 or 800/841-1879
This ultrachic getaway will feel like a haven for couples who prefer the privacy and relative anonymity of a boutique hotel to the more social environment of a small bed-and-breakfast. Standing at the water's edge in the middle of Cannery Row, the Spindrift Inn is European in its styling and architecturally impressive throughout. To get the most out of your experience here, we suggest you splurge on a waterfront room, where the fresh scent of salt water drifts through the air and you can hear the soothing sound of crashing waves just below your room. Binoculars and window seats encourage you to spend leisurely hours watching seals and otters at play in the kelp beds. The wood-burning fireplace that casts an amber glow on the hardwood floors, stylish carpets, and sumptuous fabrics enhances the ambience. All 42 rooms here feature down comforters and feather beds (some sleigh beds, some canopies), TV/VCRs hidden in armoires, and spacious marble bathrooms. If it's a warm evening, only one thing could possibly tempt you out of this heavenly lair: a short stroll along the silvery moonlit beach. In the morning, a newspaper and a breakfast of fruit, orange juice, croissants, and sweet rolls await outside your door on a silver tray. Wine and appetizers are served every afternoon in the lobby, where they can

be enjoyed in the company of other guests or taken up to the rooftop garden for a panoramic picnic.

$$$$ *AE, DC, DIS, MC, V; checks OK; www.spindriftinn.com.*

Romantic Restaurants

CAFE FINA
❂❂

47 Fisherman's Wharf / 831/372-5200 or 800/THE-FINA
Although Cafe Fina doesn't look very promising from the outside—its yellow facade blends into the other seafood vendors on the pier—you'll be pleasantly surprised by its handsome interior. Vintage black-and-white photos depicting hardworking fishermen and members of the owner's seafaring family adorn the walls both upstairs and downstairs, and stylish halogen lights spotlight each photo as well as each table. Mauve cloth napkins bring a splash of color to the white tablecloths draping each table. The elongated downstairs dining area isn't our first choice for romance because the tables are set too close together, and only four come with decent views. Instead, head upstairs, where fewer than a dozen tables—all with views—create an intimate dining experience. For an extraspecial rendezvous, request the table for two in the upstairs corner; it has the best view in the house. You'll be treated to the sight of clear turquoise water below, sea lions sunning themselves on the rocks along the water's edge, and anchored sailboats bobbing in the background. Cafe Fina uses a wood-burning oven for its meat dishes and crispy gourmet pizzas. If it's seafood you're fishing for, try the sautéed mussels or the deep-fried Monterey calamari. Fish can be blackened Cajun-style or broiled over mesquite charcoal, depending on your desires. Cafe Fina also offers Italian favorites, including pasta dishes such as linguine with clams, garlic butter, prawns, and Pernod, and the flavorful Pasta Fina (linguine with baby shrimp, white wine, olives, clam juice, olive oil, tomatoes, and green onions). Finish with any of the classic Italian desserts and call the evening a success.

$$ *AE, DC, DIS, MC, V; no checks; lunch, dinner every day; full bar; reservations accepted; www.cafefina.com.*

CIBO
❂❂

301 Alvarado St / 831/649-8151
Cibo may translate as "food" in Italian, but in this case, it also means elegance, romance, jazz, and wonderful Sicilian cuisine. The Italian-owned and operated Cibo offers creative interpretations of traditional Sicilian recipes as well as more California-style fare, with a menu that includes tempting pizzas and pastas along with grilled meat and seafood dishes. The open

kitchen, which spans the entire back wall of the restaurant, favors locally grown herbs and vegetables. Daily seafood specials, such as seared monkfish on a bed of roasted-corn mashed potatoes surrounded by a luscious bacon-beurre blanc, are usually a good bet, but desserts can be uneven, so don't count on, say, flawless tiramisu. Cibo's decor handsomely blends neoclassic, modern, and rustic elements. The burnt sienna–hued walls are adorned with classical architectural drawings and niches that hold blown-glass vases; ivy trails from pots near the entryway; and ornate metalwork and mirrors decorate the various rooms. The lighting could be more atmospheric, and some of the dark wood tables are placed a little too near each other. A lively mix of jazz, soul, funk, reggae, and Latin dance music keeps things upbeat Tuesday through Saturday—but for the most romantic musical accompaniment, dine here on Sunday to the strains of live jazz.
$$ *AE, DIS, MC, V; no checks; dinner every day; full bar; reservations recommended; www.cibo.com.*

FRESH CREAM
✿✿✿❨
99 Pacific St / 831/375-9798
Long considered the crème de la crème of French dining in Monterey, Fresh Cream's spectacular views of the harbor through floor-to-ceiling windows create a romantic backdrop in three of the separate dining rooms (a fourth dining area does not offer a view). Well-spaced tables covered with tasteful linens, fresh bouquets, and glass oil lamps are more than conducive to amorous conversation. The simple architectural design gives the restaurant a sophisticated yet warm feel, and the service definitely complements it; Fresh Cream has one of the most gracious and refined wait staffs we've encountered. Hearty portions of classic French dishes with California accents are artistically presented and so delicately scrumptious you will savor every bite. We highly recommend the appetizer of lobster ravioli, a creation akin to eating a lobster soufflé stuffed inside handmade pasta. Even the salad included with dinner—fresh greens with goat cheese and toasted pecans tossed with light balsamic vinaigrette—is well above garden variety. The tempting entrée choices range from grilled filet mignon surrounded by roasted portobellos and a truffle-Madeira sauce to roasted duck with black-currant sauce to delicate poached salmon in saffron-thyme sauce. Desserts are culinary works of art. Two straws come with the frothy mocha milkshake topped with billows of freshly whipped cream; you'll have to get close enough to kiss in order to share this cool sensation, so naturally we highly recommend it.
$$$ *AE, DC, DIS, MC, V; checks OK; dinner every day; full bar; reservations recommended; www.freshcream.com.* &

MONTRIO
♥♥

414 Calle Principal / 831/648-8880
Locals throng to Montrio's lively, tightly packed dining room, where tables are jammed almost on top of each other. Though the crowds are a black mark in the book of romance, the restaurant's snazzy interior and artistically presented seafood dishes and desserts make it kiss-worthy. The sky-blue ceiling is frescoed with billowing white clouds, and twisted metal sculptures and artwork embellish the dining room's alcoves and corners. Black track lights dangle from exposed ceiling pipes, illuminating tables covered with white linens and furnished with brightly colored crayons and blank paper—when was the last time you composed a passionate haiku for your beloved? A second dining room upstairs is slightly less funky but equally noisy, due to similarly crowded tables and an adjacent open bar. Nevertheless, the service is gracious and the California-style cuisine is better than average, with enticing seafood dishes such as grilled salmon over beans and black rice with citrus-cumin broth or grilled gulf prawns served with caramelized-leek risotto. For dessert, share the white-nectarine pecan crisp with vanilla-bean ice cream.
$$$ *AE, DIS, MC, V; no checks; dinner every day; full bar; reservations recommended; www.montrio.com.* &

STOKES RESTAURANT AND BAR
♥♥♥

500 Hartnell St / 831/373-1110
The charm of downtown Monterey is best enjoyed by strolling the pretty streets to admire the historic Spanish Colonial buildings and homes. The architecture oozes romantic potential, and the promise is perfectly fulfilled by Stokes, which is set inside one of the prettiest buildings in town: a large, sunset-pink stucco home built in 1833. The simple beauty of its exterior continues inside, where shimmering gold-leaf stencils adorn the graceful columns and archways. The appealing entry is warmed by a wood-burning fireplace, and the spacious interior is divided into several airy dining rooms with terra-cotta floors and bleached-wood plank ceilings. Unique wrought-iron chandeliers and large modern paintings enhance the historic setting. The main dining room exudes a rustic Mediterranean ambience, with banquette seating covered in blue, teal, and tan fabrics; wooden chairs and tables; and small-paned windows. While some tables are much too close together, the corner tables are well suited for intimate repasts. The California-inspired menu offers a few Spanish twists, including some excellent tapas, such as crispy polenta with mushrooms and Tuscan white-bean bruschetta. Combine these affordable plates with the homemade sourdough bread and oil-cured olives brought to your table, and you have a light meal—but that would mean missing out on the other outstanding appetizers, such as the

layered tower of house-made mozzarella and ripe heirloom tomatoes or the outstanding sweet white-corn bisque. Hearty entrée choices include a grilled pork chop served with savory bread pudding and pear chutney or seared hanger steak with a spinach-cheese tart. Save room for dessert; the enticing prospects include warm ginger cake with strawberry-rhubarb compote or molten chocolate lava cake.

$$ *AE, MC, V; no checks; lunch Mon-Sat, dinner every day; full bar; reservations recommended; www.stokesrestaurant.com.* &

PACIFIC GROVE AND PEBBLE BEACH

ROMANTIC HIGHLIGHTS

You can still find a measure of peace and quiet in the enchanting ocean-front town of **Pacific Grove,** unlike neighboring Monterey and Carmel, which can get overcrowded at peak times. Exquisite **Victorian mansions** line Ocean View Boulevard, where the tide laps at the seemingly endless stretch of sandy shoreline. Not only is Pacific Grove's quiet charm a welcome change of pace, but also the bevy of bed-and-breakfasts and restaurants here includes some of the most impressive properties we've encountered along the Central Coast.

If leisurely mornings, quiet scenic walks, and romantic dinners are your idea of a grand time, you've come to the right place. The serene pace and the wide choice of luxury accommodations (most of which require a two-night stay on weekends throughout the year) make this an ideal romantic getaway. The attractions in Monterey, Carmel, Pebble Beach, and Big Sur are all just down the road—in fact, in geographic terms, you might as well be staying in Monterey, since the town of Pacific Grove begins at the Monterey Bay Aquarium (it ends at the 17-Mile Drive gate).

Walking the shoreline in Pacific Grove with your loved one is, no doubt about it, a four-lip experience. Take time to saunter hand in hand along **Ocean View Boulevard**, where a whisper of salt water gently caresses your faces as waves thunder against the rocks at the water's edge. You can watch sea otters splashing in kelp beds and pelicans perching in sunny spots. Depending on the time of year, you might even catch sight of a whale or two swimming by on their migration route. If you expect your walk to take you all the way to **Lovers Point Park**, at the southern tip of Monterey Bay, consider packing a picnic to enjoy beneath the shade of a tree or on one of the benches bordering the park.

For more breathtaking ocean views and a look at Monterey County's fascinating past, be sure to visit the **Point Pinos Lighthouse** (Asilomar Blvd at Lighthouse Ave; 831/648-5716; 1–4pm Thurs–Sun). Set at the northernmost tip of the Monterey Peninsula, it was built in 1855 to guide mariners past the hazards of the rocky coast. Now the oldest operating lighthouse on the West Coast, this National Historic Landmark is not only intriguing to explore, but also makes an ideal vantage point for savoring magnificent ocean vistas. If you crave seclusion, be sure to walk the glorious, windswept sands of nearby **Asilomar Beach**.

In addition to all the natural beauty of this picture-postcard little town, fine art and exquisite architecture are found here as well. The **Pacific Grove Art Center** (568 Lighthouse Ave at Forest Ave; 831/375-2208; www.pgartcenter.org) has four galleries filled with sculptures, photographs, and drawings. Each October, you can stroll through some of the town's most beautiful and artfully restored structures on the **Victorian Home Tour** (call Pacific Grove Chamber of Commerce—see Access and Information). Without doubt, the best way to visit a local Victorian home is to indulge in a romantic supper at **Robert's White House** (649 Lighthouse Ave; 831/624-9626). The restaurant, previously known as Gernot's Victoria House, was recently bought by a notable local chef who serves three-course meals in the impressive surroundings decorated in period style.

If you find yourselves planning another trip to Pacific Grove, you're not alone; **monarch butterflies** return here every year. In fact, Pacific Grove bills itself as "Butterfly Town, USA" in honor of the approximately 50,000 monarchs that migrate here from late October to mid-March. Two popular places to look at the butterflies are the Monarch Grove Sanctuary (at Lighthouse Ave and Ridge Rd) and George Washington Park (at Sinex Ave and Alder St). At the informal **Pacific Grove Museum of Natural History** (at Forest and Central Aves; 831/648-5716; www.pgmusem.org; 10am–5pm Tues–Sat), you can learn more about the life cycle of these fascinating winged creatures.

Pacific Grove is the starting point for the famous **17-Mile Drive** (from Hwy 1, take Hwy 68 west to Sunset Dr and continue west to Pacific Grove entrance gate; entrance fee is $8.25 per vehicle). The route offers such resplendent views that your tour will likely take much longer than the 17-mile length suggests. It's worth spending an entire afternoon to make this drive so you can stop wherever your hearts desire, whether you want to linger over a crescent-shaped sandy cove, photograph the famous lone cypress clinging to the side of a cliff, or gaze at the frolicking wildlife at Seal and Bird Rocks.

As the route continues and turns to the east, it enters **Pebble Beach**, a gated elite community that shelters palatial homes and estates, along with several world-class golf courses. If refreshment is in order, try one of the restaurants at **The Inn at Spanish Bay** or **The Lodge at Pebble Beach** (see Romantic Lodgings), which overlook the profoundly beautiful setting and serve food that almost equals the view. (The restaurants will reimburse the $8.25 vehicle fee required to enter Pebble Beach if you show your entrance receipt after lunch or dinner; it's a nice idea to stop for a meal here since there are no reasonably priced accommodations in this wealthy enclave.)

Otherwise, unless ogling the rich and famous is your idea of romance, continue on; soon the natural beauty of the peninsula will be all yours again. Each bend in the road reveals new vistas of the sun shimmering on the vast Pacific and white sea spray crashing dramatically against scenic coastal rocks.

Access and Information

Highway 1 provides access to Pacific Grove and Pebble Beach via exit 399A for Pacific Grove/Pebble Beach/Highway 68 West. From Highway 101, take the Highway 156/Monterey exit, which merges with Highway 1. The town of Pacific Grove is just a five-minute drive from Monterey's Cannery Row and is thus served by the **Monterey Peninsula Airport** (Hwy 68 off Holsted Rd, 4 miles from Monterey; 831/648-7000; www.montereyairport.com).

For more information, contact the **Pacific Grove Chamber of Commerce** (at Forest and Central Aves; 831/373-3304 or 800/656-6650; www.pacific grove.org).

There are five entrances to the **17-Mile Drive;** the $8.25-per-vehicle entrance fee is waived if you stay at a hotel within the gates, and Pebble Beach restaurants will also reimburse you. If you can, avoid the busy summer weekends and come midweek. Visitors may enter the 17-Mile Drive for free on foot or bike, although cyclists are required to use the Pacific Grove gate on weekends and holidays. Additional information about 17-Mile Drive and Pebble Beach can be found by contacting **Pebble Beach Resort** (831/624-3811; www.pebblebeach.com/17miledrive.html).

Romantic Lodgings

THE CENTRELLA INN
🎔❦

612 Central Ave, Pacific Grove / 831/372-3372 or 800/233-3372
Harbored in a residential neighborhood, this renovated turn-of-the-20th-century inn specializes in friendly hospitality. Every afternoon, freshly baked cookies and a carafe of cream sherry sit on an old oak table in the bright parlor, where the sun beams in through a wall of beveled-glass windows. Here you can relax by the fire and refresh yourselves after a long afternoon of window shopping or strolling along the waterfront. In the morning, the

scent of freshly brewed coffee and homemade breakfast goodies provides all the incentive you'll need to hop out of bed. Down comforters, old-fashioned wallpaper, and antique furniture create an authentic Victorian atmosphere in the 21 rooms and 5 cottages found on this property owned by the "Inns by the Sea" chain (which operates many bed-and-breakfasts along the Central Coast, including the Inn at Depot Hill in Capitola and the Babbling Brook Inn in Santa Cruz). Unfortunately, this authenticity extends to creaky floors and rickety doors and doorknobs, but these can be avoided by staying in one of the five cottage suites—with private entrances, fireplaces, and cozy sitting areas—reached by a brick walkway bordered by camellias and gardenias. The rooms on the first and second floors of the house are small, in need of minor touch-ups, and somewhat confining (especially those with shared baths), but the two spacious attic suites tucked under skylights on the third floor offer considerably more space and privacy. Last but certainly not least is the Garden Room, the Centrella's honeymoon quarters. Whether you're celebrating a honeymoon or not, this self-contained unit (attached to the main house) is your best bet for romance. A private entrance ensures seclusion in this spacious room, which comes complete with a wood-burning fireplace, pretty floral accents, and a two-person Jacuzzi tub in the black-and-white-tiled bathroom.

$$$–$$$$ *AE, DIS, MC, V; checks OK; www.centrellainn.com.*

GATEHOUSE INN
◐◑◖

225 Central Ave, Pacific Grove / 831/649-8436 or 800/753-1881
Built as a seaside "cottage" in 1884, this beautifully restored Victorian flaunts trappings and amenities its original builders might have envied. Elaborate, custom-designed, hand-silk-screened wallpapers adorn the walls and ceilings in the homey parlor and snug, antique-filled guest rooms—you'll want to lie in bed together just to admire the intricate Middle East–inspired patterns above your heads. In the spacious Langford Suite, a beautifully appointed white-lace bed faces the bay, and a potbellied stove warms the room. The Sun Room features a white wrought-iron bed and offers a glimpse of the nearby ocean. Wine-colored curtains cast a rosy glow over the sexy Victorian Room's sumptuous burgundy linens and claw-foot tub. For those who crave privacy, five of the nine rooms have their own private entrances and three adjoin secluded brick patios. The owners do everything possible to make this feel like your home away from home. Freshly baked cookies, fresh fruit, and tea and coffee are available at all hours, or you can help yourselves to the fully stocked refrigerator, filled with juices, sodas, and milk (to go with the cookies, of course). In the morning, a full breakfast buffet of specialties such as pumpkin-cornmeal pancakes and cheese strata provide

the perfect start to a romantic day by the sea; and when you return in the afternoon, you'll find an enticing array of wine and appetizers.
$$$ *AE, DIS, MC, V; checks OK; www.sueandlewinns.com/gatehouse.*

GOSBY HOUSE INN
🌢🌢
643 Lighthouse Ave, Pacific Grove / 831/375-1287 or 800/527-8828
Since its early life as a boardinghouse, this yellow and white Victorian inn has undergone several renovations—while retaining all of its charm. (The home's history is illustrated in a series of black-and-white photographs mounted inside.) Of the 22 rooms here, 20 are in the main house (and 5 of these have private entrances); the other 2 are located in the Carriage House. The guest rooms come in all sizes, shapes, and lighting moods; some are a bit dark, while others are flooded with sunshine. Floral wallpaper, antique wood furnishings, and white embroidered bedspreads are found in each; other amenities vary—10 rooms have fireplaces; only 6 rooms have TVs; and all but 2 rooms have private baths. Private balconies in the second-floor Gosby and Holman Rooms are enticing, and rooms in the Carriage House come equipped with whirlpool tubs and separate showers. The floral parlor in the main house is a beautiful setting in which to enjoy a delicious country breakfast or afternoon tea. If you'd rather have breakfast in your room, it's an extra $5 per person. As with all of the comfortable West Coast lodgings that are part of the Four Sisters group of inns, every effort has been made to make your stay as comfortable as possible, right down to the teddy bears placed on each of the beds. In fact, if there is any hesitation at all in our enthusiasm about the Gosby House Inn, it is that the decor may be a bit too flowery. Also, some of the first-floor rooms are too close to the busy kitchen and dining room.
$$–$$$ *AE, DIS, MC, V; checks OK; www.gosbyhouseinn.com.*

GRAND VIEW INN
🌢🌢🌢🌢
557 Ocean View Blvd, Pacific Grove / 831/372-4341
The blue and white 1910 Grand View Inn is the sister property of Pacific Grove's famous Seven Gables Inn (see review), is managed by the same discriminating owners and shares Seven Gables's spectacular oceanfront setting. Not surprisingly, it also shares a well-deserved four-lip rating. In the words of the innkeepers: Seven Gables is ornate, and the Grand View is more sedate. The Grand View is an Edwardian mansion (versus its Victorian sister next door), so the interior tends toward the handsome side, with natural woods, square shapes, and large, comfortable furnishings. Notable for their simple elegance and sleek lines, the 10 ample guest rooms boast high ceilings, blond-wood detailing, and marble bathrooms. Chandeliers cast a formal light on brass and canopied beds and other enticing period touches

such as antique armoires. A beautifully handcrafted wood staircase spirals to the top of the house, where bay windows in the Rocky Shores Room showcase the best views on the property. Non-oceanside rooms overlook the Grand View's lovely rambling gardens; a small creek trickles through boulders and greenery in the beautifully landscaped front yard. Afternoon hors d'oeuvres and an all-you-can-eat breakfast of baked egg dishes, muffins, pastries, fruit, yogurt, and more are served at two large tables in the lovely oceanfront dining room. After filling up, take time to explore the wondrous section of California coast that's right outside your door. $$$$ *MC, V; checks OK; www.7gables-grandview.com.*

GREEN GABLES INN
❤❤❤

104 5th St, Pacific Grove / 831/375-2095 or 800/722-1774
From the moment you step inside this Queen Anne Victorian, you'll know you are in for an enchanting experience. The Green Gables Inn, as its name suggests, is a multigabled structure with leaded-glass windows that afford dreamy views of Monterey Bay. A collection of antiques decorates the parlor, where a carousel horse stands behind a sofa, stained-glass panels frame the fireplace, and freshly cut flowers are arranged about the room. Each of the 11 rooms—6 in the main house and 5 in a carriage house—are decorated in cheerful paisley with country floral accents. But couples beware: aside from the Lacey Suite and Jennifer Room, all the rooms in the main house share bathrooms, which in our opinion is not conducive to uninterrupted kissing. Be sure to request a room with private facilities. The Lacey Suite has romantic appeal, and not just because of its marble bathroom, equipped with an antique claw-foot tub; located adjacent to the parlor, it's the largest room, and beautifully appointed, too, with hardwood floors, a four-poster canopy bed, and a tiled fireplace. Other, smaller rooms in the main house might include sloped ceilings, bay windows, comfortable sitting areas, fireplaces, and ocean views. One room with angled ceilings and a love-seat bench resembles a tiny chapel (which might or might not be romantic, depending on your religious views). The five rooms in the Carriage House are all spacious, but the ocean view isn't as grand. Nevertheless, these rooms will entice you with their fireplaces and private baths; four offer Jacuzzi tubs for two. In the morning, indulge in a full country-style breakfast served beside a fireplace and expansive windows that face the shimmering sea. In the afternoon, trays of house-made appetizers, cheeses, and vegetables are served alongside a selection of wine; there's also tea and hot coffee accompanied by a sweet treat. Sherry and dessert are set out in the evenings. $$–$$$ *AE, DIS, MC, V; checks OK; www.foursisters.com.*

THE INN AT SPANISH BAY
❂❂❂❂
2700 17-Mile Dr, Pebble Beach / 831/647-7500 or 800/654-9300
Although the exclusive Inn at Spanish Bay looks like a condominium complex and feels like a country club, in fact it's an excellent spot in which to indulge your most affectionate inclinations. Not only does this world-class resort cater to your every imaginable need, but it also has breathtaking ocean views beyond its rolling, emerald-green golf course bordered by windswept grasslands and sand dunes. A bagpiper dressed in traditional Scottish garb walks along the inn's perimeter at dusk, playing melodies that drift in with the sea breeze. In addition, the resort has a full-service fitness club, a tennis pavilion complete with eight championship courts, a golf course par excellence, several choice restaurants, and an exemplary staff that will pamper you. Guest rooms with ocean vistas are preferred, naturally, but they are also considerably more expensive, naturally. Many rooms command refreshing views of cypress forests instead and are more reasonably priced (keep in mind that "reasonable" is relative here). The 270 elegant rooms are equipped with gas fireplaces, deep soaking tubs with separate glass-enclosed showers, and all the amenities you'd expect from a luxury resort. Once you've arrived at this prime locale, you probably won't want to leave. Luckily, on-site dining options include the well-respected Roy's at Pebble Beach (see Romantic Restaurants), and the resort recently added an upscale Italian restaurant, Peppoli (831/647-7433), which serves rich Tuscan fare in a cozy dining room overlooking the ocean. In addition, drinks and snacks are served in the evenings on the spacious outdoor patio overlooking the windswept dunes and golf course; strategically placed fire pits ward off the chill.
$$$$ *AE, DC, MC, V; checks OK; www.pebblebeach.com.* ♿

THE INN AT 213 SEVENTEEN-MILE DRIVE
❂❂❂
213 17-Mile Dr, Pacific Grove / 831/642-9514 or 800/526-5666
Any address on wildly scenic 17-Mile Drive has major kissing potential, and this exquisite inn, which opened in 1999, definitely lives up to the promise of its romantic location. Rooms are housed in an elegantly restored 1920s Craftsman home and adjacent structures and surrounded by stunning flower gardens and lawns. The mood inside is one of meticulous elegance: the original 1926 beam floors have a lustrous glow, gorgeous orchids bloom on the table before an impressive stone wood-burning fireplace, and lots of large windows and French doors allow in natural light. Each of the 14 rooms is named after a shorebird and offers different amenities and decor. The rooms in the main house are immaculately clean and pretty. Couples flock to the Blue Heron Room, which boasts a king-size brass bed, Oriental rugs, a sitting room with daybed, and a balcony overlooking the bay. The bright

and cheerful Turnstone Room, equipped with a queen-size four-poster bed swathed in colorful linens, has lots of windows and a lovely view of the bay. The Avocet Room is decorated in a handsome Oriental-style color scheme of red, cream, and black and has a small balcony. (Our only complaint about the decor here holds true for several of the rooms, in which televisions are perched in full sight on dressers or tables; the bulky electronics detract from the romantic ambience and would be better stashed in a cabinet.) Couples seeking more space and privacy can book one of the Redwood Rooms or the Pelican cottage, both set adjacent to the main home. The Guillemot Room, one of the Redwoods, is a veritable tree house, paneled entirely in glowing redwood, with towering vaulted ceilings, a cozy fireplace, nautical-inspired decor, and a brass king-size bed. The Pelican Room, set in the rose garden, has a fireplace and an enticing king-size bed made up with soft floral linens. Monarchs flutter in the trees in the Butterfly Sanctuary just 200 yards away, and a three-block stroll leads you right to the water's edge. A full buffet breakfast includes fruit, homemade breads, and morning dishes such as frittata or light crab soufflé; dine at individual tables in the home's original billiard room or on the lovely sunporch. Wine and hors d'oeuvres are served each afternoon, and in the evening, the communal hot tub set out beneath a scenic old oak tree is an enticing spot for a relaxing soak. $$$–$$$$ AE, MC, V; checks OK; www.innat17.com. &

LIGHTHOUSE LODGE SUITES
✪✪✪
1150 and 1249 Lighthouse Ave, Pacific Grove / 831/655-2111 or 800/858-1249
A large cypress shades the colorful gardens and immense rock outcroppings that surround this assembly of Craftsman-style cedar-shingled accommodations. A welcome change of pace from the ubiquitous Victorian bed-and-breakfasts found along the Central Coast, the 31 pleasantly decorated guest rooms here are perfectly designed for romantic seclusion. Private entrances and decks ensure solitude, while vaulted ceilings, rich color schemes, and standard but handsome furnishings provide charm. Everything you need for a romantic evening is at your fingertips, including a wet bar, a gas fireplace, Jacuzzi tub set in a seductive marble bathroom, and even a bedside dimmer switch to help set an amorous mood. Although it might be hard to leave this lap of luxury, the ocean is only a short walk from your front door. Every morning, guests gather in the spacious dining room, located in the middle of the property. A complimentary cooked-to-order breakfast is served at two-person tables, while fireplaces at both ends of the room help take off the morning chill. If you'd rather not venture out, have breakfast delivered to your room. In the afternoon, a noteworthy selection of complimentary appetizers and local wines invites quiet conversation after a busy day of touring. If that's not enough, the affiliated Lighthouse Lodge across the

street features a complimentary barbecue each evening for guests staying in the suites. Warning: Two separate properties comprise the Lighthouse Lodge Suites. When making your reservations, be absolutely sure that you book a suite rather than a unit in the separate lodge. Otherwise you will end up with a mediocre, motel-style room that is certainly cheaper but not remotely romantic; the lodge is generally crowded with families, to boot. $$$–$$$$ *AE, DC, DIS, MC, V; no checks; www.lhls.com.*

THE LODGE AT PEBBLE BEACH
❂❂❂❂

17-Mile Dr, Pebble Beach / 831/647-7500 or 800/654-9300
Upscale and refined, this luxury resort is designed for couples with deep pockets and a desire to play the famous course at Pebble Beach, the mecca of American golf courses. But nongolfers can easily find romance here, too. Built in 1919, this world-renowned piece of heaven has been attracting golfers and lovers alike for decades. Although the service is a bit stuffy at times, that won't keep you from enjoying the golf course, shops, fitness area, tennis club, equestrian center, and deluxe full-service spa and salon. The cream-colored lobby, decorated with paintings, sculptures, greenery, and a grand piano and anchored by vast marble fireplaces at each end, is simply breathtaking. An entire wall of immense floor-to-ceiling windows overlooks the perfectly manicured golf course and, beyond it, the dramatic ocean surf. Although the lodge itself is not intimate, the incredibly posh rooms more than compensate. Each of the 161 luxury suites and guest rooms is appointed with polished, tasteful furnishings and all the right amenities to make your stay extremely comfortable. All are decorated differently, so describing each room's deluxe decor might fill up the rest of this book. Forty-seven rooms offer fantastic ocean views—with nothing at all standing between you and the sea. Sixty-five have what management calls garden views, which really means they overlook the expansive main lawn and the golf course. Rooms with "scenic vistas" have partial views of the ocean. After a day on the course, retire to your suite and relax in the Jacuzzi tub or deep soaking tub or cuddle in front of a wood-burning fireplace. If all those indoor and outdoor sports have worked up your appetite, culinary gratification can be had just steps away. For a quick, casual meal before teeing off, opt for Stillwater Bar and Grill (831/925-8524), which offers a menu of seafood, steak, and hamburgers. The most notable of the property's four restaurants is Club XIX (831/625-8519), an intimate French dining room with an upscale ambience (men are required to wear jackets). The restaurant's windows face Carmel Bay and the celebrated Pebble Beach Golf Course, and tables are set with white linens, gold-rimmed china, and candles. The mix of French and Californian cuisine served here is impressive, featuring dishes such as

aged prime New York sirloin with truffle sauce or wild white salmon with tarragon sauce; the house-made desserts are like tiny works of art. $$$$ *AE, DC, DIS, MC, V; checks OK; www.pebblebeach.com.* ⅓

THE MARTINE INN
◐◐◐

255 Ocean View Blvd, Pacific Grove / 831/373-3388 or 800/852-5588
This turn-of-the-20th-century pink Mediterranean villa set by the sea is a haven for kissing couples, thanks to its splendid water views and romantic rooms. Set directly across the street from the ocean and just four blocks from Monterey's bustling Cannery Row, the location is equal parts charm and convenience. Each of the 24 old-fashioned rooms features a private bath and ornate antiques, and many have claw-foot tubs and wood-burning fireplaces. Rooms face either the ocean or the garden courtyard, which has a delightful dragon fountain. In the spirit of romance, there are no televisions to distract you from each other; a large pool and hot tub are accessible to all guests. If you like snuggling in bed together, book the Maries Room, which is furnished with a five-piece 1880 English oak Sheraton-style bedroom set, including queen bed; you can watch the coast just outside the window from the splendor of the bed. There's also a claw-foot tub and shower. The biggest splurge is the Parke Room, at the very top of the house, which has three window-walls of ocean views, a sitting area, a claw-foot tub, a massive white-brick corner fireplace, and a grand antique bedroom set complete with four-poster canopy bed. Lovebirds on a budget aren't left out, either, since the courtyard-view rooms (some with shower-only bathrooms) are more affordable. Our favorite is the California room, which has an open beamed ceiling and a rare and exotically painted bedroom set from the 1880s. In the rest of the inn, several intimate sitting rooms offset three large common areas: the library, the main dining room (with a dazzling view of the bay), and the breakfast parlor. The personable innkeeper will be happy to show you his collection of five vintage roadsters, including a 1925 MG, which he races. In the morning, an elaborate and delicious breakfast served on antique silver, crystal, and lace is offered in the waterfront dining room; each afternoon, relax in the Victorian parlor with wine and hors d'oeuvres. $$$–$$$$ *AE, DIS, MC, V; checks OK; www.martineinn.com.*

THE OLD ST. ANGELA INN
◐◐◐

321 Central Ave, Pacific Grove / 831/372-3246 or 800/748-6306
This 1910 Cape Cod–style home, originally built as a summer residence, retains that fresh, airy feel associated with warm-weather retreats. Large windows and numerous skylights throughout let ample amounts of sunshine flood the country-inspired common rooms; sea breezes flow through the ocean-facing rooms; and a colorful garden affords a pleasant place to sit and

watch birds splash about in the birdbath. Although the home is located in a residential neighborhood along a somewhat busy street, the tranquility of Monterey Bay, and its long walking path, are just one block west. Recently redecorated, all nine delightful rooms are bright and comfortable. Amenities include skylights and ceiling fans, large windows, lovely linens, and hardwood floors laid with decorative rugs. Our romantic favorites are the four rooms upstairs: the nautically inspired Crow's Nest, the blue and white Whale Watch with its private deck, the roomy Garden Gable, and the Bay View, which boasts the best ocean views. Most of the rooms are warmed by fireplaces, and many have one-person jetted tubs in the bathrooms (thanks to the owner's foresight in putting the water faucet in the tub's center, two people can usually squeeze in . . . but we do mean squeeze). Otter's Cove, a cozy room off the garden, is small, but it offers a charming curtain-enclosed window seat perfect for snuggling up with a book (or each other). It's also the least expensive room and ideally suited for those seeking privacy at a reasonable price. A small sunroom overlooking the garden is where guests gather to partake of the full breakfast of juices, homemade muffins, bagels, fruit, and a delicious main course. Potato pancakes chock-full of toasted pecans, egg casseroles filled with crab or Canadian bacon, and strawberry-stuffed French toast topped with homemade whipped cream are just some of the possibilities. The decadent delights don't end in the morning, either. Come evening, a generous wine and cheese hour brings plenty of appetizers to the living-room table, and later on, brownies, cookies, or a cheesecake take care of your sweet tooth. Some people who stay here don't even bother going out for dinner.
$$–$$$ DIS, MC, V; checks OK; www.sueandlewinns.com.

SEVEN GABLES INN
🌢🌢🌢🌢
555 Ocean View Blvd, Pacific Grove / 831/372-4341
Truly a sight to behold, this immense yellow and white Victorian mansion holds court on a rocky promontory in Pacific Grove. Every plush, stately room at this celestial bed-and-breakfast offers views, ranging from satisfactory to outstanding, of the glistening ocean and rugged coastal mountains. Built in 1886, the house has been painstakingly renovated, and an extensive collection of fine art and museum-quality antiques sets it off to perfection. Tiffany glass windows, Persian carpets, 18th-century oil paintings, marble statues, and crystal chandeliers are just some of the collector's items crowded into the inn's opulent common areas—which, as a consequence, aren't necessarily homey. Luckily, the 14 guest rooms are all inviting, cozy retreats with private, albeit standard bathrooms. Broad windows trimmed with lace and balloon valances make the rooms bright and sunny by day; at night, classic lighting fixtures shed a soft, warm glow. Oriental carpets, canopy beds, and classical artwork add to the historical flavor of every

room. We especially liked the eight rooms spread out between three cottages and a guest house behind the main building, which enjoy enhanced privacy and similar ocean views. On most weekends, you will find at least one or two couples spending their wedding night at the Seven Gables Inn. But even if it doesn't happen to be your honeymoon, all that romance is sure to rub off. Breakfast, served family-style, is a grand affair of freshly baked muffins, croissants, and special egg dishes. A generous, proper high tea, also served in the exquisite dining room, features tortes, homemade fudge, and a large assortment of pastries, all accompanied by a stunning view of the water. $$$$ *MC, V; checks OK; www.7gables-grandview.com.*

Romantic Restaurants

FANDANGO
❤❤❤

223 17th St, Pacific Grove / 831/372-3456
Explore a taste of the sultry Mediterranean at this festive restaurant, where the cooking captures the robust flavors of Spain, Italy, and France. The decor is charming whether you are seated in one of the three front rooms or in the cozy wine cellar, with its thick rock walls, vintage wine bottles, and copper pots hanging from the rafters. Colorful curtains frame the windows, bottles of olive oil and magnificent flower arrangements grace each white-linen-draped table, and the worn wood floors and numerous fireplaces make for cozy warmth. Near the back of the restaurant, a more informal—and noisy—environment awaits in the glass-roofed terrace, where the open grill issues the delicious scent of seafood and poultry being cooked over mesquite and fruitwood. There's also a sunny outside patio fronting the road that is perfect for a casual lunch or Sunday brunch. For a taste of North Africa, try the outstanding couscous *Algérois,* made according to a century-old family recipe. France is represented by rack of lamb *à la Provençale,* Spain and Italy by wonderful paellas and pastas. Swordfish, salmon, and scallops are examples of the sea's bounty taken advantage of here. These are but a handful of Fandango's creatively prepared dishes; you'll delight in discovering the rest on your own.
$$$ *AE, DC, DIS, MC, V; no checks; lunch Mon–Sat, dinner every day, brunch Sun; full bar; reservations recommended; www.fandango restaurant.com.*

JOE ROMBI'S LA MIA CUCINA
❤❤

208 17th St, Pacific Grove / 831/373-2416
For those hoping to find a warm, welcoming, yet stylish Italian trattoria in an upscale town like Pacific Grove, Joe Rombi's is heaven-sent. The dining

room is sleek and spare, and tables are dressed in white linens, but there's nothing stuffy about the ambience—or the satisfying Italian food—at this small, lively restaurant. Advertisement posters from the late 1800s add color to the white walls, which are illuminated by track lights; despite the restaurant's small size, the tables are spaced adequately far apart. La Mia Cucina means "my kitchen," and you might wish it were your own kitchen once you taste classic Italian dishes such as tomato and fresh mozzarella Insalata Caprese and pasta dishes such as puttanesca and three types of savory ravioli. Heartier dishes such as grilled steak topped with basil butter, as well as lighter fare such as chicken piccata and fresh fish specials, round out the menu. With its easy ambience and tasty dishes, Joe Rombi's is a delightful slice of small-town Italy.
$$–$$$ AE, MC, V; no checks; dinner Wed–Sun; beer and wine; reservations recommended.

OLD BATH HOUSE RESTAURANT
✦✦✦✦

620 Ocean View Blvd, Pacific Grove / 831/375-5195
This time-honored establishment is a favorite for special occasions—or when you're simply in the mood to splurge. Set at the edge of Lovers Point Park, the restaurant is known for its intimate oceanside dining and its scrumptious desserts. The dark-wood interior with a low, carved ceiling, the romantic lighting, and the gracious service create an enticing ambience. Cozy tables, softly illuminated by candlelight, line the large picture windows that overlook the crashing surf. The views are mesmerizing at sunset, but it's also enjoyable to watch the distant flicker of city lights across the water once darkness falls. The continental fare is fresh, seasonal, and well prepared. Begin your meal with a creamy lobster bisque or artichoke and Gorgonzola cheese ravioli with a lemon-nutmeg cream sauce. An appropriate main dish for the evening might be the Lovers Point Lamb, two marinated and grilled porterhouse chops served with almond-herb couscous; an array of fresh seafood, poultry, and steak also entices. For those who'd like a taste of the good life without breaking the bank, the Old Bath House offers four-course early-bird dinners at moderate prices. (If you time it right, the sunset will be waiting for you after dinner at nearby Lovers Point.) Chocolate lovers will want to dive into the Oceans of Chocolate dessert, a bittersweet chocolate brownie with espresso cream cheese, vanilla or chocolate ice cream, and warm chocolate sauce.
$$$ AE, DC, DIS, MC, V; no checks; dinner every day; full bar; reservations recommended; www.oldbathhouse.com.

PASTA MIA TRATTORIA
♥♥

481 Lighthouse Ave, Pacific Grove / 831/375-7709
Set in the heart of Pacific Grove, this renovated Victorian from the outside looks more like a private residence than an Italian restaurant. Inside, the only elements carried over from the house's domestic past are the polished hardwood floors and the windows curtained with lace. Twisted ropes of garlic and chilis and colorful ceramics adorn the walls, and freshly cut red roses accent tables draped with white linen; the mood is casual and friendly. For the most privacy, request a table in the cozy window alcove that overlooks Pacific Grove's charming store-lined streets. If you've brought your appetites, you won't be disappointed, as the portions here are generous (if not, you can always share a few dishes). However, the not-too-speedy service means you shouldn't plan on hurrying through your meal. Hearty homemade soups and pastas are the kitchen's specialties; try the half-moon pasta stuffed with pesto in a zesty lemon cream sauce with chicken and sun-dried tomatoes or prawns sautéed in a champagne cream sauce. Entrée options also tempt, including veal marsala or breast of chicken with a garlic, wine, and rosemary sauce or a light and satisfying daily fish preparation. For dessert, Pasta Mia serves up some of the best tiramisu in town. The restaurant is an evening destination only, but a recently opened second restaurant under the same ownership, Pizza Grotto (1244 Munras; 831/647-1133) serves many of the delicious pasta dishes from the Pasta Mia menu, as well as a full menu of tempting pizzas, at both lunch and dinner.
$$ *AE, MC, V; no checks; dinner every day; beer and wine; reservations recommended.*

RED HOUSE CAFÉ
♥♥♥

662 Lighthouse Ave, Pacific Grove / 831/643-1060
With the appeal of a pretty country home and food that would draw praise from the toughest big-city food critics, the Red House Café is a longtime favorite in Pacific Grove. The closely spaced tables and acoustics weren't designed for romantic privacy, but there's no doubt that this restaurant, housed in a century-old red brick house, is an extremely cozy spot. The most popular meals are breakfast and lunch, and on sunny days you can catch ocean breezes as you eat on the porch at a wicker table for two. Inside both of the snug dining rooms, walls painted robin's-egg blue and soft green, plus sturdy wooden tables, create a charmingly rustic picture. The front room, warmed by a fireplace, has a handful of tables, but this seating option is less pleasant at peak times when the space fills with hungry diners waiting for open tables. Crowds do flock to the Red House Café, so reserve your table in advance or prepare to wait—but even if patience is required, the delicious food will be your reward. Even simple dishes such as Irish oatmeal, Belgian

waffles, pastries, a mixed green salad, or a roast beef sandwich on sour-dough taste unusually delicious when they come from this kitchen, which uses only the finest ingredients. In the evening, dine on local salmon or other Monterey Bay seafood; crab-cake lovers will swoon when they taste these pillowy treats stuffed full of succulent crab. Should you be looking for an afternoon pick-me-up, the restaurant also houses the only Mariage Frères (France's most prestigious and time-honored tea house) tea salon and shop on the Monterey Peninsula. It's a lovely spot to linger over one of the finest and most aromatic cups of tea you've ever tasted, paired with the Red House Café's scrumptious fresh pastries.

$ *No credit cards; no checks; breakfast, lunch Tues–Sun, dinner Thurs–Sat; beer and wine; reservations recommended; www.redhousecafe.com.*

ROY'S AT PEBBLE BEACH
❂❂❂
2700 17-Mile Drive (The Inn at Spanish Bay), Pebble Beach / 831/647-7423

If you're looking for a nice place to stop for lunch during a scenic sojourn along 17-Mile Drive, look no further than Roy's. Couples staying at the posh Inn at Spanish Bay (see Romantic Lodgings, above) will almost certainly find themselves in this famous dining room at some point during their stay. During our romantic travels, we've dined at all of Roy's restaurants in Hawaii and at the Seattle location. While each of these—all founded by star chef Roy Yamaguchi—has many redeeming features, there's no doubt that this Roy's has the most inspiring views. The split-level restaurant commands million-dollar panoramic vistas of The Links golf course, windswept dunes, and the sparkling Pacific through floor-to-ceiling windows. Sleek blond-wood floors and architectural details are enhanced by colorful rugs and upholstered chairs, peaked copper ceilings, and art deco–style chandeliers and sconces. A bustling open kitchen, common to all Roy's restaurants, can be a distraction, but the friendly and efficient service will keep your experience smooth. The restaurant's popularity means intimate tables are hard to come by, but the splendid ocean scenery and faultless pan-Asian cuisine will take your minds off the crowds. Our recommendation is to take advantage of your proximity to the sea and sample any of the seafood creations, which range from hibachi-style salmon and blackened rare ahi to delicious wok-steamed clams and mussels. If you're more in the mood for a hearty meat dish, you can't go wrong with the island-style honey-mustard garlic-grilled short ribs. Order the melting-hot chocolate raspberry cake before your main course (so the kitchen has time to prepare it), and there's no doubt your meal will end on a high note.

$$$ *AE, MC, V; checks OK; breakfast, lunch, dinner every day; full bar; reservations recommended; www.roys-restaurants.com.*

TASTE CAFE & BISTRO

❂❂❂

1199 Forest Ave, Pacific Grove / 831/655-0324

Sometimes romance is found in unexpected places, and that's the case with this popular restaurant set inside an unremarkable minimall near the busy junction of one of Pacific Grove's main streets and Highway 68. Fortunately, the moment you step inside, the pretty dining room welcomes you in Mediterranean style, with textured yellow walls trimmed in green, terracotta-tiled floors, and soaring vaulted ceilings frescoed with angels. Gorgeous fresh flowers, wrought-iron plant stands overflowing with greenery, and skylights create an appealing garden mood. Gauzy curtains and tasteful fabric treatments on the large front windows conceal the busy street outside, while tables set with white linen and crystal add elegance. The only potential drawback to your romantic meal here is that the dining room can get noisy on crowded weekend nights. But this is minor in comparison to the benefits, which include some of the finest food in the region. The menu combines rustic French, Italian, and California cuisines, and dishes are made with the freshest local produce, seafood, and meats. For a savory lunch, order warm grilled shrimp salad or tasty chicken-apple sausage, both served with a heavenly side dish of potatoes au gratin, decadently creamy inside and topped with crispy browned cheese. For dinner, start with house-cured salmon carpaccio with mustard-dill dressing or a classic Caesar salad. With enticing entrée options such as juicy roasted half chicken with mashed potatoes or grilled steak with horseradish and crispy *pommes frites*, the decision isn't easy. Desserts such as the warm brioche pudding with apricot coulis and the bittersweet chocolate torte are divine. This spot is a favorite with locals enjoying a special celebration, so be sure to call well ahead for reservations, especially if your date falls on the weekend.

$$ *AE, MC, V; checks OK; lunch, dinner Tues–Sun; beer and wine; reservations recommended; www.tastecafebistro.com.* &

CARMEL AND CARMEL VALLEY

ROMANTIC HIGHLIGHTS

Artists, poets, and playwrights congregated in **Carmel** at the turn of the 20th century, drawn by its spectacular setting on the coast. Today, the town retains much of its bohemian charm, although it has taken on an undeniably ritzy tinge. Upscale boutiques, fashionable art galleries, expensive inns, and fine restaurants share flower gardens with the rows of storybook cottages clustered within Carmel's one-square-mile city limits. There are no streetlights, and in the evenings, the town's narrow boulevards are illuminated solely by the soft glow emanating from cozy neighborhood restaurants and storefronts. Streetlights aren't the only big-city amenities missing in Carmel, either—you won't see billboards, parking meters, neon signs, or street addresses. (We list street junctions rather than formal addresses in our reviews because that's all you'll need to find your destination.)

If Carmel sounds idyllic, however, the unfortunate thing is you're not the only ones who think so. It is the Central Coast's most popular destination, which means that most weekends it gets disturbingly crowded. During the summer, the town is full to the point of bursting. It's not just people filling the streets, either; Carmel is renowned as a pet-friendly city (many local inns welcome dogs, and in many shops, man's best friend is allowed in to browse). Because the crowds are almost certain to detract from the romantic mood, we highly recommend timing your visit on a weekday or in the off-season. If you want to visit during the high season but avoid the fray—and you can afford to splurge—venture 4 miles south to **Carmel Highlands**, which offers unparalleled views of the Pacific and posh hotels such as the **Highlands Inn** (see Romantic Lodgings). Farther inland, you can escape the hordes by setting up romantic headquarters in serene and beautiful Carmel Valley.

Keep in mind, however, that when the crowds aren't bad and the sun is shining, Carmel's romantic appeal is as clear as its crystalline coastal waters. Naturalists and romantics will appreciate the beautiful white sand beaches. The local paper, the *Carmel Pine Cone*, lists the time the sun will set each day. Armed with this information, walk down Ocean Avenue to **Carmel Beach City Park** a half hour before the spectacular sunset unfolds. More solitude can be found by driving a mile south on **Scenic Drive** (the street running alongside the beach) to **Carmel River State Beach**.

Without doubt, the best way to see Carmel's delightful sights is on foot. Even those who have never heard of the poet Robinson Jeffers will be inspired by his ocean-view homestead, the **Tor House** (26304 Ocean View Ave, at Stewart Way; 831/624-1813; www.torhouse.org). This rustic stone cottage, completed in 1919, is where Jeffers wrote most of his poetry. (*Tor* is

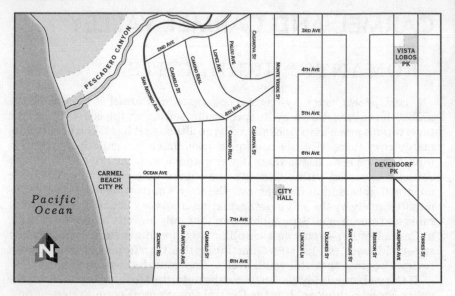

an old Irish word for "craggy knoll.") You can also visit the four-story Hawk Tower, which Jeffers built by hand for his wife out of huge rocks he hauled up from the beach below: guys, take note. More in-depth tours are available through **Carmel Walks** (831/642-2700; www.carmelwalks.com), which offers a fascinating two-hour guided walk Tuesdays through Fridays of more historic homes, as well as secret gardens and courtyards.

Don't miss the chance to discover the beauty of **Point Lobos State Reserve** (on Hwy 1 approximately 3 miles south of Carmel; 831/624-4909; pt-lobos .parks.state.ca.us/; no pets allowed). This beach makes an epic setting for a kiss. The barking of sea lions drifts through the salt-scented air as you hike one of the dozen trails leading to ocean coves, where you might spot harbor seals, sea otters, and, between December and May, migrating California gray whales. Nearby are tide pools you can explore together, searching out scrambling crabs and purple sea urchins. Seclusion and spectacular scenery are yours for the hiking, particularly if you follow one of the less-traveled trails that hug the cliffs of this rugged coastline. (For more nearby hiking recommendations, see the Big Sur chapter.)

Romance away from the coast abounds in beautiful **Carmel Valley** (from Carmel, take Hwy 1 to Carmel Valley Rd). Few drives are as romantic as the one that passes through this valley, where vineyard-covered hills, pastoral meadows dotted with grazing horses, and well-tended golf courses make for endlessly scenic views. The valley's wineries are popular destinations; especially fine kissing grounds can be found at **Chateau Julien Wine Estates** (8940 Carmel Valley Rd, about 5½ miles upvalley; 831/624-2600; www.chateaujulien.com; open every day), where a French-style chateau is set amid scenic vineyards and lavish gardens. After sipping chardonnay, cabernet sauvignon, and merlot in the high-ceilinged tasting room, adjourn to the cobblestone courtyard for a romantic picnic. Buy goodies beforehand at the organic deli and bakery at the valley's famous **Earthbound Farm** (7250 Carmel Valley Rd, approximately 3½ miles upvalley; 831/625-6219; www.ebfarm.com; open every day). To enjoy wine tasting without worrying about driving, contact a local tour company such as **Your Maître D'** (831/624-1717; www.yourmaitred.com) and cozy up in the back of a limousine as you are transported in grand style to wineries around the valley.

Carmel Valley's **Garland Ranch** (roughly 9 miles upvalley) is outdoor romance at its best: you cross the sparkling Carmel River over a scenic wooden bridge to reach the hiking trails, which wind through an open valley with views of the Santa Lucia Mountains. Bring a picnic lunch and make a day of it; you're almost certain to encounter sunshine here, unlike in Carmel, which can be shrouded in coastal fog. The community exudes a distinctly relaxed, ranchlike mood, but establishments such as **Bernardus Lodge** (see Romantic Lodgings) are ultraluxurious and romantic. Don't miss the chance to wander hand in hand around sunny **Carmel Valley Village**. The tiny town with a Western ranch feel harbors a number of antique and garden shops, wine-tasting rooms, and charming restaurants, such as **Café Rustica** (see Romantic Restaurants), where you can dine alfresco on the sunny garden patio.

Access and Information

Highway 1 provides direct access to Carmel. From Highway 101, take the Highway 156/Monterey exit, which merges with Highway 1. The region is served by the **Monterey Peninsula Airport** (831/648-7000; www.monterey airport.com; Hwy 68 off Holsted Rd, 4 miles from Monterey).

For more information about Carmel, call or visit the **Carmel Visitor Information Center** (831/624-2522; www.carmelcalifornia.org; upstairs on San Carlos St between 5th and 6th Aves; 9am–5pm Mon–Fri), which is amply stocked with maps, brochures, and publications on area attractions and lodgings. It's a good place to find out more about Carmel's annual events, such as the monthlong **Carmel Bach Festival** (831/624-2046; www.bach festival.com), which begins in mid-July; tickets go on sale as early as January. More information about **Carmel Valley** can be found by going online (www.carmelvalleycalifornia.com) or by contacting the **Carmel Valley Chamber of Commerce** (831/659-4000; www.carmelvalleychamber.com).

Romantic Lodgings

BERNARDUS LODGE
❤❤❤❤

415 Carmel Valley Rd, Carmel Valley / 831/658-3400 or 888/648-9463
The owners of Bernardus Winery also created this lodge and spared no
expense in crafting a romantic haven. Even your arrival is plush: a cour-
teous staff member greets you with glasses of Bernardus wine. The 57 guest
rooms and suites are housed in the lodge's terra-cotta- and lemon-colored
buildings, set on a scenic terraced hillside dotted with ancient oaks and
pines and offering vistas of the surrounding Santa Lucia Mountains. Every
resort amenity you could hope for is here, including two excellent restaurants, a beautiful outdoor pool surrounded by chaise lounges and private
pool cabanas, tennis and croquet courts, a small fitness center, and a full-
service spa (if you crave a relaxing couples' massage, book in advance, as
appointments fill up early). The rooms are all upscale, elegant, and comfortable; our favorites are those on the top floor, where the pale carpets,
vaulted white ceilings, large windows, and private decks create a feeling of
space and light, while tasteful wooden furnishings add warmth. Relax on
the sumptuous brown fine-wale corduroy sofa and elegant armchair set in
front of the gas fireplace with its simple, art deco–style mantel. One tasteful
armoire contains the television; the other holds your plush robes and slippers. The king-size beds are heavenly, piled high with down comforters
and fabulous Frette linens. Other conveniences include a CD player (bring
your own CDs) and a wet bar (where complimentary Bernardus wine and a
gourmet cheese plate await your arrival). The elegant bathrooms have pristine white soaking tubs large enough for two, spacious white tiled showers,
double sinks, luxury Kiehl's bath products, and—a romantic dream—truly
flattering light. Only two rooms have Jacuzzi tubs; the rooms are 100 square
feet larger, and the private tubs are outdoors. These rooms are located by
the incredibly romantic wedding garden, where wisteria-draped arbors,
rose gardens, and a stone fountain provide the perfect backdrop for those
tying the knot. The two restaurants on the property have distinctly different
moods; a jacket and tie are optional in both. Wickets Bistro (831/658-3550)
has a more casual feel, and you'll fall in love with the outdoor patio, where
you can indulge in delicious, fresh seasonal dishes (don't miss the portobello
mushroom soup) as a fire roars in the large, rustic stone hearth and the stars
twinkle above you. The more formal restaurant, Marinus (831/658-3550),
serves a sophisticated mix of California and French cuisine; the impressive
menu even offers the option, between the first and second courses, of an
"indulgence" course: dishes such as red abalone risotto or soft-boiled eggs
with osetra caviar. Couples can enjoy the gourmet experience in an elegant

dining room anchored by a majestic fireplace or the lovely outdoor terrace surrounded by lush landscaping.
$$$$ *AE, DC, DIS, MC, V; no checks; www.bernardus.com.* &

CARMEL VALLEY RANCH
❂❂❂

1 Old Ranch Rd, Carmel Valley / 831/625-9500 or 800/422-7635
Even if you've never won the Masters, you'll feel like a golf celebrity as you pass through the gated entrance of this exclusive estate, a haven for golf and tennis enthusiasts (and corporate retreaters). Upon arrival, you are greeted by name and chauffeured via golf cart to your secluded, luxurious suite (an especially nice touch if you haven't mastered the art of packing light). Nestled in the rolling hills of the Carmel Valley, this 1,700-acre wooded property has kept 1,200 acres pristine, with deer and wild turkeys roaming the sprawling grounds. A series of contemporary ranch-style guest buildings house the 144 supremely private and upscale suites; seven room styles are available. Each room features a private entrance, a deck, and tasteful earth-tone decor accented by burgundy and green. Cathedral ceilings soar above modern appointments, and white shutters open to reveal stunning views of the valley. A gas fireplace radiates warmth, and a second fireplace in the bedroom promises late-night romance. Sparkling white tiled bathrooms hold separate showers and extralong soaking tubs, many of which are fronted by a window. If you have the good fortune to be able to reserve a spa suite (our top romantic pick), you can indulge in a romantic soak beneath the stars: the private hot tub, set on a wraparound deck high in the trees, is a true nest for lovebirds. Set farther away from the main accommodations are 44 more-recently built suites with similar decor and larger bathrooms, all equipped with double vanities and jetted tubs. Nightly turndown service delivers freshly baked cookies to your room. Exclusive almost always translates into expensive, and Carmel Valley Ranch is no exception. Fortunately, you get what you pay for here. Your comfort is the ranch's top priority, and the gracious staff is only a phone call (and a golf cart) away. Other amenities cater to the athletically inclined: golfing on an 18-hole championship course, playing tennis, horseback riding, hiking, and swimming. A variety of specialty golf, tennis, spa, and romance packages are also worth looking into (a couples' massage followed by champagne and chocolate-covered strawberries will certainly set the mood). The ranch has three restaurants, including the elegant Oaks, which serves refined American regional cooking in a formal room graced by Old California antiques, a towering stone fireplace, and a phalanx of windows affording a panoramic view of the oak-covered hills.
$$$$ *AE, MC, V; checks OK; www.wyndham.com.* &

COBBLESTONE INN
♨◀

Junipero between 7th and 8th, Carmel / 831/625-5222 or 800/833-8836
Affordable rooms are hard to find in Carmel, and when you do find them, they tend to be in motor lodge–type settings far from the water. So it's not surprising, given that the Cobblestone Inn has some of the more reasonable rates in town, that its rooms are clustered around a central courtyard that doubles as a parking lot. All the same, lovebirds seeking romance on a shoestring will be pleased to hear that there are some benefits to staying here. To start with, the inn is professionally run by the well-regarded Four Sisters group of inns. White shutters ensure privacy in the 24 simple guest rooms, each decorated with floral wallpaper, watercolor paintings, and plaid linens. The inexpensive furnishings are slightly worn, but you will find antique brass beds and river-rock fireplaces in every room. The lower-priced rooms are quite small but comfortable and clean. The larger rooms have couches set in front of the fireplaces (though if you're going to splurge, we recommend looking elsewhere). All of the rooms, regardless of price, feature plain standard private bathrooms. The inn's real strength is its pleasant common areas, including the clean, cheerful lobby adorned with country curios and teddy bears and the adjacent breakfast room with sunny yellow walls, inviting sofas, and a massive stone fireplace. This is where the morning buffet and afternoon hors d'oeuvres are served each day. On a warm morning, adjourn with your breakfast to the outdoor patio in the courtyard, where cobblestones and wisteria-draped arbors transform the motor lodge–setting into a quaint alfresco nook.
$$–$$$ *AE, DIS, MC, V; checks OK; www.foursisters.com.*

CYPRESS INN
♨♨◖

Lincoln St at 7th Ave, Carmel / 831/624-3871 or 800/443-7443
With its Moorish Mediterranean architecture, the Cypress Inn makes a pretty picture of arches, white stucco walls, and a red tile roof. This stately 43-room inn wraps around a lovely garden courtyard overflowing with flowers and greenery. Movie star Doris Day owns the inn, and posters from her career adorn the walls of the elegant main lobby, which is decorated in shades of pale apricot and features a white marble fireplace; this might seem too fancy for pets, but, in fact, four-footed guests are welcome here and in the rooms (dog beds are even on hand should you need one). The well-maintained guest rooms match the refined elegance of the lobby and feature tasteful yet simple decor. No two rooms are alike, but all are equipped with plush robes, cable television, CD players, and a flask of complimentary sherry. Colorful ceramics, Turkish rugs, and copper bowls decorate the stucco walls and wide windowsills; wrought-iron and wicker furniture complement the earth-toned interiors. Black-and-white photographs

Puppy Love

Some couples just don't consider a getaway romantic unless they can bring along their beloved golden retriever or adored calico kitty. If you are one of them, you'll be glad to hear that Northern California offers an array of romantic lodgings that will also accommodate your pet. San Francisco's **Hotel Monaco** (501 Geary St; 415/292-0100 or 800/214-4220) welcomes pets with open arms. Upon arrival, your four-legged friend will score biscuits and a water bowl; if you need to duck out for a short pet-free interlude, there's a good chance that one of the notoriously pet-friendly staff members will take your dog for a walk. There are even all-inclusive packages designed with your pet in mind, with perks such as chew toys, plush doggie towels, cute dog tags, and a pet-walking service. At Union Square's elegant **Campton Place Hotel** (340 Stockton St; 415/781-5555 or 800/235-4300), cats and dogs receive a friendly reception along with treats in the fancy marble lobby. At the **Hotel Palomar** (12 4th St; 415/348-1111 or 877/294-9711), it's a dog's life (cats aren't allowed)—including a gourmet canine dinner, chew toy, and luggage tag, as well as grooming and doggie daycare for an additional charge. From this or other downtown hotels, such as the pet-friendly **Hotel Triton** (342 Grant Ave; 415/394-0500 or 800/433-6611), it's just a short walk to **Yerba Buena Park**, where you can all enjoy the park's grassy lawns and waterfalls.

If splendid ocean views are at the top of your wish list, head north to the village of Mendocino, where **The MacCallum House** (45020 Albion St; 707/937-0289 or 800/609-0492) welcomes pets of all varieties in its charming ocean-view suite cottages. At Mendocino's **Stanford Inn by the Sea** (Comptche-Ukiah Rd and Hwy 1; 707/937-5615 or 800/331-8884), the rooms of pet owners are replenished each day with food and water bowls, sleeping beds, and ribbon-tied doggie biscuits; the expansive, scenic property is perfect for on-leash exploration.

Perhaps the best place to commune with nature—and your pooch—is the famously pet-friendly town of Carmel. Many shops allow dogs inside to browse, and some restaurants even permit you to dine with your canine companion! Carmel's **Cypress Inn** (Lincoln St at 7th Ave; 831/624-3871 or 800/443-7443) welcomes four-footed guests in its elegant lobby and rooms and offers dog beds should you forget Fido's at home. The **Vagabond's House Inn** (4th and Dolores; 831/624-7738 or 800/262-1262) also allows pets. While you're here, don't miss a stroll at the dog-friendly, leash-free **Carmel City beach**, an enticing stretch of sandy shoreline that offers prime exploring for pets; meanwhile, the humans in your party can entertain themselves with the breathtaking ocean views. (For more information on pet-friendly romantic lodgings, see the index at the back of the book.)

embellish the lovely marbled bathrooms, which feature glass-enclosed showers and deep soaking tubs. All the rooms in the deluxe category offer fireplaces, wet bars, jetted tubs, and plenty of space. In this category, just two rooms offer far-off glimpses of the blue sea: the Tower Suite, a unique two-level accommodation, and Room 215, a favorite honeymoon suite featuring a Jacuzzi tub, fireplace, king-size bed, and small ocean-view balcony. Ten additional luxury rooms were completed in June 2004; none have ocean views, although two have balconies overlooking the quaint streets of Carmel. Additional results of the renovation include an expansion of the cozy bar where the complimentary breakfast buffet is served: it now also offers lunch and light evening snacks, in addition to the afternoon tea (reservations recommended) and the evening happy hour. A small workout facility and conference room are also new.
$$$–$$$$ *AE, DIS, MC, V; checks OK; www.cypress-inn.com.*

HIGHLANDS INN
◗◗◗◖
Hwy 1, Carmel Highlands / 831/620-1234 or 800/682-4811
Some places you have to see to believe, and this exclusive inn is one of them. Views of the coastline from the Highlands Inn will literally take your breath away. The unparalleled panorama takes in windswept trees, white surf breaking over sharp rock outcroppings, and an occasional pod of spouting whales on the distant horizon. Happily, all of this splendor is located just 4 miles south of downtown Carmel. Most of the 142 sleek rooms, clustered in small groups and terraced into the hillside, share the same incredible view. You can even glimpse the ocean from the beautifully tiled, jetted tubs in the spa-equipped suites—the tubs are enclosed behind sliding doors that open to the bedroom and the views beyond. Wood-burning fireplaces and dimming lights give every room a romantic glow, and modern furnishings create a comfortable atmosphere. Most guest rooms have the added conveniences of a full kitchen, TV/VCR, CD player, and binoculars. We highly recommend requesting a room without anyone above you. Suffice it to say the soundproofing could be improved (a bit disappointing, considering this is a Park Hyatt property). Outside, a sloping staircase winds past cypress trees and gardens to a heated outdoor pool surrounded by patio furniture and umbrella-shaded tables. You won't have to wander far for superb meals. The inn's exceptional restaurant, Pacific's Edge (see Romantic Restaurants) serves outstanding views along with seasonal California cuisine for lunch and dinner, while the California Market draws those seeking a more casual breakfast, lunch, or dinner in the comfortable dining room or on the adjoining redwood deck. The staff at the California Market also packs picnic baskets in case you're heading off to Big Sur.
$$$$ *AE, DC, DIS, MC, V; checks OK; www.highlandsinn.hyatt.com.* ⚘

LA PLAYA HOTEL
ⓞⓞⓒ

Camino Real, Carmel / 831/624-6476 or 800/582-8900
At the sprawling pink La Playa Hotel, the Pacific Ocean is visible through pine and cypress trees, and the sound of the dramatic surf echoes in the distance. This Mediterranean-style villa offers a tranquil setting and all the amenities of a full-service hotel. La Playa's lobby is warmed by an enormous fireplace and decorated with hand-loomed area rugs and lovely antiques. A sweeping staircase, accented by vivid tile work, winds upstairs to 75 basic guest rooms filled with hand-carved furnishings, including whimsical mermaid-motif headboards. Peach tones add warmth to the sunny interiors, which feature wooden shutters and recessed lighting. While the standard rooms are certainly nice, we were a little disappointed by the stark white bathrooms and the absence of certain creature comforts—namely, robes. Some accommodations in the main building are small—possibly perfect for couples who are looking to get close—and some offer stunning ocean views. Our favorite rooms are situated on the lower floor, with private terraces that open onto the property's lush inner courtyard and 2 acres of beautiful, award-winning formal gardens filled with a profusion of colorful flowers (the gardens are a popular wedding site). Not far away, you'll also find a heated pool encircled by orange poppies swaying on slender stems. Five storybook cottages nestled in a nearby garden grove offer all the privacy in the world; naturally, they are also the most expensive units at La Playa. Each has a full kitchen or wet bar, a terrace or garden patio, and a wood-stocked fireplace; however, the rustic interiors, furnished with eclectic antiques, lack the upscale elegance of the resort's other accommodations. Although breakfast is not included with your stay, it is available at the hotel's restaurant, the Terrace Grill (831/624-9010). Dine alfresco on the heated open-air terrace overlooking the fabulous gardens, and indulge in seasonal fare that highlights Monterey County produce and fresh seafood.
$$$-$$$$ AE, DC, MC, V; checks OK; www.laplayahotel.com. &

MISSION RANCH
ⓞⓒ

26270 Dolores St, Carmel / 831/624-6436 or 800/538-8221
Worth visiting for its gorgeous setting alone, the Mission Ranch looks as if it was transported here straight from the ranchlands of Texas. Given the Western-themed surroundings, it might not surprise you to hear that this down-home getaway is owned by actor and former Carmel mayor Clint Eastwood. The renovated 1850s farmhouse, along with a handful of white cottages with green trim, are surrounded by cypress trees, sheep pastures, and rolling hills that reach down to the fringes of the ocean. (The "Bonanza" ambience is so complete that the six championship tennis courts, exercise room, and banquet facilities seem out of place.) The ranch's 31 guest rooms

are more comfortable than charming, furnished with a mix of eclectic antiques, old-fashioned fabrics, and a few rather unsightly details, such as exposed electrical cords. These are redeemed somewhat by the queen- or king-size beds draped with floral or country-style patchwork quilts and the picture windows surveying enticing views of lush green meadows. The Meadow View Room and the Hay Loft Bedroom feature gas fireplaces and one-person whirlpool tubs. The Bunkhouse Cottage is equipped with a full kitchen in case cooking together is one of your favorite romantic pursuits. Our favorite spots are the six guest rooms in the picturesque farmhouse. These rooms feature hardwood floors and lovely antiques and share a wide wraparound veranda entwined with trailing bougainvillea. The informal and Western-themed Restaurant at Mission Ranch (831/625-9040), which operates under separate management, serves hearty American-style fare; look elsewhere for intimate dining. Be sure to request a room away from the restaurant; the piano bar can get a little rowdy, and if your room is nearby, you may find the noise less than romantic. $$–$$$$ AE, MC, V; checks OK. &

QUAIL LODGE RESORT AND GOLF CLUB
●●●

8205 Valley Greens Dr, Carmel Valley / 831/624-2888 or 888/828-8787
Although this 600-acre resort is especially tailored to please golf lovers, even nongolfers will be charmed by passing through a private gate into your own secluded patio, where you'll feel worlds away from everything and everybody. Adorned with native plants and a Japanese rock pool filled with floating flowers, the entry is designed to draw nature into your immediate surroundings. And if you're active but golf is not your thing, you might be tempted by the resort's tennis facilities, jogging and hiking trails, European-style spa with steam rooms, two outdoor pools, a fitness center, and a large hot tub. A major $25 million renovation completed in summer 2003 added new amenities and heightened the luxury in the resort's 100 rooms, all of which are inviting and contemporary, with Asian-style furnishings, blond-wood accents, and beds swathed in plush, stylish linens. Bathrooms are big, bright, and beautiful, with garden-facing windows and shutters opening into the bedrooms. After a day on the green, place your shoes in the two-way butler's pantry for cleaning (one of the many distinctive touches here) and then ease into the extralong tub for a soak. More relaxation can be found on the cozy couch fronting the fireplace or on your private patio with views of the lakes, gardens, or golf course. Eight room categories are available, ranging from superior to fireplace king to two-bedroom suites, and none come cheap. The Covey Restaurant (831/620-8860) offers wine-country cuisine, such as venison osso buco, sweetbread salad, and crab-crusted halibut, with an emphasis on fresh, local products. Well-prepared California cuisine is served at the resort's clubhouse restaurant, Edgar's (831/620-8910). Set

about a half mile down the road from the main lodge, its top-floor location allows for excellent views of the course.
$$$$ *AE, DC, MC, V; checks OK; www.quaillodge.com.* ♿

STONEPINE
◐◐◐◐

150 E Carmel Valley Rd, Carmel Valley / 831/659-2245
Lined with gnarled oaks, a milelong access road that crosses a wooden bridge over a creek and passes corrals full of horses leads to the aristocratic estate of Stonepine. As the wrought-iron reception gate swings open, a formidable French country manor covered with ivy comes into view. If you opt to be picked up from the Monterey Airport, you'll first lay eyes on this splendor from the backseat of Stonepine's own Phantom V Rolls Royce. Such first-class service is the norm at this hotel that caters to the rich and famous. In the spacious foyer and living room of the main house (dubbed Chateau Noel), a gallery of windows, damask-covered sofas and love seats, hardwood floors laid with a hand-woven Chinese rug, and an oversize limestone hearth create a picture of elegance. In the evening, this room is often graced by the music of a string ensemble. Eight of Stonepine's fashionable accommodations are located in the main house; elegant wallpaper, lavish draperies, fireplaces, tastefully framed prints, and polished wooden furnishings surround guests with old-world style and modern comfort. A sexy Roman marble bath with a Jacuzzi tub and an intimate sitting room are two of the enticing features found in the Taittinger Suite. The Don Quixote Room has a king-size bed, two bathrooms, and French doors that lead to a private garden and patio. Even the petite Dong Kingman Suite captivates, thanks to its peaches-and-cream color scheme and full marble bath, overlooking the rose garden. Fireplaces and canopy beds in many of the rooms are romantic grace notes. About a mile away, the four suites in the ranch-style Paddock House have Jacuzzi tubs and access to a fully equipped country kitchen. The most secluded unit of all is the self-contained, two-bedroom Briar Rose Cottage, with a rustic stone fireplace and its own porch overlooking a fragrant rose garden. Also on the property you'll find a 5,000-square-foot French country villa called the Hermes House and a mini-estate called Gate House, which appeals more to families. Stonepine prides itself on its gracious European-trained staff, which will cater to your every desire—expect to be thoroughly indulged. Afternoon tea and a complimentary gourmet breakfast are served in the formal dining room, which features cathedral ceilings, burnished oak paneling, and an immense fireplace. A superb and extremely expensive five-course dinner is also served here but is not included with your stay. If you like to ride, you can saddle up two horses at Stonepine's equestrian center. $$$$ *AE, MC, V; checks OK; www.stonepinecalifornia.com.* ♿

TICKLE PINK INN
◐◐◖

155 Highland Dr, Carmel Highlands / 831/624-1244 or 800/635-4774
You'd be forgiven for imagining that this inn, with a name like Tickle
Pink Inn, couldn't be anything more than a horror of pastels. But forget
the name: there is nothing pink in sight. (The inn, actually beige in color,
is named after former State Senator Edward Tickle.) Perched atop rugged
shoreline cliffs, Tickle Pink Inn overlooks miles of the Pacific coast, and all
but 1 of the 35 rooms share this colossal view. The vistas help compensate
for the outdated decor in the rooms. Our advice is to avoid the less-expensive rooms (a relative term here, given the exorbitant prices), since they
have particularly lackluster appointments. The minisuites will induce more
romantic thoughts, with their river-rock fireplaces, wrought-iron king-size
beds, blond-wood furnishings, black-tiled bathrooms, and semiprivate and
private decks. Four suites have two-person Jacuzzi tubs (we prefer the three
in which the tub sits in the living room). There is also a communal outdoor
Jacuzzi tub. A separate stone cottage set lower on the hillside offers the
most seclusion, along with two bedrooms, a fireplace, an outdoor deck, and
a jetted tub in the bathroom. Check-in brings fresh cookies, and later in the
evening, complimentary fruit, wines, breads, and cheeses are served on the
glass-enclosed wood patio overlooking the crashing waves. When the wind
is blowing, guests congregate in the plush fireside lobby furnished with
comfy, overstuffed sofas. A continental breakfast is also served here, unless
you ask to have it delivered to your room.
$$$$ MC, V; checks OK; www.ticklepink.com.

VAGABOND'S HOUSE INN
◐◖

4th Ave and Dolores St, Carmel / 831/624-7738 or 800/262-1262
A large, gnarled oak stands guard in the center of the Vagabond's small
interior courtyard, where a waterfall spills over a rock garden surrounded
by potted camellias, rhododendrons, and ferns. Many of the guest rooms
in this unpretentious English Tudor–style lodging face this tranquil scene.
Amenities in the 11 modestly decorated rooms include kitchenettes, wood-
burning fireplaces, and a decanter of sherry beside each bed. Knotty-pine
walls lend rustic charm to several rooms, while marbled bathrooms add
a touch of elegance. The first sight you'll see upon stepping out of your
room is the courtyard's massive oak, which is adorned with tiny white
lights. In the morning, an extended continental breakfast of fruit, freshly
baked breads, and egg dishes can be brought directly to your room. But
the best thing about the Vagabond's House is that the price is right. If you
are seeking absolute privacy, you can inquire here about the Lincoln Green
Cottages, under the same ownership. We can't wholeheartedly recommend
these four country cottages: while the exteriors have quaint English charm,

the exorbitant prices are not justified by the dated, utilitarian interiors. The peaceful setting is certainly romantic, but considering that Carmel's legendary beachfront is just blocks away from the Vagabond, there are few compelling reasons to pay the higher price tag of the cottages.
$$$–$$$$ *AE, DIS, MC, V; checks OK; www.vagabondshouseinn.com.*

Romantic Restaurants

ANTON & MICHEL
✿✿✿
Mission St between Ocean and 7th Aves, Carmel / 831/624-2406 or 866/244-0645
Classic continental cuisine and a traditional romantic atmosphere make this restaurant an appealing date destination, although the food can be uneven. The neoclassical decor is very pretty; oil paintings featuring fair ladies and flowers embellish the peach- and cream-colored walls, Corinthian columns separate the dining rooms from one another, and an entire wall of windows in one room looks out upon a lovely courtyard. Candle lanterns placed on linen-draped tables cast a soft, romantic glow, inspiring intimate conversation. Our advice is to stick with the signature dishes, such as ostrich scaloppine crusted with pink and black peppercorns, Black Angus filet mignon, or the tableside presentations of rack of lamb or chateaubriand. (The specials tend to be less reliable.) Don't miss the chance to enjoy one of the traditional French desserts, such as crêpes suzette; for a dramatic finish, order the cherries jubilee or the bananas Foster, both flambéed right before your eyes.
$$$ *AE, DC, DIS, MC, V; no checks; lunch, dinner every day; full bar; reservations recommended; www.carmelsbest.com.*

CAFÉ RUSTICA
✿✿❶
10 Delfino Pl, Carmel Valley Village / 831/659-4444
When the coast is shrouded in chilly fog, it's a good time to escape to reliably sunny Carmel Valley for a meal at this charming Italian restaurant. From the moment you swing open the white picket-fence gate and step beneath the pink rose-draped arbor, you'll find yourselves relaxing amid the cheerful surroundings and warm hospitality. The most romantic seats are on the lovely garden patio, open nearly every month of the year, thanks to the cooperative valley climate. During the heat of the day, green umbrellas shade the patio, decorated with lush potted plants and flowers. In the evenings, the patio is nothing short of magical, warmed by heat lamps and flickering candles on the rustic wooden tables. The restaurant's interior is pleasantly countrified, with walls of knotty pine, low exposed-stone ceilings, a collection of rooster china, and other farmhouse touches. The

bustling open kitchen does create some distraction, so request a table off to the side. Fortunately, you'll have nothing but appreciation for the kitchen once you taste what emerges from its wood-fired oven. Specialties include pizzas such as the Lorraine, topped with caramelized sweet yellow onions, maple-smoked bacon, and Gruyère cheese, and the Pasta Rustica, laden with delicious and tender grilled eggplant, sweet roasted peppers, kalamata olives, and fresh basil. The assortment of entrées includes the fresh fish of the day and a hearty Hungarian Paprika Beef Goulash. Remember to save room for dessert; options range from a moist lemon pudding cake and crème brûlée to country apple galette with house-made caramel sauce and whipped cream. Service is energetic and efficient, and local wines are well represented on the extensive wine list.
$$ MC, V; checks OK; lunch, dinner every day; beer and wine; www.carmelvalleycalifornia.com.

CASANOVA RESTAURANT
♥♥€

5th Ave between San Carlos and Mission Sts, Carmel / 831/625-0501
Tucked away on one of Carmel's quiet side streets, this charming restaurant bills itself as the town's most romantic dining establishment. (Perhaps the name gave this away.) Such a claim may or may not be true, depending on where you sit. When the weather's nice, the small brick patio fronting the restaurant would be an ideal spot—if it weren't for its proximity to the entrance. The interior courtyard is divine on a summer's day—but the tables are so close together you could kiss your neighbor without even stretching your neck. (And that's undoubtedly not the kind of kissing you have in mind.) Inside, the ambience definitely improves. A romantic repast accompanied by lively mood-setting music can be had in any of the three cozy dining rooms, each of which is decorated on a unique theme (we like the 30-seat Alpine chalet–style Milagro Room; the 75-seat Harvest Room is elegant but less intimate). Throughout, the decor is a subdued version of country rustic: striped curtains adorn the windows, low hanging lamps add just the right amount of light, and pastoral odds and ends decorate the earthy straw and clay walls. There's also the Fountain Patio (with heat lamps) for alfresco dining. Drawing on the country cuisines of France, Italy, and Spain, entrées include paella for two, seafood linguine tossed in a white wine and lemon cream sauce, and thyme-seasoned pork tenderloin au jus accompanied by onion marmalade and confit of tomato. The dinners are not inexpensive, but all come with three courses, including a variety of scrumptious appetizers. Among Casanova's many superb desserts are a Basque-style pear tart and a chocolate custard pie with whipped cream, nuts, and shaved dark and white Belgian chocolate.
$$ MC, V; no checks; lunch, dinner every day, brunch Sun; full bar; reservations recommended; www.casanovarestaurant.com. &

FLYING FISH GRILL
●●
Mission St between Ocean and 7th Aves, Carmel / 831/625-1962
A redwood-planked den filled with bright flying-fish sculptures might seem an unlikely find on the ground level of the Carmel Plaza shopping center. But this dark, downstairs hideaway is full of surprises, from the innovative Asian-fusion creations to the cozy decor, which includes a fireplace. The intimate booths encourage a romantic mood. Blue linens make a splash on the bare wood tables, accented with a fan of chopsticks, and candles illuminate the whimsical papier-mâché fish overhead. Creative East-West fusion is always on the menu, including dishes such as Yin-Yan Salmon—a plate of roast salmon on angel hair pasta sprinkled with sesame seeds and served with a soy-lime cream sauce. Other tempting choices include the pan-fried almond-crusted Chilean sea bass served with whipped potatoes, a Chinese cabbage and rock shrimp stir-fry, and the house specialty, rare peppered ahi tuna on angel hair pasta. If you like to be entertained at dinner, try the seafood clay pot for two, a steaming medley of seafood, vegetables, tofu, noodles, sauces, and rice that you cook at the table yourselves. Then, cool off by dipping your spoons into one of three different sundaes: traditional hot fudge, basic banana, or a luscious green tea creation.
$$ *AE, DIS, MC, V; no checks; dinner Wed–Mon; beer and wine; reservations recommended.*

GRASING'S COASTAL CUISINE
●●●
6th Ave at Mission St, Carmel / 831/624-6562
Set off a quaint brick courtyard adorned with window boxes bursting with flowers, this bistro combines charm and sophistication in a quintessentially Carmel manner. The modern interior is inviting, with cathedral ceilings, warm textured walls, gorgeous floral bouquets, and track lighting that illuminates colorful paintings and sculptures. Tables set with white linens, crystal, and fresh flowers make a pretty backdrop for the excellent dishes turned out of the kitchen. The excellent contemporary California-Mediterranean fare is the result of teamwork by two notable Bay Area chefs. Fresh, seasonal dishes are on the menu for both lunch and dinner. At the midday meal, choose from superb pastas, salads, sandwiches, and entrées such as bronzed salmon with grilled portobellos, roasted potatoes, and garlic. Dinner is a slightly more upscale affair, and you can celebrate the occasion by choosing a special bottle from the thoughtful wine list. As you nibble on savory appetizers such as crispy potato pancakes with house-cured salmon and crème fraîche or savory three-onion tart with balsamic syrup, mull over the enticing main courses, such as a wild-mushroom stew with creamy polenta, roast duck with an orange-port glaze, or local swordfish with orzo

pasta and Asian vegetables. On a warm evening, request a table on the small patio and kiss alfresco.

$$ AE, DC, MC, V; local checks only; lunch, dinner every day; beer and wine; reservations recommended; www.grasings.com. &

PACIFIC'S EDGE
◖◖◖◖

Hwy 1 (Highlands Inn), Carmel Highlands / 831/622-5445 or 800/682-4811
Every table at this peerless spot offers at least a glimpse of the ocean through expansive floor-to-ceiling windows that front two sides of the restaurant. If you are ready to break the bank for one special evening, this is the place, since the acclaimed California cuisine is as inspired as the setting. Even if you opt for drinks only, the contemporary fireside lobby is a wonderful place to watch the sun sink in the west. The spacious, light-filled dining room is elegant yet understated, decorated in rich earth tones accented by natural wood and stone. Dinner plates resembling colorful, sea-worn beach glass adorn the tables, each of which is illuminated by a pretty oil lamp. The feel is of an extremely tasteful hotel dining room, which is appropriate; if you wanted cozier quarters, after all, you wouldn't come to a Park Hyatt hotel. Appetizers such as roasted-beet salad with fresh asparagus, farm-fresh artichokes with basil mayonnaise, or potato-wrapped ahi tuna will start your meal on an elegant note. Entrées on the three- to five-course menu range from grilled Monterey Bay salmon in an onion-rosemary sauce to roasted rack of lamb with white-truffle potatoes. The vast wine list has garnered many awards. It's doubtful you'll have much room for dessert, but the decadent molten chocolate cake is a treat that should not be missed. If you want to time your meal to enjoy the sunset together, book your table well in advance, as this time of day is understandably popular.

$$$ AE, DC, DIS, MC, V; checks OK; lunch, dinner every day, brunch Sun; full bar; reservations recommended; www.highlands-inn.com.

TUTTO MONDO TRATTORIA
◖◖

Delores between Ocean and 7th Aves, Carmel / 831/624-8977
This bucolic Italian trattoria looks as though it belongs in the rolling hills of Tuscany rather than in downtown Carmel. A fire in the dining room softly illuminates the brick floor and the ceiling, where open beams are bedecked with wine bottles, large copper pots, and long garlic braids. The ambience is as cheerful as the owner, who has had the chance to pose with various movie stars and sports figures, as you'll see from the plethora of photographs on the walls. A large wrought-iron chandelier crowns the room, which is furnished with a handful of dark wooden tables. Although some of these are set too close together for our romantic preferences, cozy floral booths set against the wall are a good bet. The kitchen serves up delicious Northern

and Southern Italian fare, and the extensive menu offers nine varieties of savory bruschetta along with more than two dozen pasta creations, all topped with freshly grated Parmesan and Romano cheese. There are also traditional antipasto platters, generously sized salads, flat-bread pizzas, and several seafood specials, as well as hearty entrées such as herb-roasted chicken. Mondo's dessert tray, loaded with creamy Italian creations, is too tempting to pass up. We couldn't resist the cool panna cotta topped with fresh strawberries. *Perfetto!*
$$ MC, V; checks OK; lunch, dinner every day; beer and wine; reservations recommended; www.mondos.com.

BIG SUR

ROMANTIC HIGHLIGHTS

The rugged seaside cliffs, aquamarine waters, and mist-shrouded forests of Big Sur have inspired countless visitors to raptures. This region, which encompasses a 90-mile stretch of coastline that begins about 30 miles south of Carmel, is revered for its incredible natural beauty and its laid-back atmosphere. (Despite the New Age mood, however, the prices at the upscale lodgings will have you seeing dollar signs.) Traffic can also slow down the fun during the busy summer season. Our favorite time to visit is spring—April through early June—when the windswept landscape is brightened by **California poppies** and **purple lupine** and the crowds have not yet descended.

The **scenic drive** through Big Sur provides some of the most breath-taking views you may ever experience together in a single afternoon. Plan to go slowly: an experience of this magnitude should be approached with patience (and attention at the wheel). There's no real destination to rush to, since there's no actual town in Big Sur. The places where you will want to pull over are the various parks and viewpoints that dot the rugged coast. We recommend seeking out an isolated beach or a secluded spot in the wilderness and enjoying a private showcase of the views.

Riding horses side by side along the beach is wildly romantic, and you can indulge yourselves with a little help from **Molera Horseback Tours** (831/625-5486 or 800/942-5486; www.molerahorsebacktours.com), located in **Andrew Molera State Park** (on Hwy 1, 21 miles south of Carmel; 831/667-2315). If you don't know how to ride, you're in luck: no experience is necessary to take one of these jaunts, which wind through bay laurel and redwoods and climb a scenic ridge before reaching that promised beach. Rides are offered every day, weather permitting (except Jan–Apr) and it's OK to call at the last minute; they might be able to accommodate you. Horseback riding isn't the only romantic pursuit you can enjoy in this sprawling 4,800-acre state park, the largest on the Big Sur coast: more than 15 miles of trails zigzag through grasslands and redwood forests and along the Big Sur River—in summer, many of them frequented by the avid bicyclists who flock to the park. (Many trails are closed in winter.) For a relaxed stroll, try the milelong walk from **Creamery Meadow** to **Molera Beach**, which passes through a meadow laced with wildflowers to a 2-mile-long beach harboring the area's best tide pools.

Because **Pfeiffer–Big Sur State Park** (831/667-2315; www.bigsurcalifornia .org) is one of California's most popular parks, we advise romance seekers against visiting it, unless you are mountain bikers specifically drawn by the trails. In summer, the park can get exceedingly crowded and is simply not suited to intimate moments. You'll find much more romantic solitude if you can locate the unmarked **Sycamore Canyon Road** (the only paved, ungated road west of Hwy 1 between the Big Sur Post Office and Pfeiffer–Big Sur State Park). This is the hidden route to the exhilaratingly beautiful **Pfeiffer Beach** (follow the road until it ends at a parking lot, about 2 miles from Hwy 1). Hemmed in by scenic cliffs and haystack rocks that you can approach at low tide, Pfeiffer Beach is one of Big Sur's most epic seascapes. Watching the sunset from this vantage point is so amazing, it almost feels as though it could change your lives (or at least inspire a life-changing proposition . . .).

Do not confuse the Pfeiffer–Big Sur State Park mentioned above with the highly romantic **Julia Pfeiffer Burns State Park** (831/667-2315; www.big surcalifornia.org). "Julia" is 11 miles south of the other park and offers what feels like 100 percent more privacy in its natural wonderland of more than 3,000 acres. Enchanting waterfalls, sequestered beaches, and spellbinding views are to be enjoyed throughout. Luckily for slow-paced romantics, one of the shortest trails in this hiker's paradise is also one of the most beautiful: the fairly level **Waterfall Trail** is just a quarter mile long, but its ocean views go on forever. As you follow the path that winds through redwoods to chaparral on the cliff, set high above the water, salty ocean spray and the fresh scent of California sage fill the fresh air. Benches—shaded by bay laurel and redwoods and with terrific views of the water and stunning 80-foot **McWay Falls** below—await you at the end of the trail. Keep an eye out for California sea lions and sea otters frolicking in the surf in the cove below.

Despite Big Sur's popularity—summer weekends mean slow traffic on the two-lane highway—the area has remained sparsely populated, and restaurants are few and far between. It's a good idea to come equipped with a picnic, especially if you are planning to take advantage of the many hiking trails that lead to secluded romantic spots in the region. Another option is to follow in the footsteps of many other visitors and stop for lunch and the legendary views at **Nepenthe** (see Romantic Restaurants).

Access and Information

Big Sur Valley is located 26 miles south of Carmel on Highway 1. If you're traveling from San Francisco, take Highway 101 South to Highway 156 West, connect to Highway 1 South, and continue through Monterey and Carmel to Big Sur (the total distance is about 150 miles). The two-lane section of Highway 1 that winds through Big Sur can become very crowded in the summer and on holiday weekends. It will help if you come either off-season or midweek, when traffic is fairly light. No matter what time of year you visit, it's a good idea to start driving early, fill your tank, take a camera and binoculars, bring a jacket, and wear good hiking shoes. Traveling in Big Sur can be a bit confusing: some of the park names sound similar (too many Pfeiffers!), and it's hard to watch the road, take in the scenery, and still be ready to stop in time when you come to a park or gallery of interest.

The **Big Sur Chamber of Commerce** offers helpful information (831/667-2100; www.bigsurcalifornia.org; 9am–1pm Mon, Wed, Fri) and an excellent Web site, although the office hours are limited. The **Big Sur Ranger Station** (831/667-2315; open every day) can give additional information about hiking and camping.

Romantic Lodgings

POST RANCH INN
✦✦✦✦
Hwy 1 / 831/667-2200 or 800/527-2200
Environment-conscious design meets exclusive luxury at the Post Ranch Inn, set high atop the coastal cliffs of Big Sur 30 miles south of Carmel. The unusual glass-and-wood units blend discreetly into spectacular surroundings of California redwoods and oaks, dramatic sea cliffs, crashing waves, and rolling mountains. Given the prime location, upscale atmosphere, and full-service resort amenities, it is not surprising that this inn has become a sought-after destination (many rooms book up a year in advance). The inn's 30 accommodations are spread across the cliff-side acreage; some are hidden in the trees, while others perch on the cliff. Setting and layout vary, but all of the interiors are stylish yet subtle, incorporating natural wood and stone elements. Huge picture windows allow the surrounding natural beauty to pour in from every angle, and each room has its own terrace, king-size bed with denim duvet, cushioned wicker chairs, wood-burning fireplace, slate-tiled bathroom with Japanese-style spa tub, and pull-out massage table for in-room treatments. There are no TVs, but a state-of-the-art CD stereo system provides 30 channels of musical programming via satellite. A small refrigerator is stocked with complimentary snacks and nonalcoholic beverages, and a lavish continental breakfast is presented in the inn's

breathtaking restaurant, Sierra Mar (see Romantic Restaurants). The free-standing Ocean House units are built right into the side of the bluff and have curved-beam sod roofs upon which grass and wildflowers grow. Prices for these rooms go beyond unbelievably expensive, but the ocean views from the bed, bath, window seat, and terrace are some of the best in Northern California. Another place to savor the view is from the heated cliff-side pool, where you can soak your cares away amid breathtaking scenery. If your romantic experience would be enhanced with a few outdoor activities, join in the guided morning nature walks (available on select mornings) or head to the yoga yurt to stretch your muscles. A final note: It will cost you to stay here, as the management makes very clear. A sign at the bottom of the long driveway posts the unbelievably expensive rates and states that the restaurant is "by reservation only." While a bit unwelcoming, this does deter the general public, making Post Ranch Inn all the more private, quiet, and delightful.

$$$$ AE, MC, V; checks OK; www.postranchinn.com.

VENTANA INN & SPA
🌀🌀🌀

Hwy 1 / 831/667-2331 or 800/628-6500

The rocky slopes of the Santa Lucia Mountains form the end of Big Sur's astonishing coastline, which creates the illusion that these high peaks are tumbling directly into the sea. Ventana Inn, set on 243 acres of forested mountainside, offers a ringside seat for this exhilarating scene, and its amenities will satisfy every other need you could possibly have for a special weekend away. Soothe your senses in two Japanese hot baths, two heated pools, a sauna, and a Jacuzzi tub; then don a fluffy robe and retreat to your room. Rustic elegance is the name of the game here. All of the 62 accommodations, which are spread out among a dozen or so buildings, feature wood-burning fireplaces, interiors richly paneled in wood, cedar furnishings with touches of pastel, and private patios facing either the forest and towering mountains or the endless ocean in the distance. The cedar-lined Vista Suites, among the most luxurious accommodations, include an oversize bathroom with a slate shower and an ocean-view deck with private outdoor spa tub—talk about a prime kissing spot! In the afternoon, a wine and cheese buffet is offered in the lobby; in the morning, a continental breakfast buffet is presented here or in the library adjacent to the outdoor patio. (Breakfast can also be delivered to your room for no additional charge.) For lunch and dinner, follow the wooded path to Cielo (see Romantic Restaurants), which delivers panoramic patio views of 50 miles of coastline—and dinner prices that can also take your breath away. Consider treating yourselves to an in-room massage or venturing to the spa for one of the 2½-hour couples' massage treatments, aptly named "intimate ocean experience," "intimate earth experience," and "intimate aromatherapy experience." Whether you opt for

a massage or not, the relaxation that will wash over you during a stay at this lovely retreat is quite likely to surpass your every expectation.
$$$$ *AE, DC, DIS, MC, V; checks OK; www.ventanainn.com.*

Romantic Restaurants

CIELO
◐◐◐◖

Hwy 1 (Ventana Inn & Spa) / 831/667-2331 or 800/628-6500
The long-established, eco-stylish Ventana Inn claims to inspire a sense of tranquility that will "nourish your spirit," and we might add that its wonderful restaurant nourishes the body equally well. The natural colors and textures that characterize the inn's decor are echoed in its elegantly rustic restaurant. An abundance of cedar is found everywhere, from the high, open-beamed ceiling down to the polished floor. A cozy bar area sits off to one side of the restaurant, and expansive windows face an outdoor terrace and, beyond that, the stunning natural beauty all around. White linens, single flowers, and little candle lanterns at each table add romantic flair, but when the restaurant is full (a regular occurrence on summer weekends), the tables are a little too close to one another for comfort. If the weather allows, less-crowded seating and spectacular ocean views are available on the fireside terrace fronting the restaurant. It is here that you will truly find *cielo* (heaven). Although the decor and ambience of the restaurant are undoubtedly delightful, a revolving-door parade of chefs has meant a relatively frequent changing of the culinary guard. Fortunately, one thing that never changes is the kitchen's reliance on fresh, organic ingredients, often from Cielo's own gardens. The current menu offers California cuisine with a twist; for example, caramelized Maine Diver scallops with baby carrots, asparagus, basmati rice, and red Thai curry coconut-milk broth; summer-vegetable risotto with English peas, sweet corn, summer squash, and asparagus; and oak-grilled Kansas City steak au poivre with a side of grilled Castroville artichoke and mashed potatoes. There's also a chef's tasting menu featuring a choice of three or four courses. Desserts, such as apple tarte Tatin topped with honey crème fraîche sorbet, are delectable and beautifully presented. Exemplary service enhances the dining. If you are staying at the inn, the quiet walk back to your room on the well-lit forest path offers the chance to pause for a kiss beneath the leaves rustling in the evening breeze.
$$$$ *AE, DC, DIS, MC, V; checks OK; lunch, dinner every day; full bar; reservations recommended; www.ventanainn.com.*

NEPENTHE RESTAURANT
◐◖

Hwy 1 / 831/667-2345
Nepenthe is hardly a secret destination—you might even call it a landmark or tourist attraction of sorts. Interesting metal sculptures cover the expansive landscaped grounds; a gift shop sells an array of earth-friendly mementos; and wind chimes play a soft melody in the breeze. In fact, there are two restaurants on the premises: Café Kevah (closed Jan–Feb) is located one level below and serves breakfast and brunch at a walk-up counter; the casual fare is enjoyed at canvas umbrella-shaded tables on a spacious patio overlooking the Big Sur coast. But Nepenthe itself is the true destination here, and you can't miss it. The restaurant is set at the top of an outdoor staircase, and the entry is marked by a massive redwood carving of a phoenix. A student of Frank Lloyd Wright's designed the building, and the fact that this was the honeymoon cottage of Rita Hayworth and Orson Welles adds to the mystique. Inside, the atmosphere is relaxed and earthy, the menu typical American cuisine, the food average and plentiful, and service merely standard. What makes Nepenthe such a good place to kiss is its location, perched on a breathtaking cliff that soars 800 feet above the Big Sur shoreline. This feature alone is enough to make an otherwise ordinary meal here memorable. The word *nepenthe* is derived from a Greek word meaning "no sorrow," and we agree that sorrow would be hard to feel here, especially if you come with your loved one around sunset. The fiery display of the sun sinking into the ocean shows nature using its most exquisite palette, from the drifting pale lavender-blue clouds to the intense crimson and amber sky at sunset. Window seats are perfectly arranged to take advantage of the brilliant moment, and the outdoor seating is equally good.
$$ *AE, MC, V; no checks; lunch, dinner every day; full bar; reservations required for parties of 5 or more; www.nepenthebigsur.com.*

SIERRA MAR
●●●◐

Hwy 1 (Post Ranch Inn) / 831/667-2800
Simply put, Sierra Mar boasts the best vantage point on the entire Central Coast. The exclusive restaurant of the Post Ranch Inn (see Romantic Lodgings, above) perches on a cliff 1,100 feet above the sparkling ocean. From almost any seat, floor-to-ceiling windows allow you to look straight down onto the rocky shoreline and kelp beds; southern views take in much of the rugged coastline beyond. On the outdoor deck, you can train the telescope on migrating whales, lounging seals, and magnificent hawks flying *below* you. The views are heart-stopping (fortunately, a kiss ought to resuscitate you in no time). Even if the weather turns gray, this restaurant is a breathtaking place to dine. The decor of slate floors, peeled log beams, and simple blond-wood chairs is sleek. Votives in natural stone holders and exotic

little floral arrangements brighten each table, while track lighting overhead imparts a warm glow. Elegantly prepared regional California cuisine is typically served in a four-course, prix fixe format, but any appetizer or entrée can be ordered à la carte. While the menu changes nightly, you might start by ordering grilled quail topped with fig compote, followed by a radicchio salad with shaved Parmesan and balsamic dressing. Entrée choices range from roasted pheasant breast served with rich foie gras gravy to tender lamb chops with porcini–lamb shank risotto. Desserts spanning the taste horizons, from tart lemon mousse to a heavenly crème brûlée, are beautifully presented. If the sun is still above the horizon when you've finished dinner, linger over a cappuccino or after-dinner drink—you simply don't want to miss watching the day come to a close in one of the coast's most spectacular settings.

$$$ *AE, MC, V; local checks only; lunch, dinner every day; full bar; reservations recommended; www.postranchinn.com.* &

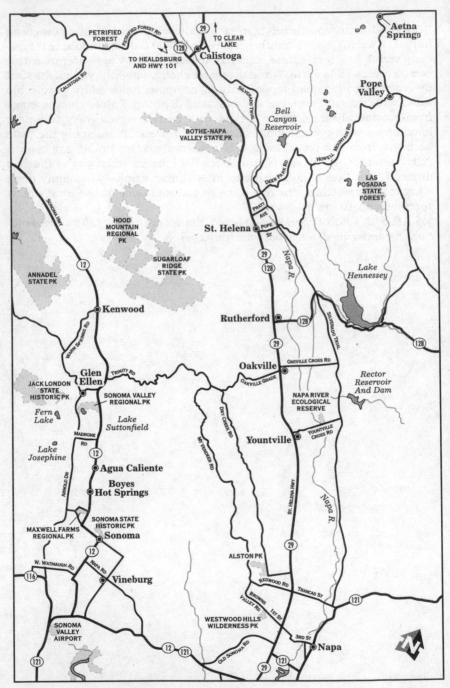

"Let him kiss me with the kisses of his mouth:
for thy love is better than wine."
—SONG OF SOLOMON

♡ NAPA

Napa truly has its own romantic character, defined not just by its world-famous wineries, but also by its robust regard for living life to the fullest. The 35-mile-long stretch of grape-strewn real estate surrounding the Napa Valley's rural Highway 29 offers an enormous selection of bed-and-breakfasts, gourmet restaurants, luxury spas, and, of course, wine-tasting rooms. There are also wonderful trails to explore and parks that harbor shady picnic spots and scenic overlooks of the golden, rolling hills.

Regardless of the time of year, Napa is tightly packed with visitors. In the high season (March through November), the traffic can be truly loathsome. In winter, crowds are fewer and reservations are easier to make, but many establishments close or have limited hours, particularly in January, and the weather is difficult to predict. Despite all this, don't be deterred—an excursion to Napa offers memories to last a lifetime. And once you visit, you will understand why this vineyard-rich region has become one of California's most popular tourist destinations. It's not just the wine—it's also the pleasure-seeking spirit of the place itself.

Some of Napa's wineries are less-than-romantic tourist magnets, while others are scenic wonders. The following three chapters feature **Romantic Wineries** sections highlighting places that hold special interest for couples seeking more-intimate wine-country moments. (The list is not meant to indicate which wines in the region are best—a highly subjective matter in any case.) It's a good idea to pick out beforehand the four or five wineries you'd like to visit during your weekend stay, and stick with your itinerary. Please know your limits, and do not drink and drive. One option that is not only safe but also lots of fun is to hire a chauffeured limousine for the afternoon. Two-person tours available from **Antique Tours Limousine Service** (707/226-9227; www.antiquetours.net; 3-hour minimum) can easily become a daylong affair to remember, complete with gourmet picnic lunch for an additional fee.

NAPA AND ENVIRONS

ROMANTIC HIGHLIGHTS

You might expect the region's namesake town of **Napa** to be a peaceful wine-country village but, in fact, this sprawling city located at the southernmost end of Napa Valley is anything but. About half the county's 73,000-plus residents live here, and the city serves as the local commercial hub. Consequently, on your first visit, you may notice more shopping plazas, fast-food chain outlets, and gas stations than wineries (most of the tasting rooms are located a few miles out of town). But once you proceed into the town's historic central district, laced with shady boulevards lined with stunning Victorian homes (some of which house romantic bed-and-breakfasts), you'll begin to get a sense of Napa's charms.

Lovers of good food and wine will find something to kiss about at **Copia: The American Center for Wine, Food & The Arts** (500 1st St; 707/259-1600 or 888/51-COPIA; www.copia.org; closed Tues). "The good life is a religion in Northern California. Now it finally has a temple," one publication wrote about this $70 million facility. Although crowds flock here to see the unique food-related art exhibits, attend cooking demonstrations or wine-tasting classes, and enjoy live music at the center's 500-seat concert terrace on the scenic Napa River, the 13-acre property is so roomy that it rarely feels overcrowded. You're especially likely to find a quiet moment if you stroll around the beautiful grounds, which include sloping, plush green lawns and a flourishing organic garden. The casual on-site café is usually noisy and packed, but the food at the expensive restaurant, **Julia's Kitchen** (named after Julia Childs), is as elegant as you would expect from this lavish facility.

Come evening in Napa, when you are ready to take a break from food and wine, other cultural offerings await. Downtown Napa boasts a lovely jewel-box theater that makes for an intimate evening date. The **Magrit Biever Mondavi Opera House** (1030 Main St; 707/226-7372; www.nvoh.org) presents a wide array of performances of theater, opera, dance, and more. This 1879 national historic landmark, which in its heyday hosted everything from readings by famed local author Jack London to vaudeville shows and masquerade balls, reopened in 2003 with its first performance since 1914. Taking part in literary history with your loved one ought to be good for a kiss.

It's easy to while away the afternoon browsing in downtown Napa, which is located along a placid riverfront. In the **Historic Napa Mill** (500 Main St; 707/251-8500; www.napamill.com), a charming 19th-century brick building, you'll find an upscale boutique hotel, shops, restaurants, and an adorable bakery. For a quick and tasty lunch, stop at **ABC**, also known as the **Alexis Baking Company** (1517 3rd St; 707/258-1827), for freshly made sandwiches and slices of rich chocolate-caramel cake. Also downtown, **Bounty Hunter Rare Wine and Provisions** (975 1st St; 707/255-0622; www.bounty hunterwine.com) is a sleek and sexy place to cozy up to the sophisticated Western-inspired bar, sip or buy wines, and snack on gourmet appetizers any time of day or late into the evening.

Although it is without doubt the most touristy excursion in the region, the **Napa Valley Wine Train** (1275 McKinstry St; 707/253-2111 or 800/427-4124; www.winetrain.com; closed first week of Jan; reservations required) can also be a lot of fun. The train's line of 1915 Pullman cars, each beautifully restored with glowing mahogany paneling, polished brass, stenciled ceilings, etched-glass partitions, and gold and burgundy velvet draperies, makes a lovely setting for the ride along the Napa Valley. In the dining car, everyone has a window seat, and polished silver, fine bone china, pressed white linens, silver candle lanterns, and single red roses bedeck the tables. A lunch or brunch excursion is the best way to view the scenery of—what else?—pretty rolling vineyards (although the train's route parallels Highway 29, so if you have already driven through the valley, you have probably seen these sights). The dinner train is best enjoyed in summer, when the days are longer.

If you'd like to counteract all that wine tasting and gourmet dining with some energetic hand-in-hand hiking, you're in luck. Just 2 miles east of downtown Napa is the pristine mountain escape of **Skyline Wilderness Park** (2201 Imola Ave; 707/252-0481; www.ncfaa.com/skyline/about.htm; follow Imola Ave east of downtown). Once you pay the $4 to park, 26 miles of hiking trails await. The wide, even trails are ideal for easy strolling, as well as for bicycling (mountain bikers are required to wear helmets). In whatever way you explore here, many places may inspire a kiss, from the beautiful mountain lake to secluded spots with gorgeous valley views. Be sure to bring sunblock and water—it gets hot and dry in these parts.

Of course, the ultimate pastime is visiting the finest local **wine-tasting rooms.** If battling traffic on busy Highway 29 doesn't fit into your romantic plans, try the Silverado Trail, a serene stretch of highway that follows the east side of the Napa Valley. The Romantic Wineries section for this chapter suggests several lovely wineries within easy driving distance of the town of Napa. You can also travel farther north (for wineries north of Napa, see the Romantic Wineries sections in the Napa Valley Wine Towns chapter and the Calistoga chapter).

Access and Information

The most popular way to tour this largely rural area is by car. Driving from San Francisco, you will likely hit some traffic: Take Highway 101 across the Golden Gate Bridge, then continue on Highway 101 North. Exit onto

Highway 37, then take a left onto Highway 121 North (Sears Point Raceway will be on your left). Stay on 121, following signs for Napa until you reach Highway 29, which then follows the length of the valley. Travel time to Napa from San Francisco International Airport is approximately 2 hours; add an extra hour or more during rush hour.

If you're traveling from the East Bay or Oakland International Airport, take Highway 80 North to Vallejo, then take the Highway 37/Marine World exit going west. This will take you to Highway 29, where you go right (north) to Napa. As you approach Napa, the road splits; for downtown Napa, keep to the right and follow the signs that say Lake Berryessa/Downtown Napa. (You can also take one of four downtown Napa exits off Highway 29.) For the rest of the Napa Valley, stay to the left and follow signs for 29 North.

Napa's wineries are clustered mainly along **Highway 29** and the **Silverado Trail**, two parallel roads running the length of the valley. The place is a zoo on weekends—especially in the summer and early fall, when the traffic on narrow Highway 29 rivals rush hour in the Bay Area. Most wineries these days charge a tasting fee, which can range from $5 for sips of three or more current releases to $25 for a single glass at Opus One. Some wineries also require reservations for tours, but don't let that deter you—the smaller establishments need to be able to control the number of visitors at any one time and to make sure someone will be available to show you around.

Helpful information and walking-tour maps are available through the **Napa Valley Conference and Visitors Bureau** (1310 Town Center Mall; 707/226-7459; www.napavalley.com).

Romantic Wineries

ARTESA VINEYARDS & WINERY
❤❤❤

1345 Henry Rd / 707/224-1668
Artesa is off the beaten track, but of the hundreds of wineries in the valley, few can boast as many good reasons to make a long drive. The absolutely magical grounds feature vast valley views, modern sculptures, and fabulous fountains. The winery, built into a grassy hillside, harbors a sleek, minimalist tasting room with soaring ceilings and impressive columns. Although at its 1991 inception Artesa, owned by Codorníu of Spain, was dedicated solely to *méthode champenoise* sparkling wine production, six years later it underwent a name change and a $10 million investment to focus on award-winning premium still wines. Today you can taste about a dozen wines, including various region-specific chardonnays and pinot noirs, a sauvignon blanc, cabernet sauvignon, zinfandel, and two sparklers. There's also a fantastic gift shop, the Carneros Center, which pays tribute to this famous

appellation's special growing conditions, and a small historical museum featuring winemaking casks, presses, and implements that date to the 16th century. Artesa's permit does not allow for food to be sold or enjoyed on the picnic-perfect property but, fortunately, there is no rule against kissing. *10am–5pm every day; tours 11am and 2pm every day; tasting fee $2 per 2-ounce pour or $6 for any 6 wines, $3 per 2-ounce pour of reserve wines or $6 for all 3 reserves; www.artesawinery.com.*

DARIOUSH WINERY
UNRATED
4240 Silverado Trail / 707/257-2345
It's impossible for us to guess the romantic caliber of the new Darioush Winery; construction was still underway at this edition's deadline, but it was scheduled to open by late 2004. We can say that it has major kissing potential and that the ambitious final structure will include traditional Persian gardens, state-of-the-art facilities, and impressive buildings situated to take advantage of sweeping views of the vineyards. A courtyard built of the same large stone blocks that make up the winery's imposing exterior leads to a tasting room with towering ceilings, columns, and a tasting bar where you can sample the winery's reds (cabernet, shiraz, and merlot) and whites (chardonnay, viognier, and vin gris). It's a nice touch that every wine taster receives a bottle of Evian or juice. You'll also have the chance to learn about the winery's commitment to classic Bordeaux varietals and techniques (they even handpick their grapes). With its winning combination of great wines and stunning architecture, Darioush has the potential to become one of the most romantically inspired wineries in Napa Valley. *10:30am–5pm every day; tasting fee $5, credited toward purchase; www.darioush.com.*

DOMAINE CARNEROS BY TATTINGER
●●
1240 Duhig Rd / 707/257-0101
Visitors traveling on Highway 12/121 to and from Napa or Sonoma often don't realize that they're passing by some worthwhile destinations along the way. Domaine Carneros, an impressive winery that specializes in sparkling wines, is one such place—that is, if you're in the mood for an elegant and somewhat formal tasting experience. Perfectly trimmed hedges and stately stone fountains line the stairway leading to the château, which has marble floors and crystal chandeliers. Inside, the old-world illusion falls short in the rather corporate-style tasting room and gift shop; nonetheless, if it's sparkling wine you're interested in, they've got delicious examples here. Tastes are accompanied by light hors d'oeuvres and crackers; caviar is also on offer. If it's not too hot, enjoy your bubbly on the terrace. Tour buses frequently make stops at this popular winery, so be prepared for crowds;

during the high season, it's best to visit either early or quite late. Those who want to know more about *méthode champenoise,* France's traditional sparkling wine-making process, can drop in on the free 40-minute tour, which includes an educational film and glimpses of the aging cellar and production line.

10:30am–6pm every day; tours 11am–4pm every day, call for winter hours; tasting fee $5–$10 by the glass; www.domainecarneros.com.

THE HESS COLLECTION WINERY
❂❂❂

4411 Redwood Rd / 707/255-1144
A fine wine should be lingered over, and so should this exceptional winery, which also harbors an acclaimed art collection. Located in a dramatic turn-of-the-20th-century building with thick stone walls and set on a quiet side road far removed from the rush of Highway 29, this secluded winery will seduce you into slowing down your pace with its self-guided tour. A short audiovisual presentation explains the Hess philosophy of grape cultivation and wine making, while three floors showcase Donald Hess's fabulous art collection, including works by such contemporary artists as Francis Bacon, Frank Stella, and Robert Rauschenberg. As you pass through the gallery, peek through the windows for a look at the wine-making operation. Picnic tables are not provided, but you can take a leisurely walk through the tranquil garden courtyard before tasting chardonnay, cabernet sauvignon, and zinfandel in the tasting room, an impressive high-ceilinged space with exposed-stone walls.

10am–4pm every day, excluding major holidays; tasting fee $5; www.hesscollection.com.

JARVIS
❂❂

2970 Monticello Rd / 707/255-5280 or 800/255-5280
Jarvis is a stunning example of what someone with a vision, a passion for wine, and an unlimited budget can create. Come here to see how the other half—or, perhaps more appropriately, the other 1 percent—lives. The tour begins at the imposing entrance to the wine caves. The entrance looks like something out of a James Bond movie, with massive arched doors opening to the caves and modern bronze sconces lining the walls. Toward the center of the tunnels, waterfalls plummet into a stream, which serves both entertainment and practical purposes—the running water helps maintain the cave's natural humidity. The tour continues into the property's main building to a grand room called the Crystal Chamber. Immense, dazzling amethysts and crystals on display at each end of the room are a sight to behold. Finally, after stopping for a glimpse of the fiber-optic chandelier in the ladies' room (yes, men get to peek in for just a moment), you'll be taken to a formal

tasting room furnished with a long marble table and elegant royal-blue chairs trimmed in gold. Here, gourmet cheese and crackers accompany wine tastings of four (the Bacchus Tasting Tour) or six (the Vintage Tasting Tour) Jarvis wines such as cabernet sauvignon, chardonnay, and cabernet franc. Touring this winery is a one-of-a-kind experience, but come prepared to endure the serious and somewhat pretentious tone that characterizes the tour, which lasts at minimum about an hour. If you are aware of this one drawback in advance and still want to visit, be sure to contact the winery as early as possible: the tours book up quickly, especially during the height of the season.

By appointment only; tour fee $20–$30; www.jarviswines.com.

MONTICELLO VINEYARDS
●●

4242 Big Ranch Rd / 707/253-2802 or 800/743-6668
In this bustling valley, Big Ranch Road is a road less traveled and, to paraphrase the poet Robert Frost, taking it to the peaceful country setting of Monticello Vineyards can make all the difference. Flanked by acres of vineyards on either side, a long driveway leads to a stately mansion—modeled after Monticello, Thomas Jefferson's home—and its adjacent informal tasting room. After touring and sipping award-winning chardonnay, merlot, and pinot noir in the tasting room, check out the picnic area, which is surrounded by quaint white lattice. A rose garden lends a gorgeous backdrop for the picnic tables, and several old walnut trees provide shade on sunny days. If you plan ahead and bring your own lunch, all you'll need is a bottle of wine, available for sale in the tasting room. Isn't life in Wine Country wonderful?

10am–4:30pm every day; www.corleyfamilynapavalley.com.

SILVERADO VINEYARDS
●●●

6121 Silverado Trail / 707/257-1770
As you ascend the steep, narrow, curving drive that leads to this impressive hilltop winery, you might just feel as though you've landed in one of the hill towns of Italy. Of course, once you glimpse the large parking lot at the summit, you'll remember that you're in Napa—and that this 30,000-square-foot facility, which opened in 2001, draws quite a few visitors. But the crowds will quickly fade when you escape outside to the beautifully landscaped patio that overlooks the entire northern half of the Stags Leap District. Inside, the winery is elegant, understated, and refreshingly clean of gift-shop items. Within the airy new 4,000-square-foot tasting room (complete with huge fireplace), you can sample four of the winery's six or seven current releases, which include cabernet, sangiovese, chardonnay, sauvignon blanc, and merlot. Step into the hallway to peek through French doors

at the enormous new barrel room, where 1,000 oak barrels contain aging cabernet and merlot. No picnics are allowed on the terrace, but enjoying a glass of *vino* in the late afternoon on the patio with views of the winery's 95 acres of vineyards makes for a blissful consolation.
10:30am–5pm every day; tasting fee $7; www.silveradovineyards.com.

WILLIAM HILL WINERY
✿✿❀

1761 Atlas Peak Rd / 707/224-4477
Lots of wineries in Napa Valley have gorgeous surroundings that simply beg to be enjoyed in privacy, but many of them are mobbed with visitors. Touring William Hill Winery is by appointment only, so fewer crowds congregate here, and a stroll through the beautiful grounds can be enjoyed in relative solitude (and usually you can get a same-day appointment for tasting). It's worth the phone call to experience this small winery set on top of a grassy embankment overlooking verdant hills lined with symmetrical rows of grapevines and sprawling shade trees, with mountains rising majestically in the distance. It's an inspiring panorama, and the lawns and gardens are yours to enjoy once you've landed an appointment. Inside the attractive tasting room, faux-antique-painted walls and a terra-cotta floor create a lovely atmosphere for tasting the well-regarded cabernet sauvignon, merlot, and chardonnay; massive windows look down on hundreds of wooden barrels filled with aging wine.
By appointment only; tasting fee $5; www.williamhillwinery.com.

Romantic Lodgings

BLUE VIOLET MANSION
✿✿✿

443 Brown St / 707/253-2583 or 800/959-2583
The accommodations in this aptly named lavender Queen Anne Victorian were definitely designed with romance in mind. Of the 17 guest rooms spread out on four floors, 14 feature single or double whirlpool tubs, all but 2 have fireplaces, and 6 have king-size beds. The ambience and decor reflect a unique combination of turn-of-the-20th-century elegance and fanciful whimsy. The rooms on the first two floors contain an eclectic mix of antiques and are decorated in Victorian style. The home's lofty top floor, called the Camelot Floor, holds four of the home's most private and unique accommodations. These are decorated with a King Arthur theme, complete with hand-painted murals, but exquisite antiques and stained-glass windows maintain a sense of Victorian decorum. Romantic perks include CD players, gas fireplaces, and two-person whirlpool tubs in the bathrooms. Once you are ensconced in one of these private rooms, pour some of your complimen-

tary bottle of wine into the two silver goblets provided and make a toast to the timelessness of romance. Three grand rooms on the main floor are the newest accommodations on the property. While they aren't as private as the rooms on the Camelot Floor, they are lovely—particularly the Empress Parlor, which has charming views of the pool and garden. A full, two-course breakfast, served in the main-floor dining room, might include fresh fruit and cinnamon rolls to start, followed by an egg dish, vanilla French toast, or crepes filled with artichoke hearts and sun-dried tomatoes. Before your morning meal, wander through the grounds to take in the fresh air and the scents of blooming flowers. If it's hot, cool off in the outdoor pool and spa surrounded by a lush green lawn and gorgeous flower gardens. The prime kissing spot is an immaculate white gazebo in front of the house. If playing lord and lady of the manor appeals to your "Masterpiece Theatre" sensibilities, the innkeepers will happily play along. A five-course candlelit dinner can be served in your room or in the eclectically decorated dining room known as Violette's at the Mansion (ask the innkeepers for complete details; reservations required). If an occasion calls for something truly romantic, it's possible to arrange a private alfresco dinner for two in the gazebo.
$$$–$$$$ *MC, V; checks OK; www.bluevioletmansion.com.*

CEDAR GABLES INN
❤️❤️❤️

486 Coombs St / 800/309-7969
The romance of Renaissance England radiates from this impressive dark-brown-shingled mansion, trimmed in white and sheltered by immense cedar trees. Stepping through the large front doors, guests are immediately engulfed by the sheer grandeur of the rich burgundy carpeting, dark redwood walls, tall leaded-glass windows, and Gothic-style antiques. Though the mansion is enormous, there are several cozy "conversation corners" tucked away here and there. Don't miss the opportunity to kiss in the mezzanine level's quaint seating area; the only witness will be the armored knight standing guard. All of the nine guest rooms are on the second and third floors, up a wide carpeted stairway lined with bold wooden banisters. Each room is decorated with exquisite antiques, lush carpeting, and opulent fabrics in rich, warm tones. All of the rooms have queen-size beds and private baths (five include two-person jetted tubs), and four rooms feature gas fireplaces. The handsome Churchill Chamber, done in shades of black, gray, and cream and complemented by Italianate-style mahogany furnishings, has a whirlpool tub that will seduce you in seconds: this two-person jetted tub is surrounded by a dark wood canopy—as if it were a bed. Also boasting a luscious bubbling bath is Count Bonzi's Room, the largest room in the house. To properly enjoy this pool-size jetted tub, bring a bottle of wine to sip beneath the dimmed lights of the chandelier. Count Bonzi's Room also boasts the largest walnut headboard we've ever seen (8 feet tall,

to be exact) on its inviting bed. One of the most private accommodations is Lady Margaret's Room: tucked away from the others, this spacious room is equipped with its own "secret entrance." Perhaps the most romantic of all the rooms is the Gables Suite, the only one with a two-person Jacuzzi tub at the foot of the beautiful walnut queen bed. Special touches such as the evening wine and cheese reception, nightly turndown service, and having your bed made while you're enjoying breakfast add to the home's gracious atmosphere. Breakfast is served in a bright, black-and-white-tiled sun room at two-person tables clothed in crisp white linens. A variety of homemade baked goods, fresh fruit, and a hot entrée of French toast soufflé or chili-sausage-cheese-egg bake are just some of the delectable treats you may find on offer.

$$$–$$$$ *AE, MC, V; checks OK; www.cedargablesinn.com.*

CHURCHILL MANOR
❂❂❂
485 Brown St / 707/253-7733
Tall, perfectly trimmed hedges effectively enclose this stately historic mansion in delicious privacy. The pretty fountain, the immaculate lawn, and the towering white columns on the majestic building create a lasting first impression, one that may remind you of plantation mansions of the Deep South. You know your stay will be a grand one once you glimpse the two elegant parlors on the main floor; both feature high ceilings, ornate chandeliers, intricately carved columns, velvet-draped windows, original fireplaces, and stunning antiques. Victorian opulence—nicely balanced with masculine and feminine motifs—continues in the 10 upstairs guest rooms, which feature antique bedroom sets and private baths. Many have fireplaces as well. Our two favorites are the second-floor Edward Churchill Room (No. 5), the largest room, and the third-floor Mary Wilder Room (No. 8). The former features a stunning walnut king-size bed from France, a gold-leaf-tiled fireplace, pretty floral motifs, and a giant cast-iron bathtub crowned by a crystal chandelier. There's also a two-person shower. Grape-motif wallpaper and deep hunter-green carpeting define the handsome Mary Wilder Room, with its king-size bed, gas fireplace, and sunny corner location. Although the green-tiled bathroom has a lovely claw-foot tub, the real gem here is the walk-in shower room (yes, it is so large we must call it a room!). Other accommodations throughout the house vary in decor, from violet motifs to golf themes. Most will do for romance, although some are rather snug. The only accommodation we can't wholeheartedly recommend is Adam's Room (No. 1), a ground-level room that's too close to the common areas for romance. Step into the marble-floored sun room for a full breakfast of baked apples or poached pears, muffins or croissants, and your choice of a cooked-to-order omelet or orange French toast. On warmer days, this morning feast can be enjoyed on the huge veranda that lines the entire front

of the house. Freshly baked cookies in the afternoon, wine and cheese in the evening, and the availability of croquet gear make your stay exceedingly comfortable. Thanks to its popularity as a wedding venue, this beautiful mansion has limited opportunities to enjoy it during summer weekends. On most Friday and Saturday nights, the entire mansion is booked by wedding parties; however, call ahead and ask about any openings—you may just be lucky.

$$ AE, DIS, MC, V; checks OK; www.churchillmanor.com.

THE HENNESSEY HOUSE
❂❂❂

1727 Main St / 707/226-3774
This multicolored Queen Anne Victorian housing a pleasant and well-maintained bed-and-breakfast stands out among the ordinary buildings on Main Street. A well-tended lawn and colorful flower beds flank the main residence, where six guest rooms are offered; all are decorated with a combination of beautiful English and Belgian antiques, and most are furnished with four-poster or canopy beds. Other features include high ceilings, fireplaces (in some), cozy feather beds with down pillows, marble bathrooms, stained-glass windows, and claw-foot tubs (in most). It's the adjacent Carriage House, however, that holds the most romantic accommodations on the property. All four of these suites offer more privacy and considerably more space than the rooms in the main house, along with separate entrances, whirlpool tubs for two, fireplaces, double vanities, and lovingly restored antiques. Sport and hunting themes give these rooms a rather masculine mood: the second-floor Bridle Suite has an equestrian theme, while the first-floor Fox's Den was decorated with an English hunt in mind. Vaulted ceilings and skylights lend an airy feel to the two upstairs suites, while the two downstairs suites feature huge doors that open onto private patios. For all guests, a full gourmet breakfast is served in the dining room beneath a beautiful hand-painted, stamped-tin ceiling. Soft classical music provides the auditory backdrop. Creatively prepared entrées such as caramel or blueberry-stuffed French toast or spicy baked eggs with chiles await each morning, along with homemade granola, fruit plates, yogurt, and freshly baked goodies. It all goes perfectly with a cup of the inn's house-blended coffee. In the evening, sample wine and hors d'oeuvres on the shaded back patio while listening to the bubbling fountain and the birds. Unwind even further with a visit to the sauna, available to guests 24 hours a day.

$$$ MC, V; checks OK; www.hennesseyhouse.com.

LA BELLE EPOQUE
⚫⚫

1386 Calistoga Ave / 707/257-2161 or 800/238-8070
Situated in a quiet residential neighborhood, this colorful Queen Anne–style home has a beautifully maintained exterior that speaks volumes about the love and attention that goes into the upkeep here, both inside and out. A consistent and opulent Victorian theme runs through the six guest rooms located on the first and second floors of the home, while the Champagne Suite has a more contemporary look. High ceilings, hardwood floors covered with Oriental rugs, beautiful Victorian antiques, ornately patterned wallpapers, floral linens, and sitting areas showcasing authentic stained-glass windows are a few of the romantic features found in the six elegantly decorated Victorian-style rooms. All have standard private baths (one with a jetted tub), and two feature wood-burning fireplaces. The Champagne Suite is located on the ground floor, near the common area and small wine-tasting room: it has a more modern feel, with floral linens, dark green carpeting, a small sitting area, and an elevated king-size bed, along with a spacious bathroom with a shower big enough for two. Even though this suite is close to the common area—where vintage wines and hors d'oeuvres are served nightly—it is by far the most spacious and private room in the inn. Plus, after the wine and cheese hour ends at 7pm, you'll have the entire common area to yourselves. At breakfast, guests gather at a magnificently decorated table in the regal dining room. What comes your way can only be called gourmet: apples baked in pastry with crème fraîche, roasted beef tenderloin in a merlot sauce, Grand Marnier French toast, and Southern spoon bread with fresh Napa corn.
$$$$ *MC, V; checks OK; www.labelleepoque.com.*

LA RÉSIDENCE COUNTRY INN
⚫⚫⚫

4066 Hwy 29 / 707/253-0337
Casual refinement and great kissing potential abound at La Résidence. Two impressive buildings—a cedar-shingled manor called the French Barn and a stately Victorian named the Mansion—hold 23 beautifully appointed guest rooms. The rooms in the French Barn feature French and English pine antiques, soft and pleasing color schemes, and rich designer linens and bedspreads with matching window treatments and slipcovers. Fireplaces and balconies (or patios) are highlights in these rooms. Rooms in the Mansion live up to the building's elegant exterior and feature high ceilings, polished dark wood furnishings, chandeliers, and white plantation shutters. Standard but beautiful private bathrooms contain all the usual comforts. Our favorite Mansion room is No. 31, a ground-level hideaway with its own entrance. Inside, an enormous four-poster bed is tucked into the alcove of a bay window, and the fireplace, CD player, and deep soaking tub further

enhance the room's romantic appeal. The most recent addition to the property is the single-story Cellar House, where three large, spacious suites have king beds, cable TVs, fireplaces, wet bars, and terraces overlooking the beautiful gardens. The most private accommodation of all is the small cottage next to the vineyards. From its semiprivate patio, French doors open into a spacious two-room suite that's simply a divine place to spend the night. Brick paths meander throughout the property, inviting you to admire the well-tended grounds embellished with rose trellises, grape arbors, an ancient oak tree, and two towering fountains. A casual wine and cheese hour is held nightly on the back patio (or in the second-floor salon, depending on the weather). You might consider a dip in the pool on hot afternoons, but an even more kiss-worthy option would be a moonlit soak in the Jacuzzi tub behind the Mansion, where you can stargaze and luxuriate any time of year. In the morning, a three-course breakfast is served at individual tables in the French-country dining room or, if the sun shines, on the backyard terrace. Those especially sensitive to noise should take into account the inn's location along busy Highway 29; although road noise is hardly noticeable inside the guest rooms (especially in rooms facing away from the highway), traffic can be heard from the outside patios. Fortunately, a wall of tall trees fronting the property conceals the road from your view.
$$$$ *AE, DC, DIS, MC, V; no checks; www.laresidence.com.*

MILLIKEN CREEK INN
❀❀❀❀
1815 Silverado Trail / 707/255-1197 or 888/622-5775
For lovers seeking an extremely stylish and luxurious nest, this recently opened inn is the answer. With just 10 rooms, the inn's small size encourages an intimate mood similar to that of a bed-and-breakfast, yet it offers a sky-high level of service, privacy, and amenities that is more often associated with exclusive resorts. Set on 3 beautifully landscaped acres on the banks of the serene Napa River, the mood here is one of tranquility and escape, despite the location on a busy road linking the world-famous Silverado Trail to downtown Napa and its attractions (only minor noise makes it through the thorough soundproofing). Most of the beautifully decorated rooms, which are scattered among three riverfront buildings on the property, have every imaginable romantic touch, from flickering fireplaces and sparkling new hydrotherapy tubs to luxurious beds and private decks with scenic river views. The decor is a soothing blend of khaki, chocolate, and cream brightened by exotic Indonesian accents; polished hardwood floors are softened by tasteful rugs. The Italian linen–swathed king-size beds alone are worth four kisses. Upon checking into your room, you'll find a deliciously indulgent chocolate-cabernet cake waiting, along with orchids and fresh seasonal flowers. It won't be long before you dive into the hydrotherapy tub, where you can relax amid the bubbles and watch the fire or,

on a warm evening, enjoy the gauzy curtains billowing in the breeze off the river and the palm-frond fans turning lazily overhead. A slate-tiled shower with a "rain" showerhead, plush robes and soft towels, and luxury bath amenities wait in each of the private bathrooms. In the inn's main lobby you'll find a generous wine and cheese tasting each afternoon, and its plush leather chairs provide an enticing place to plan out the next day's itinerary—the winery-lined Silverado Trail is just moments away. You won't be leaving the modern world behind: Internet access, TVs, and DVD players are in each room. The on-site spa offers a couples' massage in the cozy spa room or, more romantically, outdoors in a riverside gazebo hung with filmy curtains. An elegant breakfast is delivered to your door in a charming wicker basket; savoring the freshly baked scones and delicious quiche on your private deck as the morning breeze caresses your faces is the perfect start to a wine-country morning.

$$$$ *AE, MC, V; checks OK; www.millikencreekinn.com.*

OAK KNOLL INN
❷❷❷❷

2200 E Oak Knoll Ave / 707/255-2200
Oak Knoll Inn is an embodiment of everything that is appealing in bed-and-breakfasts. A country road leads to the tree-lined property surrounded by nothing but fertile vineyards, lush meadows, and abundant birdlife. You enter through the cozy living room, which has charming decor, a large book collection, and a wood-burning fireplace; French doors open into the courtyard area. Here, two wings of suites overlook a long swimming pool, steaming spa, and spectacular scenery. Each of the four spacious suites has a remarkable 17-foot-tall vaulted ceiling, double-stone walls (for soundproofing), and a wood-burning fireplace with a comfortable sofa set before it for snuggling. The marble bathrooms are full of light, and the plush king-size beds are smothered in soft pillows and fine linens. Fresh flower bouquets are everywhere, and French doors open onto the courtyard. Rooms come stocked with a complimentary bottle of wine and bottled cold drinks, and you'll also find bird-watching guides and binoculars that encourage a closer look at the wildlife outside your window. All of the rooms are wonderful; however, the two end units both feature a dramatic 12-foot cathedral window facing neighboring vineyards. Personal service is another of Oak Knoll Inn's specialties, and the innkeepers are eager to make your visit to Napa Valley memorable. If you've never been to the area before (or even if you come here regularly but would like to see some different wineries and restaurants this time), put your schedule in their capable hands. You won't be disappointed with the detailed itinerary they put together for you. The evening wine-and-cheese hour is a Napa treat in itself. Almost every evening, a local winemaker comes to pour his or her wines and personally answer questions. It's a perfect way to educate your palate by sampling

what the smaller wineries produce—and you don't even have to get in your car. There's also a bounty of delicious breads, cheeses, vegetables, and dips, beautifully presented by the gracious innkeepers. The gourmet breakfast offerings, served at the fireside dining room table, include dishes such as Anaheim chili quiche spiced with fresh salsa and sweet creations such as apple crisp topped with lavender ice cream or chocolate tacos filled with tropical fruits. On warmer mornings, the outside deck serves as the dining room, and hot-air balloons occasionally float by overhead. Such serenity isn't found just anywhere. $$$$ *MC, V; checks OK; www.oakknollinn.com.*

Romantic Restaurants

ANGÈLE
♥♥❤

540 Main St / 707/252-8115
By the time you learn to say the name of this restaurant correctly (it's pronounced "AHN-zhel"), you probably will have fallen under its spell. This family effort by Claude Rouas—founder of the famed Auberge du Soleil (see Romantic Lodgings in the Napa Valley Wine Towns section)—and daughters Bettina and Claudia offers classic French-country cuisine in truly captivating surroundings. The interior is accented by a wood-beam ceiling and lighting that gives everyone that special glow; candles on the tables, a sleek bar, and colorful paintings on the walls round out the inviting decor. The restaurant's quarters are cozy, but if you prefer more space, request a seat on the heated riverfront patio, which on a late summer evening can provide the restaurant's most inspired romantic backdrop. A freshly made baguette and creamy butter, along with gracious and prompt attention from your server, set the stage for the meal. The menu mainly offers French classics but has a California flair: you'll find everything from oxtail and lentil salad with tangy ravigote dressing to steamed mussels in braised-fennel broth. Don't miss the decadent pile of crisp, glistening, lightly salted *pommes frites* or the best gourmet hamburger in Napa. Despite the chic atmosphere, the restaurant is family friendly, but not so much so that romantic duos will feel out of place. Don't miss the house-made sorbet or creamy coffee-flavored pot de crème for dessert. $$–$$$ *AE, MC, V; local checks only; lunch, dinner every day; full bar; reservations recommended; www.angele.us.*

BISTRO DON GIOVANNI
❂❂
4110 Hwy 29 / 707/224-3300
The warm, inviting interior of Don Giovanni, which has earned a reputation for its fine food and wine, has rustic Tuscan charm with sunny yellow walls, terra-cotta-tiled floors, antique copper cookware, and a large gas fireplace in the corner. The tables are too packed in for our romantic sensibilities, and the noise level can get out of hand on busy nights; happily, dining outdoors here is nearly perfect year-round, thanks to an abundance of heat lamps and the valley's naturally warm climate. One patio features a wood-burning fireplace; the other has lovely views of the groomed lawns, a fountain, and the surrounding vineyards. The ambience is a bit more private and romantic on this second patio, though the noise from the nearby highway is not ideal. Begin the meal with a savory appetizer of *fritto misto* for two before enjoying other delights, which include superb thin-crust, crisp pizzas with exotic toppings such as fig and prosciutto flavored with balsamic vinegar; a beet and haricots verts salad; delicious homemade pastas; and grilled or wood oven-roasted meats and fish. For a fitting finale, try the tiramisu topped with whipped cream.
$$ *AE, DC, DIS, MC, V; local checks only; lunch, dinner every day; full bar; reservations recommended; www.bistrodongiovanni.com.*

COLE'S CHOP HOUSE
❂❂❂
1122 Main St / 707/224-6328
This recently opened steakhouse offers the most upscale restaurant environ-ment in this often-casual wine-country town, making it an ideal destina-tion for a dress-up date. Its deluxe retro decor has charm, and the classic menu is certain to make meat lovers swoon. Located in a restored historic building that dates to 1886, the dining room is a bright, high-ceilinged affair with exposed rustic stone walls, glowing hardwood floors, and dark wood tables adorned with white linens. It can get noisy, so your best bet inside is to request one of the cushioned booths. Without a doubt, however, the charming courtyard patio (open May–Oct) is the most romantic spot. This outdoor setting, within view of central Napa's quaint century-old buildings and just steps from the serene river that flows through town, is an enticing spot to while away the evening together. It's a good idea to come prepared for the sky-high prices; the tempting old-school side dishes, such as creamed spinach, are ordered à la carte. You need not stick with steak: additional menu classics include a tangy Caesar salad, rich oysters Rockefeller, veal, lamb, and a few vegetarian dishes thrown in as a nod to modern tastes. The

wine list emphasizes expensive reds, but the beautifully prepared classic cocktails may tempt you away from wine for the evening.

$$$ *AE, DC, MC, V; local checks only; dinner every day; full bar; reservations recommended; www.coleschophouse.citysearch.com.*

LA BOUCANE
●●

1778 2nd St / 707/253-1177
In a valley where hot new French bistros regularly make the headlines, it's nice to come upon a charming, unpretentious, classic French restaurant. Nestled in a cozy Victorian home along a residential street, La Boucane has been a Napa mainstay for more than two decades. Its formula for success: straightforward and sinfully rich French fare, with a menu that's easy to understand. Straightforward also describes the decor in the dining room, where each table is laid with white linens, surrounded by simple wooden chairs, and topped off with a single red rose and candles. Soft classical music and a stunning orchid centerpiece provide pleasures for the ears and eyes. There's not much here to distract you from each other—except, of course, the food. We started by savoring a creamy lobster bisque so decadent it should be called a dessert, followed by rack of lamb that proved simple and satisfying. Couples may want to indulge in the crisp-roasted duckling *à l'orange*, a dish that's made for two. And to finish, a taste of homemade crème brûlée, sealed by a golden caramelized crust, will leave you feeling nothing short of *magnifique!*

$$$ *MC, V; local checks only; dinner Tues–Sat (closed Jan).*

ZUZU
●◖

829 Main St / 707/224-8555
The tables are close together, the bar is packed, and a no-reservations policy means you might have to wait for a table if there's a line out the door. Romantic? Not necessarily. But far be it from us to deny the charms of this bright and bustling jewel-box restaurant, especially since we always want to dine here at least once when we're in town. Just be forewarned that this is downtown Napa's favorite neighborhood dining room, and come prepared to overlook the noisy atmosphere in favor of the remarkably good (and well-priced) tapas and wine. Fortunately, the fun and convivial mood will most likely catch you up in its spell. The comfortable-yet-chic ambience is classic California wine country: you'll fit right in whether you're wearing khakis and a T-shirt or dressier attire. Tables are set along the compact wine bar in the small downstairs dining room (very noisy) or upstairs in the loft (much quieter). The most difficult part is deciding which of the small, European-style plates to order from the enticing menu: don't miss the Moroccan barbecued lamb chops with a sweet-spicy sauce; tangy paella topped with braised

meats, shellfish, and a dollop of aioli; or the satisfying apple empanadas. The eclectic wine list should have something to tempt you, even after a day of touring wineries.

$ AE, MC, V; no checks; lunch Mon–Fri, dinner every day; beer and wine; no reservations; www.zuzunapa.com.

NAPA VALLEY WINE TOWNS

ROMANTIC HIGHLIGHTS

Heavily trafficked Highway 29 provides a straight shot through the Napa Valley. The best-known and most-frequented part of the route passes through the center of the valley, which is home to some of Napa's most famous wineries. Along the route are a handful of small towns—from ritzy St. Helena to blink-and-you'll-miss-it Oakville—that harbor the region's most exclusive accommodations and beloved restaurants. Since it's unlikely that you would visit one of these towns without making an excursion to the others nearby, we include them all in this chapter for your romantic convenience.

Located 9 miles north of Napa off Highway 29, **Yountville** is one of the few places around here where the two of you can veer off the crowded roads and enjoy a slice of small-town tranquility. In fact, Yountville's distinctive, quiet charm makes it one of our top picks for places to kiss. Stop in the heart of town to check out the shops and restaurants housed in **Vintage 1870** (6525 Washington St; 707/944-2451), a pretty brick complex that was originally constructed as a winery back in 1870. Another good spot to find special mementos of your trip is the French-inspired **Antique Fair** (6512 Washington St; 707/944-8440), where you can daydream about furnishing your love nest at home with some of the gorgeous imported 18th-, 19th-, and 20th-century antiques or simply pick up some great French-milled soap or silver accessories.

Yountville is also headquarters for one of the wine country's most beloved romantic adventures: a hot-air balloon ride that provides enthralling views of the vineyard-laced landscape. The excursions usually commence at sunrise, when the air is still and cool (yes, that means somewhere between 5 and 9am). But while the rise-with-the-birds launch time may seem like a drawback at first, it's more than worth it—views of the day's first rays spilling over the golden hills are simply a lovely sight to wake up your senses. Some balloon companies cram lots of people into one balloon basket, but **Above the West Hot-Air Ballooning** (6525 Washington St; 707/944-8638 or 800/627-2759; www.nvaloft.com; rates start at $195 per person; reservations required) limits the number of passengers allowed on every flight (maximum is eight), a touch that is after our own romantic hearts. Private flights, including weddings aloft—talk about cloud nine!—can be arranged for a price. After floating through the morning, you'll return to earth for a gourmet champagne brunch. Remember that your trip is at the mercy of nature: balloons are launched only when the weather is optimal.

Other than its world-class wineries, the town of **Oakville**'s main claim to fame is the **Oakville Grocery Co.** (7856 Hwy 29 at Oakville Cross Rd, 707/944-8802; www.oakvillegrocery.com). This famous old-fashioned country market becomes nearly claustrophobia-inducing at noontime, when hordes of tourists arrive for lunch; however, the gourmet picnic goodies are fabulous—and worth it. More picnic supplies can be found farther down the road, just south of St. Helena, at **Dean & Deluca** (607 S Hwy 29; 707/967-9980; www.deananddeluca.com), which sells a dizzying array of cheeses, wines, and other picnic items. Our advice is not to wait until you're hungry to navigate the crowded aisles at these stores, but to buy your picnic fixings early and then head for the wineries in the hills. The town of **Rutherford**, neighboring the towns of Oakville and St. Helena, has no commercial center but it does boast a number of excellent wineries and highly regarded lodgings such as Auberge du Soleil (see Romantic Lodgings).

Upscale **St. Helena** is the most popular destination of all the towns along Highway 29. This picturesque hamlet embodies everything there is to love about the wine country: a handful of sophisticated boutiques, cafés, restaurants, and art galleries is surrounded by countryside dotted with wineries and bed-and-breakfasts. Although St. Helena offers a vast selection of places in which to explore, eat, stay, and kiss, you'll pay a price to stay here, and not just in financial terms. The highway runs through town and traffic is often bumper to bumper during peak hours; intimate moments are not always easy to find. Fortunately, the town's charms more than outweigh these drawbacks. If your timing is right, the **St. Helena Farmers Market** (Crane Park; 7:30am–noon Fri, May–Oct; off Hwy 29, east on Sulphur Springs Ave, right on Crane Ave) is a lovely spot to stock up on picnic provisions. Lunch goodies will come in handy should you want to head out of town to the quieter environs of **Bale Grist Mill State Historic Park** (Hwy 29, 3 miles north of St. Helena; 707/963-2236 or 707/942-4575), a cool, forested park where you'll find tranquil paths, one of which leads to a restored wooden grist mill with a 36-foot waterwheel.

Parallel to Highway 29 is the world-renowned **Silverado Trail**, Napa's most fabulous wine road. Here you'll find wineries with a higher romantic quotient than those set along crowded Highway 29. Our top picks are listed below in the **Romantic Wineries** section.

Romantic Wineries

BURGESS CELLARS
●●◖

1108 Deer Park Rd, St. Helena / 707/963-4766
There are many reasons for visiting one winery rather than another. If you are a consummate oenophile, the exceptional quality of the wines at Burgess Cellars, which produces excellent, award-winning zinfandel, syrah, and cabernet sauvignon, is its most alluring feature. If you delight in discovering charming, less-crowded wineries in the midst of touristy Napa Valley, you won't fail to be pleased by Burgess Winery's intimate size and exquisite views of the vineyard-laced countryside. Tastings are by appointment only, but you can easily make them on the weekends (10am–4pm Sat–Sun) by dropping by the winery in person; on weekdays, it's essential to call in advance. No matter when you visit, it's worth the effort to sample the delicious wines and enjoy the views—without the company of hordes of other visitors.
By appointment only; www.burgesscellars.com.

DOMAINE CHANDON
●●●

1 California Dr, Yountville / 707/944-2280
If you don't plan to dine at this winery's legendary romantic restaurant (see Romantic Restaurants, below), it's worth stopping here anyway for the beautiful surroundings and refreshing bubbly. Although it is located just off Highway 29, the spectacular winery is set behind a hillside that completely conceals the road from view, and the route to the grounds passes vineyards and a flower-rimmed pond. Tours do not include tasting, but you can purchase champagne by the glass or by the bottle in the Salon, a comfortable outdoor seating area that looks out to vineyards and oak-covered hills. Cabaret performances and evening concerts are also sometimes offered at the winery; call beforehand.
10am–6pm every day, 11am–5pm Nov–Apr; www.chandon.com.

JOSEPH PHELPS VINEYARD
●●◖

200 Taplin Rd, St. Helena / 707/963-2745 or 800/707-5789
Drive on a winding road up, up, and away from the busy Silverado Trail to this large, unpretentious winery with lovely Asian-style landscaping and beautiful views. Set on a verdant, secluded hillside, Joseph Phelps Vineyard is one of the only wineries along the Silverado Trail that escapes traffic noise completely. Wine tastings are served solely as part of a tour, but to join in you need only make a reservation. An adjacent outdoor terrace presides over a stunning view of a sparkling lake surrounded by vineyards and

rolling hills; it's an inspiring spot for a post-tour picnic. (Tables are filled on a first-come, first-served basis with members of the Phelps Preferred, the wine club, getting first dibs.) On weekends, it's a good idea to schedule your tour three to four days in advance; less-busy weekdays, you can often get a same-day appointment.
By appointment only; www.jpvwines.com.

MERRYVALE VINEYARDS
🌑🌗

1000 Main St (Hwy 29), St. Helena / 707/963-7777 or 800/326-6069
There is nothing particularly outstanding about the location or picnic facilities at Merryvale Vineyards. But the entertaining and highly informative two-hour seminar ($15 per person) held on weekend mornings, which includes extensive tasting, is well worth a visit here. Guests learn how to understand and appreciate the different components in wine, such as tannins and sugar content, and also learn about the barrel-aging process. If you are not in the mood for a two-hour-long seminar, visit the attractive tasting bar, which features a nice array of Merryvale wines. On your way out, you may want to stop in the charming gift shop, which is filled with delightful souvenirs of the valley.
10am–6:30pm every day, call for seasonal hours; seminars 10:30am Sat–Sun; tasting fee $5–$12; www.merryvale.com.

MUMM NAPA VALLEY
🌑🌑

8445 Silverado Trail, Oakville / 707/942-3434 or 800/686-6272
If you have grown a bit weary of chatting with fellow wine enthusiasts and listening to discussions of different blending and crushing techniques, you might find Mumm Napa Valley a refreshing change of pace. In other words, come here if you are looking for a hands-off experience. Mumm's tasting room is run like a restaurant, so you can sit at your own table and quietly enjoy a variety of sparkling wines (for a price) while looking out at the vineyards and mountains. The patio area, set beside lush rows of grapes, makes for a lovely summer setting. What we like most about Mumm is that no one interrupts you after the champagne is poured.
10am–5pm every day; tasting fee $3 and up; www.mummcuveenapa.com.

OPUS ONE
🌑🌑🌑

7900 Hwy 29 at Oakville Cross Rd, Oakville / 707/944-9442
A visit to this prestigious winery would be enjoyed most by couples who share a true passion for world-class wine (and aren't afraid of the prices that come with it). Opus One, a collaboration between the late Baron Philippe de Rothschild and Robert Mondavi, is dedicated to producing the single

and outstanding cabernet blend that is also called Opus One. You can tour without tasting or taste without touring, but the winery's high-tech winemaking practices will doubtless intrigue wine buffs, and the stunning neoclassical architecture is another good reason to take the hourlong free tour. Tastings are expensive ($25 per 4-ounce glass) and the atmosphere is quite serious, as is the extraordinary wine. If you want the whole experience, schedule your tour well in advance; weekend spots book up a month ahead of time. Needless to say, in such buttoned-up and formal surroundings, the real romance resides in your wine glass.

10am–4pm every day; tours 10:30am every day by appointment only; tasting fee $25; www.opusonewinery.com.

RUTHERFORD HILL WINERY
❤❤❤❤

200 Rutherford Hill Rd, Rutherford / 707/963-1871
The impressive (and kiss-inspiring) Rutherford Hill wine caves are carved deep into the cliffs behind the winery. It's well worth taking one of the three daily tours ($10, includes tasting) to learn the interesting facts about these caves, which are among the valley's most extensive—the tunnels, galleries, and passageways stretch nearly a mile in length and harbor more than 8,000 oak barrels. When you emerge, blinking in the sunlight, warm up with a stroll around the scenic grounds or enjoy a picnic at tables sheltered by shady oaks or set amid a sprawling century-old olive grove. Sip a glass of merlot, enjoy the views of the valley, and relish the beauty of the wine country together.

10am–5pm every day; tours 11:30am, 1:30pm, 3:30pm every day; tasting fee $5; www.rutherfordhill.com.

S. ANDERSON/CLIFF LEDE VINEYARDS
❤❤❤❤

1473 Yountville Crossroad, Yountville / 707/944-8642 or 800/428-2259
As you tour the wine country, you will hear terms such as "mossy," "chewy," or, our personal favorite, "barnyard" used to describe the taste and smell of a fine wine. At S. Anderson Vineyard, these humorous terms are recognized as such. This is not to say that the people at S. Anderson don't take wine seriously—on the contrary, this endearing, family-owned and -operated winery would not be where it is today if they did not take their business extremely seriously. Nevertheless, the hourlong tour, complete with generous tastes of the winery's famous champagnes and wines, is as entertaining as it is insightful. The highlight of the twice-daily tours is the dramatic champagne caves. These ancient-looking caves, boasting 18-foot-high ceilings, exposed volcanic rock walls, uneven cobbled floors, and more than 400,000 bottles of some of the finest champagnes in the area, are by far the biggest you'll see on any tour in the valley. The darkness is alleviated by bare light bulbs strung

on a single black wire and softened by the glow of candles flickering against the barren walls. You might enter these magical caves under the impression that champagne is only for special occasions, but after sipping S. Anderson's latest vintage, you'll be convinced that it is the other way around—that fine champagne makes any occasion special. Even if you don't take the tour, you'll be delighted by sipping wines in the new tasting room, which opened in 2004. The gardens are also beautiful: don't forget to purchase your own bottle of bubbly, sit at one of the picnic tables surrounded by fragrant roses, and toast your special time here.
10am–5pm every day; tours 10:30am, 2:30pm every day; tasting fee $5 and up; www.4bubbly.com.

ST. CLEMENT VINEYARD
♥♥♥
2867 Hwy 29, St. Helena / 707/967-3033 or 800/331-8266
Neatly tended vineyards climb up to this picturesque Victorian house perched at the crest of a hillside; the home's antique-filled original living quarters serve as a quaint tasting room. Once you've filled your glasses, wander outside to the porch swing or to one of the picnic tables arranged around the patio and terraced grounds, and drink in lovely views of the surrounding countryside along with your wine. You must call ahead to reserve one of the picnic tables, which are available by reservation only (for parties of up to 10 people). It's worth the forethought if you are exploring the wine country with a group of friends to bring gourmet goodies and enjoy a leisurely picnic on the romantic, well-manicured grounds.
10am–4pm every day; tasting fee $5; www.stclement.com.

Romantic Lodgings

AUBERGE DU SOLEIL
♥♥♥♥
180 Rutherford Hill Rd, Rutherford / 707/963-1211 or 800/348-5406
If the words "splurge" and "pamper" come to mind when planning your romantic getaway, Auberge du Soleil is the place for you—especially if the emphasis is on "splurge." This upscale resort, perched on a forested hillside overlooking the rolling Napa Valley, has some of the most well-known, heart-stirring, and certainly first-class accommodations in the area. Each of the 50 rooms is outrageously beautiful, inviting, and spacious. Forty-eight of the suites are spread throughout 11 French country–style cottages, creating a sense of privacy and exclusivity that has resulted in the resort's worldwide reputation as a premier escape. Many rooms have Jacuzzi tubs (or oversize tubs) where candles and fragrant bath salts await; all have wood-burning fireplaces and private terraces with stupendous views. Blond-wood

furnishings fill the sun-kissed interiors, which are further brightened by tasteful modern artwork throughout. Lavish California king size beds, embellished with sunny yellow pillows and fuchsia-colored bedspreads, are yet another delight; the brilliant fabrics are matched by rustic decor touches such as terra-cotta-tiled floors and warm taupe walls. It all adds up to evoke the sensory delights of a Mediterranean hill town. Two additional guest rooms, located in the main building, are slightly smaller and lack fireplaces. In-room massage treatments are available, there is 24-hour room service, and your suite is equipped with a stereo, TV/VCR, and gourmet wet bar. In fact, every convenience you can imagine is merely a phone call away. Stroll around the grounds and you'll find a full-service spa, a swimming pool and sundeck, and a quiet path leading through an olive grove and sculpture garden.
$$$$ *AE, DIS, MC, V; checks OK; www.aubergedusoleil.com.*

HARVEST INN
❂❂
1 Main St, St. Helena / 707/963-9463 or 800/950-8466
Lovely flowering gardens and manicured lawns flank the meandering brick walkways that lead to the Harvest Inn's cluster of English Tudor–style buildings. The lobby boasts high ceilings and a vast cobblestone hearth, and brick chimneys, iron lanterns, and wood beams enhance the Olde English atmosphere; tall trees completely conceal the inn from Highway 29. The 54 recently renovated rooms come in a choice of seven categories, ranging from Cozy Queen Rooms to two-story Executive Suites. Some of the names are certain to appeal to romantics with funny bones: Earl of Ecstasy, Count of Fantasy, Duchess of Delight. Interiors vary, but Olde English decor dominates, with hardwood floors, heavy draperies, wood-beam ceilings, and enormous brick fireplaces. Furnishings tend to be a mix and match of antiques and, despite the renovations, some pieces look indeed like they've been here since time began. As everywhere, romantic amenities, views, and location improve as prices increase. Luckily, most rooms have a wood-burning fireplace that helps enhance the mood (assuming you know how to start the fire yourselves), and many feature patios or balconies. Noteworthy romantic possibilities include the rooms with patios/balconies adjacent to the 14 acres of vineyards behind the inn, as well as the Executive Suites, which boast two-person jetted tubs in their upstairs loft bedrooms. If you don't get a room with a view, don't despair—vineyard vistas can also be enjoyed from the coffee shop, where a continental breakfast buffet is presented every morning. Featuring stained-glass windows and warmed by a large brick fireplace, the coffee shop makes for a nice morning retreat; or you can head to the outdoor deck for an alfresco breakfast. The property's

178

two outdoor swimming pools, Jacuzzi tubs, and complimentary mountain bikes are also available for guests.
$$$$ *AE, DIS, MC, V; checks OK; www.harvestinn.com.*

THE INK HOUSE BED AND BREAKFAST
♥❤

1575 Hwy 29, St. Helena / 707/963-3890
Authenticity is the hallmark of this gorgeous yellow Italianate Victorian, built in 1884. Wrought-iron gates and landscaped gardens surround the home and lend privacy to the wraparound veranda, although noisy Highway 29, which fronts the property, is both visible and audible. Inside, the noise seems to recede, perhaps due to the ornate decor, which nearly overwhelms the senses. But while the inn is known for its 19th-century detail, some say its real claim to fame is the fact that Elvis Presley filmed *Wild in the Country* here in 1959 (if you are not partial to the King, don't fret—there is no Elvis paraphernalia in sight). On the main floor, two cozy parlors brim with antiques. The seven guest rooms on the main and upstairs floors are all individually decorated with soft colors; lace half-canopies and curtains; queen-size antique wood, brass, or wrought-iron beds; eclectic antiques; and Oriental carpets. All but two rooms feature private baths, and none have TVs or telephones (all the better for a romantic getaway). Some touch-ups and structural improvements are needed here and there, but if you're a lover of Victorian decor, this won't matter. For the best views—and the best kissing—climb upstairs to the observatory at the top of the house. Furnished with comfortably worn wicker chairs and area rugs covering hardwood floors, this room is encircled by windows that give panoramic views of the vineyards below. In the morning, a delicious array of freshly baked breads and muffins, a hot entrée, and coffee and tea are served in the dining room at one large table or by the fireplace in one of the parlors.
$$$ *MC, V; checks OK; www.inkhouse.com.*

INN AT SOUTHBRIDGE
♥♥♥

1020 Main St, St. Helena / 707/967-9400 or 800/520-6800
Although it is the younger sibling of the celebrated Meadowood property (see review), the Inn at Southbridge is in no way overshadowed by its big sister. Set near the heart of St. Helena on Highway 29, this Mediterranean-style inn has inherited the same stylishness, high quality, and excellent service as its older counterpart (which is saying a lot). All 21 spacious guest rooms boast California-French decor, with modern walnut furnishings, wrought-iron lamps, down comforters, wood-burning fireplaces, and butter yellow walls with sage green accents. The overall look is clean-lined and modern, a refreshing change of pace for this region. Upper-level rooms have vaulted ceilings, and some bathrooms are illuminated by skylights. If

your hearts are set on a quiet country ambience, the Highway 29 location is a definite drawback. (If your budget allows, consider Meadowood instead.) However, guest rooms are soundproofed, and continuous landscaping efforts around the property block out some of the traffic noise. On the plus side, the inn is within easy walking distance of downtown St. Helena, numerous wineries, and many restaurants. And as an added bonus, the inn's guests have complimentary use of the beautiful Health Spa Napa Valley (1030 Main St; 707/967-8800; www.napavalleyspa.com) adjacent to the inn. This recently built facility features an outdoor lap pool and Jacuzzi tub, a spacious workout room, steam rooms, and some very soothing spa treatments. Enjoy a massage on a private patio bordering the peaceful aromatherapy gardens, or treat yourselves to a healthy grape-seed mud wrap, the spa's signature treatment. There's even a couples' room, where the two of you can delight in a massage simultaneously. This is one of the most kissworthy spas we've seen in Napa Valley. *$$$$ DC, MC, V; checks OK; www.innatsouthbridge.com.*

MAISON FLEURIE
❤❤❤

6529 Yount St, Yountville / 707/944-2056 or 800/788-0369
Green ivy covers the brick-and-stone exterior of Maison Fleurie, a comfortable getaway that offers countrylike ambience at an in-town location. The Main Building, a charming 1873 hotel, holds seven guest rooms, along with the dining room, lobby, and kitchen area. More rooms are found next door in two small brick buildings named the Old Bakery and the Carriage House. Charming French-country details such as hand-painted murals, elegantly rustic antiques, warm color schemes, and floral linens appoint each of the 13 rooms. Four of the most spacious rooms are found in the Old Bakery, and each boasts a king-size bed, a one-person whirlpool tub in the bathroom, and a gas fireplace. Guests in these rooms can enjoy the bottle of complimentary wine on their small patio or deck surveying the outdoor pool, spa, and nearby restaurants. The two Carriage House rooms feature private entrances, and one has a gas-log fireplace. The seven rooms in the Main Building, some of which are extremely tiny, are located on the upper floor; they have easy access to the expansive sundeck overlooking acres of nearby vineyards. The Main Building's most romantic room, a deluxe queen room, features the inn's only double Jacuzzi tub. However, its location next to the lobby and the resultant noise are detracting factors. Whichever room you select, afternoon wine and hors d'oeuvres as well as evening turndown service are part of the package. In the morning, venture to the teddy bear-filled lobby of the Main Building, where a full breakfast is served buffet style. Down some steps, you'll find a crackling fire warming the terra-cotta-

tiled floors in the provincial dining room; here, tables for two allow for a semiprivate morning affair as you plan your wine-country excursions. *$$$ AE, MC, V; no checks; www.foursisters.com.*

MEADOWOOD NAPA VALLEY
✪✪✪✪

900 Meadowood Ln, St. Helena / 707/963-3646 or 800/458-8080
This grande dame of the wine country is reminiscent of an elegant Cape Cod resort, with tiers of gables, gray clapboard siding, and sparkling white trim and balustrades. And although the address is in St. Helena, this exclusive getaway is discreetly tucked into the forested foothills of the Napa Valley, nowhere near a highway or any other source of potential noise. Meadowood believes in the three R's—refinement, relaxation, and rejuvenation, that is. Neatly trimmed croquet lawns, 2 miles of hiking trails, a nine-hole golf course, seven tennis courts, two swimming pools, a state-of-the-art fitness center, and a full-service health spa are all available to guests. The 85 guest rooms are scattered among the resort's 250 wooded acres. Room styles vary from studios to cozy cottages all the way up to multiroom suites, but none can be considered a bargain; even the smallest studios are astronomically expensive. Some rooms overlook the croquet lawns; several Hillside Terrace rooms provide the ultimate in privacy. The Oakview Terrace cottages, conveniently located above the pool and spa area, are light-filled retreats with private decks overlooking the hillsides. Most rooms offer private entrances, stone hearths, wood-burning fireplaces, private balconies, dimming lights, cathedral ceilings with skylights, and subtle, softly hued interiors—it all adds up to a wonderful sense of serenity. Down comforters, gourmet honor bars, and air-conditioning ensure comfort. Even the tile floors in the bathrooms are heated, so your feet will stay toasty when you pad in barefoot. This is one of the most expensive places to stay in the Napa Valley, but if you are celebrating a special occasion or just want to splurge, Meadowood justifies the expense; best of all, you don't even have to leave if you don't want to. At this edition's press time, the formal Restaurant at Meadowood had been closed for nearly a year (and the reopening date had not yet been set); since it received romantic accolades in our previous edition, we look forward to seeing its doors open again. In the meantime, hungry guests can visit the casual Grill at Meadowood for tempting California cuisine: the lunch menu includes dishes such as grilled pear salad or savory portobello mushroom sandwich, while heartier dinner fare offers entrées such as goat-cheese ravioli, pan-seared halibut, or grilled rib-eye steak with blue-cheese polenta. In warm weather, the Grill's spacious outdoor terrace is a lovely spot to linger over a romantic alfresco lunch. *$$$$ AE, DC, DIS, MC; checks OK; www.meadowood.com.*

PETIT LOGIS
♦♦

6527 Yount St, Yountville / 707/944-2332 or 877/944-2332

Petit logis is French for "small, temporary lodgings," a term that fits this unique inn situated in the middle of town. A long shingle-style building, fronted by a vine-covered trellis and a small lawn, is home to five side-by-side rooms. For those seeking a reprieve from flowery, overstyled decor, the French-country minimalist feel here should soothe your senses. All rooms are similar in size, and each has simple furnishings, rough-textured walls painted pale yellow, and a hand-painted mural depicting a garden scene (the only art on the otherwise bare walls). Romantic highlights in each room include a queen-size bed fronting a gas fireplace and a cavernous bathroom where a 6-foot-long Jacuzzi tub and separate tiled shower await. TVs are hidden away in wall cabinets, and small semiprivate patios offer views of a nearby restaurant, the town, and the mountains beyond. Our favorite rooms are Room No. 3, with its pine bed and matching furniture, and Room No. 1, which, although it's closest to the road, best captures the sun's rays and boasts a four-poster bed in the corner. As the name states, Petit Logis is a lodging, not a bed-and-breakfast. However, if you choose to pay the "with breakfast" rate, the innkeepers will arrange for your breakfast at one of two participating local restaurants. Simply walk over to the restaurant of your choice and order whatever suits your fancy.

$$$ AE, MC, V; checks OK; www.petitlogis.com.

VILLAGIO INN & SPA
♦♦♦

6481 Washington St, Yountville / 707/944-8877 or 800/351-1133

A clean and classic Mediterranean look of earthy stucco finishes, tiled roofs, and bubbling fountains sets the Villagio apart. This inn is the younger sibling of the Vintage Inn (see review) and affords the same standards, luxury, and features; the only thing that isn't on a par with its predecessor is the landscaping, but that's only because it's newer. This inn is a delightful retreat, complete with a full spa, a workout room, two pools, and a lovely, sun-filled lobby where afternoon and morning treats are offered. Like those at the Vintage Inn, guest rooms at Villagio are clustered in small buildings spanning the property; a long fountain running through the center of the grounds generates a soft, comforting sound that helps you forget about nearby traffic noise. . . somewhat. Unfortunately, this clustered building design often doesn't afford the best views, and depending on your room location, you might see more of your neighbor than of an inspiring vista. This neighbor also might be talking on a cell phone or wearing a name tag, considering that the hotel's amenities tend to draw conferences. Luckily, the rooms' interiors are wonderfully warm and appealing, with dimming lights, soothing earth tones, luxurious linens and towels, and plantation-style

shutters. Some suites boast two-person whirlpool tubs in their slate and marble bathrooms, and a bottle of complimentary wine is yours to share. Each guest room has a patio or deck as well as a fireplace. Like many other inns in town, Villagio parallels noisy Highway 29, and earplugs may be necessary if you don't want to wake up to the sounds of traffic. A continental breakfast buffet, complete with champagne, a half dozen pastry choices, and plenty of fruit, should get those taste buds prepared for wine tasting. And if you have no zip after a day spent sipping, be sure to take advantage of the soothing spa services on the property.
$$$$ *AE, DC, DIS, MC, V; checks OK; www.villagio.com.*

VINEYARD COUNTRY INN
❤❤❦

201 Main St (Hwy 29), St. Helena / 707/963-1000
If only this pleasant French-country inn was set just a little farther away from the highway, it would be prime kissing territory, for other than its poor location, no detail has been overlooked. If you are seeking the intimacy of a bed-and-breakfast, you should look elsewhere than this corporate-owned retreat, but otherwise, this small and efficiently run hotel makes an enticing place for weary wine tasters to rest their heads. All 21 guest rooms are gracious two-room suites situated in a complex of one- and two-story stucco and tiled buildings. The simply decorated rooms have full baths, four-poster or sleigh beds, and sumptuous down comforters; the sitting areas are attractive and comfortable, with wet bars, large brick fireplaces, and light mauve and soft-white color schemes. Some rooms even offer private patios and balconies that overlook neighboring vineyards. A generous continental breakfast is served at two-person tables in the sun-filled communal dining room. From this vantage point, you can take in views of the vineyards on one side and of the brick courtyard with outdoor pool and Jacuzzi tub on the other. Before the rates are hiked up in April, it's worth checking the Web site for the frequently offered—and very reasonable—winter Internet specials.
$$$ *AE, DC, MC, V; checks OK; www.vineyardcountryinn.com.*

VINTAGE INN
❤❤❤

6541 Washington St, Yountville / 707/944-1112 or 800/351-1133
Outside the Vintage Inn, beauty awaits at every turn: fountains, reflecting pools, and flowers embellish the apartment-like complex of brick and clapboard buildings. Inside, soft classical music breezes through the serene lobby, which features plum-colored chairs, a brick hearth, and a high, peaked, open-beam ceiling. In the 80 inviting guest rooms, wood-burning fireplaces, warm neutral tones, plantation-style shutters, small shallow jetted bathtubs (that are due for an upgrade), and private patios all help make for a suitably romantic stay. A complimentary bottle of wine joins

hotel-like amenities such as TVs, refrigerators, and coffeemakers in every room. Room service and a concierge are also available. We prefer the spacious minisuites and the upstairs rooms with vaulted ceilings—particularly the ones in the inner courtyard, where you are less likely to be bothered by road noise from Highway 29. These Inner Court rooms are more costly, but in our opinion a good night's sleep is worth the extra money. A continental champagne breakfast is served fireside in the lobby every morning. If a bubbly mimosa with breakfast doesn't get you going, a dip in the inn's heated outdoor pool should.

$$$$ *AE, DC, DIS, MC, V; no checks; www.vintageinn.com.*

WINE COUNTRY INN
◐◐

1152 Lodi Lane, St. Helena / 707/963-7077
Situated on a beautifully landscaped knoll overlooking tranquil acres of tree-edged vineyards, this large inn has all the makings for a romantic country getaway. The 24 guest rooms, spread throughout three different buildings, are individually decorated with old-fashioned country accents, including calico and floral wallpapers, handmade patchwork quilts, homespun local art, and white wainscoting in the bathrooms. Most of the rooms feature wood-burning fireplaces and small balconies or decks that look out upon the pastoral surroundings. Three rooms have outdoor hot tubs set on private decks, and one sports a whirlpool tub in its bathroom. Need we say that we recommend these four rooms most highly for romantic purposes? The five recently added cottages are luxurious (and expensive) enough to nearly rate a separate category: each of the beautifully designed 800-square-foot getaways has hardwood floors, sitting area with fireplace, reading nook, and enticing king-size bed. You'll also find convenient amenities in the cottages such as a wet bar, refrigerator with ice maker, coffeemaker, and stereo. The opulent bathrooms decorated with stained glass are a highlight and feature jetted two-person tubs, three-headed walk-in showers, and heated tile floors. Landscaping designed to shield your love nest surrounds the patios, which are furnished with teak chairs and bright potted flowers. The outdoor swimming pool, bordered by flowers and greenery, affords the best views of the vineyards and stunning evening sunsets. We can't think of a better spot in which to enjoy a newly purchased vintage as you dip your toes in the cool, sparkling water. Mornings feature an extensive buffet breakfast of hot scones and croissants, a hot egg dish, and fresh fruit served in the main house's parlor.

$$$–$$$$ *AE, MC, V; checks OK; www.winecountryinn.com.*

YOUNTVILLE INN
◐◐
6462 Washington St, Yountville / 707/944-5600 or 800/972-2293
Set on the quieter edge of town (although still not far enough away from the noisy highway), the Yountville Inn offers 51 roomy accommodations spread throughout seven buildings. The New England–style inn, with a stylish river-rock facade and white-trimmed windows and balconies, has a charming setting on a creek. It's here, near the water's edge, that you'll find the most romantic rooms on the property. Not only are the patios off these superior rooms just a stone's throw from the pretty creek, but also you'll find vaulted ceilings and more peace and quiet than in other locations. All of the rooms are brightened by a French-country flair and warmed by fieldstone fireplaces. The decor includes attractive and upscale country-style furnishings that appear to have jumped out of the Pottery Barn catalog, a tempting snack basket, plus conveniences such as coffeemakers and TV/VCRs. Bathrooms are fabulous, with Italian tile, double sinks, and comfortable robes. The beds are extremely comfortable, and overall there's a quality of sparkling newness to this accommodation, which is a relatively recent arrival among St. Helena's many inns. Adjacent to the lodgelike lobby, where a continental breakfast buffet is served, you'll find a heated pool and spa.
$$$ AE, DC, DIS, MC, V; California checks only; www.yountvilleinn.com.

ZINFANDEL INN
◐◐
800 Zinfandel Lane, St. Helena / 707/963-3512
Set on a relatively quiet street between Highway 29 and the Silverado Trail, this stone-and-wood Tudor-style home is enhanced by its forested surroundings, which enclose 2 acres of gardens, an aviary, two gazebos, a small swimming pool, a hot tub, and a fish pond and waterfall. The three guest rooms exude homespun European ambience. The fabric swags and rather ornate decor may be too flowery for some; others will revel in its colors and patterns. The ground-floor Chardonnay Room features a large stone fireplace, a wood-beam ceiling, a large jetted tub, and bay windows overlooking the garden. Oak furnishings, a tiled Jacuzzi tub, fireplace, private deck, and stained-glass window enhance the upstairs Zinfandel Suite. The third room, Petite Sirah, is indeed petite and not the best option, especially due to its detached bath. Cozy down comforters, a complimentary chocolates-and-champagne basket upon arrival, and a lavish full breakfast (served family-style every morning) are nice extras. While not as upscale as many wine-country properties, the Zinfandel Inn gives travelers a taste of the old-fashioned bed-and-breakfast experience.
$$$–$$$$ MC, V; checks OK; www.zinfandelinn.com.

Romantic Restaurants

AUBERGE DU SOLEIL
●●●●

*180 Rutherford Hill Rd (in the Auberge du Soleil resort), Rutherford /
707/963-1211 or 800/348-5406*
Perched high on a ridge above the Napa Valley, Auberge du Soleil commands
a sweeping view of the countryside. Ensconced in hills covered with flour-
ishing olive groves, the restaurant and its neighboring buildings are so well
integrated with the landscape that they seem to be organically linked. Walls
of taupe-colored stucco, light pine-paneled ceilings, wooden tables, and
a Spanish-style hearth all add to this elegantly natural effect. The dining
room and lounge were designed to supply premium viewing pleasure from
every nook and cranny, and tables in the lounge are positioned near a fireplace large enough to generate ample warmth. However, the absolute best
place to kiss at Auberge du Soleil Restaurant is on the expansive outdoor
deck. A properly timed evening visit will allow you to bask in the warm hues
of day yielding to night. The view is a hard act to follow, but the kitchen
does a fine job of keeping up. Although the restaurant's name is French, the
menu offers an international array of dishes, with a focus on fresh, regional
ingredients. The Seven Sparkling Sins is, as its name implies, a decadent
appetizer for two, featuring caviar and other delicacies. For more innocent
starters, try the cumin-chervil crab cakes or tempura ahi-salmon sashimi.
Entrées include seafood, meat, and poultry dishes, as well as a three-course
vegetarian tasting dinner. Whether you indulge in a dining adventure here
or simply toast each other in the bar, the potential for romance is more than
likely—it's guaranteed.
*$$$$ AE, DIS, MC, V; no checks; breakfast, lunch, dinner every day; full
bar; reservations recommended; www.aubergedusoleil.com.*

BISTRO JEANTY
●●●

6510 Washington St, Yountville / 707/944-0103
Comparisons between the California wine country and France are a dime
a dozen—and not always accurate—but the comparison is justified at the
warm and inviting Bistro Jeanty, beloved for its French comfort staples
such as cassoulet and *entrecôte frites* (steak with fries). This spot has all the
charming authentic details down pat, from the window boxes with geraniums
outside to the antiques and specials chalkboard inside. A large "community
table" by the front door seats the diners without partners or reservations
and is a favorite with locals who drop by. Vintage French posters and
butcher paper-topped tables add further charm. We suggest you bypass the
front dining room, which tends to be quite noisy due to the waiting crowd,
communal eating table, and casual bar. The back room, next to the fireplace,

affords a little more peace and quiet—but not much more when the place gets busy. Even if the ambience is not the most intimate, your taste buds will certainly fall in love with the classic French fare: lamb tongue salad, the signature tomato and puff-pastry soup, delicate sole meunière, and the robust and hearty coq au vin. For the finishing touch, share the silky crème brûlée, which includes a surprise layer of chocolate mousse, or the traditional crepe topped with delicious orange butter. Recently, the acclaimed owner of Bistro Jeanty opened a new restaurant, Père Jeanty (6735 Washington St, Yountville; 707/945-1000; www.perejeanty.com). Designed to evoke a French-country cottage and offering a menu with mesquite-grilled items and other dishes that are slightly less formal than those at its bistro cousin, this restaurant is certain be an appealing place to kiss as well.

$$$ *MC, V; no checks; lunch, dinner every day; full bar; reservations recommended; www.bistrojeanty.com.*

CINDY'S BACKSTREET KITCHEN
❤❤❤

1327 Railroad Ave, St. Helena / 707/963-1200
The dining scene in St. Helena involves something of a revolving door, but there's no doubt that this delightful restaurant, which opened in 2003, is here to stay. Set a block away from the Old West Victoriana of St. Helena's main drag, this restaurant is the latest creation of the acclaimed chef behind Mustards Grill—just down the road in Yountville. The creative American comfort food is equally as delicious as that of its predecessor, and a variety of dining rooms—some more intimate than others—provides even better grounds for romantic encounters. Old-fashioned moldings adorn the dining rooms, white linens and candles top the tables, and service is prompt, yet the mood is distinctly laid-back and friendly. You'll feel at home the moment you step into the bustling entry room, with its sleek zinc bar and adjacent cushioned banquette lined with tables. Request a table in the quieter downstairs dining room away from the bar or upstairs, where tables are scattered in yet another dining room with high peaked ceilings. Seats are situated rather close together, but you'll forget about the minor lack of privacy once the food arrives. You'll find the same tempting (and temptingly affordable) menu of small plates, hearty salads, entrées, and sandwiches for both lunch and dinner. Lighter fare includes a delicious crispy flatbread adorned with local cheeses, smoked heirloom tomatoes, roasted corn, and basil and salads that range from an excellent classic Caesar to the curried chicken salad with sugar snap peas, butter lettuce, and crispy bacon. For the main event, the wild-mushroom tamales with creamy grits and chard and house-made salsa or the grilled pork with rum marinade are surefire bets. As scrumptious as everything on your plate will be, do save room for the seasonal desserts, such

as warm peach and berry cobbler topped with melting scoops of vanilla-bean ice cream.
$-$$ *DIS, MC, V; no checks; www.cindysbackstreetkitchen.com.*

DOMAINE CHANDON
◐◐◐◖

1 California Dr, Yountville / 707/944-2892
Domaine Chandon is surely one of the most beautiful places to dine in all of Northern California. Secluded on the grounds of a country winery, this immense, three-terraced dining room spares no expense in its luxuriousness. Inlaid stone walls, arched-wood-beam ceilings and doorways, and views of well-tended lawns and gardens combine to create a sensuous, elegant dining experience. If it weren't for the dining room's overwhelming popularity, large size, and poor acoustics, we would have awarded this restaurant four lips without a second thought. Despite these shortcomings, the restaurant is still a stunning place to eat, and the sparkling wines only enhance the experience. The ultradeluxe menu brings forth an assortment of delicacies, starting with the appetizers. If you crave caviar, are tempted by tartare, or favor foie gras, you'll find quite a generous selection with the starters. Past winners from the ever-changing menu have included an exquisite appetizer of alder-smoked trout served on a bed of curly endive and a Japanese eggplant soup that arrives not as the customary puree but as a multicolored mélange streaked with basil and red and yellow peppers. Anything from the grill—including beef, rabbit, or the divine pancetta-wrapped salmon—is meltingly tender. Be sure to finish with one of the seasonally inspired decadent desserts, such as the ground-almond shortcake with strawberries or warm "gooey" chocolate cake topped with vanilla ice cream. If you can get a reservation before the busiest dinner hours, you're likely to find the experience rapturous.
$$$ *AE, DC, DIS, MC, V; no checks; lunch, dinner Thurs–Mon (closed Jan); wine only; reservations recommended; www.chandon.com.*

THE FRENCH LAUNDRY
◐◐◐◐

6640 Washington St, Yountville / 707/944-2380
Housed in a lovingly renovated two-story brick building that could easily be mistaken for a private country home, this world-renowned restaurant is Napa Valley's finest. Several dining rooms make up the interior, including one upstairs, and the elegantly adorned tables provide plenty of elbow room. Subdued colors and a simple French-country decor give prominence to the real artwork here: that which arrives on your plate. First and foremost, The French Laundry is a food lover's paradise. Romance comes second—although a close second, we admit. The superlative chef's-choice menu changes daily and is the most popular option, although an additional prix

fixe menu lets you choose from among several selections for each course. The menu may include such exotic and superbly executed dishes as chilled cauliflower panna cotta topped with sevruga caviar; a Maine lobster pancake surrounded by a delicate carrot-ginger butter; a New Zealand venison chop with red wine–braised cabbage; or herb-roasted monkfish served with a ragout of wine-braised oxtail, glazed pearl onions, and pan-roasted salsify (oyster plant). For dessert, you may be offered a luscious chocolate soufflé or the chef's signature "coffee and doughnuts," a cappuccino semifreddo served alongside two hot-from-the-fryer sugar doughnuts. Service is faultless, although if you're trying to have an intimate conversation, the constant replacement of silverware may be an unwelcome interruption. Due to The French Laundry's popularity, reservations are almost impossible to obtain, usually requiring 60 days' advance booking for limited seatings. Most innkeepers in the area are well aware of this fact and try to make advance reservations for you when you book a stay at their inn. (They deserve a kiss for this!) While spontaneous romance is always a big plus in our book, planning ahead is a must in this case.

$$$$ *AE, MC, V; local checks only; lunch Fri–Sun, dinner every day; beer and wine; reservations required; www.frenchlaundry.com.*

GREYSTONE RESTAURANT
✿✿✿

2555 Main St, St. Helena / 707/967-1010

Discussions about the CIA occur frequently in the Napa Valley, but not because of any overabundance of covert activities. Rather, people are talking about Napa's famous Culinary Institute of America. Located at the northern reaches of the Napa Valley, this destination—formerly the Christian Brothers Greystone Winery—is housed in a monumental 1889 Gothic stone structure. Today, after extensive remodels, Greystone serves as a continuing education center for chefs from around the world and (luckily for all of us) a first-rate restaurant. The atmosphere here is festive and usually noisy, with voices resonating off the thick stone walls and high ceiling, but the experience as a whole is memorable and charming. Copper hanging lamps illuminate colorful chairs and beautifully adorned wooden tables, and an open "show" kitchen allows you to watch the chefs in action. Two acres of organic gardens on the premises provide the freshest produce available, and local products (including area wines) are used in abundance. The Mediterranean-influenced menu is designed so guests can enjoy a variety of dishes. Call them tapas, small plates, or mezes, but most of all, call them delicious. The reasonably priced options range from Spanish potato tortillas to dolmas to pork kebabs sprinkled with North African spices. If you're in the mood to share, try the signature paella entrée for two. As the seasons change, so does the menu, so you might have to visit at least four times! During the winter months, comforting dishes such as Portuguese

white-bean stew with shellfish or roasted rack of lamb marinated in pomegranates and red wine are featured. Desserts are the perfect finale, from
lavender flan with brandied orange slices to pear-and-date tart with walnut
ice cream. It is not always easy to get a reservation at Greystone, but your
efforts will reap great culinary (and kissing) rewards.

$$$$ *AE, DC, MC, V; local checks only; lunch, dinner every day; full bar;
reservations recommended; www.ciachef.edu/greystone.*

LA TOQUE
●●●

1140 Rutherford Cross Rd, Rutherford / 707/963-9770
This recent arrival to the Napa Valley restaurant scene is making a splash
among food aficionados, and its intimate dining room is making waves
among those seeking romance. The large, one-room dining area echoes the
simple Southwest look of its environs, the Rancho Caymus Inn, which is
styled like a classic hacienda. Fifteen large, linen-covered tables are well
placed around the room's perimeter, and a soaring floral arrangement holds
court in the center. High ceilings and a stone fireplace are the only other
embellishments besides the wall sconces. If only the lights were dimmed a
bit more, the austere room would be cozier. This is not the place to come if
you need flexibility in your dining time: with only 15 tables, seating times are
understandably limited to twice an evening (first seating 5:30pm–6:30pm,
second seating 8pm–9pm; dinner lasts 2½–3hours). A set menu featuring five
courses changes nightly but always delivers uncomplicated, well-balanced
French dishes with local flair. Line-caught local salmon with beets and red
wine, duck breast with peppered Bosc pear in red wine, and veal tenderloin
with potato gratin are just a sampling of the delectable delights. While the
dinner prices are high, the generous portions won't disappoint, so make sure
you eat only a light lunch.

$$$ *AE, MC, V; no checks; dinner Wed–Sun; full bar; reservations required;
www.latoque.com.*

MARTINI HOUSE
●●●●

1245 Spring St, St. Helena / 707/963-2233
Since it opened in 2001, the Martini House has been a wonderfully intimate
alternative to the nearly endless supply of boisterous gourmet dining rooms
filling up Napa. Located in a beautifully renovated and spacious Cali-
fornia Craftsman bungalow, the Martini House's every design aspect radi-
ates elegance and polish. Beamed ceilings, dark wood paneling, authentic
Craftsman details, jewel-toned fabrics, and intimate lighting all contribute
to the inviting ambience. (The dining room is yet another feather in the cap
of the restaurant's famous designer, Pat Kuleto, who helped create many of
San Francisco's most acclaimed restaurants, including Boulevard, Farallon,

and Jardinière.) Equally enticing on a warm evening is the greenery-lined garden patio, furnished with shaded tables; however, you can hear passing traffic here, unlike inside. This restaurant is one of the finest places to dine in Napa, and the menu is a showcase of wine-country fare, incorporating top-notch local ingredients that include farm-raised meats, wild game, and the freshest seasonal produce available—with some produce and herbs picked directly from the kitchen gardens. There's a tempting prix fixe menu, or you can order à la carte. It's the creative touches that make each entrée so delectable: try the roasted lamb and creamy polenta with porcini sauce and wild mushrooms (direct from local foragers) or bay scallops with saffron gnocchi, sautéed spinach, and Parmesan cream. Wine pairings are suggested on the menu, or you can speak directly with the down-to-earth yet highly knowledgeable sommelier for one or two brilliant suggestions. The desserts are delicious concoctions, including chocolate soufflé cake with blood-orange ice cream and caramel crème brûlée with chocolate shortbread and spiced pecans. The Wine Cellar bar downstairs is home to one of Napa Valley's only full wine bars, featuring an unequaled 600-bottle international wine list (although it's a bit too popular, and thus crowded, for romance). **$$$** *AE, MC, V; no checks; lunch, dinner every day; beer and wine; reservations recommended; www.kuleto.com.*

MUSTARDS GRILL
❤

7399 Hwy 29, Yountville / 707/944-2424
This boisterous, popular restaurant is not even remotely intimate. Still, the delicious and hearty dishes are so good that in a more romantic setting, this place would garner far more than one smooch from us. The atmosphere is clamorous and casual—there's a big open kitchen, white walls, dark wood wainscoting, and a black-and-white checkerboard floor—but the extensive wine list and inventive menu of comfort food inspired by spices and flavors from all over the world will appeal to those looking for a fun lunch spot. If you don't mind an audience, you might even be able to sneak in a kiss across the table. Dinner might not be in the cards (don't even try it without reservations). Don't miss the giant crispy onion rings or the tasty chili relleno appetizer to start. For the main event, try the ever-changing specials from the grill, which might include lemon and garlic chicken with a heaping pile of garlic mashed potatoes or chipotle-rubbed quail with wild-mushroom tamale on the side.
$$ *AE, DC, MC, V; no checks; lunch, dinner every day; full bar; reservations recommended; www.mustardsgrill.com.*

PINOT BLANC
❤❤◖

641 Main St (Hwy 29), St. Helena / 707/963-6191
Pinot Blanc offers an inspired backdrop for dining and kissing. The sensational interior, painted in shades of yellow and pale green, features upscale French decor and richly upholstered chairs and booths. This highwayside restaurant has undergone several makeovers since it first opened several years ago, and we hope this choice of decor is here to stay. Although the restaurant is rather large, the eating area is divided into a number of rooms, including several "salons" that accommodate about only four or five tables each. All of the dining areas are quite romantic, although we're especially partial to the small room off the main entrance, which has only four linen-topped tables set against bright red walls and picture windows. During summer, the outdoor patio, sheltered by trees and hidden from the highway, is a divine place to enjoy a leisurely lunch. While the decor is a complete success, the French-influenced cuisine is more hit-and-miss. Fortunately, if you stick with the basics, you're less likely to be disappointed. Good bets include the slow-roasted chicken with roasted potatoes, a bountiful bowl of risotto with wild mushrooms, and grilled rib-eye steak *frites* with cabernet-shallot butter. The wine menu suggests, naturally, trying a bottle of pinot blanc, but it also features more than 350 other possibilities, and the lengthy list of whites comes to the rescue of those suffering from chardonnay burnout.
$$$ *AE, DC, DIS, MC, V; no checks; lunch, dinner every day; full bar; reservations recommended.*

TERRA
❤❤❤◖

1345 Railroad Ave, St. Helena / 707/963-8931
Housed in a noble century-old stone building with high ceilings and arched windows, Terra's evocative surroundings are well balanced by the restaurant's charming and unpretentious ambience, and it all adds up to an ideal backdrop for enjoying each other's company. Best of all, the excellent food, which showcases the cuisines of southern France and northern Italy, is faultless without being over the top. The chef has recently won many notable awards, but despite this pedigree—or perhaps as a result of it—the kitchen turns out refreshingly simple and original food that is free of trendy extravagance. Though the menu changes with the seasons, tried-and-true standbys include fried rock shrimp with organic greens and chive mustard sauce; broiled sake-marinated rock cod with shrimp dumplings; spaghettini with tripe, tomato, and butter beans; and grilled, dry-aged New York strip steak with sautéed vegetables and anchovy-garlic sauce. The outstanding desserts created by the restaurant's acclaimed pastry chef might include strawberries drenched in a cabernet-and-black-peppercorn sauce served with vanilla ice cream or a dramatically sculpted tiramisu. For the most

intimacy, request a table in the dining room to the left of the entrance, as the main room receives a fair amount of traffic. Wherever you sit, we have no doubt you will call an evening here one of your favorites in the wine country.

$$$$ *DC, MC, V; local checks only; dinner Wed–Mon; beer and wine; reservations recommended; www.terrarestaurant.com.*

TRA VIGNE
●●◖

1050 Charter Oak Ave, St. Helena / 707/963-4444

The Italian-style courtyard dining at Tra Vigne is pure heaven, the Tuscan-inspired food is exceptionally fresh, and the surroundings are certainly grand. Unfortunately, in all other respects, this restaurant is a perfect example of how it's possible for one of the most popular dining rooms in Napa to lack the warmth and intimacy that are necessary for a truly romantic evening out. Reservations are nearly impossible to get on weekend nights, and even if you can get a table, the noise level in the dining room prohibits sweet nothings. Furthermore, the chefs have changed several times over the past two years, and as of late the food can range from great to merely good. Nevertheless, the setting is truly impressive: trailing ivy covers the handsome brick exterior, and wrought-iron gates open to a brick courtyard. Inside are 25-foot-tall ceilings, a stunning oak bar, and towering wrought iron–embellished French windows. The tables are individually spotlighted from above, and every detail, including the food, is attended to with sophistication and panache. The menu is seasonal, but you can usually find excellent *fritti* of fried prawns and vegetables or expert wood-fired pizza specials, such as a classic Margherita. Pastas range from traditional to more experimental plates, such as ravioli with eggplant ricotta, mozzarella, tomato *conserva,* and warm oregano crumbs. Hearty entrées might include grilled wild king salmon with fresh chickpeas, Blue Lake beans, and Meyer lemon sauce; roasted organic chicken breast with roasted carrots, potatoes, escarole, and garlic-lemon jus; and a savory grilled lamb sirloin with rapini and olive jus. For a lighter lunch, food to go, or wine tastings, head to the less-expensive Cantinetta Tra Vigne (707/963-8888) and indulge in the focaccia pizza, gourmet sandwiches, and tasty soups and salads. As you peruse the list of about 100 wines by the glass, you'll have no trouble remembering where you are.

$$$ *CB, DC, DIS, MC, V; no checks; restaurant: lunch, dinner every day; cantinetta: lunch every day; full bar; reservations recommended; www.travignerestaurant.com.*

CALISTOGA

ROMANTIC HIGHLIGHTS

There is no place in the United States quite like Calistoga, California. The entire town, it seems, is dedicated two the rejuvenation of the body and spirit through an ingenious variety of treatments. Of particular romantic interest is the abundance of natural hot springs and mineral pools, where the two of you can soak until supreme relaxation sets in. Several of the spas also offer services designed especially for couples. In addition to spending a day at a spa, you'll want to devote some time to exploring the town, which has a charmingly laid-back atmosphere (even in the height of tourist season) and a fun mix of places in which to stay, eat, and shop. Of course, this being wine country, you'll also find wine-tasting rooms within easy driving distance.

One of the most popular—and charmingly historic—day spas in town is **Indian Springs** (1712 Lincoln Ave; 707/942-4913; www.indiansprings napa.com), to which urban couples flock for massages and the legendary mud baths. Since Calistoga is also an extremely popular wedding destination, it's not unusual to encounter an entire family or bridal party crowding into the Mission-style entry hall to register for spa appointments as an antidote to prewedding jitters. Indian Springs is not inexpensive, but it's worth every penny to soak up the authentic atmosphere. (If, when you arrive, you have the urge to hold your nose, don't worry: that's the aroma of authentic mineral water, and before long, as the other sensory delights of your spa treatment distract you, it will go unnoticed.) One reason we are so fond of Indian Springs is its grand mineral pool, the best and largest in town. (Take our word for it: you might encounter a family—or three—at the poolside here, but the other pools in town attract many more, and during high season some of them resemble nothing so much as your local YMCA during a kiddie swimming lesson.) You'll appreciate the higher measure of serenity at Indian Springs—often it's so quiet that you can hear the steam from one of the geysers feeding hot mineral water into the pool.

Fortunately, in a town with as many spas as Calistoga has, you can find just about anything, including a place for total escape: in this case, a spa that specializes in treatments for couples. That heavenly destination is **Lavender Hill Spa** (1015 Foothill Blvd (Hwy 29); 707/942-4495 or 800/ 528-4772; www.lavenderhillspa.com). Privacy and intimacy are the top priorities here, and you'll find a calming atmosphere and a variety of treatments to choose from for rejuvenation and renewed peace of mind. We highly recommend the volcanic-mud bath, which is actually a wonderful mixture of soft ash, sea kelp, and essential oils, followed by a warm blanket wrap and light foot massage. Side-by-side mineral bathtubs and two massage tables make the experience perfectly couple-friendly. The treatments take place in the bath-house, which is fully insulated for noise protection and warmth. We also urge you to try the hourlong massage, which will be everything you hope for, and then some. The professional staff works wonders on tense muscles, and the overall result is simply amazing. An hour or a day at Lavender Hill Spa is something you and your bodies will remember for a long time to come.

Once you're completely relaxed, it's time to enjoy lunch or browse in the shops lining the quaint downtown. Or head over to the **Calistoga Inn**'s (1250 Lincoln Ave; 707/942-4101; www.calistogainn.com) pretty outdoor patio for a tall, cool drink—try one of the house-brewed beers or ales. Once you're refreshed, stroll down the main street and browse through the many intriguing shops marketing everything from silk-screened T-shirts and salt-water taffy to luxurious French soaps and antique armoires.

High in the hills above Calistoga, a hike through the beautiful redwood canyons and oak-madrona woodlands in **Robert Louis Stevenson State Park** (off Hwy 29, 8 miles north of Calistoga; 707/942-4575; www.parks.ca.gov) is certain to inspire some alfresco kissing. If your idea of romance includes extremely vigorous activity and splendid views, we highly recommend the route to the 4,343-foot summit of Mount St. Helena along **Mount St. Helena Trail** (located within the park; difficult; 9 miles round trip). It's not a hike to be taken lightly: this steep climb is the premier challenge for hikers looking to make a day of it in the Napa Valley. Fortunately, the summit offers one of the finest views of the California wine region to be found anywhere. The trail is best tackled during the spring wildflower season—not only because it's so pretty, but also because summers at high noon are intolerably hot. The mountain is slated for development as a state park sometime in the future, but for now it is more of a wilderness area, with few recreational improvements beyond trail cuts.

Access and Information

If you're traveling from the Bay Area and need detailed directions to the region, see Access and Information in the Napa and Environs chapter. Calistoga, located at the northern end of Napa Valley, is accessed via Highway 29.

For additional information, contact the **Calistoga Chamber of Commerce** (1458 Lincoln Ave, No. 9, Calistoga, CA 94515; 707/942-6333; www.calistoga chamber.org).

Romantic Wineries

CHÂTEAU MONTELENA WINERY
✪✪✪

1429 Tubbs Lane / 707/942-5105
A visit to this majestic winery nestled in a wooded dell on a scenic, quiet road north of Calistoga promises a feast for more than just the palate: just downhill from the winery, you'll discover a beautifully landscaped park that includes a lake with colorful pagoda, charming footbridges, and beautiful weeping willow trees; it's almost no surprise when the gorgeous white swans adrift on the water's surface catch your eye. Much of the parklike setting is off-limits, but the views are yours for the taking, and you'll find plenty of secluded spots for kissing in the section you are allowed to explore. The winery itself, a stunning French château-style structure built of stone, is known for its chardonnay. Other wines poured in the tasting room include a zinfandel blend and an estate cabernet sauvignon.
10am–4pm every day; tasting fee $10; www.montelena.com

SCHRAMSBERG VINEYARDS
✪✪✪

1400 Schramsberg Rd / 707/942-6668
Schramsberg is one of the most distinctive wineries in all of Napa Valley. Set high on a scenic wooded ridge, this beautiful 1862 estate is full of both historical and oenological interest. The stone buildings of the winery are located far enough away from the traffic of the main road to provide quiet refuge, and because only private tours are allowed (no fee), your introduction to the world of champagne will be sparklingly intimate. After you roam through the labyrinth of underground cellars that were tunneled into the rocky ground as long ago as the 1870s, it's worth it to participate in the tasting (not offered without the tour), despite the considerable fee. Schramsberg's delicious sparkling wines will make it crystal clear to you why bubbly is the preferred beverage of romance. With future celebrations in mind, you might want to stop at the wine shop—by this point, you will have learned almost all the secrets of *méthode champenoise* and may wish to own a bit of effervescent history to share.
10am–4pm every day; tours by appointment only; tasting fee $20; www.schramsberg.com.

Romantic Lodgings

CHELSEA GARDEN INN
◐◐◖

1443 2nd St / 707/942-0948 or 800/942-1515
At the Chelsea Garden Inn, located in a residential neighborhood just two blocks from downtown Calistoga, you'll find the intimacy of a bed-and-breakfast with the added bonus of a pool and poolside lounging room with a vaulted ceiling and French doors. Five newly remodeled private suites are delightfully clustered around the pool and garden courtyard—three in the main home's bed-and-breakfast, two in newly remodeled separate cottages. Each individually decorated accommodation has a private entrance and features a spacious sitting area with cozy fireplace, as well as comforts such as a mini refrigerator, coffeemaker, TV, and full air conditioning. In the main house, the most private accommodation is found upstairs in the Palisades Suite (named after the Palisade Mountains, which can be seen from the sitting room and bedroom). Here, you'll find a queen-size four-poster bed as well as a daybed for lounging and a small balcony overlooking the pool. The main-floor Lavender and Palm Suites can be opened up to each other if you happen to be traveling with another couple. The tasteful tropical-theme fabrics, rattan sofa and chairs, and dark wood accents give the Palm Suite a subtle island flavor; it holds both a daybed and queen-size bed. The Lavender Suite's cheerful decor includes warm peach-colored walls, blue gingham and chintz furnishings, and a queen-size bed; the spacious bathroom also has a claw-foot tub. Of the two accommodations found in separate structures on the property, our favorite is the Garden Room, which boasts a pretty color scheme of pale green and rose, white wicker furnishings, a king-size bed, and a lovely private patio. The Cottage, with a queen-size bed and a retro Western design theme (the walls are painted with a trompe l'oeil mural to look like wood cabin walls), is the only accommodation with a small kitchen, making it a good choice for longer stays. On a sunny morning, lounge by the pool for a few hours before you head out to tour wineries (or simply stay put and wait for the inn's afternoon wine and cheese hour). Full breakfasts are served at individual bistro tables in the main house's dining room.
$$$ *AE, DIS, MC, V; checks OK; www.chelseagardeninn.com.*

CHRISTOPHER'S INN
◐◐◐

1010 Foothill Blvd (Hwy 29) / 707/942-5755
Although Christopher's Inn is set not far from a jam-packed intersection of Highway 29, its many charms outweigh the drawbacks of its busy location. The architect-innkeeper went to great lengths to reduce the traffic's impact when he turned these three buildings into an English-country inn

and, thanks to the many soundproofing efforts, once you settle into your delightful accommodations for a quiet evening, you will find that the street sounds are hardly noticeable. Most of the 22 beautiful guest rooms have private entrances, high ceilings, intriguing antiques, and gas or wood-burning fireplaces. The French-country decor includes tasteful floral linens and window treatments. The inn's nine newest rooms, all of which have fireplaces and seven of which include fabulous jetted tubs, all receive rave kissing reviews. Those on the ground floor feature enclosed garden patios as well. Our romantic favorites include Room 16, known as simply "The Room." Gracing this beautiful blue-and-white retreat is a glass-enclosed jetted tub (with head pillows) that fronts the fireplace, as well as a carved four-poster bed. Another fantastic jetted delight, a two-person sunken tub, is found in Room 11. Room 12, done in light apricot tones, is another good bet, thanks to its enclosed patio, jetted tub, and snug daybed. If the steep price tag of these new beauties is beyond your budget, opt for the Secret Garden Room. Off on its own, this pocket-size room has a wonderful enclosed patio overflowing with camellias and star jasmine. Mornings are leisurely at Christopher's, with an expanded continental breakfast delivered to your door in a basket.

$$$–$$$$ *MC, V; checks OK; www.chrisinn.com.*

COTTAGE GROVE INN
❀❀❀❁

1711 Lincoln Ave / 707/942-8400 or 800/799-2284
Located in an old elm grove at the edge of town, these 16 cottages offer loads of both privacy and charm. All of the cottages have impressive features such as hardwood floors, Jacuzzi tubs, wet bars, dimming lights and skylights in both bedroom and bath, and soft robes. Slip in a mood-setting CD (available for complimentary use from the front desk), light a candle, and bubble your cares away in the relaxing hot water. The shaded porches are perfect for lounging the day away. While each cottage is decorated with its own theme (ranging from Victorian to fly-fishing motifs), all come with the same *accoutrements d'amour*; beds are either king or queen size. The roadside location is not ideal, but all windows and porches face inward to the quiet court-yard—honestly, these cottages could be in the middle of Manhattan and we wouldn't mind; that's how charming they are. A wine and cheese reception, featuring several choices of reds and whites, is served in the common area each evening, and an expanded continental breakfast buffet is served in the fireside dining room or, if the weather's good, on the outdoor patio. Better yet, take a tray back to your cottage and enjoy the morning on your front porch. Later, work off that buttery croissant by riding through town on the inn's two complimentary 1950s coaster bikes.

$$$$ *AE, DC, DIS, MC, V; checks OK; www.cottagegrove.com.*

THE ELMS
❍❍

1300 Cedar St / 707/942-9476 or 888/399-ELMS
If wandering around downtown Calistoga is at the top of your wish list, this sparkling-white French Victorian bed-and-breakfast offers a good central location, right next to a quiet residential park and a block away from the main shopping street. Upon arrival, guests are welcomed into the snug parlor, which has a glowing fireplace and elegant French Victorian antiques. A steep, curved staircase ascends to the second and third floors, where four of the seven guest rooms are located. All of these rooms are a bit on the small side, but you will be extra comfy at night tucked between a fluffy feather bed and a billowy down comforter. Authentic Victorian decor fills every room, and some have special romantic touches such as canopy beds with white eyelet covers and floral linens, private balconies, window seats, and high ceilings covered with pounded tin. All but two rooms have fireplaces. The three other rooms available at The Elms are located in the separate Carriage House, near the main building. The Honeymoon Cottage in this building is the largest guest room of all and features a private entrance and patio, kitchenette, and wonderful two-person Jacuzzi tub framed by black and white tiles. Even more enticing is the king-size bed overlooking the Napa River, right outside your door. The two other rooms here, although small, pack a romantic punch with private entrances, one-person Jacuzzi tubs, antique furnishings, and French-country charm. A full breakfast is served downstairs in the main house each morning. Later in the day, a generous assortment of wines and cheeses are offered beside the fire or outside on the patio.
$$$ DIS, MC, V; checks OK; www.theelms.com.

FOOTHILL HOUSE
❍❍❍

3037 Foothill Blvd (Hwy 128) / 707/942-6933 or 800/942-6933
Some bed-and-breakfasts have a way of immediately making you feel right at home, and Foothill House is one such place. Perhaps it's the innkeeper's warm welcome, maybe it's the smell of freshly baked cookies in the air, or it could be the way the world seems to slow down the moment you reach the tucked-away-from-the-road property. Or all three. Regardless, the flowery decor and quiet pace of this traditional bed-and-breakfast make it a serene harbor for old-fashioned, unpretentious romance. The exterior of the inn is modest, but the rooms are extremely comfortable, and the three rooms in the main house all feature fireplaces or stoves complete with chopped wood. Our top pick is the incredibly spacious Evergreen Suite, which features a beautiful private redwood deck surrounded by trees. The whirlpool tub in the bathroom could use an update, but you can also adjourn to the outdoor hot tub, available to all guests, and listen to the wind rustle the leaves.

Throughout, the Laura Ashley–style fabrics and pink-and-green or bur-gundy-and-green color schemes are a bit outdated; if you strongly prefer the modern Pottery Barn look, this isn't the place for you. Atop the property's steep hill is a separate cottage, which is also the most spacious and private accommodation. The Quail's Roost is the picture of old-fashioned comfort enhanced by modern amenities, including a double-sided fireplace and glass-enclosed whirlpool tub for two. Within this 1,000-square-foot space there's also a lovely little kitchen, four-poster bed, and reading alcove. The homey decor includes teddy bears and fabrics in a mix of rosy plaids and flo-rals, and there's also a sheltered backyard patio with serviceable (if slightly worn) patio furniture. Appetizers and wine are served each afternoon. When you return from dinner, you'll find the bed neatly turned down and a con-tainer of the Foothill House's signature chewy chocolate chip cookies and a miniature book about love on your pillow. Breakfast is a highlight, deliv-ered to your door in a basket packed with everything from freshly squeezed orange juice and hot coffee to baked goods, fruit, and a hot egg dish. As you linger over the last morsel of the French toast soufflé, you will be revitalized for another day of wine-country exploring. The superhospitable innkeeper will gladly help you plan your day if you request it.
$$$-$$$$ AE, DIS, MC, V; checks OK; www.foothillhouse.com.

LA CHAUMIÈRE
♥♥《

1301 Cedar St / 707/942-5139 or 800/474-6800
If you aren't looking closely enough, you might pass right by this charming Cotswold-style home, hidden behind lush foliage and a majestic, vine-cov-ered cedar. With its white-stucco exterior and thatched roof, the home is simply charming. In fact, the entire scene will make you feel as if you're in the countryside rather than just a block from downtown Calistoga. Upon arrival, guests are greeted with wine and hors d'oeuvres in the dining area, which is filled with the owner's collection of elephant-themed art and eclectic antiques. Of the three rooms at the inn, the two located in the main home have private baths and copious antiques. The handsome and dark Downstairs Room features an exquisite Louis XV bed, a private porch, and a black and lavender bathroom with fixtures and tiles from the 1930s. The sun-filled Upstairs Room is actually a small suite with two rooms, one of which houses the owner's collection of porcelain clowns. Even if you aren't newlyweds, the Honeymoon Cottage, set behind the house, is the accommo-dation to book. Built in the early 1900s, this cottage retains many original rustic touches, such as rough-hewn redwood walls and support beams and a wood-burning fireplace with a petrified-wood hearth. Country-style furnishings, landscape paintings, and hardwood floors covered by South-west-style rugs create a cozy atmosphere. There is a small, sunny kitchen for guests to use, and the private bath (shower only) reminds you you're

in Napa with its walls covered with wooden wine crates. One of the best features of La Chaumière sits next to the cottage and is open to all guests: a towering redwood is surrounded by a large deck romantically furnished with both a hot tub and hammock. A staircase leads up to a second deck (called The Treehouse) set in the tree's boughs, where, in warmer months, soothing massage treatments can be scheduled for a fee. Breakfast begins with a fruit course and then moves on to such hearty dishes as Italian sausage frittata, homemade lemon pancakes, or Grand Marnier French toast with chicken-apple sausage. This morning repast can be savored either at the dining room table with other guests or outside on the brick patio, where the burbling fountain provides background music and hummingbirds offer fly-by entertainment.
$$$ *MC, V; checks OK; www.lachaumiere.com.*

MOUNT VIEW HOTEL AND SPA
❀❀❀

1457 Lincoln Ave / 707/942-6877 or 800/816-6877
This National Historic Landmark hotel, located smack in the middle of downtown Calistoga, is not exactly off the beaten path, but amazingly, the rooms here can be quieter than other lodgings in town directly on Foothill Boulevard (Highway 29). The moment you step inside this two-story 1914 hotel, you'll notice its style and polish; the high-ceilinged lobby is an inviting picture, complete with potted palms, plush sofas, gleaming hardwood floors, and fresh flowers. The 20 rooms and 9 suites, which tend to be on the small side, are cheerfully decorated with tasteful ivory-and-gold wide-striped wallpaper, colorful country-style textiles, overstuffed furnishings, feather beds, fresh flowers, and homey accouterments such as coffeemakers and sparkling water. (Alas, less attention in detail is paid to room elements such as the old and rather small televisions and the general wear and tear.) Each morning, as the rooms brighten with wine-country sun, a continental breakfast is delivered to your door. The three cottages located across the parking lot from the courtyard (and its large outdoor pool and hot mineral whirlpool) are preferred by honeymooners. Each cottage is fenced in for privacy and has a tiny outdoor patio (with hot tub) and wet bar. Rooms may be on the expensive side here, but this is Calistoga's only true full-service hotel. Stomp, described as a stylish French-cuisine restaurant, opened in summer 2004 to replace the former dining establishment (the popular Southern-themed Catahoula) just as this edition was going to press; call the hotel for details. The full-service Mount View Spa (707/942-5789) offers everything from massage to reflexology, body wraps, stone therapies, and facials. For couples more interested in spending quality time together than gallivanting all over town, this makes an appealing package.
$$$$ *AE, DIS, MC, V; checks OK; www.mountviewhotel.com.*

THE PINK MANSION
♦♦♦

1415 Foothill Blvd (Hwy 128) / 707/942-0558 or 800/238-7465
This turn-of-the-20th-century Victorian is not quite as pink as its name implies, though the exterior is indeed painted a rosy shade. Inside, the decor is marked by a bright and airy country elegance. The main parlor, which the new owners remade in neoclassical fashion with Bradbury & Bradbury wallpapers, pays tribute to the style of the inn's previous owner, "Aunt" Alma Simic, decorated with her intriguing Asian art pieces and collection of antique angels and cherubs. A curved window seat in the turret is a prime kissing spot. The six guest rooms on the main and second floors are all outfitted differently, but all have lovely decor, private baths, and TV/VCRs. Views range from garden vistas to stunning panoramas of the mountains. The recently remodeled Honeymoon Room and Master Room each offer 800-plus square feet of space, 12-foot-high vaulted ceilings, king-size beds, wood-burning fireplaces, and Jacuzzi tubs *à deux*. In the Honeymoon Room, the neoclassical decor includes a gleaming wooden canopy bed, marble statuary on the mantel, a crimson color scheme, and a tiny private deck with views of the distant hills. The Master Room is the largest accommodation, with an entertainment center, private sitting room, and so much space that there's an additional bed. There is no Jacuzzi tub in the Rose Room, but it is nevertheless an outstanding choice for romance, with its high, intricately decorated ceilings, gleaming walnut floors, and beautiful king-size bed. A chandelier sparkles above the sunken sitting room, where you can cozy up together in front of the raised fireplace; there's also a private redwood deck. If you want the maximum privacy and space, book the Carriage House, an airy hideaway with master bedroom and a large loft (both with queen beds), fireplace, modest kitchenette, a tumbled-stone bathroom with Jacuzzi tub, and a fabulous private redwood deck. To entice you out of your warm bed, a bountiful breakfast of fresh scones, baked apples or poached pears, and Norwegian pancakes or baked French toast is served in the homey dining room. There's an inviting indoor lap pool, attractively set in an airy sun room equipped with a fireplace to keep things toasty—and even toastier environs outside, where a hot tub tucked among the backyard greenery awaits.
$$$–$$$$ *DIS, MC, V; checks OK; www.pinkmansion.com.*

Romantic Restaurants

ALL SEASONS CAFE
♦♦◗

1400 Lincoln Ave / 707/942-9111
With its delightful menu and classic interior, this 1940s-style storefront café is an enchanting place to enjoy a romantic dinner for two. Large windows,

an old-fashioned bar, colorful art pieces, white linen-topped tables, and a black-and-white checkerboard floor lend depth to the cozy interior. Tables are packed in quite tightly around the edges of the room; try the tables in the restaurant's center instead. Entrées are exceptionally light and fresh, and portions are more than generous. You won't have any trouble deciding what wine to order with your dish, since pairing recommendations are featured on the seasonal menu. Try a salmon tartare appetizer with sauvignon blanc, dig into a hearty plate of oven-roasted lamb with potato gratin alongside a glass of merlot or cabernet, or sip a pinot noir as you dine on crispy-skin chicken with butternut-squash puree. A rich espresso pot de crème ended our meal on an up note. If the complicated and ever-changing menu is a bit too dazzling, ask for recommendations from the knowledgeable servers, and if you don't have time for a meal here, head to the rear of the restaurant, where a retail wine store with a tasting bar allows you to check out the hundreds of first-rate foreign and domestic wines offered at remarkably reasonable prices. You'll find the perfect bottle for a romantic celebration.
$$ *DIS, MC, V; local checks only; dinner every day, lunch Fri–Sun; beer and wine; reservations recommended; www.allseasonswineshop.com.*

WAPPO BAR & BISTRO
🔴🔴
1226-B Washington St / 707/942-4712
Come here on a warm summer day, since Wappo's courtyard patio is the most romantic in town. Tucked between two buildings, the brick-lined patio profits from the cool covering of trees and a vine-covered trellis; it's also sheltered enough that sweet nothings won't get lost in background noise. If the day is gray, the interior will do for a quiet dinner. The building's history is evident in the wood-beam ceiling, large multipaned windows, and mirrors framed by old barn wood; henna-painted lampshades round out the rustic look. For better or worse, the banquette seats—set against the wainscoting, without back cushions—will have you sitting up straight to eat. The small menu changes often and offers a cheerful excursion through cuisines from around the world, from the Middle East to Europe to Asia to South America to the good old USA. For example, your culinary journey might begin with delicate Vietnamese spring rolls dipped in a hot and spicy *nam pla* sauce. Next, you might try the flavorful Lebanese lemon chicken or an Indian dish of Chilean sea bass with *garam masala*, mint chutney, and basmati rice. End your tour in traditional American fashion, with a cool slice of coconut cream pie topped with whipped cream.
$$ *AE, MC, V; local checks only; lunch, dinner Wed–Mon; beer and wine; reservations recommended; www.wappobar.com.*

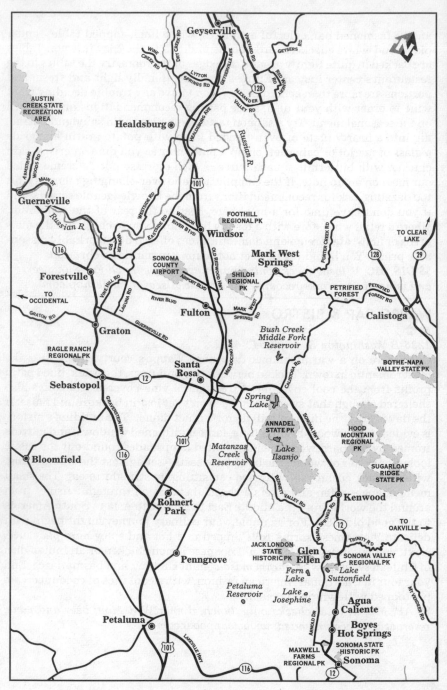

*"Where kisses are repeated and the arms hold
there is no telling where time is."*

—TED HUGHES

♡ SONOMA

We agree with those who say that when it comes to comparing Sonoma Valley's wine country with Napa's, less is definitely more: Sonoma is less congested, less developed, less commercial, and less glitzy than its rival. But despite its more bucolic qualities, this region is still home to some of California wine country's most renowned restaurants and elegant retreats. And, though Sonoma is less trafficked than Napa, don't make the mistake of imagining that Sonoma's winery tasting rooms (or lodging rates, for that matter) are unaffected by high season: the town of Sonoma is particularly crowded with tourists in the summer, and our recommendation is to visit during the spring or fall.

For kissing purposes, the Sonoma wine country is informally divided into several regions: the quaint, historic town of **Sonoma** and environs, including the nearby hamlets of **Glen Ellen** and **Kenwood**, a tightly woven area that is home to about 40 wineries; the sprawling city of **Santa Rosa**, with easy proximity to the wooded hills and pastoral vineyards of the neighboring town of **Sebastopol** and the **Russian River Valley** at the northern end of the county; and the towns of **Healdsburg** and **Guerneville**. Though any of these destinations will do if wine tasting is the order of the day, each offers a unique experience in itself.

Each of the following chapters includes a **Romantic Wineries** section that highlights places where couples are most likely to enjoy intimate moments. (The list is not meant to indicate which wines in the region are best—a highly subjective matter in any case.) Please know your limits, and do not drink and drive. One option that is not only safe but also lots of fun is to hire a chauffeured limousine for the afternoon. A reputable company in Sonoma County is **Style 'N Comfort Limousine** (707/578-3001 or 800/487-5466; www.snclimos.com), which includes in its fleet a spotless white 1966 Austin Princess that's perfect for two.

SONOMA AND ENVIRONS

ROMANTIC HIGHLIGHTS

Quieter than Napa, Sonoma Valley is our favorite place for an intimate wine-country escape: nothing beats sitting in the sunshine at a beautifully landscaped winery (relatively free of crowds) and enjoying a kiss to the serenade of songbirds. Add a gourmet picnic and two glasses of chilled sauvignon blanc to the picture, and you're certain to agree with us that Sonoma is tops. One thing that sets Sonoma apart from Napa is its layout: unlike the wine towns of Napa Valley, all of which are bisected by Highway 29, Sonoma Valley towns are set in the countryside.

At the heart of the valley is its namesake town of **Sonoma**. Despite its bustling popularity, it's a prime spot for a romantic rendezvous. The village itself wraps around a parklike square shaded by sprawling oak trees and sculpted greenery. This central square is laden with park benches, flower-lined walkways, and a sparkling fountain and duck pond. Beyond the square's perimeter is an array of charming shops, restaurants, and wineries. However, as is the case in most wine-country towns, summer crowds in Sonoma can range from overpowering during the week to unbearable on the weekends. Off-season is the best time to find both a degree of solitude and cooler, more comfortable weather.

When you arrive, you'll definitely want to spend at least one afternoon exploring Sonoma. A stroll around the plaza area offers interesting shopping and an excellent bookstore, **Reader's Books** (127 Napa St E; 707/939-1779; www.readersbooks.com). If you're planning a daylong excursion, you can acquire all the gourmet goods necessary at the **Sonoma Cheese Factory** (2 W Spain St; 707/996-1931; www.sonomajack.com): we suggest filling up your basket with some of the award-winning sourdough bread, local deli meats and mustards, and scrumptious pesto jack cheese. If the timing is right, you can supplement your treats with the freshest of organic fruits and vegetables at the **Sonoma Farmer's Market**. In summer, you can catch this colorful affair, which takes place in the town's central plaza, in the cool of dusk (Sonoma Plaza; 5:30pm–dusk Tues, Apr–Oct). A year-round market is held on Friday mornings (Depot Park, 1 block north of Sonoma Plaza; 9am–noon Fri). No matter when you visit, it's fun to mingle with the locals and take advantage of the area's natural bounty.

You can also spend a leisurely day in town and do your wine tasting without ever getting into the car. Downtown Sonoma offers a wide array of wine-tasting locales. The generously stocked **Wine Exchange** (452 1st St E; 800/938-1794; www.wineexsonoma.com) offers wine and beer tastings every day. You'll find takeout gourmet fare, wine tasting, and an espresso bar at **Cucina Viansa** (400 1st St E; 707/935-5656). For the most romantic wine tasting, however, head to the new and extremely polished **Ledson Hotel and Harmony Club** (480 1st St E; 707/996-9779; www.ledson.com) for a late-night version. The elegant ambience includes live jazz and a tasty menu of appetizers.

After all that eating and drinking, you may feel inspired to pedal together along the scenic trails of Sonoma Valley. **Sonoma Valley Cyclery** (20093 Broadway, at Newcomb St; 707/935-3377) rents bikes and doles out maps for a handful of wonderful, easy trails, all about a mile long. Another, even less-strenuous, option for revitalization is an outing to the tiny town of **Kenwood** for a luxury treatment at the **Kenwood Inn & Spa** (see Romantic Lodgings).

North of the town of Sonoma, Highway 12 passes through the town of **Boyes Hot Springs**; little more than a thoroughfare with ramshackle businesses, the town is mainly noteworthy as the home of one of California's most renowned and most expensive spa resorts, the **Fairmont Sonoma Mission Inn & Spa** (see Romantic Lodgings). North of here is **Glen Ellen,** a quiet rural community located just off Highway 12. The relaxed atmosphere of this tiny, charming hamlet is a welcome change from the tourist bustle of the larger wine-country towns. A culinary fixture in the town of Sonoma, **the girl & the fig restaurant** (see Romantic Restaurants), recently opened **the fig cafe & winebar** in Glen Ellen (13690 Arnold Dr; 707/938-2130). This and a few other appealing places, along with some of our favorite Sonoma Valley bed-and-breakfasts, make Glen Ellen an ideal place to stop and savor the quiet.

Glen Ellen's best-known attraction is **Jack London State Historic Park** (2400 London Ranch Rd, off Hwy 12; 707/938-5216; www.jacklondon park.com). Alas, this 800-acre spread, built by the writer and originally (and aptly) named Beauty Ranch, can feel more like a zoo than a park in the summer, when tourism is at its peak and the kids are out of school. But if you come at a quieter time of year, you'll find many spots perfect for kissing, including lovely picnic sites scattered around the grounds, as well as wooded paths suitable for an old-fashioned stroll after lunch. Also on this historic site is a grand stone house-turned-museum that contains London's art collection and memorabilia from the exotic travels he and his wife embarked upon together over the years.

Access and Information

The most popular way to tour this largely rural area is by car. Driving from San Francisco, it's difficult to avoid traffic (whatever you do, don't drive during rush hour): from the airport, head north on **Highway 101** toward San Francisco and continue to the Golden Gate Bridge. Cross the bridge, then continue on Highway 101 North. Just past Novato, exit onto Highway

37. For the town of Sonoma, head east on Highway 37 for about 8 miles. Take a left onto Highway 121 North (Sears Point Raceway will be on your left). Stay on 121 and then turn onto Highway 12 North to reach the valley towns of Sonoma, Glen Ellen, and Kenwood. For other Sonoma County destinations, such as Santa Rosa or Healdsburg, remain on 101 and continue north.

Thanks to the increased number of visitors, many Sonoma vintners now charge a small fee to taste their wines (in general, however, the cost of wine tasting is less prohibitive here than in Napa). Some wineries require reservations for tours, but don't let this deter you—the smaller establishments just need to control the number of visitors at any one time and to make sure someone will be available to show you around.

More information about the Sonoma Valley is available from the **Sonoma Valley Visitors Bureau** (453 1st St E; 707/996-1090; www.sonoma valley.com), which has a helpful concierge program (707/996-1090; sonoma concierge@sonomavalley.com) that offers referrals and reservations for hotels, restaurants, balloon rides, limos, and spa treatments.

Romantic Wineries

BARTHOLOMEW PARK WINERY
●●●●
1000 Vineyard Lane, Sonoma / 707/935-9511
Tucked in 400-acre Bartholomew Memorial Park and surrounded by old vines and gnarled oak trees, this historic, colonial-style boutique winery harbors one of the most beautiful settings in the valley. It also happens to be an exceptional picnicking spot, complete with tables, seclusion, and hiking trails. But there are plenty of reasons to go indoors, including the limited-production wines. A museum showcases Victorian photographs documenting viticulture practices from the 19th century and information about Agoston Haraszthy, the winery's eccentric former owner. Tours, available for a fee, include a spin around the museum and a private tasting, as well as a 10 percent discount off all purchases.
11am–4:30pm every day, closed major holidays; tours by appointment; tasting fee $3; www.bartholomewparkwinery.com.

BUENA VISTA WINERY
●●●◖
18000 Old Winery Rd, Sonoma / 707/938-1266
Gather your picnic goodies in Sonoma Plaza before heading off to this historic 1857 winery. Once you arrive, a chilled chardonnay and a peaceful picnic spot are all you'll need for the classic Buena Vista experience. Rugged stone walls covered with tangles of ivy lend a strong sense of history to this

winery, one of California's oldest. Picnic tables are set by a woodsy creek and on a hillside terrace, and all are shaded by sweet-scented eucalyptus trees. The air-conditioned tasting room offers a small selection of fine gifts, and a mezzanine gallery showcases local art. Tours of the stone winery and the hillside tunnels are available.

10am–5pm every day; tasting fee $5; www.buenavistawinery.com.

CHATEAU ST. JEAN
❶❷❸

8555 Sonoma Hwy (Hwy 12), Kenwood / 707/833-4134 or 800/543-7572
Getting stuck in a huge tour group is never romantic, which is why we love Chateau St. Jean. This elegant winery estate allows you to take a self-guided tour at your own pace, and during harvest time, you can witness the wine-making process. Regardless of when you visit, be sure to climb up to the observation tower. From this perspective, you have a wonderful view of the expansive vineyards, rolling green hills, and beautifully tended property. If you forgot to bring picnic supplies, visit the shop to find edible delights from the on-site kitchen and an assortment of fresh, local, gourmet special-ties. Purchase a bottle of Chateau St. Jean's highly acclaimed wine, choose a prime picnic spot on the lush lawn, and then kiss to the marvelous concept of the two-person tour group.

10am–4:30pm every day; tasting fee $5; www.chateaustjean.com.

CLINE CELLARS
❶❷❸

24737 Arnold Dr, Sonoma / 707/935-4310
After all those chateau-style wineries in Napa, the country-farm setting of Cline Cellars is a refreshing change of pace. And unlike those stuffy environs that discourage picnics, this winery offers lovely picnic tables surrounded by more than 5,000 rosebushes. The property offers sweeping views of the Carneros Valley, and you can't help but relax at the sight of the large, old-fashioned porch that wraps around the turn-of-the-20th-century farmhouse. In the casual, laid-back tasting room, you can taste a variety of complimentary nonreserve wines, including our favorite, the Cline Zinfandel.

10am–6pm every day; tasting fee $1 per reserve wine–$5 for reserve flight; www.clinecellars.com.

GLORIA FERRER CHAMPAGNE CAVES
❶❷❸

23555 Hwy 121, Sonoma / 707/996-7256
As the name suggests, the focus here is on that most romantic of drinks, champagne. Whether it's a special occasion or not, any afternoon here is sure to be wonderful. Gloria Ferrer's stunning Spanish-style villa is set a

half mile from the highway at the base of gently rolling hills. After taking a tour of the caves and learning how fine champagne is created, you can purchase a full glass of sparkling wine in the spacious tasting room, where plenty of two-person marble-topped tables await beside a crackling fire. Or you can sit, sip, and smooch outside on the vast veranda, which faces acre upon acre of grapes.

10:30am–5:30pm every day; wines sold by the glass; www.gloriaferrer.com.

VIANSA WINERY AND ITALIAN MARKETPLACE
◐◐

25200 Hwy 121, Sonoma / 707/935-4700
Viansa, run by the established Sebastiani winery family, offers not only fine wine but also an extensive Italian market where you can purchase gourmet picnic supplies and plenty of edible mementos of your time spent in wine country. (The picnic area is reserved for people who purchase their picnic items from Viansa.) Fresh herbs and vegetables complement pâtés, salads, and other tasty Italian treats, all made right on the premises. Try one of the freshly baked focaccia sandwiches and a luscious dessert, followed by a smooth cappuccino. You can enjoy this small feast inside the casual, brightly lit market, but the attractive grounds outside also beckon. Numerous picnic tables are set beneath a grape trellis overlooking young grapevines and a 90-acre waterfowl preserve. There's also, of course, wine tasting (complimentary unless you wish to taste the special reserve wines).
10am–5pm every day; www.viansa.com

Romantic Lodgings

BELTANE RANCH
◐◐

11775 Sonoma Hwy, Glen Ellen / 707/996-6501
A working farm, vineyard, and down-home bed-and-breakfast are effectively combined at this wine-country destination, making it a truly countrified place to stay. A dusty driveway off the main road winds up to the yellow wood-frame farmhouse set in the midst of gentle hills and green pastures. The setting of this 1,600-acre ranch is the real attraction here—it is ideal for long, lazy afternoons and peaceful evenings. Although none of the five rooms in the century-old, modestly renovated main home are particularly sophisticated, they do offer unmistakable coziness and country-style comfort; the three upstairs rooms are the most desirable. On warm summer mornings, guests in the main home can sit on the wraparound deck and eat a hearty breakfast while surveying the front yard's lush garden. In chilly weather, breakfast is served in the country-style dining room, complete with a red brick fireplace. No matter where you sit, you won't leave hungry after

indulging in seasonal fruit dishes and hot entrées made with ingredients from the on-site garden or nearby farms. The newer Garden Cottage is more appealing (and more romantic) than the other rooms, thanks to its private separate location, tucked-away garden, colorful decor, and, best of all, a two-way butler pantry where breakfast is left for you in the morning. After the morning indulgence, pitch a game of horseshoes in the garden, or hike the trails that wind through the estate's vineyards and hills.
$$ *No credit cards; checks OK; www.beltaneranch.com.*

EL DORADO HOTEL
●●

405 1st St W, Sonoma / 707/996-3030 or 800/289-3031
What the El Dorado Hotel lacks in warmth and personality, it makes up for in privacy, comfort, and convenience. Located at the edge of Sonoma's town square, this hotel has 27 modestly proportioned rooms furnished with four-poster iron beds under pale peach bedspreads and TVs displayed on dressers; the floors are hardwood or terra-cotta-tiled and the walls are bare except for mirrors uniquely framed by branches. The rooms are not so much intentionally minimalist as simply lacking in decoration, which gives them a not-quite-intimate feel. French doors in most rooms open to small patios that overlook either the hotel's inner courtyard and its heated pool or the nearby town square. The rooms facing the town square provide great views but can be extremely noisy (the vocal rooster in the town square doesn't help, either). If you are light sleepers, we highly recommend a courtyard-view room and/or bringing along heavy-duty earplugs. A split of wine is included with your stay, and the hotel-level amenities, such as the pool and the courtyard, do provide some creature comforts; the courtyard in particular is a pleasant, sunny spot to enjoy the complimentary continental breakfast. Piatti Restaurant (707/996-2351), located in the hotel, is a chain restaurant known for its bustling atmosphere and fresh, well-prepared Italian cuisine. This location is no different from the others—except that it is incredibly convenient if you are guests at the hotel.
$$$ *AE, MC, V; checks OK; www.hoteleldorado.com.* &

FAIRMONT SONOMA MISSION INN & SPA
●●●

18140 Sonoma Hwy, Boyes Hot Springs / 707/938-9000 or 800/862-4945
With its serenely ethereal grounds and elegant pink stucco buildings, the Sonoma Mission Inn feels worlds away from the hustle and bustle of regular life—and that's exactly the point. Thanks to the dazzling array of European-style spa treatments and a state-of-the-art fitness facility, the only limit on your spa experience is your budget. The recently renovated spa offers everything from aerobics classes and Swedish massages to aromatherapy facials, seaweed wraps, and tarot card readings—all in perfectly groomed

surroundings. You'll also find exercise rooms, saunas, Jacuzzis, a salon, yoga and meditation classes, and two swimming pools, one of which is filled with artesian mineral water. The inn even recently reacquired its historic golf course, which had been sold during the Depression. Given all these options, you probably won't be spending a lot of time in your room—which is a good thing, since many of the guest accommodations are tasteful but standard upscale hotel fare. Bathed in shades of light peach and pink, each of the more than 230 rooms features plantation-style shutters, ceiling fans, and down comforters. Some units have wood-burning fireplaces and deluxe granite or marble bathrooms big enough for an all-afternoon kissing session. Especially pleasing are the Fairmont Heritage rooms in the historic building that underwent a $12 million renovation in 2004: the elegant French-country decor includes toile fabrics and custom-made furnishings; the rooms overlook the inn's swimming pool; and a favorite, Room No. 232, is located in a turret. The inn's two restaurants, Santé and the Big 3 Diner, both offer Californian fare. The elegant Santé is one of the most expensive restaurants in Sonoma, with a national reputation for its French-inspired seasonal cuisine; the less-expensive Big 3 Diner offers light pastas, pizzas, and grilled items, as well as hearty breakfasts.
$$$$ AE, DC, DIS, MC, V; checks OK; www.fairmont.com.

GAIGE HOUSE INN
●●●●
13540 Arnold Dr, Glen Ellen / 707/935-0237 or 800/935-0237
"Stunning" is the only word to describe the rooms inside this impressive Italianate Victorian. Skillfully blending the beauty and simplicity of Balinese and Southeast Asian decor with a varied collection of antiques and modern artwork, the innkeepers have transformed the Gaige House into one of the finest luxurious boutique inns in the Sonoma Valley. Guests are greeted by the concierge and escorted to their room to settle in, after which they can visit the fireplace-warmed parlor for an excellent array of appetizers and wine. The 15 guest rooms are located throughout the main house, the attached Garden Annex, and the separate Pool House. All are spacious retreats with private entrances. In the main house, the corner Gaige Suite is the grandest room, complete with its own expansive deck, a king-size carved mahogany bed, and an immense blue-tiled bathroom with an enticing whirlpool tub. A raised teak bed takes center stage in Room No. 10, which also includes a cozy adobe fireplace, a private deck overlooking the tranquil garden, and a steamy double shower and bubbling Jacuzzi tub. Our favorite accommodation is the Creekside Suite, located in the Pool House. Sophisticated Asian-inspired touches, beautiful orchids, natural-fiber rugs covering concrete floors, dimming lights, a gas fireplace, and a wall of windows looking onto your own creek-side patio are offerings too romantic to pass up. The carved glass sink in the bathroom is a work of art,

and the two-person Jacuzzi tub works wonders. Need we mention there's a two-person shower, too? Equally sleek and more private, if a bit less grand, is the Woodside Suite, which features a raised king-size bed with a striking headboard made of sea grass, a silver-toned Japanese soaking tub, and a small, private outdoor deck area enclosed by bamboo. After a day spent tasting wine, return to the inn to refresh yourselves with a dip in the pool or nearby Jacuzzi tub. Then sink into the garden furniture on the communal creek-side patio and steal a kiss or two. In the morning, start off with a brisk walk along country roads, then return to enjoy a two-course breakfast served in the elegant sun room. The creative chef whips up such delights as Creole eggs in a spicy tomato sauce, chocolate-chip pancakes with banana compote, and apple-Gruyère-ham crepes. With amenities like this and such splendid surroundings, one night here definitely won't be enough. Scheduled to open in fall 2004 are eight new spa suites overlooking the property's serene creek; they will be equipped with huge granite soaking tubs opening to private spa gardens, providing even more deluxe accommodation options for kissing couples.
$$$ *AE, DIS, MC, V; checks OK; www.gaige.com.*

GLENELLY INN
❤❤
5131 Warm Springs Rd, Glen Ellen / 707/996-6720
This 1916 inn is a legacy of Glen Ellen's heyday as an invigorating getaway for San Franciscans, who flocked here via train. The inn's setting is as enchanting as ever, nestled at the base of a steep hill and shaded by the gnarled branches of century-old oak and olive trees. A brick courtyard and soothing Jacuzzi tub are found in the lower rose garden, and a double hammock swings lazily in the breeze on the less formally landscaped upper terrace. Although the architecture hails from an era when standard rooms were smaller, the country decor, Norwegian down quilts, and claw-foot tubs in most of the eight rooms help make up for their smallish size. Wood-burning stoves in two of the rooms enhance the coziness. All rooms open onto either a large common veranda or a patio where chairs are waiting. A full breakfast, served fireside in the spacious upstairs common room, always includes freshly squeezed juice, baked goods warm from the oven, and a seasonal fruit dish. A tasty, filling main dish, such as a salsa jack soufflé or hash-brown decadence, varies from day to day. If the weather permits, enjoy breakfast on the oak-shaded patio out back.
$$$ *AE, DIS, MC, V; checks OK; www.glenelly.com.*

THE KENWOOD INN & SPA

✿✿✿

10400 Sonoma Hwy (Hwy 12), Kenwood / 707/833-1293 or 800/353-6966

You might think you've stumbled through a portal into old-world Tuscany when you arrive at this villa-style hillside destination, one of Sonoma's most acclaimed (and expensive) luxury destinations. Ivy-draped walls, blossoming rose gardens, and tall hedges and palm trees create the sense of a verdant oasis. Thick walls conceal the archway-lined courtyard, which harbors a central fountain, aqua-colored swimming pool, and inviting hot tub. Although it was built in the latter half of the 20th century, the property's centerpiece villa has an ancient patina. The recent multimillion-dollar expansion (which closed down the resort for a time) added several new buildings that continue the Italian style of architecture, and these and the property's original structures house the 30 opulent guest rooms. Decor and amenities vary from room to room, but throughout you'll find features such as wrought-iron chandeliers, plush feather beds with brocade headboards, wood-burning fireplaces, and rich fabrics in olive, cream, and rose. Some of the original rooms have small, ivy-framed stone balconies that face the lovely garden and pool (unfortunately, they also face nearby Highway 12). The Italian theme continues in the breakfast room, with its trompe l'oeil murals and tapestry-covered high-backed chairs. Here, an Italian-accented three-course gourmet breakfast is served at intimate two-person tables. Since you're splurging, you'll no doubt want to take advantage of the services offered at the Caudalie Spa (707/833-6326), which is associated with a world-renowned French spa known for pioneering the world's most exclusive *vinothérapie* treatments. These make use of the latest scientific discoveries involving the miraculous anti-aging qualities of grapevine and grape-seed extracts. (And you thought grapes just made a good drink!) Schedule an in-room "Togetherness Massage," complete with candlelight and champagne. Another result of the expansion is a new on-site restaurant that provides dining for guests only.

$$$$ *AE, MC, V; checks OK; www.kenwoodinn.com.*

MACARTHUR PLACE

✿✿✿◖

29 E MacArthur St, Sonoma / 707/938-2929 or 800/722-1866

This lush, magnificent property holds two stunning buildings: a circa 1860 Victorian manor house (reputed to be one of the oldest homes in Sonoma) and its adjacent barn, both of which have recently been marvelously restored. Add to these authentic surroundings a handful of charming new buildings, mature gardens, a small swimming pool, and a quiet, in-town setting, and you have a worthy romantic getaway. The 64 guest accommodations are scattered throughout the Manor House, cottage duplexes, and two single-suite cottages. Each room displays an individual style, though

Spa
Sparks

Relaxation is an art form in Northern California and, thanks to an array of fabulous spas that cater to couples, you'll find no shortage of places to enjoy a luxurious side-by-side massage with your sweetheart. San Francisco's finest urban refuge for couples is the **Nob Hill Spa at the Huntington Hotel** (1075 California St; 415/345-2888), where you can take in majestic views of the city skyline while you soak in the spa's indoor pool and Jacuzzi surrounded by floor-to-ceiling windows. Carefully arranged according to the ancient Chinese theories of feng shui, the spa's layout includes treatment rooms decorated with unique artwork, rich fabrics, lovely design details, and even fireplaces. In the spa room specially designed for couples, unwind together with pampering massages; afterward, retire to the intimate outdoor terrace for an alfresco spa lunch and more sparkling city vistas.

If you're craving a luxurious country getaway, retreat to the beautiful, sunny Carmel Valley and the **Bernardus Lodge Spa** (415 Carmel Valley Rd; 831/658-3560). Located on the exquisite, manicured grounds of the Bernardus Lodge, just steps away from its large turquoise outdoor pool lined with cabanas and lounge chairs, the spa offers a vast array of treatments, including ancient Hawaiian massage techniques. Before or after your spa treatment, you'll find further relaxation with a soak in the open-air warming pool (always 101°F) surrounded by delightful gardens and accessible to spa patrons only. In the Vineyard Room, devoted to couples' relaxation and enjoyment, you'll find dual oversize treatment tables, a shower built for two, and French doors leading outside to a private therapy bath and garden.

If you want a little bit of adventure along with your relaxation, set your compass north to Sonoma County and take the back roads to the tiny hamlet of Freestone, where you'll discover a whole new kind of serenity at the Japanese-style spa **Osmosis** (209 Bohemian Hwy; 707/823-8231). The specialty here is unique cedar enzyme baths, a deeply relaxing heat therapy you'll experience side by side in cozy redwood tubs; your visit also includes tea served overlooking the property's exquisite Japanese gardens.

For days of wine and roses in the heart of the California wine country, retreat to the oasis of **Fairmont Sonoma Mission Inn & Spa** (18140 Sonoma Hwy; 707/938-9000 or 800/862-4945), where the sight of the lush landscaping, beautifully tended grounds, and bubbling fountains will relax you before your treatment even begins. Inside the spa, you can soak for hours in pools surrounded by palms and filled with healing thermal mineral spring waters, step into a private whirlpool, or retreat to the couples' spa room for an afternoon of very relaxing togetherness.

upscale country decor, soothing solid color schemes, magnificent beds with designer floral duvets, and plenty of windows are common to all. Furniture ranges from antique pine to whitewashed woods, and signature bathroom features include taupe and white ceramic-tiled floors and walk-in showers. Guest rooms in the duplex cottages (four rooms to a two-story cottage, in most cases) are similar in size and layout but offer more privacy. The classic Manor House's selling points are many: unique room layouts, private patios off some rooms, enormous windows, and a sense of history not found in the more modern structures. We fell in love with the second-floor Burris Suite, a spacious room done in a soft dusty rose color. Two French doors lead to a balcony overlooking the gardens, classical botanical art adorns the walls, and an elegant four-poster bed resides next to a comfortable sitting area. You can also survey the garden from the window-side claw-foot tub in the bathroom. For couples seeking the utmost in luxury and privacy (and willing to pay the price), the top-of-the-line accommodations are the two recently completed premium cottage suites, which offer spacious bathrooms with hydrotherapy tubs, wood-burning fireplaces, wet bars, and high-tech amenities including flat-screen televisions and DVD/CD players with six-speaker surround sound. Natural light floods these spacious accommodations, highlighting the enticing king-size beds. Other nice touches are the cathedral ceilings and the romantic interior shutters that open to reveal the hydrotherapy tub to the rest of the suite and the fireplace. Saddles (707/933-3191), the property's upscale steakhouse restaurant, has high ceilings and rustic wood floors and offers an authentic Western-inspired ambience. On a warm evening, the terrace overlooking the gardens is a lovely place to dine (and kiss) alfresco. Saddles Martini Bar beckons with a "shaken-not-stirred" respite from the valley's ubiquitous wines. After enjoying the continental breakfast in the Saddles dining room, lounge by the pool that serves as the property's centerpiece, stroll along the grounds to smell the flowers, or rent a bicycle for a journey through nearby neighborhoods. When you return, try a massage at The Spa (707/933-3193), located adjacent to the pool.

$$$$ *AE, MC, V; checks OK; www.macarthurplace.com.*

RAMEKINS
❤❤

450 W Spain St, Sonoma / 707/933-0452
If cooking together sounds like the right romantic recipe, you'll delight in this unique bed-and-breakfast, which offers a variety of cooking classes geared to cooks of all skill levels. The large, unadorned Mediterranean-style building sits just a few blocks from Sonoma's town square. Inside, you'll find a culinary school downstairs and six delightful and luxurious guest rooms upstairs. Not surprisingly, the decor is food themed throughout the building and ranges from colorful modern prints of eggplants and

tomatoes to whimsical banisters sculpted and painted to resemble asparagus; there are also lovely English-country antiques and old-fashioned
cooking utensils and gadgets. Whipping up some romance is easy in one of
the spacious, sunny, yellow-painted guest rooms. Elegant English-country
furnishings, highlighted by beautiful wood or four-poster beds, pine chests,
and rich floral duvets, are complemented by modern bathrooms featuring
tiled walk-in showers and oversize ceramic sink bowls. Some rooms also
feature balconies and most come with either king- or queen-size beds. Make
sure you don't book the one room with two twin beds. A continental breakfast, including pastries made by Ramekins' official pastry chef, is served
at a quiet upstairs dining table. Downstairs, there's a flurry of activity as
apron-clad culinary students head from kitchen to kitchen with notebooks
in hand. Cooking topics range from kitchen survival to soups and stocks to
pastry preparation (call for a class catalog and more details).
$$$ *MC, V; checks OK; www.ramekins.com.*

THISTLE DEW INN
♥♥♥

171 W Spain St, Sonoma / 707/938-2909 or 800/382-7895
Just a block from Sonoma's busy town center, two turn-of-the-20th-century
homes comprise this restful retreat. In the main house, the common area
and dining room are appointed with Arts and Crafts–style antique furniture
mixed with contemporary effects; both are warmed by a wood-burning fire-
place. The five guest rooms, divided between the two homes, are filled with
more Arts and Crafts antiques and also have handmade Amish patchwork
quilts, queen-size beds, bright sponge-painted walls, and private bathrooms.
Set behind the main home and farther from the road, the rear house is where
real romance (or, at least, the rooms with the most romantic perks) can be
found. All four accommodations here boast private entrances; one has a gas
fireplace, another has a whirlpool tub for two, and the remaining two offer
both gas fireplaces and whirlpool tubs, for a warm, bubbling combination.
The most spacious option is Mimosa, which features charming decor of jade
green walls offset by forest green carpeting, a weathered brick mantel over
the fireplace, and a comfortable porch swing on a large deck overlooking
the rear garden. The sole room in the main home is a budget-friendly choice
but also comfortable, with rosy sponge-painted walls, a queen-size bed, and
simple oak furnishings. Mornings at the inn are a treat that might feature
banana-buckwheat pancakes, fruit-filled oven-baked Dutch babies, mush-
room-and-Brie omelets, or cinnamon-raisin French toast. After breakfast,
inspect the inn's greenhouse, where the innkeeper has collected hundreds
of different species of cactus. You can also borrow two of the inn's compli-
mentary bikes for a day of exploring Sonoma and its environs. Evenings at
Thistle Dew Inn bring hors d'oeuvres and pleasant conversation near the
warmth of the stone fireplace. If you are just passing through town, you'll

be pleased to hear that one-night stays are always possible here (most other wine-country accommodations have two-night minimums). $$$–$$$$ *AE, DIS, MC, V; checks OK; www.thistledew.com.* &

TROJAN HORSE INN
🖤🖤

19455 Sonoma Hwy (Hwy 12), Sonoma / 707/996-2430 or 800/899-1925
Weary wine tasters immediately feel welcome upon entering this pleasant turn-of-the-20th-century Victorian farmhouse. The spacious, sun-filled parlor holds a mixture of contemporary and antique country furnishings, and the glowing hearth creates warmth as you visit with the hospitable inn-keepers over freshly baked cookies or scones. Even though the house borders Highway 12, the surroundings are so clean, comfortable, and colorful that you'll soon forget the outside world entirely. The six guest rooms, all with private baths and contemporary and antique furnishings, vary in decor and mood. All received an update thanks to new owners who arrived in 2004; redecorated in a classical Victorian style and renamed for jazz legends, the rooms now feature all-new Frette duvet covers and new mattresses among other improvements. Three standouts include the charming Ellington Room, with a chandelier dangling from the ceiling and a woodstove in the corner; the inviting Veloso Room, with a king-size brass bed and decor in shades of soft green; and Sarah Vaughn's Room, romantically equipped with both a queen-size bed fronting a gas fireplace and a two-person jetted tub in the bathroom. In the morning, a full gourmet country breakfast ensures a hearty start to a day of wine tasting. Savory and sweet dishes rotate daily and may include mushroom and asparagus quiche, decadent chocolate pancakes, or oven-baked cream-cheese French toast. If the sun cooperates, you'll want to linger on the garden patio after indulging in evening hors d'oeuvres and local wines (Thurs–Sat). Last, but definitely not least, there's an outdoor Jacuzzi tub sheltered by an ancient bay tree in the backyard. $$$ *AE, DIS, MC, V; checks OK; www.trojanhorseinn.com.*

VICTORIAN GARDEN INN
🖤🍷

316 Napa St E, Sonoma / 707/996-5339 or 800/543-5339
The diminutive grounds enveloping the Victorian Garden Inn include lush bowers of roses, azaleas, and camellias encircling inviting little tables and chairs as well as flowering fruit trees bending low over white Victorian benches. These are the pleasurable sights in view as you traverse the trel-lised brick walkway that leads to the front door of this modest retreat, set in a peaceful Sonoma neighborhood only blocks from the town square. Much attention has been lavished on the garden, which, as the name implies, is the centerpiece here. We only wish as much attention had been lavished on the house, a lovely Victorian farmhouse in need of touch-ups and a fresh coat of

paint. Four comfortable guest rooms are available on the property; however, we recommend only the three detached units, since the room in the main house does not have its own bath. Top o' the Tower, housed in an old water tower, is the least expensive of the detached units. Although this room is quite small and equipped with only a shower, it is ultraprivate and has high ceilings and well-chosen pastel blue decor. The pretty Garden Room located on the lower level of the water-tower structure features a gas fireplace, a cut-lace duvet, wicker furnishings, and a claw-foot tub. Most spacious is the handsome, cabinlike Woodcutter's Cottage (adjacent to the water-tower building), with its high, open-beam ceiling, hunter-green interior, claw-foot tub, and wood-burning fireplace. A California-style continental breakfast, featuring locally grown fruit, granola, fresh cherry juice, and pastries, is set out in the main dining room every morning. Guests are welcome to take their breakfast back to their room or enjoy it on the patio next to the garden. On summer afternoons, a swim in the pool behind the house should cool you off, or you can simply retreat to your air-conditioned room. Sign up in advance and you can reserve up to an hour of private time in the garden hot tub, the perfect spot for a romantic evening soak.
$$$ *AE, DC, MC, V; checks OK; www.victoriangardeninn.com.*

Romantic Restaurants

DELLA SANTINA'S
❀❀

133 Napa St E, Sonoma / 707/935-0576
This little slice of Italy is tucked behind a stone facade not far from Sonoma's main square. Opera music fills the tiny front dining room, where 11 tables are packed in tight, each adorned with crisp white linens and a yellow rose. Whitewashed walls feature framed antique lace, while above the gas fireplace, beautiful portraits of the owner's children give the restaurant a homey feel. The family atmosphere is pervasive here: the owner greets locals with a kiss on the cheek. For couples who'd rather kiss one another, try requesting one of the four tables in the second dining area, hidden within a covered interior courtyard. Summertime dining on the large outdoor patio out back is another good choice, although tables are tight here, too. Straightforward and traditional Italian dishes, ranging from pesto tortellini to spit-roasted chicken garnished with fresh herbs, fill the menu. Prices are reasonable, and they become even more so if you order the Della Santina Cena, a special dinner for two featuring salad, pasta, and your choice of a rotisserie entrée. Desserts dazzle, especially the rum-soaked panna cotta.
$$ *AE, DIS, MC, V; local checks only; lunch, dinner every day; beer and wine; reservations recommended.*

THE GENERAL'S DAUGHTER
●●◖

400 W Spain St, Sonoma / 707/938-4004
A massive yellow Victorian building set in the heart of Sonoma Valley
houses this showstopping restaurant. Inside, large plants and half walls
help separate the three dining rooms. Soothing shades of yellow, cream,
or peach brighten up each dining space, while life-size paintings of farm
scenes and animals add a whimsical touch. After sunset, twinkling chandeliers provide a soft, soothing glow. In the warmer months, you can enjoy
your meal on the outdoor patio (which, unfortunately, faces the parking lot)
or at a more private table on the restaurant's wraparound porch. The eclectic
menu of small plates, sandwiches, and hearty entrées has an international
flair, from an appetizer of seared rare ahi tostadas with spiced avocado and
salsa fresca to entrées such as grilled pork chops with apple-mango chutney
and scalloped potatoes or spicy jambalaya with blackened prawns, andou-
ille sausage, and chicken. You'll find plenty of Sonoma County vintages on
the wine list. As with the menu itself, what's for dessert is anyone's guess,
but it's likely that you'll enjoy it; if the cheese blintzes with fresh blueberry
sauce are on the menu, they make a refreshingly unusual choice.
*$–$$ MC, V; no checks; lunch, dinner Tues–Sat, brunch Sun; full bar; reser-
vations recommended; www.thegeneralsdaughter.com.*

THE GIRL & THE FIG
●●

110 W Spain St (Sonoma Hotel), Sonoma / 707/938-3634
The motto of this well-loved wine country restaurant is "country food with
French passion," which seems like an appropriate destination for any couple's wine-country getaway. The dining room is painted a cheerful yellow
with wood paneling; alas the tables are packed in too tightly, but while this
might not permit much privacy, it will allow you to sneak a peek at your
neighbor's plate. What you see is likely to entice, especially if it's the signature fig salad with arugula, dried figs, pecans, chèvre, pancetta, and fig-port
vinaigrette. After this tasty starter, move on to the aromatic steamed mussels with Pernod, garlic, leeks, fresh herbs, and croutons, or sample a savory
pan-seared striped bass with roasted-shallot-and-chive vinaigrette and
mashed potatoes. Cheese lovers should splurge on the cheese menu, which
features local productions. Save room for the refreshing and delicious desserts, such as the unusual lavender crème brûlée or delicate chilled Meyer
lemon soufflé with whipped cream and fruit compote. The trend-setting
wine list offers an array of Rhône-style California wines. Though everything
is wonderful here, if you're seeking a truly intimate tête-à-tête, plan your

visit for the warmer months, when the lovely seasonal patio is open for alfresco dining (and kissing).

$$ AE, MC, V; checks OK; lunch, dinner every day; full bar; reservations recommended; www.thegirlandthefig.com.

MERITAGE
🌹🌹

522 Broadway, Sonoma / 707/938-9430

It seems only natural to discover this charming Mediterranean-inspired restaurant, which serves an appealing blend of southern French and northern Italian cuisines, in the sunny wine-country environs of Sonoma. In fact, it's this style of cooking rather than the famous French wine blend that gives the restaurant its name. However, the dining room's wrought-iron grapevine railing, distressed surfaces, and plentiful wood and copper accents are pure California wine country. Whether seated at a cozy booth inside or on the garden patio, diners are treated to a changing daily menu that accentuates the freshest local ingredients. A signature dish such as the crispy polenta with wild mushrooms and Gorgonzola sauce is sure to please, while those who prefer the classics might be more drawn in by the napoleon of escargots with champagne and wild thyme or the classic Caesar salad. Oysters have been called an aphrodisiac, so you might be enticed to order a few fresh and briny selections from the raw bar. Main courses include options such as thin spaghetti with sautéed chicken breast, baby spinach, and roasted tomatoes in a spicy garlic sauce or the clean flavors of fresh salmon poached over spinach with roasted potatoes and aromatic herb aioli. The takeout deli and marketplace are fabulous should you need gourmet treats to go, and breakfast and brunch feature classic eggs Benedict and omelets.

$$ AE, MC, V; no checks; breakfast Wed–Sun, lunch, dinner Wed–Mon, brunch Sat–Sun; beer and wine; reservations recommended.

SANTA ROSA AND THE RUSSIAN RIVER VALLEY

ROMANTIC HIGHLIGHTS

The most charming destination in northern Sonoma County is not necessarily the city of Santa Rosa itself, but the wooded towns and hamlets in its environs, such as Sebastopol. The **Russian River Valley,** also within easy driving distance, has many outstanding rural wineries. Fortunately for couples in need of a relaxing retreat, the many heart-warming accommodations here provide easy access to all the local attractions, and there are some wonderful restaurants as well.

Historically, **Santa Rosa** has been more a countrified suburb than a big city, but in recent years it has started to explode with growth and, unfortunately, sprawl. However, its abundance of affordable accommodations and its proximity to a wide range of attractions mean Santa Rosa can make a comfortable, if not peaceful, headquarters for exploring the area. If the timing is right, be sure to wander together through the wildly successful **Santa Rosa Downtown Market** (4th St from B St to D St; 707/524-2123; www.srdowntown market.com; 5pm–8:30pm Wed, late May–late Aug). It's not exactly intimate, but the anything-goes mood at this bazaar, filled with music, magicians, and a plethora of fresh-from-the-farm food, will certainly provide amusement—and plenty of goodies for your wine-country picnic basket.

If you're in the mood to really get away from it all, escape to the skies with an excursion in a hot-air balloon. Rides for parties of two are available from Santa Rosa's **Above the Wine Country Ballooning** (707/829-9850 or 888/238-6359; www.balloontours.com; from $195 per person, plus $250 fee for private flight for two); we think you'll agree this is a far more appealing option than traveling with a standard balloon-ride crowd of eight or more. From the comfort of your sturdy two-passenger basket dangling below the brightly colored balloon, you'll enjoy a bird's-eye view for thousands of acres, including redwoods, the Russian River, the Geyser Mountains, the Pacific Coast, and the San Francisco skyline. If weather conditions are good, the ride begins in Santa Rosa early in the morning, includes at least an hour in the air, and unwinds with a champagne picnic brunch at a local café.

West of Santa Rosa at the crossroads of Highway 116 and Highway 12 is the quiet town of **Sebastopol**, the gateway to the Russian River Valley. The hamlet's friendly and appealing downtown is filled with pleasant shops, new age bookstores, and restaurants. If you love to shop hand in hand for antiques, you'll be in heaven browsing through the dozens of **antique shops** in the area (the Sebastopol Chamber of Commerce has more information; for details see Access and Information).

Sebastopol is also home to **Flying Horse Carriage Company** (707/849-8989; www.flyinghorse.org; Apr–Oct, weather permitting; from $85 per person), purveyors of one of the finest romantic excursions in Sonoma wine country: an authentic horse-drawn carriage tour that includes wine tasting, cold drinks, and refreshments. Riding in the white Cinderella-style carriage drawn by powerful draft horses is unique enough but becomes even more delightful with stops at beautiful wineries (bring your own gourmet picnic and enjoy lunch on the grounds) and the chance to visit local wine caves. The ultimate experience has to be the full-moon ride on a warm summer night. With moonlight illuminating the vineyards and just your carriage on the quiet back roads, it's nothing short of magical (not to mention the perfect setting for a proposal).

From Sebastopol, **country roads** lined with apple orchards and vineyards head in all directions, perfect for scenic drives. Some of these roads lead to fine restaurants worth stopping for (with advance reservations). If you venture to the tiny adjacent town of Graton, don't miss the chance to dine at the **Underwood Bar and Bistro** (9113 Graton Rd; 707/823-7023), an elegant European-style bistro with delicious tapas, fresh oysters, specialty cocktails, and well-prepared French-inspired entrées. In the equally small nearby town of Forestville, the stately **Farmhouse Inn** (see Romantic Lodgings) set along River Road—a pretty route paralleling Highway 116—is a romantic and hidden-away place to enjoy dinner.

From Graton, you can travel the gorgeous, narrow, winding Graton Road to the Bohemian Highway, passing through the town of **Occidental** along the way. Don't be fooled by the looks of this humble, one-street burg—it's home to one of the region's most intimate retreats, the **Inn at Occidental** (see Romantic Lodgings). Should you be looking for some pampering, call ahead and book appointments at the famous spa in these parts, **Osmosis Enzyme Bath and Massage** (209 Bohemian Hwy, Freestone; 707/823-8231; www.osmosis .com). This is the only place in California that offers the unique cedar-enzyme "bath" for two, which includes tea served overlooking a beautiful Japanese tea garden.

At the northern edge of the Russian River Valley is the wooded town of **Guerneville**, set on the banks of the Russian River itself. (Many routes lead here, including Highway 116, the Bohemian Highway, and River Road, so it's easy to make a loop if you are planning a scenic driving trip.) While the summer crowds and assortment of cheap cabins and motels in Guerneville's shopworn downtown are not very romantic, it nonetheless boasts some restful haunts. One such haven is **Armstrong Woods State Reserve** (17000 Armstrong Woods Rd; 707/869-2015), a peaceful grove of spectacular ancient redwoods threaded with a variety of hiking trails. If a horseback ride in the shade sounds heavenly, you can saddle up at **Armstrong Woods Pack Station** (707/887-2939; www.redwoodhorses.com), which offers 1½-hour and half- and full-day horseback rides, along with gourmet lunches. If you don't mind joining flocks of young and old alike, go for a dip at one of the small swimming beaches on the Russian River itself, or paddle away together on a canoe trip. Be sure to toast to your romantic getaway at **Korbel Champagne Cellars** (see Romantic Wineries). You won't have this place to yourselves, but it's worth the trip to sip some of the delicious bubbly and enjoy the beautiful views of the vineyards and the Russian River.

Access and Information

Santa Rosa is north of San Francisco on Highway 101. Traffic on this thoroughfare is often slow and nearly comes to a standstill for most of rush hour.

From Highway 101, Guerneville is easily accessed by taking the Highway 116/River Road exit and following it west into town. Because the Russian River parallels Guerneville's main road (River Road), it won't take long to familiarize yourself with the area.

For more information, contact the **Santa Rosa Convention and Visitors Bureau** (9 4th St at Wilson; 800/404-7673; www.visitsantarosa.com; from Hwy 101 take 3rd St exit, turn right on Wilson). Other good sources of regional information include the **Sebastopol Chamber of Commerce & Visitor Center** (265 S Main St; 707/823-3032 or 877/828-4748; www.sebastopol.org). For more information about Guerneville and the Russian River, contact the **Russian River Chamber of Commerce & Visitors Center** (16209 1st St, Guerneville; 707/869-9000 or 877/644-9001; www.russianriver.com).

Romantic Wineries

KORBEL CHAMPAGNE CELLARS
❂❂❂

13250 River Rd, Guerneville / 707/824-7000
Set in an ivy-covered brick building nestled in a redwood forest with a view of the Russian River, the Korbel tasting room is one of the grandest in the Sonoma area: a spacious, elegant chamber, complete with a crystal chandelier. Before tasting, take a tour of the winery or the stunning gardens. The deli offers gourmet food items, and the colorful flowers and towering shade trees enhance the picnic area (although the grounds themselves suffer from proximity to a noisy nearby street). Toast your time in wine country over glasses of the delicious bubbly.
9am–5pm every day, 9am–4:30pm Oct-Apr; www.korbel.com.

MATANZAS CREEK WINERY
❂❂❂❂

6097 Bennett Valley Rd, Santa Rosa / 707/528-6464 or 800/590-6464
What's so special about Matanzas Creek Winery? How about 2 million lavender stems blanketing the front hills of the sprawling property? Often compared with the lavender hills found in Provence, their scent and sensual appearance are simply breathtaking. If you happen to visit in June or July (lavender harvest time), the fragrance in the air is nearly as intoxicating as the wines produced here. The main building and wine-making facility are set back behind the lavender fields and hidden by tall trees and shrubs. Daily tastings of the winery's latest triumphs are offered; purchase a bottle and stroll through the lavender fields arm in arm, or set up a picnic lunch at one of the two tables located at the back of the property in a serene wooded area. If you want to take more than memories back home with you, visit the

store, where you'll find a whole range of Matanzas Creek lavender products, including bath oils, bath salts, potpourri, sachets, and soaps.
10am–4:30pm every day; tasting fee $5, refunded with wine purchase; www.matanzascreek.com.

Romantic Lodgings

APPLEWOOD INN
●●●●
13555 Hwy 116, Guerneville / 707/869-9093 or 800/555-8509
Built in 1922, this Mission-style pink stucco inn once served as a private family estate. Today the European allure and historic elegance of the property, set 1 mile south of Guerneville, enchant guests in search of romantic accommodations. Winding footpaths lead past beautiful landscaping and a stone courtyard adorned with a lion's-head fountain to a large outdoor swimming pool set among stands of trees. Eight of the inn's 19 guest rooms are located in the spacious original building; they exude historic authenticity, with English-style antiques, dark wood accents, and brightly colored fabrics. Several rooms in this building have private balconies, and most offer lovely views of the landscaped grounds. However, nice as these rooms are, we can't wholeheartedly recommend them after having seen the seven rooms in the Piccola Casa, which are much more stylish, light, and contemporary. Here, eye-catching artwork hangs on pastel walls, and thick down comforters drape sensuous queen-size sleigh beds. All of these rooms have gas fireplaces, as well as Jacuzzi tubs or double-headed showers in spacious, modern bathrooms inlaid with gorgeous tile work. As an added pleasure, each ground-level room has a private patio and fountain. The Gate House, completed in 1999, offers three additional contemporary deluxe suites with bedside fireplaces, whirlpool baths, couples' showers, and private decks. In the morning, indulge in the vast array of hot breakfast entrées, such as sautéed apples, Brie omelets, and eggs Florentine, served with pastries and fresh fruit. With its rustic yet elegant dining room, the Applewood Restaurant is a delightful place to relax after spending the day playing at the riverfront or touring the Sonoma Valley. You can linger over a romantic candlelit dinner here and expect to find excellent, sophisticated cuisine that incorporates the freshest local ingredients along with organic bounty from the inn's own 2-acre garden and fruit orchard.
$$$–$$$$ AE, MC, V; no checks; www.applewoodinn.com. &

AVALON LUXURY BED AND BREAKFAST
✪✪✪

11910 Graton Rd, Sebastopol / 707/824-0880 or 877/3AVALON
The road to this charming Tudor-style bed-and-breakfast, opened in 2001, passes through sunlit meadows and groves of trees, but you might be convinced that it actually travels back in time: with its magical themes and deeply forested, mist-shrouded setting, this property seems to emerge from a romantic legend. Fortunately, there are plenty of luxuries to keep your feet on the ground here. All three suites feature separate entrances, colorful and whimsical decor, gas fireplaces with thermostats, king-size beds, fine linens, large private baths, and local handmade soaps. The two suites on the lower level of the main home both set the stage for a few magical kisses. Our favorite is the Enchanted Forest Suite, which features decor in champagne and chocolate hues, with elegant wall sconces and tasteful wrought-iron accents. You can cozy up in the plush chairs set before the fireplace or enjoy the quiet with a nap on the enticing bed piled high with pillows and cushions and swathed in sumptuous linens; the spacious, tumbled-marble bathroom has double stone basin sinks, stacks of fluffy towels, and an expansive glassed-in shower. The adjacent Magician's Suite is done in a rich blue color scheme and features a tranquil forest view, sleek three-sided fireplace, spacious steam-room shower, and bright-blue-glass vessel sinks. Well-lit steps and pathways lead to each suite's private entrance, so you may come and go as you wish. (These paths also make it easy to find your way to the inn's sparkling clean outdoor hot tub, nestled beneath the soaring trees.) As charming as these suites are, the splendid Guenevere's Tower is even more romantic. Set adjacent to the main home, this upper-level suite is nothing short of a kissing refuge, with a spacious sitting area, antique claw-foot soaking tub, and two Romeo and Juliet–style balconies (one for each lover, of course). Delicious, freshly baked cookies and tea welcome you upon arrival, and all sorts of restaurant and wine-touring tips can be gleaned from the helpful owners, a husband-wife team who live on the premises with their young son (as you may guess from the sight of the kiddie play structure on the grounds). The wonderfully peaceful atmosphere is especially gratifying in the mornings, when sunlight streams through the leafy foliage. This is the time to stroll along the pretty garden paths and listen to the babbling creek before breakfast, a beautifully prepared gourmet indulgence.
$$$$ *AE, DC, MC, V; checks OK; www.avalonluxuryinn.com.*

FARMHOUSE INN
✪✪✪✦

7871 River Rd, Forestville / 707/887-3300 or 800/464-6642
This luxurious and newly remodeled Sonoma Valley escape, set on a busy but scenic wine-country road, has a lovely, century-old farmhouse as its centerpiece. The beautiful grounds include a glistening outdoor pool, a nearby

pool-room spa where massages and facials are available, a croquet course, and English gardens. The eight accommodations are found in a single-story building opposite the house and parking lot, and while the structure appears modest and unobtrusive from the outside, each of the rooms features an upscale interior with impressive kissing potential. Open the door and you'll discover an array of features designed to encourage intimacy, including wood-burning fireplaces, spacious two-person Jacuzzis, gorgeous in-room saunas, and bathrooms with European "rain" showerheads and thick robes. Down comforters and fine linens adorn the king- and queen-size feather beds. Each suite is individually decorated, with plush carpet, rich brocade fabrics, upholstered settees, and tasteful color schemes that range from pomegranate and tangerine in Room No. 3 to elegant gold, ivory, and taupe in Room No. 8. Every convenience, including CD players, TVs, and air conditioning, has been seen to. The only potential drawback: the parking lot is just outside your window, so there's no view and the curtains will remain closed for privacy; fortunately, with such a fine-feathered love nest, you probably won't mind. Request a room at the back of the property to put some distance between yourselves and the busy road. Guests gather in the morning for fruit, cereal, and hot dishes such as huevos rancheros or eggs Florentine in the conservatory-style dining room or outdoors on the terrace. Just to make sure all needs are taken care of, the property also has a fantastic European country-style restaurant, with formal dining room and outdoor sundeck, which is also open to the public for dinner Thursday through Sunday.

$$$–$$$$ *AE, MC, V; checks OK; www.farmhouseinn.com.* ♿

THE GABLES

✿✿✿

4257 Petaluma Hill Rd, Santa Rosa / 707/585-7777 or 800/GABLES-N

Because 3½ acres of picturesque farmland surround this gabled Victorian Gothic Revival home, we were tempted to call it a country getaway; unfortunately, the traffic zooming along on the nearby highway convinced us otherwise. However, once you step inside this lovely inn, you will be won over by the beauty of the main parlor and by the aroma of the freshly baked treats that come with the afternoon tea. The Gables offers seven remarkable rooms to choose from, plus a cozy cottage next door. The Parlor Suite, located on the main floor, is the largest and most elegant accommodation. Decorated in hunter green and burgundy, it is equipped with a king-size bed, down comforter, and Italian marble fireplace. The other guest rooms are reached via a curving mahogany staircase. The house's exterior features 15 gables that crown keyhole-shaped windows, which are incorporated into each room's decor. Floral wallpapers, richly colored linens, attractive antiques, and private bathrooms accompany every room, and three also have wood-burning fireplaces to warm your toes on cold nights. The most enticing (and most private) accommodation of all is the self-sufficient cottage. You'll find a loft bedroom with a feather bed and down comforter, a double whirlpool tub, and a full kitchen for your convenience. Knotty pine walls, a Franklin stove, and attractive handcrafted wood furniture are endearing touches. After a day of wine tasting, return to the cottage, snuggle up in your plush bathrobes, and watch a classic romantic movie (provided in-room) for some kissing inspiration. To lure you out of your snug bed in the morning, a gourmet country breakfast is served in the formal dining room. The meal includes fresh fruit, home-baked breads with homemade jam, and an ever-changing hot entrée, such as French toast with caramelized bananas. $$$ *AE, DIS, DC, MC, V; checks OK; www.thegablesinn.com.*

THE INN AT OCCIDENTAL
◐◐◐◐
3657 Church St, Occidental / 707/874-1047 or 800/522-6324
A visit to this perfectly luxurious getaway, full of unusual antique collections, feels a little like stepping into a piece of imaginative artwork. Set high on a redwood-covered hillside overlooking the small historic town of Occidental, the property's main home is a beautifully restored gabled Victorian brimming with charm. Oriental carpets cover the hardwood floors, and tasteful antiques fill common areas where guests can lounge in overstuffed sofas and enjoy the warmth of a crackling fire in the brick hearth. Outside, the flower-laden veranda, furnished with comfortably cushioned white wicker furniture, is a perfect place to sip wine. No detail has been overlooked by the highly professional innkeepers, and even the smallest of the inn's 16 guest rooms is convincingly elegant. Gorgeous, fresh color schemes and striking, well-chosen artwork fill each room, many of which feature creative themes and unique antique collections, from cut glass to Tiffany silver and even antique marbles that set the imagination alight. Fluffy down comforters cover sumptuous feather beds, and rich chocolates await on the bedside tables. Though all of the rooms in the main house have their own extraspecial touches, we do have a few favorites: the Cut Glass Room is just right for romance, with sliding French doors opening onto a private patio, garden, and full-size hot tub (alas, we're not the only ones who find this room terribly romantic, so book it well in advance). A mahogany four-poster canopy queen-size bed, set in front of a brick fireplace, distinguishes the Tiffany Room, which offers the most privacy (no neighboring rooms on either side). Another standout is the Marble Suite, which delights with the aforementioned antique marble collection, not to mention its king-size bed, fireplace, spa tub for two, and sunny yellow walls. An additional building behind the main home harbors eight more recently added—and highly romantic—rooms, all of which feature unique and charming decor, private entrances, private decks or shared balconies, fireplaces, and spa tubs with the romantic addition of dimmer lights. The spacious bathrooms all

have glassed-in showers and double sinks. Each room has its own personality: among our favorites is the Safari Room, with a king-size bed veiled with yards of translucent mosquito netting, antique leather traveling cases stacked to form end tables, and a giraffe peering out from the floor-to-ceiling wall mural. Awaken in the morning to the enticing aromas of freshly baked pastries, orange-thyme pancakes, homemade granola, and other gourmet delights served family-style in the wine cellar. When the weather is warm, you can enjoy this repast outside on the attached patio. With such beautiful accommodations and such a lovely setting, you and your beloved might just forget about touring the wine country altogether and decide to stay put.
$$$$ *AE, DIS, MC, V; checks OK; www.innatoccidental.com.*

VINTNERS INN
◆◆

4350 Barnes Rd, Santa Rosa / 707/575-7350 or 800/421-2584
On the drive to Vintners Inn, which is surrounded by well-groomed rows of grapevines, you'll feel as though you've passed through a magic portal into southern France. The hotel itself seems more like a vintner's private estate than a hotel—even though the freeway is in sight. A fountain splashes in the central plaza, and brick pathways lead to the Mediterranean-style, sand-colored buildings with red tile roofs. The 44 spacious, uncluttered guest rooms are appointed with contemporary and antique-reproduction pine furnishings. French doors open to brick patios or iron grillwork balconies that overlook either 50 acres of surrounding vineyards or the inner courtyard's fountain. Upper-story rooms have high, peaked ceilings, and all of the rooms feature oversize oval tubs in their standard bathrooms. Sip a mellow cabernet by the wood-burning fireplace if you are in a fireplace suite. In the common-area library, overstuffed chairs provide comfy fireside snuggling; a huge Jacuzzi spa is also available for all guests' use, but it is set so close to the road that the traffic noise can be distracting. A deluxe continental breakfast is served at tables for two in the reception building. You can enjoy home-baked breads, cereals, yogurt, fruit, and even waffles made to order in the bright sun room overlooking the lawns or on the outdoor terrace. As for dinner, you won't have to venture far to find excellent food—the highly acclaimed restaurant John Ash & Co. (see Romantic Restaurants) is on the property.
$$$$ *AE, DC, MC, V; checks OK; www.vintnersinn.com.*

Romantic Restaurants

JOHN ASH & CO.
● ● ●

4330 Barnes Rd (Vintners Inn), Santa Rosa / 707/527-7687

You won't find a much better view of the vineyards than the one you'll enjoy while sitting in this restaurant located at the Vintners Inn (see Romantic Lodgings). Clusters of candlelit, linen-covered tables overlook the panoramic country scene through floor-to-ceiling windows; tables on the outdoor brick patio offer the same magnificent view. In the evening, an inviting fire casts a warm glow in the restaurant, which is an ideal showcase for Sonoma Valley foods and wines. The menu changes seasonally but always offers an enticing California-style hybrid of French, Italian, and Asian cuisines. Start the meal on a light note with fresh English pea soup with tarragon and mint, or indulge together in a plate of crispy fried calamari with Thai dipping sauce. Entrées such as seafood risotto with mussels, spicy scallops, and slow-roasted roma tomatoes or grapevine-smoked roasted pork chop with sweet potato puree, poached red pear, and cranberry-tangerine salsa are as colorful and creative as they are delicious. For dessert, chocolate lovers shouldn't miss the warm, flourless chocolate cake with a gooey chocolate-truffle center, topped with a unique combination of vanilla syrup, mint oil, and crème anglaise. This restaurant is always busy (make reservations early!) and be forewarned that decibel levels can rise accordingly. Service is prompt, friendly, and professional—and, of course, you'll find all your favorite Napa and Sonoma wines on the reasonably priced and expansive wine list.

$$$ *AE, MC, V; local checks only; lunch, dinner every day, brunch Sun; full bar; reservations recommended; www.vintnersinn.com.*

STELLA'S CAFE
● ● ◖

4550 Gravenstein Hwy N, Sebastopol / 707/823-6637

You'll find this little gourmet gem just before Forestville, adjacent to Mom's Apple Pie. Though Stella's Cafe, a rural favorite that opened in 1999, is a far cry from the grand, pretentious restaurants so prevalent in other parts of the wine country, the excellent food here is as good, if not better, than what you'll find in such acclaimed places. The friendly, casual restaurant seats 50 and includes a bar space; while it may not offer soft candlelight and red roses, it does offer an intimate country dining experience and the chance to dig into something satisfying. The owner trained at renowned culinary institutions, and plenty of creative and international touches enhance the comfort food–style cooking. The ever-changing menu ranges from classics such as old-fashioned rib-eye steak and pan-roasted chicken with Dijon and truffled mashed potatoes to spicier fare, such as coconut lentil soup or

spicy grilled prawns with red jalapeño mango puree and pineapple cous-cous salad; an array of vegetarian dishes also tempt. Finish with the divine strawberry shortcake. Scoring a reservation can be difficult, and you'll soon know why locals fill the place night after night. Excellent wines, many from nearby vineyards, make it tempting to share a whole bottle (you can always bring what's left back to your room).
$$ *MC, V; checks OK; lunch Mon, Wed–Sat, dinner Wed–Mon; beer and wine; reservations recommended.* &

SYRAH
◐◐◖

205 5th St, Santa Rosa / 707/568-4002
The best time to dine at this casual restaurant, housed in a historic building in downtown Santa Rosa, is in warm weather, when you can take advantage of the patio. The interior, though airy and charming, is not exactly quiet or intimate, with its towering wood-beam ceilings, flagstone floors, and exposed kitchen complete with lots of hanging copper pots and cookware. The French-inspired American fare on the dinner menu is divided into smaller plates and larger plates, and both present some enticing options for food lovers. The lighter options might include steamed mussels with *pommes frites* and saffron cream, shallots, and garlic or decadent seared Sonoma foie gras and black beluga lentils with smoky bacon. As for the full meals, the lamb chops have a pomegranate glaze and a side dish of goat cheese and eggplant risotto, while the duck breast is served with pear reduction sauce and baby bok choy. Also, four- or seven-course "at-the-chef's-whim" tasting menus can be paired with wine. For dessert, order the pudding in three creamy layers of chocolate, caramel, and coffee, and ask for two spoons.
$$$ *DIS, MC, V; no checks; lunch, dinner Tues–Sat; beer and wine; reservations recommended; www.syrahbistro.com.*

WILLI'S WINE BAR
◐◐

4104 Old Redwood Hwy, Santa Rosa / 707/526-3096
Come to this popular restaurant and wine bar if you're interested in an adventurous sort of mealtime encounter: rather than your typical selec-tion of appetizers and entrées, this menu pairs more than 30 international "small plates"—call them tapas, mezes, or hors d'oeuvres, if you like—with an extensive wine selection, so you can sample a dizzying array of food-and-wine combinations. The low-slung, weathered gray building is unspec-tacular from the outside, and the tables are packed in tightly inside, but the food is so good it outweighs the not-particularly-romantic ambience. You'll find slightly more privacy (but not much less noise) if you can score the table set into a nook at the back of the 14-seat wine bar. The patio offers

additional seating, but it's not your typical fancy wine-country affair: the views are of lawn and highway, and it's heated with plastic siding so it stays warm year-round. The owners of the restaurant hail from the sophisticated world of San Francisco restaurants, and it shows in the vast number of intriguing options: you can try Hog Island oysters on the half shell with fresh coriander mignonette, Dungeness crab "tacos," mac 'n' cheese laced with caramelized cauliflower and black truffle fonduta, Sonoma rabbit rillettes with walnut crostini, braised beef short ribs with Indian spices on butternut-squash orzo pasta, or duck barbecue on white cheddar polenta. Finish with a warm chocolate hazelnut cake with spiced hazelnuts and tiramisu-flavored ice cream, and you'll be ready to adjourn to more private quarters. Reservations are accepted up to two months in advance.
$-$$ *AE, DIS, MC, V; no checks; lunch, dinner Wed–Mon; beer and wine; reservations recommended; www.williswinebar.net.*

ZAZU
●●◖

3535 Guerneville Rd, Santa Rosa / 707/523-4814
Only a modest sign marks this red roadhouse, formerly the site of the well-loved Willowside Café. Yet plenty of people have managed to discover this much-talked-about little treasure, and finding it is half the fun. Polished copper tabletops, hardwood floors, and an assortment of ornately framed mirrors and soft-toned lights create a cosmopolitan atmosphere that is unexpected in this rural setting. The menu is a blend of hearty American comfort food and Italian classics, all with that fresh, seasonal spin so common to restaurants in the wine country. There are Asian influences, too. You might start by sharing a crisp poppyseed-crusted soft-shell crab with ruby grapefruit, avocado, and poppyseed dressing. For the main event, try a rich and moist duck flavored with star anise and served with exotic sides, including apricot sambal, crispy rice cake, and bok choy. If you're in the mood for a hearty classic, try the juicy, naturally raised flatiron steak with Point Reyes blue-cheese ravioli and roasted garlic or the legendary slow-roasted balsamic pork shoulder with caramelized onions and mashed potatoes. It's hard to resist the retro-inspired dessert of homemade "nutter-butter" cookies with Scharffenberger chocolate fondue. Wines focus on varietals made within a 50-mile radius, including lots of affordable options.
$$$ *MC, V; local checks only; dinner Wed–Sun; beer and wine; reservations recommended.*

HEALDSBURG AND GEYSERVILLE

ROMANTIC HIGHLIGHTS

The romantic attractions of Healdsburg are twofold: first, there's the charming and sophisticated town itself; second, the scores of wineries nearby. Many of these are found in the Russian River Valley, a vast bucolic region to the west of town that is dotted with quiet, scenic, off-the-beaten-path wineries that are a pleasure to discover together. North of Healdsburg is the tiny, modest hamlet of **Geyserville,** which is surrounded by some glitzy and world-renowned wineries. Nature-loving couples should keep in mind that all kinds of outdoor adventure and hiking in Guerneville is just a scenic wine-country drive away (see the Santa Rosa and the Russian River Valley chapter).

You might be surprised to discover that **Healdsburg** is more charming and sophisticated than some of its better-known southern neighbors. This is partly because, unlike the wine towns of the Napa Valley, most of which are set directly on a busy thoroughfare, Healdsburg is more in the country-side. Its allure, though certainly slanted toward tourists, seems completely unforced, and the upscale shops and restaurants in the area are all in the best of taste. In fact, once upon a time, this town entirely lacked preten-tiousness; that's not quite true anymore, especially now that star New York chefs are drawn here specifically to open new restaurants, and there's an elegant boutique hotel set directly on the town's once-rustic square. But somehow all the attention has not diminished Healdsburg's charm, instead only adding to its appeal.

Shopping is not necessarily a romantic activity, and we generally don't recommend it: it involves simply too many distractions from each other. However, more than any other wine-country plaza, Healdsburg's trans-forms browsing into a charming pursuit that can be considered romantic. The plaza's periphery is packed with upscale galleries and shops that will interest you both with their eclectic selections of food, drink, home furnish-ings, jewelry, and artwork. For one-of-a-kind artistic mementos of your trip, head to **Art and All That Jazz** (119A Plaza St; 707/433-7900; www.artand allthatjazz.com), which has a nice selection of jewelry, art glass, paintings, and ceramics.

You'll understand that a store can be romantic the moment you open the old-fashioned screen door of the **Jimtown Store** (6706 Hwy 128 at Alexander Valley Rd; 707/433-1212; www.jimtown.com; from Healdsburg Plaza go north on Healdsburg Ave past Simi Winery, turn right on Alexander Valley Rd, continue 3.7 miles). Not only is this adorable, picture-perfect country store the ideal place to stock up on wine-country goodies (such as their famous olive spread), but it's also the best spot in this completely rural area to stop for lunch: after ordering an espresso drink and gourmet sandwich from the deli, you can adjourn to the picnic tables on the funky, supercasual outdoor patio. You'll find yourselves spending longer than planned as you delight in the store's quirky selection of retro gifts. The adjoining barn is filled with affordable antiques.

For a truly romantic means of exploring the wine country, rent a tandem bicycle and pedal away under your own combined power. **The Healdsburg Spoke Folk Cyclery** (249 Center St at Mill St; 707/433-7171) rents tandems and touring bikes and provides maps to great riding trails as well as the best winery routes (and the ones that require the least effort). If you visit in summer, be sure to ride early in the morning or late in the evening, or your ride will be more about heat exhaustion than wine tasting and romance.

Hot-air ballooning is a popular activity in the wine country, and each of these lofty rides offers something unique. If you choose to rise with the sun in Healdsburg and embark on this daring experience with **Aerostat Adventures** (707/433-3777 or 800/579-0183; www.aerostat-adventures.com; from $195 per person), the reward is an unparalleled view of the Russian River canyon. You can book for a party of two or, less romantically, make the excursion with as many as eight other people. The only catch is that you must embark early to ensure the best weather conditions. However, if the thrilling ride across Russian River, Dry Creek, and Alexander Valley doesn't wake you up, the aromas of the sparkling-wine breakfast with made-to-order omelets, fresh fruits, breads, orange juice, coffee, tea, and plenty of bubbly served at a local café afterward will get you going. You'll even receive one digital photo of your balloon ride over the vineyards and another digital photo of your departure from the ground, which are forwarded via e-mail upon your return.

Access and Information

The town of Healdsburg is just east of Highway 101, while the majority of its wineries are in the Russian River Valley to the west. Other wineries are north of Healdsburg, in Geyserville. All of the area wineries are shown on a helpful map available from the **Russian River Wine Road** (707/433-4335 or 800/723-6336; www.wineroad.com); it's a good idea to request one before your trip.

You can also find the map at the **Healdsburg Chamber of Commerce & Visitors Bureau** (217 Healdsburg Ave; 707/433-6935 or 800/648-9922; www.healdsburg.org), along with plenty of additional information on local lodgings, restaurants, and activities. Their Web site is an excellent source of area information.

Romantic Wineries

A. RAFANELLI WINERY
⬢⬢⬢

4685 W Dry Creek Rd, Healdsburg / 707/433-1385
Tours and tasting are available by appointment only at this family winery set deep in the countryside, but the experience is worth the effort, if only to experience a refreshing departure from the touristy approach of so many of California's wineries. Although there is no picnic area, you'll enjoy sipping wine in the wood-barn tasting room or wandering around the grounds, which are hemmed by lovely grape arbors. The views of Dry Creek Valley are stunning, and it's likely you'll get to meet members of the Rafanelli family; they've been growing grapes and making wine here for generations. It's no small treat to taste the zinfandel, cabernet sauvignon, and merlot, either (the top-quality wines are not available in retail outlets and can be purchased only at the winery).
By appointment only; www.arafanelliwinery.com.

DRY CREEK VINEYARD
⬢⬢⬢

3770 Lambert Bridge Rd, Healdsburg / 707/433-1000 or 800/864-9463
You'll have to make a small detour off West Dry Creek Road (where most of the other wineries we recommend are located) to get here, situated as it is on a flatland surrounded by vineyards and sloping hills deep within the countryside. But, believe us, the trip is worth it. Stained-glass windows adorn ivy-covered stone barns that serve as tasting rooms. Once you've selected your wine, head outdoors to the picnic tables set beneath shade trees on a manicured lawn surrounded by flower gardens.
10:30am–4:30pm every day; www.drycreekvineyard.com.

EVERETT RIDGE VINEYARDS & WINERY
⬢⬢⬢

435 W Dry Creek Rd, Healdsburg / 707/433-1637
Follow a winding farm road and a long gravel drive to get to this long-established Sonoma winery, where two picnic tables sit next to an old red barn overlooking lush vineyards and rolling golden hills. Roaming chickens and weathered antique farm equipment enhance the rural setting. The winery, which uses sustainable farming methods to grow certified organic grapes, produces small lots of award-winning wines. Depending on what's on offer, you might be able to taste anything from sauvignon blanc and chardonnay to zinfandel, syrah, pinot noir, and port.
11am–4:30pm every day; www.everettridge.com.

FERRARI-CARANO WINERY
❍❍❍

8761 Dry Creek Rd, Healdsburg / 707/433-6700 or 800/831-0381
No trip to the area would be complete without a stop at this popular winery, which oozes classic California wine country. Formal flower gardens with perfectly trimmed shrubs line the path to the Italianate mansion, where a lovely gift shop and tasting room await. Unfortunately, because this is one of the most upscale (and also one of the most crowded) wineries in Sonoma Valley, there is no picnic area. However, you can stop and smell the roses while strolling along the brick walkways that wind through the gardens. *10am–5pm every day; www.ferraricarano.com.*

HOP KILN WINERY
❍❍❍❍

6050 Westside Rd, Healdsburg / 707/433-6491
At this memorable winery, you'll find one of the most romantic picnic spots in all of Sonoma County. Gravel pathways lead to sun-soaked picnic tables set next to a country pond surrounded by vineyards. More tables are to be found in the cozy, shaded garden. Wine tasting takes place in the impressive stone building—a historic landmark—that was once a hop kiln and now doubles as a small art gallery. *10am–5pm every day; www.hopkilnwinery.com.*

LAMBERT BRIDGE WINERY
❍❍

4085 W Dry Creek Rd, Healdsburg / 707/431-9600 or 800/975-0555
A roaring fire in the massive stone fireplace warms the large, barnlike building that houses the Lambert Bridge tasting room, where rows of barrels line one wall. The mood is casual here, and the staff is delightfully unpretentious. A gazebo and eight picnic tables are set in a lovely fenced garden; here you can snack on gourmet cheese and salami from the tasting-room shop or, better yet, bring your own goodies and unwind over a leisurely lunch and a glass of wine. *10:30am–4:30pm every day; www.lambertbridge.com.*

ROCHIOLI VINEYARDS & WINERY
❍❍❍

6192 Westside Rd, Healdsburg / 707/433-2305
This is yet another Healdsburg-area winery with an intoxicating picnic setting. Spend a lovely afternoon lingering at a table on the shaded patio with ambrosial views of lush, mature vineyards—some of the oldest in the Sonoma area—with a backdrop of undulating mountains. Continuously rotating art shows adorn the tasting room, where you'll find the real stars of

the show: the award-winning Russian River Valley wines include sauvignon blanc, chardonnay, and pinot noir.
11am–4pm every day.

Romantic Lodgings

BELLE DE JOUR INN
❀❀❀❀

16276 Healdsburg Ave, Healdsburg / 707/431-9777
The four cottages and the separate Carriage House Suite at the fabulous Belle de Jour Inn are all equally irresistible, but there are just enough differences to make choosing one difficult. The four cottages stand out against the property's gentle green hills, tall eucalyptus and olive trees, and bright flowers. Although they are connected, each one is a private hideaway offering hardwood floors and modern furnishings mixed with plenty of country charm. Romantic bonuses include private entrances and sumptuous linens and robes. With the exception of the Morning Hill Room, with its two-person shower/steam unit, all have whirlpool tubs. Of the cottages, our favorite is the Terrace Room, which features a high vaulted ceiling, private patio, wood-burning stove, and whirlpool tub with a stunning view of the surrounding vineyards and lush greenery. Running a close second is the Caretaker's Suite, a large yet cozy room with a king-size canopy bed. The pièce de résistance, however, is the inn's newest suite, in the second story of the Carriage House. Its interior is decorated in creamy whites and highlighted by redwood salvaged from an old barn. Enhancing the wonderful space are luscious crimson- and gold-toned linens, a four-poster king-size bed, a fireplace, a two-person whirlpool tub decorated with green tile, and a large glass shower. Privacy is guaranteed, thanks to its out-of-the-way location, and the sunrise views are exceptional. Breakfast at Belle de Jour is a cornucopia of ever-changing daily delights, including fresh fruit and yogurt, Parmesan-baked eggs, cranberry scones, and fresh muffins. The innkeeper will also whip up your favorite coffee drink, be it a full-strength espresso or a double latte. This morning feast is enjoyed in the breakfast room of the main house. Belle de Jour Inn also offers a unique opportunity: touring the wineries in grand style from the back of the innkeeper's 1925 Star Touring Car. Personally chauffeured tours are available April through October for guests (reservations required; 3-hour minimum). You're certain to turn heads kissing in the backseat of this beauty.
$$$ *AE, MC, V; no checks; www.belledejourinn.com.*

CALDERWOOD INN
♥♥€

25 W Grant St, Healdsburg / 707/431-1110 or 800/600-5444
Nestled in a quiet residential neighborhood and secluded behind old-growth cypress and spruce trees, this Queen Anne Victorian inn offers relaxed refinement in a beautiful setting. Sip a refreshing glass of lemonade with your honey as you unwind on the front-porch swing, or enjoy the cool shade by the koi pond. Savor the splendor of the parlor, complete with period furnishings, elegant fireplace, and baby grand piano. Wine and cheese are served here every afternoon, complemented by the sounds of a player piano that's wired to stereo speakers. Custom-designed Bradbury & Bradbury silk-screened wall and ceiling papers enhance the Victorian mood throughout the home, including the six guest rooms. Cozy alcoves and sloping ceilings, attractive linens and plush robes, and period antiques highlight each room; most offer claw-foot tubs in their private baths (one room has a detached bath), and one room features a Jacuzzi tub. An opulent full breakfast is served in the formal dining room each morning. The tasty special of the day might be eggs Benedict or croissants stuffed with mascarpone cheese; accompaniments include home-baked breads, seasonal fruits, and breakfast meats.
$$$ MC, V; checks OK; www.calderwoodinn.com.

CAMELLIA INN
♥♥€

211 North St, Healdsburg / 707/433-8182 or 800/727-8182
The Camellia Inn combines Victorian elegance with modern amenities, including a refreshing swimming pool in the backyard. The two parlors of this 1869 Italianate Victorian home are trimmed with intricate, leaf-motif plasterwork and furnished with Oriental carpets, floral-patterned sofas, eclectic antiques, tapestry-covered chairs, and marble fireplaces. These parlors are lovely, if visually busy, places in which to enjoy complimentary afternoon wine and hors d'oeuvres. The inn's nine individually decorated guest rooms will appeal to almost any bed-and-breakfast connoisseur. All rooms have private baths (one is down the hall but still private), and four feature Jacuzzi tubs. Beautiful antiques and family heirlooms are mixed with modern furnishings, and you'll also find pretty linens, comfy sitting areas, and gas-log fireplaces. Our favorite rooms are Royalty, with its Scottish canopy bed, and Tiffany, which sports Bradbury & Bradbury wall coverings, a four-poster queen-size bed, and a large Jacuzzi tub for two. A full buffet breakfast, served at one large table in the dining room, includes a hearty main dish such as quiche or huevos Mexicanos, cinnamon rolls or rhubarb torte, and plenty of fresh fruit. Afternoon refreshments are served outside near the pool in the summer months. The inn offers some nice romance packages, ranging from simple seductions to elaborate

productions. Visit midweek to sign up for a package called "Chocolate-Covered Wednesday," when you'll be treated to in-room chocolates, a pairing of dessert with chocolate port in the evening, and chocolate treats at breakfast. (Chocolate body frosting and chocolate tattoos are also available for more daring types.)
$$–$$$ *AE, DIS, MC, V; checks OK; www.camelliainn.com.*

GRAPE LEAF INN
❂❂❂
539 Johnson St, Healdsburg / 707/433-8140 or 877/547-4654
This beautifully refurbished Queen Anne Victorian, painted lavender with bright purple trim, stands out as a winsome highlight in its otherwise ordinary neighborhood. Attention to detail and Victorian elegance are the hallmarks of your stay here. Accommodations are spread around the property, with seven suites in the main house and five additional suites in a more recently added luxury wing. When you look at the main house from the outside, it's hard to believe it harbors more than one suite—much less seven—but the well-designed accommodations are more than ample. Features include sloped ceilings with skylights in the four upstairs rooms, multicolored leaded-glass windows throughout, separate sitting areas, hardwood floors, and double whirlpool tubs (in five of the rooms). The decor is unique in each room, including tasteful designer wallpapers, luscious linens, and matching bed skirts and window treatments. The five elegantly appointed suites in the new wing are designed to be kissing havens, and each is furnished with a huge and pillowy king-size bed. In some rooms, amorous extras include lovely antiques, majestic fireplaces, and Jacuzzi tubs for two. For a memorable romantic escape, try the Mourvedre room, located in an eight-sided Victorian turret with soft blue walls, a high coved ceiling adorned with a hand-painted mural, an antique fireplace with marble accents, and a bathroom equipped with two-person spa tub. The innkeepers take advantage of their location in the heart of wine country by incorporating local wines and produce into their breakfast treats: results might include pears poached in zinfandel or apricots cooked in a late-harvest wine. Corn and cheddar pancakes, as well as other homemade goodies, fresh fruit, and juices, are served in the two living rooms or on the patio, when weather permits. Add to this lavish meal the early-evening wine tastings, and the Grape Leaf Inn more than lives up to its wine-country name and setting.
$$$–$$$$ *AE, MC, V; local checks; www.grapeleafinn.com.* &

HAYDON STREET INN
❂❂
321 Haydon St, Healdsburg / 707/433-5228 or 800/528-3703
Harbored on a quiet residential street, this lovely inn, set in a gabled Queen Anne Victorian home and two-story cottage, allows you to easily explore

Healdsburg by day and relax in elegant comfort by night. The cottage, located behind the house, offers the two most desirable accommodations: the Victorian Room, which has cathedral ceilings, restored antiques, a queen-size wicker bed dressed in country florals, and a two-person whirlpool tub; and the Pine Room, which features whitewashed walls, a Battenburg lace canopy over the queen-size bed, and a skylight above its whirlpool tub. The six antique-filled guest rooms in the main house are smaller, less private, and not particularly romantic. One standout, however, is the Turret Room—its bed is tucked under the eaves and a claw-foot tub sits beside a fireplace. Breakfast, served in the main dining room, is a full country affair with home-baked breads and muffins, fresh fruit and juice, and a hot entrée such as quiche or oat-nut pancakes.
$$$ *AE, DIS, MC, V; checks OK; www.haydon.com.*

HEALDSBURG INN ON THE PLAZA
🌢🌢🌢

110 Matheson St, Healdsburg / 707/433-6991 or 800/431-8663
The entrance to the Healdsburg Inn on the Plaza is located in an art gallery and gift shop on the ground floor. (Yes, you're in the right place.) Be sure to admire the work of the talented local artists featured here as you pass through; you may even find the perfect memento to take home. A staircase leads to the bed-and-breakfast area on the second floor, where 10 guest rooms adjoin a mezzanine. Every room has a private bath, some feature gas fireplaces and bay windows, and three rooms share a lovely outdoor balcony. Detailing original to the turn-of-the-20th-century building, such as crown moldings, wainscoting, and pressed-wood walls, is found throughout. The very lovely Garden Suite, also known as the Honeymoon Suite, is the most romantically equipped room, featuring a whirlpool tub for two, corner gas fireplace, and king-size iron and brass bed. All rooms are decorated with American antiques, down comforters and quilts, firm canopy beds adorned with handmade rag dolls or teddy bears, and cozy sitting areas trimmed in pastel colors and textured country fabrics. There's more artwork upstairs; the hallways and guest rooms double as minigalleries for local artists. One of the most outstanding features of this inn is its rooftop garden and solarium set above the plaza—a charming setting for the savory buffet breakfast and afternoon wine-and-popcorn reception. A champagne brunch is served on Saturdays and Sundays, and if you happen to get hungry midday, freshly baked treats are always in the cookie jar.
$$$ *MC, V; no checks; www.healdsburginn.com.*

THE HONOR MANSION

❍❍❍❍

14891 Grove St, Healdsburg / 707/433-4277 or 800/554-4667

Once in a while, we come upon a place that is so close to perfect it reminds us why we do what we do. The Honor Mansion is one of those places. Beauty and grace emanate from the very foundations of this white Italianate Victorian home, set next to a 100-year-old magnolia tree in a quiet residential neighborhood. Your first glimpse of elegance is found in the guest parlor, with its deep burgundy wallpaper, period antiques, and crackling fire in the hearth. Five rooms, seven suites, and a private cottage all offer thoughtful touches and varied decor. All of the accommodations include feather beds with richly colored down comforters, private bathrooms (many with claw-foot or spa tubs), and exquisite antiques. Amenities designed for your comfort and pleasure include CD players and CDs, fluffy robes and soft slippers, lap desks, turndown service with chocolates, and even garment steamers. Accommodations range from the outrageously luxurious suites to the more quietly romantic rooms in the main home, such as the ground-floor Rose Room, which has a delightful private porch and a claw-foot tub in the spacious bathroom. If you're on a budget, we recommend the cozy Angel Room, which is decorated with a cherub mural in the corner above the bed and a handmade patchwork quilt on the inviting bed. Certainly one of the most private options is the self-contained Squire's Cottage, situated near the koi pond. A vaulted ceiling with clerestory windows, a sparkling whitewashed interior, and jewel-toned linens add charm and romantic ambience. Snuggle up on big pillows next to the gas fireplace or relax on your own garden patio. There's also a TV/VCR and video library, a king-size canopy bed fronting the fireplace, and a claw-foot tub for two framed by stained-glass windows. The seven luxury suites in various duplex structures around the gorgeous property compete with the cottage for the most kissing appeal. Amorous offerings in these suites include cozy sitting areas, corner fireplaces, two-person showers, and outdoor jetted tubs tucked into enclosed gardens. The most recently constructed suite, Vineyard Suite One, is a fabulous getaway with a private patio that boasts a lavish, fabric-draped, outdoor whirlpool tub that's a vision of fairytale romance. Early-evening refreshments are served in the dining room of the main house. If the weather cooperates, take your drink to the outdoor deck, which is furnished with green wrought-iron tables and chairs and surrounded by colorful gardens and a pond full of "kissing koi" (they'll actually "kiss" your finger). In the back of the home, an outdoor swimming pool promises recreation and relaxation for worn-out wine enthusiasts. An easy-to-use espresso maker is available for guests who need their lattes early in the morning. At a later hour, breakfast is presented in the grand dining room and might include freshly baked cranberry-apricot scones, sweet poached pears, and hearty crepes filled with scrambled eggs, zesty salsa, and fresh avocado. The helpful concierge can direct you to

241

wineries and make reservations for dinner, and the spa services will make you feel more pampered than royalty.
$$$–$$$$ *MC, V; checks OK; www.honormansion.com.*

HOPE-MERRILL HOUSE
●●●

21253 Geyserville Ave, Geyserville

HOPE-BOSWORTH HOUSE
●●

21238 Geyserville Ave, Geyserville / 707/857-3356 or 800/825-4233
Staying at this elaborately restored turn-of-the-20th-century Victorian is like going back in time: the Eastlake Stick–style Hope-Merrill House showcases lavish period detail (alongside modern amenities) in its eight beautiful guest rooms. Stunning silk-screened Bradbury & Bradbury wall coverings and ceiling papers add flourish to the Sterling Room, while the romance of a whirlpool tub for two enhances both the beautiful Peacock Room and the Carpenter's Gothic Room. In the Peacock Room, gaze up at images of gold, rose, and gray-blue peacocks strutting around the ceiling border as you get cozy in front of the gas fireplace, or open the French doors to step into the marble-topped tub for a relaxing soak. The Vineyard View Room has a fireplace and a beautifully restored antique armoire, not to mention a shower ample enough for two. In the morning, you're sure to enjoy the full, country-style breakfast of fresh fruit, pastries, a hot egg dish, and breakfast meats. Afterward, take a dip in the refreshing outdoor swimming pool (available only in the warm months) set behind the home, near a latticed gazebo and a vineyard. Couples on a budget may be intrigued by the property's less-expensive cousin across the street, the Hope-Bosworth House: this cheery, informal Queen Anne-style Victorian inn has four bedrooms, all with queen-size beds, views of the neighborhood, and private baths (one is private but situated across the hall). The Oak Room deserves special mention; it is the only room furnished with a Jacuzzi tub for two and has a charming country ambience to boot. The Sun Porch Room, accented by wicker furnishings and hardwood floors, is another good option. Guests here are treated to the same elaborate breakfast as their neighbors, and they have access to the pool and other facilities at the Hope-Merrill House.
$$$ *AE, DIS, MC, V; checks OK; hope-inns.com.*

HOTEL HEALDSBURG
●●●

317 Healdsburg Ave, Healdsburg / 707/431-2800 or 800/889-7188
Located right on the central plaza, this chic new boutique hotel is the latest see-and-be-seen destination in Healdsburg. If you are seeking hyperstylish, gleaming modern luxury, you will find it here. Plush rooms, spa services,

a hip (and noisy) restaurant, and instant access to downtown's adorable old-fashioned square are just a few of the benefits to staying in this full-service luxury hotel (Healdsburg's only one). The 55 cheerful rooms are all similarly furnished, evoking the pages of a Pottery Barn catalog with clean, airy decor elegantly accented by colorful Tibetan rugs and dark wood furnishings. Enticing features include goose-down duvets, CD players, Frette bathrobes, large glittering bathrooms that beckon with walk-in showers and two-person tubs, and French doors opening to private balconies overlooking the plaza. Though plaza shopping and dining are right outside the front door, there's plenty of reason to hang around—especially a grappa bar, an enormous garden pool, a full-service spa, a fitness room, and the excellent and expensive Charlie Palmer's Dry Creek Kitchen (707/431-0330), which serves seasonal cuisine accentuating pure flavors and local ingredients. A continental breakfast, included in the rates, is served in the hotel lobby.
$$$$ *AE, DC, MC, V; checks OK; www.hotelhealdsburg.com.* &

MADRONA MANOR
❤️❤️
1001 Westside Rd, Healdsburg / 707/433-4231 or 800/258-4003
A royal crest adorns the white arch that welcomes you to this landmark inn and restaurant. The setting is truly one of the most majestic and peaceful in Healdsburg: beautifully landscaped gardens and surrounding woods completely hide the stately 1881 mansion from any sign of the nearby city and highway. Though many of the accommodations have been recently redecorated, it's still difficult for them to live up to the splendor outside. Of the numerous rooms and suites distributed throughout the three-story Victorian mansion, the adjacent Carriage House, the Garden Cottage, the Meadow Wood Complex, and the newly renovated School House, only a handful are truly suited to kissing couples. The most romantically oriented accommodations are the two School House Suites, set in a renovated historic building at the property's edge and completed in 2000. Here you'll find sponge-painted walls, king-size beds, separate sitting rooms, Jacuzzi tubs for two, and fireplaces in the bedrooms, as well as a private decks overlooking gardens and hills. Other good romantic choices are the second-floor rooms in the mansion, most of which are outfitted in classic pink-and-green flowery decor and have period antiques, tall ceilings and windows, spacious bathrooms, ornate window treatments, large fireplaces, and queen- or king-size beds backed by massive wooden headboards. A buffet breakfast of baked scones, fresh fruit, cereals, and coffee and tea is served to guests in the main house's beautiful dining room. Come evening, the gourmet restaurant is a haven for kissing couples, with its high ceilings, lace curtains, rose-colored wallpaper, and several dining rooms furnished with intimate tables draped in white linens.
$$$ *AE, MC, V; checks OK; www.madronamanor.com.*

Romantic Restaurants

BISTRO RALPH

♥♥❤

109 Plaza St E, Healdsburg / 707/433-1380
It's not always the case that the restaurants that are easiest to find are also among the best, but it's that delightfully simple in Healdsburg. Located right on the plaza, the stylish Bistro Ralph is one of the best choices in town, and it's heartening to see that this longtime favorite continues to thrive in a town where restaurants have been afflicted with the revolving-door syndrome as an ever-newer-and-hipper ambience descends. Housed in a slender storefront on the square, the restaurant has a cozy, slightly industrial feel, with white brick walls and a dozen or so linen-topped tables. The small open kitchen does create a small amount of noise, but food-minded couples will delight in the chance to sit at the long concrete counter and watch the chef perform culinary magic. And it is magic indeed: what emerges from the kitchen here is consistently excellent. The focus is on fresh, local ingredients in bistro-style fare. Choice starters include grilled portobello mushrooms with white truffle oil and crispy Sichuan pepper calamari. The lamb dishes are always good, particularly the hearty spring lamb stew à la provençal and the lamb shanks with crème fraîche–horseradish mashed potatoes. The lunch menu sticks to upscale salads and sandwiches, such as a grilled ahi or salmon sandwich and the popular lamb burger on a fresh roll, all three served with a pile of irresistible shoestring fries.
$$ *MC, V; local checks only; lunch, dinner Mon–Sat; beer, wine, and martinis; reservations recommended.*

RAVENOUS

♥♥♥

420 Center St, Healdsburg / 707/431-1302
Back in the day, before this now-glitzy town was famous enough to have boutique hotels, the sole outpost of Ravenous was a funky little eight-table spot next to the Raven movie theater. We adored it then for its excellent food and fun ambience, and now there is even more to love, since the restaurant has a bigger location but is still just a few blocks from Healdsburg's central square. Best of all, you can now make reservations, so the table for your romantic tête-à-tête is assured. The new location is far more spacious and elegant than the former setting but has some of the same artsy charm. The dining room exudes Mediterranean warmth while beautifully incorporating an airy modern flair with its warm orange walls, polished hardwood floors, fresh flowers, and black wrought-iron fixtures. Light and lively California cuisine is the name of the game here. Offerings from the ever-changing seasonal menu might include beef short ribs in a red wine–brandy sauce, grilled pork tenderloin quesadilla topped with an avocado-melon salsa, or smoked

salmon on corn cakes. The plentiful portions here mean one thing is certain: you definitely won't be ravenous when you leave. Since first love dies hard (as every kiss expert knows), we can't help but note that the restaurant's first outpost is still in town under the apt name Ravenette (117 N St, Healdsburg; 707/431-1770).

$$ *MC, V; no checks; lunch, dinner Wed–Sun; full bar; reservations recommended.*

ZIN
●●
344 Center St, Healdsburg / 707/473-0946
Located just off Healdsburg's main plaza, this restaurant has plenty of urban polish, thanks to towering ceilings with broad wooden beams, a poured-concrete floor, and metal tables. Unfortunately, the decor provides absolutely no buffer between you and the boisterous dinner parties beside you. Nevertheless, the food here is fantastic, and since top-notch culinary indulgence is one essential component of any romantic weekend in the wine country, it's definitely worth a visit. The vast choice of zinfandels here—an apt theme, considering the Sonoma area is prime zin country—and the fact that the restaurant specializes in dishes that are particularly well suited to pairing with zinfandels will make fans of this full-bodied red wine think they've arrived in heaven. The menu is peppered with updated versions of hearty American classics, and each day features a blue-plate special, such as meatloaf or St. Louis–style barbecued ribs. The hush puppies with red pepper make a great starter—a mountain of them served hot, fluffy, and grease-free. Entrées include a succulent sliced duck breast served on a bed of garlic mashed potatoes topped by sautéed spinach. Grilled lamb chops come with asparagus and a giant helping of roasted new potatoes. Portions tend to be huge, so arrive with hearty appetites—or consider ordering just one main dish with two forks. Just remember that on busy weekend evenings, you should arrive ready to shout rather than whisper your sweet nothings.

$$$ *AE, MC, V; local checks only; lunch, dinner every day; beer and wine; reservations recommended.*

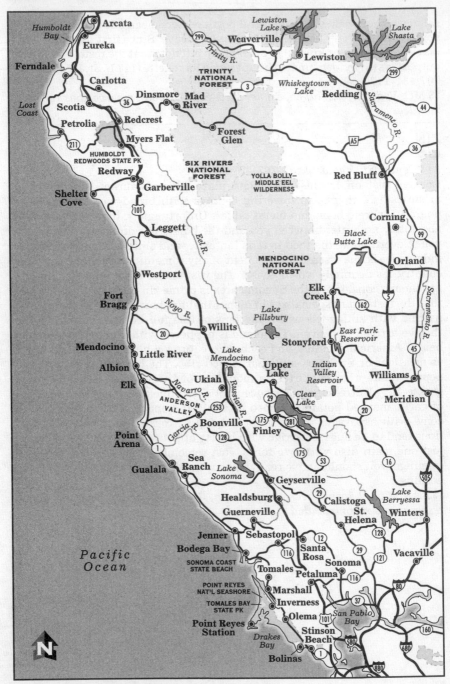

*"What of soul was left, I wonder, when the
kissing had to stop?"*

—ROBERT BROWNING

♡ NORTH COAST

If you've never witnessed the North Coast's incredibly dramatic and arresting scenery, be prepared for the experience of a lifetime. Unlike the more populated coastline south of the San Francisco Bay Area, this rugged shoreline remains relatively isolated—and pristine. The variety of romantic surroundings ranges from dramatic coastal towns where turbulent white-caps thunder up against tall, rocky cliffs to quiet beaches where sand dunes, overgrown with grass and wildflowers, beckon. Just a few miles inland, thousands of acres of beautiful pastoral farmland offer a serene contrast to the dynamic coast.

Not surprisingly, the region offers many superlative places to stay, eat, and hike, though not in such abundance as to detract from the region's natural beauty. We can hardly think of a better setting for romance—kissing here seems inevitable. Some destinations in the area, such as the northern hamlet of Mendocino, are tourist havens for exactly the reasons we describe above; therefore, kissing couples who seek privacy should take peak season into account when planning travel. Spring and late fall are excellent times to avoid the crowds, and some of the smaller and quieter destinations along the coast—towns you may never have heard of, such as Elk or Albion—provide quieter surroundings all year long. Keep in mind that many of the Romantic Lodgings options in this chapter are situated on Highway 1. In some cases, traffic noise is a drawback, but a location on Highway 1 can also mean a remarkable oceanfront setting. Throughout this chapter, we describe an establishment's relation to the highway (when applicable) and specifically note whether road noise is a romantic distraction.

The Northern California Highway 1 is an exhilarating roller-coaster ride of a lifetime. A compact two-lane roadway, it writhes along terrain that seems impassable. Hugging the ocean from atop towering cliffs, each turn capriciously switches back on itself, following the edge so closely that you might feel as though you're hang-gliding instead of driving. It is imperative that you allow yourselves enough time to travel this highway at a leisurely, touring pace. With this highway's myriad coiled turns and a minimum of passing lanes, maneuvering is difficult and speeding is impossible. Scads of scenic turnoffs will demand your attention, so go slowly and stop at any point that intrigues you to take in the visual glory. Each corner and each turn unfolds views so astonishing that a warning seems in order: driving and kissing don't mix! Before you indulge, pull over and park the car; you can return to negotiating the narrow turns later. Highway 1 breaks off from Highway 101 just north of the Golden Gate Bridge in Marin County and continues northward to the town of Leggett, about 80 miles south of Eureka. If you are in a hurry to get somewhere, do yourselves and the rest of the traffic on Highway 1 a favor: take Highway 101.

MARIN COAST AND POINT REYES NATIONAL SEASHORE

ROMANTIC HIGHLIGHTS

Travel across the Golden Gate Bridge and drive just an hour north of San Francisco, and you'll arrive at some of California's most scenic— and relaxed—romantic destinations: the towns and villages of West Marin County. The journey along **Highway 1** passes through eucalyptus groves and along high bluffs with spectacular ocean views until it drops to sea level at the tiny town of **Stinson Beach**, home of the popular Stinson Beach State Park. Although this 3-mile stretch of white sand beach is often packed with crowds in summer, there's always enough room for two more: so take off your shoes, close your eyes, and bask in the sun with your sweetheart. There are few places near here to rest your head for the night, however, which is why we suggest a final destination farther north, around **Point Reyes National Seashore**. This 71,000-acre sanctuary of forested hills, deep green pastures, and undisturbed beaches is a paradise for couples seeking romance and seclusion.

There are four towns in and around the Point Reyes National Seashore boundary: Olema, Point Reyes Station, Inverness Park, and Inverness. **Olema**, with its Highway 1 location, offers some wonderful accommodations and provides convenient access to the coastal area. The other three villages, all of which are situated within easy reach of the shore of **Tomales Bay**, boast numerous waterfront and hillside retreats. The region is sparsely populated and quiet during the winter months, but it's well traveled in the spring and summer. Fortunately, there's enough wilderness here to go around, and you can escape the crowds with some careful planning—but, as always, you'll find even more privacy if you travel in the off-season. A stay at one of the romantic bed-and-breakfasts in this area will be memorable at any time of year, but if you do come in summer or on a holiday, be sure to make your reservation far in advance. Also, come prepared for small-town quirks; for example, Point Reyes area restaurants tend to close their kitchens early, around 8:30 or 9pm at the latest. And don't forget to pack layers: Point Reyes gets chilly at night regardless of the season.

This region offers some of the world's most **romantic walks**, and you often will find yourselves alone on incredibly scenic trails. Whether your hike begins on a rolling, grass-covered dune or on a densely forested knoll, it almost always ends with a spectacular ocean view. Many area lodgings offer maps and hiking guides. The array of trails is nearly endless; among the most kiss-worthy destinations are **Kehoe Beach** and **McClures Beach**. Both are reached via a scenic 45-minute excursion (via Pierce Point Rd) through windswept meadows and working dairy ranches—watch out for cows on the road! Any amount of driving would be worth it for the vast stretches of remote white sand beach and crashing ocean surf—in fog or in sun, this experience is unforgettable. At the westernmost tip of the Point Reyes Peninsula, you can visit the popular **Point Reyes Lighthouse** (415/669-1534; 10am–4:30pm Thurs–Mon, weather permitting) via a windy 0.4-mile walk and thigh-burning 308-step staircase. When the fog burns off, the lighthouse and the headlands provide a fantastic lookout point for gray whales on their yearly migration, December to March. Our advice: find a comfortable position, snuggle close, and be patient.

Don't miss out on the many smaller parks around the area, either. One particularly romantic destination is the aptly named **Heart's Desire Beach**, located on the west side of Tomales Bay in **Tomales Bay State Park** (small entry fee required). While this stretch of sand (and the parking lot) fill up quickly on summer weekends, the views of the tranquil, sparkling bay live up to the beach's name.

You can paddle a kayak around scenic Tomales Bay with **Blue Waters Kayaking** (415/669-2600; www.bwkayak.com). Based in **Inverness**, this romantically minded paddling outfitter offers guided moonlight kayak tours on the weekends (from $59 per person). It's a perfect way for the two of you to see what the night brings to Tomales Bay. Another option is to hire a pair of horses at **Five Brooks Stables** (8001 Hwy 1; 415/663-1570; www.five brooks.com; reservations required), located 3½ miles south of Olema. This fabulous horse ranch offers hourly rentals as well as half-day trips around Point Reyes National Seashore and the beach.

The town of **Point Reyes Station** holds an appealing, if small, selection of restaurants and shops where you can refresh yourselves or explore on a rainy day. A rail town in the 1890s, Point Reyes Station is steeped in dairy-farming tradition—which explains why one of California's best small cheese makers, **Cowgirl Creamery**, churns out delicious, award-winning rounds for all to see at **Tomales Bay Foods** (80 4th St; 415/663-9335). This delightful converted barn specializes in gourmet foods to go, but you can also shop for handmade crafts or sip cappuccinos or wine at one of the small tables. Stock up here on delicious picnic goodies such as cured salmon, smoked trout, roasted-eggplant sandwiches, or smoked chicken with potato salad; or keep it simple with an array of excellent local cheeses, handmade crackers, artisan breads, and California wines. Then nab your kissing partner and head out to the beach. Other tasty treats can be found at **Bovine Bakery** (11315 Hwy 1; 415/663-9420) and the adorable **Pine Cone Diner** (60 4th St; 415/663-1536).

For something decidedly different, drive 10 miles north to the tiny, scenic hamlet of **Marshall** and the historic **Hog Island Oyster Company** (9 miles north of Point Reyes Station; 415/663-9218; www.hogisland oyster.com; 9am–5pm Tues–Sun). It's a working farm, not a restaurant, but it does offer the chance to enjoy bivalves plucked fresh from their nearby beds: for a small fee you're provided with shucking gloves and knives, barbecue kettles, hot sauces and fresh lemon slices, and a waterfront picnic table where you can enjoy your feast (tables are first-come, first-served on weekdays and by reservation only on weekends). The reputation oysters enjoy as a powerful aphrodisiac might just inspire you to make the trip.

Access and Information

Two major highways provide access to the North Coast: **Highway 1**, the only route that runs along the coast, and **Highway 101**, the central artery that connects to Highway 1 via two main scenic roads. To enjoy the full-blown coast experience, take the Stinson Beach/Highway 1 exit from Highway 101 north (about 7 miles north of the Golden Gate Bridge) and head west. This is the quickest route to Muir Woods and Stinson Beach. For the quickest route to Point Reyes and Tomales Bay, exit from Highway 101 at Sir Francis Drake Boulevard, which takes you through West Marin to Olema, where Highway 1 and Sir Francis Drake Boulevard intersect.

Finding lodging in the busy summer months around Point Reyes can be difficult if you don't reserve well in advance. If you're having trouble finding a vacancy, contact **Point Reyes Lodging** (415/663-1872 or 800/539-1872; www.ptreyes.com) or the **Inns of Marin** (800/887-2880 or 415/663-2000; www.innsofmarin.com) for information on available lodgings. The **West Marin Chamber of Commerce** (415/663-9232; www.pointreyes.org) is also a good source for lodging and visitor information. You can pick up a free map and hiking trail guide at the **Bear Valley Visitor Center** (Bear Valley Rd; 415/464-5100; www.nps.gov/pore/; follow signs from Olema; open every day).

Romantic Lodgings

THE BEACH COTTAGE
🌢🌢🌢

Stinson Beach (call for street address) / 415/868-0474
With the closure of Casa del Mar, one of the few romantic accommodations in Stinson Beach, it was beginning to look like the only way to spend a few days here was to stay with local friends, if you were lucky enough to have them, or to rent an entire vacation home. Fortunately, one of the former innkeepers of the Casa del Mar has saved the day with the Beach Cottage, a cozy retreat located just steps from the breathtaking Pacific. The small one-bedroom studio has a lovely cedar interior complete with warm hardwood floors and beam ceilings; the sparse furnishings are arranged with Japanese-style simplicity. Stowed neatly away in a closet are a tea kettle, gourmet tea, and coffee; there's also a mini refrigerator for storing any goodies you'd like to bring with you. A queen-size bed laden with a plush down comforter takes center stage, and a wrought-iron gas-lit woodstove adds ambience. In the morning, a breakfast of freshly squeezed juice, seasonal fruit, and home-baked goods arrives on your doorstep. In the simple tiled bathroom, a window next to the shower opens to let in fresh sea breezes. By far the most incredible aspect of this retreat is its splendid location, and you can enjoy it on the oceanfront deck, which offers perfect sunset views. Your stay is accompanied by the music of crashing surf; just a few steps bring you to a beautiful sandy beach. In the evening, you can stroll to the town of Stinson Beach and its handful of restaurants within about five minutes.
$$$$ No credit cards; checks OK; www.stinsonbeachfront.com.

BLACKTHORNE INN
🌢🌢🌘

266 Vallejo Ave, Inverness Park / 415/663-8621
Like a tree house, only better, the Blackthorne Inn is a four-story fantasy nestled high in the woods. Twin turrets, peaked gables, stained-glass windows, and a firefighter's pole that descends to the driveway below (just in case you don't feel like using the stairs) augment more-practical features at this inn, such as the main floor's expansive redwood deck and the nearby hot tub nestled among the trees. Inside the common room, the immense stone hearth, vaulted open-beam ceiling (including beams salvaged from a San Francisco pier), and numerous windows create a feeling of light and warmth. The five guest rooms feature skylights, mix-and-match antiques, and knotty wood walls. Rooms have CD players but no TVs or phones, in keeping with the concept of a serene getaway. We recommend bypassing the two ground-floor rooms, which share a detached bath; instead, ascend the narrow spiral staircase that leads to the more private accommodations. The Lupine Room is divinely cozy, with a sloping ceiling and its own entrance.

The larger Overlook Room has a small outdoor terrace offering forest views, as well as a rather odd Juliet-style balcony overlooking the living room; the private bathroom is a few steps down the hall. Head higher into the treetops for one of Northern California's most unusual rooms, appropriately named the Eagle's Nest. This dazzling aerie with windows on all sides occupies the top of the octagonal tower; a steep ladder leads to a private sundeck (or stargazing deck, depending). Come prepared for an adventurous jaunt to your bathroom—it lies across a 40-foot-high outdoor walkway. The jetted hot tub, which fronts the Eagle's Nest's bathroom facilities, is available to all guests until 10pm, after which it is designated for the exclusive use of Eagle's Nest occupants. The full breakfast buffet served every morning can be enjoyed on the deck, weather permitting, or in the sunny breakfast room at your own table for two.
$$$$ *MC, V; checks OK in advance; www.blackthorneinn.com.*

COTTAGES ON THE BEACH
❂❂❂

12788 Sir Francis Drake Blvd, Inverness / 415/663-9696
Beachfront cottages make ideal settings for romance, and these little gems are no exception, despite their location just steps from a busy road. Both cabins are surrounded by newly landscaped grounds and have pleasantly painted exteriors, but you'll truly fall in love the moment you step inside. Richly colored Oriental carpets lie on gleaming hardwood floors, and French doors open onto private decks overlooking tranquil Tomales Bay. In both cottages, contemporary, stylish artwork graces the sponge-painted walls, and dried flowers, baskets, and antiques lend additional charm to the living areas. A ladder in one cottage leads to a snug sleeping loft; plush down comforters drape the beds in both units. Complimentary breakfast fixings are stocked in the fully equipped modern kitchens, where copper tea kettles sparkle against clean white tiles.
$$$ *MC, V; checks OK; www.ptreyescountryinn.com.*

DANCING COYOTE BEACH GUEST COTTAGES
❂❂

12794 Sir Francis Drake Blvd, Inverness / 415/669-7200
Nestled on the shore of Tomales Bay, this getaway is perfect for those in search of quiet time together. Dancing Coyote rents three adjoining beach-front cottages, all sheltered from the busy road by a stand of sturdy pine and cypress trees that climb a small hillside. A lovingly landscaped garden surrounds a small outdoor deck furnished with wooden lounge chairs, where guests can enjoy close-up views of pelicans swooping down to the water's edge. Decorated in pastel shades of peach and green, Birch and Beach are weather-worn, two-story cottages with all the right romantic touches: wood-burning fireplaces, cozy loft bedrooms, two private decks, abundant

skylights, and floor-to-ceiling windows. Touch-ups are needed here and there, but for the most part this shouldn't interfere with your enjoyment of the surroundings. Skye, a less expensive, slightly more rustic studio cottage, has rough-hewn wood beams and walls, a small sleeping loft (just big enough for a bed) with a glimpse of the bay, and a funky but surprisingly invigorating outdoor shower. Breakfast supplies are provided for guests to enjoy at their leisure in the privacy of their own small kitchens. Each cottage has access to a private beachfront a few feet from the front door; your sense of privacy might be minimized when all cottages are occupied and neighboring guests are trekking past to reach the beach. If this is a romantic distraction, take advantage of the fact that all the windows are equipped with Venetian blinds.
$$$ *No credit cards; checks OK.*

HOLLY TREE INN & COTTAGES
❤❤❤

3 Silverhills Rd, Inverness Park / 415/663-1554 or 800/286-4655
This family-friendly bed-and-breakfast offers four pleasant guest rooms, but for romantic purposes, we recommend staying at one of the three secluded cottages set in various locations around Inverness. On the same grounds as the bed-and-breakfast—but tucked into a far-off, private corner—you'll find Cottage-in-the-Woods, a two-room hideaway with a small fireplace, a king-size bed, and an old-fashioned bathtub situated so that you can gaze at the garden as you bathe. Two other options have more secluded locations. The first is the Sea Star Cottage, built on stilts over Tomales Bay; a 75-foot-long wooden walkway over the tidal waters is your charming—not to say unusual—entryway. Simplicity reigns inside the cozy, casual living room with woodstove, bedroom with four-poster queen-size bed, and small bathroom. The absolute best place to kiss here is in the sun room, which spans the front of the cottage; soak in the large bubbling hot tub and watch seabirds float by. (The only trace of humans appears via the long dock of the Inverness Yacht Club, next door.) In both cottages, a breakfast basket with fresh fruit, quiche, and home-baked scones is left for you in the kitchen. For couples who prefer even more space and total self-sufficiency, there's the two-bedroom Vision Cottage, set atop a quiet hillside adorned with old-growth bishop pines. Although the shores of Tomales Bay are nowhere in sight, neither is the highway, which creates a sense of peaceful seclusion. Inside, you'll find floor-to-ceiling windows, knotty pine walls, a cozy woodstove, eclectic antiques, a full kitchen stocked with breakfast fixings, and two separate bedrooms simply furnished with antique pine beds. Two decks survey views of the surrounding forest, and the oversize outdoor Jacuzzi tub invites you to soak for hours. If you choose to stay at the bed-and-breakfast itself, Mary's Garden Room has a private entrance and a cozy fireplace. Guests here can sign up for a private soak in the outdoor hot tub and, come

morning, enjoy a full breakfast in the dining room with treats such as vanilla French toast topped with fresh local berries.
$$$–$$$$ *AE, MC, V; checks OK; www.hollytreeinn.com.*

MANKA'S INVERNESS LODGE
⬢⬢⬢⬢

Calendar Way at Argyle St, Inverness / 415/669-1034 or 800/58-LODGE
Since Manka's Inverness Lodge runs one of the sexiest restaurants in all of Northern California (see Romantic Restaurants), it's no surprise that the overnight accommodations are also seductive at this legendary turn-of-the-20th-century hunting lodge, set on a densely forested hillside and complete with furry rugs and big-game trophies. Eight rooms and six distinctive cottages are available in and around the lodge. The four rooms in the lodge feature massive tree-limb bedsteads, rough-hewn wooden walls, cozy fireplaces, and bold hunting prints and plaids. Located above the restaurant, they are vulnerable to noise during dinnertime, but become entirely intimate after hours or on nights when the restaurant is closed. The Redwood Annex houses four additional handsome rooms. Two cabins on the grounds continue the hunting-lodge theme and offer romantic touches, such as two-person antique tubs; we especially like Fishing Cabin, with its private deck including outdoor shower and redwood hot tub. At the edge of Tomales Bay, two cabins called the Boatman's Quarters and the Boathouse offer wonderful rustic-nautical decor, king-size beds, and decks on the water. For a retreat deep in the woods, you can't go wrong with 125, a Craftsman-style cottage set four blocks from the lodge with an utterly private redwood deck complete with hot tub, separate living room and kitchen, and partial bay view. The other Craftsman-style cottage, Perch, is a larger, two-bedroom retreat. Breakfast is not included with your stay, but the restaurant is open for guests every morning. You'll be more than ready to set off on a hike after a morning meal of, say, eggs scrambled with shiitake mushrooms and local goat cheese, accompanied by homemade wild boar sausage and cream biscuits. (Don't worry; lighter options are also available.) If you're impressed with what the kitchen produces in the morning, plan ahead by making reservations for dinner, when Manka's chefs really shine.
$$$$ *MC, V; checks OK; www.mankas.com.*

MARSH COTTAGE
⬢⬢◗

Point Reyes Station (call for street address) / 415/669-7168
As you might deduce from the name, this small, weathered, Cape Cod–inspired getaway sits on the edge of a marsh on Tomales Bay. Although the cabin is situated just off a fairly busy road, a fence effectively deflects most of the traffic noise. Cattails, wildflowers, and long, honey-colored grass flourish around the cabin. Country prints and fabrics, a wood-burning fire-

place, and French doors that open onto a sundeck overlooking the marsh enhance the natural setting. In warm, sunny weather, a two-person hammock set up outside provides the perfect vantage point for bird-watching or enjoying the sunset over the rolling hills across the bay. By design, there is no TV or telephone to distract you from the peaceful setting, although you will find a CD player, so bring along your favorite romantic CDs. The retreat can be rented as a straight vacation cottage, in which case you must bring your own provisions, or as a bed-and-breakfast. We prefer the latter, because it's so cozy to arrive and find the fully equipped kitchen already stocked with a more-than-generous selection of fresh orange juice, home-baked bread or muffins, butter and jam, seasonal fruits, milk and granola, as well as a basket of eggs, tea, and coffee. Your only complaint here will be that you can't stay longer.
$$$ *No credit cards; checks OK; www.marshcottage.com.*

THE NEON ROSE
✿✿✿❀
76 Overlook Rd, Point Reyes Station / 415/663-9143 or 800/358-8346
Thankfully, the only neon to be found at this private country retreat is in the form of a single red rose, set above the bedroom's arched door frame. Situated in a serene neighborhood, the geometrically inspired Neon Rose, despite its name, caters to lovers who want to escape the city—neon lights included. Pass through a flourishing flower garden into the self-contained one-bedroom cottage, which commands sweeping views of the Point Reyes National Seashore and the bay beyond. The simply decorated and uncluttered interior features hardwood floors, white walls softened by a few pastel accents, and modern appointments. Organic foods are highlighted in the continental breakfast fixings, and the cabin features an abundance of skylights and windows that allow natural light to shine in, with the idea that it's essential for one's health to experience the sun's daily cycle. No curtains cover the living room windows, but with undisturbed meadows before you, lack of privacy isn't a problem. The conveniences of home, such as a full kitchen, stereo system, and telephone, are all here, plus a living area warmed by a gas-lit woodstove, a small bedroom with a queen-size bed and plush down comforter, and a jetted tub in the bathroom. You can prepare breakfast at your own pace; come equipped with groceries should you want to whip up your own private dinner as well. Neon Rose provides peace, quiet, light, and a healthy dose of relaxation. You might never want to go back to the city.
$$$ *No credit cards; checks OK; www.neonrose.com.*

OLD POINT REYES SCHOOL HOUSE COMPOUND
✿✿✿

11559 Hwy 1, Point Reyes Station / 415/663-1166
Several kiss-worthy accommodations dot this scenic property, each with its own unique romantic appeal. The most spacious option is Gray's Retreat, in a renovated two-story cedar barn that was the original Point Reyes schoolhouse. Today the lower floor of this building, framed by flower gardens, has been beautifully transformed into an idyllic country retreat, just right for two. Sunshine streams through expansive windows in the living room and adjacent spacious kitchen, highlighting the gold and forest green color scheme and terra-cotta-tiled floors. Soothing artwork, eclectic furnishings, floral fabrics, and a wood-burning fireplace create a stylish, cheerful ambience. Cozy up in the antique four-poster bed covered with rich, inviting linens, or dazzle your beloved with your culinary prowess in the fully equipped gourmet kitchen (provide your own provisions). French doors in the bedroom and the dining area open onto a private wooden deck that overlooks a lovely horse pasture. Another lodging that caters to couples is the appealing Jasmine Cottage, surrounded by herb, flower, and vegetable gardens. The crisp, clean interior has white linen curtains, terra-cotta-tiled floors, sage green accents, a wood-burning Franklin stove, and a full kitchen stocked with tasty breakfast items. Both Jasmine Cottage and Gray's Retreat have TV/VCRs (only Gray's Retreat has cable and a private phone). Far more romantic, both also boast *chimeneas*—freestanding Mexican terra-cotta fireplaces—so you can lounge together before the fire on the outdoor patio and watch for shooting stars. Located above Gray's Retreat is the Barnloft, a small unit with big views; 8-foot-high windows offer lovely vistas of the Point Reyes landscape, and there's even a double window seat to enjoy them in (there's no TV—but you won't miss it). A ship's ladder leads to a sleeping loft under a skylight, perfect for gazing at the stars before you fall asleep. There's also a sofa that converts to a cozy double bed, a full bath, and a private kitchen (bring groceries; only milk, coffee, and granola are provided). The hot tub secluded behind a latticed-wood fence is available to all guests, as are the lovely garden patio and well-groomed boccie ball court. The innkeeper's home is just on the other side of the garden, and the in-town location offers easy access to shops and restaurants—but a getaway here still feels like a country retreat.
$$$–$$$$ *AE, MC, V; no checks; oldpointreyesschoolhousecompound.com.*

OLEMA DRUIDS HALL
✿✿✿✿

9870 Hwy 1, Olema / 415/663-8727 or 866/554-4255
This striking 1885 building, deftly remodeled into an exquisite bed-and-breakfast, was once a meeting hall for the Druids Association—but today, it's hearts and minds that meet inside the grand structure. A gorgeous main

room welcomes you inside with towering ceilings, elegant sofas set before the fireplace, a beautiful marble statue and original paintings, and double French doors opening onto a hand-laid brick patio surrounded by lush gardens. Among the four rooms in the main house and the adjacent cottage, two are clear choices for romance: the Grand Suite and the private Cottage. (Keep in mind that both are also splurges.) The Grand Suite, on the hall's second floor, is an apartment-size getaway that is the ultimate in luxury (and price) and includes a gorgeous, fully equipped gourmet kitchen and spacious living room with fireplace. A dramatic metal and glass wall partitions off the bedroom, where you'll want to immediately dive onto the lavishly made-up king-size bed. You can also soak for hours in the double Jacuzzi tub, sip wine on your private deck overlooking gardens and parkland, or descend the deck's private staircase to the vine-covered gazebo in the property's lovely back garden. In the Cottage, simple, elegant Japanese style is layered onto a Craftsman bungalow. Here, you'll find warm-hued, hand-milled wood throughout, terra-cotta floors with radiant heat, vaulted ceilings, a fully equipped kitchen, and an open-hearth fireplace in the living room. Several steps lead up to the bedroom and an inviting king-size bed; the gold-toned marble bathroom features a Jacuzzi spa tub with double showerheads. Fresh pastries and fruit, plus the day's newspaper, arrive at the front door of the Cottage and the Grand Suite each morning; guests in the remaining rooms enjoy an expanded continental-style breakfast of local organic goodies, which they can partake of on the sunny front porch (it does face Highway 1, however, within earshot of passing traffic). Of the two main-house ground-floor bedrooms, the spacious Olema room is by far the more seductive, with a king-size bed, French doors to the front porch and garden, and a picture-perfect tile and marble bathroom with double Jacuzzi tub and shower. The sunny second-floor Nest room, just big enough for its queen-size bed, is best for couples who don't mind close quarters. Plush robes, Aveda products in the gorgeous bathrooms, and breathtaking flower displays throughout add even more elegance to this top-notch retreat. $$$–$$$$ *AE, MC, V; checks OK; www.olemadruids.com.*

ONE MESA BED & BREAKFAST
♥♥♥
1 Mesa Rd, Point Reyes Station / 415/663-8866
The scenic charm of the Point Reyes countryside gets a dose of French-country style in the rooms and cottage at this nicely priced getaway. We applaud the emphasis on romantic privacy; all three rooms in the property's main building—a rambling, single-story structure—and the charming cottage offer private decks, mini- or full kitchens, stereos with romantic music choices, and either a garden setting or beautiful countryside views. The charming decor is characterized by glowing wood floors, butter yellow walls hung with tasteful botanical prints, huge comfy chairs set before small,

gas-lit white iron stoves, and, best of all, luxurious feather bed–topped mattresses piled high with soft linens and plump, colorful throw pillows. In the bathrooms of the Moonlight and Sunlight Rooms, you'll find an oversize claw-foot tub with handheld shower set behind an embellished screen; a sink set into an antique vanity; and a toilet in a small water closet. Both rooms also boast French doors opening onto a deck with peaceful views of the countryside. The Starlight Room is located on the opposite side of the house, so its deck overlooks the well-tended front garden instead of the rolling hills; it boasts a similarly charming interior, with the addition of a larger, two-person soaking tub. For the height of romantic privacy, book the bright, welcoming Sunset Cottage, complete with a private redwood porch, cozy woodstove, full kitchen stocked with breakfast fixings, vividly painted blue bedroom with down comforter–topped queen bed, and spacious sky-blue bathroom. You'll find a TV/VCR and a selection of movies in each room. After the self-check-in, enjoy a nibble on the delicious treats stocked in your kitchen, including fresh bread, delicious locally made cheese, home-made cookies, granola and yogurt, and a selection of gourmet coffee and tea. It's helpful to remember that One Mesa isn't a standard hotel: maid service is not provided, so unmade beds will remain that way; you'll find European-style handheld showers; and the full hot breakfast is served only on weekends—on weekday mornings, simple fresh pastries are delivered to your door. In our opinion, these quirks only enhance this destination's charm (it's also what keeps the rates affordable). Don't forget to stroll through the garden and take a dip in the hot tub; a road runs nearby, but you may not even notice the occasional passing car if you're gazing up at the stars. We recommend making reservations well in advance to secure your stay at this alluring and increasingly popular spot. $$–$$$ *MC, V; checks OK; www.onemesa.com.*

POET'S LOFT
♥♥●

19695 Hwy 1, Marshall / 415/453-8080
Even if you're not poets, a weekend here just might inspire the two of you to pen a few love poems. Poet's Loft is set just off the highway, but the otherwise spectacular setting is worth a thousand words. Perched on stilts, the angular, multilevel wood house juts out over the placid waters of Tomales Bay. Skylights and floor-to-ceiling glass windows infuse the interior with light and showcase views of the bay. Throw rugs accent the hard-wood floors, and contemporary pastel furnishings fill the living room and kitchen, located on the main floor. A wood-burning fireplace will keep you toasty warm, as will the spacious outdoor hot tub, which offers a sweeping panorama of the bay and Point Reyes Peninsula. If this doesn't fuel your poetic inclinations, nothing will! The master bedroom and smaller guest bedroom are located upstairs. Since this is a vacation rental, not a bed-and-

breakfast, guests provide their own food and linens. However, if you are from out of town and don't have your own at the ready, linens and towels can be provided for an extra charge.
$$$ *No credit cards; checks OK; www.poetsloft.com.*

TEN INVERNESS WAY
◕◕

10 Inverness Way, Inverness / 415/669-1648
This traditional bed-and-breakfast has billed itself "the inn for hikers and readers," although, given its location—within easy driving distance of some of Tomales Bay State Park's most wildly beautiful trails and beaches—we would add romance-seekers to the list. While the inn's book-lined downstairs living room, anchored by a large fireplace, is an inviting place to dive into a novel, the inn works best as a headquarters for active couples with plenty of outdoor plans (read: the small rooms are neither luxurious nor designed for all-day lounging). It's also one of the very few affordable accommodations in this overpriced region. The five rooms feature pleasant country motifs, queen-size beds, and private baths. First choice for romance is Room 1, a small, sun-filled corner room with sloping ceilings and a pleasant window seat. A more spacious accommodation is found downstairs in the ground-floor Garden Suite, which has a full kitchen, dining area, and private patio (beware: you may hear guests' footsteps overhead). Breakfast is delivered to your door when you stay in this suite, but we see nothing wrong with joining the other guests to dine in the toasty, woodstove-heated living room; here you'll feast on treats such as pecan Belgian waffles or savory quiche. The hot tub is situated in a worse-for-the-wear wooden shelter and affords no view, so we recommend visiting it at night, when all you'll notice is how the soaking soothes your tired muscles. On sunny mornings, lounge on the patio in Adirondack chairs facing herb gardens and fruit trees.
$$–$$$ *DIS, MC, V; no checks; www.teninvernessway.com.*

Romantic Restaurants

MANKA'S INVERNESS LODGE
◕◕◕◕

Argyle St, Inverness / 415/669-1034 or 800/580-LODGE
Dinner at Manka's is a once-in-a-lifetime romantic dining experience, though if you're lucky it will turn out to be more than once. Although this turn-of-the-20th-century hunting lodge is set alongside a steep residential street, the dense greenery surrounding the inn makes you feel as though you're nestled deep within the forest. A fire blazes in the first of three seductively lit dining rooms, while candles flicker on white linen-cloaked tables. The fire also serves as the kitchen's grill, filling the room with

delicious cooking aromas. Dark wood paneling in one dining room contributes to the coziness of the lodge surroundings; the largest room has a massive flower arrangement as its center. Tables are nicely spaced for intimate conversation, and tranquil melodies from the grand piano provide mood-making music. Manka's kitchen prides itself on using regional ingredients and locally caught fish, so much so that the menu each night is determined by what the farmers and fishing boats bring in that day. Grilled game is the house specialty, but what it will be—venison, quail, or rabbit—remains a nightly surprise. Flavorful vegetarian options and fresh seafood dishes are also featured, changing daily. An evening feast might include appetizers such as a delicious clam and mussel soup with fennel and cilantro puree or grilled polenta with local wild mushrooms and entrées such as house-cured grilled pork chops served with mashed potatoes, Italian black cabbage, and pear-kumquat chutney or the fireplace-grilled wild sturgeon served with smoky sweet-pepper broth. Desserts made from scratch, such as creamy cheesecake with warm caramel sauce and toasted pecans, are almost sweeter than a kiss. Each evening has one seating for dinner (7pm; 4pm on Sunday). Menu options vary: the restaurant presents a five-course prix fixe menu on Thursday through Sunday; an à la carte menu is available on Monday. *$$$$ MC, V; checks OK; dinner Thurs–Mon; beer and wine; reservations recommended; www.mankas.com.*

OLEMA INN RESTAURANT
⚫⚫⚫
10000 Sir Francis Drake Blvd, Olema / 415/663-9559
Housed in a yellow Victorian-style farmhouse surrounded by a wraparound porch, white picket fence, and gardens and orchards, this restaurant is the picture of country elegance. Diners travel frequently from Marin or the Bay Area to enjoy the beautifully prepared food, upscale yet relaxed ambience, and top-notch service. (The inn's rooms located upstairs are tastefully decorated and comfortable, but their proximity to the busy restaurant and its crowds prevents them from feeling truly romantic.) The dining room's interior is bright and airy, with high ceilings, skylights, and large windows overlooking the gardens. Warm pine floors, pastel-hued woodwork, antique wall sconces, candles, and a soundtrack of soft jazz bring a romantic coziness to the room. Well-spaced two-person tables strategically line the windows, but come prepared: this restaurant's understandable popularity can create a rather noisy atmosphere on busy weekend nights. In warm weather, opt for a seat outside on the pretty garden patio overlooking the orchard. The menu features seasonal local produce and meats. Start things off with a salad of grilled scallops and fresh heirloom tomatoes or local Tomales Bay oysters with your choice of eight toppings, including classic French champagne vinaigrette or Sterling Sturgeon Caviar and lemon crème fraîche. Main courses are equally tempting, from a dish of pan-roasted organic chicken

with savory romesco sauce to grilled Niman Ranch steak (hormone-free) or the daily fresh fish special. The sweet finale could be a seasonal dessert such as white nectarine-strawberry crisp or a satisfying bread pudding with butterscotch sauce and whipped cream.

$$$ *AE, MC, V; checks OK; lunch Fri–Sun, dinner Wed–Mon, brunch Sun; beer and wine; reservations recommended; www.theolemainn.com.* &

THE STATION HOUSE CAFE
🌶️🌶️

11180 Shoreline Hwy, Point Reyes Station / 415/663-1515
In warm weather, the brick terrace at this time-honored Point Reyes spot—beloved for decades by West Marin residents and San Francisco day-trippers—is a lovely, climbing-rose- and arbor-bedecked place for a sunny breakfast, casual lunch, or alfresco supper. But while the wainscoted interior is welcoming and pleasant, don't expect a quiet romantic meal here; the casual dining room serves with equal enthusiasm families with children, large groups of friends, and quiet couples. What you *can* expect to find is consistently tasty food, along with a good selection of wines. The menu changes weekly, featuring local produce, seafood, and organic beef from Niman Ranch. Breakfast items range from French toast made with Il Fornaio bakery's sweet challah to buckwheat pancakes and roasted-vegetable frittatas. For dinner, the Station House standbys, such as fish-and-chips with country fries and coleslaw, always satisfy; or, you can take the fancier route, starting with a platter of local oysters and mussels, followed by a braised lamb shank (made with Guinness Stout) or salmon with roasted-yellow pepper sauce. No matter what you decide to order here, it's hard to leave the Station House feeling anything but satisfied.

$$ *DIS, MC, V; local checks only; breakfast, lunch, dinner every day; full bar; reservations recommended.* &

SONOMA COAST

ROMANTIC HIGHLIGHTS

The Sonoma Coast, with beautiful scenery and golden beaches, offers a 50-mile stretch of isolated shoreline, a few small towns, and a handful of romantic accommodations. If you're looking for a swanky vacation complete with fancy restaurants and boutique shopping, look elsewhere on the North Coast—you won't find it here. However, the Sonoma Coast lies within only a few hours' drive from the Bay Area (a good two to three hours closer than Mendocino). **Bodega Bay**, with its active docks complete with rusty fishing boats and begging sea lions, is, for the most part, still a working-class fishing village. (The town of **Bodega** is a few miles southeast of Bodega Bay off Highway 1.)

Bodega Bay's attractions include nearby **Bodega Head** (from downtown Bodega Bay, turn west on Eastshore Rd, go right at the stop sign onto Bay Flat Rd, and follow it to the end). This small peninsula, which shelters Bodega Bay, harbors two superb walking trails that follow the ocean at the head. The first, a 4-mile round-trip trail, starts from the west parking lot and ends at the sand dunes of **Salmon Creek Beach**. An easier 1½-mile round-trip walk begins in the east parking lot and encircles the edge of Bodega Head. From December through April, Bodega Head also doubles as one of the premier whale-watching points along the California coast.

As you travel through the region, watch for the "coastal access" signs from Highway 1, which will direct you to the region's long, windswept, and—need we say it—exceedingly romantic beaches. Farther north, the town of **Jenner** is little more than an exquisitely scenic bend in the road where the Russian River meets the sea. But if taking quiet walks on the beach and breathing in the salty air without any distractions sound like your idea of romantic heaven, this is the place for you. Jenner makes a nice stop, with its calm river waters, sandy shoreline, and views of the sparkling Pacific. There aren't many kiss-worthy overnight options here, but consider stopping for a meal at **River's End** (1104A Hwy 1; 707/865-24840) to get your fill of this incredible scenery. Perched at the edge of the Russian River estuary, the restaurant—with a small outside deck—has wonderful ocean views. Lunch offers reasonably priced burgers and sandwiches; dinner fare is more eclectic and expensive (and slightly less reliable). Hours tend to vary as much as the menu does; be sure to call ahead if you're planning to dine here—for maximum romance, time your dinner for sunset.

Another kiss-worthy stop in Jenner is **Goat Rock State Park** (watch for signs from Hwy 1). This dramatic location would get four lips—and then some—except that, like many other state parks, it is so packed with people during the summer and on weekends that privacy is nearly impossible to find. Still, this place is so gorgeous that in the end you shouldn't let the crowds deter you. Here, the milky green and blue waters of the Pacific crash into the surf and meet the mouth of the Russian River. Water laps on both sides of the small strip of beach at this estuary, and massive rocks protrude from the sea—colonies of sea lions and seals often bask here in the sun. On busy weekends, you might find more seclusion at **Shell Beach**, just south of Goat Rock State Park. A well-used trail leads down to this little section of sand, which is best visited at low tide, when there are diverse tide pools to gaze into.

Sea Ranch is undoubtedly one of the most beautiful seaside destinations in the nation, due mostly to rigid adherence to environmentally harmonious architectural standards. A wide selection of vacation rental homes, some quite grand, are available in this renowned secluded community (rates are generally lower on the east side of Highway 1). Return visitors often sample different locations—woods, meadows, ocean bluffs—and you can take your pick by browsing the offerings of **Bodega Bay and Beyond Vacation Rentals** (see Romantic Lodgings). The only hotel accommodations in the area are found at **Sea Ranch Lodge** (see Romantic Lodgings). Also in the area is the award-winning **Sea Ranch Golf Links** (located along Sea Ranch's northern boundary at entrance to Gualala Point Regional Park; 707/785-2468; open every day), a challenging Scottish-style 18-hole course open to the public that was designed by Robert Muir Graves.

Access and Information

Two major highways provide access to the North Coast: **Highway 1**, the only route that runs along the coast, and **Highway 101**, the central artery that connects to Highway 1 via two quieter, more scenic roads. To drive to the Sonoma coast via Highway 1, take the Stinson Beach/Highway 1 exit from Highway 101 north (about 7 miles north of the Golden Gate Bridge) and head west. Keep in mind that driving is always slow along the coast. To save time, travel farther north on Highway 101 before heading west to the coast (of course, this will save you time only if you avoid rush hour, which is very congested on this particular freeway). The easiest route to Bodega Bay and Jenner: Traveling north on Highway 101, exit at Petaluma/Highway 116 west. Follow Bodega Avenue to Petaluma Valley Ford Road and continue on to Bodega Highway.

First-time visitors to Bodega Bay will want to stop by the **Sonoma Coast Visitors Center** (850 Hwy 1; 707/875-3866; www.bodegabay.com, www.visit sonomacoast.com), a good place to load up on free maps, guides, and brochures, including the "Bodega Bay Area Map & Guide."

Romantic Lodgings

BODEGA BAY AND BEYOND VACATION RENTALS
❂❂❂
575 Hwy 1, Bodega Bay / 707/875-3942 or 800/888-3565
It's hard to believe that the owners of these spectacular custom-built homes don't live here year-round, but their absence is your romantic gain. One of these dream houses or cozy cottages can become your reality with just a simple phone call to Bodega Bay and Beyond. The rental properties are scattered in and around Bodega Harbour, a community of stylish, contemporary homes with water views, and many hug an 18-hole golf course. Currently, 80 attractive homes and cottages are on the list, all nicely furnished and

equipped with everything you could ever need, and more: full kitchens, TV/VCRs, wood-burning fireplaces, firewood, and even barbecue grills. Listen to the distant blare of the foghorn from the deck of the Sea Cottage, a rustic little number that overlooks the 15th green and onward to the beach and bay. More water views, ample sunlight, stylish decor, and extra touches such as double-headed showers and plush linens are some of the enticing features of Cedar Cove. On the contemporary side is the Bay Haven, complete with nautical accents, an outdoor Jacuzzi tub off the second bedroom, and an expansive deck with views of the bay. Fisherman's Cottage may not have ocean views, but the creekside location is a plus, and the sea is only seconds away. This bright two-bedroom cottage with knotty pine walls and comfortable furnishings offers a woodstove, CD player, three decks, and an outdoor Jacuzzi tub. Couples might also want to try the aptly named Love Shack, located a couple of miles north of Jenner. This tiny one-bedroom cottage built among the sand dunes offers an inviting deck with terrific views of the ocean; you'll want to soak all day in the outdoor hot tub. With all of the rentals, two-night minimums are required, but we recommend staying longer and taking advantage of the generous midweek specials (four nights for the price of three). If you're looking for self-sufficiency and seclusion enhanced by proximity to the magnificent Pacific, these options are too good to pass up.

$$$–$$$$ *MC, V; checks OK; www.sonomacoast.com.*

BODEGA BAY LODGE AND SPA
♥♥☽

103 Hwy 1, Bodega Bay / 707/875-3252 or 800/368-2468
Bodega Bay Lodge offers far more romance and personality than you would guess from its motor-lodge exterior. A closer examination reveals wondrous water views, a highly comfortable interior, and a charming restaurant. The inviting lobby is outfitted with floor-to-ceiling bookshelves and overstuffed sofas placed next to a large fieldstone fireplace (it becomes even more inviting near dinnertime, when you can partake of the complimentary wine reception here). The lodge's 84 spacious guest rooms and suites are situated atop an oceanfront bluff, from where they enjoy gorgeous views of Bodega Bay along with the windswept grasslands of the adjacent Doran Beach Regional Park and nearby bird sanctuary. Only the occasional sound of the harbor horn interrupts the peace of this sprawling property. Distinctive touches such as shell lamps and seascape sculptures add charm to the hotel-style rooms, which are done up in shades of hunter green and cardinal red, accented by nautical motifs, and comfortably furnished. Most rooms offer the romantic luxury of wood-burning fireplaces; TVs, coffeemakers, plush white towels and robes, and the convenience of refrigerators and wet bars are appreciated amenities. Best of all, every room features a private deck overlooking the water. If your budget can stretch, spring for one of the five

Executive Whirlpool Suites—and in particular the ground-level Trumpeter Swan Suite, situated adjacent to the restaurant. This corner suite dazzles lovebirds with its king-size bed, CD player, and an ultradeluxe bathroom complete with two-person whirlpool tub and a glass-enclosed shower brightened by a skylight. In addition, you'll have nature right outside your private patio. A walk to the beach takes only five minutes, but if you want to stay on the property, there's plenty to do here, too. Pretty dune grasses border trails that meander to an exercise room, sauna, heated outdoor pool, and glass-enclosed whirlpool with an open-top gazebo and ocean views. If, after all that, you still need to unwind, try the spa's offerings, which include massages, body treatments, and facials. The on-site Duck Club restaurant (see Romantic Restaurants) is a good choice for an upscale dinner date.
$$$$ AE, DC, DIS, MC, V; checks OK; www.bodegabaylodge.com. &

SEA RANCH ESCAPE
❤❤❤
60 Sea Walk Dr, Sea Ranch / 707/785-2426 or 888/SEA-RANCH
Views of the surf crashing onto Sea Ranch's rugged, rocky shoreline can best be appreciated from the seclusion of your very own luxury rental home, we think you'll agree. Sea Ranch Escape's vacation properties, scattered along more than 10 miles of exquisite coastline, are some of the prettiest we've seen, ranging from cozy cottages tucked among trees to enormous oceanfront homes equipped with every imaginable luxury and amenity. You're sure to find something to match your budget and tastes. Many of the houses are newly built and stylishly outfitted, while others can best be described as the archetypal simple beach cabin. No matter which property you choose, all come stocked with the basic necessities (a full kitchen and cooking utensils, towels, linens, blankets, firewood). Many have spectacular ocean views, decks, fireplaces or wood-burning stoves, and even Jacuzzi tubs. Homes are categorized as oceanfront, hillside, cluster, ocean-view meadow, and forest, so decide which setting fires your romantic imagination, and then go make your vacation dream come true. Here are a few romantic suggestions: Couples often gravitate to the rustic one-bedroom Honeymoon unit, a small post-and-beam home with honey-colored wood-paneled walls, comfortable furnishings, a woodstove, and TV and stereo. Enjoy the lovely ocean view from the hot tub; you're just a short walk to the beach. If you're looking for waterfront accommodations with a more affordable price tag, consider the Pacific Edge; this one-bedroom condominium unit lacks a hot tub, but the comfy queen bed, freestanding fireplace, TV/VCR, stereo, and gorgeous view of a quiet cove make up for it. Lovers of the woods will want to head to the hills to the Treehouse, a one-bedroom wonder that's hidden in the forest. This multidimensional home's interior features wood paneling, large windows, a loft bedroom, and a hot tub on its deck.
$$$–$$$$ MC, V; checks OK; www.888searanch.com.

SEA RANCH LODGE
◗ ◗ ◖

60 Sea Walk Dr, Sea Ranch / 707/785-2371 or 800/732-7262
The endless drama of the Pacific Ocean offers plenty of romantic inspiration, and the closer your accommodations are to this magnificent shoreline, the better. They don't get much closer than Sea Ranch Lodge, set on a bluff directly above the grassy dunes and ocean. Architecturally interesting and angular in shape, the lodge offers gorgeous views from most guest rooms—in fact, the 20 rooms are simply (though elegantly) furnished so that nothing competes with the incredible scene outside the picture windows. Stylish taupe colors, natural fibers, woven chairs, dried-vine wreaths, and knotty pine walls free from unnecessary adornments help bring nature indoors. (None of the rooms contains a TV, and with these vistas, you won't miss it.) Cozy window seats and wood-burning fireplaces turn Room Nos. 1 and 7 into popular picks, while No. 11, a corner room, boasts the most wide-reaching views. If a soaking tub is more important to you than a sweeping vista, Room No. 20 has a dandy of a hot tub in its private backyard, plus a wood-burning stove indoors. There's no ocean view, but you can watch the stars sparkle at night while you soak. A buffet-style breakfast with fresh fruit and hot entrées, included with your stay, is served in the Sea Ranch Restaurant (see Romantic Restaurants), where outstanding ocean vistas are served up daily along with breakfast, lunch, and dinner. Couples tying the knot, take note: A barn might not be your first idea for a wedding venue, but the one at Sea Ranch will change your minds. Located on a seaside bluff, this weathered old barn has been transformed into a study in rustic elegance. For weddings (summers only), fabrics are draped from the rafters, and hay-covered floors add just the right country touch to your special day.
$$$–$$$$ *AE, MC, V; checks OK; www.searanchlodge.com.*

SONOMA COAST VILLA
◗ ◗

16702 Hwy 1, Bodega Bay / 707/876-9818 or 888/404-2255
Nestled among 60 acres of rolling hills dotted with oak trees, grazing cattle, and roaming horses, Sonoma Coast Villa's red-tiled roofs, terra-cotta and stucco exteriors, and beautifully terraced grounds are the picture of Mediterranean tranquility. Located in the town of Bodega, Sonoma Coast Villa is just a hop, skip, and a jump from the Pacific. Movie fans will be interested to know that Hitchcock's *The Birds* was filmed here in 1961, and you will enjoy a bird's-eye view of the hauntingly familiar Potter School House and St. Teresa's Church. In the villa's courtyard, a shaded and landscaped walkway proceeds past an inviting outdoor swimming pool framed by elegant cypress trees. Surrounding the pool are the inn's six original guest rooms; six newer rooms are located around back. The rooms' interiors are not especially romantic or impressive, with a hodgepodge of furnishings, draperies, and

decorations—which is disappointing, given the prices. However, tempting amenities such as private entrances, wood-burning fireplaces, slate floors, stucco walls, and private baths may outweigh this drawback. Skylights, recessed ceilings with dimming lights, Jacuzzi tubs, and private patios also enhance some of the rooms. To spice up the villa's romantic potential, we recommend visiting the on-site spa for a massage, sharing a late-night dip in the indoor communal Jacuzzi tub, or taking a moonlit walk through the lavish property. You can also explore inside: a wonderful circular staircase in the lobby leads to the tower library, which is brimming with dog-eared novels and homey knickknacks; panoramic windows showcase lovely views of the surrounding countryside. A hot, country-style breakfast is included with your stay; it's served each morning at two-person tables in an open and airy dining room with large windows looking onto the courtyard.
$$$–$$$$ *AE, MC, V; checks OK; www.scvilla.com.* &

Romantic Restaurants

THE DUCK CLUB
❀❀❀
103 Hwy 1 (Bodega Bay Lodge and Spa), Bodega Bay / 707/875-3525 or 800/368-2468
After a day spent exploring the beautiful Sonoma coast, a candlelight dinner at this inviting restaurant is the icing on the cake. An immense river-rock fireplace warms the bay-view dining room, which is decorated with duck sculptures and paintings. Large (a little too much so) round tables are draped in white linens. The chef is known for creative, award-winning dishes that star game, seafood, and produce from Sonoma County; creations include roasted Petaluma duck with Valencia orange sauce, farm-fresh asparagus strudel bathed in a mild curry sauce, and seared Sonoma foie gras. *Le poisson du jour* comes straight from the docks down the street, temptingly incarnated in the seafood sampler that features crab cakes, cured salmon, cornmeal-crusted oyster, and day boat scallops. Large windows overlook the bay, so be sure to request a table with a view when making the required reservations. The Duck Club also offers a lengthy wine list, with an extensive selection of Sonoma County labels. Picnic lunches are available upon request. If you stay the night at the lodge and breakfast here too, be sure to bring binoculars to watch the birdlife in the wetlands below.
$$$ *AE, DC, DIS, MC, V; no checks; breakfast, dinner every day; beer and wine; reservations recommended; www.bodegabaylodge.com.* &

SEA RANCH RESTAURANT

❤❤

60 Sea Walk Dr (Sea Ranch Lodge), Sea Ranch / 707/785-2371 or 800/732-7262
Much like the Sea Ranch Lodge itself (see Romantic Lodgings), this restaurant showcases the magnificent beauty of its setting by keeping the interior decoration to a minimum. From the restaurant's towering wall of windows, you can look out upon acres of windswept grasslands that slope down to the shoreline. Although fresh flowers and crisp white linens adorn every table, the dining room exudes an exceedingly casual, lodge-style ambience. If you come for dinner, make sure your reservation time corresponds with the sunset. The menu offers flavorful California cuisine made with the freshest local seafood and produce; if you're in the mood to splurge, order the chef's multicourse tasting menu paired with wine. Start things off with Tomales Bay oysters or a creamy potato-leek soup drizzled with truffle oil; main courses include such temptations as roasted Niman Ranch pork loin with fig and caramelized apple compote or herb-roasted wild salmon served with ragout of grilled artichokes and chanterelle mushrooms. Save room for the heavenly desserts, such as the chocolate-espresso pot de crème with crisp almond biscotti and a dollop of fresh whipped cream. After you've finished eating, head to the fireside room, where you can relish the warmth of a fire flickering in the stone fireplace, or take in more delicious ocean views in the adjacent solarium.
$$$ AE, MC, V; checks OK; breakfast, lunch, dinner every day, brunch Sun; full bar; reservations recommended; www.searanchlodge.com.

MENDOCINO COAST FROM GUALALA TO LITTLE RIVER

ROMANTIC HIGHLIGHTS

Of all the coastal destinations in Mendocino County, the northern village of Mendocino is definitely the most famous (see the next chapter). But lovebirds seeking privacy (or a shorter drive from the Bay Area) might want to explore some of the smaller—and often overlooked—seaside destinations on the stretch of the North Coast from Gualala, in the southern part of the county, to Little River, just south of Mendocino (and rather a suburb of it).

The same rugged coastal beauty that has made Mendocino such a tourist mecca is apparent everywhere. The smallest towns in the region can be missed in the blink of an eye when you're driving, especially given the distraction of spectacular coastal scenery. Dining is often limited in these remote locations, and your activities may be restricted to enjoying the ocean views and walking hand in hand on the beach—but then again, that's exactly the kind of seclusion many couples hope for.

Gualala's situation on the Pacific is breathtaking, and although the town's developed main strip lacks charm, excellent parks, beaches, and hiking trails—not to mention romantic accommodations—await on the outskirts of town. As for the often mispronounced name of Gualala, don't worry. Locals won't give you a hard time if you say it wrong, but the correct pronunciation is "wah-LA-la." (This Native American word means "water coming down place," referring to the town's location at the junction of the Gualala River and the sea.) Gualala is well known for kayaking, and **Adventure Rents** (Cantamare Center; 888/881-4386 or 707/884-4386; www.adventurerents.com) can provide everything you need. Whether you brave the ocean waves (best for those with experience) or just explore the scenic Gualala River (fine for beginners), an excursion on the water is sure to inspire a kiss. If you paddle upriver, you can spot ospreys, great blue herons, brown pelicans, and maybe even river otters at play. Canoes and double kayaks are also available. Afterward, wind down over dinner and top-notch views at **Top of the Cliff** (39140 S Hwy 1; 707/884-1539; call for seasonal closures), a casual upstairs restaurant tucked into a small shopping center. The tasty clam chowder makes a perfect midday meal, while dinner brings a hearty selection of pastas, steak, and fresh seafood.

For uninterrupted exploring by land or by sea, pack a lunch from **The Food Company** (Hwy 1 and Robinson Reach; 707/884-1800). Located right off the highway in Gualala, this picnic heaven offers an array of carry-out goodies, from spicy tamale pie and barbecued pork ribs to green bean–artichoke salad and rich chocolate cake (plus a good selection of wine). Such treats will be the perfect refreshment after a romantic coastal hike. One of our favorite places to explore in this area is the 195-acre **Gualala Point Regional Park** (42401 Hwy 1, approximately 1 mile south of Gualala; 707/785-2377; $3 fee). In fact, of the six public beach access points along Highway 1 between Sea Ranch and Gualala, this one offers the most bang for the buck. The park has 10 miles of trails weaving through coastal grasslands, redwood forests, and river canyons, in addition to picnic sites, camping areas, and excellent bird- and whale-watching opportunities along the mostly deserted beaches.

Fifteen miles north of Gualala is tiny **Point Arena**. The real attraction here is not the quiet, three-block stretch of town but the **Point Arena Lighthouse** (end of Lighthouse Rd; 707/882-2777; www.mcn.org/1/palight; about 5 miles northwest of downtown Point Arena off Hwy 1; 10am–4:30pm Apr–Sept, 10am–3:30pm Oct–Mar; $5 admission). On a clear day, it's worth the hike up the six-story tower's 145 steps to enjoy the standout view of the coast.

Located about 7 miles north of Point Arena, Manchester is less a town than a series of wildly scenic windswept grasslands and bluffs; its romantic perk is the 760 acres of wide beaches, meadows, and sand dunes at beautiful **Manchester State Park** (half mile north of town on Hwy 1; 707/882-2463; www.parks.ca.gov). The 15-minute walk across the dunes from the parking lot is a leg-burner, but your reward is an utterly secluded and beautiful 5-mile sweep of coastline.

The town of **Elk** is not much bigger than Point Arena, but its wonderful, romantic inns—and its breathtaking seascape—boost its kissing quotient. Even if you don't spend the night here, consider stopping for supper at the authentic Irish-style **Bridget Dolan's Pub** (5910 Hwy 1; 707/877-1820). In the cozy dining room, you'll find crisp white walls accented by warm wood wainscoting and a handful of tables set around a pot-bellied cast-iron stove. White tablecloths and flowers are the backdrop for casual fare such as fish-and-chips or three-cheese lasagne.

Elk is a good jumping-off point for exploring the wineries of Mendocino County, known as the **Anderson Valley wineries**. Reach them by driving inland via Philo-Greenwood Road, a scenic route that climbs Greenwood Ridge before dropping down into the tiny town of Philo, home to some big-name wineries. Among the most wildly romantic of the wineries in this area is scenic **Husch Vineyards** (4400 Hwy 128, Philo; 707/895-3216); sample the delicious sauvignon blanc and other wines in the rustic tasting room, and afterward picnic beneath oak trees. Champagne is the traditional drink of romance, and plenty of it can be found in these parts: **Pacific Echo** (8501 Hwy 128, Philo; 707/895-2065) is a French-owned winery that makes delicious bubbly and offers a lovely front porch for sitting and sipping; the large and well-known **Roederer Estates** (4501 Hwy 128, Philo; 707/895-2288) offers a more traditional tasting-room experience along with incredible views of the surrounding region. For maps or more information on area wineries, contact **Mendocino Coast Wine Growers Alliance** (707/468-9886; www.mendowine.com).

North of Elk are **Albion** and **Little River;** the latter, just 2 miles south of Mendocino, offers more affordable lodgings than its neighbor and handles Mendocino's tourist overflow. This quiet location is a good place to set up your romantic headquarters, since Mendocino's dining and shopping are still at your fingertips. Little River's other major asset is one of the finest outdoor kissing spots on the Mendocino coast: **Van Damme State Park** (707/937-5804). This 2,337-acre preserve filled with ferns and second-growth redwoods contains a small beach, a visitor center, and a campground, but the main attraction is the 15 miles of spectacularly lush trails. Ideal for a romantic walk, the trails start at the beach and wind through the redwood-covered hills. **Fern Canyon Trail** is the park's most popular route; it's an easy and incredibly scenic 2½-mile hiking and bicycling path that crosses over the Little River.

Romantic Lodgings

ALBION RIVER INN
◖◖◖◖

3790 Hwy 1, Albion / 707/937-1919 or 800/479-7944

Spontaneity is the soul of romance, but sometimes it pays to plan ahead. If you're thinking of taking a trip to the North Coast, we suggest you make reservations at the Albion River Inn immediately (or at least two months in advance). Everybody wants to stay at this sprawling, slightly ramshackle New England–style inn, and if you're lucky enough to get a room, you'll immediately see why. It sprawls across 10 secluded acres and offers resort-style amenities, yet it possesses the charm of an intimate, cozy inn. And fortunately, the inn's popularity in no way diminishes its romantic virtues. Set on a precipice towering above Albion Cove and the Pacific, the inn offers 20 stunning ocean-view units. All boast wood-burning fireplaces, elegant country touches, floral linens, down comforters, cozy robes, and complimentary wine and coffee. All but two rooms have private decks with superlative views. Six of the luxury rooms feature Jacuzzi tubs with ocean vistas, while several others have two-person soaking tubs. Take the time to stroll along the inn's private headland pathway, which leads to expansive vistas of water and sky. If, after a long day of touring, you're looking for a first-class spot to watch the sky turn fiery red as the ocean thunders against the shore below, this is the place. In the morning, enjoy a generous complimentary breakfast of fresh breads, homemade granola, eggs cooked to order, potatoes au gratin, fresh fruit, and juices, served in the inn's waterfront restaurant (see Romantic Restaurants). Dinner here is another romantic must; the food is as delicious as the view.

$$$–$$$$ AE, DIS, MC, V; checks OK; *www.albionriverinn.com.* ⚹

AUBERGE MENDOCINO
◖◖◖

8200 N Hwy 1, Little River / 707/937-0088 or 800/347-9252

The year 2003 brought new ownership and renewed romantic shine to this charming accommodation, formerly known as Rachel's Inn. Its location on busy Highway 1 belies the tranquility within, where comfortable elegance reigns. Conveniently, the popular hamlet of Mendocino is just 2 miles away (and the reasonable prices are also convenient). An array of tempting room options for couples includes accommodations in the historic main home, adjacent restored barn, or private cottage. The nine immaculately clean, beautifully decorated rooms and suites each have a queen or king bed, fluffy comforter, and private bath; many of the rooms also have fireplaces. The inn's location, between Van Damme State Park and the Mendocino headlands, gives guests easy access to the region's most magnificent outdoor kissing destinations. The budget-minded should consider the small but charming

rooms on the main home's top floor: the Blue Room, set farthest from the highway, is decorated in azure shades and has a large bathroom with clawfoot tub (the shower is handheld); the Grey Room offers a peekaboo glimpse of the ocean, but it's also closer to the highway. The price tags increase for the larger, more lavishly appointed rooms downstairs, such as the Parlor Suite and Garden Room: both are striking in their comfort and elegance but are a bit too close to the home's common area. In the renovated barn, try the top-floor Upper Suite, which has a spacious sitting room, a private balcony, a fireplace, and a separate bedroom with white linens accented by pastel florals. (Steer clear of the Mezzanine Suite, as the windows overlook the parking lot.) For the utmost in privacy, book the Parkside Cottage and enjoy a huge private sitting room, king-size bed, and porch overlooking the pleasant lawn. If you're traveling with another couple, or just want more views, check into the two-bedroom Little River Cottage, a charming 1880 historical cottage with phenomenal ocean views. Spectacular breakfasts are served in the elegant dinning room; homemade cookies, biscotti, and sherry are available for guests to help themselves.
$$$ MC, V; checks OK; www.aubergemendocino.com.

COAST GUARD HOUSE HISTORIC INN
🖤🖤

695 Arena Cove, Point Arena / 707/882-2442 or 800/524-9320
Formerly a lifesaving station, the Coast Guard House Historic Inn has been transformed into a comfortable, unpretentious getaway proudly overlooking the pier and Arena Cove. The five various-sized guest rooms in this venerable, weather-beaten, Cape Cod–style home and two separate cottages are simply decorated, with an emphasis on Arts and Crafts furnishings and accents. In the main house, couples who can't bear to be apart can snuggle up in the ultracozy Flag Room. Although its location near the living room isn't the best, this nautical-inspired hideaway charms with its sitting nook for two and queen-size bed tucked into a windowed alcove with ocean views. The other four rooms in the main house are pleasant but lack the Flag Room's romantic character. For the most seclusion, we recommend either of the two cottages. The Boathouse is charming and cozy, with gold sponge-painted walls, high ceilings, tiled floors, a potbellied stove, a jetted two-person tub in the living room, and a sunny private patio. In the spacious Cypress Cove, you can relax on the ocean-view front porch, cozy up to the wood-burning stove in the living room, or slip into the two-person spa tub set next to a gas fireplace. It's all shipboard romance upstairs in the sleeping quarters, where you'll find a queen-size captain's bed overlooking Arena Cove. With the wet bar, refrigerator, microwave, and coffeemaker, you might be tempted to move in. Breakfast is served at the dining table in the main

house (but can be delivered to the cottages) and includes tasty dishes such as spinach soufflé, potato pie with Gruyère cheese, and berry pancakes. **$$–$$$** *DIS, MC, V; checks OK; www.coastguardhouse.com.*

ELK COVE INN
❂❂❂❂

6300 S Hwy 1, Elk / 707/877-3321 or 800/275-2967
Set on a bluff with spectacular views of sea stacks jutting up from the blue Pacific, Elk Cove Inn's views will leave you breathless. The property, once merely pleasant, has become a highly romantic destination thanks to the new owner's improvements, which include room renovations and a new on-site, intimate spa. Guests receive a complimentary basket of delicious cookies and a split of wine before they adjourn to their quarters: options include cottages, rooms in the main house, and an adjacent complex with four luxury suites. The cottages and rooms are being remodeled one by one, and we can't wait until the entire property is transformed. The recently redone Bavarian cottage beckons with buttery yellow walls, pale green trim, a redwood ceiling with skylight, a cherry sleigh bed draped with lavish linens, and armchairs set into a window alcove with an ocean view. The other cottages that have not yet been remodeled feature interiors more rustic than elegant, but they have equally incredible views. The luxury suites, which enjoy a secluded location just a few steps from the ocean-view gazebo and the path to the beach, are *the* places to pucker up. Decorated in authentic Craftsman style, all are similar in design and amenities and feature hunter green decor, redwood vaulted ceilings, ocean-view decks, inviting king-size beds (one downstairs suite has a queen) swathed in luscious linens, and roomy bathrooms with jetted tubs, glass-enclosed showers, and heated floors. In the morning before breakfast, whip up a latte with your own espresso machine and sip beside the fireplace. Among the rooms in the main house are some less-expensive options: Molly's Garden is small and lacks an ocean view, but its newly renovated blue and ivory interior won't fail to charm. All guests are welcome to sign up in advance to use the hot tub (unfortunately, it's located just steps from Highway 1, so you can hear passing cars). The spa, which opened in summer 2003, offers tandem massage for couples; there's also a wet room with aromatherapy shower, sauna, and hydrotherapy tub. Mornings bring a bountiful breakfast buffet of savory egg dishes, hot corn pudding with spicy salsa, fresh fruit, crispy bacon, French toast, coffee cake, hot biscuits with jam, and bread pudding with rum sauce. With advance notice, it's possible to arrange special romance packages ranging from dinner for two in the gazebo at sunset to spa treatments with extra romantic touches.
$$$–$$$$ *AE, DC, DIS, MC, V; checks OK; www.elkcoveinn.com.*

THE HARBOR HOUSE INN
❤❤❤

5600 S Hwy 1, Elk / 707/877-3203 or 800/720-7474

A favorite destination of fine food lovers because of its outstanding restaurant (see Romantic Restaurants), this 1916 oceanfront redwood inn offers six tasteful, luxurious guest rooms and four cottages as well. The views, of sea stacks and timeworn rock arches rising from the Pacific, are unique to this section of coast. The rooms differ in style, but all have a chic contemporary look, with soft carpeting, crisp linens, and fireplaces. The small, standard baths are not equipped with jetted tubs, but the lodging's other extraordinary features, such as the restaurant, far outweigh this minor drawback. The tiny Lookout Room remains a kissing favorite, due to its private location, wonderful balcony, and outstanding views—it doesn't have a fireplace, but a little romance would quickly heat up these cozy quarters. Larger and more stately is the bright Harbor Room, which comes with a positively regal king-size bed. Seclusion is ensured in the self-contained, casually rustic Seaview and Oceansong Cottages, which have semiprivate decks, king-size beds, fireplaces, and full ocean views. You can't help but eat like royalty here: a full breakfast and four-course dinner for two are included in the rates (unless you visit in December or January, when weeknight stays include breakfast only and rates are heavily discounted). The breakfast is an extraordinary gourmet affair, including hot baked entrées, fresh fruit, pastries, coffee, tea, and juice. After dining, we recommend taking a romantic walk hand in hand along the property's cliff-side vegetable gardens or soaking up the ocean views from one of the numerous lookout benches. $$$$ MC, V; checks OK; www.theharborhouseinn.com.

INN AT VICTORIAN GARDENS
❤❤❤❤

14409 S Hwy 1, Manchester / 707/882-3606

Victorian Gardens is a striking gray and white Victorian farmhouse tucked so completely among 92 acres of meadows and forest that you can't see it at all from the road. Quiet serenity envelops you from the moment the gracious hosts welcome you like personal friends into their beautifully appointed residence (guest accommodations are offered only Thursday through Sunday). The exterior is thoroughly Victorian, but the interior is a refreshing mix of old and new, with a marked Italian accent. Polished hardwood floors, hand-loomed Italian rugs, hand-stenciled wallpapers, and exquisite artwork from the innkeepers' world travels characterize the main floor, and the same stylish elegance continues in the three guest rooms upstairs. Sloped ceilings, hardwood floors, and gorgeous artwork prevail in all of the guest rooms, which are spaced reasonably far apart. The spacious Master Bedroom is the premier suite. Distant ocean views can be enjoyed from its comfortable sitting area, the claw-foot tub fronts an elegant etched-glass window, and a fluffy down quilt warms the queen-size bed. (Note the color of this bed frame: it's painted with the *very* same paint used on that famous bridge by the bay.) The Northwest Bedroom, another favorite, has a queen-size bed with sumptuous linens and a down comforter, an enormous tiled bath, and ocean and pastoral views from the large soaking tub for two. The other bedroom, Golden, has a detached bath; however, it's still a fine choice for romance, with its wrought-iron queen-size bed and wicker chairs set beside a bay window that showcases the awe-inspiring sunsets. A lavish, multicourse breakfast, featuring eggs from resident hens, is served in the elegant dining room beside a crackling fire or in the adjacent sunny sitting room. Early evening brings wine and hors d'oeuvres, which you can enjoy on the wraparound porch if weather permits. The Inn at Victorian Gardens is a complete little world: if it's rainy, browse in the formal library or watch a classic movie in the parlor (there are no TVs in the rooms). Sunny weather invites you to breathe deeply in the meditation garden or flex those leg muscles along various trails on the property. And you absolutely shouldn't miss the opportunity to dine here (see Romantic Restaurants). *$$$ MC, V; checks OK; rooms available Thurs–Sun only; www.innat victoriangardens.com.*

NORTH COAST COUNTRY INN
❂❂
34591 S Hwy 1, Gualala / 707/884-4537 or 800/959-4537
Set at the edge of busy Highway 1, this cluster of terraced, weathered red-wood cottages—six suites in all—scales a forested hillside and provides many of the essentials for a romantic escape. The four original suites are our favorites. All have private decks, and two offer peekaboo ocean views (across the busy highway). The Sea Urchin suite is especially adorable. High peaked ceilings and open beams give all of the suites a feeling of spacious-ness, while walls adorned with country collectibles, antique logging tools, and botanical art provide old-fashioned authenticity. Bright throw rugs warm the wood floors, and patchwork quilts dress the antique four-poster beds. All four also feature fireplaces, skylights, and fully equipped kitchen-ettes. A few steps up the beautifully landscaped hillside, a modern building contains two deluxe suites, the Southwind and the Evergreen. These are comfortably outfitted with brass king-size beds, fireplaces, sitting areas overlooking floor-to-ceiling windows, and one-person Jacuzzi tubs in the bathroom. In the Southwind, you'll find a telescope for viewing sea lions and whales, plus a French-country theme with yellow and white walls accented by blue carpeting. The Evergreen overlooks huge redwood trees and fea-tures walls and ceiling of knotty pine. A delicious breakfast for all guests is offered in the cheerful downstairs room of the modern building; round tables for two and the gas fireplace contribute a cozy feel. One of the proper-ty's best features awaits at the end of a charming lighted pathway trimmed

with flowers. Here, sequestered among the pines, is an enclosed hot tub and outdoor shower. Lock the wooden gate and let the bubbles take you away. If you continue on to the hillside's crest, you'll discover a meadow in which sits a gazebo, comfortable lounge chairs, and a small fountain. While road noise is audible from this retreat, the seclusion is so seductive you'll forget civilization and let the forest sounds and distant ocean roar engulf you.
$$$ *AE, MC, V; checks OK; www.northcoastcountryinn.com.*

SEACLIFF
♥€

39140 S Hwy 1, Gualala / 707/884-1213 or 800/400-5053
Seacliff's four modern cedar structures sit on an oceanfront bluff overlooking the confluence of the Gualala River with the Pacific Ocean. From the parking lot, they look like nothing more than an ordinary apartment complex, but once you step inside and gaze at the extraordinary view, you'll know why this is a fabulous place to kiss the day away. The eight rooms on the first floor will appeal to your wallets, but the eight second-floor rooms will steal your hearts, thanks to their vaulted ceilings, large windows, and superior views from corner decks. Since the decor in all the units can only be described as hotel standard (uninspired bathrooms, modest furniture, and drab color schemes), we highly recommend spending the additional $20 per night to perch on the second floor. All of the rooms have a gas fireplace, a king-size bed, and a two-person whirlpool tub in the bathroom; from your private patio, you can revel in the perfectly unobstructed ocean views and use the provided binoculars to spot wildlife. Even if the room decor doesn't send you into raptures, the reasonable cost and romantic amenities of these rooms make them worthy of a toast with the complimentary sparkling wine or cider.
$$–$$$ *MC, V; checks OK; www.seacliffmotel.com.*

ST. ORRES
♥♥€

36601 Hwy 1, Gualala / 707/884-3303
Across the highway from a cloistered sandy cove 2 miles north of Gualala, this fascinating structure appears suddenly, seemingly out of nowhere: a hand-carved, wood-and-glass, Russian-style chalet. Stained-glass windows in two intricately crafted towers twinkle in the daylight; inside, prismatic light bathes the interior in a velvety amber glow. The 8 inexpensive rooms with shared baths in the main house are not designed for romance, but the 13 small cottages scattered about the grounds have far more potential. The cottages, with their rustic furnishings, small kitchens, and varying color schemes, all have their own distinct characteristics. Some feature unobstructed ocean views, while others have skylights, sundecks, fireplaces, and sunken tubs. Some interiors are more rustic than romantic, but couples

should find something to please them among the eight "Creekside" cottages, which share exclusive use of a spa facility with hot tub, sauna, and sundeck. You might try the Blue Iris Cottage, which has a spacious tiled bathroom with a two-person private sauna and Jacuzzi tub set before windows with a serene forest view. Come morning, a full breakfast, including homemade granola and freshly baked bread, arrives at your door in a large basket. Cottages book up to eight weeks or more in advance during the summer, and dinner reservations at St. Orres Restaurant (see Romantic Restaurants) are often hard to come by—we recommend booking far in advance if this is your destination of choice.

$$$–$$$$ *MC, V; checks OK; www.saintorres.com.* &

WHALE WATCH INN
◗◗❦

35100 Hwy 1, Gualala / 707/884-3667 or 800/942-5342
Witnessing the migration of the earth's largest animals from the comfort of your own private balcony is a vacation indeed, and couples migrate to this oceanfront destination even outside whale-watching season. In almost all of the 18 rooms and suites, the sound of crashing surf is as clear as a bell, and it's only 134 steps to the beach below. The accommodations, which are housed in five wooden buildings spread throughout the cliff-side property, offer more comfort than elegance—unappealing elements in some of the rooms include dated furnishings, nondescript artwork, and slightly garish floral-print fabrics. However, the amenities in the eight suites in the Pacific Edge Building and the two rooms in the Quest House may outweigh the less-than-stylish decor for many couples; all have extraordinary views and wood-burning fireplaces, and some offer private decks and whirlpool tubs for two. Ocean Sunrise and Crystal Sea, both located in the Quest House, have pleasant wooded surroundings; the second-floor Crystal Sea enjoys the best ocean views. Rooms in the Sea Bounty and Cygnet House buildings are not as well put together. In keeping with the romantic theme, none of the rooms have TVs or phones. At the hour you designate, a delicious gourmet breakfast is served in your room. As you enjoy your food, you can savor ocean views—and hopefully the sight of a whale pod from your perfect vantage point.

$$$–$$$$ *AE, MC, V; checks OK; www.whalewatchinn.com.* &

Romantic Restaurants

ALBION RIVER INN RESTAURANT
●●

3790 Hwy 1, Albion / 707/937-1919 or 800/479-7944
A glorious cliff-top setting and expansive ocean views help make this stylish dining room a worthwhile romantic destination. Although the profusion of tables limits privacy and the dining room is filled to capacity most days, the intimate mood is undeniable from the moment you enter. The interior is awash in soft lighting and flanked by floor-to-ceiling windows affording incredible views. The menu focuses primarily on deftly executed fresh seafood dishes. Start with bites of fennel-crusted ahi tuna or a rich soup of butternut squash, caramelized leeks, and fresh fennel. For main dishes, options include a roasted duck breast with a tangy orange, ginger, and rice wine-vinegar reduction served with maple-whipped yams and zucchini strings; pan-roasted halibut served with creamy polenta and a Meyer lemon butter sauce; and oven-roasted, marinated quail wrapped in honey-cured bacon. The produce is all local and impeccably fresh. Though the dishes are thoroughly satisfying, the chef's light touch should leave you with enough room for dessert. You'll be sweetly tempted by the refreshing seasonal fruit desserts, such as a rhubarb-and-wild-berry cobbler, or the popular caramelized coconut bananas topped with warm rum-caramel sauce and scoops of vanilla ice cream.
$$$ AE, DIS, MC, V; checks OK; dinner every day; beer and wine; reservations recommended; www.albionriverinn.com. ⎣

THE HARBOR HOUSE RESTAURANT
●●●

5600 S Hwy 1 (Harbor House Inn), Elk / 707/877-3203 or 800/720-7474
Nonguests of the Harbor House Inn are invited to partake of dinner here; however, reservations are extremely limited when the inn is full, and the only seating is at 7pm. Harbor House Inn guests, on the other hand, have reservations nightly (a four-course dinner and full breakfast are included with your stay). The contemporary dining room is warmed by a wood-burning fireplace and enhanced by enormous windows; to take full advantage of the restaurant's spectacular view, beg for a window table (alas, you can't reserve any particular table). Fortunately, the dining room is small enough that you can glimpse the ocean from nearly every seat in the house. The four-course prix fixe dinners change nightly but may start with such delicacies as smoked duck dumplings surrounded by a mango-sesame sauce, traditional crab cakes followed by grilled filet mignon on a potato-mushroom cake, or seared rare ahi tuna served with a zing of horseradish cream. Dinners always begin with a small, hot-from-the-oven loaf of bread that goes perfectly with the chef's delicious soups, such as the tomato-basil

or Indian spice-spinach. The salad, made from homegrown vegetables, might be a combination of greens tossed with herb vinaigrette or sprouts mixed with olives, water chestnuts, and a toasted sesame-seed dressing. Expect to find entrées such as ravioli stuffed with crab, fennel, and shiitakes in a Pernod cream sauce or seared sea scallops on roasted yellow-pepper rouille with Spanish basmati rice pilaf. The seafood is harvested from local waters, and the meats and cheeses come from nearby farms. Many of the fine wines on offer are locally produced.

$$$$ *AE, MC, V; checks OK; dinner every day (Fri–Sat only Dec–Jan); beer and wine; reservations required; www.theharborhouseinn.com.*

INN AT VICTORIAN GARDENS
⬢⬢⬢⬢

14409 S Hwy 1, Manchester / 707/882-3606

Reservations are required at the Inn at Victorian Gardens (no drop-ins allowed), but it's well worth the extra effort to experience the romantic surprises that await you when you dine at this lovely, intimate destination with three guest rooms (see Romantic Lodgings). The resident chef/innkeeper creates outstanding five-course gourmet Italian meals that evoke a bygone era of elegance. Designed to resemble a dinner party, the experience allows you to savor the lost art of dining, when meals were enjoyed throughout the evening and accompanied by fine wine and conversation. Your innovative Italian host prepares delicious renditions of classics such as succulent roasted pork loin; thin slices of ham rolled around diced potatoes, carrots, and green beans with homemade mayonnaise; and *vincisgrassi,* hand-rolled pasta stuffed with savory wild mushrooms. Desserts are equally mouthwatering. A new, hand-printed menu is presented daily, and many of the ingredients are plucked straight from the garden. Each course is served family-style in the fireside dining room, but if you'd rather dine alone (and you reserve early enough) you can book a table *à deux.* As you would expect from the attention to detail here, fine Italian china, linens, crystal, and silver accompany the meal, as do top-notch wines and after-dinner drinks. Dinner is also open to nonguests on the same basis. Dinners start at 7:30pm and last as long as your hearts desire.

$$$$ *AE, MC, V; checks OK; dinner Thurs–Sun, one seating only; beer and wine; reservations required; www.innatvictoriangardens.com.*

THE LEDFORD HOUSE RESTAURANT
⬢⬢◗

3000 Hwy 1, Albion / 707/937-0282

It's a rare thing when an ocean-view restaurant's food and ambience are as good as the vistas, but that's the case with the Ledford House Restaurant, situated alone on a bluff with stunning ocean views. Soft jazz filters in from the mellow bar area, single long-stemmed flowers adorn every table, and

candlelight casts flickering shadows on whitewashed walls, infusing the dining room with warmth. When the coast is shrouded in fog (which occurs more often than some would like to admit), Ledford House becomes even more cozy and inviting. The simple French bistro–inspired menu tempts with dishes such as cassoulet (lamb, pork, garlic sausage, and duck confit slowly cooked with white beans) and braised rabbit, as well as more traditional California cuisine such as grilled swordfish; Dijon-herb-encrusted rack of lamb; and a hearty risotto with roasted-vegetable ragout, shiitake mushrooms, and Asiago cheese. The romantic atmosphere and gracious wait staff make this a wonderful place to spend an evening together. After dinner, sidle up to the bar and listen to the live music, featured nightly.
$$$ *AE, MC, V; checks OK; dinner Wed–Sun (closed 3–4 weeks Feb–Mar— call for details); full bar; reservations recommended; www.ledford house.com.* &

PANGAEA
◐◐
39165 S Hwy 1, Gualala / 707/884-9669
When this well-loved local restaurant migrated south from Point Arena to a new location in Gualala in summer 2003, its legions of fans followed—and so do we. With its expanded hours, a more romantic setting, and food as delicious as ever, there's never been a better time to spend an evening at Pangaea. The three intimate, interconnecting dining rooms are painted in rich colors that create a jewel-box feel; one is chili red, another is blue with decoupage maps on the ceiling, and another is filled with warm hues of yellow and orange. Beaded votive candles and ever-changing paintings by local artists add character. Operated by a husband-and-wife team, the restaurant has an artistic bent, as is shown in the dramatic (and generous) food presentations, not to mention the bold flavors. Visit for lunch to try the duck tacos on homemade corn tortillas or a rich, satisfying bowl of homemade soup. But dinner is when the restaurant really shines. The addition of a wood-burning oven in the kitchen gives the dish of oven-roasted mussels and clams a flavorful authenticity; other options on the ever-changing menu may include braised lamb shanks, savory rabbit terrine, or rare seared ahi with wild mushrooms, fingerling potatoes, and savory black-olive tapenade. For dessert, the warm, bittersweet chocolate cake provides a melt-in-your-mouth finish.
$$ *MC, V; checks OK; lunch Fri–Sat, dinner Wed–Sun; beer and wine; reservations recommended; www.pangaeacafe.com.*

ST. ORRES RESTAURANT
❤❤❤
36601 Hwy 1 (St. Orres Inn), Gualala / 707/884-3335
The Russian-inspired architecture of St. Orres is refreshingly unusual (see Romantic Lodgings), and the restaurant, housed in a three-story-high wooden tower, is similarly unique. Filled with stained-glass windows, stenciled woodwork, and trailing plants, the dining room has a formal yet comfortable atmosphere and holds clusters of intimate, candlelit tables. The only letdown is that tables are wedged tightly together in spots. The restaurant's constantly changing prix fixe dinner menu is a three-course delight of soup, salad, and entrée, offering unusual dishes such as wild boar stuffed with dates and walnuts, savory pheasant breast over wild-mushroom risotto cakes, or grilled Sonoma County quail marinated in tequila and served with yam pancakes, pheasant wontons, and a blood orange–jalapeño pepper glaze. If you can't tell already, the specialty here is wild game of the North Coast served with a French-country twist, and vegetarians might want to eat elsewhere. Save room for the delicious desserts. The house-made Jack Daniels ice cream with roasted pecans and maple syrup proves to be a delightfully mellow and creamy surprise.
$$$ MC, V; checks OK; breakfast (inn guests only), dinner every day (call ahead in winter); beer and wine; reservations recommended; www.saint orres.com. ♿

MENDOCINO

ROMANTIC HIGHLIGHTS

A magnificent view of the rugged headlands and the Pacific is the main attraction of this historic village, although Mendocino's white spire church and pristine New England–style seaside streets are also full of charm. Because the town is so alluring, it is also very crowded, especially in the late spring and summer. Its many bed-and-breakfasts are frequently booked on weekends—often months in advance. A good option is to visit in early spring, when climbing tea roses and wisteria begin to blossom and vibrant green grasses spread across the bluffs. In the off-season—late fall and winter—the crowds are less prevalent but, alas, so is the sun. Nevertheless, the fog also has its charms. When everything is shrouded in a veil of misty white, you can snuggle up in a cozy bed-and-breakfast—and enjoy off-season discounts, which generally begin in November.

You don't need a map to explore Mendocino's quaint shopping district, which includes old-fashioned storefronts housing art galleries and specialty shops. Just grab your beloved's hand and set off. Some of our favorite romantic discoveries include **Garden Bakery** (10450 Lansing St; 707/937-3140), where you can sit outside in the sunshine over cups of steaming coffee and delicious cinnamon buns. Steal a kiss behind a shelf at the **Gallery Bookshop** (45098 Main St; 707/937-BOOK; www.gallerybooks.com), one of the best independent bookstores in Northern California. **Mendocino Jams & Preserves** (440 Main St; 707/937-1037 or 800/708-1196; www.mendo jams.com) is a town landmark that offers free tastings of its luscious marmalades, dessert toppings, mustards, chutneys, and other spreads. Stop by the **Fetzer Tasting Room** (45070 Main St; 707/937-6190; www.fetzer.com; 10am–6pm every day) to sample the excellent wines—it might just inspire you to plan a day trip to the **Anderson Valley wine country**, about an hour's drive away. (For more information on these wineries, see Romantic Highlights in the preceding chapter.)

Perhaps more than any other attraction, **Mendocino Headlands State Park** (707/937-5804; free admission) lures visitors—the coastal headlands and the park surround the town on all sides. This protected, flawless curve of land offers several miles of accessible paths that wind along the edge of the heather-covered bluffs. On calm, sunny days, the glistening ocean reveals hidden grottos, sea arches, and tide pools as foamy white surf encircles the rocky boundary of Mendocino. If you happen to be here December through March, you may see whales migrating along the coast. Even on days when the thick ocean fog enfolds the area in a pale cloak, this is still a wonderful place to explore (and you'll have a great excuse to snuggle close). The headlands' main access point for those on foot is at the west end of Main Street—or, if you'd rather drive, take the motorist's scenic route along Heeser Drive off Lansing Street. **Mendocino State Park Visitor Center** is located at Ford House (735 Main St; 707/937-5397). When the sun is shining, begin your walk armed with supplies from **The Mendocino Bakery** (Lansing at Ukiah; 707/937-0836) and find a secluded place on the bluffs to spread out your picnic. There's something for everyone among the to-go items, including several types of frittatas, focaccia pizzas, and bakery goods.

Traveling approximately 8 miles north of Mendocino brings you to the beautiful **Mendocino Coast Botanical Gardens** (18220 Hwy 1; 707/964-4352; www.gardenbythesea.org; $7.50 admission fee; open every day—call for seasonal closures). Fronted by a rustic garden shop and a country café on the west side of the highway, the entrance gives little indication of the 47 acres of botanical wonders to be found inside. Follow walkways festooned with rhododendrons that lead to formally landscaped annuals, hillsides laced with hydrangeas, and meadows mellow with heather. No matter what time of year you visit, something beautiful will be in bloom. Wander to the westernmost reaches of the garden to find a stunning seascape with welcoming benches perched high above the crashing surf. In the winter you might even see a whale pass by in the distance, its breathing spout rising against the vast horizon. If you've worked up an appetite after exploring the gardens, consider heading into Fort Bragg for a hearty meal at the casual **North Coast Brewing Company** (444 N Main St, Fort Bragg; 707/964-3400)—don't forget to order a glass of their famous beer.

Another reason to stray north of the town of Mendocino is the spectacular array of parks you will find, all of which beckon energetic couples to engage in some rugged outdoor exploration. About 2 miles north of Mendocino, off Highway 1, is **Russian Gulch State Park** (707/937-5804). This is a veritable paradise for campers, hikers, and abalone divers, but privacy can be found in parts of the 5½-mile round-trip hike along **Falls Loop Trail** to the Russian Gulch Falls, a misty 35-foot waterfall secluded in the deep old-growth forest. Another appealing trail located between Mendocino and Fort Bragg on Highway 1, 1½ miles north of the town of Caspar, is the **Jug Handle State Reserve's Ecological Staircase Trail** (707/937-5804). This 5-mile round-trip trail gets surprisingly little traffic and has an intriguing attraction: a series of naturally formed, staircaselike bluffs—each about 100 feet higher and 100,000 years older than the one below it—that differ dramatically in ecological formation. You'll climb from beaches to headlands to an amazing pygmy forest filled with waist-high, century-old trees.

Our favorite spot for kissing also involves the longest drive—but it's worth it. About 3 miles north of Fort Bragg off Highway 1, **Mackerricher State Park** (707/937-5804; free admission) offers a wondrous assortment of nature's delights: waterfalls at the ends of forested trails, grass-covered headlands overlooking the Pacific, 8 miles of white sand beaches, rolling sand dunes, and haystack rocks where harbor seals spend the day lounging in the sun. The best thing about this state park is its distance from Mendocino; the extra few miles make it less popular, which gives it a definite kissing advantage. Upon your return to town, finish the day on a high note with a visit to the **Mendocino Hotel and Restaurant** (see Romantic Lodgings); the elegant bar and lounge are perfect spots to relax in over a nightcap or hot cocoa in front of the fireplace.

Access and Information

Depending on your route, it takes between 3½ and 5 hours to reach Mendocino from the Bay Area; there are several Highway 1/Highway 101 routes to consider. Driving is always slow along the coast, and you should make your route decision based on your time constraints and your tolerance for what is truly a driving challenge. Countless hairpin turns on Highway 1 require slowing to 10 miles per hour, and traffic can further impede your progress. However, this coast highway offers its own well-known scenic rewards, so here are a couple of options should you choose this path (avoid commuting hours like the plague if you want to make good time on Highway 101). First option: travel north on Highway 101 and exit at Sebastopol/Highway 12 west, which connects with the Bodega Highway. Second option: traveling north on Highway 101, exit at Petaluma/Highway 116 west. Follow Bodega Avenue to Petaluma Valley Ford Road and continue on to Bodega Highway. Once you exit Highway 101, you will be rewarded with scenic drives through idyllic pastoral settings. Third option: the fastest route to Mendocino is the one that avoids Highway 1 the most. This entails taking Highway 101 north just past Cloverdale to the Mendocino/Highway 128 West exit. Travel west on Highway 128 through Boonville and Anderson Valley to connect to Highway 1, then go north 10 miles to Mendocino. Highway 128 supplies plenty of curves of its own but straightens out around the town of Boonville; after Boonville, it winds through magnificent old-growth forest to the ocean.

Expect fog, wind, and cold weather to increase as you travel north along the coast. The **National Weather Service** (831/656-1725) provides updated weather reports; call **Caltrans** (800/427-7623) for highway conditions. Stock up on provisions for the drive and bring layers of clothing—and don't forget the binoculars and wide-angle lens.

Contact the **Fort Bragg–Mendocino Coast Chamber of Commerce** (332 N Main St, Fort Bragg, CA 95437; 707/961-6300 or 800/726-2780; www .mendocinocoast.com) for more information about the Mendocino area.

Romantic Lodgings

AGATE COVE INN
♥♥❅

11201 N Lansing St, Mendocino / 707/937-0551 or 800/527-3111
Ensconced among lovely gardens on a bluff across the street from the ocean, this historic 1860s farmhouse enjoys extraordinary views of the Pacific. The best part about staying here is breakfast in the glass-enclosed dining room, one of the most charming breakfast experiences in all of Mendocino—thanks both to the spectacular vistas and to the scrumptious morning goodies, which are prepared on a century-old wood-burning stove. Trays are available to take the fixings back to your room, but after you drink in the view, you'll want to stay right here. From this room, you can also witness spectacular sunsets by the fireside hearth—or, if you're lucky, catch a glimpse of migrating whales. The 10 guest rooms do not quite live up to the view or the gardens. All are located in either country-style cottages or in a duplex cottage, and all differ in size and style. If noise bothers you, inquire about the location of your cottage—several of the smaller ones at the back of the property sit just yards from an adjacent highway. Generally, you can expect four-poster or sleigh queen- or king-size beds, amenities such as TVs and CD players, and private patios with views that vary in quality.

Gas-burning fireplaces warm all but one room. The Emerald Room and the Obsidian Room, located in the duplex cottage, feature the most space and amenities, with extralarge tubs for two, double-headed showers, private decks, king-size beds, and fireplaces. It's fortunate that the extraordinary ocean views distract the eye from the fussy, flowery decor. One of the more recently redecorated accommodations, the Jasper cottage, has more appeal: here you'll find a pleasant, neutral decor of warm-hued wood and taupe linens, a queen-size sleigh bed, a fireplace, a private bath with shower, and a deck with an ocean view.
$$$-$$$$ *AE, MC, V; checks OK; www.agatecove.com.*

BREWERY GULCH INN
❤❤❤❤
9401 Hwy 1, Mendocino / 707/937-4752 or 800/578-4454
The most noteworthy romantic destination to arrive on this stretch of coast in years, Brewery Gulch is a secluded, dramatic, lodge-style inn set high on a bluff just a mile south of the village of Mendocino. Opened in March 2001 and constructed of 150-year-old redwood timbers salvaged from nearby waterways, this strikingly beautiful spot is nothing short of heart-stirring. It's on the opposite side of the highway from the Pacific, but the high bluff setting offers water views nonetheless, and you can still hear waves crashing in the distance. Step inside and the soaring ceilings, massive beams, flagstone floors, enormous fireplace, and vast windows fronting lovely woodland will take your breath away. The 10 rooms are stylish, fabulously comfortable, and marvelously private. Each one offers comfortable leather club chairs set before a gas fireplace, a down comforter, a CD player, a TV hidden in an armoire, and a spacious bathroom with a granite-topped redwood vanity; for a romantic occasion, it's definitely worth the splurge for a bathroom with a Jacuzzi or soaking tub. All of the accommodations are lovely, but the corner rooms with private outdoor decks set our hearts beating faster. On the second floor, the Raven boasts a beautiful soaking tub for two; a small, charming deck with ocean views; a king-size bed with plush, deep red linens; and handsome furniture with a mahogany finish. When you open the windows, you can hear the surf. Of the first-floor corner rooms, we are partial to Madrone, with its soft green color scheme and spectacular Jacuzzi tub in the bathroom. Other choices include the two loft rooms, the Lookout and the Smuggler's Cove, located on the top floor and accessed by private short staircases; while these lack private decks or extra-luxurious bathrooms, they boast the inn's finest ocean views and give you the cozy feeling of staying in a tree house. The rooms are impeccably clean, the service is highly professional, and nearly anything is possible if you arrange it in advance, from hot-stone massages to gourmet backpack picnics supplied with a hiking map of nearby waterfalls. (Check the Web site for a wonderful variety of romance packages.) Each afternoon brings

complimentary wine and hors d'oeuvres. Delicious, creative, and bountiful breakfasts are prepared by a French-trained chef and served at private tables in the fireside dining room; in warm weather, dine on the flagstone patio while basking in the sunshine.
$$$–$$$$ *AE, MC, V; checks OK; www.brewerygulchinn.com.* &

C. O. PACKARD HOUSE
❍❍❍❶
45170 Little Lake St, Mendocino / 707/937-2677 or 888/453-2677
This establishment has always boasted a more elegant interior than many other B&Bs in town, yet the new owners who arrived in 2004 have infused this inn with even more sophistication. Each of the four rooms in this landmark 1878 Carpenter's Gothic–style Victorian has a delightful romantic ambience. Despite the Victorian facade, there is nothing remotely fussy here; inside, sophistication prevails, along with a collection of contemporary artwork from San Francisco art galleries. Each room boasts all the romantic must-haves: cozy bedside gas fireplaces, two-person jetted tubs, luxurious bath products, robes and slippers, glass-enclosed showers, and beautiful big beds covered by lush linens and pillows. There are also flat screen TVs with cable and DVD players, and Bose radios and CD players. Creamy neutral hues, large paned windows, and sparkling marbled baths add elegance to each room. If you stay in the Pacific View Room, you can peer over the rooftops to the sea. This is the largest room, complete with a king-sized Parisian sleigh bed and an arched entrance leading to the magnificent bathing area. Speaking of baths, the loo is even lovelier in the Garden Court Room; this stunning light-filled bathroom features a jetted tub framed by a large window opening to garden views. Privacy prevails in the Chapman Point Room. Just be careful not to knock yourselves out on the hallway's sloping ceilings, which add character to these tucked-away quarters. The king-sized pine and iron sleigh bed has a feathered comforter and plenty of pillows to prop yourselves up for viewing the sea beyond. Two luxurious bedrooms downstairs have gorgeous interiors, although the location closer to common areas doesn't offer the prime privacy of some of the other quarters. If you are planning a longer stay, ask about the two freestanding cottages with private entrances also on the property that are available to rent for a month or longer. In the morning, a full two-course breakfast, highlighting rich dishes such as puff pear pastries, Dutch babies with berries, and espresso flan, is served at the dining room table. There's also the heartwarming option of having a continental breakfast delivered to your room in a basket (if you would rather kiss than socialize with fellow guests). In the evening, gather for complimentary wine hour with savory snacks in the living room. Although noise from the adjacent school is sometimes noticeable, the central location—nearby the local art center and community theater—more than makes up for it: at dinnertime, you can stroll

hand in hand to any one of Mendocino's restaurants since all are within walking distance of C. O. Packard House. For a weekend of fun with no fuss, consider the romance package, which includes dinner at a charming nearby restaurant; chilled wine awaits you in your room on arrival.
$$$ *DIS, MC, V; checks OK; www.packardhouse.com.*

COAST RETREATS
◑◑◑◉

Mendocino (call for street addresses) / 707/937-1121 or 800/859-6260
Having traveled the world looking for romantic retreats of their own, the owners of this impressive rental company finally found their slice of heaven in Mendocino. Fortunately, they're eager to share. Some of Mendocino's most dramatic ocean views are to be had from the decks, porches, and front yards of Coast Retreat's six sensational, ultraprivate rental properties. Four of these rental homes, perched atop steep bluffs that jut out over the incoming tide, are built as close to the ocean as is possible. We especially liked the Jameson House, where French doors open onto a spacious water-view deck showcasing seagulls and ospreys sailing by at eye level. A large hot tub, a walk-in shower for two, a beautiful jade-colored tile kitchen, and a telescope are other romantic features here. Just down the road, the artistically decorated Bungalow shares the same breathtaking oceanfront stage, plus a hot tub and a deck that wraps around three sides of the house. Copper countertops in the kitchen, mosaic tiles in the bathrooms, and other hand-worked details give the one-bedroom house personality. All of the homes have fully equipped kitchens, so bring provisions to whip up meals for your sweetheart. No matter which property you decide on, all have amenities and views designed to cater to your romantic desires—you're in for a treat.
$$$$ *MC, V; checks OK; www.coastretreats.com.*

CYPRESS COVE & OCEAN SPLENDOR
◑◑◑◑

THE HAYLOFT
◑◑◑◉

Mendocino (call for street addresses) / 707/937-1456 or 800/942-6300
Believe us when we say it is worth the effort to plan your special get-away around the availability of these outstanding rental properties. Ocean Splendor, perched on a magnificent bluff a few miles south of Mendocino in Little River, is the newest and most splendid, offering complete seclusion and luxury. Relax in the hot tub on the deck, get cozy in front of one of two fireplaces, or relax amid decor that tastefully mixes antiques with clean, modern furnishings. It's definitely a splurge, but for a special occasion you can't go wrong. Cypress Cove, a mile south of Mendocino, is a two-story beach house with wraparound floor-to-ceiling windows showcasing

spectacular views of town and the bay. The two suites here are decorated in a contemporary Scandinavian style, and both feature amenities such as private decks, indoor whirlpool tubs for two, separate showers, wood-burning fireplaces, and complete entertainment systems. In both suites, the beds face seaward, and the ambience is easily adjusted by dimming lights. The second-floor Pacifica is decorated in shades of teal, with large bouquets of fresh flowers and terra-cotta-tiled floors. The ground-level Cove Suite's color scheme is subdued gray and sea green, and it boasts a corner window seat with magnificent views—in fact, this has to be one of the absolute best places to kiss in all of California. Coffee, tea, brandy, and chocolates are provided, but breakfast is not; however, each suite is equipped with a kitchen. One further option is the Hayloft, a beautifully maintained one-bedroom retreat surrounded by cypress and fir trees about 5 miles from the ocean and 2 miles from Mendocino. It occupies the second story (a garage is below) and has some memorable romantic touches, including a hidden hot tub on the back deck and skylights over the inviting queen-size bed. There's also a fully equipped kitchen, tiled wood-burning fireplace, and armoire stocked with TV/VCR, CD player, and a selection of music and movies. The soft white and beige interior, accented by natural woods, is immaculately clean. From the bedroom, French doors open onto a small balcony, which overlooks the driveway and the owner's home nearby. A generous basket of fruit and bakery goods comes with the cottage, and such appliances as a coffeemaker and juice squeezer make mornings easy.
$$$–$$$$ *MC, V; checks OK; www.mendocinopreferred.com.*

THE JOSHUA GRINDLE INN
❤❤

44800 Little Lake Rd, Mendocino / 707/937-4143 or 800/GRINDLE
Set on the edge of town, this 1879 Victorian farmhouse—a rather large and traditional bed-and-breakfast—offers some romantic room choices. All 10 rooms feature period and country antiques and new but standard bath-rooms; some of the rooms have wood-burning fireplaces. Our favorites for romance are the two rooms in the Saltbox Cottage and the Watertower II, a small, sunny room featuring a unique location—as the name implies, in a historic water tower. The spacious Master Suite in the main house is another fine choice. In the bedroom, you'll find tasteful antiques and a four-poster queen-size bed that faces a lovely fireplace with a wooden mantel; the spacious, light-filled bathroom features a deep whirlpool tub. All rooms are devoid of TVs and phones but loaded with treats, including chocolate chip cookies and a split of wine. A bountiful breakfast is served in the country-style dining room or in-room, if you request this service the night before.
$$$ *MC, V; no checks; www.joshgrin.com.*

THE MACCALLUM HOUSE
🖤🖤🖤
45020 Albion St, Mendocino / 707/937-0289 or 800/609-0492
How does a room in a greenhouse sound for your romantic getaway? Or a room in a historic livery stable? Both are possible at the MacCallum House, as are rooms in a former water tower, gardener's shed, gazebo playhouse, or garage, as well as the original 1882 Victorian mansion—love has many homes on these grounds. Taken over in 2002 by locals with a vision, the MacCallum House is better than ever after improvements to the grounds and garden; all of the rooms have been renovated. Two of the cottages offer the most intimacy: the Greenhouse has a private garden area with wisteria and roses, as well as a private two-person Jacuzzi tub that invites soaking under the stars. The spacious, bright room has two beds, a king and a double, along with south-facing skylights and a Franklin wood-burning stove. The Carriage House is a bit smaller but offers similar amenities, including king-size bed and private, outdoor hot tub. Both have cable TV/DVD players, CD players, and refrigerators, and microwaves. Lovebirds on a budget might be happy to kiss in the Gazebo Playhouse; this steep Japanese pagoda–style structure is tiny, and its location in front of the main house isn't extremely private, but the old-growth fir paneling sets a cozy mood and the deck with a view of the water is inviting. In the main house, we recommend the large, bright, tastefully furnished Rooms 1 and 2, equipped with claw-foot tubs *à deux*. Room 18, an upper unit in the restored Barn, features a brass queen-size bed fronting a massive stone fireplace plus a double whirlpool tub in the bathroom. Though the room tends toward the small side, the semiprivate patio in front, overlooking the property, town, and sea, helps compensate. CD stereos are offered in most rooms, as are TVs (some with high-tech flat screens), cable, and DVD players. Don't miss dinner at the MacCallum House Restaurant—a delightfully intimate experience (see Romantic Restaurants).
$$$–$$$$ MC, V; no checks; www.maccallumhouse.com. ♿

MENDOCINO HOTEL & GARDEN SUITES
🖤🥂
45080 Main St, Mendocino / 707/937-0511 or 800/548-0513
Transport yourselves to a bygone era as you cuddle next to the fire in the Mendocino Hotel's elegant lobby, among tapestry-upholstered settees and Persian carpets. Built in 1878, this historic destination's bar is one of the best spots in town for a predinner warm-up or after-dinner drink, and once you see the lobby, it's tempting to book a room here without a thought. However, many of the basic rooms in this hostel-style hotel share bathrooms, and even the ocean-view suites in the main building are a bit too worn for romance. The 25 self-contained Garden Suites, surrounded by beautiful rose gardens, are far more inspiring. Many offer parlors, fireplaces,

balconies, private baths, and soaking tubs; however, they lack ocean views, and the prices are steep. In the authentic Victorian dining room downstairs, flickering candles cast a soothing glow on dark wood accents, deep red wall coverings, and faceted glass partitions. The soft lighting and dark, cozy quarters are highly romantic, while the traditional menu offerings, of California-style cuisine such as pan-seared ahi tuna, double-baked pork chops, and prime rib au jus, are best described as ordinary. One irresistible option is to share an order of deep-dish olallieberry pie topped with homemade ice cream before the parlor's roaring fireplace. Breakfast is not included with your stay, but tempting morning meals are available in the hotel's Garden Cafe and Bar, a gloriously lush greenhouse setting that's especially inviting when the sun streams in.
$$–$$$$ *AE, MC, V; checks OK; www.mendocinohotel.com.* &

THE STANFORD INN BY THE SEA
🌢🌢🌢🌔
Hwy 1 and Comptche-Ukiah Rd, Mendocino / 707/937-5615 or 800/331-8884
A harmonious marriage of luxury and rustic elegance, this expansive redwood lodge takes advantage of its beautiful setting and offers an eco-conscious haven. All 33 rooms and suites feature private decks where you can enjoy views of the sun setting on the distant horizon and the nearby Pacific, as well as of the inn's sloping lawn, gardens, and llamas grazing in corralled pastures. If the evening is chilly, as it usually is in this region, cuddle by the fire in your knotty pine–paneled room and slide a mood-setting CD into your stereo. All of the rooms, even the smallest, have fireplaces, stereos, TV/VCRs, and sleigh or four-poster beds covered with richly colored plush linens; decor varies from room to room and ranges from dark-wood walls and burgundy furnishings to sun-streaked pine-wood interiors and country antiques. If you want to surround yourselves with lots of space, we recommend the large suites at the end of the property. Another standout choice for couples is the secluded River Cottage, set on the water's edge. In the morning, visit the alluring greenhouse-enclosed pool, spa, and sauna—this bright and humid solarium and its abundance of tropical plants, orchids, and ceiling fans might make you feel as though you're actually in the tropics. After you've warmed yourselves thoroughly, enjoy a complimentary, cooked-to-order vegetarian breakfast—tempting, creative egg dishes or delicious blue-corn waffles along with organic, shade-grown coffee—presented in the sunny dining room. Afternoon snacks and evening wine and hors d'oeuvres are also included in the price. Come dinnertime, you won't have to wander far to enjoy the fruits (and vegetables) of Stanford Inn's meticulous organic gardens. The beautiful, window-filled restaurant, the Ravens (see Romantic Restaurants), showcases some of Northern California's best gourmet vegetarian cuisine. Down where the river meets the sea, the inn's recreational

outfitter, Catch a Canoe and Bicycles, Too (707/937-0273), offers state-of-the-art mountain bikes to guests on a complimentary basis. If pedaling isn't your passion, rent a canoe, kayak, or outrigger and paddle away to a private picnicking spot to smooch.
$$$$ *AE, DC, DIS, MC, V; checks OK; www.stanfordinn.com.*

WHITEGATE INN
❂❂❂

499 Howard St, Mendocino / 707/937-4892 or 800/531-7282
In some towns, Victorian-style bed-and-breakfasts are so abundant they all start to look alike, but that's not the case in Mendocino. The Whitegate Inn, a milky white Victorian with black trim, stands out—with its elegant crystal chandeliers, antique furnishings, claw-foot tubs, and floral and textured wall coverings—as one of the few traditionally Victorian places to stay in town. It also stands out as an excellent example of why some people fall in love with the bed-and-breakfast experience. A warm greeting (including a personalized hello from Violet, the welcoming kitty), friendly hospitality, and lavish breakfasts and snacks are just a few of the treats you can expect from the very gracious hosts. Outside, an expansive redwood deck, charming gazebo, and garden benches provide prime kissing spots; smell the flowers, gaze at the clear blue sea, and then venture back inside to the parlor for afternoon wine and cheese. Six comfortably elegant guest rooms await in the main house, each with ocean or village views, cozy down comforter, unremarkable bathroom, and gas or wood-burning fireplace. The most romantic choice is the separate cottage set behind the house that has its own private garden deck, king-size bed, corner woodstove, and claw-foot tub; guests staying here can opt to have breakfast delivered. The multicourse gourmet meal, which might include apple-caramel French toast or an artichoke frittata, is served family-style in the formal dining room. With advance notice, a table for two can be arranged in the parlor for breakfast.
$$$ *MC, V; checks OK; www.whitegateinn.com.*

Romantic Restaurants

CAFE BEAUJOLAIS
❂❂❂❂

961 Ukiah St, Mendocino / 707/937-5614
Some say Cafe Beaujolais is the most romantic restaurant in Mendocino; others argue that the tables are too close together. Either way, we're delighted with the recent remodel, which switched out the busy Victorian florals and fussy pink wallpaper and lamps that were contributing to the cramped atmosphere. The interior is now very sleek yet still warm enough to be romantic: crisp white wainscoting accents moss green walls hung

with black-and-white photographs. Soft track lighting from above and candles, white linen, and crystal on the tables add to the ambience. Even if you're closer to other diners than you would prefer, the incredible cuisine and professional service more than make up for the compact seating. A casual, glassed-in porch overlooking the gardens holds additional tables; this is a lovely spot to dine on a pleasant day, but it can get too hot when the sun beats down. Despite the French name, Cafe Beaujolais specializes in creative seasonal cuisine with Mexican and Asian influences. Portions are generous, so be careful not to fill up on the hearty breads made daily at the on-site bakery, a basket of which is brought to your table before your meal. Using fresh, quality seasonal ingredients is the kitchen's top priority, and the chefs' dedication is apparent in dishes such as pan-roasted sturgeon fillet with truffle emulsion sauce or roasted free-range chicken served with saffron-chanterelle sauce and mashed yellow potatoes. The desserts are delicious—try the dark chocolate and sour cherry cake with billows of freshly whipped cream or the tasty raspberry bread pudding; in fact, even if you eat dinner elsewhere, consider stopping by this gem of a restaurant for a sweet finish.

$$$$ *AE, DIS, MC, V; checks OK; dinner every day; beer and wine; reservations recommended; www.cafebeaujolais.com.*

MACCALLUM HOUSE RESTAURANT
✪✪✪✪

45020 Albion St, Mendocino / 707/937-5763

Housed on the ground floor of a lovely turn-of-the-20th-century mansion, this restaurant is our favorite place for a romantic dinner in Mendocino. The only difficulty is deciding where to enjoy your meal: in the evening, the redwood-paneled dining room, warmed by a cobblestone fireplace, will beckon, but if you arrive around sunset, the more casual café, located in the home's delightfully old-fashioned enclosed porch surrounded by windows, offers spectacular views of the Pacific. Either way, you'll find a menu bursting with outstanding seasonal dishes that rely heavily on fresh local seafood, organic meats, and produce from neighboring farms and ranches. Start by dipping warm slices of bread into a trio of locally made olive oils, or if you're in the mood for decadence, try the Liberty Farm duck confit with grilled radicchio, cranberry vinaigrette, Humboldt Fog cheese, and toasted pine nuts. For the main course, consider the melt-in-your-mouth wild-mushroom risotto cakes with creamy mozzarella centers, grilled butternut squash, sautéed chard, and a rich port wine sauce. Equally satisfying is a dish of day boat scallops topped with a reduction of shiitake mushrooms and Anderson Valley sparkling wine or the grilled steak served with zinfandel-braised shallots and porcini butter mashed potatoes. In the café, you can order anything from the tempting formal restaurant menu or choose from more casual options, including the delicious MacTwins—two

Niman Ranch burgers with caramelized onions, Point Reyes Farmstead blue cheese, applewood-smoked bacon, and sun-dried tomato mayo on poppyseed buns. Everything on the menu changes seasonally. For dessert, expect sweets enriched by the restaurant's signature homemade ice creams, such as the taco-shaped praline cookie filled with six scoops of the heavenly stuff. On the other hand, you won't want to miss the dessert specials, such as the light-as-air lemon soufflé that we sampled. Sandwiched between the two dining rooms is the Grey Whale Bar and Café, an inviting spot to enjoy snacks, a quick meal, or cocktails while seated on the couch next to the fireplace. If you are guests at the inn (see Romantic Lodgings), it's just a short stroll from here to your cozy, romantic room.
$$$ *MC, V; no checks; dinner every day; full bar; reservations recommended; www.maccallumhousedining.com.* &

THE MOOSSE CAFÉ
♦♦●

390 Kasten St, Mendocino / 707/937-4323
Sparking up a little romance is easy at this casually intimate café, where a meal at a fireside table is the perfect antidote to a chilly, foggy afternoon or evening. The interior of the restaurant is sleek, with plenty of modern artwork on the walls and large windows overlooking the garden and street. The small outdoor deck offers just a handful of tables, but all have lovely ocean views. Nighttime brings an even cozier atmosphere, with sparkling window lights setting the dining room aglow. In spring 2004, the arrival of new owners and a new chef from San Francisco brought changes to the menu, which now changes frequently—with the seasons—and relies more then ever on natural meats, local and organic produce, and products from small purveyors. At lunch, try the flank steak sandwich on rosemary bread with blue cheese and balsamic onions, or house-made macaroni and cheese with sharp cheddar and crispy breadcrumbs. Dinner options on a summer evening might include a dish of roasted chicken with olive oil–mashed potatoes and sautéed summer vegetables, or a pan-fried pork chop with sage, creamed corn, sautéed greens, and fried crispy carrots. Local seafood appears in a cioppino of fresh fish and shellfish simmered in a saffron fennel tomato broth, as well as daily seafood specials—there's also an ever-changing pasta special. Save room for the decadent house-made desserts, which range from chocolate pudding with whipped cream and bittersweet chocolate shavings to homemade lemon buttermilk pie. The wine list, which has been broadened under the guidance of the new owners, offers a wide array of fine wines and includes local vintages. Directly above the restaurant is The Blue Heron Inn (707-937-4323; www.theblueheron.com) with offers three rooms, two of which share a bath. The noise of the restaurant downstairs makes it less appealing for quiet romance, although the inexpensive

price (which includes a continental breakfast) may convince budget-minded couples to give it a shot.

$$$ MC, V; checks OK; lunch, dinner every day; beer and wine; reservations recommended; www.theblueheron.com. &

955 UKIAH STREET RESTAURANT
❸❸❹

955 Ukiah St, Mendocino / 707/937-1955

When it comes to dinner recommendations in Mendocino, 955 Ukiah is on the tip of every local's tongue. A long boardwalk bordered with greenery leads to the entrance of this casual restaurant, as popular with groups of friends and families as with couples. The dining room overlooks a garden of small leafy trees draped with tiny white lights. A 20-foot vaulted ceiling in the split-level dining room absorbs some (but not all) of the sounds coming from the busy open kitchen. Local artwork and trailing plants accentuate wood-paneled walls. Adequately spaced tables covered with white linens, fresh flowers, and votive candles create a comfortable atmosphere in which to enjoy the delicately flavored California cuisine. Some of the tempting menu items include giant ravioli filled with five cheeses, slow-roasted duck, or Pacific red snapper accented with pesto and wrapped in phyllo dough; there are also nightly seafood specials. Grandpa's favorite bread pudding with huckleberry compote is a must for dessert.

$$$ MC, V; checks OK; dinner Wed–Sun; beer and wine; reservations recommended. &

THE RAVENS RESTAURANT
❸❸❹

Hwy 1 and Comptche-Ukiah Rd (The Stanford Inn by the Sea), Mendocino
707/937-5615 or 800/331-8884

For a unique dining experience, travel a mile south of Mendocino to the environmentally friendly Stanford Inn by the Sea (see Romantic Lodgings). The elegantly rustic dining room serves gourmet vegetarian and vegan dishes only, and these delicious creations are definitive proof that satisfying meals without meat do exist. The menu varies monthly to take advantage of seasonal organic produce, some of which derive from the lodge's own gardens. Dishes range from lighter fare—the fantastic herbed Asiago polenta cakes sautéed in a roasted garlic-chardonnay sauce with local organic shiitake mushrooms—to hearty entrées such as the Forbidden Moroccan Curry made with baby portobello mushrooms, spiced vegetables, a rice pyramid, and cooling cucumber-yogurt sauce. We took a chance on the Seapalm Strudel and delighted in this flaky phyllo-dough creation stuffed with locally harvested sea palm and caramelized carrots and onion, accompanied by wasabi and plum sauces, and served with a savory Asian-inspired stir-fry. Service can be shockingly slow, but it's worth the wait to savor these masterfully crafted dishes. Request a table by the windows and book your reservation at sunset, and the view will seduce you on first sight.

$$ *AE, DC, DIS, MC, V; checks OK; breakfast Mon–Sat, dinner every day, brunch Sun; full bar; reservations recommended; www.stanfordinn.com.*

THE LOST COAST AND EUREKA

ROMANTIC HIGHLIGHTS

Nrth of Mendocino, the Pacific coast becomes even more remote and wild, lined by some of the most impressive and extraordinary coastal forests in the world. You'll also find a handful of luxurious inns and comfortable bed-and-breakfasts, along with towns such as Ferndale and Eureka, which boast some wonderful old Victorian architecture. You can explore the mysterious **Lost Coast**, a remote, 850-square-mile area south of Ferndale and north of Westport, where you'll find more than 75 miles of virtually uninhabited coastline; backpackers love the beaches, pristine tide pools, and abundant wildlife. Mornings are more likely to bring chilly fog than warm sunshine, but the fog usually burns off by the afternoon.

Places characterized by this type of remote wilderness are usually lacking in creature comforts, and this holds true here—come prepared, for example, for limited dining options. Also, in some of the towns along Highway 101, development in the form of cheap motels and fast-food chains detracts from the scenery. Nonetheless, no matter what brings you to this neck of the redwoods—whether you are drawn here by the region's wild remoteness or because it makes a convenient stopover during a long trip up the coast— you'll be glad to know that we found some wonderful places to kiss.

If you arrive via Highway 101 and **Garberville**, we recommend that you tour the magnificent **Avenue of the Giants**, a 31-mile stretch of former stage-coach road that parallels Highway 101. It's worth braving the tacky tourist attractions—such as the Chimney Tree and the Shrine Drive-Thru Tree—to experience this road, which winds along the Eel River through stunning groves of coast redwoods. A highlight is the half-mile, self-guided loop foot trail through **Founders Grove** (4 miles north of Humboldt Redwoods State Park Visitor Center, Weott; 707/946-2263; www.humboldtredwoods.org). These staggeringly massive redwoods, some of which have been around for more than 2,200 years, were described by John Steinbeck as "ambassadors from another time." It is truly romantic to gaze up at the world's largest trees hand in hand with your sweetheart.

The Victorian village of **Ferndale**, which hugs the hills of the Eel River Valley, is a little bastion of romance in the region. Beautifully preserved

Victorian homes line the residential streets of this State Historic Landmark, and dozens of boutiques, antique stores, and art galleries lure visitors from the busy highway. Not only does this out-of-the-way town have great old-fashioned appeal, but it's also the home of the famous **Gingerbread Mansion Inn** (see Romantic Lodgings). Take a trip back in time by strolling past the village's memorabilia at the **Ferndale Museum** (515 Shaw St at 3rd St; 707/786-4466). The **scenic drive** along Centerville Road is a 5-mile excursion that starts at the west end of Main Street downtown and passes by several ranches and dairy farms on the way to **Centerville Beach County Park**. If you continue beyond the park and past the retired naval facility, you'll be rewarded with an incredible view of the Lost Coast to the south. In the evening, take in a play at the **Ferndale Repertory Theatre** (447 Main St; 707/786-5483; reservations recommended).

Set on pretty Humboldt Bay, **Eureka** is the largest town in northwestern California and, as a former 19th-century seaport, lumber town, and gold-mining region, boasts a fascinating history. (It's named after the popular gold-mining expression *Eureka!*—Greek for "I have found it.") The picturesque **Old Town** (between 1st and 3rd Sts and C and M Sts) offers a 13-block stretch of shops, restaurants, and hotels. You can kiss in front of one of the state's most-photographed houses, the multigabled and turreted **Carson Mansion**, which features a three-dimensional, ornately patterned edifice that took more than 100 men two years to construct (2nd and M Sts; privately owned, not open to the public), or explore Old Town history at the **Clarke Memorial Museum** (240 E St at 3rd St; 707/443-1947), which showcases more than 1,200 examples of Hupa, Yurok, and Karok Indian basketry, dance regalia, and stonework. For lunch, sample the tasty sandwiches and sweets at **Ramone's Bakery** (209 E St in Old Town; 707/445-2923; www.ramonesbakery.com); then tour Humboldt Bay Harbor on the oldest passenger vessel on the Pacific Coast, the *Madaket* (departs from the foot of C St; 707/445-1910). Fresh pints of ale and pub food can be had at the **Lost Coast Brewery** (617 4th St between G and H Sts; 707/445-4480), but by far the most romantic meal in town is to be found at the outstanding **Restaurant 301** (see Romantic Restaurants).

During summer, consider a short jaunt north of Eureka to the college town of **Arcata**, home to California State University at Humboldt. Here, you can stroll the scenic, perfectly groomed lawns of **Arcata Plaza** or enjoy the award-winning bagels at **Los Bagels** (403 2nd St at E St in Old Town; 707/442-8525). In summer, the vibrant **Arcata Plaza Farmer's Market** (contact North Coast Growers Association, 707/441-9999, for more information; 9am–1pm Sat, Apr–Nov) is also a draw, with exotic, colorful produce and live music starting at 10am. Though this region offers quiet pursuits rather than glamorous Napa-style romance, couples who enjoy exploring will be rewarded with some memorable romantic experiences.

Access and Information

The easiest way to reach this region is by car via Highway 101, which follows an inland route through northern Mendocino County and eventually turns west to arrive at Eureka on the coast. It can be reached in several hours from San Francisco, though the trip is much longer if you drive along the coast on Highway 1. The seldom-visited Lost Coast can be reached by the **Mattole Road**, which starts just north of Weott at the southern boundary of the Avenue of the Giants, runs north and west to the hamlets of Honeydew and Petrolia, and reaches the coast just south of Cape Mendocino. From there it continues north to Ferndale, 16 miles south of Eureka. The **Arcata/Eureka Airport** in McKinleyville (11 miles north of Eureka) is served by Alaska Airlines/Horizon Air (800/252-7522; horizonair.alaskaair.com) and United Express (800/241-6522; www.united.com). **Rental cars** are also available there.

Tourism is the area's number-two revenue generator, gaining fast on timber, and information about tourist destinations is plentiful. Contact the **Humboldt County Convention and Visitors Bureau** (1034 2nd St, Eureka; 707/443-5097 or 800/346-3482; www.redwoodvisitor.org) or the **Crecsent City–Del Norte County Chamber of Commerce** (1001 Front St, Crescent City; 707/464-3174 or 800/343-8300; www.northerncalifornia.net) for more information. You can also check on upcoming events and activities in **Ferndale** (www.victorianferndale.org/chamber).

Romantic Lodgings

BENBOW INN
♥♥

445 Lake Benbow Dr, Garberville / 707/923-2124 or 800/355-3301
Mile after mile of ancient, towering redwoods draw tourists north on Highway 101 but, surprisingly, there are few overnight accommodations for the romantically inclined. Luckily, this National Historic Landmark, set just off the highway and surrounded by stands of oak and redwood, provides a kiss-worthy place to cozy up from mid-April through December. Built in 1926, the Tudor-style hotel in its glory days hosted dignitaries such as Eleanor Roosevelt and Herbert Hoover. Today the Benbow is a little worn around the edges but still elegant, filled with old-world antiques and accents. Complimentary hors d'oeuvres (in addition to afternoon tea and scones) are served every afternoon in the spacious, rustic lobby, where Oriental carpets cover hardwood floors and rocking chairs near the hearth beckon. Although the hotel's 55 small rooms have all been renovated, they retain a historic feel; you'll find antiques and old-fashioned wallpaper, red velvet lounge chairs, Oriental carpets, paisley linens, and nicely tiled but otherwise standard

baths. We especially like the Terrace Rooms, which have private patios that overlook the landscaped grounds and nearby river, as well as TV/VCRs (there's a large movie library at the front desk); the Fireplace Rooms offer these amenities and handsome wood-burning hearths. The Garden Cottage is the most luxurious of all, with a canopied king-size bed, private patio overlooking the gardens, fireplace, Jacuzzi spa, and walk-in tiled shower. Other delightfully quirky touches include a basket of mystery novels in each guest room, bikes to explore the outlying grounds, and a film projector in the lobby showing classic black-and-white flicks starring Charlie Chaplin and Clara Bow. In the Tudor-style dining room, chandeliers and candle lanterns cast an intimate glow while large-paned windows provide a great view of the river and gardens. The menu changes frequently but always features seafood, beef, pasta, and poultry dishes. Relax at one of the two-person tables and indulge in fresh salmon, grilled chicken breast marinated in lime and herbs, or honey-miso-roasted pork loin served with black-eyed peas. On Sunday the Benbow offers a sumptuous champagne brunch. **$$-$$$$** *AE, DIS, MC, V; checks OK; closed Jan–mid-Apr; www.benbowinn.com.*

GINGERBREAD MANSION INN
❂❂❂❂
400 Berding St, Ferndale / 707/786-4000 or 800/952-4136
With its elaborate trim, turrets, manicured shrubs, and towering palm tree, the magnificent peach and yellow Gingerbread Mansion Inn is one of Northern California's most photographed homes—not surprising, since it's indeed as pretty as a picture. Built in 1899 as a private residence, this three-story Victorian now operates as an 11-room bed-and-breakfast. The owner of this marvelous home has attended to every detail with painstaking care. Each elegant room has been individually decorated with period wallpaper, beautiful antiques, a romantic fireplace, and luscious linens and fabrics; whimsical touches include two claw-foot tubs placed side by side in several of the rooms. Choosing from among the different but equally gorgeous rooms can be difficult, but if a splurge is in your plans, the extraordinary Empire Suite should be your first choice. Situated at the top of the house, this converted attic suite has peaked 12-foot ceilings, alcoves, and walls adorned with rich gold and black Regency Revival wallpaper. White Ionic columns frame an enormous king-size bed draped with luxurious, sexy black and gold Egyptian-cotton linens. A claw-foot tub and an oversize glass-enclosed shower (with five massage jets and three showerheads) face a gas fireplace at one end of the suite; at the other end, a cozy love seat fronts a second fireplace and a corner alcove holds a sumptuous, gigantic reading chair big enough for two. Once you sink into such splendor, the only hard part will be climbing back out. Other choices for romantic escapes include the second-floor Fountain Suite (home to the side-by-side tubs and two

fireplaces); the Rose Suite, furnished with a magnificent four-poster bed; and the main-floor Garden Suite, with French doors opening onto the well-tended gardens. Evening turndown service with house-made chocolates, as well as prebreakfast coffee service outside your door, are welcome touches. Downstairs in the regal dining room, enjoy the morning's lavish spread of fruits, freshly baked cakes and pastries, and satisfying breakfast entrées. This may even hold you until afternoon tea time, when an appetizing array of hors d'oeuvres, tea sandwiches, and petit fours are served on silver platters and hand-painted china in the formal sitting room, which is brimming with turn-of-the-20th-century antiques.

$$$–$$$$ *AE, MC, V; checks OK; www.gingerbread-mansion.com.*

HOTEL CARTER, BELL COTTAGE, CARTER COTTAGE, CARTER HOUSE
◕◕◕
301 L St, Eureka / 707/444-8062 or 800/404-1390

You might just shout "Eureka!" yourselves as you enter the warm, sun-filled lobby of the Hotel Carter, a Northern California destination in itself. Relax on the inviting couches and chairs next to the crackling fireplace and enjoy the complimentary afternoon wine and hors d'oeuvres as you revel in the comfort, style, and gracious service everywhere in evidence. Twenty-three rooms with soothing taupe interiors, dimming lights, Southwest-style couches or chairs, weathered pine furnishings, plantation-style shutters, and entertainment centers hidden in antique pine armoires are spread out over three floors. The most luxurious rooms, on the third floor, feature marble wood-burning fireplaces, jetted tubs for two, and double-headed showers; some have massive pine four-poster beds. While the hotel's rooms are truly exceptional, the ultimate romantic retreat awaits across the street in the Carter Cottage. This restored Victorian is decorated with French-country flair and filled with lots of natural light from an abundance of windows. In addition to the gourmet kitchen, fireplace in the living area, and romantic lighting, there's a dreamy bedroom with a wrought-iron four-poster bed enclosed by white curtains that fronts a gas fireplace. French doors lead to the large bathroom, which features a two-person whirlpool tub (with head pillows for extra comfort) and a double-headed shower. As an extra bonus, there's an enclosed back deck for your private pleasure with a lovely view of sparkling Humboldt Bay. There's no need to leave this love nest when hunger strikes; upon prior arrangement, a multicourse dinner can be prepared and served in the cottage. The adjacent Bell Cottage holds three guest rooms; though not as extravagant or as private as the Carter Cottage, each room has a double whirlpool tub and two have fireplaces. These rooms have a modern edge, with dimming halogen lamps, black leather furniture, parquet wood floors, and boldly printed fabrics in shades of gray, taupe, and black. Kitty-corner to the Hotel Carter is the Carter House, an

impressive dark brown Victorian with towering brick chimneys that offers five guest rooms. Though these are pleasant, we prefer the more romantic character of the two cottages and the Hotel Carter. Come evening, enjoy a sweet moment before bedtime in the hotel's lobby, with warm homemade cookies and soothing herbal tea. The best restaurant in town, Restaurant 301, is located on the hotel's main level (see Romantic Restaurants), and you should definitely reserve a table for dinner. A delicious gourmet breakfast, included with your stay, is served in the restaurant. If you wish to explore Eureka and its surroundings, don't hesitate to ask the gracious innkeepers for advice—their enthusiasm for their hometown is infectious.
$$$–$$$$ *AE, DC, DIS, MC, V; checks OK; www.carterhouse.com.* &

Romantic Restaurants

CURLEY'S GRILL
❤❤
400 Ocean Ave (Victorian Inn), Ferndale / 707/786-9696
Romantic restaurants are few and far between in this area, but Curley's would stand up even to stiff competition. Casual but classy, this bright and inviting one-room restaurant features a handful of nicely spaced tables topped with whimsical salt and pepper shakers. Vivid local artwork adorns the walls, illuminated by track lighting. For the most privacy (and the best kissing), request one of the tables tucked into a window alcove; in warm weather, be sure to sit at one of the tables on the shaded back patio. The menu is on the casual side, with an abundance of entrée-size salads, grilled sandwiches, and seafood. Everything is superbly prepared and delicious. Be sure to start off your meal with the restaurant's signature dish: savory grilled polenta topped with mushrooms, sage, and sautéed tomatoes. Main courses range from a hearty plate of meat loaf with garlic mashed potatoes to grilled steelhead with a pesto and crumbled roasted-almond topping. At the end of the meal, house-made desserts are showcased on a tray brought to your table; save room, because all are irresistible!
$$ *DIS, MC, V; checks OK; breakfast Sat–Sun, lunch, dinner every day; beer and wine; reservations recommended; www.restaurant.com/ curleysgrill.* &

RESTAURANT 301
❤❤❤
301 L St (Hotel Carter), Eureka / 707/444-8062 or 800/404-1390
Restaurant 301 at the Hotel Carter (see Romantic Lodgings) raises dining in Eureka to a whole new level, thanks not just to its outstanding food but also to its exquisitely sophisticated dining room. Stylish tapestries hang from the high ceiling, modern artwork adorns the warm beige walls, and pale

pine furnishings lend European flair. Candles and little lanterns flicker at every white linen–covered table, and tall windows look out to the street and the harbor in the distance. (If you want to whisper those sweet nothings in total privacy, book the one and only table tucked into the hotel's cozy wine shop, where the two of you will be surrounded by hundreds of vintages. Rest assured—wine bottles don't talk.) The regionally influenced à la carte menu changes weekly but consistently features local seafood, meat, and produce; we highly recommend several prix fixe menus, too. Many ingredients are picked fresh from the hotel's own organic garden, including the aptly named "salad of garden-gathered greens." The main courses are satisfying and delicious: pan-roasted pork chops with pear chutney, potato gnocchi with chanterelles and oven-dried tomatoes, and pan-seared salmon bathed in a fresh lemon verbena tomato sauce are some of the choice entrées on offer. The kitchen focuses on keeping flavors clear and full, and the presentation is lovely. The wine list has won awards. Top off your meal with an unforgettable dessert—perhaps the bread pudding drenched in warm caramel sauce.

$$–$$$ AE, DC, DIS, MC, V; checks OK; breakfast, dinner every day; full bar; reservations recommended; www.carterhouse.com. ♿

SIERRA NEVADA

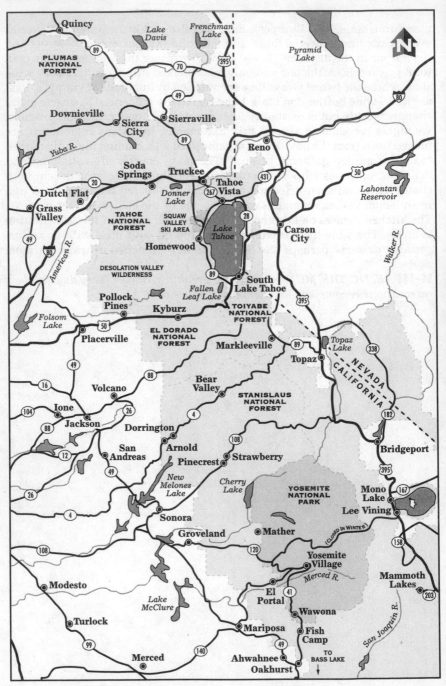

"Soul meets soul on lovers' lips."
—PERCY BYSSHE SHELLEY

♡ SIERRA NEVADA

The Sierra Nevada range is home to two of California's most popular vacation spots: Lake Tahoe and Yosemite. Both destinations have the potential to be tremendously romantic. Glistening in the foothills of the High Sierra peaks, Lake Tahoe is the largest alpine lake in North America, 22 miles long and 12 miles wide with 72 miles of shoreline. The area's alpine climate results in warm, dry summers and cold, snowy winters. Spring and fall can be a little of both. The area's breathtaking scenery, fishing, swimming, skiing, hiking—and yes, gambling—lure tourists of all stripes. To the south, Yosemite's allure is mainly the magnificent natural sights, which include the much-photographed rock formation of Half Dome, as well as endlessly scenic views of mountains, meadows, and glacial lakes. If you're looking for some great spots for overnight kissing, a diverse range of romantic accommodations can be found in both regions.

Lake Tahoe is commonly referred to in terms of its north and south shores (the California-Nevada border actually bisects the lake lengthwise, so its west side is in California and its east side is in Nevada). The North Shore has long been the ritzier area, home to upscale recreation communities such as Incline Village and Squaw Valley, and its towns, such as Tahoe Vista and Tahoe City, both set along the lake, harbor first-rate restaurants and luxurious lodgings. Smaller hamlets such as Homewood and Carnelian Bay offer welcome peace and quiet, even during the busy summer season. The South Shore is more populous and urban, filled with neon-topped casinos, high-rise hotels, and the echoes of ringing slot machines.

Despite all its terrific ski resorts, Tahoe is actually most crowded in the summer, when thousands flock here to cool off at the lake and enjoy warm-weather activities such as boating and hiking. Yosemite essentially closes down for much of the winter, so it too is a crowded summer destination. If you have your hearts set on summertime kissing at Lake Tahoe or in Yosemite Valley, just remember: lots of other folks do too. If you visit Lake Tahoe in winter, be sure to inquire about ski-package deals.

The spring and the fall are when you're most likely to find moments of privacy in these breathtaking natural settings. If you're coming during the

LAKE TAHOE

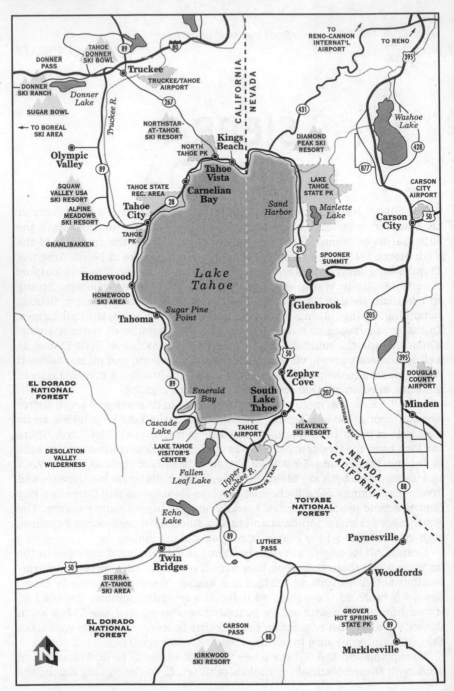

summer and you really want to avoid the crowds but still escape to the mountains, simply travel farther north, to the isolated and beautiful Mount Shasta region.

NORTH SHORE OF LAKE TAHOE

ROMANTIC HIGHLIGHTS

No matter the season, your chances for outdoor kissing abound on the North Shore, which is quieter and more romantic than its flashier neighbor to the south. The best-known towns here are the lakeside **Tahoe Vista** and **Tahoe City**, bustling lakefront communities filled with a mix of quaint shops and useful places such as grocery stores. Luckily for those seeking a place to smooch, each town offers a handful of excellent restaurants and some very kiss-worthy bed-and-breakfasts. Smaller blink-and-you'll-miss-it hamlets such as **Homewood** and **Carnelian Bay** also harbor romantic hideaways. And, of course, the ski resorts—even fancy ones such as **Squaw Valley** and **Incline Village**—and wonderful lakeside parks offer plentiful opportunities for outdoor kissing. One of the best—and least-frequented—lakeside parks is the lovely beach at **Sand Harbor State Park** (on Hwy 28, 3 miles south of Incline Village; 775/831-0494; parks.nv.gov).

One of the High Sierras' most picturesque settings is nestled at the base of jagged peaks on the North Shore at **Squaw Valley USA** (off Hwy 89; 530/583-6985 or 800/545-4350; www.squaw.com). With some of the most challenging ski terrain in the area, the largest choice of upscale accommodations, and a seemingly endless array of perfectly groomed slopes, Squaw is a popular destination for skiing couples. After a recent, massive expansion, Squaw Valley's core is now an upscale alpine village (similar to the renowned Whistler and Blackcomb Ski Resorts in British Columbia). Complete with a central square lined with outdoor fireside patio restaurants, one-of-a-kind boutiques (rather than chain stores), and towering Craftsman-meets-alpine-style condo buildings, the village also sponsors live music, fire jugglers, and summertime food and wine festivals. Restaurants include upscale options such as **PlumpJack Balboa Cafe** (530/583-5850; www.plumpjack.com). Whether all this is romantic is up to you to decide, but there's no doubt about one thing: ever-increasing crowds. Of course, ever since this first-class ski resort made a name for itself hosting the Winter Olympics back in 1960, it hasn't exactly been the place to go to find privacy. Come here for the alpine sports or warm-weather pastimes such as horseback riding, biking, hiking, and golf.

One of Tahoe's must-see views, whether you visit in winter or summer, is also to be had at Squaw Valley. Take the cable car to the Olympic Ice Pavilion at **High Camp**, which departs from the main building at the base of Squaw Valley Ski Resort. The ride is an adventure in itself, as the tram soars above hawks and swings over rocky pinnacles to Squaw Mountain's 8,200-foot summit. Come at sunset and watch the rosy light spread across the peaks and the twinkling lights of Tahoe's small towns emerge in the distance. If you want to do more than lock lips and look at the view, High Camp has an outdoor skating rink and an enormous heated swimming pool (you can dive into the steaming water as early as still-freezing-cold March). Several restaurants are also available. The best date option is **Alexander's** (530/581-7278), which offers mountaintop twilight dinner specials and floor-to-ceiling windows overlooking the valley.

The hot summer weather brings a phenomenal array of lakeside activities, which take on an especially romantic glow at beautiful **Sugar Pine Point State Park** (on Hwy 89, 10 miles south of Tahoe City; 530/525-7982; www.parks.ca.gov) on the west shore of Lake Tahoe. Picnic on the beach with gorgeous views of the lake or explore the hiking trails shaded by pine, fir, aspen, and juniper. This park is the starting point for North Tahoe's 15-mile-long paved trail, which stretches from here north along the lake to Dollar Point on the North Shore. This is a great place for an easy stroll, although there will be plenty of others traveling by foot, bike, or in-line skates. In winter, visit the park to enjoy more than 20 kilometers of marked cross-country ski trails.

Of the three developed shores of Lake Tahoe, the smallest—the west shore—remains the most pristine. You won't find big hotels, flashy casinos, or shopping centers here—just the tiny town of **Homewood**. A few romantic establishments are set among the towering pines, and you'll also find a summer paradise at **D. L. Bliss State Park** (on Hwy 89, 17 miles south of Tahoe City; 530/525-7277 or 800/444-7275; www.parks.ca.gov). Located a couple of miles north of beautiful but busy **Emerald Bay**—one of the most photographed sights in the world—Bliss is a fitting name for this park, which hugs the lakeshore. The best place to kiss in all of Tahoe is located here, at **Rubicon Point**, a quarter-mile hike from the last accessible parking lot. Views of the lake grow more magnificent at every turning of the well-worn path that weaves along the shore and into the rocky cliffs. Though Rubicon Point is not well marked, you'll know when you've arrived: the view becomes a splendid panorama of the lake's transparent waters with a backdrop of snowcapped Sierra peaks.

While the parks and the ski gondolas provide magnificent views of the area, there's a third option: **Mountain High Balloons** (530/587-6922 or 888/462-2683; from $175 per person). With the wind guiding your craft high above treetops and the shimmering lake below (you can even see the reflection of your balloon), it manages to be both a thrilling and peaceful adventure.

Access and Information

Many highways lead to Lake Tahoe, but among the most traveled are **Interstate 80**, from Sacramento to Truckee and Reno; **US 50**, from Sacramento to South Lake Tahoe and Carson City; and **Highway 88**, from Jackson to Kirkwood and the Hope Valley. **Reno/Tahoe International Airport** (www.renoairport.com) is approximately 45 miles from Lake Tahoe, and **Sacramento International Airport** (www.sacairports.org) is approximately 100 miles from the lake.

The best source for information about the North Shore is the **North Lake Tahoe Resort Association Visitors and Convention Bureau** (530/583-3494 or 888/434-1262; www.tahoefun.org). This is also the place to call if you're having trouble finding a hotel room or campsite (a common problem during peak season) or would like information on ski packages. The Lake Tahoe region is serviced by dozens of other Web sites loaded with information (www.skilaketahoe.com, www.laketahoeconcierge.com, www.virtual tahoe.com, www.tahoereservations.com, www.tahoesbest.com, www.tahoe vacationguide.com).

During the off-season, when the weather is still too cold for summer activities but too warm for good snow, some establishments close, especially on the North and West Shores, where there are no casinos. Always call in advance to make sure your desired destination is operating at the time you hope to visit. Such efforts may even be rewarded by the more-than-reasonable accommodation rates that tend to spring up in the off-season.

Romantic Lodgings

CHANEY HOUSE
♦♦

4725 W Lake Blvd, Homewood / 530/525-7333
Driving along West Lake Boulevard, with its mesmerizing water views, it's easy to cruise past this stately home sheltered by large native pines. Only a small sign announces the home's location, so keep your eyes peeled. Built in 1928 by Italian masons, this impressive stone structure has much to offer those looking for something other than Western-style lodge decor. You can't help but get into a medieval mood as you step through the enormous front door, where in the living room the blazing fire casts a warm glow on the 18-inch-thick stone walls, cathedral ceilings, Gothic doors, and original pine woodwork. The Honeymoon Hideaway lives up to its name. Located behind the main home, this two-story stone cottage features all that's necessary for romance: a queen-size bed tucked into an alcove, a flip-on gas fireplace for instant ambience (not to mention heat), and an oval jetted tub complete with bubble bath. If you request it, the innkeepers will even serve

your breakfast on a semiprivate patio located between the Hideaway and the main house. Three more guest rooms, all with private baths, are found in the main house. The best is the handsome Russell's Suite, accessed by a unique spiral staircase. This hidden-away room is simply decorated with knotty-pine walls and plaid motifs (animal lovers should come prepared for the stuffed deer head mounted above the queen-size bed). The inn's brochure states that there is a "lake view" from this room and that is true—if you get down on the floor and look out through the knee-high windows. The remaining two rooms, the second-floor Master Suite and the main-floor Jeanine's Room, are slightly less private and more standard. A formal breakfast buffet is served in the equally formal dining room or on the kitchen-side patio, when weather permits. Enjoy fresh fruit, scrumptious egg dishes served with homemade sauces, and the house specialty: oven-stuffed French toast topped with hot, homemade blackberry sauce.
$$ DIS, MC, V; checks OK; www.chaneyhouse.com.

THE COTTAGE INN
❤❤❤
1690 W Lake Blvd, Tahoe City / 530/581-4073 or 800/581-4073
Far from the glitz of the casinos and the sterility of the high-rise hotels, the Cottage Inn embraces nature instead of trying to overwhelm it. Set in a half-circle, the 15 duplex cabins here are designed for privacy. All units feature private entrances, and some even have front porches. Each cottage is unique, but all share a rustic, Western feel accentuated by hardwood floors, knotty-pine walls, charming decor, and local artwork. For kissing purposes, we highly recommend the aptly named Romantic Hideaway, featuring a massive river-rock waterfall that descends into a deep Jacuzzi tub. The nearby Evergreen Heaven Suite is also overflowing with romantic goodies, including a thermal massage tub for two set into a cozy alcove. All of the rooms, from the most basic studio style to the deluxe units, have gas fireplaces, modern private baths, tucked-away TV/VCRs, and—uniquely—flannel nightshirts perfect for keeping you warm on nippy nights. If you can tear yourselves away from your cozy little cottage, sit by the fire in the 61-year-old main cottage, where home-baked treats are laid out in the evening and a full country breakfast is served in the morning. (If you're in the mood for a secluded start to the day, you can request that breakfast be left on your doorstep.) After a day of hiking or skiing, indulge in an evening sauna or stroll to the nearby beach, where you can dig your toes into the cool sand and kiss to the lullaby of Lake Tahoe's gently lapping waters.
$$ MC, V; checks OK; www.thecottageinn.com.

MAYFIELD HOUSE
🌑🌑

236 Grove St, Tahoe City / 530/583-1001 or 888/518-8898
Highly trafficked Tahoe City can be a bit of a hassle to drive through, but this traditional bed-and-breakfast is located on a side road away from the hustle and bustle. The 1932 all-stone Mayfield House retains many of its original features and caters to those who enjoy a sense of yesteryear mixed in with their romance. While the historical element is strong, new owners have brought a breath of fresh air to the interior. All of the common areas and rooms have a comfortable, mountain-country look. Baskets hang from the rafters in the sunny living room, creatively displayed pinecones and country antiques line the bookshelves, white lights trim the river-rock fireplace, and antique crates and suitcases have been turned into functional side tables in some of the bedrooms. Hardwood floors accented by vibrant throw rugs and large paned windows provide splashes of color, texture, and light. Three of the six guest rooms have private detached bathrooms; one of these, called the Alpine Alcove, is so charming that the journey to the bath is easily forgiven—especially once you see the tempting steam shower surrounded by glass and slate (robes and slippers are also provided). Romantic twosomes adore the Alpine Alcove's tucked-away, mezzanine-level location. For those who desire attached bathrooms, the Angler Suite, the Mountain Hideaway Room, and the Cottage all deliver. Although it's tight on space, the Cottage, located behind the main house, offers the most privacy. Skylights over the queen-size bed and in the bathroom are bonuses. In the main home, the upstairs Mountain Hideaway Room ranks high for romance with its country-and-western theme, deep jetted tub in the bathroom, king-size bed, and enough room for some (slow) country dancing. The downstairs Angler Suite has a fly-fishing motif, with plenty of "gone fishin'" gear as well as a king-size bed that's very inviting after a day on the lake or on the slopes. After a morning walk about town, along the lake, or across the street to the golf course, return to find waffles topped with fresh whipped cream and strawberries, apple-walnut pancakes, and chocolate-chip banana bread. *$$$–$$$$ MC, V; checks OK; www.mayfieldhouse.com.*

PLUMPJACK SQUAW VALLEY INN
🌑🌑🌗

1920 Squaw Valley Rd, Squaw Valley / 530/583-1576 or 800/323-7666
This two-story, wood-shingled lodge, strategically situated at the base of the mountain next to Squaw Valley Resort's gondola and parking lot, is Grand Central Station during ski season. Still, if you don't mind the crowds, PlumpJack is a very convenient and stylish place to stay. The extraordinary decor—best described as medieval-meets-modern—is unlike that of any other ski lodge for miles. The interiors of the 61 guest rooms and suites harbor swirling metal accent lamps and sconces and artsy furnishings such

as couches shaped like fluffy clouds and side tables resembling seashells. All regular guest rooms feature similar decor and amenities, including one king-size or two queen-size beds with thick down comforters, and subtle color schemes of burnished steel, taupe, olive, and cream. Just to keep you guessing, the San Francisco–chic decor is accompanied by a selection of beautifully framed paintings. The six pricier specialty suites are worth the extra cash, especially if you have romance on your minds. Luxurious amenities abound, including Jacuzzi tubs (in four of the suites), wet bars, magnificent beds, big-screen TVs (in some), and separate sitting areas. We especially like the two third-floor penthouse suites, where prominent granite slabs surround the heated pool and two hot tubs on the spacious outdoor patio. The direct mountain view from this spot is definitely worthy of a kiss . . . if you don't mind company. Breakfast isn't included in your stay, but guests can enjoy a morning meal at the two restaurants; for a more private option, try room service (available 7am–10pm). The adjoining PlumpJack Cafe and nearby PlumpJack Balboa Cafe (530/583-5850) offer upscale cuisine and service regardless of your attire (this is, after all, a ski resort) and a tempting menu of modern American dishes: milk-brined double-cut pork chop with Yorkshire pudding and summer vegetables; spicy Maine soft-shell crab with pickled ginger vinaigrette and chili *tobiko* (flying fish roe); or duckling served two ways—roasted breast and confit leg with lime mashed sweet potatoes and huckleberry sauce. Those already familiar with PlumpJack in San Francisco will know that the reasonably priced wine list is among the nation's best.

$$$ *AE, DC, DIS, MC, V; checks OK; www.plumpjack.com.* &

RESORT AT SQUAW CREEK
❀❀❀

400 Squaw Creek Rd, Squaw Valley / 530/583-6300 or 800/327-3353
This massive resort of black-tinted glass looks out of place against the rolling golf meadows and craggy mountains that surround it. However, once you step inside the building, you'll no longer mind. The dramatic lobby alone is worth a peek, with its wall of cathedral-high windows showcasing the mountain face. The resort's grounds are even more spectacular, with a waterfall cascading past the skating rink (basketball court in summer) down to three outdoor Jacuzzi tubs, two swimming pools, and one 110-foot-long water slide. Every amenity is within your reach, from a shopping arcade to a spa and health center to five restaurants to airport shuttle service. Unfortunately, all of this is also within reach of the wealthy families who pack in here for vacations. However, the resort's large scale and lack of intimacy may just be outweighed by its benefits, which include ski-in/ski-out access from the lift beside the resort. Be sure to ask about the midweek package deals, which can knock a hefty amount off the normally exorbitant rates. Surprisingly, the 403 unbelievably expensive guest rooms are merely

standard, with a comfortable but unimaginative feel. What sets these rooms apart from others in Squaw Valley are the unsurpassed mountain views (especially from the Valley View Rooms), which get better the higher you go. While the resort has long been a paradise for skiers, golfers, and tennis players, the $3 million refurbishment of the 10,000-square-foot spa has also made it a destination for couples seeking state-of-the-art relaxation with body wraps, mud baths, and massage. The hotel offers plenty of dining options for hungry couples (800/327-2525 ext 15 for reservations): The continental restaurant Cascades Sierra Grille and the comfortable Bull-whackers Pub are the more casual offerings for breakfast and lunch. The resort's upscale bistro, Ristorante Montagna, is a good place to relax with lunch or dinner for two; here you can indulge in wood-oven-baked pizzas and juicy rotisserie-grilled meats while enjoying stunning mountain views from the large outdoor deck.

$$$$ *AE, DC, DIS, MC, V; checks OK; www.squawcreek.com.* &

ROCKWOOD LODGE

♦♦

5295 W Lake Blvd, Homewood / 530/525-5273 or 800/538-2463
You will immediately feel at home upon entering this stone "Old Tahoe"-style house, so take off your shoes (required) and relax a while. Honey-colored knotty-pine walls, hand-hewn open-beam ceilings, and soft cream carpets (hence the no-shoes policy) provide a soothing, homey ambience. If the cozy atmosphere doesn't take the chill off snow-kissed cheeks, then snuggling by the roaring fire in the living room should do the trick. Although the home's interior has a rustic feel, the five guest rooms are quite stylish. Each is decorated with floral linens and window treatments and filled with Shaker-style antiques such as a 19th-century workbench and an old New England cobbler's bench. Cozy down comforters cover puffed-up feather beds, and fresh flowers brighten the mood. Each room has its own private bath and comes with warm, terry-cloth bathrobes. Both the Secret Harbor and the Rubicon Bay Rooms offer filtered views of the lake, as well as tiled tubs with dual showerheads. We especially like Secret Harbor's Russian wedding bed—a hand-painted, four-poster wood canopy. The third-floor Zephyr Cove Room offers views of the surrounding forest and a nearby building and provides the most seclusion for sweethearts. Although the Emerald Bay Room is tiny, it boasts the best bathroom of all: its 7-foot-long Roman tub (equipped to hold 100 gallons of water) comes with two shower-heads for double the fun. Unfortunately, you'll be doing a hallway dash to get to this wonder. When weather permits, an ample full breakfast is served in the backyard beneath tall pines or, if the road noise doesn't bother you, on the front patio next to the outdoor stone fireplace. On chill mornings, treats are served at a large table in the simple dining room.

$$-$$$ *MC, V; checks OK; www.rockwoodlodge.com.*

SHOOTING STAR B&B
❂❂❂
315 Olive St, Carnelian Bay / 530/546-8903 or 888/985-7827
This recently opened bed-and-breakfast provides a quiet oasis even during
Tahoe's busy summer season. Located in quiet Carnelian Bay among a
cluster of residential homes across a busy road from the lake, the setting
is modest. From the simple exterior of this two-story wooden lodge-style
home, you wouldn't guess at the color, style, and comfort found in the
three luxurious and individually decorated guest rooms. The ground-level
entryway welcomes you with flagstone floors and fresh flowers, and on this
floor you'll find two of the rooms. The "C" room is the smallest, done in a
vibrant blue-and-white color scheme with a gas fireplace you can gaze at
from the bed. The "B" room has even more amorous features. You'll immediately want to dive into the antique white bed draped with striking red
linens; red candles, gold-framed mirrors, and a gas fireplace set into the wall
are romantic accents. At the table for two in the alcove surrounded by windows, you can catch a very distant view of the lake. The gorgeous bathroom
has aqua blue-tiled floors and walls and a sparkling two-person Jacuzzi
tub. The most private love nest, however, is the spacious "A" room upstairs.
The breakfast room and common area are also upstairs, but you have to
go through a heavy solid pine door and down a short hallway to reach this
haven, so it feels sequestered and private. Since it's located on the opposite
side of the house from the road, no traffic is audible; best of all, it's above
a garage and has no neighbors. Lofty ceilings, pale lilac walls, and dusty
blue trim create a soft backdrop for the dark wood furnishings, your own
private table for two, and a sitting area furnished with a cushioned loveseat
and armchair. Potted palms, antique prints, and the enticing king-size bed
piled high with pillows complete the scene. The spacious tiled bathroom,
done in a delightful soft green and lavender color scheme, has a giant tiled
walk-in shower with double showerheads so you can get squeaky-clean
together. Throughout the rooms, luxurious details such as Aveda products,
knit robes, stacks of fluffy towels, and fresh flowers will make you feel pampered. Downstairs you'll find a cozy room for watching movies (we applaud
the romantic mood created by eschewing TVs and telephones in the rooms).
In the morning, breakfast is served upstairs in the open common area, which
contains the charming yellow-and-blue kitchen and dining area. Each
afternoon, hors d'oeuvres are also served here.
$$$ *AE, DIS, MC, V; checks OK; www.shootingstarBandB.com.*

THE SHORE HOUSE
❂❂❂◖
7170 N Lake Blvd, Tahoe Vista / 530/546-7270 or 800/207-5160
The charming Shore House certainly lives up to its name. Located right
on the shore of Lake Tahoe, it is one of the only bed-and-breakfasts in the

area that can truly be classified as waterfront. (Most bed-and-breakfasts take the liberty of describing themselves as "waterfront" even when a road separates them from the water.) At the Shore House, unobstructed views of the lake are part of the package. On a beautiful summer day, the fabulous lakefront lawn, dotted with cushioned furniture, is as inviting as can be. When snow caps the mountains, soak in Tahoe vistas from the comfort of the bubbling outdoor hot tub. Lakefront views continue inside the cozy dining room, where several log-pole tables and a river-rock fireplace create a minilodgelike setting. Wine and hors d'oeuvres are served here nightly, and come morning, guests are treated to such scrumptious delights as Belgian waffles topped with blackberries, French toast stuffed with Neufchâtel cheese, or the innkeeper's award-winning Monte Cristo sandwiches. All nine deliciously inviting rooms have private entrances, gas-log fireplaces, and bright, beautifully tiled bathrooms. Custom-built log furnishings and beds, down comforters, and locally painted watercolors give each room a rustic finish. (They're not truly rustic, though: all have CD players, high-tech LCD TVs, hair dryers, coffeemakers, mini refrigerators, and irons). Not all of the rooms have direct lake views, so be sure to specify your preference when making your reservations. The main building houses seven of the rooms, including the Lakeview Room, which, as its name suggests, affords wonderful lake views from the comfort of the queen-size bed. Snuggle up in the large, dark Moon Room, complete with a step-up jetted tub in the bathroom and a king-size bed. Of all the rooms here (and perhaps in all of Lake Tahoe), the self-contained Honeymoon Cottage is the place to kiss and kiss and kiss some more. Set a few feet from the lapping waters, this one-room wonder comes romantically equipped with a two-person jetted tub affording sensational water views and a queen-size bed set against the lake-front windows. The self-contained Studio Cottage is another smart choice for romance-seeking couples. Although it doesn't have much of a view—or a jetted tub—the Studio is just as private as the Honeymoon Cottage. Get creative on the provided artist's sketchboard, and perhaps the owners will place your masterpiece on the wall next to those of previous guests. $$$–$$$$ DIS, MC, V; checks OK; *www.tahoeinn.com.*

SUNNYSIDE RESTAURANT & LODGE
♦♦

1850 W Lake Blvd, Tahoe City / 530/583-7200 or 800/822-2754
A true gabled mountain lodge built of wood and stone, Sunnyside takes full advantage of its perch on Lake Tahoe's forested northwest shore. In the warmer months, its expansive, sun-soaked wooden deck is an enticing spot to relax and enjoy views of the lake, beach, and boat-filled marina. In winter, a blazing fire crackles in the large river-rock fireplace in the lounge. The 23 comfortable and airy guest rooms all have high ceilings and walls decorated with nautical or Audubon-inspired artwork and photographs.

You'll find simple, comfortable furnishings, including vintage wooden chests that function as coffee tables. Five rooms feature fireplaces surrounded by river rock and topped with wooden mantels. With the exception of the four garden-view rooms, all rooms are oriented toward the sparkling lake; all have balconies. In the morning, enjoy a complimentary continental breakfast, and later on, savor afternoon tea. The lodge is also home to a pleasant waterfront restaurant. You can venture here for summertime lunches on the deck or an evening meal in the dining room. Even if the weather isn't on the "sunny side," this lodge is one place that will certainly brighten up any romantic getaway.
$$$ *AE, MC, V; no checks; www.sunnysideresort.com.*

THE VILLAGE AT SQUAW VALLEY
🌣🌣◖

1985 Squaw Valley Rd, Squaw Valley / 530/584-1000 or 888/805-5022
Maybe it was the whirlpool tubs that won us over—eight of them altogether, all located off one of the three fitness centers and accessed via heated walkways with views of the snowy peaks outside. Or maybe it was the 286 spacious luxury condominiums done in tasteful Craftsman-meets-alpine style housed in the five towering redwood beam–accented buildings. Whatever it was, we're sold. As you enter its sophisticated lobby, this retreat seems exactly like a regular hotel. But unlike a regular hotel, these units are condos that are rented out as hotel rooms when they're not being occupied by their owners. While all the units feature the same tasteful furnishings and color schemes, keep in mind that decor details may vary depending on the owner. (Fortunately, to be part of the rental program, condo owners must agree to make few alterations to the interiors, and top-quality linens and towels are part of the package, increasing the hotel feel.) In any case, you select a suite by layout rather than by decor. The one-bedroom suites are perfect for one couple, and it's definitely worth the extra money to get a place with mountain views (some units overlook the endless asphalt parking lot). The picture-perfect interiors we saw featured a sitting room with cushy sofa, armchair, and Craftsman-style fireplace; a bedroom with king-size bed, pale yellow walls, and tastefully framed Ansel Adams prints; and a spacious bathroom with oversize deep soaking tub and heated tile floors. Book far in advance for a one-bedroom, since the majority of the rentals are two- and three-bedroom suites, and their high prices definitely will require sharing with others. All rentals include fully equipped kitchens (right down to the silverware), gas fireplaces, balconies, heated floors, TV/DVDs, daily housekeeping service, and access to sports/ski lockers downstairs. Above all, the location couldn't be better, set in the middle of Squaw's newly developed, pedestrian-only, restaurant-and-boutique-filled European-style resort village. Squaw's slopes are just steps away; if your toes get cold in your ski boots, you can simply swoosh off the mountain straight to your room. With

all the fire jugglers, snow-making contests, après-ski fire pits, and other festival-type events happening in the village event plaza right outside your door, it's hardly quiet—but then again, that's not why couples come to this type of ski resort to begin with.

$$$$ *MC, V; checks OK; www.thevillageatsquaw.com.*

Romantic Restaurants

CHRISTY HILL
❍❍❍

115 Grove St, Tahoe City / 530/583-8551
Reflections of the glorious Lake Tahoe sunset dance on the waters outside Christy Hill most evenings. Make your reservations for a presunset dinner and, if you time it right, you'll be lingering over dessert when the fiery colors light up the lake and distant mountains. If the sun isn't cooperating, don't fret, because this dining room has romantic appeal rain or shine. Picture windows take in unobstructed views of the lake in all its glory, watercolor paintings enhance the cushioned booths and tables, and a two-way fireplace in the center of the room warms up winter nights. Tall birch branches adorned with holiday lights and placed alongside the windows bring a little of the alpine scenery inside. The menu changes seasonally but always offers a wide selection of fresh seafood—Fanny Bay oysters, broiled salmon, and Alaskan halibut oven-baked with garlic-bread crumbs—plus choice-cut meats such as Australian lamb. Christy Hill's experienced servers (most have been here for 10 years or more) know the menu and extensive wine list well, so don't hesitate to seek their advice. Dessert is a wonderful excuse to extend your evening here; try the warm summer-fruit cobbler with house-made vanilla ice cream or the decadent chocolate pot de crème. Christy Hill also has one of the finest outdoor patios in town, and making reservations for alfresco dining by the lake is highly recommended.

$$$ *AE, MC, V; checks OK; dinner Tues–Sun; beer and wine; reservations recommended; www.christyhill.com.*

GRAHAM'S
❍❍❍❍

1650 Squaw Valley Rd, Squaw Valley / 530/581-0454
After a day spent swooshing down the slopes, few things sound more appealing than sitting with your favorite ski partner in front of a blazing fire, sharing a bottle of wine, and replenishing yourselves with hearty, country-style food. Graham's is an excellent choice for doing all three, and you won't even have to venture far from the slopes. Located in the upper reaches of Squaw Valley, this shingled building (one of the oldest in the area) holds a divinely cozy dining room with fewer than a dozen candlelit

tables. Although it's intimate, you won't feel scrunched. Pine-planked vaulted ceilings, skylights, and a massive stone fireplace set directly opposite an equally enormous mirror contribute to the restaurant's sense of spaciousness. Textured butter-colored walls and Italian-scene artwork lend a distinct Tuscan touch. Mediterranean "country cuisine" best describes the robust, flavorful dishes that arrive at your table. Pine nut–crusted rack of lamb served alongside mint-mustard sauce, Muscovy duck breast with blackberry port-wine sauce, and plump lobster-stuffed ravioli in sage-scented brown butter should more than satisfy. The fresh catch of the day is grilled and topped with fresh herbs from the garden, and sometimes Moroccan dishes (such as lamb shank with couscous) and Spanish specialties (such as paella) are showcased as nightly specials. Whatever you order, end dinner by splitting a generous slice of tiramisu, and don't worry about all those calories . . . they'll quickly be used up kissing. *$$$ MC, V; checks OK; dinner every day (call for summer hours); full bar; reservations recommended; www.dinewine.com.*

LE PETIT PIER
◗◗
7238 N Lake Blvd, Tahoe Vista / 530/546-4464
This gem of a French restaurant is, as its name suggests, perched at the water's edge. Inside, the three intimate dining rooms emanate cozy country warmth. A lantern glows at each table, and the contemporary decor is enhanced by white linens and modern artwork. The classic French dishes on offer here are exquisitely prepared. Begin the meal with such mouth-watering appetizers as escargots in Roquefort butter, warm foie gras with truffle sauce, or oysters on the half shell. Enticing entrées include lavender honey-glazed duck breast; peppercorn-crusted filet mignon au Roquefort; and New Zealand venison topped with a garlic rub and accompanied by a shiitake, portobello, and burgundy reduction. Le Petit Pier's wine list has garnered prestigious awards, so you won't have any trouble finding a bottle to celebrate your special occasion. When making a reservation, request a table by the window and be sure to arrive before sunset—you don't want to miss this view, which extends clear across Lake Tahoe. *$$$ AE, DC, DIS, MC, V; local checks only; dinner Wed–Mon; full bar; reservations recommended; www.lepetitpier.com.* &

SWISS LAKEWOOD RESTAURANT
◗◖
5055 W Lake Blvd, Homewood / 530/525-5211
Old Swiss photographs, cowbells, and other Alpine-style memorabilia fill every nook and cranny of Swiss Lakewood's dining room, all with a backdrop of bright red walls. Sound a little garish? You might think so at first, but after being greeted by the charming international staff and enjoying your scrumptious meal, you might decide instead that the place is just "tastefully

cluttered." French continental cuisine graces the menu year-round, and cheese fondue for two is a specialty during the winter; it's a rare treat to feed this tasty meal to each other. In general, sauces are a highlight, whether it's the caper-lemon-mustard sauce drizzled over a delicate crab cake appetizer or the tasty Madagascar green-pepper sauce poured over the hearty Black Angus pepper steak flambé, prepared at your table in fiery style. For dessert, consider the Grand Marnier soufflé or the cherries jubilee flambé for two. Sure, it's all sinfully high in calories, but during those cold winter nights it takes a rich, hearty meal—and plenty of kisses, of course—to keep you warm. There's an extensive wine list as well.

$$$ *AE, MC, V; no checks; dinner Tues–Sun; full bar; reservations recommended; www.swisslakewood.com.* &

WILD GOOSE
◒◒◒◒

7320 N Lake Blvd, Tahoe Vista / 530/546-3640
It was inevitable: a true four-star restaurant on the shores of Lake Tahoe. Without a trace of fanfare or a hint of pretension, executive chef John Tesar quietly opened in 2003 what has already become Lake Tahoe's finest restaurant. As if the panoramic views of the lake weren't stunning enough, the interior is fashioned after classic lake cruisers of the 1920s, with glowing wood paneling and a profusion of finely polished mahogany, metal, and granite—the overall effect is sleek, sexy, and very inviting. The contemporary American cuisine is on a par with the Bay Area's finest restaurants: fried squash-blossom appetizer stuffed with herbed goat cheese, roasted tomato sauce, and tomato-basil sorbet; curried blue-claw crab with sunflower sprouts, mango crème fraîche, and chili oil; wild mushroom-crusted halibut with purslane salad and creamy mashed potatoes; and hoisin-barbecued salmon with braised bok choy and shiitake mushrooms, topped with a coconut-green curry sauce. Everything is expertly prepared, beautifully arranged, and properly presented by a well-trained staff. In the winter, request a table near the custom-built fireplace; in other seasons, you'll want a table on the terraced outdoor dining area overlooking the lake. With a prelude like this, your evening is certain to be filled with kisses.

$$$–$$$$ *AE, DC, DIS, MC, V; no checks; dinner Wed–Sun; full bar; reservations recommended; www.wildgoosetahoe.com.* &

WOLFDALE'S
◒◒◒

640 N Lake Blvd, Tahoe City / 530/583-5700
Lake Tahoe embraces the knotty-pine, rustic-lodge look, and so the sleek decor of Wolfdale's comes as a welcome change of pace. The casually elegant main dining room has hardwood floors and tables adorned with white tablecloths, exotic orchids, and hand-thrown Japanese-style plates; the

walls here and in the pleasant second dining room are hung with a collection of provocative modern art. The restaurant is known for dishing up innovative California cuisine often accented with Asian touches. The small, frequently changing menu offers an intriguing mix of truly one-of-a-kind, light, and beautifully arranged dishes that range from very good to absolutely delicious. Everything served in the restaurant—from the herb-kissed focaccia to the savory sausages, smoked fish, and divine desserts—is prepared on the premises. You might begin your meal with a soft-shell crab tempura or a vegetable spring roll with a Thai curry-ginger sauce, followed by grilled Columbia River sturgeon with mushroom duxelles and tomato coulis, barbecued ribs with white-corn bisque, or roasted quail stuffed with fennel sausage and onions served on a bed of kale. There's no direct view of the lake, but in the summertime you can sit outdoors and enjoy catching a sparkling glimpse of water through the trees.

$$$ MC, V; no checks; dinner Wed–Mon (every day July–Aug); full bar; reservations recommended; www.wolfdales.com. &

SOUTH SHORE OF LAKE TAHOE

ROMANTIC HIGHLIGHTS

If you happen to be looking to elope, South Lake Tahoe is the place for you—so long as you don't mind pledging "I do" in a roadside wedding chapel surrounded by an endless sea of neon lights and strip malls. Not to mention casinos: the top guns on this side of the lake are Harrah's, Caesars Tahoe, Harveys, and the Horizon, all squeezed next to each other on Highway 50 in Nevada. Needless to say, Tahoe's South Shore, which sits astride the California-Nevada state border, is better known for its gamblers, economy hotels, and traffic jams than its romance quotient. "No thanks," you say? Don't tune out yet. There's something here for downhill ski enthusiasts, too: Heavenly Ski Resort, one of America's largest, encompasses 4,800 acres of terrain and dazzling panoramic views of Lake Tahoe. And within easy driving distance of South Shore are more off-the-beaten-path resorts such as Kirkwood and the majestic natural splendor at Carson Pass.

Heavenly Ski Resort (off Hwy 50; 775/586-7000 or 800/2-HEAVEN; www.skiheavenly.com) is so immense that it actually straddles both California and Nevada, and its recent multimillion-dollar expansion has resulted in even more development. For some of Lake Tahoe's most inspired views, hop aboard the brand-new, $20-million-dollar, state-of-the-art **Gondola at Heavenly** (half block west of Stateline; 775/586-7000; www.skiheavenly.com). The trip up the steep mountainside in your eight-passenger cabin car provides such gorgeous views that you may want to come back and try it in every season. As you ascend 2.5 miles into the sky, the views of Lake Tahoe, Carson Valley to the east, and Desolation Wilderness to the west become more and more stunning. The ride ends at a huge observation deck, which takes full advantage of this plane-pilot's vantage point of 9,000-plus feet. The serenity of the mountain air and views of the crystalline lake set the stage for a kiss.

Lake Tahoe's brilliant blue waters are so deep that they never freeze over, so it's navigable even during the dead of winter. This is a boon for romance seekers, who can enjoy the sights year-round from the **Tahoe Queen** (530/541-3364 or 800/238-2463; www.laketahoecruises.com; reservations required), an authentic Mississippi stern-wheeler. The winter views are splendid, but summer is the most romantic time of year for a boat trip, as you can lounge out on the deck enjoying the warm sunshine and the breeze. Many of the Emerald Bay sightseeing tours are crowded with families, and your best romantic bet is the three-and-a-half-hour cruise at sunset. After a meal of continental cuisine and California wine, there's music and dancing; be sure to take a stroll on the moonlit deck as well.

Long stretches of sandy beach are one thing with which the South Shore trumps its more subdued northern counterpart. Unfortunately, during the height of the summer season, a private walk by the shore can be difficult to come by, since families, boaters, and tourists of all stripes flock to the most accessible lakeside beaches. Fortunately, many of the views here are so breathtaking you may not even notice the crowds: try **Nevada Beach** (on Elk Point Rd, 1 mile east of Stateline, Nevada), which has spectacular views of Lake Tahoe and the Sierra Nevada, or **Zephyr Cove** to the north. If you can visit during a quieter time, such as spring or late fall, you're more likely to find moments of romantic solitude. Whether you're spending a day at the beach, on the hiking trails, or even on the slopes, a picnic basket will come in handy. In South Lake Tahoe, the best place to pick up gourmet sandwiches and freshly squeezed juices is at **Sprouts** (3123 Harrison Ave; 530/541-6969; corner of Hwy 50 and Alameda St).

If the summer crowds—or the winter lift lines—are getting you down in South Lake Tahoe, it's time to journey 30 miles south to **Kirkwood** (off Hwy 88; 209/258-6000; www.kirkwood.com; free shuttle service to and from South Lake Tahoe). When the skiing conditions at Tahoe are good, the snow is often deepest at this resort and the skiing is some of Tahoe's best. The **Kirkwood Cross Country Ski Center** (209/258-7248), one of the best such centers in California, offers lessons for all ages and skill levels. The resort also offers some very tempting ski and lodging packages, should you decide that the South Shore is entirely too crowded for your getaway.

Getting to Kirkwood from South Lake Tahoe requires a considerable pilgrimage over passes along Highway 88. But the route also happens to turn incredibly scenic once it escapes the congested South Shore area. In summer, you'll pass by gorgeous sunlit meadows and craggy granite cliffs, which should inspire you to stop by the **Carson Pass Information Station** (at summit of Carson Pass on Hwy 88; www.fs.fed .us/r5/eldorado; open every day in summer) for information about the vast number of exquisite hikes to be had in this area, such as the flat 5-mile round trip to **Scotts Lake**, which departs from the **Big Meadow Trailhead** (from Carson Pass Information Station, drive east about 9 miles on Hwy 88 to its junction with Hwy 89). Shimmering alpine lakesides and wide meadows provide ample grounds for hand-in-hand nature walks and picnics, too.

Access and Information

Many highways lead to Lake Tahoe, but among the most traveled are **Interstate 80,** from Sacramento to Truckee and Reno; **US 50**, from Sacramento to South Lake Tahoe and Carson City, Nevada; and **Highway 88**, from Jackson to Kirkwood and the Hope Valley. **Reno/Tahoe International Airport** (www.reno airport.com) is approximately 45 miles from Lake Tahoe, and **Sacramento International Airport** (www.sacairports.org) is approximately 100 miles from the lake.

For more information, stop by the **South Lake Tahoe Chamber of Commerce** (3066 Lake Tahoe Blvd; 530/541-5255; www.tahoeinfo.com) to get free maps, brochures, and guidebooks to the area. If you're having trouble finding a room, contact **Lake Tahoe Visitor Authority** (800/210-3459; www .virtualtahoe.com) or log onto www.tahoereservations.com for assistance.

Romantic Lodgings

BLACK BEAR INN BED & BREAKFAST
🌢🌢🌢🌢
1202 Ski Run Blvd, South Lake Tahoe / 530/544-4451 or 877/232-7466
The Black Bear Inn, located on the road to Heavenly Ski Resort, is likely to leave you breathless. Modeled after some of the West's great lodges, this seven-room inn manages to capture all their majesty and rustic style, but without the crowds, fanfare, or enormous size. One look at the impressive Great Room and you'll want to stay: the centerpiece—a 34-foot-high river-rock fireplace—is enhanced by magnificent rough-hewn log poles stretching up to the cathedral ceilings and a river-rock wall with French doors that open to the backyard patio. Museum-quality country and farm antiques fill the interior; you'll see vintage sleighs, snowshoes, and some interesting conversation pieces, such as a pie safe (designed to keep sweet tooths from sampling the goods) and spikes from the old Truckee railroad. During the evening wine-and-cheese hour, tempting treats are set out on an antique

workman's bench fronting the fireplace. Of the five impressive rooms in the main lodge, we recommend the second-floor Fallen Leaf Room, where you can kiss on the private balcony, and the spacious Sequoia Room, a tucked-away retreat for those desiring complete privacy. All rooms are delightfully decorated in lodge style and feature private entrances, TV/VCRs hidden in armoires, king-size beds with firm and soft pillows, private bathrooms done in slate and pine, and glass-enclosed showers big enough for two. Create instant romantic ambience anytime by flipping on the gas fireplace via a bedside switch. More kissing spots await in the backyard, including the sheltered hot tub, perfect for nighttime soaks. There's also a charming duplex cabin that holds two equally lovely rooms. Ultimate privacy is found (if you can afford it) in the private and luxurious Snowshoe Thompson cabin, which has vaulted ceilings with log beams, a three-sided river-rock fireplace, a kitchenette, and a huge bath complete with a two-person Jacuzzi tub and large walk-in tile shower. Come breakfast time, freshly baked muffins are presented on an antique grocery counter, and an old-fashioned washbasin is filled with glass bottles of orange juice and milk. Enjoy such treats as eggs Benedict; blueberry strudel; or (our favorite) a green apple, walnut, and Brie omelet. Guests in the cabins can have their breakfast delivered and enjoy it in bed.
$$$-$$$$ *MC, V; checks OK; www.tahoeblackbear.com.* &

INN AT HEAVENLY
✿❂

1261 Ski Run Blvd, South Lake Tahoe / 530/544-4244 or 800/692-2246
The Inn at Heavenly may look like a motel from the outside, with its two long buildings separated by a parking lot, but take a closer look and you'll be pleasantly surprised. Each of the 14 guest rooms is individually decorated in traditional alpine motifs—such as black bears, canoes, and trout. Hand-stenciled walls, queen- or king-size beds covered by quilts, and some of the more impressive river-rock fireplaces we've seen round out the decor. Most rooms have kitchenettes and all feature private though unremarkable bathrooms. Space is at a premium in many of the rooms, so if you and your honey bring along all your recreational gear, expect a tight fit. One area of the inn has been converted into a sauna, hot tub, and steam bath sanctuary; reservations are required, which may squelch your spontaneity. No reservations are required, however, for kissing on the 2 acres of park behind the inn or pedaling to your hearts' content on the complimentary bikes (available in summer only). An expanded continental breakfast is served daily in the homey gathering room. The Inn at Heavenly also offers a number of cabins; each features a hot tub and full kitchen, while some offer fireplaces and porches. You can rent a single bedroom in one of the cabins or take over an

entire three- or four-bedroom cabin, although we must say the latter choice is better suited to groups than to cuddling couples.
$$–$$$ *AE, DIS, MC, V; checks OK; www.innatheavenly.com.*

TAHOE SEASONS RESORT
🌣🌣🌢

3901 Saddle Rd, South Lake Tahoe / 530/541-6700 or 800/540-4874
What could be nicer than rolling out of bed in the morning and walking just a few steps to the slopes? Well, how about returning to your room after a day on the hill and sinking into your own private whirlpool tub? All this and more is possible at this sumptuous resort, situated across the street from Heavenly. Each of the 160 minisuites features a pleasantly appointed living room and bedroom separated by an oversize whirlpool tub enclosed by shoji screens. A gas fire flickers in the hearth of nearly every guest room, while microwaves and refrigerators make inventive snacks a romantic possibility. Request one of the upper mountain-facing rooms for the best views; the lake-facing rooms offer only peekaboo glimpses over the neighborhood rooftops. For the absolute best views, grab your tennis racket and favorite partner and journey to the rooftop, where several courts—and fabulous vistas—await. Back on earth, a small pool and hot tub are unromantically located next to the bar and lounge area, so you're better off soaking in your room. There's also a pleasant, casual restaurant on-site, free valet parking, 24-hour front desk, and room service.
$$–$$$ *AE, DIS, MC, V; checks OK; www.tahoeseasons.com.*

Romantic Restaurants

CAFE FIORE
🌣🌣🌣

1169 Ski Run Blvd, No. 5, South Lake Tahoe / 530/541-2908
You don't have to worry about distractions at Cafe Fiore—with only seven tables, it doesn't get more intimate than this. Candles glow at each of the window-side tables in the cozy, wood-paneled dining room. In the summer, more tables are set up outside, but the view of the parking lot isn't particularly attractive. The northern Italian cuisine features seafood and traditional pastas, numerous chicken dishes, and plenty of veal specialties. Unlike the extensive entrée menu, dessert choices are limited—happily, they're also out of this world. Dig into the homemade white-chocolate ice cream or share a unique and delicious ice cream sundae creation called a snowball. The award-winning wine list is extensive and certain to have a bottle or half-bottle just right for your celebration; there's also a selection of

nearly 20 wines by the glass. Because Cafe Fiore has so few tables, reservations are hard to come by, so be sure to call ahead.

$$$ MC, V; no checks; dinner every day; beer and wine; reservations required; www.cafefiore.com.

EVAN'S AMERICAN GOURMET CAFÉ
◐◐◐◖

536 Emerald Bay Rd, South Lake Tahoe / 530/542-1990

The food at Evan's is so divine that after dinner, the two of you might not remember anything but the succulent flavor of your expertly prepared meal. This is especially the case because the interior is really just a backdrop for the incredible food rather than an attention-getter in its own right. You'll relax the moment you enter the small, softly lit dining room of this 1930s vintage house, where you'll find soft colors and fresh flowers at every table. The ever-changing menu features an eclectic and impressive blend of cuisine from around the world (the owners were serving chic fusion cuisine before it had a name). The philosophy here is to use only the finest, freshest ingredients and not to overwhelm them with heavy sauces or overstylized culinary technique. The wine list, with nearly 300 labels, is as engaging as the food. You'll swoon over dishes such as house-smoked duck-breast salad with microgreens and papaya vinaigrette, perfectly grilled halibut topped with a citrus beurre blanc, and roast lamb with crispy ginger-orange bread crumbs and coconut jasmine rice. After dinner, try one of the lavish desserts, such as the tiramisu with coffee crème anglaise. Seating is limited, so be sure to call ahead for reservations—and come with an appetite so you can savor every last bite of your impeccably delicious meal.

$$$ DIS, MC, V; no checks; dinner every day; beer and wine; reservations required; www.evanstahoe.com.

NEPHELES
◐

1169 Ski Run Blvd, South Lake Tahoe / 530/544-8130

This restaurant has an appeal completely different from any other restaurant in this book. In fact, it is the only restaurant we've encountered that provides the option of taking an on-site hot tub spa before you start dinner. Given its unique offering, along with the funky redwood exterior with a huge stained-glass window of a smiling sun, this restaurant is definitely an only-in-Tahoe type of establishment. In the dining room, you'll find standard decor and straightforward California cuisine. Dinner includes soup of the day or freshly tossed salad with house-baked sourdough bread and entrées such as roasted lamb with a Dijon mustard crust, dark-ale-and-honey-marinated free-range chicken breast with a sun-dried cherry and smoked chipotle chili roasted-corn sauce, or stuffed and grilled portobello mushroom topped with Asiago cheese. Once dinner is over, the memory that

will probably stay with you and your sweetheart is of the predinner soak. You'll get into hot water in one of the several private hot tubs behind the restaurant sheltered within a fenced-in courtyard. Under clear or snowy skies, listen to piped-in stereo music while enjoying full cocktail service. Reservations are required, and showers and towels are provided. Unusual, yes. Totally Tahoe? Also yes.
$$ *AE, DIS, MC, V; no checks; dinner every day; full bar; reservations recommended; www.nepheles.com.*

ST. IVANO'S

605 Hwy 50, No. 4, Zephyr Cove / 775/586-1070
The place to come for your own little slice of Italy on the lake is this, the best Italian restaurant in South Lake Tahoe. You'll feel immediately welcomed by Ivano Costantini, the charismatic owner and maitre d'; the enticing aromas of garlic, olive oil, and fresh basil wafting through the air hint at the flavors to come. It requires a bit of work to find this place, as it is located on the southeastern shoreline in Nevada and recessed into a tiny business complex right off the highway. The intimate dining room holds only about 10 tables, each bedecked with a white tablecloth and fresh flowers. Entrées range from reasonably priced pasta standards—linguine puttanesca, tortellini di Parma, fettuccine al bolognese—to *secondi* classics such as scaloppine parmigiana (veal with fresh tomato sauce, prosciutto, and mozzarella) and filetto di Giovanni—thinly sliced tenderloin marinated in olive oil, vinegar, and rosemary, then quickly seared to lock in the juices (no fusion confusion at this restaurant). The wine list offers more than 100 wines from Italy and California. Only a kiss can top this meal.
$$–$$$ *AE, DIS, MC, V; no checks; dinner every day; beer and wine; reservations recommended.* ♿

YOSEMITE

ROMANTIC HIGHLIGHTS

To say that Yosemite National Park is paradise on earth is not an exaggeration, and adjectives are of little use in trying to describe the region's glory. No matter which entrance you take to get into the park, your first views will literally take your breath away. Towering rock formations that soar thousands of feet above lush valleys and meadows, cascading waterfalls, and alpine lakes are just a few of the magnificent sights at hand. The 4,500-foot-high exposed granite face of **El Capitan** will inspire you to clasp

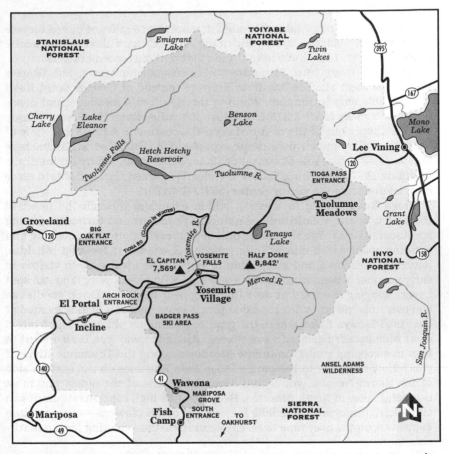

hands and gaze up (and up) in wonder, and the 2,425-foot-high **Yosemite Falls** is the highest waterfall in North America.

Winter, spring, summer, or fall—there's beauty every season at Yosemite. Snowfall brings a host of activities, including downhill or cross-country skiing at **Badger's Pass** (Glacier Point Rd; 209/372-8430; www.yosemite park.com), ice skating at the outdoor rink at **Curry Village** (209/372-8319; winter only), or snowshoeing and snow camping in more pristine areas. During the warmer months, when the valley is awash in brilliant colors, outdoor enthusiasts come to camp, ride horseback, climb immense rock faces, bike, and hike. With 840 miles of trails, Yosemite is prime hiking territory, and options for every ability level are marked on the visitor's map. One of the easiest hikes, the **Mirror Lake/Meadow Trail** (2 miles round trip, 5 miles if you circle the lake), is also one you won't want to miss for its magnificent view of **Half Dome**'s massive rock face (209/372-0200 for information about trails and conditions; www.nps.gov/yose). Another good way to sightsee on the valley floor is by pedaling through it; more than 8 miles of paved bicycle paths wind through the eastern end of the valley. Curry Village and **Yosemite Lodge** (209/372-1208) have bike stands that rent one-speed cruisers.

At nearly every turn, Yosemite yields spectacular views, but **Glacier Point** tops them all. The one-hour drive to the end of Glacier Point Road is accessible only in summer, winding through fertile meadows and dense forest to a rocky ledge 3,215 feet above the valley floor. Here, you'll enjoy what is simply one of the best vistas on the continent: a bird's-eye view of the entire valley and the panoramic expanse of the High Sierra. Kissing here is especially memorable at sunset or under a full moon. Many hiking trails originate at Glacier Point; follow the clearly marked signs or obtain more information from the **visitor center** (559/372-0200).

Tioga Road (closed in winter), which meanders through the heart of the valley, boasts a multitude of natural attractions and turnouts offering spectacular vistas. You'll want to pull over at many points on this long and winding road, which climbs high into the Sierras past forested hillsides, luxuriant meadows, and steep granite slopes. The ideal time to visit is in early summer, when the meadows are dotted with wildflowers. You can spot hawks winging overhead or deer lingering near the lakes. Bring goodies so you can stop and enjoy the roadside picnic areas, one of which is located at beautiful **Tenaya Lake**, where the granite mountains plummet right into a clear blue lake fringed with evergreens. Along the way you'll also want to stop at sweeping sunlit **Tuolumne Meadows**, along the Tuolumne River. If you follow the route to the park's Tioga Pass Entrance on the eastern side of the Sierra Nevada, you'll find **Mono Lake**, one of the oldest and most beautiful lakes in North America. Because of its high concentrations of salt and alkali, this crystal blue lake is encircled by tufa towers—white calcium deposits sculpted over time to resemble sand castles—making for a remarkable landscape.

At the southern entrance to the park, 35 miles south of the valley, lies **Mariposa Grove**, home to some of the planet's largest and most ancient living things. This massive grove of giant sequoias is right out of a storybook—you half-expect the trees to start talking. You can even kiss beneath the world's oldest sequoia, the 2,700-year-old Grizzly Giant. (To get a sense of its size, just imagine that it takes 27 fifth-graders to reach around the trunk of this monstrous tree.) Shuttle buses are allowed here, but cars are not, so wander on foot through the hushed forest to your hearts' content.

Surrounding Yosemite National Park, you'll find a handful of towns that, while not exactly destinations in themselves, harbor some lovely accommodations for couples. Some of the most remarkable options are in modest towns you may never have heard of, such as **Oakhurst**. Most people pass through it without blinking an eye on their way to the park, but this is a four-lip destination, thanks to the presence of **Château du Sureau** (see Romantic Lodgings) and **Erna's Elderberry House** (see Romantic Restaurants). A better-known town is **Bass Lake**, located 14 miles outside of the park. Although parts of the lakeshore are crowded with residences and lodges, the sizable lake itself, surrounded by evergreens and Sierra Nevada peaks, is ruggedly beautiful. A little farther afield is **Groveland**, located 23 miles west of Yosemite National Park; this town sprang to life during the 1849 California gold rush, and today the wooden sidewalks and Old West–style buildings are visible reminders of its historic past.

Access and Information

This area is accessed only by car, and the roads within the park can be very congested in summer. During winter, snow and ice limit access to the park, and many of the eastern passes are closed; call for **highway conditions** (800/427-ROAD). If you're flying in, the closest airport is **Fresno-Yosemite International Airport** (559/251-7554; www.flyfresno.org), located approximately 65 miles from Yosemite.

Entering Yosemite National Park requires a $20-per-car entrance fee (individuals 17 years and older traveling alone by bicycle, motorcycle, or on foot pay $10), no matter which entrance you use. In return, you receive a seven-day pass, a detailed park map, and the "Yosemite Guide," a handy tabloid featuring the park's rules, rates, attractions, and current exhibits. Unless bumper-to-bumper traffic is your idea of a vacation in the woods, skip Yosemite Valley during summer weekends. It's also good to keep in mind that the millions of tourists who visit each year are taking a toll on the park. Wherever your Yosemite adventure takes you, remember to tread lightly and disturb the land and the wildlife as little as possible.

A word about reservations at the lodges within the park: due to Yosemite's popularity—more than 4 million people visit each year—reservations for accommodations within the park can be hard to come by, especially during the popular summer months. Your best strategy for visiting the natural splendor is to plan ahead, making **reservations** (559/252-4848; www.yosemitepark.com) even up to a year in advance. Other options include visiting from November through March, which has the added benefit of midweek rates dropping as much as 25 percent.

For additional information about the park, contact the **Yosemite Valley Visitors Center** (Village Mall, Yosemite Valley; 209/372-0200; www.nps.gov/yose); this is also where you can pick up the **Yosemite Road Guide** if you're partial to touring the park by car. Other good sources of regional information include the **Tuolumne County Visitors Bureau** (800/446-1333; www.thegreatunfenced.com) and **Yosemite Area Travel Information** (www.yosemite.com).

Romantic Lodgings

AHWAHNEE HOTEL

♥♥€

Yosemite Valley, Yosemite National Park / 209/372-1407 (hotel) or 559/252-4848 (reservations)

Even if you've never been to Yosemite, you're probably familiar with pictures of the legendary Ahwahnee Hotel. Built in 1927, this landmark six-story hotel, made of native granite boulders and redwood-hued concrete, is an architectural masterpiece, beautifully set beneath Yosemite's majestic Royal Arches. Inside, Native American mosaics, rugs, and artwork adorn the many common areas. Huge fireplaces warm a colossal lounge where wrought-iron chandeliers hang from cathedral ceilings and floor-to-ceiling windows capture the vertical sweep of Yosemite's craggy rock walls. Tall windows in the bright solarium provide the perfect place to kiss while taking in stunning views of Glacier Point. The 99 standard guest rooms are more modest than the grand common areas; these are essentially nice hotel accommodations decorated with Native American motifs. The rooms offer basic amenities: comfortable sitting areas, TVs hidden in armoires, king-size beds with standard linens, walk-in closets, robes, and standard baths. Location, not ambience, is what you are paying for here—and, while the prices are very high, you definitely get what you pay for. If kissing in the heart of Yosemite is your desire (and if you have a credit limit higher than Half Dome), we suggest you reserve one of the six Penthouse Suites located on the hotel's private-access top floor. These palatial wonders vary in design and decor, although they all feature separate sitting areas and elegant appointments. One has mahogany paneling, a fireplace, and leaded-glass windows reminiscent of a Swiss chalet; another offers a Jacuzzi tub with shutters that open onto a sunken living room. An option between the high-end Penthouse Suites and the standard guest rooms is one of the hotel's four Parlor Suites, which are appointed with subtle color schemes, European-style furnishings, wood-burning fireplaces, and lots of windows. These suites can be rented as either two- or three-room units. Also on the property, in the wooded area behind the main building, are 24 cottages that form a series of duplexes and pentaplexes. Although they are much more rustic than the rooms in the main building, they boast surprisingly large bathrooms and innovative headboards created by a local artist. For a special getaway, look into the Ahwahnee's romance packages, which may include such extras as champagne and roses upon arrival, down comforters, satin sheets, and breakfast in bed or a special in-room candlelight dinner for two. Although the Ahwahnee attracts an overabundance of tourists year-round and reservations are hard to come by, there's no arguing that this is

the only accommodation in the park where your lips will be satisfied. At the Ahwahnee, you are in for a classic Sierra experience.
$$$–$$$$ *DC, DIS, MC, V; checks OK; www.yosemitepark.com.* &

CHÂTEAU DU SUREAU
●●●●
48688 Victoria Lane, Oakhurst / 559/683-6860
A 4-lip rating system fails us when we run across a property like Château du Sureau, which warrants 10 lips (if not more). In fact, we were tempted to revise our entire rating system, because nothing we've seen compares to the luxurious grandeur of this authentic French Provincial country estate. Wrought-iron gates swing open to reveal a luminous white stucco castle with a stone turret and red tiled roof ensconced in 9 acres of wooded hillside. Stone walkways meander past a murmuring fountain, a stream-fed swimming pool, lovely gardens, and even a life-size chessboard. Inside the manor walls, you are greeted like royalty and ushered past common areas brimming with luxurious appointments to the palatial comfort of your room. Soon after, a plate of delicious appetizers arrives at your door, the first of many pampering touches. Chandeliers add elegance to each of the 10 guest rooms, which are appointed with fine European antiques, richly colored linens, fresh flowers, and French doors that open onto private balconies or patios. CD players are tucked discreetly in antique cabinets, fires crackle in the stone hearths in colder months, and every light switch has a dimmer to set the right romantic mood. Nearly as large as bedrooms themselves, the beautiful bathrooms feature handmade French tiles, soaking tubs, and luxurious robes. Rooms located on the second floor offer both more expansive views and more privacy. Extraordinary doesn't begin to describe the service here, which caters to your every desire and whim (*almost* to the point of excess). Long-stemmed roses and decadent chocolates appear on your pillows after turndown service. You can even ask to have your bags unpacked and your pajamas laid out! For a small fee, a picnic lunch can be prepared for you to enjoy on a day hike; upon your return, the staff will be happy to oblige you with some "magic to pamper tired feet"—a foot massage. (Fortunately, gratuities are added to your bill to save you the trouble of tipping along the way.) In the morning, freshly squeezed orange juice, banana-bread French toast, corn cakes stuffed with smoked salmon, and melt-in-your-mouth croissants, among other delicacies, await guests in the sunny terracotta-tiled breakfast room. When weather permits, your morning repast may be served at wrought-iron tables on the outdoor breakfast patio. Just as our four-lip rating fails to illustrate the grand opulence of the château, our highest price category fails to accurately reflect the cost of staying at the château's pièce de résistance, the Villa Sureau. Nestled among the pine trees, this Paris Manor–style home can be yours and yours alone—if you're willing to pay the $2,000-plus-a-night price tag. There's no doubt that this

is an absolutely incredible place to kiss. Fourteen-foot ceilings rise above an impressive collection of European antiques and original 19th-century paintings, while two bedrooms, two bathrooms, a minikitchen, a library and drawing room with a baby grand piano, and a breakfast balcony complete the picture. Enormous bathrooms come equipped with freestanding steam showers, whirlpool tubs, bidets, and elegant marble accents. One of the bedrooms features a raised bed set below a stained-glass window and enclosed by thick floor-to-ceiling draperies. Outside the villa is a private Roman spa where you can soak under the stars or receive a massage. You'll want for nothing here, but if you do, simply push a button in any of the rooms to summon your own personal butler, who lives downstairs. (If you feel you can do without a 24-hour butler, you are welcome to rent only half the villa.) Once you've kissed like royalty here for a day, returning to reality may be almost too much to bear.

$$$$ *AE, MC, V; no checks; seasonal closure Jan; www.chateaudu sureau.com.* &

DUCEY'S ON THE LAKE
♥♥

39255 Marina Dr, Bass Lake / 559/642-3121 or 800/350-7463
Reminiscent of a ski lodge, Ducey's on the Lake features 20 suites, most with lake and marina views. Though the decor is fairly standard, featuring pine armoires, green carpeting, pink walls, and floral bedspreads, choice romantic amenities such as private balconies, wet bars, sitting areas, wood-burning fireplaces, and bathrobes make this an extremely comfortable place to call home for a night or two. In addition, two-person spa tubs in some of the rooms are sure to appeal to weary outdoor enthusiasts. Those who aren't yet weary can take advantage of the resort's tennis courts, sauna and hot tubs, outdoor swimming pool, and lake recreation (boating, waterskiing, fishing, and swimming). Of course, there's also Yosemite National Park, a mere 14 miles away. For evening entertainment, try dinner at the on-site restaurant: it's the only game in town as far as romance is concerned. Glowing candles at every table and knotty-pine walls decorated with antique skis and snowshoes lend rustic warmth to the two-tiered dining room overlooking Pines Marina on Bass Lake. The restaurant doesn't qualify as fine dining, but the cozy booths and tables with sparkling water views are a fine place to enjoy the menu's steaks, seafood, or pasta (for this type of food, the prices are rather steep). Live entertainment is also on hand, with jazz on the lakeside deck every Friday night in the summer. Go for the complimentary continental breakfast (a better option than the alternative, a discount certificate for the causal and mediocre Pines Restaurant on the upper part of the property). While we're doling out romantic warnings, we might add that Ducey's on the Lake shares property and facilities with the Pines Chalets.

These 84 duplex-style cabins with dated furnishings are geared mostly toward families; we recommend only the Ducey's suites for romance. $$$ *MC, V; checks OK; www.basslake.com.*

GROVELAND HOTEL
❍❍❶

18767 Main St, Groveland / 209/962-4000 or 800/273-3314
There may not be much gold left in California's Gold Country, but one precious gem remains: the Groveland Hotel. Set alongside Highway 120, it makes a fine stop on the way to Yosemite—or even a headquarters: the park's entrance is only about an hour's drive away. The original adobe section of this historic inn was built in 1849. The other half, a Queen Anne-style building, was added around the turn of the 20th century. Today, after being saved from demolition and undergoing a massive restoration, this pastel yellow hotel combines romance with plenty of historic charm. Upon arrival, you'll receive a coupon for a complimentary glass of wine, served either in the authentic gold-rush saloon or in the Victorian Room restaurant (see Romantic Restaurants). Take in some California sunshine in the peaceful courtyard, or unwind on the inn's expansive wraparound porch (which, unfortunately, allows easy glimpses into many of the guest rooms). Four modest guest rooms are located on the second floor of the original house; the other 13 are in the Queen Anne next door. Country-style Victorian florals and 19th-century furnishings grace every room, while modern couches, down comforters, and carpeting ensure comfort. Some rooms have the cozy charm of Grandma's house, while others feature elegant appointments. The three suites with separate sitting areas, gas fireplaces, and spa tubs are especially popular with romantic travelers. Another frequently requested unit is Lyle's Room, said to be the dwelling place of the resident ghost. (Apparently, this friendly spirit sneaks mints from guests' pillows from time to time. Ask anyone at the hotel about Lyle; he's the talk of the inn.) The European-style continental breakfast, a buffet of cereals, fruit, bagels, English muffins, cinnamon rolls, coffee, teas, and juices, is served in the main building's dining room. For special occasions, the hotel also offers a romance package, featuring a welcome basket full of goodies, an in-room gourmet dinner, and other pampering touches.
$$$ *AE, DC, DIS, MC, V; checks OK; www.groveland.com.* &

THE HOMESTEAD
❍❍❍

41110 Rd 600, Oakhurst / 559/683-0495 or 800/483-0495
Set on 160 wooded acres outside Oakhurst, the Homestead's four sophisticated cottages are surrounded by ancient oak trees and enfolded in country quiet. While the setting appeals primarily to naturalists who are looking to escape the city, the high-ceilinged cabins are beautifully appointed and

offer plenty of modern comforts: gas fireplaces, TV/VCRs, comfy robes, and private full baths. Knotty-pine walls and *saltillo*-tile floors lend rural style, and inviting linens cover four-poster or canopy beds in the separate bedrooms. You'll be amazed to learn that these adobe, stone, and cedar cottages were designed and built by the amiable innkeepers themselves. Although the cabins are all similar in design and amenities, each has its own distinct decor. Cowboy hats, lariats, and other memorabilia give the Ranch Cottage its Western look (there's even a horseshoe over the front door for good luck), while the Garden Cottage is as fresh as spring with its lovely wall stenciling, floral fabrics, and ivy-entwined four-poster bed frame. An equestrian theme enlivens the Country Cottage, and indigenous artwork distinguishes the Native American Cottage. A basket of baked goods and fresh fruit awaits in each fully equipped kitchen, so once you arrive you're on your own and your privacy is ensured. A gas barbecue and accompanying picnic table are also available for use by all guests. Set on the upper level of a barn-style structure, the Star Gazing Loft is the fifth—and least expensive—accommodation on the property. Though it's slightly smaller than the cabins, this one-room studio offers similar privacy (the only thing below the suite is a storage space) and amenities: a private entrance, a kitchenette stocked with breakfast goodies, a TV/VCR, handcrafted pine furniture, and views of the countryside (and the stars in the evening) through a large picture window. Its wicker furnishings and eclectic decor make it a casual and cozy hideaway. The new two-bedroom Ranch House, completed in the summer of 2004, offers a haven for couples traveling together.
$$–$$$ *MC, V; checks OK; www.homesteadcottages.com.*

HOUNDS TOOTH INN
♥✿€
42071 Hwy 41, Oakhurst / 559/642-6600 or 888/642-6610
This sprawling, Victorian-style home, painted cream with dark green trim, sits 12 miles from Yosemite's south entrance. Highway 41 borders one side of the property, but you descend a steep driveway to the inn, leaving the road mostly out of sight (although not completely out of hearing). Once inside, start things off with complimentary cookies and wine served at a lovely bar area next to a glowing fireplace. Twelve distinctly decorated guest rooms fill the first and second floors of the home. We like the spaciousness of the second-floor rooms, with their vaulted ceilings and large windows, although the five rooms on the ground floor offer private entrances via the wraparound cement patio. All guest rooms feature private baths, ceiling fans, feather-top mattresses, and sunny dispositions. Five have whirlpool tubs and one room comes equipped with a refrigerator, wet bar, and microwave. (Unfortunately, visible air-conditioning units and TVs set out on the most convenient pieces of furniture detract from the otherwise attractive rooms.) The Hounds Tooth Room, done up in a striking taupe and black color

scheme, is our favorite. A sumptuous king-size bed covered with handsome linens faces the mantel, where a TV is discreetly tucked away above the gas fireplace. In one corner of the bedroom, you'll find a two-person whirlpool tub set next to a window affording views of the treetops. This room also features a couch perfect for snuggling, a handsome cherrywood desk, and a large bathroom. We also like the Tower Room, otherwise known as the Honeymoon Room, for its whimsical wrought-iron bed frame encircled with sheer netting and ivy. This bright room features a whirlpool tub just steps from the queen-size bed. Those looking for a masculine touch will prefer the Firelight Room, with its cherrywood furniture, wingback chairs, and maroon linens covering a king-size bed. Road noise is only a problem if you venture outside to relax on the flower-filled patio or stroll around the 2½-acre property. A buffet-style breakfast of quiche, cereal, pastries, sweet breads, fresh fruit, and coffee is served in the sunny main-floor breakfast nook each morning.
$$–$$$ *AE, DIS, MC, V; checks OK; www.houndstoothinn.com.*

TENAYA LODGE AT YOSEMITE

1122 Hwy 41, Fish Camp / 559/683-6555 or 888/514-2167
The fact that awe-inspiring Yosemite National Park is located just 2 miles north of Tenaya Lodge might be incentive enough to stay in this large hotel. Set just off the highway, Tenaya commands views of a luscious valley hemmed by trees rising in succession to the horizon—this view would be heavenly if it weren't for the sprawling parking lot that surrounds the hotel. You might not have uninterrupted views of Yosemite's splendor, but you get what you pay for here in terms of service and amenities. Enormous iron chandeliers trimmed with candles hang from cathedral ceilings in the large, slightly dated lobby, where a fire crackles in an immense stone fireplace and canoes and hunting trophies adorn the dark wood walls. A recent renovation has given the 244 guest rooms new furnishings, attractive bedspreads, and Native American patterns in shades of green, burgundy, and tan. All rooms feature standard baths and TVs hidden in armoires. For slightly higher prices, the Luxury and Honeymoon Suites offer hand-carved four-poster beds, private balconies, soaking tubs, and extra space. Treat yourselves to a massage and then dine at one of the hotel's three restaurants. An indoor pool, a fitness center, a sauna, a Jacuzzi tub, and rental bicycles are available for guests who still have energy after Yosemite.
$$$ *AE, DC, DIS, MC, V; checks OK; www.tenayalodge.com.* &

Romantic Restaurants

AHWAHNEE DINING ROOM
❀❀

Yosemite Valley (Ahwahnee Hotel), Yosemite National Park / 209/372-1489
Finding good food and a romantic dining ambience in Yosemite Valley is
almost as difficult as making the steep climb to the top of Bridalveil Falls.
Fortunately, if the park's splendor has aroused your passion for romance,
you can wine and dine your sweetheart at the Ahwahnee Dining Room.
Grand sugar-pine trestles and granite pillars give the enormous dining
room a rustic elegance, and 34-foot ceilings soar above pink linen-swathed
tables, plus rugs and draperies in bright shades of yellow, green, and red.
Be certain to arrive well before nightfall to admire the view: full-length
windows showcase the splendid sights of Yosemite Falls and Glacier Point.
Once darkness falls, the soft light of the chandeliers suspended from the
cathedral ceiling and slim candles in wrought-iron holders at your table
create a cozy mood. Meals are presented on the Ahwahnee's signature
china—which comes off as slightly more touristy than attractive, alas.
The menu features mostly meat and seafood dishes, from filet mignon and
braised lamb shank to pan-seared salmon and broiled ahi. Both food and
service are mediocre, but at least you have that spectacular view and your
special someone to keep your mind on romance.
*$$$–$$$$ DC, DIS, MC, V; checks OK; lunch, dinner every day; full bar;
reservations recommended; www.yosemitepark.com.* &

ERNA'S ELDERBERRY HOUSE
❀❀❀❀

48688 Victoria Lane, Oakhurst / 559/683-6800
People drive for hours just to dine at Erna's Elderberry House. You might
wonder why a restaurant in such an obscure location merits so much time
in a car, but once you've spent a blissful evening at this luxurious French
restaurant, you'll know (and you might find yourselves driving for hours
to come back). Nestled among elderberry trees adjacent to the Château du
Sureau (see Romantic Lodgings), this is a restaurant with a view—of the
castle itself, the magnificent gardens, and at sunset a splendid sky awash
with color behind towering ponderosa pines. Large chandeliers softly illu-
minate the main dining room, a beautiful interior of cathedral ceilings, rich
red walls, tapestries, paintings, and ornate gold-framed mirrors. Beauti-
fully upholstered chairs adjoin white linen-swathed tables adorned with
flickering candles, while a fire crackling in the hearth fans the flames of
romance in the cooler months. Erna's exquisitely presented six-course prix
fixe dinners change daily and are served by an exceedingly formal and gra-
cious wait staff. (If you prefer a more casual meal, the chateau has a smaller
bistro-style menu downstairs, but in our opinion, it's inconceivable to come

all the way here without splurging on the whole romantic experience.) Characteristic offerings might include a poached quail egg topped with caviar, delicious tuna tartare with miso-basil sauce, unusual and savory New England clam chowder laced with curry, Sonoma lamb noisettes with tarragon-tomato essence sauce, a crisp salad topped with apples and Roquefort cheese, and a chocolate terrine with fresh fruit and homemade ice cream for the sweet finale. You're certain to have a fabulous evening.

$$$$ AE, DIS, MC, V; no checks; dinner every day, brunch Sun; full bar; reservations recommended; www.elderberryhouse.com. &

VICTORIAN ROOM
❂❂❂

18767 Main St (Groveland Hotel), Groveland / 209/962-4000 or 800/273-3314

The Victorian Room is the only fine-dining establishment in these parts, and it is definitely worthy of your romantic consideration. Set on the main floor of the historic gold-rush hostelry Groveland Hotel (see Romantic Lodgings), this casually elegant restaurant consistently turns out artistically presented gourmet cuisine prepared with local seasonal ingredients. The interior is subtly lit by brass chandeliers; pale pink walls provide the backdrop for three whimsical angels who hover in flight above a stream of gold gauze, while mauve-colored wainscoting and window treatments create rosy warmth. Each of the cozy tables in the dining room is topped with a white tablecloth, fresh flowers, and a glowing candle, and some tables look out onto the hotel's veranda. On a warm evening, the seating here is definitely romantic, complete with lovely gardens, candlelit tables, and nostalgic lamppost lighting. The award-winning wine list has plenty of special bottles to choose from, and warm hospitality and swift service make dinner here an enjoyable experience. Seafood lovers won't want to miss the incredible snow crab bisque, followed by the aptly named yum yum shrimp: giant shrimp sautéed in a cross-cultural blend of Indian ginger ghee, sake, garlic, cilantro, scallions, lime, and tomatoes. The rack of lamb is a house specialty, and other favorites include rib-eye steak and grilled salmon. Those who wouldn't mind death by chocolate will come close to heaven with the dessert known simply as "chocolate suicide." Should you want to saddle up for a nightcap, there's also an authentic gold rush–era saloon.

$$$ AE, DC, DIS, MC, V; no checks; dinner Thurs–Sun in winter, every day in summer; full bar; reservations recommended; www.groveland.com.

MOUNT SHASTA REGION

ROMANTIC HIGHLIGHTS

Magnificent, snowcapped Mount Shasta, standing alone on the horizon and soaring 14,162 feet into the sky, is without doubt the romantic highlight of California's remote northern region. The sight of its glacial white peak cutting into the blue skies that so often grace this scenic region in summer is certain to inspire a kiss. Nestled below the peak are the towns of Dunsmuir, McCloud, and Mount Shasta, and while these former railroad, mill, and lumber towns are modest destinations, they do harbor some lovely romantic surprises along their quiet streets. While it's often thought of as a stopover for people on the way to or from Oregon, this region's splendid natural beauty and its increasing number of romantic accommodations make it worthy of a trip in its own right. Unless you have skiing in mind, summer is the best time for a romantic getaway here, since winter's snow and ice often create difficult driving conditions. No matter the season, all throughout your stay, you'll feel the enduring power of this mountain.

For couples seeking as many chances as possible to gaze at this icy peak, the major attraction in the area is the **Shasta Sunset Dinner Train** (530/964-2142 or 800/733-2141; www.shastasunset.com; year-round, reservations recommended in summer; from $75 per person), which follows a historic turn-of-the-20th-century logging route. Unlike so many touristy train rides, this one has authentic charm, from the handsomely restored vintage rail cars complete with mahogany paneling and antique brass to the journey itself, which follows the train's original route of breathtaking steep grades, sharp curves, and switchbacks. As you enjoy a well-prepared four-course dinner on white linens and china in your railcar, you'll be treated to views of Mount Shasta, Castle Crags, and the Trinity Alps. The 40-mile, three-hour journey allows plenty of time for kissing.

The tiny mill town of **McCloud**, home to the dinner train, bills itself as "the quiet side of Mount Shasta." Once you arrive, you'll see that the motto is appropriate, since the two-block downtown is pretty sleepy indeed. However, McCloud is also home to the region's most romantic bed-and-breakfasts and provides easy access to surrounding nature trails. Staying here will appeal to anyone who loves to spend their waking hours outdoors; it also makes a wonderful getaway for urban couples looking to drop off the map for a quiet weekend. If you don't want to drive into the town of nearby Mount Shasta for dinner (and even if you are staying elsewhere), be sure to reserve a table at the intimate restaurant at the **McCloud Hotel** (see Romantic Lodgings).

Mount Shasta, a quaint mountain hamlet with a new age ambience, has a handful of attractions and charming restaurants. The small downtown is

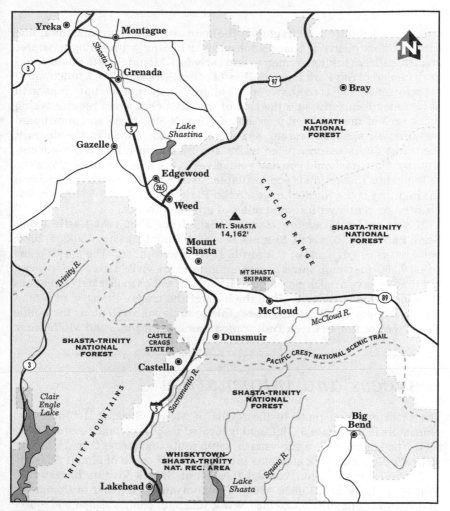

lined with bookstores, cafés, and galleries, and browsing here is an appealing way to spend an afternoon. If you're planning to do any hiking—or simply want some snacks for your room—stop by the **Berryvale Grocery** (305 S Mt Shasta Blvd; 530/926-1576) for fresh organic produce, gourmet sandwiches, and a colorful gift and clothing selection from around the world.

The tiny historic railroad town of **Dunsmuir** is also nearby. The main romantic attraction here is the wonderful **Cafe Maddalena** (see Romantic Restaurants), although if you stop in Dunsmuir on your way to a nearby hiking adventure, you can pick up lunch, espresso, and delicious pastries and cookies at the **Cornerstone Bakery & Café** (5759 Dunsmuir Ave; 530/235-4677).

Above all, nature in all its glory is the main attraction here, and the alpine climate offers plenty of chances for outdoor kissing, with skiing in winter and magnificent hiking in summer and early fall. **Mount Shasta Board & Ski Park** (at end of Ski Park Hwy, off Hwy 89, 10 miles east of I-5; 530/926-8610 ski resort, 530/926-8686 snow report) offers mostly intermediate runs with nary a mogul in sight, and the cost of the lift ticket won't require taking out a second mortgage on your home. There's also a ski and snowboard rental/repair shop, restaurant, snack bar, and ski school. In the summer, the resort offers naturalist-led walks and mountain-biking trails—accessible by chairlift should you find yourselves in the mood to rocket down the hilly terrain (bike rentals are available, too). About a quarter mile down the highway is the **Nordic Lodge** (on Ski Park Hwy; 530/926-8610), a cross-country ski center with several miles of groomed tracks.

If you prefer to admire Mount Shasta from afar, visit **Castle Crags State Park** (off I-5, about 13 miles south of Mount Shasta; 530/235-2684; www.parks.ca.gov), one of California's geologic wonders. The park's enormous 6,500-foot-high spires of ancient granite are visible from the freeway, but they deserve a much closer look. Hike up the park's moderately strenuous 2.7-mile **Summit Dome Trail** to the base of the crags—the view of Mount Shasta alone is worth the trip. Less athletic souls can stroll along the 1-mile **Root Creek** or **Indian Creek Trail** or picnic among the pines and wildflowers.

Access and Information

The most common route to the towns of Mount Shasta, McCloud, and Dunsmuir is **Interstate 5**. McCloud is located a short distance east of Interstate 5 on Highway 89, a curvy north-south route that passes through Lassen Volcanic National Park and joins Interstate 5 just south of Mount Shasta.

For more information, contact the **Mount Shasta Visitors Bureau** (300 Pine St at Lake St; 530/926-4865). The **Dunsmuir Chamber of Commerce and Visitors Center** (800/386-7684; www.dunsmuir.com) is also a good source for information on the area. The **Shasta Cascade Wonderland Association** (800/474-2782; www.shastacascade.org) offers information on Lassen, Modoc, Plumas, Siskiyou, Shasta, and Trinity Counties.

Romantic Lodgings

MCCLOUD GUEST HOUSE
♥♥

606 W Colombero Dr, McCloud / 530/964-3160 or 877/964-3160
The stunning emerald green lawns and towering oak and pine trees that surround this stately, two-story mansion are nothing short of astonishingly beautiful. The property also boasts a fascinating history, since the home was built in 1907 for one of McCloud's timber barons and in the 1920s and 1930s served as a retreat for such luminaries as Herbert Hoover and Jean Harlow. All the more reason to be disappointed, then, that the rooms inside live up to neither this ritzy legacy nor the impressive exterior. This establishment got its start as a country inn and restaurant in the early 1980s, and more recently, new owners have arrived with plans for improvements. However, while the interior does have lovely historic features, including a lobby and dining room with beveled glass, antique wallpaper, and a massive stone fireplace, the furnishings are sparse and the overall feel is dark, chilly, and dated (at the time of our visit, the carpet desperately needed replacing). Also needing an update are the inn's five large guest rooms, which have the same aforementioned carpet, bare walls that could use some artwork, and linens that should be upgraded. Features such as four-poster beds and antique furnishings do add charm; the two best rooms upstairs have claw-foot tubs (if you're especially interested in soaking, the sole room downstairs has a two-person Jacuzzi tub). A multicourse breakfast is served in the morning. With plans for refurbishment underway, we think this inn will soon come closer to kissing perfection. In the meantime, you can't go wrong with lounging on the white wicker furnishings on the home's gorgeous wraparound veranda, where the true old-fashioned charm and beautiful views will keep the mood romantic.
$$ *AE, MC, V; no checks.*

MCCLOUD HOTEL
♥♥♥

408 Main St, McCloud / 530/964-2822 or 800/964-2823
Lush grass pathways lined with fragrant rosebushes, cozy sitting areas with Adirondack chairs amid a profusion of potted plants, even a secluded nook with seats before a gently bubbling fountain: the romantic gardens surrounding this historic inn offer an endless array of places to kiss. To add to the charm, the hotel's restaurant can deliver wine and appetizers anywhere on the grounds, so if you've selected your favorite kissing spot and don't want to budge, you can linger for hours with refreshments. Gorgeous as they are, the grounds don't for a minute overshadow the stately 1915 hotel, which is on the National Register of Historic Places. The hotel was meticulously restored in 1995, although ongoing work and additions

continue to create the most romantic environment possible. The hotel's 17 elegant guest rooms vary in size and amenities (each has a private bath), with simpler accommodations on the ground floor and more rooms plus four luxury suites upstairs. For romance, we highly recommend the suites. These spacious and tasteful love nests offer two-person tiled Jacuzzi tubs, fluffy robes, and beautiful four-poster beds; the two suites at the front of the hotel have access to a shared balcony. You can also have the delicious gourmet breakfast delivered to your door in the morning. Guests staying elsewhere can descend to the warm wood-paneled lobby area for a gourmet morning meal of fresh fruit, house-made bread, and a hot breakfast dish. Saturday afternoon brings a lavish spread of tea and scones, and lunch and dinner are also available in the restaurant, an intimate 10-table affair with white linens and well-prepared continental cuisine. If you're looking for a special getaway, the Sweetheart Package offers chilled wine in your room, plus dinner at the restaurant. After spending the day exploring outside in the fresh mountain air, you'll be delighted to collapse on the lobby's enticing sofa and chairs, sip a glass of wine, and cozy up before the crackling fire in the majestic fireplace.
$$–$$$ AE, DIS, MC, V; checks OK; www.mccloudhotel.com. &

MCCLOUD RIVER INN
♥♥♥

325 Lawndale Ct, McCloud / 530/964-2130 or 800/261-7831
The owners of this country Victorian-style bed-and-breakfast, set right in the middle of the charming town of McCloud, have an avocation that's after our own hearts: they claim to be in the "relationship renewal" business. It's certainly true that the moment you step in the door, you'll feel well taken care of and able to concentrate entirely on each other. Built at the turn of the 20th century as headquarters for the McCloud River Lumber Company, this inn has five individually decorated guest rooms, all with private bathrooms and filled with period-style furnishings. While the decor is a bit incongruous in some places and slightly worn in others (namely, the hallway carpet), the warm hospitality and romantic perks in the rooms are sure to outweigh these minor drawbacks. Without a doubt, the best choice for kissing is Room 4, an upstairs hideaway with a four-poster queen-size bed and an enticing Jacuzzi tub with lace drapes. Enjoy views of the town's quaint main street through the windows, or relax in the sitting area—where you can also have breakfast in the morning. Nearly as enticing is Room 5, with a crisp green and white color scheme, an elegant wrought-iron bed, and a claw-foot soaking tub in the bathroom. In keeping with the inn's mission, there are no TVs or telephones to distract you from each other. The inn has a gift shop with snacks, T-shirts, and mugs; the ample breakfast offers fresh fruit, pastries, and frittatas.
$–$$$ AE, DIS, MC, V; checks OK; www.mccloudriverinn.com.

Romantic Restaurants

CAFE MADDALENA
❁❁❁

5801 Sacramento Ave, Dunsmuir / 530/235-2725
This tiny, historic railroad town in the mountains may seem an unlikely setting for a fine restaurant, but as soon as this dining room was opened by chef/owner Maddalena Sera, it was hailed by food critics from Shasta to San Francisco for its authentic Italian fare. The beloved institution recently changed hands, and fortunately the new owners—who established the wildly popular Trinity Café in Mount Shasta—are carrying on the tradition of excellence. The charm of the restaurant is intact, from its sunny yellow exterior to its intimate dining room that embodies charming Shaker-style simplicity with knotty-pine walls, large windows, and tables set with white linens and crystal. The new owners have expanded the previous menu, which was predominantly Sardinian, to include authentic dishes from southern France, Spain, and North Africa. Offerings may include *zarzuela* (a Spanish shellfish stew in a tomato-saffron broth); herb-roasted lamb rack with ratatouille; an exotic couscous with a tagine of yam, carrots, and prunes; or a pan-seared filet mignon with sauce *vin de minervois*. The menu changes seasonally, and everything is made fresh daily, including the bread and the desserts. The wine list includes Italian, French, and Spanish labels to complement the entrées. During the summer months, request a table outside under the grape arbor.
$$ DIS, MC, V; checks OK; dinner Thurs–Sun (closed Jan–Feb); beer and wine; reservations recommended; www.cafemaddalena.com.

LILY'S
❁❁

1013 S Mt Shasta Blvd, Mount Shasta / 530/926-3372
There's a reason this restaurant is popular with locals: the very good California cuisine—with an ethnic flair—is fresh, delicious, and creative. An interior with quaint farmhouse charm and a pretty outdoor patio for warm-weather dining contribute to the restaurant's romantic appeal. The location fronts a wide, busy street, which creates an unwanted soundtrack of passing cars if you're dining alfresco—fortunately, the traffic in this mountain town is quite light. Start your dinner with spicy jalapeño pasta or baked Brie and follow with an entrée of prime rib, Chicken Rosie (a chicken breast browned in butter and simmered with raspberries, hazelnut liqueur, and a hint of cream), or the terrific enchiladas *suizas* stuffed with crab, shrimp, and fresh

spinach. Lunch offerings are equally varied and imaginative, and if you're looking for an unusual breakfast, try Lily's cheesy polenta fritters.
$ *AE, DIS, MC, V; local checks only; breakfast, lunch Mon–Fri, dinner every day, brunch Sat–Sun, holidays; beer and wine; reservations recommended; www.lilysrestaurant.com.*

SERGE'S RESTAURANT
◆◆◆
531 Chestnut St, Mount Shasta / 530/926-1276
When was the last time you dined with views of a towering dormant volcano? That's what we thought. The view here is especially memorable because you will enjoy it while dining alfresco on the open-air deck. And don't worry about an unplanned side dish of hot lava; Mount Shasta hasn't blown its snowy stack since the late 1700s. Even if the weather is chilly and you dine inside without the 3-D vistas, this classical French-continental restaurant is one of Mount Shasta's best. The country-cozy interior is enhanced with lace curtains, and the mood is relaxed. The menu changes seasonally, and starters often range from garlicky escargots and prawns sautéed with Pernod to a classic Caesar salad. Entrées might include a perfectly grilled 9-ounce New York steak with provençal herbs or scallops and prawns in a light chablis sauce served over a puff pastry shell. Mount Shasta is a hotbed of vegetarianism, so the menu usually offers at least one meatless dish, such as manicotti stuffed with toasted walnuts, mushrooms, and eggplant and drizzled with a lemon-thyme tomato sauce. Desserts whipped up daily might include a rich, heavenly chocolate mousse or a cheesecake topped with a delicious berry sauce.
$$ *AE, DIS, MC, V; checks OK; dinner Wed–Sun; beer and wine; reservations recommended.*

TRINITY CAFÉ
◆◆◆
622 N Mt Shasta Blvd, Mount Shasta / 530/926-6200
You can't see the snowcapped peak of Mount Shasta from the tiny dining room at the Trinity Café, but once you taste the food that arrives on your table, it's doubtful that you'll mind. The recently arrived new owners, formerly of Napa Valley, have brought a classic wine-country trio to this little mountain town: sophisticated fare, casual mood, and seasonal ingredients. The decor is simple and the tightly packed interior can get a bit noisy on weekend evenings, but couples craving a gourmet meal will find this restaurant to be one of Mount Shasta's most appealing options for a special night out. The menu combines the flair and eclecticism of wine-country cooking with the Mount Shasta penchant for healthfulness, using fresh produce from the local farmer's market and locally raised game. Try the cabernet-braised lamb with mint pesto, grilled Pacific king salmon on panzanella salad,

whole roasted tilapia with saffron risotto, or grilled vegetables stacked with polenta and fresh mozzarella. The wine list is predominantly Californian, with featured wines to complement the nightly specials.

$$ *MC, V; checks OK; dinner Tues–Sat; beer and wine; reservations recommended.* &

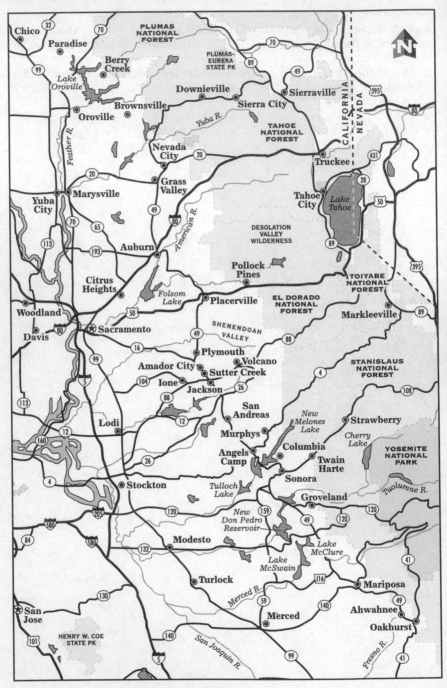

"Every kiss provokes another."
—MARCEL PROUST

SACRAMENTO AND GOLD COUNTRY

The heart of the Central Valley and the capital city of California, Sacramento is a former gold-rush boomtown. Today, with its skyscrapers, upscale restaurants, and swanky hotels, this once-small destination is brimming with urban sophistication. While some busy couples might whiz past on their way to Lake Tahoe, those traveling at a more relaxed pace can consider a weekend getaway exploring Sacramento's attractions. Geographically, Sacramento is located in the middle of the Central Valley's great plain—at nearly 300 miles long and 50 miles wide, the largest expanse of flatland west of the Continental Divide—and is bordered by the Sierra Nevada to the east. In the foothills of this magnificent range lie the many small, charming towns known collectively as Gold Country.

Gold Country was born in 1849, when news spread that the precious substance had been discovered in the Sierra Nevada. People from all over flocked to the promised land of California, and hordes of settlers determined to find riches flooded the area, turning it into something of a ruthless outlaw region. Few made fortunes in pursuit of the mother lode, but this wild, heady time changed the Golden State forever. Although the gold rush is long since past, the heritage of the Sierra still captures our imaginations, and the romance still thrives in historic towns such as Nevada City: at the height of the California gold rush, this destination in northern Gold Country was as important on the California map as Sacramento is today. Nevada City isn't the only romantic destination here, and tucked amid rolling golden hills and valleys, you'll find numerous quaint towns to explore. Farther south in Amador and Calaveras Counties, acres upon acres of well-tended vineyards grace the sloping Sierra Nevada foothills, creating a wondrous setting for bed-and-breakfasts and award-winning wineries—not to mention kissing.

SACRAMENTO

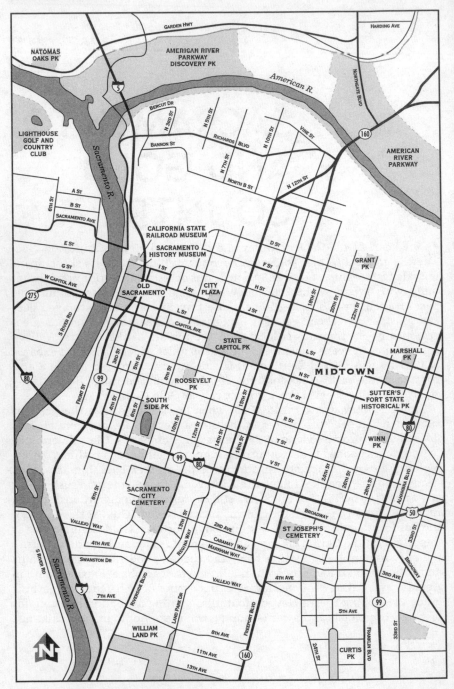

SACRAMENTO

ROMANTIC HIGHLIGHTS

Though Sacramento is one of the fastest-growing cities in the nation, the capital of the Golden State still exudes an amiable charm. Year-round sunshine graces its wide streets, which are lined with tall shade trees and renovated turn-of-the-20th-century homes. Coffeehouses, antique stores, stylish restaurants, and a handful of elegant Victorian bed-and-breakfasts enhance its friendly allure. But even though the city may in places feel like a small town, keep in mind that it is not. Traffic does clog the streets and surrounding freeways during rush hour, and most of the inns and bed-and-breakfasts in the area cater to business clientele during the week. However, these romantic drawbacks should have no disagreeable impact on your stay, especially if you plan your getaway for a weekend.

Many of Sacramento's best kissing locales are found in the heart of the city, and one such draw is free tours of the magnificent, turn-of-the-20th-century **California State Capitol Building** (10th St between L and N Sts; 916/324-0333; 9am–4pm every day); tickets are given out a half hour beforehand in the basement of the building. Even if you don't go inside the capitol itself, don't miss the opportunity to stroll the surrounding grounds of **Capitol Park**, where more than 340 varieties of trees from around the world tower in leafy majesty. Refresh yourselves with iced mochas at **Java City** (1800 Capitol Ave; 916/444-5282) and then explore the surrounding neighborhoods on foot; the tree-lined streets of Midtown (between 19th and 30th Sts) are pleasant for a shady walk, and the main retail corridor along **J Street** (particularly between 17th and 23rd Sts) harbors many inviting cafés, boutiques, and a number of Sacramento's most charming restaurants.

Our vote for the best daytime date in the entire city, however, goes to the **Crocker Art Museum** (216 O St at 3rd St; 916/264-5423), located in an exquisitely restored Italianate mansion. Home to the region's largest art collection, the museum houses a stunning display of European masters' drawings, as well as a fine selection of contemporary California art. Ornate ceilings of robin's-egg blue and gold, spiral staircases, lushly carpeted rooms filled with Crocker family heirlooms, and sleek modern galleries in the newer wing provide plentiful grounds for exploration—and inspiration for kissing. (Look upstairs in the California Gallery for paintings depicting Sacramento in the 1800s.) Art lovers might also check out **La Raza Galleria Posada** (704 O St at 7th St; 916/446-5133), a Chicano, Latino, and Native American arts center located in a beautifully restored Victorian house.

The touristy streets of Old Sacramento (a.k.a. Old Sac), the historic district running along the Sacramento River, are lined with restored Western-style facades and cheap shops. While the area is not particularly romantic, do consider lunch at one of the waterfront restaurants: **Rio City Café** (1110 Front St; 916/442-8226) has a pleasant outdoor patio and a light, airy, attractive dining room where Southwestern fare with a dash of California flair is featured. The horse-drawn carriages touring the neighborhood cater more to families than to kissing couples, but if you simply can't resist, try **Classic Coach Carriage Service** (916/834-3481; usually parked at 2nd and J). Our recommendation is to request the "park ride," which leaves Old Town behind and journeys along the Sacramento River and through the park by the Crocker Art Museum. History buffs may enjoy a visit to the popular **California State Railroad Museum** (2nd and I Sts; 916/323-9280; open every day).

If you want to explore a less-traveled but artsy part of the city, check out the latest goings-on in **Uptown**, also known as North Sacramento: this warehouse-lined neighborhood is more industrial and less pretty than other parts of the city but, as home to a growing arts scene—including the intriguing **Phantom Galleries** program that invites the public in for art viewing (second Sat; www.northsacramentochamber.org)—it makes an intriguing side trip. For fine dining, romantics will want to stop in at **Enotria Café and Wine Bar** (see Romantic Restaurants), a sophisticated eatery that boasts one of Sacramento's most expansive wine lists.

If a bit of romantic gift giving (and receiving) is in order, Sacramento's most upscale shopping mall, **Pavilions**, is the place. Located on the outskirts of the city, the mall features a series of open-air courtyards so you don't have to forsake the sunshine. A must-have treat here is sharing a gourmet lunch at the tables scattered outside **David Berkley** (515 Pavilions Lane; 916/929-4422); pair the savory smoked-chicken salad with a crisp sauvignon blanc, or consider the takeout dinner menu and bring treats back to your room for a romantic evening in.

Couples with a cultural bent will delight in Sacramento's many opportunities to get dressed up and take in a show, including those of the **Sacramento Philharmonic** (916/264-5181), which draws big-name jazz and classical performers. The city also has a thriving theater scene, and two top venues are the **Sacramento Theater Company** (1419 H St; 916/446-7501) and the **B Street Theatre** (2711 B St; 916/443-5300). The **California Musical Theatre** (916/557-1999) presents a Broadway Series from September through May, featuring as many as nine top-notch Broadway shows. For late-night drinks and intimate conversation, visit **Tapa the World** (2115 J St; 916/442-4353), an extremely popular and busy restaurant that serves until midnight. You can't go wrong with the sangria, tapas, live Spanish and flamenco guitar, or the divine "chocolate addiction" dessert.

Sacramento's two rivers—the boat-filled, bustling, muddy Sacramento River and the raft-filled, sparkling blue American River—are attractions in their own right. For athletic couples, nothing beats the **American River**

Parkway, a 5,000-acre nature preserve with a 22-mile-long, pothole-free bike trail, which starts in Old Sac and follows the water all the way to the town of Folsom. You can rent a bike at **City Bicycle Works** (2419 K St; 916/447-2453). If you are visiting during the sweltering Sacramento summer, you'll probably find it more romantic to opt for a leisurely raft trip down the American River with **American River Raft Rentals** (11257 S Bridge St, Rancho Cordova; 916/635-6400).

If a day trip is in order, consider the wildly romantic wineries in the hills above the historic town of Placerville, approximately 40 miles north. Stop first in downtown **Placerville** to pick up gourmet picnic provisions at **Dedrick's Main Street Cheese** (312 Main St; 530/344-8282). We highly recommend **Boeger Winery** (1709 Carson Rd; 530/622-8094 or 800/655-2634; www.boegerwinery.com), nestled amid lush, sloping vineyards in a historic gold-rush setting. The spacious, elegant tasting room, completed in fall 2002, offers outstanding wines—don't miss the award-winning Barbera. Unpack your picnic at the shady tables set by the creek, or peek at the museum inside one of this historic winery's original structures, which were built in 1872. Visit during the week to experience the best this lovely spot has to offer; on weekends—particularly in September and October when crowds flock to this region, known locally as "Apple Hill," for produce and family fun—the tasting room can be quite a mob scene. Another option is to travel a bit farther down back roads to **Lava Cap Winery** (2221 Fruitridge Rd; 530/621-0175 or 800/475-0175; www.lavacap.com). Named after the unique rock formations formed millions of years ago in this area, the winery's views over vineyards and the American River Canyon—with misty blue foothills in the distance—is simply breathtaking. The equally impressive wines make the perfect accompaniment to a picnic in this natural splendor.

Access and Information

Interstate 5 and Highway 99 are the primary north-south routes through the Central Valley. Among the many east-west arteries are Highway 152 between Los Banos and Merced and Highway 132 between the Altamont Pass and Modesto in the south; to the north, Highway 20 serves as an artery from the foothills near Grass Valley to Clear Lake. Interstate 80 takes you east to the Reno-Lake Tahoe region or west to San Francisco. There is no region-wide public transportation system (though there are options within the cities), so it is best to explore this area by car. However, take note that the Central Valley is often blanketed with thick fog during the winter months (worst is Dec-Feb). Driving can be hazardous; check on current **road conditions** (800/427-ROAD;www.dot.ca.gov) throughout the Central Valley and the state. Interstate 5 provides easy access to **Sacramento International**

Airport (www.sacairports.org), but flights are often delayed due to poor visibility. Always call the individual airline to confirm schedules.

Romantic Lodgings

AMBER HOUSE
◆◆◆◖

1315 22nd St / 916/444-8085 or 800/755-6526

Poets, artists, and musicians inspired the decor at Amber House, and you in turn will be inspired here. Set on a quiet residential street just eight blocks from the capitol, the inn consists of three turn-of-the-20th-century homes, called the Poet's Refuge, the Artist's Retreat, and the Musician's Manor. Guests are typically greeted in the parlor at the Poet's Refuge, a welcoming Craftsman-style home with comfortable furnishings, a dark brick hearth, and beautiful hardwood accents. After initial introductions, guests are escorted to their quarters for an in-room check-in, quite a fancy touch for a bed-and-breakfast. Of the 14 guest rooms, 11 have Jacuzzi tubs in bathrooms; the 3 remaining rooms feature elegant antique tubs. In the Poet's Refuge, the Lord Byron Room is of special romantic interest, with its wrought-iron canopy bed draped with floral linens and white fabric, not to mention the circular two-person Jacuzzi tub in the marble bathroom. Large windows fill the airy Emily Dickinson Room with sunlight, and the romantic mood is enhanced by a double-sided fireplace that faces both the bedroom and the bathroom's double Jacuzzi tub. Accommodations in the neighboring Artist's Retreat are bright and cheerful; all the rooms feature reproductions of masterpieces by their respective namesakes. In the lovely Van Gogh Room, a stunning, bright yellow bedroom opens to a solarium-like bathroom with a double Jacuzzi tub and a glass-enclosed shower. Rose-patterned linens drape a king-size wrought iron–canopy bed in the Renoir Room, which also has a double whirlpool tub. Musician's Manor, a yellow and purple colonial-style home, boasts some of our favorite rooms. Hide away in the upstairs Vivaldi Room, which features a four-poster bed, a snug little gas fireplace, and a bathroom with an oval Jacuzzi tub. There's also a private balcony where you can breakfast (and kiss). Another winner is the first-floor Mozart Room, which comes complete with all the romantic amenities of the Vivaldi Room plus a heart-shaped Jacuzzi tub. A full, delicious breakfast can be enjoyed anywhere you'd like, from the backyard garden of the Musician's Manor to your own room. Don't worry if you have the temptation to overeat: bicycles are on hand so you can burn off those extra calories as you pedal through the old-fashioned neighborhoods. Many of Sacramento's trendiest and best restaurants are within a few blocks of Amber House. For an extraspecial romantic touch, ask the innkeeper about arranging a horse-drawn carriage ride to and from dinner (approximately $50 round-trip per couple).

$$$–$$$$ *AE, DC, DIS, MC, V; checks OK; www.amberhouse.com.*

HYATT REGENCY SACRAMENTO
◐◐◐

1209 L St / 916/443-1234 or 800/233-1234

This is the only lodging in Sacramento that truly feels like a big-city hotel. While that may not make it the most personal or intimate destination, it is ideal for couples who are seeking a luxurious urban experience. As you walk through the vaulted marble entryway, you are ushered into a world of pampering, and you'll find the service excellent and professional. The outstanding artwork displayed throughout the hotel—murals, paintings, and wrought-iron railings and banisters—is all by local artists, a welcome personal touch in this large hotel. The sumptuous, light-filled atrium lounge is an ideal spot to relax. Many of the 503 well-appointed guest rooms offer pretty views of palm tree–lined Capitol Park; request one of these and you should be pleased with the views out the window. While the hotel is too large to be considered intimate, the rooms do feature welcome hotel amenities, including individual climate control and cable TV. The decor is what you'd expect from a Hyatt: the tasteful yet business-friendly furnishings include desks but also things that everyone can appreciate, such as extremely comfortable beds. The popular restaurants include Dawson's (916/321-3600), a chophouse that caters mostly to meat eaters with its prime rib, pepper steak, and filet mignon; and Vines Café (916/321-3610), which offers a seasonally changing menu of morning and lunchtime favorites along with a champagne brunch on Sundays. Weather permitting, the restaurant's outdoor Fountain Patio is a lovely place to enjoy an alfresco meal. Located downtown near the capitol building, this hotel draws plenty of politicos and business types during the week, but that shouldn't detract from the romantic benefits you'll find here.

$$$ *AE, DC, DIS, MC, V; checks OK; www.hyatt.com.*

STERLING HOTEL
◐◐◑

1300 H St / 916/448-1300 or 800/365-7660

This baronial Victorian mansion, set in the heart of downtown, serves many needs. During the week, business executives flock here to take advantage of its central location. On weekends, the Sterling caters primarily to couples in search of relaxation and wedding parties who take over the stunning Victorian ballroom. No matter when you visit, the understated Victorian elegance of this hotel is sure to please. Each of the 17 handsome guest rooms features nicely framed artwork, a four-poster or canopy bed topped with floral linens, and a marble-tiled double Jacuzzi tub. Sunlight streams through stained-glass windows in most of the bathrooms. Views range from fair (the neighborhood street) to poor (a nearby rundown building). If you are going to splurge here, we suggest booking the spacious Bridal Suite. The bedroom, though it is enormous, isn't anything extraordinary, but the bathroom certainly is. An elevated double Jacuzzi tub flanked by tall white Grecian columns is surrounded by floor-to-ceiling Italian gray marble. If that's not enough, there's also a glass-enclosed double-headed shower. Even if you're not really newlyweds, why not pretend? An expanded continental breakfast consisting of cereals, fruits, homemade pastries, and breads is served in the sparse breakfast room downstairs; it can also be taken back to your room. Guests also have the added luxury of ordering lunch and dinner via room service from Chanterelle (see Romantic Restaurants), the hotel's intimate restaurant.

$$$–$$$$ AE, DC, MC, V; checks OK when mailed in advance; www.sterlinghotel.com.

VIZCAYA
●●

2019 21st St / 916/455-5243 or 800/456-2019
Although there are some resemblances, you might never guess that Vizcaya, a bed-and-breakfast, is the younger sibling of the noted Sterling Hotel (see review). While both landmark Victorians play host to hundreds of weddings each year, Vizcaya lacks some of the elegance and polish of its more urbane sibling. Located in a residential city neighborhood, this property certainly shines on the outside, with its manicured gardens, flowing fountain, and brick courtyard shaded by stately trees. Also breathtaking is the Roman-esque-style Pavilion, where weddings, receptions, and meetings are held. What disappoints are some of the guest rooms that the hotel itself deems romantic. There are marble-tiled fireplaces in four of the nine rooms, and five rooms feature Jacuzzi tubs, but the rooms' decor is more often than not an eclectic mishmash of modern and antique furnishings with patterns that are out of place in such elegant surroundings. The top-floor Penthouse Suite is the prime example: it did not captivate our hearts, despite its Jacuzzi tub and tucked-away setting. The three Carriage House rooms in back are the best options, both in terms of decor and location (they are farthest from the adjacent busy street). We also like the second-floor Room No. 2, where a four-poster bed fronts a marble fireplace and a skylight brightens the double Jacuzzi tub and double shower in the spacious bathroom. If you stay in the Carriage House, you'll have to venture to the main home's dining room to partake of the full breakfast, which includes such basics as waffles and cooked-to-order eggs. Weddings are the specialty at Vizcaya, and on the weekends you're likely to see and/or hear one or two or three. (The average is about five per weekend.) Vizcaya has perfected the art of producing wedding ceremonies with all of the frills—we just wouldn't recommend spending a

honeymoon night in the room pegged for newlyweds, the drab Garden Suite. It provides plenty of space in which to get ready for your wedding, but the bedroom itself doesn't inspire any romantic thoughts.
$$$ *AE, DC, MC, V; checks OK when mailed in advance; www.sterling hotel.com.*

Romantic Restaurants

BIBA
❂❂❂

2801 Capitol Ave / 916/455-2422
Reservations are a must at this extremely busy eatery offering excellent Italian classics. Arched windows, square white pillars, surrounding mirrors, and modern artwork set the scene; fresh flowers add a dash of color, but the cozy, linen-draped tables are placed too close together to encourage intimate conversation. The food is prepared with the finest ingredients available and painstaking attention to detail. The menu changes seasonally, but whenever you visit, don't miss the superb homemade pasta specialties, which might include a goat-cheese ravioli with sage butter. The grilled pork chops served with a white-bean puree and stuffed roasted peppers are also excellent. Traditional Italian desserts dominate the menu; the creamy, delicate cannoli takes the cake. The long list of domestic and Italian wines offers a dazzling array of options. Service can be a bit stuffy and, due to the restaurant's popularity, it can also be a bit slow at times. For lovers of all things Italian, however, these are minor drawbacks compared with the food's divine authenticity.
$$$ *AE, DC, MC, V; no checks; lunch Mon–Fri, dinner Mon–Sat; full bar; reservations recommended; www.biba-restaurant.com.*

CHANTERELLE
❂❂

1300 H St (Sterling Hotel) / 916/442-0451
Set in the heart of downtown Sacramento in the popular Sterling Hotel (see Romantic Lodgings), the ground-floor Chanterelle restaurant features an eclectic menu with something for everyone. Fronted by a charming brick terrace, sunlight sifts through the restaurant's leaded-glass windows into two separate dining rooms adorned with striking modern paintings. Black metal chairs make a sharp contrast to layers of white linen on each table. The dining rooms are perfect for a dark or chilly day; however, if the sun is shining (as it usually is in the River City), dine instead at an umbrella-covered table on the patio. Start your meal with the unusual-looking green dumplings made of pesto, roasted corn, charred peppers, and fresh basil or a more classic salad or soup. Hearty entrée options include a tandoori-style

pork chop marinated in yogurt, cumin, and cayenne and served with couscous or a traditional rack of lamb with red-pepper ratatouille. Finish in style with a taste of tiramisu or a slice of chocolate decadence cake with raspberry sauce. When there is a special event at the Sterling Hotel—which occurs quite frequently—noise from the nearby ballroom can carry over into the dining room, disrupting your peace and quiet; come prepared.
$$$ *AE, DIS, MC, V; no checks; dinner every day; brunch Sun; wine and beer only; reservations recommended; www.sterlinghotel.com.* &

ENOTRIA CAFÉ AND WINE BAR
●●●

1431 Del Paso Blvd / 916/922-6792
This gem of a restaurant is located off the beaten path in a section of Uptown that is not at first glance particularly romantic. Yet this neighborhood of seemingly empty warehouses is actually home to Sacramento's Second Saturday Art Walk, at the heart of a growing arts district. For couples seeking romance, the real draw is this sophisticated Italian-inspired eatery that boasts delicious food, one of Sacramento's most expansive wine lists, and a distinctly intimate atmosphere. The cozy main dining area features a small bar, open kitchen, closely packed tables, and a whole wall of wine bottles (the restaurant sells wine retail, so you can go home with a bottle of the wine you enjoyed). For the most romantic seating, adjourn to the wisteria-draped outdoor courtyard to dine at tables covered in white linen amid garden beds of fresh herbs and shady trees, with a truly enchanting Tuscan-inspired mural as a backdrop. Another choice spot for romance is the open, airy loggia, which links the main dining room to the garden. Begin your feast with an antipasto platter of feta cheese, mixed olives, white anchovies, bresaola, marinated artichokes, and quail eggs. Main courses range from a grilled filet mignon with rich potato gratin and sautéed greens to delicate spinach and ricotta ravioli in a light cream sauce. The refreshing blackberry cabernet sorbet is a perfect antidote to the languorous heat of a Sacramento summer evening. One of the most innovative features of the outstanding wine list is its option of tasting flights, which offer three tastes of a certain varietal, such as pinot noir, for example. There's also a tempting selection of dessert wine and port.
$$–$$$ *AE, DIS, MC, V; no checks; lunch Fri, dinner Tues–Sun; full bar; reservations recommended; www.enotria.com.*

THE FIREHOUSE
●●●◖

1112 2nd St / 916/442-4772
The Firehouse, well hidden among the storefronts of Old Sacramento, revels in its rich history, which dates back to 1853. Towering cathedral ceilings are offset by red brick walls, while a wrought-iron spiral staircase cascades

down into the bar area and a brass fire pole nearby serves as a vivid reminder that this restaurant was once Fire Station No. 3. A Victorian opulence adds a finishing touch to the historical fixtures, and elaborate mirrors, life-size oil paintings in ornate gold frames, and massive floral arrangements fill the dimly lit interior. The nicely spaced tables in the two dining rooms are adorned with lamplike candles, fine linens, and gold-rimmed china. In the enchanting back brick courtyard, large trees provide ample shade for the wrought-iron tables and chairs. This is a thoroughly engaging lunch spot, and at night tiny white lights set the trees aglow; a burbling fountain cleverly drowns out street noise at all times of day. The Firehouse prides itself on its service, which we must say is excellent. The classic American cuisine, however, is of the hit-and-miss variety. While certain traditional dishes, such as the glazed duck breast and rack of lamb, succeed, others, such as the pork tenderloin covered by an apple-brandy cream, are disappointing. Fortunately, the dessert tray is a winner. Chocolate mousse swirled within a chocolate cup or the traditional tiramisu, delicious with a strong cup of coffee, should help fan the flames—of love, that is.
$$$–$$$$ *AE, DIS, MC, V; no checks; lunch Mon–Fri, dinner Mon–Sat; full bar; reservations recommended; www.firehouseoldsac.com.* &

PARAGARY'S BAR AND OVEN
❍❍❍

1401 28th St / 916/485-7100
If you feel like dining in the sunshine, head straight for this bustling, casual restaurant in Midtown and grab a courtyard table. But go early if you want to beat the crowds—it's a popular spot! Three waterfalls flowing over modern metal sculptures not only bring beauty and coolness to the courtyard, but also create enough gentle background noise to allow for private conversations. A massive outdoor corner fireplace helps heat things up after the sun goes down. The atmosphere is stylish-casual and the Italian menu features sophisticated options such as grilled asparagus with shallots, marinated beets, and capers; prosciutto-wrapped pears with warm goat cheese, hazelnuts, and arugula; a wood-fired pizza with Italian sausage, cilantro pesto, sautéed red onions, and sweet peppers with mozzarella; and a grilled lamb sirloin with garlic mashed potatoes, fava beans, and black-olive relish. The restaurant's other location (2220 Gold Springs Ct; 916/852-0214) lacks the romantic courtyard but offers similarly tempting fare; each have wonderfully imaginative menus that change frequently and feature produce from the restaurant's own gardens.
$$$ *AE, DC, MC, V; no checks; lunch Mon–Fri, dinner every day; full bar; reservations recommended; www.paragarys.com.*

SLOCUM HOUSE
♥♥♥€

7992 California Ave, Fair Oaks / 916/961-7211
Sometimes you have to travel far to strike it rich with romance. Such is the
case with Slocum House, located 16 miles northeast of Sacramento in the
suburban community of Fair Oaks (the drive from downtown Sacramento
can take between 20 and 45 minutes, depending on traffic). This 1925 bungalow, set on a forested knoll surrounded by lush, slightly wild gardens, is
filled with romantic nooks. In the large back courtyard, magnificent maples
shelter the tables, while vine-covered fences, manicured hedges, and strut-
ting roosters—which think they own the place—complete the picture. The
prime alfresco table is No. 94, hidden behind ivy and beneath lush trees
(it would be wise to reserve well in advance, since this little number was
voted the most romantic table in the Sacramento area by local press). Other
patio tables are equally nice but not as secluded. Inside, the several dining
rooms are cozy, decorated with conservative pastel wallpaper and vintage
photographs of the home and Slocum family, although the gray and mauve
table linens could use more pizzazz. Entrées come with soup or salad, fresh
vegetables, and homemade bread. Consider the seared halibut atop mashed
potatoes with Dijon-chive beurre blanc; the Pacific Rim ahi tuna with soy-
lime vinaigrette; the spicy Black Angus New York steak; or the smoked butternut squash risotto. Special dinners should always end on a sweet note,
and if you are celebrating a special occasion, have the restaurant's staff
write your heartfelt thoughts on the dessert with chocolate sauce. (Be sure
to call ahead if you want it to be a surprise!)
$$$ *AE, DIS, MC, V; no checks; lunch Tues–Fri, dinner Tues–Sun, brunch
Sun; full bar; reservations recommended; www.slocum-house.com.* &

TWENTY EIGHT
♥♥♥

2730 N St / 916/456-2800
Setting itself apart from its more casual neighbors in this leafy part of
Midtown is the luxurious and sophisticated Twenty Eight. With its elegant
taupe stucco facade and dark, intimate interior, it's a perfect spot for a
romantic evening. The decor of gold and olive green is set off by creamy
white tablecloths, tailored window treatments, and sun-shaped crystal
chandeliers. Comfortable padded booths line the windows and dominate
the dining room, offering plenty of privacy. A little alcovelike room in back
has just two tables, so request one of these for even more seclusion. Asian,
Mediterranean, and classical influences mark the small but diverse menu.
Be sure to start off with the succulent lobster pot stickers in a delicious
curry sauce. The house specialty, sesame-crusted ahi with crispy noodles
and shiitake mushrooms, is not outstanding, although the fish is incredibly
fresh; other, more robust options include grilled lamb chops with artichoke

risotto. Among the creative desserts, we recommend the luscious coconut rice pudding with mangos. The extensive wine list includes more than 200 of the best labels from California and France.

$$$ *AE, DC, MC, V; local checks only; lunch Mon–Fri, dinner Mon–Sat; full bar; reservations recommended.*

THE WATERBOY
❦❦❦

2000 Capitol Ave / 916/498-9891
The simply adorned dining room at this Midtown restaurant boasts high ceilings and large windows that showcase the beautiful tree-lined street outside. The tables, though well-spaced, are not particularly private; the romance here is in the outstanding food. The menu, inspired by the dishes of southern France and northern Italy, changes monthly to stay attuned to the seasons. The chef insists on fresh, high-quality ingredients such as naturally raised beef and lamb from Niman Ranch, and it makes all the difference. Among the starters, consider the delicious classic Caesar salad or the sweet and creamy corn soup. Standout entrées include the hearty shellfish stew—a fragrant tomato-saffron broth heaped with fresh clams, mussels, prawns, and tender chunks of sea bass—and the pan-roasted pork chop with bacon-braised endive and a decadent potato gratin. The wine list of fine California varietals offers selections by the bottle, half-bottle, or glass, and there's also a generous selection of dessert wines, from late-harvest Gewürztraminer to Italian *vin santo*. End the meal with the irresistible chocolate-almond torte with chocolate truffle ice cream.

$$–$$$ *AE, DC, DIS, MC, V; no checks; lunch Tues–Fri, dinner Tues–Sun; beer and wine; reservations recommended; www.waterboyrestaurant.com.*

NORTHERN GOLD COUNTRY

ROMANTIC HIGHLIGHTS

Northern Gold Country is home to one of the best-loved destinations in the foothills: the quaint and utterly charming town of **Nevada City**. What exactly makes it so romantic? The name might lead you to picture flashing lights, casinos, and nondescript motels; instead, this is one of the most picturesque towns in Gold Country. It's actually difficult to spot the bed-and-breakfasts here, since even the residential homes are spectacular Victorians with gingerbread trim, picket fences, and lush green lawns. The feel is reminiscent of a town in rural New England, and on crisp fall afternoons, when the leaves are brilliant shades of red, orange, gold, and purple, this comparison needs no elaboration. In fact, many of the area's earliest settlers hailed from New England, and some brought along their favorite trees as they journeyed west 150 years ago. Allow yourselves at least two days to behold the grand display of fall colors and to visit the shops and restaurants downtown. The annual blaze of autumn glory usually begins early in October and lasts about six weeks. During the winter holidays, the streets twinkle with festive lights, and in summer, the long, warm evenings are perfect for alfresco dining.

To get the lay of the land, put on your walking shoes and pick up a free "Walking-Tour Map" at the **Chamber of Commerce** (132 Main St at Coyote St; 530/265-2692). Or, for a highly romantic alternative, indulge in a horse-drawn carriage ride with **Nevada City Carriage Company** (530/265-8778; www.nevadacitycarriagecompany.com; tours for two $30). Town highlights include the **National Hotel** (211 Broad St; 530/265-4551; www.thenational hotel.com), where the cozy gold rush–era bar is ideal for a cocktail or two; the white, cupola-topped **Firehouse Number 1 Museum** (214 Main St at Commercial St; 530/265-5468; 11am–4pm every day, Sat–Sun Dec–Mar), featuring gold-rush memorabilia; and the picturesque white clapboard **Nevada City Methodist Church** (433 Broad St; 530/265-2797) founded in 1850, among this romantic town's most popular places for couples to tie the knot. Drop by the **Nevada City Winery** (321 Spring St; 530/265-9463 or 800/203-9463; www.ncwinery.com) for a taste of acclaimed zinfandel; explore the downtown's many upscale galleries and shops; or visit **Broad Street Books and Espresso Bar** (426 Broad St; 530/265-4204) and sip a latte on the shady terrace patio. (Don't be surprised to see people kissing across the street; the scenic white church there is a popular spot for weddings.)

Nearby, you'll find the town of **Grass Valley**, the most heavily mined area in Northern Gold Country. While it lacks the charm of Nevada City, its downtown is quaint, and the **212 Bistro** (see Romantic Restaurants) at the historic Holbrook Hotel is a fine spot for amorous dining.

If you want to escape towns and crowds altogether, take a hike—literally: a short drive north of Nevada City brings you to the beautiful **Independence Trail** (from Hwy 49, trailhead is on the right, just before sharp bend in road and large bridge crossing South Yuba River). This wheelchair-accessible trail is paved and extremely well maintained—not to mention beautiful. The route leads to waterfalls and pools, quenching your desire to be near clear blue water that crops up in this dry, golden landscape. Depending on your pace, the walk takes about an hour round trip.

Though some are drawn to **Coloma** for its gold rush–era trappings, more arrive looking for adventure, including opportunities for hot-air balloon rides, white-water rafting trips, hikes, and, of course, gold-panning expeditions. Coloma's setting, in Marshall Gold Discovery State Historic Park, a wooded section of the American River canyon, is certainly romantic.

Access and Information

With Interstate 5 or Highway 99 as your motoring-off point, you will find a slew of highways and county roads (marked with a "J") running east toward Highway 49. A California map or Gold Country region map is your best bet for finding the quickest route, as well as for identifying all those tempting side roads that pop up along the way. Highway 49 travels through most of the Gold Country towns. From San Francisco, take Interstate 80 east toward Sacramento. From Sacramento, continue on Interstate 80 to intersect with Highway 49 in Auburn, or take Interstate 50 to Highway 49 in Placerville.

For more information on planning a visit, contact the **Nevada City Chamber of Commerce** (132 Main St, Nevada City, CA 95959; 530/265-2692 or 800-655-6569; www.nevadacitychamber.com).

Romantic Lodgings

COLOMA COUNTRY INN
○○●

345 High St, Coloma / 530/622-6919
Though Coloma's gold rush–era trappings are designed to draw tour groups, you can avoid the crowds by checking into this picturesque gray and white clapboard-style farmhouse, bordered by flower gardens and a white picket fence in a picturesque, serene setting. Although all seven guest rooms are comfortable, the Carriage House's Geranium Suite struck us as the most romantic. Set back from the main house and enveloped by gardens, the 1898 Carriage House has a storybook appearance, with window boxes, flower-covered trellises, and an antique weathervane. With its private kitchenette, white wooden queen-size bed, and French doors that open onto a charming garden patio, the Geranium Suite is designed for couples who crave quiet time alone together. Couples traveling together will appreciate the Carriage House's other room, the Cottage Suite, which features two bedrooms and a sitting room. These rooms are nicely appointed, with French-country antiques and floral fabrics and linens. In the main farmhouse, handmade quilts, country art, and American antiques lend a homespun flavor to most of the rooms. We especially like the light and bright Lavender Room, with its quilt-covered queen-size bed and claw-foot tub in the private bath. Some rooms in the main house share a hallway bathroom and some have tiny double beds, so be sure to be specify your preferences when making reservations. In the afternoon, fresh lemonade and iced tea are served in the gazebo, and baskets are provided for guests who wish to handpick local berries. In the morning, a breakfast of home-baked breads, seasonal fruits, and hearty

granola is served in the formal dining room or, on especially warm days, outside under the pergola overlooking the pond.

$$ *MC, V; checks OK; www.colomacountryinn.com.*

DEER CREEK INN
❤❤❤

116 Nevada St, Nevada City / 530/265-0363 or 800/655-0363

Countless establishments are named after lakes or rivers, even if they are not remotely near water, but the Deer Creek Inn earns its name. This venerable blue Queen Anne Victorian sits at the edge of Deer Creek—all that separates the house from the rushing stream is a grassy backyard dotted with fountains, flower beds, and cushioned chairs and hammocks perfect for endless lounging. The five guest rooms feature private marble baths, canopy or four-poster beds with down comforters, antique furnishings, and air-conditioning. Some have their own private verandas. Although Elaine's Room is dubbed the Honeymoon Suite, no doubt due to its private entrance, patio, wrought-iron canopy bed, and Roman tub and shower for two, our favorite rooms are upstairs: Winifred's Room, dressed in violets, boasts a claw-foot tub at the foot of the bed and an excellent creek view from the patio. The decor differs in each room, but all are comfortably elegant; the only drawback is the traffic noise that filters in from the somewhat busy street that fronts the inn. Breakfast is a three-course bonanza of sweet and savory treats that may include delicious cheesy breakfast quiche, fresh fruit, and pecan French toast with orange-maple syrup. The deck overlooking the creek is the ideal place to enjoy the morning offerings, as is the formal dining room on cooler days. Complimentary afternoon wine and appetizers, along with an endless supply of the innkeeper's freshly baked cookies and brownies, will keep you satisfied all day. At the time of this writing, the ownership of this establishment was changing hands, but we have high hopes that the new proprietors will successfully carry on the tradition of romance at this wonderful inn.

$$$ *AE, MC, V; checks OK; www.deercreekinn.com.*

EMMA NEVADA HOUSE
❤❤❤

528 E Broad St, Nevada City / 530/265-4415 or 800/916-3662

Built in 1856, this picturesque Victorian was the home of 19th-century opera singer Emma Nevada, the glamorous diva of her day. Today, impressive renovations have made her former home fairly sing with romance. Outside, red roses line the white picket fence that encloses the lush yard. Inside, tall ceilings and generous windows give the home a wonderfully spacious feeling. The friendly new owner has refurbished the central rooms with beautiful period antiques and improved the level of service here impressively with her attention to detail, visible everywhere from the delicious breakfasts to the fresh flowers adorning the home. Of the six guest rooms, we prefer the three on the main floor, with their high ceilings and spaciousness (they also come with plush robes, whereas the less-expensive rooms upstairs do not). In Nightingale's Bower, you'll find a charming antique fireplace; luxurious Italian bedding drapes a queen-size bed set into bay windows that face the front yard—it's necessary to draw the drapes for privacy. The small bathroom with an oval Jacuzzi tub rounds out the romantic picture. Touted as the honeymoon suite, the light and bright Empress's Chamber features a hand-carved queen-size bed covered with pristine white linens; a Jacuzzi tub for two awaits in the lovely bathroom. For a French-country feeling, try Mignon's Boudoir, also on the main floor, which has hardwood floors, a gas fireplace, and a claw-foot tub in the pretty bathroom. The remaining three bedrooms, tucked upstairs under the gables, are slightly smaller but do have charm. Enjoy an early-morning coffee upstairs on the sunny veranda, set above the parking lot and stands of lush trees, and then adjourn to the airy sunroom for breakfast. Here, beneath the peaked cathedral ceiling and circular wall of windows, you'll enjoy a delicious breakfast of mountain-berry cobbler, savory crustless quiche, fresh fruit, and homemade scones. Afterward, descend the veranda stairs to the secluded creek-side garden, where tucked-away benches call you over for one thing: a kiss, of course. $$$–$$$$ *AE, MC, V; checks OK; www.emmanevadahouse.com.*

GRANDMÈRE'S INN
🌑🌑🌘

449 Broad St, Nevada City / 530/265-4660
Grandmère's Inn stands tall at the top of a hill, showing off its impressive white columns and Colonial Revival flair. A wrought-iron fence encloses this stately white 1856 home flanked by mature trees. The garden in back, a popular spot for weddings, is our favorite aspect of this getaway: beautifully landscaped, flower-filled terraced lawns are dotted with stone benches. Inside, the parlor has a cozy window seat and cushioned furnishings, but it feels a bit dark; wine and cheese are offered here in the afternoon. The six spacious guest rooms feature unremarkable decor of light gray walls, white trim, plantation shutters, and country-style furnishings such as antique pine pieces, handmade patchwork quilts, and baskets. The two-room Susan B. Anthony Suite boasts a private sunporch overlooking the garden; Ellen's Garden Room, secluded below the home, offers the most privacy, along with a private garden entrance and an oversize tub. The large Diplomat's Suite handsomely decorated in gray and dark blue comes with a lovely four-poster bed. A private front porch entrance leads to the two-room Senator's Chambers, where you'll find a four-poster king-size pine bed, claw-foot tub, and a rather odd sunporch (you can't get into it, but you can look at its rocking chair and teddy bear display). Our favorite is the recently opened, small but charming Cordula's Room, with a unique sun room overlooking

the garden, pretty sage green walls, and a lovely antique bedroom set. A full country breakfast is served in the dining room, but we suggest you take your trays to a secluded spot in the terraced garden. This is a wonderful place to spend some affectionate time together planning the rest of the day. $$$–$$$$ *AE, MC, V; checks OK; www.grandmeresinn.com.*

RED CASTLE HISTORIC LODGINGS
◐◑

109 Prospect St, Nevada City / 530/265-5135 or 800/761-4766
Tucked into a forested hillside above Nevada City, this imposing four-story red-brick mansion with wraparound verandas and intricate white trim offers guests a chance to travel back in time. Everything about this Gothic Revival home (one of only a handful on the West Coast) is designed to make you feel as if you are living in the Victorian era, from the stately antiques decorating every inch of space to the afternoon teas served in the parlor, to the absence of telephones, TVs, and alarm clocks. Only the ticking of the grandfather clock echoes from the hallway. After a few minutes here, you might just start believing you are in the 1800s. Traditional floral wallpaper, lace curtains fronted by heavy draperies, Oriental carpets, chandeliers, and magnificent ornate mirrors set the mood. In keeping with the character of typical Victorian homes, many of the rooms are very dark, even during the day. Luckily, ample antique lights help brighten things up. Of the seven guest rooms, we recommend the more spacious ones on the ground floor, despite their proximity to the front door and parlor. All three ground-floor rooms feature queen-size beds, high ceilings, and private bathrooms with antique or antique-reproduction fixtures. Each of these rooms also has access to either a semiprivate patio or porch. Ornate wallpapers, chandeliers, French doors, and four-poster or canopy beds provide Victorian charm at every turn. Of all the rooms, we especially like the Forest View Room, a private little hideaway on the ground level. A centerpiece claw-foot tub, a canopy bed with a dimming chandelier above it, and your own private veranda make this prime kissing territory. On the more unusual side, its bathroom features a unique toilet and shower combination in which both facilities share one space (a curtain separates the two, but they share the same tiled floor). Of the remaining three rooms, the two middle-level ones are much too small to be considered comfortable, and the top-floor two-bedroom Garret Suite has a detached bathroom down a short flight of stairs, which doesn't make it ideal for romantic interludes. A lavish five-course breakfast featuring all sorts of goodies, from a savory tomato, onion, and Gruyère tart to a sweet tarte Tatin, is served buffet-style in the entry-level foyer. Guests are welcome to savor breakfast privately in their room, on the veranda, or in a secluded spot near the garden fountain. With its half acre of lovely terraced gardens, finding an intimate site here shouldn't be difficult. Best of all, a winding pathway leads through trees and greenery to the town

below. It is only about a five-minute walk, and since the path is well lit at night, you may even want to walk to dinner. As a final note, when visiting this inn, we must warn you not to arrive before the designated check-in time. Several notes by the front door, not to mention a small clock, remind guests what time they're welcome.

$$$ *MC, V; checks OK; www.historic-lodgings.com.*

Romantic Restaurants

CITRONÉE BISTRO
✿✿✿

320 Broad St, Nevada City / 530/265-5697
Whether you have a taste for a casual lunch or an intimate candlelit dinner, this downtown restaurant delivers—along with some of the tastiest food this side of the Sierras. Citronée, one of the top restaurants in the area, offers two dining rooms, each with its own distinctive appeal. The decor in the street-facing front dining room is best described as Tuscan chic. Textured butter-colored walls are adorned with framed posters; blond wood tables and chairs top tiled floors; and a long bar, offset by a brilliant floral display, commands the space on one side of the window-filled room. This is the perfect place to enjoy lunch, especially on a glorious sunny day. Those who want to hit the mother lode when it comes to romance, however, should make their way to the back dining room. Here, the rough-hewn beams, wood-planked ceiling, and aged brick walls will make you feel as though you're descending into a gold mine. Little tea candles, modern artwork illuminated by halogen lamps, and white linen-covered tables contribute softness and elegance to the cozy, rustic space. Citronée may be situated in a small town, but its menu spans the globe. The sea bass with wasabi mashed potatoes and caramelized lemongrass sauce is superb, as is the stuffed pork chop filled with mushroom duxelles served over polenta. Other interesting entrées include braised garlic short ribs or vegetarian phyllo purses filled with wild mushrooms and baby spinach. The desserts don't rate high on originality or selection, but that didn't prevent us from quickly consuming the cream-filled profiteroles covered in chocolate sauce and accompanied by vanilla ice cream.

$$$ *AE, MC, V; local checks; lunch Mon–Fri, dinner Mon-Sat; beer and wine; reservations recommended.*

THE COUNTRY ROSE CAFÉ
◑◑

300 Commercial St, Nevada City / 530/265-6252

Historic brick buildings abound in these little gold-rush towns. One of them, right in the heart of Nevada City, houses the charming Country Rose Café. The mood is distinctly casual and there's usually a crowd at lunchtime, but this little spot has plenty of appeal nonetheless. High ceilings, exposed-brick walls, floral table linens, and carved oak chairs create a casual, coun-trified setting; high-backed booths along one wall provide some privacy. On a summer day, try to secure a table on the shady deck. Lunch consists of soups, sandwiches, and salads, while dinner offers a hearty variety of French-influenced fare, from five types of ravioli to *poulet Escoffier* to roast game hen with jalapeño-tequila sauce. The menu, presented simply on a dry-erase board, changes daily. Service is friendly but rushed at times due to the cafe's popularity.

$$$ *AE, DC, MC, V; local checks only; lunch, dinner every day, brunch Sun; beer and wine; reservations recommended.*

NEW MOON CAFE
◑◑◑

203 York St, Nevada City / 530/265-6399

The pretty but unremarkable cedar exterior of this restaurant doesn't quite hint at the level of sophistication you'll find inside. Tasteful blue and yellow lamps hanging from the ceiling in the spacious dining room cast a romantic glow, colorful bold paintings by local artists adorn the walls, and lovely arrangements of fresh flowers make this restaurant the most stylish in town. The only ambience problem here is the noise level; on busy nights, you might have trouble hearing each other's sweet nothings. For the most privacy, request one of the tables on the raised dais by the back windows; it's only a few steps higher than the main room but feels above the fray. Couples willing to overlook the noise will dine in high style: everything, down to the res-taurant's organic-grain bread, is made from scratch. The menu emphasizes local bounty and natural free-range meats, and portions are plentiful. Fresh vegetables are served with every entrée, including the sumptuous Navarro Scampi and the vegetarian wild-mushroom lasagne, made with New Moon's own fresh pasta, three different Italian cheeses, and a smoked tomato sauce. The daily specials are special indeed; one memorable dish was a beautifully arranged crab-cake salad including asparagus, endive, organic greens, and a generously sized, plump, moist, seared-on-the-outside crab cake topped with savory crème fraîche. Gorgeous desserts, such as house-made ice cream served in a blue martini glass and topped with whipped cream or a luscious sky-high lemon cake, will end the meal on a sweet note.

$$$ *AE, DC, MC, V; checks OK; lunch Tues–Fri, dinner Tues–Sun; beer and wine; reservations recommended.*

212 BISTRO
◆❢
212 W Main St (Holbrooke Hotel), Grass Valley / 530/273-1353
The historic Holbrooke Hotel looks and feels much as it must have in the late 1850s—rowdy saloon and all. Tucked down the hall and just past the front desk, the old-fashioned restaurant is an elegant surprise. (Although the hotel offers a variety of antiquated and timeworn rooms upstairs, we don't recommend them for a romantic encounter.) In the dining room, several globe chandeliers hang from the high ceiling, green library lamps illuminate most of the wooden tables, and brick walls and archways make cozy alcoves for intimate dining. Plantation shutters complete the antebellum scene, while rotating displays of modern artwork add a touch of sophistication. The seasonal menu offerings focus on satisfying California-influenced classics, showcasing dishes such as grilled pork tenderloin with a spicy blackberry merlot sauce served with mashed potatoes or roasted chicken stuffed with Gruyère cheese and served with spinach, prosciutto, and a white wine sauce with herbs. The shady patio out back is a pleasant spot for an alfresco lunch or dinner.
$$$ AE, DC, DIS, MC, V; checks OK; lunch Mon–Sat, dinner every day, brunch Sun; full bar; reservations recommended; www.holbrooke.com.

SOUTHERN GOLD COUNTRY

ROMANTIC HIGHLIGHTS

Welcome to the wine region where the journeys are almost as much fun as the wineries themselves. If you have traveled the back roads of Sonoma County and fallen in love with wineries off the beaten path, similar delights await you here. The velvety rolling hills and valleys, scattered with venerable oaks and grazing cattle, are beautiful in every season. Autumn leaves enhance the already golden landscape, winter brings rain (when there isn't a drought) and turns the hillsides a delicious green, and wildflowers dab color everywhere in the spring and summer. Many of the wineries offer sublime views of the countryside in addition to tastes of superb, award-winning local wines. Our list of Romantic Wineries reflects our particular favorites (for maps and winery details, pick up a free copy of the "d'Vine Wine and Visitors Guide" at local wineries and restaurants).

Though most of the unique communities that dot the landscape here are rich in history, not all of them are ideal for romantic getaways. Large towns such as Jackson have authentic Gold Country appeal but are too large and overrun with tourists to supply much romance; others draw crowds that might detract from your experience (noisy motorcyclists populate certain towns in the region on weekends). Fortunately, plenty of places are tailor-made for romance.

A lovely place to begin your explorations is **Amador County**; for maps and a complete guide to local wineries, contact **Amador Vintners** (209/267-2297; www.amadorwine.com). The region is best known as the home of the fertile **Shenandoah Valley**—a true wine-country paradise—and here the town of **Sutter Creek** is a good choice for your romantic headquarters. This former gold-rush community has retained its Western-style storefronts, beautiful 19th-century buildings, whitewashed overhanging balconies, and balustrades. Boardwalks lined with antique shops, gift boutiques, and casual cafés invite a relaxing stroll together. However, we do feel the need to warn romance seekers that all the inns and bed-and-breakfasts in Sutter Creek face Highway 49, and traffic here picks up in the mornings, so noise can be a problem (you might request a room far back from the road). A typical day here might involve exploring the town then driving the scenic roads to **Amador City** and **Plymouth** for an afternoon of wine tasting (see Romantic Wineries). Another scenic drive is to take Sutter Creek–Ione Road (from Sutter Creek, watch for signs off Hwy 49) and wind through the enchanting countryside to the beautiful **Clos du Lac winery** (see Romantic Wineries) near **Ione**. South of Sutter Creek, the town of **Jackson** is where folks from surrounding towns do their shopping. We recommend stopping here for provisions and then moving on to the delightful accommodations found in the surrounding countryside.

A bit farther south is **Calaveras County**, which Mark Twain put on the map when he wrote "The Celebrated Jumping Frog of Calaveras County" in 1865. In our opinion, a few of the destinations here will make amorous hearts leap, as well. The most kiss-worthy spot is the quaint town of **Murphys**. Set at an elevation of 2,200 feet, "above the fog and below the snow," as the locals like to say, it's a refreshing destination during the region's hot summers; as you ascend, pine trees become more prevalent and the air grows cooler—although the sun remains just as powerful, so bring a hat. The main street, with its raised wooden boardwalks and Western-style facades, segues into pretty residential streets lined with gingerbread Victorian homes, white picket fences, and tall locust trees. After browsing in upscale boutiques such as **Piazza** (219 Main St; 209/728-0707) or **Hudson Classics** (237 Main St; 209/728-8391), indulge in a light lunch or gourmet snacks from the **Alchemy Market and Wine Bar** (191 Main St; 209/728-0700; www.alchemymarket .com). The wine bar, with its vaulted ceilings, tiled floors, old-fashioned bar, and glitzy chandeliers, is also a great spot to linger over appetizers and wine; the summer months bring live jazz or flamenco music on Saturday nights.

Many of the finest wineries in Calaveras County have tasting rooms right in the heart of the quaint town of Murphys, but by far the better option is to explore the back roads and visit the working wineries themselves (see Romantic Wineries). Many establishments in town offer maps to the nearby wineries; for a complete list of wineries, contact the **Calaveras Wine Association** (866/806-9463; www.calaveraswines.org). Touring here offers an excellent opportunity both to see the countryside and to enjoy some vintage sips: it's one of the oldest wine-growing regions in California, and although the wineries are ensconced in rural seclusion, the vintners are very serious about wine making. One of our favorite wineries in the area, **Stevenot** (see Romantic Wineries) is the site of a summer outdoor theater festival, **"Theatre Under the Stars,"** run by the **Murphys Creek Theatre** (209/728-8422; www.murphyscreektheatre.org).

More vigorous outdoor activity can be found 18 miles northeast of Murphys on Highway 4 in **Calaveras Big Trees State Park** (209/795-2334; www.parks.ca.gov), a popular summer destination for camping, swimming, hiking, and fishing along the Stanislaus River. It's the perfect opportunity for an energetic walk—and a lazy picnic—among giant sequoias. Couples should keep in mind that various events are scheduled almost every summer weekend in Murphys, overloading this tiny community. As charming as it is, on a busy weekend you might feel like getting out of town.

In **Tuolumne County,** the gateway to Yosemite, the setting is distinctly alpine as the foothills lead to full-fledged mountains. We highly recommend a quiet getaway to the heart-stirring **McCaffrey House Bed & Breakfast Inn** (see Romantic Lodgings), located at approximately 4,000 feet elevation in the tiny hamlet of **Twain Harte** (named after writers Mark Twain and Bret Harte). Twain Harte is the gateway to the **Stanislaus National Forest** (209/532-3671; www.fs.fed.us/r5/stanislaus), home to 1,100 miles of hiking trails, 78 lakes, and, of course, millions of alfresco kissing spots. You might also consider a visit to **Sonora** and **Columbia**; at the latter, you'll find narrow streets lined with Old West storefronts and overhanging balconies. **Columbia State Historic Park** (209/532-0150; www.parks.ca.gov), the best-restored and most unusual of Gold Country's portals to the past, is filled with touristy shops, but there are plenty of diversions. Pick up some rich, old-fashioned chocolate creams from **Nelson's Columbia Candy Kitchen** (Main St; 209/532-7886) as you check out the stagecoach (vehicles not allowed inside the park), the shopkeepers in period costume, and the fiddlers and banjo players in the street. Tourist attractions might not be very intimate, but they can certainly be entertaining, and these deliver.

Access and Information

If, like most visitors to the area, you decide to drive, there are several ways to travel to the region. With Interstate 5 or Highway 99 as your motoring-off point, you will find a slew of highways and county roads (marked with a "J") running east toward Highway 49. A California map or Gold Country region map is your best bet for finding the quickest route, as well as for identifying all those tempting side roads that pop up along the way. The easiest way to explore the towns on and off Highway 49 is by automobile.

For information on Calaveras County, contact the **Calaveras Visitors Bureau** (800/225-3764; www.visitcalaveras.org). The **Murphys Business Association** (www.visitmurphys.com) has lots of helpful information about the town's shops and restaurants. Helpful information about Tuolomne County can be found via the **Columbia Chamber of Commerce** (209/536-1672; www.columbiacalifornia.com) or the **Tuolomne County Visitors Bureau** (800/446-1333; www.thegreatunfenced.com).

Romantic Wineries

AMADOR FOOTHILL WINERY
◐◖

12500 Steiner Rd, Plymouth / 209/245-6307 or 800/778-WINE
Perched high on a hillside, the Amador Foothill Winery offers exquisite views of the orchards, vineyards, and shimmering lakes in the valley below. This scene is set off by the distant Sierras, snowcapped in the winter and spring. Despite its outstanding view, this working winery is not the best spot for a picnic: it doesn't make an effort to hide its industrial wine-making equipment, and you can see machinery from the sun-drenched picnic tables outside. Nevertheless, training your eyes on the views to the east and tasting the award-winning zinfandel and fumé blanc make for a winning romantic combination.
12pm–5pm Fri–Sun; www.amadorfoothill.com.

CLOS DU LAC CELLARS
◖◖◖

3151 Hwy 88 at Jackson Valley Rd, Ione / 209/274-2238
This majestic winery's setting is as enticing as the tasting room's list of award-winning wines. The drive to the winery meanders past hills of vineyards and a serene duck pond to a stately stone structure that resembles a French country manor. In the modern tasting room, sunlight pours through multipaned windows set high near the cathedral ceiling, casting a golden glow over the wood paneling. Outside, picnic tables set in natural greenstone outcroppings and shaded by old oak trees overlook edenic fields and Bacchus Pond. Beyond is a stretch of Miwok Indian land. Enjoy this dreamy vision with a picnic lunch and a bottle of the winery's finest—the only trouble you'll have is choosing between the award-winning zinfandel and the sangiovese.
10am–5pm Wed–Sun.

GERBER VINEYARDS/LARAINE
❂❂❂

3675 Six Mile Rd, Murphys / 209/736-4766
The winding back roads that lead to this tiny boutique winery are wildly scenic, and there's no doubt that, once you arrive, the placid views of sloping vineyards and grazing cows, accompanied by birdsong and the wind rustling the leaves, set the stage for romance. Sips of tasty chardonnay and much more await upon your arrival in the tasting room, housed in a beautifully restored 1880s ranch house. Outdoor tables shaded by an old-growth maple tree offer an ideal spot for a secluded picnic (bring your own provisions). *10am–5pm Sat–Sun; www.gerbervineyards.com.*

IRONSTONE VINEYARDS
❂❂

1894 Six Mile Rd, Murphys / 209/728-1251
Hordes of visitors and a parking lot almost as long as an airport runway detract from the intimacy at this winery and "entertainment complex." But there's certainly plenty to do, from wine tasting to strolling through the jewelry shop and small museum with its 44-pound crystalline gold-leaf specimen. Colorful gardens lead to massive iron doors that open to the tasting room and gift shop, a vast room with a stone fireplace and cathedral ceiling. Here, a full gourmet deli offers salads, sandwiches, and fresh breads for hungry couples. You can enjoy your treats, along with a glass of wine, outside on the shady patio—just don't expect to have the place to yourselves. *10am–6pm every day; www.ironstonevineyards.com.*

KARLY
❂❂

11076 Bell Rd, Plymouth / 209/245-3922
A long, winding, and dusty drive past sprawling oaks and rows of grapevines brings you to Karly's beautifully landscaped winery. Views of the surrounding country are almost as delicious as the robust zinfandels. Only one picnic table is set within the sunny courtyard, so the chances of snagging it are slim. *12pm–4pm every day; www.karlywines.com.*

SOBON ESTATE
❂❂

122250 Steiner Rd, Plymouth / 209/245-4455
The family behind the exceptional Sobon Estate also runs the nearby winery, Shenandoah Vineyards (12300 Steiner Rd). Among the standout wines you'll want to try from the two wineries are crisp whites such as sauvignon blanc and viognier and reds including zinfandel and sangiovese. Browse in the

contemporary art and ceramics gallery set among the wine barrels and, on sunny days, admire views of the vineyards from the cozy picnic tables situated beneath a stand of trees.

10am–5pm every day (both wineries); www.sobonwine.com.

STEVENOT WINERY
❂❂❂

2690 San Domingo Rd, Murphys / 209/728-0638

Stevenot Winery is an extraordinary place to discover together. The steep, winding route here is not for the faint of heart, but the exquisite setting and excellent wines are well worth the trip. In the rustic elegance of the sod-roof tasting room, don't miss the delicious Spanish *tempranillo* or the award-winning zinfandel. You can purchase your favorite bottle, along with gourmet items such as specialty mustards, jams, cheeses, and breads, and then adjourn outside to enjoy your picnic at one of the tables beneath the lush arbor. Except for the winery buildings themselves, all you'll see are acres of idyllic vineyards and forested rolling hills.

10am–5pm every day; www.stevenotwinery.com.

STORY WINERY
❂❂❂❂

10525 Bell Rd, Plymouth / 209/245-6208 or 800/713-6390

Far off the beaten path, this family-operated winery takes pride in its more-than-50-year-old vineyards, which continue to produce extraordinary vintages. Sip wine to your hearts' content as you bask in the visual splendor of the gorgeous Cosumnes River canyon. Plenty of picnic tables nicely spaced apart under the oaks make this our favorite winery for a picnic with a view.

12pm–4pm Mon, Thurs–Fri, 11am–5pm Sat–Sun; www.zin.com.

VILLA TOSCANA
❂❂❂

10600 Shenandoah Rd, Plymouth / 209/245-3800

This winery's Tuscan-inspired architecture seems to have been designed with romance in mind. In addition to the outstanding wines, there is a wonderful little bistro where you can indulge in a delightful meal while sipping a favorite bottle of wine purchased from the winery. The lovely garden setting with a fountain provides the perfect backdrop for a leisurely afternoon together.

10am–5pm every day; www.villatoscano.com.

YOUNG'S VINEYARDS
❂❂❂❂

10120 Shenandoah Rd, Plymouth / 209/245-3005
One of the most picture-perfect winery settings in the region is found at Young's Vineyards, where couples can sip their favorite vintages surrounded by well-tended lawns and sprawling vineyards. California poppies, blooming roses, and other flowering delights adorn the grounds around the renovated barn that houses the tasting room. Journey down the gravel pathway to the stone fence that encloses a lawn; here, two picnic tables set beneath the oaks let you sit in the shade and admire the nearby pond. *10:30am–5pm Sat–Sun.*

Romantic Lodgings

AMADOR HARVEST INN
❂❂

12455 Steiner Rd, Plymouth / 209/245-5512 or 800/217-2304
Nestled among vineyards in the heart of the Shenandoah Valley, this picturesque white farmhouse bed-and-breakfast offers one of the most stunning settings in Gold Country. A massive black walnut tree partially embraces the gray and white home, set among sprawling manicured lawns. Just below the inn, a fully stocked lake (catch-and-release only) awaits, bordered by weeping willows, stately oaks, and hilly vineyards. Deaver Vineyards (209/245-4099; www.deavervineyard.com; 11am–5pm every day) has a tasting room on-site, and numerous other wineries are a grape's throw away. For those interested in sips, this is your place—those more interested in lips will find satisfaction here as well. The inn's four guest rooms, located upstairs, are of the standard variety: clean, comfortable, and simply decorated with oak furnishings, rocking chairs, and a painting here and there. The smallest room, Chardonnay, is our favorite because it has both an attached bathroom and access to a shared deck with million-dollar views. For more space, book the Zinfandel Suite, complete with a king-size bed and private bathroom. (One guest room has a bath down the hall.) Though Amador Harvest Inn's rooms may not inspire overwhelmingly amorous thoughts, the surroundings certainly will. It's one of the most peaceful spots in the region—the motto here is "the loudest noise you're likely to hear is a frog croaking or a cork popping." The bucolic surroundings are so authentic, in fact, that you should come forewarned that modern conveniences such as restaurants and shops are about a half-hour's drive away, along country roads and Highway 49. A full breakfast is served in the dining room each morning. Come evening, take in spectacular views of the lake as you sit on the back porch and enjoy hors d'oeuvres.
$$ MC, V; checks OK; www.amadorharvestinn.com.

DUNBAR HOUSE
✿✿✿✿

271 Jones St, Murphys / 209/728-2897 or 800/692-6006

Touted as the crown jewel of Gold Country, this 1880 Italianate Victorian is truly a sight to behold. A white picket fence and lovingly tended flower gardens envelop the home's expansive grassy yard, where hummingbirds flit above a water fountain and a large hammock swings gently beneath the trees. Each of the four beautiful, countrified guest suites has a wood-burning stove, so you can get toasty as you toast each other with the complimentary bottle of wine kindly provided by the innkeepers. A welcome plate of appetizers awaits you in your room upon arrival, and chocolates are left on your pillows at turndown. Antiques, hardwood floors graced with Oriental carpets, and queen-size beds covered with lush down comforters add to the romantic ambience. The pleasant Ponderosa Room, though less impressive than the other accommodations here, offers a claw-foot tub in the bathroom and views of the gardens. In the handsome Sequoia Room, settle into a bubble bath in the claw-foot tub set next to the woodstove. The upstairs Sugar Pine Room is beautifully adorned with country pine furnishings. Views from this second-story delight can be enjoyed from two vantage points: the claw-foot tub overlooking the garden and the charming little balcony just above the home's entryway. In the spacious Cedar Suite, commonly reserved by couples looking for an extraspecial romantic get-away, you can cuddle on the white brass bed in front of a warm woodstove, relax on your private sunporch in the late afternoon, or pamper yourselves in the two-person whirlpool bathtub surrounded by candlelight. There's also a private patio. This suite is adjacent to the dining room, which may prove bothersome if everyone else in the inn decides to eat an early break-fast there. The gourmet breakfast of freshly baked treats, fresh fruit, and entrées beautifully adorned with edible flowers is an affair to remember, served at the time and place of your choosing, be it the dining room, your own room, or on the patio. Later in the day, plan a picnic for two. Dunbar House provides the basket, blanket, cooler, and even sun hats for a day of touring the countryside.

$$$ AE, MC, V; checks OK; www.dunbarhouse.com.

THE FOXES BED AND BREAKFAST INN
✿✿✿

77 Main St (Hwy 49), Sutter Creek / 209/267-5882 or 800/987-3344

This bed-and-breakfast is one of the best finds in Gold Country. Set in the heart of Sutter Creek, the beautifully restored 1857 New England–style farmhouse is tucked far enough away from the road to ensure privacy but is so centrally located that guests can walk to restaurants, shops, or the theater. A shaded garden with lots of nooks surrounds the house, and a bubbling fountain keeps the ears occupied. Elegantly simple country and

Victorian furnishings throughout the inn are arranged with a designer's touch. In the large country kitchen, polished silver tea sets gleam in the sunlight, hinting at the lovely gourmet breakfasts that are delivered to your room each morning (unlike other bed-and-breakfasts, meals here are cooked to order, so you will have several dishes to choose from). Walk through a private garden entrance to the spacious Honeymoon Suite, which features an antique claw-foot tub and a half-canopy bed warmed by a wood-burning fireplace. (The cozy private library in the Fox Den and the two-room Hideaway Suite also have wood-burning fireplaces.) The two upstairs suites in the main home—the Anniversary Suite and Victorian Suite—are especially appealing for lovebirds. Even if it's not your anniversary, we recommend inventing a celebration in order to claim the Anniversary Suite. A magnificently carved 9-foot-tall headboard and an equally astounding dresser and armoire take center stage in the light, window-filled room, which has vaulted ceilings. A claw-foot tub set by the window lets you soak as you look out upon gardens below. Unfortunately, this room faces the street, so traffic noise might be a problem. A quieter option is across the hall in the Victorian Suite, a handsome room done up in the warm colors of fall. This suite offers cuddling couples a queen-size bed fronting a gas fireplace. The tiled, sun-filled bathroom features a step-up claw-foot tub, a walk-in shower, two comfortable robes, and dimming lights. The inn's other rooms are located at the back of the house, sheltered from direct street noise. All the rooms have CD players and all but two rooms—the Victorian Suite and the Hideaway—have TV/VCRs; an ample selection of CDs and videos is available should you want to play romantic music or cozy up in front of a movie. Breakfast is served at the hour you request.

$$$ *DIS, MC, V; checks OK; www.foxesinn.com.*

GATE HOUSE INN
❤️❤️

1330 Jackson Gate Rd, Jackson / 209/223-3500 or 800/841-1072
Set deep in Jackson's countryside, the Gate House Inn is a truly quiet escape. Rosebushes trim the walkway leading up to the turn-of-the-20th-century beige and green Victorian, whose historic elegance has been brought back to life by meticulous renovations, securing the inn a spot on the National Register of Historic Places. Guests are encouraged to explore the colorful grounds (flower identification maps are provided), wander past the trickling water fountain, and enjoy a refreshing dip in the unheated waters of the large outdoor pool. Inside the house, beautiful antiques and impressive architectural touches keep the eyes entertained. Oriental rugs in the dining room and entry hall accent the mahogany-inlaid oak parquet floors. In the living room, you'll find a French rosewood center table with a carved urn at its base, among other imposing antiques. Attention to those who are not inclined to like knick-knacks: the owners have a penchant for angels and

this creates a marked visual theme. A 7-foot angel ornaments the chimney's exterior, and the living room and dining room areas are adorned with cherubs. Thankfully, the angel theme is not obvious in the inn's four guest rooms and additional cottage. Some of the rooms are plainer than others, but all of them are comfortable, with private baths, queen-size beds, and interesting antiques. The upstairs French Room is the most impressive, with its commanding views of the north garden and its Louis XIV bedroom set trimmed in gold. The first-floor Parlor Room sports an extralong antique tub for extralong soaks together. Secluded in the backyard, a renovated woodshed has been converted into the charming, self-contained Summer House. Rustic and cozy, the cottage features knotty cedar walls, a wood-burning stove, and a two-person Jacuzzi tub. Breakfast is served by candlelight in the formal parlor at one large antique dining table.
$$ *AE, DIS, MC, V; checks OK; www.gatehouseinn.com.*

GREY GABLES INN
❀ ❀ ❀

161 Hanford St (Hwy 49), Sutter Creek / 209/267-1039 or 800/473-9422
You'll find a dash of the English countryside in Gold Country at the Grey Gables Inn. This sprawling gray and white Victorian, encircled by flowering gardens, sits along Highway 49 just outside Sutter Creek's town center. Comforts such as private baths, air-conditioning, and gas-log fireplaces are found in the eight delightful rooms, each of which is named after an English poet. As an extra touch, a poem composed by the room's namesake is beautifully framed above the fireplace. The very elegant Byron Room has light mauve walls, hunter green appointments, and rich mahogany furnishings. Country Victorian antiques beautify the Browning Room, with its brass bed, lace curtains, and claw-foot tub. Tucked away on the inn's top floor is the pretty Victorian Suite, with arched ceilings, soft pink walls, lace curtains, and a claw-foot tub. Windows in all of these picture-perfect rooms are soundproof, so road noise should not be a problem. In proper British tradition, afternoon tea is presented daily by the English innkeepers, and wine and hors d'oeuvres are served in the formal parlor each evening. At breakfast, fine china and complete silver service enhance a satisfying gourmet meal. Individual tables are set up in the dining room, so you can enjoy breakfast at a table for two; if you want to ensure privacy, you can request that breakfast be delivered to your room. It is options like these that make an establishment truly romantic.
$$$ *AE, DIS, MC, V; checks OK; www.greygables.com.*

THE HANFORD HOUSE BED AND BREAKFAST INN
❂❂❹

61 Hanford St (Hwy 49), Sutter Creek / 209/267-0747 or 800/871-5839
As you drive southbound into Sutter Creek, you can't help but admire the Hanford House's beautiful brick building. Wrapped in ivy, the historic building radiates charm both inside and out. An air of clean spaciousness fills the simply decorated rooms, which feature high ceilings, California pine furnishings, country antiques, and peach, sage, and taupe color schemes. Of the 10 guest rooms, our two favorites are the most expensive (though they're still reasonably priced) and the most spacious. A gorgeous cherrywood king-size canopy bed bedecked with white draperies and warm blue linens welcomes you in the Gallery Suite, which also has a fireplace, a comfortable seating area, and plenty of room for falling in love. Romantics will appreciate the two-person Jacuzzi tub and private sundeck in the Gold Country Escape, not to mention the beautiful pewter and brass queen-size bed surrounded by ivory drapes and covered by tapestry-style linens. Dimming rose-hued lights in both suites help set an amorous mood, and their tucked-away, upstairs locations ensure the utmost privacy. If you stay in the suites, hot morning beverages, home-baked treats, and a newspaper are brought to your door before breakfast. Although both of these rooms are close to perfect, they do front Highway 49, so light sleepers should take note. Even if you opt for one of the other rooms, you'll find plenty of space in each, plus pleasant decor, private baths, Ralph Lauren linens, and fluffy robes. Baked goods and coffee are set out in the common hallway prior to breakfast. For outdoor kissing, head up to the sunny redwood deck overlooking the town's rooftops and the oak-knobbed hills or relax on the sun-dappled patio on the west side of the inn. A full breakfast is served in the cheerful breakfast room, where guests have left their names and appreciative comments on every inch of the walls and ceiling. (Definitely different, but guests think it's a fun touch.) Savor such treats as vegetable quiche, basil crepes with creamy eggs, or fruit-topped Belgian waffles, all of which incorporate organic and/ or local products. If you get hungry later on (which is highly unlikely after such a feast), venture to the guest pantry, where you'll find such goodies as low-fat biscotti, specialty iced teas and lemonades, and a carafe of wine. **$$–$$$** *AE, DIS, MC, V; checks OK; www.hanfordhouse.com.*

MCCAFFREY HOUSE BED & BREAKFAST INN
❂❂❂

23251 Hwy 108, Twain Harte / 209/586-0757 or 888/586-0757
From the golden valley of Gold Country, you'll climb up, up, up to 4,000 feet above sea level to reach this bed-and-breakfast nestled among the trees. Located off Highway 108 and bordered by a forest of cedar, pine, and oak, this seven-room inn is well worth the 10-minute drive from Sonora—its proximity to beautiful Stanislaus National Forest is especially

advantageous for couples who appreciate outdoor kissing. You'll be greeted by three friendly dogs and one cat, who escort you into the large, contemporary home filled with the innkeepers' family photos, treasures from world travels, and a well-chosen and varied art collection. In the common living room, sit on soft couches and sip a glass of wine. If the weather's nice, head outside to the home's most outstanding feature: a series of terraced decks furnished with shaded tables that look out into the dense woods. On one such deck sits the communal hot tub, perfect for bubbling beneath the moonlight. Two guest rooms are tucked away downstairs and the rest are located upstairs on the second floor; of course, the latter offer better forest views. Done up in a mix of floral prints and solid colors, each lovingly decorated room exudes country elegance, including pine queen-size beds (in four-poster or sleigh styles), matching armoires, and vibrant quilts. All rooms feature down pillows, fluffy robes, lovely bay windows or patios, and gas fireplaces equipped with timers so you can fall asleep together in warm comfort. Each room has a TV/VCR hidden within the armoire, and guests can choose from hundreds of videos in the innkeepers' extensive collection. While all of the rooms are wonderful, we particularly recommend the Green Room, which has a private, forest-facing balcony. When the morning sun starts filtering through the trees, enjoy your coffee on the deck or take a prebreakfast walk through the woods. When you return, breakfast will be waiting in the dining room at a series of two- and four-person tables. (Request a table for two if you wish to breakfast alone.) Morning entrées rotate from sweet to savory and include a fruit starter course, minimuffins, juice, and plenty of robust coffee. After breakfast, be sure to explore the world of recreational opportunities waiting just minutes away. $$$ *AE, MC, V; checks OK; www.mccaffreyhouse.com.*

THE WEDGEWOOD INN
❤❤

11941 Narcissus Rd, Jackson / 209/296-4300 or 800/933-4393

"Country" is the operative word at the Wedgewood Inn, set about 8 miles outside downtown Jackson. Antiques and country artifacts fill the homey parlor and common rooms in this Victorian replica, which was custom-built to serve as a bed-and-breakfast. There's also a store overflowing with Victorian collectibles as well as an art gallery featuring the works of Thomas Kinkade. When the weather is warm and beautiful (which is most of the time in Gold Country), take advantage of the paths that cover the carefully landscaped grounds. Walk through a rose arbor to a Victorian gazebo, a perfect place for kissing. Nice touches at the Wedgewood include chocolate truffles at turndown and plush robes in the rooms. The five comfortable and spacious guest rooms, all of which have TV/VCRs and private baths, continue the country-Victorian theme. Interesting antiques, vintage clothing and accessories, shelves filled with old and new books, black-and-white

photographs, and family heirlooms abound. In the Wedgewood Cameo Room, a family wedding dress is on display, and a white embroidered bedspread covers a hand-carved queen-size bed. There's also a private balcony and a double whirlpool tub set against a greenhouse-style window. At the top of the house, Granny's Attic lives up to its name, with cozy peaked ceilings, a brick hearth, a handmade patchwork quilt, and a picture of "Granny" herself. The self-contained, two-room Carriage House Suite adjacent to the inn offers the most space and seclusion, with its private entrance, sitting room, and enclosed patio overlooking the forest. Cathedral ceilings enhance the sense of space, floral-patterned embroidered linens drape a wooden bed, and a pink-tiled two-person whirlpool tub sits in a bright window alcove. Stepping into this suite is a little like entering a museum: a loft area displays a staged collection of children's toys; dozens of antique kitchen items reside on a vintage stove; and an assortment of dolls rest in a wooden case. Breakfast, which consists of several courses on elegant china, is considered "conversational," which means it is served at one large table. If you'd rather not engage in conversation with anyone except your sweetie, breakfast can be delivered to the larger guest rooms upon request.
$$ *MC, V; checks OK; www.wedgewoodinn.com.*

Romantic Restaurants

GROUNDS
❤️◖

402 Main St, Murphys / 209/728-8663
Although Grounds is an extremely casual little spot, we found it quite charming—and the food is excellent. Pale hardwood floors laid with Turkish rugs, bare birch tables and chairs, modern art, and mirrors framed with salvaged barn wood give this dining room an open, airy, contemporary feeling. You can just stop in for espresso at a walk-up counter at the front of the restaurant, or you can sit in the back dining room or on the outside patio. Morning pastries are rich and delicious, lunches are fresh and healthy, and dinners are some of the best in town. The pasta creation we sampled, a mix of spinach, grilled chicken, and portobello mushrooms in a chardonnay-black pepper sauce, was wonderfully tasty. Other pasta, steak, and seafood dishes fill the small but flavorful menu. For dessert, indulge in the "chocolate suicide" cake. As our waitress put it, "It's rich, it's creamy, it's an oh-so-dreamy chocolate cake to die for."
$$ *AE, DIS, MC, V; checks OK; breakfast, lunch every day, dinner Wed–Sun; beer and wine; reservations recommended.*

IMPERIAL HOTEL RESTAURANT
❂❂❂

14202 Hwy 49 (Imperial Hotel), Amador City / 209/267-9172 or 800/242-5594

It's hard to escape the past in historic Gold Country, and the Imperial Hotel is one of the few places that actually encourages you to feel at home in the present. The brick interior of this gold-rush mercantile-establishment-turned-hotel lends warmth to the airy dining room, which is enhanced by high ceilings and elaborate local artwork. The linen-covered tables are embellished with fresh flowers, and sunflowers adorn the hanging lamps. If you enjoy fresh-air dining, sit outside under Japanese lanterns on a charming patio made of native stone, surrounded by plants, flowers, and a murmuring fountain. Ambience isn't the only thing the Imperial gets right—the food here is heavenly. The menu changes seasonally, so everything is as fresh as possible. Portobello mushrooms stuffed with spinach and blue cheese atop garlic mashed potatoes is one succulent choice, as is the filet mignon served with porcini mushroom butter. More on the hit-and-miss side is the thick, somewhat heavy, breadcrumb-encased pork loin surrounded by a tart cherry sauce. Entrées come with soup or salad and can be ordered in full- or half-size portions, the latter being a smart choice if you also plan on choosing a decadent slice of chocolate torte or the Grand Marnier crème brûlée. The hotel offers six upstairs guest rooms, but they directly overlook busy Highway 49. However, with brick interiors, hardwood floors, private baths, air-conditioning, and a reasonable price tag (even on weekends and holidays), they are worth knowing about if you're traveling on a budget. **$$$** *AE, DC, DIS, MC, V; checks OK; dinner Wed–Sun; full bar; reservations recommended; www.imperialamador.com.*

SUSAN'S PLACE WINE BAR AND EATERY
❂❬

15 Eureka St, Sutter Creek / 209/267-0945

Casual yet charming, this bistro is set in the back of the lively Eureka Street outdoor courtyard along with gift shops and several other restaurants. Enjoy the open air outside at one of the picnic tables shaded with purple umbrellas and covered with gingham tablecloths, or if you prefer more privacy, sit inside where wine bottles surround you and the scent of freshly baked goods wafts through the country-style dining room. It's all about choice here. You can order a create-your-own wine and cheese board, which includes samples of wine, cheese, pâtés, and meats, served with an array of vegetables; or try the interesting mix-and-match menu. You choose a main course—the catch of the day, chicken, Black Angus steak, pork tenderloin, or a vegetable—and then select an accompanying sauce, such as orange-ginger teriyaki, garlic honey mustard, or Southwestern salsa. A soup or salad and your choice of starch come with it.

$$ MC, V; no checks; lunch Thurs–Sun, dinner Thurs–Sat; beer and wine; reservations recommended.

ZINFANDELS AT SUTTER CREEK
🖤🖤

51 Hanford St (Hwy 49), Sutter Creek / 209/267-5008

Set smack-dab on the edge of Highway 49, this blue and white country-farmhouse-turned-restaurant is our favorite spot for a romantic meal in Sutter Creek. The home's original living areas have been transformed into several small, pleasant dining rooms decorated in burgundy and green, with zinfandel bottles serving as candle holders on each table. In one of the rooms, an exposed industrial refrigerator detracts from the atmosphere, and in general, you can't avoid the noise of traffic passing outside. Fortunately, the adept and creative kitchen more than makes up for these minor drawbacks. One of the only fixtures on the ever-changing menu is well worth ordering: the appetizer of hot grilled polenta topped with mushrooms, garlic, shallots, roasted sweet red peppers, fresh herbs, and cheese. You'll also find risotto, fresh fish, and pasta, along with more exotic dishes, such as a spicy North African ragout with chicken, ginger, and fresh mint served on toasted almond couscous. Entrées, served with soup or salad, include options such as rib-eye steak marinated in red wine, rosemary, and garlic and served with garlic mashed potatoes or chicken served with caramelized onions, Gorgonzola cheese, and toasted pecans. Any of these dishes would go well with a glass of the restaurant's namesake.

$$ MC, V; local checks only; dinner Thurs–Sun; beer and wine; reservations recommended.

Wedding Index

Pet Index

List of accommodations that accept pets in one room or more:

SAN FRANCISCO
Argonaut Hotel
Campton Place Hotel
Hotel Monaco
Hotel Palomar
Hotel Triton
The Prescott Hotel

CARMEL AND CARMEL VALLEY
Cypress Inn
Vagabond's House Inn

NAPA VALLEY WINE TOWNS
Harvest Inn
Vintage Inn

MENDOCINO
The MacCallum House
The Stanford Inn by the Sea

YOSEMITE
Groveland Hotel

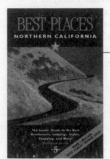

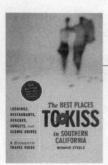